ARCHAEOLOGY
ESSENTIALS

ARCHA

ESSENT

Colin Renfrew • Paul Bahn

EOLOGY
IALS

SECOND EDITION

Theories, Methods, and Practice

with 220 illustrations

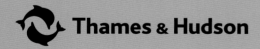
Thames & Hudson

First published in 2007 in paperback in the United States of America by
Thames & Hudson Inc., 500 Fifth Avenue, New York, New York 10110

thamesandhudsonusa.com

Second edition 2010

Library of Congress Catalog Card Number 2010928155

ISBN 978-0-500-28912-9

Printed and bound in China by Midas Printing International Ltd

Contents

DIGITAL RESOURCES

We offer additional resources for instructors and students on the *Archaeology Essentials* webpage at

thamesandhudsonusa.com/college/welcome.htm

Our website for instructors provides a test bank and images in Jpeg format to be shown in class. New for this edition are projects to support key learning objectives. Our student website offers chapter summaries, self-test quizzes, flash cards to revise terminology and concepts, a glossary, and useful internet links.

EBOOK

Archaeology Essentials is also available as an ebook. Visit nortonebooks.com for more information.

Preface

Archaeology Essentials is designed for college students taking an introductory course in archaeology. This book aims to convey some of the excitement of archaeology in the 21st century and to give students a concise and readable account of the ways in which modern archaeologists investigate and understand our remote past. Archaeologists usually make the headlines when they find something spectacular: in 2003, for example, archaeologists announced the discovery of a new, entirely unpredicted, and only recently extinct human species, *Homo floresiensis*, on the island of Flores in Indonesia. However, most archaeologists spend their time engaged in research that rarely makes the news, but is nevertheless vitally important for our understanding of the past.

Archaeology is still often a matter of painstaking excavation of an ancient site, but today archaeologists can use new techniques that sometimes avoid the need for excavation altogether. Advances in the methods for analyzing and evaluating archaeological finds mean that archaeologists can reach conclusions that would have been impossible just 10 or 20 years ago.

This book will introduce students to the methods, new and old, used by archaeologists: from the traditional shovel and trowel to satellite imaging and ground-based remote sensing. New technology has affected the work of archaeologists in the laboratory as well as in the field: we cover, for example, the use of genetic evidence. But the story of modern archaeology is not just about technology. There have been enormous advances in the questions archaeologists ask and in the assumptions and theoretical models they apply to archaeological evidence. Some questions, which an earlier generation of archaeologists might have considered closed, have now been opened up for new examination.

In other words, whatever the focus of an individual college course, it is our intention that students will find in this book an authoritative, concise, and clear explanation of modern archaeological practice.

Introduction
The nature and aims of archaeology

About 5300 years ago a 40-year-old man made his last journey, on a mountain path in the European Alps. He lay undisturbed until his body was discovered by hikers in September 1991. Archaeologists were able to determine not only his age, but also the contents of his last meal: meat (probably ibex and venison), plants, wheat, and plums. The Iceman suffered from arthritis, and analysis of a fingernail showed that he had suffered serious illness 4, 3, and 2 months before he died. At first it was thought that he died from exhaustion in a fog or blizzard. However, later analysis revealed what may be an arrowhead in his left shoulder and cuts on his hands, wrists, and ribcage, as well as a blow to the head, so he may well have died a violent death. These observations are just a sample of what archaeologists were able to learn about this long-dead man.

The thrill of discovery and the ability of **archaeology** to reveal at least some of the secrets of our past have been the theme of many famous novels and movies: notably Steven Spielberg's Indiana Jones series. Many discoveries in archaeology are far less spectacular than that of the Iceman, perhaps a collection of broken pieces of pottery, but these kinds of remains too can tell us a lot about the past through careful collection and analysis of the evidence.

Archaeology is unique in its ability to tell us about the whole history of humankind from its beginnings over 3 million years ago. Indeed for more than 99 percent of that huge span of time archaeology – the study of past **material culture** – is the only source of information. The archaeological record is the only way that we can answer questions about the **evolution** of our species and the developments in **culture** and society which led to the emergence of the first civilizations and to the more recent societies which are founded upon them.

This book provides a brief introduction to the ways in which archaeologists uncover and collect evidence about our past, how they analyze it (often using sophisticated scientific methods), and how they interpret it (both for fellow scholars and members of the public).

The Discipline of Archaeology

Many archaeologists consider themselves as part of the broader discipline of **anthropology**. Anthropology at its broadest is the study of humanity – our physical characteristics as animals, and our unique non-biological characteristics. Anthropology is thus a broad discipline – so broad that it is often broken down into different fields:

- **Physical** *or* **biological anthropology**: the study of human biological or physical characteristics and how they evolved.
- **Cultural anthropology**: the study of human culture and society.
- Linguistic anthropology: the study of how speech varies with social factors and over time.
- Archaeology: the study of former societies through the remains of their material culture and, in the case of literate cultures such as those of Mesopotamia or Mesoamerica, such written records as have survived.

Archaeologists who are interested in the societies of ancient Greece and Rome, their empires and neighboring territories, consider themselves Classical archaeologists. They study the material remains of the Greek and Roman worlds, but can also take into account the extensive written records (literature, history, official records, and so on) that survive.

Similarly, biblical archaeologists work in much the same way as anthropological archaeologists, but with reference to the events set out in the Bible.

Archaeology has some aspects in common with both history and with science. Like history, archaeology is concerned with documenting and understanding the human past, but archaeologists operate in a time frame much larger than the periods studied by historians. Conventional historical sources begin only with the introduction of written records around 3000 BC in Western Asia, and much later in most other parts of the world (not until AD 1788 in Australia, for example). The period before written records and history (meaning the study of the past using written evidence) is known as **prehistory**.

Although archaeologists spend much of their time studying **artifacts** and buildings, it is worth emphasizing that archaeology is about the study of humans and, in that sense, like history is a humanity. But it differs from the study of written history – although it uses written history – in a fundamental way. Historical records make statements, offer opinions, and pass judgments (even if those statements and judgments themselves need to be interpreted). The objects that archaeologists discover, on the other hand, tell us nothing directly in themselves. It is *we* today who have to make sense of these things. In this respect the practice of archaeology is rather like a science. The scientist collects data, conducts experiments, formulates a hypothesis (a proposition to account for the data), tests the hypothesis against more data, and then devises a model (a description that seems best to summarize the pattern observed in the data). The archaeologist has to develop a picture of the past, just as the scientist has to develop a coherent view of the natural world. It is not found ready made.

Archaeology, in short, is a science as well as a humanity. That is one of its fascinations as a discipline: it reflects the ingenuity of the modern scientist as well as the modern historian. The technical methods of archaeological science are the most obvious, from **radiocarbon dating** to studies of food residues in pots. Equally important are scientific methods of analysis: archaeology is just as much about the analytical concepts of the archaeologist as the instruments in the laboratory.

The Important Questions of Archaeology

Because the evidence of archaeology cannot speak for itself, it is important that archaeologists ask the right questions of the evidence. If the wrong questions are asked, the wrong conclusions will be drawn. For example, early explanations of the unexplained mounds found east of the Mississippi river assumed that they could not have been built by the indigenous American peoples of the region; it was assumed instead that the mounds had been built by a mythical and vanished race of Moundbuilders. Thomas Jefferson, later in his career the third President of the United States, decided to test this hypothesis against hard evidence and dug a trench across a mound on his property. He was able to show that the mound had been used as a burial place on many occasions and found no evidence that it could not have been built by the indigenous peoples. In other words, Jefferson asked questions about what the evidence suggested: he did not simply reach a conclusion that fitted his prejudices and assumptions.

One of the most important tasks of the archaeologist is to ask the right questions about the evidence. Traditional approaches tended to regard the objective of archaeology mainly as reconstruction: piecing together the puzzle. But today it is not enough simply to recreate the material culture of remote periods: how people lived and how they exploited their environment. We also want to know *why* they lived that way, why they had certain patterns of behavior and how their material culture came to take the form it did. We are interested, in short, in explaining change.

How to Use This Book

This book is organized around some of the most important questions that archaeologists ask, and in response to suggestions from a number of teachers this new edition has twelve chapters instead of ten. Chapter 1 looks at the history of archaeology, the kinds of questions asked by archaeologists in the past and the methods they used.

In Chapter 2 we ask the question What Is Left?: the evidence with which archaeologists work. The next chapter examines the important question Where? Archaeologists can learn a good deal from the **context** in which evidence is found and have developed many techniques for locating and recovering evidence. In Chapter 4 the question is When?: how can we know whether something dates from a few hundred years or many thousands of years ago? Chapter 5 examines the fascinating question of How Were Societies Organized? In Chapter 6 we look at the world in which ancient people lived: What Was the Environment and What Did They Eat? Technology was an important factor in changing society and the lives of our ancestors, as were contact and trade with other ancient peoples: the key question for Chapter 7 is How Were Artifacts Made, Used, and Distributed?

Chapter 8 looks at the archaeology of people: What Were They Like? The next chapter addresses some of the more difficult questions that modern archaeologists are trying to answer: the ways ancient peoples thought about their world and issues of identity. In other words, What Did They Think? An equally difficult question is Why Did Things Change?, the subject of Chapter 10. In Chapter 11 we address the often controversial question: Whose Past? The past may be remote in time but it can be very relevant today if it touches on the beliefs, identity, and wishes of the descendants who lived long ago. Finally, in the new Chapter 12 we look at both the practice of applied archaeology, a profession that now employs more people than the academic archaeology pursued in universities, and more generally The Future of the Past.

If you follow the questions examined in this book you will understand how archaeologists work, think, analyze, and seek to understand the past. You will also discover that not all questions can be answered or perhaps that there might be more than one answer.

To help you understand how archaeology works, we have provided some special features in this book. Case studies, designed as box features, show you archaeology in action and will help you understand the issues that archaeologists deal with in their research and fieldwork. Key Concept and Key Fact boxes summarize and review important concepts, methods, or facts about archaeology. These boxes are usually placed at the end of a section to help you reinforce what you have learned, but sometimes we have positioned them at the beginning of a discussion to help you understand technical concepts as you read about them. At the end of every chapter there is a summary to recap what you have read and a suggested reading list that will guide you to the most important and helpful publications if you want to research any subject further. Archaeological terms in the text that are defined in the glossary are highlighted in bold (e.g. **excavation**) when they first occur in a chapter.

The Searchers
The history of archaeology

THE SPECULATIVE PHASE

The First Excavations

THE BEGINNINGS OF MODERN ARCHAEOLOGY

The Antiquity of Humankind and the Concept of Evolution

The Three Age System

Ethnography and Archaeology

Discovering the Early Civilizations

19th-Century North American Pioneers

The Development of Field Techniques

CLASSIFICATION AND CONSOLIDATION

The Ecological Approach

The Rise of Archaeological Science

A TURNING POINT IN ARCHAEOLOGY

The Birth of the New Archaeology

The Postprocessual Debate of the 1980s and 1990s

The Widening Field

The Development of Public Archaeology

Indigenous Archaeologies

Study Questions
Summary
Further Reading

1

The history of archaeology is commonly seen as the history of great discoveries: the tomb of Tutankhamun in Egypt, the lost Maya cities of Mexico, the painted caves of the Old Stone Age such as Lascaux in France, or the remains of our human ancestors buried deep in the Olduvai Gorge in Tanzania. But even more than that it is the story of how we have come to look with fresh eyes at the material evidence for the human past, and with new methods to aid us in our task.

It is important to remember that just a century and a half ago, most well-read people in the Western world – where archaeology as we know it today was first developed – believed that the world had been created only a few thousand years earlier (in the year 4004 BC according to the then-standard interpretation of the Bible), and that all that could be known of the remote past had to be gleaned from the earliest historians, notably those of the ancient Near East, Egypt, and Greece. There was no awareness that any kind of coherent history of the periods before the development of writing was possible at all.

But today we can indeed penetrate the depths of the remote past. This is not simply because new discoveries are being made. It is because we have learned to ask some of the right questions, and have developed some of the right methods for answering them. The material evidence of the archaeological record has been lying around for a long time. What is new is our awareness that the methods of archaeology can give us information about the past, even the prehistoric past (before the invention of writing). The history of archaeology is therefore in the first instance a history of ideas, of theory, of ways of looking at the past. Next it is a history of developing research methods, employing those ideas and investigating those questions. And only thirdly is it a history of actual discoveries.

In this chapter and in this book it is the development of the questions and ideas that we shall emphasize, and the application of new research methods. The main thing to remember is that every view of the past is a product of its own time: ideas and theories are constantly evolving, and so are methods. When we describe the archaeological research methods of today we are simply speaking of one point on the trajectory of the subject's evolution. In a few decades' or even a few years' time these methods will certainly look old-fashioned and out of date. That is the dynamic nature of archaeology as a discipline.

THE SPECULATIVE PHASE

Humans have always speculated about their past, and most **cultures** have their own foundation myths to explain why society is how it is. Most cultures, too, have been fascinated by the societies that preceded them. The Aztecs exaggerated their Toltec ancestry, and were so interested in Teotihuacán, the huge Mexican city abandoned hundreds of years earlier which they mistakenly linked with the Toltecs, that they incorporated ceremonial stone masks from that **site** in the foundation deposits of their own Great Temple. A rather more detached curiosity about the relics of bygone ages developed in several other early civilizations, where scholars and even rulers collected and studied objects from the past.

During the revival of learning in Europe known as the Renaissance (14th to 17th centuries), princes and people of refinement began to form "cabinets of curiosities" in which curios and ancient **artifacts** were displayed rather haphazardly with exotic minerals and all manner of specimens illustrative of what was called "natural history." During the Renaissance also scholars began to study and collect the relics of ancient Greece and Rome. And they began too in more northern lands to study the local relics of their own remote past. At this time these were mainly the field monuments – those conspicuous sites, often made of stone, which immediately attracted attention, such as Stonehenge. Careful scholars, such as the Englishman William Stukeley, made systematic studies of some of these monuments, with accurate plans which are still useful today. Stukeley and his colleagues successfully demonstrated that these monuments had not been constructed by giants or devils, as suggested by local names such as the Devil's Arrows, but by people in antiquity. He was also successful in phasing field monuments, demonstrating that, since Roman roads cut barrows, the former must have been built after the latter.

The First Excavations

In the 18th century more adventurous researchers initiated **excavation** of some of the most prominent sites. The Roman city of Pompeii in Italy was one of the first of these. Buried under meters of volcanic ash after the cataclysmic eruption of nearby Mount Vesuvius, Pompeii was only rediscovered in 1748. Although to begin with the motivation of the excavators was to find valuable ancient masterpieces, it wasn't long before published finds from Pompeii were attracting enormous international attention, influencing **styles** of furniture and interior decoration, and even inspiring several pieces of romantic fiction. Not until 1860, however, did well-recorded excavations begin.

The credit for conducting what has been called "the first scientific excavation in the history of archaeology" traditionally goes to Thomas Jefferson (later in his career third President of the United States), who in 1784 dug a trench or section across a burial mound on his property in Virginia. Jefferson's work marks the beginning of the end of the Speculative Phase.

"THE FIRST EXCAVATION"

- Thomas Jefferson, later to become President of the United States, conducted the "first scientific excavation" in Virginia in 1784

- By carefully digging a trench across a Native American burial mound he was able to observe different layers and to draw reasoned conclusions from the data

In Jefferson's time people were speculating that the hundreds of unexplained mounds known east of the Mississippi river had been built not by the indigenous Americans, but by a mythical and vanished race of "Moundbuilders." Jefferson adopted what today we should call a scientific approach, that is, he tested ideas about the mounds against hard evidence – by excavating one of them. His methods were careful enough to allow him to recognize different layers (or **stratigraphy**) in his trench, and to see that the many human bones present were less well preserved in the lower layers. From this he deduced that the mound had been reused as a place of burial on many separate occasions. Although Jefferson admitted, rightly, that more evidence was needed to resolve the Moundbuilder question, he saw no reason why ancestors of the present-day Native Americans themselves could not have raised the mounds.

Jefferson was ahead of his time. His sound approach – logical **deduction** from carefully excavated evidence, in many ways the basis of modern archaeology – was not taken up by any of his immediate successors in North America. In Europe, meanwhile, extensive excavations were being conducted, for instance by the Englishman Richard Colt Hoare, who dug into hundreds of burial mounds in southern Britain during the first decade of the 19th century. None of these

Early excavations: Richard Colt Hoare and William Cunnington direct a dig north of Stonehenge in 1805.

excavations, however, did much to advance the cause of knowledge about the distant past, since their interpretation was still within the biblical framework, which insisted on a short span for human existence.

THE BEGINNINGS OF MODERN ARCHAEOLOGY

It was not until the middle of the 19th century that the discipline of archaeology became truly established. Already in the background there were the significant achievements of the newly developed science of geology. The study of the **stratification** of rocks (their arrangement in superimposed layers or strata), established principles which were to be the basis of archaeological excavation, as foreshadowed by Jefferson. It was demonstrated that the stratification of rocks was due to processes which were still going on in seas, rivers, and lakes. This was the principle of "**uniformitarianism**," that geologically ancient conditions were in essence similar to, or "uniform with," those of our own time. This idea could be applied to the human past also, and it marks one of the fundamental notions of modern archaeology: that in many ways the past was much like the present.

The Antiquity of Humankind and the Concept of Evolution

These advances in geology did much to lay the groundwork for what was one of the significant events in the intellectual history of the 19th century (and an indispensable one for the discipline of archaeology): the establishment of the antiquity of humankind. It had become widely agreed that earth's origins extended far back into a remote past, so that the biblical notion of the creation of the world and all its contents just a few thousand years before our own time could no longer be accepted. The possibility of a **prehistory** of humankind, indeed the need for one, was established.

This harmonized well with the findings of Charles Darwin, whose fundamental work, *On the Origin of Species*, published in 1859, established the concept of **evolution** to explain the origin and development of all plants and animals. The idea of evolution itself was not new – earlier scholars had suggested that living things must have changed or evolved through the ages. What Darwin demonstrated was how this change occurred. The key mechanism was, in Darwin's words, "natural selection," or the survival of the fittest. In the struggle for existence, environmentally better-adapted individuals of a particular species would survive (or be "naturally selected") whereas less well-adapted ones would die. The surviving individuals would pass on their advantageous traits to their offspring and gradually the characteristics of a species would change to such an extent that a new species emerged. This was the process of evolution. The implications were clear: that the human species had emerged as part of this same process. The search for human origins in the material record, by the techniques of archaeology, could begin.

Charles Darwin in a cartoon from the 1860s.

Darwin's work on evolution also had an immediate impact on archaeologists who were laying the foundations for the study of artifacts and how they develop over time. But his influence on social thinkers and anthropologists has been even more significant. The principles of evolution can also be applied to social organization, for culture can be seen as learned and passed on between generations, albeit in a more general way than in biological evolution.

The Three Age System

As we have noted, some archaeological techniques, notably those in the field of excavation, were already being developed. So too was another conceptual device which proved very useful for the progress of European prehistory: the **Three Age System**. As early as 1808, Colt Hoare had recognized a sequence of stone, "brass," and iron artifacts within the barrows he excavated, but this was first systematically studied in the 1830s by the Danish scholar C.J. Thomsen. He proposed that prehistoric artifacts could be divided into those coming from a Stone Age, a Bronze Age, and an Iron Age, and this **classification** was soon found useful by scholars throughout Europe. Later a division in the Stone Age was established between the **Paleolithic** or Old Stone Age and the **Neolithic** or New Stone Age.

These terms were less applicable to Africa, where bronze was not used south of the Sahara, or to the Americas, where bronze was less important and iron was not in use before the European conquest. But it was conceptually significant. The Three Age System established the principle that by studying and classifying prehistoric artifacts, they could be ordered chronologically. Archaeology was moving beyond mere speculation about the past, and becoming instead a discipline involving careful excavation and the systematic study of the artifacts unearthed. Although superseded by modern dating methods, the Three Age System remains one of the fundamental divisions of archaeological materials today.

Ethnography and Archaeology

Another important strand in the thought of the time was the realization that the study by ethnographers of living communities in different parts of the world could be a useful starting point for archaeologists seeking to understand something of the lifestyles of their own early native inhabitants who clearly had comparably simple tools and crafts. For example, as early as the sixteenth century, contact with native communities in North America provided antiquarians and historians with models for tattooed images of Celts and Britons.

And soon ethnographers and anthropologists were themselves producing schemes of human progress. Strongly influenced by Darwin's ideas about

Frederick Catherwood's accurate, if somewhat romantic, drawing of Stela A at Copán; at the time of his visit to the site in 1840 Maya glyphs had not been deciphered.

evolution, the British anthropologist Edward Tylor, and his American counterpart Lewis Henry Morgan, both published important works in the 1870s arguing that human societies had evolved from a state of savagery (primitive hunting) through barbarism (simple farming) to civilization (the highest form of society). Morgan's work was partly based on his great knowledge of living Native Americans.

Discovering the Early Civilizations

By the 1880s, then, many of the ideas underlying modern archaeology had been developed. But these ideas themselves took shape against a background of major 19th-century discoveries of ancient civilizations in the Old World and the New.

The splendors of ancient Egyptian civilization had already been brought to the attention of an avid public after Napoleon's military expedition there of 1798–1800. It was the discovery by one of his soldiers of the Rosetta Stone that eventually provided the key to understanding Egyptian hieroglyphic writing. Inscribed on the stone were parallel texts written in both Egyptian and Greek scripts. The Frenchman Jean-François Champollion used this bilingual inscription finally to decipher the hieroglyphs in 1822, after 14 years' work. A similar piece of brilliant scholarly detection helped unlock the secrets of cuneiform writing, the script used for many languages in ancient Mesopotamia.

Egypt and the Near East also held a fascination for the American lawyer and diplomat John Lloyd Stephens, but it was in the New World that he was to make his name. His travels in Yucatán, Mexico, with the English artist Frederick Catherwood, and the superbly illustrated books they produced together in the early 1840s, revealed for the first time to an enthusiastic public the ruined cities of the ancient Maya. Unlike contemporary researchers in North America, who continued to argue for a vanished white race of Moundbuilders as the architects of the earthworks there, Stephens rightly believed that the Maya monuments were, in his own words, "the creation of the same races who inhabited the country at the time of the Spanish conquest." Stephens also noted that there were similar hieroglyphic inscriptions at the different sites, which led him to argue for Maya cultural unity – but no Champollion was to emerge to decipher the glyphs until the 1960s.

19th-Century North American Pioneers

In North America, two themes dominated 19th-century archaeology: the enduring belief in a vanished race of Moundbuilders; and the search for "glacial man" – the idea that human fossils and Stone Age tools would be found in the Americas in association with extinct animals, as they had been in Europe.

Ephraim Squier, for example, an Ohio newspaperman who excavated over 200 mounds in the 1840s, considered them beyond the capabilities of any Native Americans, who were "hunters averse to labor," maintaining the myth of the Moundbuilders. Their work does still have some use, though, since the plans and records they made are now the best record there is of the many mounds which were destroyed as settlers moved westward.

Part of a 348-ft long painting illustrating a 19th-century mound excavation. Such excavations were often part of the futile search for a vanished race of Moundbuilders.

Ephraim Squier.

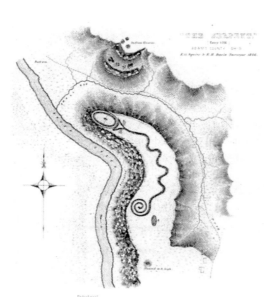

Plan of Serpent Mound, Ohio, as prepared by Squier (with the help of Edwin Davis, an Ohio physician) in 1846.

Samuel Haven.

John Wesley Powell.

Cyrus Thomas.

Samuel Haven, Librarian of the American Antiquarian Society, produced a remarkable synthesis in 1856, *The Archaeology of the United States*, which is considered a foundation stone of modern American archaeology. In it, he argued persuasively that the Native Americans were of great antiquity, and, through cranial and other physical characteristics, he pointed to their probable links with Asiatic races. Disagreeing strongly with Squier and others, he concluded that the mysterious mounds had been built by the ancestors of living Native Americans.

Another scholar, John Wesley Powell, had spent much of his youth digging into mounds and learning geology. Eventually he was appointed director of the U.S. Geographical and Geological Survey of the Rocky Mountain region. He published a wide range of information on the rapidly dwindling Native American cultures. Moving to Washington, Powell also headed the Bureau of American Ethnology, an agency he set up to study the Native Americans. A fearless campaigner for native rights, he recommended the setting up of reservations, and also began the recording of tribal oral histories.

In 1881 Powell recruited Cyrus Thomas to head the Bureau's archaeology program, and to settle the Moundbuilder question once and for all. After 7 years of fieldwork and the investigation of thousands of mounds, Thomas proved that the Moundbuilder race had never existed: the monuments had been erected by the ancestors of modern Native Americans.

The Development of Field Techniques

It was only in the late 19th century that a sound methodology of scientific excavation began to be generally adopted. From that time, some major figures stand out who in their various ways have helped create the modern field methods we use today.

Lieutenant-General Augustus Lane-Fox Pitt-Rivers, for much of his life a professional soldier, brought long experience of military methods, survey, and

Lieutenant-General Pitt-Rivers, excavator of Cranborne Chase, and pioneer in recording techniques. To the right is his meticulous plan of a barrow on Cranborne Chase.

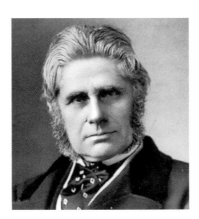

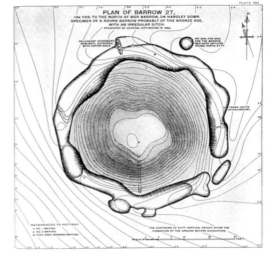

precision to impeccably organized excavations on his estates in southern England. Plans, sections, and even models were made, and the exact position of every object was recorded. He was not concerned with retrieving beautiful treasures, but with recovering all objects, no matter how mundane. He was a pioneer in his insistence on total recording, and his four privately printed volumes, describing his excavations on Cranborne Chase from 1887 to 1898, represent the highest standards of archaeological publication.

A younger contemporary of Pitt-Rivers, Sir William Flinders Petrie was likewise noted for his meticulous excavations and his insistence on the collection and description of everything found, not just the fine objects, as well as on full publication. He employed these methods in his exemplary excavations in Egypt, and later in Palestine, from the 1880s until his death.

Sir Mortimer Wheeler fought in the British army in both world wars and, like Pitt-Rivers, brought military precision to his excavations, notably through techniques such as the grid-square method of dividing and digging a site. He is particularly well known for his work at British hillforts, notably Maiden Castle. Equally outstanding, however, was his achievement as Director-General of Archaeology in India, where he held training schools in modern field methods, and excavated at many important sites.

Flinders Petrie at the Egyptian site of Abydos in 1922.

Sir Mortimer Wheeler, and one of his excavations in India, 1945.

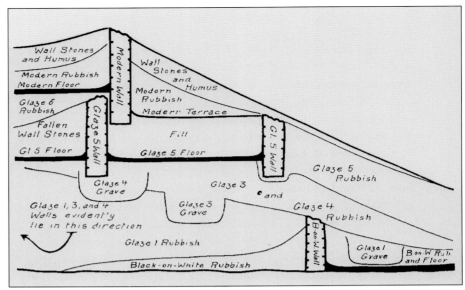

Alfred Kidder and his cross-sectional drawing of the stratigraphy at the Pecos Pueblo site.

Alfred Kidder was the leading Americanist of his time. As well as being a major figure in Maya archaeology, he was largely responsible for putting the Southwest on the archaeological map with his excavations at Pecos Ruin, a large pueblo in northern New Mexico, from 1915 to 1929. His survey of the region, *An Introduction to the Study of Southwestern Archaeology* (1924), has become a classic.

Kidder was one of the first archaeologists to use a team of specialists to help analyze artifacts and human remains. He is also important for his "blueprint" for a regional strategy: (1) reconnaissance; (2) selection of criteria for ranking the remains of sites chronologically; (3) organizing them into a probable sequence; (4) stratigraphic excavation to elucidate specific problems; followed by (5) more detailed regional survey and dating.

KEY EARLY ADVANCES

- The rejection of a literal interpretation of the biblical account of early human history and the establishment of the antiquity of humankind

- Charles Darwin's theories of evolution and natural selection

- The establishment of the Three Age System which divided prehistory into a Stone Age followed by a Bronze Age and an Iron Age

- The development of archaeological field techniques

CLASSIFICATION AND CONSOLIDATION

As we have seen, well before the end of the 19th century, many of the principal features of modern archaeology had been established and many of the early civilizations had been discovered. There now ensued a period, which lasted until about 1960, which has been described as the "classificatory-historical period." Its central concern was chronology. Much effort went into the establishment of regional chronological systems, and the description of the development of culture in each area.

It was scholars studying the prehistoric societies of Europe and North America who made some of the most significant contributions to the subject. In the United States there was a close link between anthropologists and archaeologists studying the Native Americans. The anthropologist Franz Boas reacted against the broad evolutionary schemes of his predecessors and demanded much greater attention to the collection and classification of information in the field. Huge inventories of cultural traits, such as pot and basket designs or types of moccasins, were built up. This tied in with the so-called "direct historical approach" of the archaeologists, who attempted to trace modern Native American pottery and other styles "directly" back into the distant past. By the 1930s the number of separate regional sequences was so great that a group of scholars led by W.C. McKern devised what became known as the "**Midwestern Taxonomic System**," which correlated sequences in the Midwest by identifying similarities between artifact collections.

Meanwhile, Gordon Childe, a brilliant Australian based in Britain and a leading thinker and writer about European prehistory, had almost single-handedly been making comparisons of this sort between prehistoric sequences in Europe. Both his methods and the Midwestern Taxonomic System were designed to order the material, to answer the question: To what period do these artifacts date? and also: With which other materials do they belong? This latter question usually carried with it an assumption which Gordon Childe made explicit: that a constantly recurring collection or "**assemblage**" of artifacts (a "culture" in his terminology) could be attributed to a particular group of people. This approach thus offered the hope of answering, in a very general sense, the question: Who did these artifacts belong to?

But Childe went beyond merely describing and correlating the culture sequences and attempted to account for their origin. In the late 19th century scholars had argued that all the attributes of civilization, from stone architecture to metal weapons, had spread or "diffused" to Europe from the Near East by trade or migration of people. With the much greater range of evidence available to him, Childe modified this approach and argued that

Professor Gordon Childe at the site of the Neolithic settlement at Skara Brae, Orkney, in 1930.

Europe had undergone some indigenous development – but he nevertheless attributed the major cultural changes to Near Eastern influences.

Later Childe went on to try and answer the much more difficult question: Why had civilization arisen in the Near East? Himself influenced by Marxist ideas and the relatively recent Marxist revolution in Russia, he proposed that there had been a **Neolithic Revolution** which gave rise to the development of farming, and later an Urban Revolution which led to the first towns and cities. Childe was one of the few archaeologists of his generation bold enough to address this whole broad issue of why things happened or changed in the past. Most of his contemporaries were more concerned with establishing chronologies and cultural sequences. But after World War II scholars with new ideas began to challenge conventional approaches.

The Ecological Approach

One of the most influential new thinkers in North America was the anthropologist Julian Steward. Like Childe he was interested in explaining cultural change, but he brought to the question an anthropologist's understanding of how living cultures work. Moreover he highlighted the fact that cultures do not interact simply with each other but with the environment as well. Steward christened the study of ways in which adaptation to the environment could cause cultural change "**cultural ecology**." Perhaps the most direct archaeological impact of these ideas can be seen in the work of Gordon Willey, one of Steward's graduate associates, who carried out a pioneering investigation in the Virú Valley, Peru, in the late 1940s. This study of some 1500 years of pre-Columbian occupation involved a combination of observations from detailed maps and aerial photographs, survey at ground level, and excavation and surface potsherd collection to establish dates for the hundreds of prehistoric sites identified. Willey then plotted the geographical distribution of these many sites in the valley at different periods and set the results against the changing local environment.

Quite independently of Steward, however, the British archaeologist Grahame Clark developed an ecological approach with even more direct relevance for archaeological fieldwork. Breaking away from the artifact-dominated "culture history" approach of his contemporaries, he argued that by studying how human populations adapted to their environments we can understand many aspects of ancient society. Collaboration with new kinds of specialists was essential: for example, specialists who could identify animal bones or plant remains in the archaeological record could help build up a picture not only of what prehistoric environments were like, but what foods prehistoric peoples ate.

The Rise of Archaeological Science

The other striking development of the period immediately after World War II was the rapid development of scientific aids for archaeology. We have already seen how pioneers of the ecological approach forged an alliance with specialists from the environmental sciences. Even more important, however, was the application to archaeology of the physical and chemical sciences.

The greatest breakthrough came in the field of dating. In 1949 the American chemist Willard Libby announced his invention of **radiocarbon dating**. It was not until well over a decade later that the full impact of this momentous technical achievement began to be felt, but the implications were clear: here at last archaeologists might have a means of directly determining the age of undated sites and finds anywhere in the world without complicated cross-cultural comparisons. Traditionally, prehistoric Europe had been dated by supposed contacts with early Greece and hence (indirectly) with ancient Egypt, which could itself be dated historically. The radiocarbon method now promised a completely independent chronology for ancient Europe. It also meant that to establish a date was no longer one of the main end products of research. It was still important, but it could now be done much more efficiently, allowing the archaeologist to go on to ask more challenging questions than merely chronological ones.

Archaeological applications for scientific techniques now include plant and animal studies, and methods for analyzing human remains and artifacts. Over the past decade developments in biochemistry and molecular genetics have led to the emergence of the new disciplines of molecular archaeology and archaeogenetics. Sensitive techniques in the field of chemistry are beginning to allow the precise identification of organic residues and are giving fresh insights into both diet and nutrition. The study of **DNA**, both modern and ancient, has offered novel approaches to the study of human evolution, and is now beginning to give the study of plant and animal domestication a systematic, molecular basis.

KEY DEVELOPMENTS

- The early 20th-century establishment of regional chronologies and sequences of artifacts

- The development of scientific aids for archaeology, notably radiocarbon dating

- The post-World War II development of an environmental or ecological explanation for past change

- Increasing collaboration with specialists in other disciplines such as animal or plant studies

- Gordon Childe's bold questioning of why things happened or changed in the past

A TURNING POINT IN ARCHAEOLOGY

The 1960s mark a turning point in the development of archaeology. By this time some archaeologists were dissatisfied with the way research in the subject was being conducted. These dissatisfactions were not so much with excavation techniques, or with the newly developed scientific aids in archaeology, but with the way conclusions were drawn from them – how archaeologists explain things.

The fundamental cause for dissatisfaction with the traditional archaeology was that it never seemed to explain anything, other than in terms of migrations of peoples and supposed "influences." Already in 1948 the American archaeologist Walter W. Taylor had argued for an approach which would take into consideration the full range of a culture system. And in 1958, Gordon Willey and Philip Phillips argued for a greater emphasis on the social aspect, for a broader study of the general processes at work in culture history (a "processual interpretation").

That was all very well, but what would it mean in practice?

The Birth of the New Archaeology

In the United States the answer was provided, at least in part, by a group of younger archaeologists, led by Lewis Binford, who set out to offer a new approach to the problems of archaeological interpretation, which was soon dubbed "the **New Archaeology**." Binford and his colleagues argued against the approach which tried to use archaeological data to write a kind of "counterfeit history." They maintained that the potential of the archaeological evidence was much greater than had been realized for the investigation of social and economic aspects of past societies. Their view of archaeology was more optimistic than that of many of their predecessors.

They also argued that archaeological reasoning should be made explicit. Conclusions should be based not simply on the authority of the scholar making the interpretation, but on an explicit framework of logical argument. Thus conclusions, if they are to be considered valid, must be open to testing.

These processual archaeologists sought to explain rather than simply to describe, and to do so, as in all sciences, by seeking to make valid generalizations. They tried to avoid the rather vague talk of the "influences" of one culture upon another, but rather to analyze a culture as a system which could be broken down into subsystems (like technology, trade, or ideology) which could be studied in their own right. They placed much less emphasis on artifact **typology** and classification.

In order to fulfill these aims, the New Archaeologists to a large extent turned away from the approaches of history toward those of the sciences. There was a great willingness to employ more sophisticated quantitative techniques and to draw on ideas from other disciplines, notably geography.

KEY CONCEPTS
Processual Archaeology

In the early days of the New Archaeology, its principal exponents were very conscious of the limitations of the older, traditional archaeology. The following contrasts were among those which they often emphasized:

The Nature of Archaeology:
Explanatory vs *Descriptive*
  Archaeology's role was now to explain past change, not simply to reconstruct the past and how people had lived. This involved the use of *explicit* theory.

Explanation:
Culture process vs *Culture history*
  Traditional archaeology was seen to rely on historical explanation: the New Archaeology, drawing on the *philosophy* of science, would think in terms of culture process, of how changes in economic and social systems take place. This implies *generalization*.

Reasoning: Deductive vs *Inductive*
  Traditional archaeologists saw archaeology as resembling a jigsaw puzzle: the task was one of "piecing together the past." Instead, the appropriate procedure was now to formulate *hypotheses*, constructing *models*, and deducing their consequences.

Validation: Testing vs *Authority*
  Hypotheses were to be tested, and conclusions should not be accepted on the basis of the authority or standing of the research worker.

Research Focus:
Project design vs *Data accumulation*
  Research should be designed to answer specific *questions* economically, not simply to generate more information which might not be relevant.

Choice of Approach:
Quantitative vs *Simply qualitative*
  Quantitative data allowed computerized statistical treatment, with the possibility of *sampling* and *significance* testing. This was often preferred to the purely verbal traditional approach.

Scope: Optimism vs *Pessimism*
  Traditional archaeologists often stressed that archaeological data were not well suited to the reconstruction of social organization or cognitive systems. The New Archaeologists were more positive and argued that it would never be known how hard these problems were until archaeologists had tried to solve them.

In their enthusiasm to use a battery of new techniques, the New Archaeologists drew also on a range of previously unfamiliar vocabularies which their critics tended to dismiss as jargon. Indeed in recent years, several critics have reacted against some of those aspirations to be scientific. But there can be no doubt that archaeology will never be the same again. Most workers today, even the critics of the early New Archaeology, implicitly recognize its influence when they agree that it is indeed the goal of archaeology to explain what happened in the past as well as to describe it. Most of them agree too that in order to do good archaeology it is necessary to make explicit, and then to examine, our underlying assumptions.

The Postprocessual Debate of the 1980s and 1990s

Post-modernist currents of thought in the 1980s and 1990s encouraged a great diversity of approaches to the past. While many field archaeologists were relatively untouched by theoretical debates, and the processual tradition established by the New Archaeology rolled on, there were several new approaches, sometimes collectively termed "postprocessual," which dealt with interesting and difficult questions.

Influential arguments, some of them first advanced by the archaeologist Ian Hodder and his students, have stressed that there is no single, correct way to undertake archaeological inference, and that the goal of objectivity is unattainable. However, this well-justified critique of the scientism of the early New Archaeology sometimes overlooks more recent developments in scientific methodology. It can also lead to charges of relativism, where one person's view has to be regarded as as good as another's, and where, in interpretive matters, "anything goes," and where the borderlines between archaeological research and fiction (or science fiction) may be difficult to define.

For its early proponents, postprocessual archaeology represented so radical a critique of processual archaeology as to establish a new beginning in archaeological theory. However, others saw "postprocessualism" as simply a development of some of the ideas and theoretical problems introduced by the New Archaeology. To these critics it brought in a variety of approaches from other disciplines, so that the term "postprocessual" was a shade arrogant in presuming to supersede what it might quite properly claim to complement. The term "interpretive archaeologies" (plural) has been suggested as a more positive label than "postprocessual."

In recent times, the majority of postprocessual archaeologists have taken a less aggressively anti-scientific tone, and the emphasis has instead been upon the use of a variety of personal and often humanistic insights to develop a range of different fields and interests, recognizing the varied perspectives of different social groups. Ian Hodder's work at the early farming site of Çatalhöyük in

KEY INFLUENCES
Postprocessual Archaeology

Postprocessualism is a collective term for a number of approaches to the past, all of which have roots in the post-modernist current of thought that developed in the 1980s and 1990s.

The neo-Marxist element has a strong commitment to social awareness: that it is the duty of the archaeologist not only to describe the past, but to use such insights to change the present world. This contrasts quite strikingly with the aspirations towards objectivity of many processual archaeologists.

The *post-positivist* approach rejects the emphasis on the systematic procedures of scientific method which are such a feature of processual archaeology, sometimes seeing modern science as hostile to the individual, as forming an integral part of the "systems of domination" by which the forces of capitalism exert their "hegemony."

The *phenomenological* approach lays stress on the personal experiences of the individual and on the way in which encounters with the material world and with the objects in it shape our understanding of the world. In landscape archaeology, for example, the archaeologist sets out to experience the humanly shaped landscape as it has been modified and formed by human activities.

The *praxis* approach lays stress upon the central role of the human "agent" and upon the primary significance of human actions (praxis) in shaping social structure. Many social norms and social structures are established and shaped by habitual experience (and the notion of *habitus* similarly refers to the unspoken strategy-generating principles employed by the individual which mediate between social structure and practice). The role of the individual as a significant agent is thus emphasized.

The *hermeneutic* (or interpretive) view rejects generalization, another feature of processual archaeology. Emphasis is laid, rather, upon the uniqueness of each society and culture and on the need to study the full context of each in all its rich diversity. A related view stresses that there can be no single correct interpretation: each observer or analyst is entitled to their own opinion about the past. There will therefore be a diversity of opinions, and a wide range of perspectives – which is why the emphasis is on interpretive archaeologies (plural).

Turkey provides a good example of this approach in action. It is now recognized that there is no single or coherent postprocessual archaeology, but rather a whole series of interpretive approaches and interests.

One of the strengths of the interpretive approach is to bring into central focus the actions and thoughts of individuals in the past. It argues that in order to understand and interpret the past, it is necessary to "get inside the minds" and think the thoughts of the people in question. This might seem a logical goal when examining symbolic systems (for example figurative artworks employing a complex **iconography**) but there is in reality no easy way to get into other people's minds, especially past minds.

Whatever the methodological problems, the consequence of the various debates has been to broaden the range of archaeological theory in a positive manner and to emphasize the symbolic and cognitive aspects of human endeavor in a way that the early New Archaeology failed to do.

The Widening Field

The postprocessual archaeologists are certainly right in arguing that our own interpretation and presentation of the past involve choices which depend less on an objective assessment of the data than on the feelings and opinions of the researchers and of the clients whom they aim to please. The great national museum in the United States, the Smithsonian Institution in Washington, D.C., found it almost impossible to mount an exhibition in 1995 dealing with the destruction of Hiroshima 50 years earlier, without exciting the anger both of ex-servicemen and of liberals respectful of Japanese sensibilities.

It is evident that archaeology cannot avoid being caught up in the issues of the day, social and political as well as intellectual. An example is the influence of feminist thinking and the growth of feminist archaeology, which overlaps with the relatively new field of gender studies. A pioneer in the emphasis of the importance of women in prehistory was Marija Gimbutas. Her research in the Balkans led her to create a vision of an "Old Europe" associated with the first farmers whose central focus was (or so she argued) a belief in a great Mother Goddess figure. Although many feminist archaeologists today would take issue with certain aspects of Gimbutas' approach, she has certainly helped foster the current debate on gender roles.

In an article published in 1984, Margaret Conkey and Janet Spector drew attention to the androcentrism (male bias) of the discipline of archaeology. As Margaret Conkey pointed out, there existed a need "to reclaim women's experience as valid, to theorize this experience, and to use this to build a program of political action."

The deeply pervasive nature of androcentric thinking in most interpretations of the past should not be underestimated: the gender-specific terminology of

"Man the Toolmaker," even when swept away with every reference to "mankind" corrected to "humankind," does in fact conceal further, widely held assumptions or prejudices – for instance that Paleolithic stone tools were mainly made by men rather than women, for which there is little or no evidence.

The box overleaf describes some of the more high-profile female archaeologists who have made important contributions to the discipline, but feminist archaeologists can with justice point to the imbalances between female and male professionals among archaeologists today; the goal of "political action" may be seen as justified by current social realities. In the 1990s feminist concern over androcentrism became one voice among many questioning the supposed objectivity and political neutrality of archaeology.

The Development of Public Archaeology

A further turning point came during the later 20th century in the archaeology of many countries with the development of public archaeology – that is to say archaeology supported through resources made available as a public obligation. This came with the growing realization that the potential knowledge about the historic (or prehistoric) past embedded in the archaeological record – the material remains of that past – is a resource of public importance, both nationally and internationally. And that the destruction of that past without adequate record should be avoided.

From these realizations came the widespread acceptance that these material remains of the past should be protected and conserved. Moreover, if commercial development sometimes required damage or destruction to that resource, steps should be taken to mitigate that damage through conservation and through recording. There are three key principles here:

- The material record of the past is a public resource which should be managed for the public good;
- When practical circumstances make inevitable some damage to that record, steps should be taken to mitigate the impact through appropriate survey, excavation and research;
- The developer pays: the persons or organizations initiating the eventual impact (usually through building works undertaken for economic reasons) should fund the necessary actions in mitigation.

The nations of the world have in practice developed different legal frameworks to deal with these problems. They vary from country to country. In France the approach is termed "preventative archaeology," in Britain "**rescue archaeology**," and in the United States "**Cultural Resource Management**."

These issues are worth emphasizing. In those countries with legislation protecting the material record of the past, a large proportion of the resources devoted toward archaeology come through these practices of conservation and

WOMEN PIONEERS OF ARCHAEOLOGY

Dorothy Garrod, one of the first to study the prehistoric Near East systematically.

The story of many early women archaeologists was one of exclusion and lack of recognition or promotion – or even employment. Furthermore, many brilliant academic women accepted that, after marriage, their career would no longer be a professional one, and supported the academic work of their husband with little public recognition. This has remained so until the present time, so the achievements of the following pioneers, spanning the 19th and 20th centuries, stand out all the more.

Harriet Boyd Hawes
This well-educated American majored in Classics and was fluent in Greek. Just after graduating, in her early twenties, she spent several seasons riding around Crete on muleback, in dangerous territory, alone or in the company of a woman friend, looking for prehistoric sites. In 1901 she discovered the Bronze Age site of Gournia – the first Minoan town site ever unearthed – which she excavated for the next three years, supervising a hundred local workmen. She published her findings in exemplary fashion in a lavishly illustrated report that is still consulted today.

Gertrude Caton-Thompson
A wealthy British researcher who followed courses in prehistory and **anthropology** at Cambridge, Caton-Thompson subsequently became well known for her pioneering inter-disciplinary project of survey and excavation in the Fayum of Egypt; and later, perhaps most famously, at Great Zimbabwe, where her excavations in 1929 unearthed datable artifacts from a stratified **context**, and confirmed that the site represented a major culture of African origin.

Dorothy Garrod
In 1937 Dorothy Garrod became the first woman professor in any subject at Cambridge, and probably the first woman prehistorian to achieve professorial status anywhere in the world. Her excavations at Zarzi in Iraq and Mount Carmel in Palestine provided the key to a large section of the Near East, from the Middle Paleolithic to the **Mesolithic**, and found fossil human remains crucial to our knowledge of the relationship between Neanderthals and *Homo sapiens*. With her discovery of the Natufian culture, the predecessor of the world's first farming societies, she posed a series of new problems still not fully resolved today.

Harriet Boyd Hawes (in 1892), discoverer of the Minoan town site of Gournia, Crete.

Gertrude Caton-Thompson – her work at Great Zimbabwe confirmed that the site was the work of a major African culture.

Anna O. Shepard was an acknowledged expert in the ceramics of the American Southwest and Mesoamerica.

Kathleen Kenyon was a great excavator and worked at two of the most important and complex sites in the Near East, Jericho and Jerusalem.

Tatiana Proskouriakoff – her work on Maya glyphs contributed greatly to their final decipherment.

Anna O. Shepard

An American who studied archaeology as well as a wide range of hard sciences, Shepard subsequently became a specialist in ceramics, as well as Mesoamerican and Southwestern archaeology. She was one of the pioneers of petrographic analysis of archaeological pottery, focusing on sherd paste, paint, and **temper**. She published extensively on the technology of New World pottery, and wrote a standard work, *Ceramics for the Archaeologist*.

Kathleen Kenyon

A formidable British archaeologist, Kenyon trained on Roman sites in Britain under Sir Mortimer Wheeler, and adopted his method, with its close control over stratigraphy. She subsequently applied this approach in the Near East at two of the most complex and most excavated sites in Palestine: Jericho and Jerusalem. At Jericho, in 1952–58, she found evidence that pushed back the date of occupation to the end of the Ice Age, and uncovered the walled village of the Neolithic farming community, commonly referred to as "the earliest town in the world."

Tatiana Proskouriakoff

Born in Siberia, Proskouriakoff moved with her family to Pennsylvania in 1916. Unemployed after graduating as an architect in 1930 during the Great Depression, she ended up working as a museum artist in the University of Pennsylvania. A visit to the Maya site of Piedras Negras led her to devote the rest of her life to Maya architecture, art, and hieroglyphs.

Mary Leakey

A cigar-smoking, whisky-drinking, British archaeologist who, together with her husband Louis, transformed their chosen field. They worked for almost half a century at many sites in East Africa, carrying out meticulous excavations, most notably at Olduvai Gorge, Tanzania, and at Laetoli, where she excavated the famous trails of fossilized hominin footprints, made 3.7 million years ago.

Mary Leakey worked for almost half a century at various early hominin sites in East Africa, transforming our knowledge of human development.

mitigation, as governed by national legislation. The protective system in place is influential for the way archaeology is conducted and for the way students are trained. We return to these important issues in Chapter 12.

Indigenous Archaeologies

Comparable questions have continued to emerge in the developing indigenous archaeologies in the territories of former colonies, now freed from the previous imperial power. The appropriate policy for cultural heritage management, and indeed the very nature of the cultural heritage itself, are often contested among competing interest groups, sometimes along ethnic lines. Marginalized groups, such as the Australian Aborigines, have sought to achieve more influence in the definition and management of the heritage, and have often found their interests overlooked and misunderstood.

Deeper questions arise, however, about the nature of the "globalization" process, itself the outcome of technological advances developed in the West, and whether the very notion of "cultural heritage" as commonly understood may not be a product of Western thought. The Western-conceived notion of Cultural Heritage Management has been seen by post-colonial thinkers as an imposition of Western values, with officially endorsed notions of "heritage" perhaps leading to homogenization and the undervaluation of cultural diversity. Even the UNESCO-sponsored listing of "World Heritage Sites," from the standpoint of this critique, is dominated by Western-formulated notions of "heritage."

While some aspects of archaeology at the beginning of the new millennium were inevitably controversial, they were also in some ways very positive. They emphasized the value and importance of the past for the contemporary world, and they led to the realization that the cultural heritage is an important part of the human environment, and in some ways as fragile as the natural environment. They imply, then, that the archaeologist has an important role to play in achieving a balanced view also of our present world, which is inescapably the product of the worlds which have preceded it. The task of interpretation is now seen as very much more complex than it once seemed.

STUDY QUESTIONS
• Why is the study of stratification important to archaeology?
• Why was the invention of radiocarbon dating so momentous?
• How did the New Archaeology differ from classificatory-historical archaeology?
• What are some postprocessual approaches to archaeology?
• What is feminist archaeology?
• Why has "public archaeology" become important in recent decades?

SUMMARY

- The history of archaeology is a history of new ideas, methods, and discoveries. Modern archaeology took root in the 19th century with the acceptance of three key concepts: the great antiquity of humanity, Darwin's principle of evolution, and the Three Age System for ordering material culture.

- Many of the early civilizations, especially in the Old World, had been discovered by the 1880s, and some of their ancient scripts deciphered. This was followed by a long phase of consolidation – of improvements in fieldwork and excavation and the establishment of regional chronologies.

- After World War II the pace of change in the discipline quickened. New ecological approaches sought to help us understand human adaptation to the environment. New scientific techniques introduced among other things reliable means of dating the prehistoric past. The New Archaeology of the 1960s and 1970s turned to questions not just of what happened when, but why, in an attempt to explain processes of change. Meanwhile, pioneer fieldworkers studying whole regions opened up a truly world archaeology in time and space – in time back from the present to the earliest toolmakers, and in space across all the world's continents.

- More recently a diversity of theoretical approaches, often grouped under the label postprocessual, highlighted the variety of possible interpretations and the sensitivity of their political implications.

- Precisely how archaeologists are continuing to push back the frontiers of knowledge about our planet's human past forms the subject of the rest of this book.

FURTHER READING

Good introductions to the history of archaeology include:

Bahn, P.G. (ed.). 1999. *The Cambridge Illustrated History of Archaeology*. Cambridge University Press: Cambridge & New York.

Daniel, G. & Renfrew, C. 1988. *The Idea of Prehistory*. Edinburgh University Press: Edinburgh; Columbia University Press: New York.

Fagan, B.M. 2004. *A Brief History of Archaeology: Classical Times to the Twenty-First Century*. Prentice Hall: Upper Saddle River, N.J.

Johnson, M. 2010. *Archaeological Theory, an Introduction*. (2nd ed.) Wiley-Blackwell: Oxford.

Lowenthal, D. 1999. *The Past is a Foreign Country*. Cambridge University Press: Cambridge & New York.

Trigger, B.G. 2006. *A History of Archaeological Thought*. (2nd ed.) Cambridge University Press: Cambridge & New York.

Renfrew, C. & Bahn, P. (eds.). 2004. *Key Concepts in Archaeology*. Routledge: London & New York.

Willey, G.R. & Sabloff, J.A. 1993. *A History of American Archaeology*. (3rd ed.) Freeman: New York.

What Is Left?
The variety of the evidence

The relics of past human activity are all around us. Some of them were deliberate constructions, built to last, like the pyramids of Egypt, the Great Wall of China, or the temples of Mesoamerica and India. Others, like the remains of the Maya irrigation systems of Mexico and Belize, are the visible relics of activities the aim of which was not primarily to impress the observer, but which still command respect today for the scale of the enterprise they document.

Most of the remains of **archaeology** are far more modest, however. They are the discarded garbage from the daily activities of human existence: the food remains, the bits of broken pottery, the fractured stone tools, the debris that everywhere is formed as people go about their daily lives.

In this chapter we define the basic archaeological terms, briefly survey the scope of the surviving evidence and look at the great variety of ways in which it has been preserved for us. From the frozen soil of the Russian steppes, for instance, have come the wonderful finds of Pazyryk, those great chieftains' burials where wood and textiles and skins are splendidly preserved. From the dry caves of Peru and other arid environments have come remarkable textiles, baskets, and other remains that often perish completely. And by contrast, from wetlands, whether the swamps of Florida or the lake villages of Switzerland, further organic remains are being recovered, this time preserved not by the absence of moisture, but by its abundant presence to the exclusion of air.

Extremes of temperature and of humidity have preserved much. So too have natural disasters. The volcanic eruption that destroyed Pompeii and Herculaneum in Italy is the most famous of them, but there have been others, such as the eruption of the Ilopango volcano in El Salvador in the 2nd century AD, which buried land surfaces and settlement remains in a large part of the southern Maya area.

Unfortunately most archaeological **sites** are not in areas subjected to extremes of climate or volcanic activity, and levels of preservation can vary enormously. Our knowledge of the early human past is dependent in this way on the human activities and natural processes that have formed the archaeological record, and

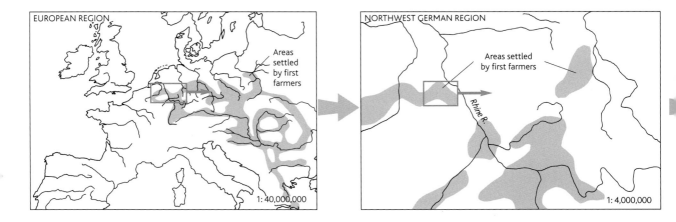

on those further processes that determine, over long periods of time, what is left and what is gone for ever. Today we can hope to recover much of what *is* left, and to learn from it by asking the right questions in the right way.

BASIC CATEGORIES OF ARCHAEOLOGICAL EVIDENCE

The evidence studied by archaeologists very often includes **artifacts** – objects used, modified, or made by people. But equally important is the study of organic and environmental remains – known as "**ecofacts**" – that, although not made by humans, can still be very revealing about many aspects of past human activity. Much archaeological research concentrates on the analysis of these artifacts and ecofacts that are found together on *sites*, which in turn are most productively studied together with their surrounding landscapes and grouped together into *regions*. Some of these different scales at which archaeologists operate, as well as the terminology they use, are illustrated above and opposite.

Artifacts are humanly made or modified portable objects, such as stone tools, pottery, and metal weapons. But artifacts provide evidence to help us answer all the key questions – not just technological ones – addressed in this book. A single clay vessel or pot can be analyzed in a number of different ways. The clay may be tested to produce a date for the vessel and thus perhaps a date for the location where it was found. It could also be tested to find the source of the clay and thus give evidence for the range and contacts of the group that made the vessel. Pictorial decoration on the pot's surface could help to form or be related to a sequence of design **styles** (a **typology**), and it could tell us something about ancient beliefs, particularly if it shows gods or other figures. And analysis of the vessel's shape and any food or other residues found in it can yield information about the pot's use, perhaps in cooking, as well as about ancient diet.

Some researchers broaden the meaning of the term "artifact" to include all humanly modified components of a site or landscape, such as hearths, postholes, and storage pits – but these non-portable artifacts are more usefully described as

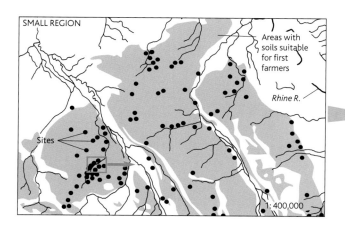

SMALL REGION

Areas with soils suitable for first farmers

Rhine R.

Sites

1: 400,000

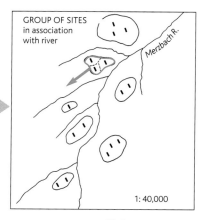

GROUP OF SITES in association with river

Merzbach R.

1: 40,000

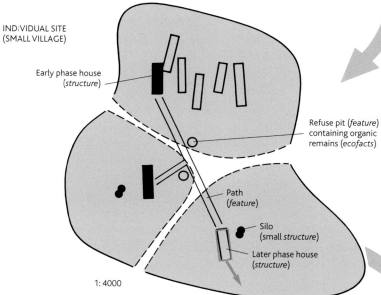

INDIVIDUAL SITE (SMALL VILLAGE)

Early phase house (*structure*)

Refuse pit (*feature*) containing organic remains (*ecofacts*)

Path (*feature*)

Silo (small *structure*)

Later phase house (*structure*)

1: 4000

Different scales and terminology used in archaeology, from the continental region (opposite page, top left) to the individual structure (right). In this representation of the pattern of settlement of Europe's first farmers (5th millennium BC), the archaeologist might study – at the broader scale – the interesting association between sites and light, easily worked soils near rivers. At the smaller scale, the association – established by excavation – of houses with other houses and with structures such as silos for grain storage raises questions, for example, about social organization and permanence of occupation at this period.

INDIVIDUAL STRUCTURE (HOUSE)

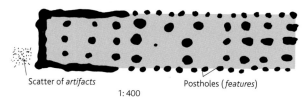

Scatter of *artifacts*

1: 400

Postholes (*features*)

Artifacts and features are found *in association with* the structure

Types of Evidence

- *Artifacts*: portable objects used, modified, or made by humans

- *Ecofacts*: organic and environmental remains not made by humans

- *Features*: non-portable artifacts

- *Sites*: places where artifacts, ecofacts, and features are found together

features. Simple features such as postholes may themselves, or in combination with remains of hearths, floors, ditches, etc., give evidence for complex features or structures, defined as buildings of all kinds, from houses and granaries to palaces and temples.

Non-artifactual organic and environmental remains or *ecofacts* include human skeletons, animal bones, and plant remains, but also soils and sediments – all of which may shed light on past human activities. They are important because they can indicate, for example, what people ate or the environmental conditions under which they lived.

Archaeological *sites* may be thought of as the huge variety of places where artifacts, features, structures, and organic and environmental remains are found together. For working purposes we can simplify this still further and define sites as places where significant traces of human activity are identified. Thus a village or town is a site, and so too is an isolated monument like Serpent Mound in Ohio. Equally, a surface scatter of stone tools or potsherds may represent a site occupied for no more than a few hours, whereas a Near Eastern **tell** or mound is a site indicating human occupation over perhaps thousands of years.

The Importance of Context

In order to reconstruct past human activity at a site it is crucially important to understand the **context** of a find, whether artifact, ecofact, or feature. A find's context consists of its immediate **matrix** (the material surrounding it, usually some sort of sediment such as gravel, sand, or clay), its *provenience* (horizontal and vertical position within the matrix), and its **association** with other finds (occurrence together with other archaeological remains, usually in the same matrix). In the 19th century the demonstration that stone tools were often associated with the bones of extinct animals in a sealed matrix helped establish the idea of the great antiquity of humankind.

KEY CONCEPTS

Context

- *Matrix*: the material surrounding a find (an artifact, ecofact, or feature)

- *Provenience*: the exact position of a find within the matrix

- *Association*: a find's relationship with other finds

- Without context, an artifact loses much of its archaeological value

Increasingly since then archaeologists have recognized the importance of identifying and accurately recording associations between remains on sites. This is why it is such a tragedy when looters dig up sites indiscriminately looking for rich finds, without recording matrix, provenience, or associations. All the contextual information is lost. A looted vase may be an attractive object for a collector, but far more could have been learnt about the society that produced it had archaeologists been able to record where it was found (in a tomb, ditch, or house?) and in association with what other artifacts or organic remains (weapons, tools, or animal bones?). Much information about the Mimbres people of the American Southwest has been lost forever because looters bulldozed their sites, hunting for the superbly painted – and highly sought after – bowls made by the Mimbres 1000 years ago.

When modern (or ancient) looters disturb a site, perhaps shifting aside material they are not interested in, they destroy that material's *primary context*. If archaeologists subsequently excavate that shifted material, they need to be able to recognize that it is in a *secondary context*. This may be straightforward for, say, a Mimbres site, looted quite recently, but it is much more difficult for a site disturbed in antiquity. Nor is disturbance confined to human activity: archaeologists dealing with the tens of thousands of years of the Old Stone Age or **Paleolithic** period know well that the forces of nature – encroaching seas or ice sheets, wind and water action – invariably destroy primary context. A great many of the Stone Age tools found in European river gravels are in a secondary context, transported by water action far from their original, primary context.

FORMATION PROCESSES

In recent years archaeologists have become increasingly aware that a whole series of **formation processes** may have affected both the way in which finds came to be buried and what happened to them after they were buried. The study of these processes is called *taphonomy*.

A useful distinction has been made between *cultural formation processes* and noncultural or *natural formation processes*. Cultural formation processes involve the deliberate or accidental activities of human beings as they make or use artifacts, build or abandon buildings, plow their fields, and so on. Natural formation processes are natural events that govern both the burial and the survival of the archaeological record. The sudden fall of volcanic ash that covered Pompeii is an exceptional example; a more common one would be the gradual burial of artifacts or features by wind-borne sand or soil. Likewise the transporting of stone tools by river action, referred to above, or the activities of animals – burrowing into a site or chewing bones and pieces of wood – are also examples of natural formation processes.

Early humans as mighty hunters (above) or mere scavengers (below)? Our understanding of formation processes governs the way in which we interpret associations of human tools with animal bones from the fossil record in Africa.

At first sight these distinctions may seem of little interest to the archaeologist. In fact they are vital to the accurate reconstruction of past human activities. It can be important to know whether certain archaeological evidence is the product of human or non-human (cultural or natural) activity. If, for example, you are trying to reconstruct human woodworking activities by studying cutmarks on timber, then you should learn to recognize certain kinds of marks made by beavers using their teeth and to distinguish these from cutmarks made by humans using stone or metal tools.

Let us take an even more significant example. For the earliest phases of human existence in Africa, at the beginning of the Old Stone Age or Paleolithic period, theories about our primitive hunting ability have been based on the association between stone tools and animal bones found at archaeological sites. The bones were assumed to be those of animals hunted and slaughtered by early humans who made the tools. But studies of animal behavior and cutmarks on animal bones suggest that in many cases the excavated bones are the remains of

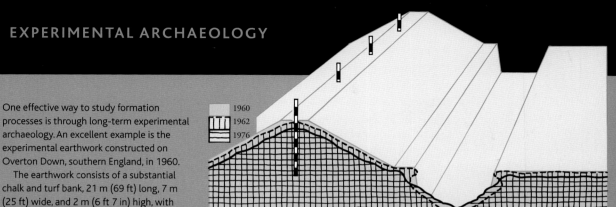

One effective way to study formation processes is through long-term experimental archaeology. An excellent example is the experimental earthwork constructed on Overton Down, southern England, in 1960.

The earthwork consists of a substantial chalk and turf bank, 21 m (69 ft) long, 7 m (25 ft) wide, and 2 m (6 ft 7 in) high, with a ditch cut parallel to it. The aim of the experiment has been to assess not only how the bank and ditch alter through time, but also what happens to materials such as pottery, leather, and textiles that were buried in the earthwork in 1960. Sections (trenches) have been – or will be – cut across the bank and ditch at intervals of 2, 4, 8, 16, 32, 64, and 128 years (in real time, 1962, 1964, 1968, 1976, 1992, 2024, and 2088): a considerable commitment for all concerned.

On this timescale, the project is still at a relatively early stage. But preliminary results are interesting. In the 1960s the bank dropped some 25 cm (10 in) in height and the ditch silted up quite rapidly. Since the

The bank and ditch as cut in 1960, together with the changes revealed by sections cut across the earthwork in 1962 and 1976.

mid-1970s, however, the structure has stabilized. As for the buried materials, tests after four years showed that pottery was unchanged and leather little affected, but textiles were already becoming weakened and discolored.

The 1992 excavations revealed that preservation was better in the chalk bank, which is less biologically active, than in the turf core where textiles and some wood had

completely disappeared. The structure itself had changed little since 1976, though there was considerable reworking and transport of fine sediment by earthworms.

The experiment has already shown that many of the changes that interest archaeologists occur within decades of burial, and that the extent of these changes can be far greater than had hitherto been suspected.

animals hunted and largely eaten by other predatory animals. The humans with their stone tools would have come upon the scene as mere scavengers, at the end of a pecking order of different animal species. By no means everyone agrees with this scavenging hypothesis. The point to emphasize here is that the issue can best be resolved by improving our techniques for distinguishing between cultural and natural formation processes – between human and non-human activity. Many studies are now focusing on the need to clarify how to differentiate cutmarks on bones made by stone tools from those made by the teeth of animal predators. Modern experiments using replica stone tools to cut meat off bones are one helpful approach. Other kinds of **experimental archaeology** can be most instructive about some of the formation processes that affect physical preservation of archaeological material (see box above).

The remainder of this chapter is devoted to a more detailed discussion of the different cultural and natural formation processes.

CULTURAL FORMATION PROCESSES – HOW PEOPLE HAVE AFFECTED WHAT SURVIVES IN THE ARCHAEOLOGICAL RECORD

We may separate these processes rather crudely into two kinds: those that reflect the original human behavior and activity before a find or site became buried; and those (such as plowing or looting) that came after burial. Now of course most major archaeological sites are formed as the result of a complex sequence of use, burial, and reuse repeated many times over, so that a simple two-fold division of cultural formation processes may not be so simple to apply in practice. Nevertheless, since one of our main aims is to reconstruct original human behavior and activity, we must make the attempt.

Original human behavior is often reflected archaeologically in at least four major activities: for example, in the case of a tool (see diagram below) there may be

1 *acquisition* of the raw material;
2 *manufacture*;
3 *use* (and *distribution*); and finally
4 *disposal* or *discard* when the tool is worn out or broken. (The tool may of course be reworked and recycled, i.e. repeating stages 2 and 3.)

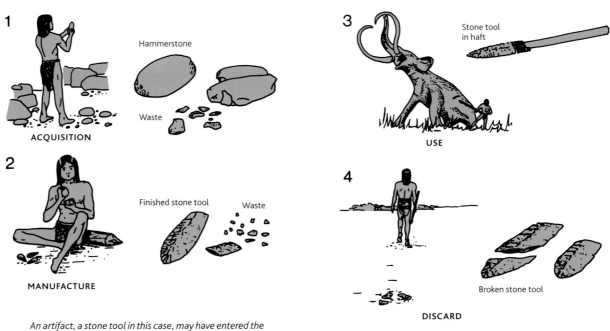

1 Hammerstone Waste **ACQUISITION**

2 Finished stone tool Waste **MANUFACTURE**

3 Stone tool in haft **USE**

4 Broken stone tool **DISCARD**

An artifact, a stone tool in this case, may have entered the archaeological record at any one of these four stages in its life cycle. The archaeologist's task is to determine which stage is represented by the find in question.

Similarly, a food crop such as wheat will be acquired (harvested), manufactured (processed), used (eaten), and discarded (digested and the waste products excreted) – here we might add a common intermediate stage of *storage* before use. From the archaeologist's point of view the critical factor is that remains can enter the archaeological record at any one of these stages – a tool may be lost or thrown out as inferior quality during manufacture, a crop may be accidentally burnt and thus preserved during processing. In order accurately to reconstruct the original activity it is therefore crucial to try to understand which of the stages we are looking at. It may be quite easy to identify, say, the first stage for stone tools, because stone quarries can often be recognized by deep holes in the ground with piles of associated waste flakes and blanks which survive well. But it is much more difficult to know beyond reasonable doubt whether a sample of charred plant remains comes from, say, a threshing area or an occupation area – and this may also make it difficult to reconstruct the true plant diet, since certain activities may favor the preservation of certain species of plant.

Deliberate burial of valuables is another major aspect of original human behavior that has left its mark on the archaeological record. In times of conflict or war people often deposit prized possessions in the ground, intending to reclaim them at a later date but sometimes for one reason or another failing to do so. These **hoards** are a prime source of evidence for certain periods, such as the European Bronze Age, for which hoards of metal goods are common, or later Roman Britain, which has yielded buried treasures of silver and other precious metals. The archaeologist, however, may not find it easy to distinguish between hoards originally intended to be recovered and valuables buried with no reclamation intended, perhaps to placate supernatural powers (placed for example at a particularly dangerous part of a crossing over a bog).

How archaeologists set about trying to demonstrate belief in supernatural powers and an afterlife will be seen in Chapter 9. Here we may note that, in addition to hoards, the major source of evidence comes from *burial of the dead*, whether in simple graves, elaborate burial mounds, or giant pyramids, usually with grave-goods such as ceramic vessels or weapons, and sometimes with painted tomb-chamber walls, as in ancient Mexico or Egypt. The Egyptians indeed went so far as to mummify their dead – to preserve them, they hoped, for eternity – as did the Incas of Peru, whose kings were kept in the Temple of the Sun at Cuzco and brought outside for special ceremonies.

Human destruction of the archaeological record might be caused by burials of the kind just described being dug into earlier deposits. But people in the past deliberately or accidentally obliterated traces of their predecessors in innumerable other ways. Rulers, for instance, often destroyed monuments or erased inscriptions belonging to previous chiefs or monarchs. Some human destruction meant to obliterate has inadvertently preserved material for the archaeologist to find. Burning, for example, may not always destroy. It can often improve the chances of survival of a variety of remains such as of plants: the conversion into carbon greatly increases the powers of resistance to the ravages of time. Clay daubing and adobe usually decay, but if a structure has been fired, the mud is baked to the consistency of a brick. In the same way thousands of clay writing tablets from the Near East have been baked accidentally or deliberately in fires and thus preserved. Timbers too may char and survive in structures, or at least leave a clear impression in the hardened mud.

Today human destruction of the archaeological record continues at a frightening pace, through land drainage, plowing, building work, looting, etc. In Chapter 10 we discuss how this affects archaeology generally and what the potential implications are for the future.

NATURAL FORMATION PROCESSES – HOW NATURE AFFECTS WHAT SURVIVES IN THE ARCHAEOLOGICAL RECORD

We saw above how natural formation processes such as river action can disturb or destroy the primary context of archaeological material. Here we will focus on that material itself, and the natural processes that cause decay or lead to preservation. Practically any archaeological material can survive in exceptional circumstances. Usually, however, inorganic materials survive far better than organic ones.

Inorganic Materials

The most common inorganic materials to survive archaeologically are stone, clay, and metals.

Stone tools survive extraordinarily well – some are over 2 million years old. Not surprisingly they have always been our main source of evidence for human

KEY CONCEPTS

Survival of Inorganic Materials

- Stone tools, fired clay, and some metals such as gold, silver, and lead, survive very well in nearly all environments

- Some metals, such as copper, can corrode depending on the soil conditions, and iron rarely survives in an uncorroded state

- Although inorganic materials, particularly stone tools and pottery, are very often found at archaeological sites, these objects may well have been equalled or superseded in abundance and importance by objects that usually do not survive, such as wooden tools or baskets

activities during the Old Stone Age, even though wooden and bone tools (which are less likely to be preserved) may originally have equalled stone ones in importance. Stone tools sometimes come down to us so little damaged or altered from their primary state that archaeologists can examine microscopic patterns of wear on their cutting edges and learn, for example, whether the tools were used to cut wood or animal hides. This is now a major branch of archaeological inquiry.

Fired clay, such as pottery and baked mud-brick or adobe, is virtually indestructible if well fired. It is therefore again not surprising that for the periods after the introduction of pottery making (some 16,000 years ago in Japan, and 9000 years ago in the Near East and parts of South America) ceramics have traditionally been the archaeologist's main source of evidence. As we saw at the beginning of this chapter, pots can be studied for their shape, surface decoration, mineral content, and even the food or other residues left inside them. Acid soils can damage the surface of fired clay, and porous or badly fired clay vessels or mud brick can become fragile in humid conditions. However, even disintegrated mud brick can help to assess rebuilding phases in, for instance, Peruvian villages or Near Eastern tells.

Metals such as gold, silver, and lead survive well. Copper, and bronze with a low-quality alloy, are attacked by acid soils, and can become so oxidized that only a green deposit or stain is left. Oxidation is also a rapid and powerful agent of destruction of iron, which rusts and may similarly leave only a discoloration in the soil.

The sea is potentially very destructive. Underwater remains can be broken and scattered by currents, waves, or tidal action. On the other hand, the sea can cause metals to be coated with a thick, hard casing of metallic salts from the objects themselves; this helps to preserve the artifacts. If the remains are simply taken out of the water and not treated, the salts react with air, and give off acid which destroys the remaining metal. But the use of **electrolysis** – placing the object in a chemical solution and passing a weak current through it – leaves the metal artifact clean and safe. This is a standard procedure in underwater archaeology and is used on all types of objects from cannons to the finds recovered from the *Titanic*.

Organic Materials

Survival of organic materials is determined largely by the matrix (the surrounding material) and by climate (local and regional) – with the occasional influence of natural disasters such as volcanic eruptions, which are often far from disastrous for archaeologists.

The *matrix*, as we saw earlier, is usually some kind of sediment or soil. These vary in their effects on organic material; chalk, for example, preserves human and animal bone well (in addition to inorganic metals). Acid soils destroy bones and wood within a few years, but will leave telltale discolorations where postholes or hut foundations once stood. Similar brown or black marks survive in sandy soils, as do dark silhouettes which used to be skeletons.

But the immediate matrix may in exceptional circumstances have an additional component such as metal ore, salt, or oil. Copper can favor the preservation of organic remains, perhaps by preventing the activity of destructive micro-organisms. The prehistoric copper (and salt) mines of central and southeast Europe have many remains of wood, leather, and textiles.

A combination of salt and oil ensured the preservation of a woolly rhinoceros at Starunia, Poland, with skin intact, and the leaves and fruits of tundra vegetation around it. The animal had been carried by a strong current into a pool saturated with crude oil and salt from a natural oil seep, which prevented decomposition: bacteria could not operate in these conditions, while salt had permeated the skin and preserved it. Similarly, the asphalt pits of La Brea, Los Angeles, are world famous for the large quantities and fine condition of the skeletons of a wide range of prehistoric animals and birds recovered from them.

Climate plays an important role too in the preservation of organic remains. Occasionally the "local climate" of an environment such as a cave preserves finds. Caves are natural "conservatories" because their interiors are protected from outside climatic effects, and (in the case of limestone caves) their alkaline conditions permit excellent preservation. If undisturbed by floods or the trampling feet of animals and people, they can preserve bones and even such fragile remains as footprints.

More usually, however, it is the regional climate that is important. *Tropical climates* are the most destructive, with their combination of heavy rains, acid

KEY CONCEPTS
Survival of Organic Materials

The main factors that determine survival are:

- Matrix: the conditions and make-up of the soil or sediment surrounding the material (which only in special circumstances preserve organic material)

- Climate: the local and regional weather conditions, which in turn affect soils, erosion, flora, and fauna

- Natural disasters, such as volcanic eruptions, and extremes of dry, cold, and wet climates

soils, warm temperatures, high humidity, erosion, and wealth of vegetation and insect life. Tropical rainforests can overwhelm a site remarkably quickly, with roots that dislodge masonry and tear buildings apart, while torrential downpours gradually destroy paint and plasterwork, and woodwork rots away completely. Archaeologists in southern Mexico, for example, constantly have to battle to keep back the jungle. On the other hand, jungle conditions can be positive, in that they hinder looters from easily reaching even more sites than they do already.

Temperate climates, as in much of Europe and North America, are not good, as a rule, for the preservation of organic materials; their relatively warm but variable temperatures and fluctuating rainfall combine to accelerate the processes of decay. In some circumstances, however, local conditions can counteract these processes. At the Roman fort of Vindolanda, near Hadrian's Wall in northern England, over 1300 letters and documents, written in ink on wafer-thin sheets of birch and alderwood, have been found. The fragments, dating to about AD 100, have survived because of the soil's unusual chemical condition: clay compacted between layers in the site created oxygen-free pockets (the exclusion of oxygen is vital to the preservation of organic materials), while chemicals produced by bracken, bone, and other remains effectively made the land sterile in that locality, thus preventing disturbance by vegetation and other forms of life.

Natural disasters sometimes preserve sites, including organic remains, for the archaeologist. The most common are violent storms, such as that which covered the coastal **Neolithic** village of Skara Brae, Orkney Islands, with sand, the mudslide that engulfed the prehistoric village of Ozette on America's Northwest Coast (see box on p. 56), or volcanic eruptions such as that of Vesuvius, which buried and preserved Roman Pompeii under a blanket of ash. Another volcanic eruption, this time in El Salvador in about AD 595, deposited a thick and widespread layer of ash over a densely populated area of Maya settlement. Work here has uncovered a variety of organic remains at the site of Cerén, including palm and grass roofing, mats, baskets, stored grain and even preserved agricultural furrows.

Apart from these special circumstances, the survival of organic materials is limited to cases involving extremes of moisture: that is, very dry, frozen, or waterlogged conditions.

Preservation of Organic Materials: Extreme Conditions

Dry Environments. Great aridity or dryness prevents decay through the shortage of water, which ensures that many destructive micro-organisms are unable to flourish. Archaeologists first became aware of the phenomenon in Egypt (see Tutankhamun box, overleaf), where much of the Nile Valley has such a dry

EGYPT

Thebes

The arid conditions that prevail in Egypt have helped preserve a wide range of ancient materials, ranging from numerous written documents on papyrus (made of the pith of a Nile water plant) to two full-size wooden boats buried beside the Great Pyramid at Giza. But the best-known and most spectacular array of objects was that discovered in 1922 by Howard Carter and Lord Carnarvon in the tomb at Thebes of the pharaoh Tutankhamun, dating to the 14th century BC.

Tutankhamun had a short reign and was relatively insignificant in Egyptian history, a fact reflected in his burial, a poor one by pharaonic standards. But within the small tomb, originally built for someone else, was a wealth of treasure. For Tutankhamun was buried with everything he might need in the next life. The entrance corridor and the four chambers were crammed with thousands of individual grave-goods. They include objects of precious metal, like the jewelry and famous gold mask, and food and clothing. But wooden objects, such as statues, chests, shrines, and two of the three coffins, make up a large part of the tomb's contents.

The grave furniture was not all originally intended for Tutankhamun. Some of it had been made for other members of his family, and then hastily adopted when the young king died unexpectedly. There were also touching items, such as a chair the king had used as a child, and a simple reed stick mounted in gold labeled as "A reed which

His Majesty cut with his own hand." Even wreaths and funerary bouquets had survived in the dry conditions, left on the second and third coffins by mourners..

The outermost of Tutankhamun's three coffins was made of cypress wood, overlaid with gold foil.

A floral collar found remarkably well preserved among the contents of the tomb of Tutankhamun.

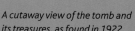

A cutaway view of the tomb and its treasures, as found in 1922.

atmosphere that bodies of the predynastic period (before 3000 BC) have survived intact, with skin, hair, and nails, without any artificial mummification or coffins – the corpses were simply placed in shallow graves in the sand. Rapid drying out, plus the draining qualities of the sand, produced such spectacular preservative effects that they probably suggested the practice of mummification to the later Egyptians of the dynastic period.

The pueblo dwellers of the American Southwest (c. AD 700–1400) buried their dead in dry caves and rockshelters where, as in Egypt, natural desiccation took place: these are not therefore true, humanly created mummies, although they are often referred to as such. The bodies survive, sometimes wrapped in fur blankets or tanned skins, and in such good condition that it has been possible to study hair styles. Clothing (from fiber sandals to string aprons) also remains, together with a wide range of goods such as basketry, feathered ornaments, and leather. Some far earlier sites in the same region also contain organic remains: Danger Cave, Utah (occupied from 9000 BC onward), yielded wooden arrows, trap springs, knife handles, and other wooden tools, while caves near Durango, Colorado, had preserved maize cobs, squashes, and sunflower and mustard seeds. Plant finds of this type have been crucial in helping to reconstruct ancient diet.

The coastal dwellers of central and southern Peru lived – and died – in a similarly dry environment, so that it is possible today to see the tattoos on their desiccated bodies, and admire the huge and dazzlingly colorful textiles from cemeteries at Ica and Nazca, as well as basketry and featherwork, and also maize cobs and other items of food. In Chile, the oldest deliberately made mummies have been found at Chinchorro, preserved again by the aridity of the desert environment.

A slightly different phenomenon occurred in the Aleutian Islands, off the west coast of Alaska, where the dead were kept and naturally preserved in volcanically warmed caves that were extremely dry. Here the islanders seem to have enhanced the natural desiccation by periodically drying the bodies by wiping or suspension over a fire; in some cases they removed the internal organs and placed dry grass in the cavity.

Cold Environments. Natural refrigeration can hold the processes of decay in check for thousands of years. Perhaps the first frozen finds to be discovered were the numerous remains of mammoths encountered in the permafrost (permanently frozen soil) of Siberia, a few with their flesh, hair, and stomach contents intact. The unlucky creatures probably fell into crevices in snow, and were buried by silt in what became a giant deep-freeze. The best known are Beresovka, recovered in 1901, and baby Dima, found in 1977. Preservation can be still so good that dogs will eat the meat and they have to be kept well away from the carcasses.

The world's oldest fully preserved human body was found in September 1991 by German hikers near the Similaun glacier, in the Ötztaler Alps of South Tyrol. They spotted a human body, its skin yellowish-brown and desiccated, at an altitude of 3200 m (10,500 ft). The Iceman is the first prehistoric human ever found with his everyday clothing and equipment; other similarly intact bodies from **prehistory** have been either carefully buried or sacrificed.

The body was placed in a freezer in Austria, but subsequent investigation determined that the corpse – called Similaun Man, Ötzi, or simply the "Iceman" – had lain c. 90 m (300 ft) inside Italy, and he has been housed there, in a museum in Bolzano, since 1998. Fifteen radiocarbon dates have been obtained from the body, the artifacts, and the grass in the boots: they are all in rough agreement, averaging at 3300 BC.

It was initially thought the Iceman was overcome by exhaustion – perhaps caught in a fog or a blizzard. After death, he was dried out by a warm autumn wind, before becoming encased in ice. Since the body lay in a depression, it was protected from the movement of the glacier above it for 5300 years, until a storm from the Sahara laid a layer of dust on the ice that absorbed sunlight and finally thawed it out.

He was a dark-skinned male, aged in his mid- to late 40s. Only about 1.56–1.6 m (5ft 2 in) tall, his size and stature fit well within the measurement ranges of Late Neolithic populations of Italy and Switzerland. Preliminary analysis of his **DNA** confirms his links to northern Europe.

The corpse currently weighs only about 54 kg (120 lb). His teeth are very worn, especially the front incisors, suggesting that he ate coarse ground grain, or that he regularly used them as a tool. When found

he was bald, but hundreds of curly brownish-black human hairs, about 9 cm (3.5 in) long, were recovered from the vicinity of the body. These had fallen out after death and it is possible he had a beard.

A body scan has shown that the brain, muscle tissues, lungs, heart, liver, and digestive organs are in excellent condition, though the lungs are blackened by smoke, probably from open fires, and he has hardening of the arteries and blood vessels. Traces of meat have been found in his colon, and his final meal seems to have consisted of meat (probably ibex and venison), wheat, plants, and plums.

Traces of chronic frostbite were noted in one little toe and eight of his ribs were fractured, though these were healed or healing when he died.

Groups of tattoos, mostly short parallel vertical blue lines were discovered on both sides of his lower spine, on his left calf and

The equipment and clothing of the Iceman are a virtual time-capsule of everyday life – over 70 objects were found associated with him.

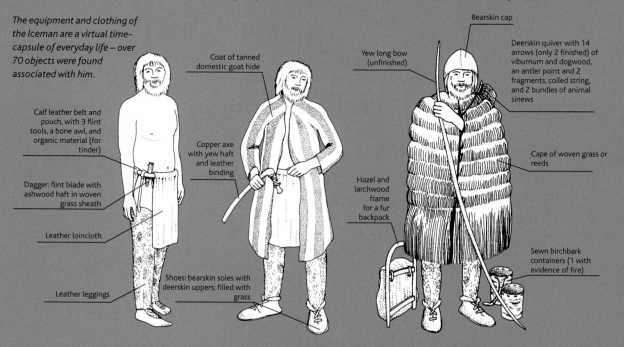

Calf leather belt and pouch, with 3 flint tools, a bone awl, and organic material (for tinder)

Dagger: flint blade with ashwood haft in woven grass sheath

Leather loincloth

Leather leggings

Coat of tanned domestic goat hide

Copper axe with yew haft and leather binding

Shoes: bearskin soles with deerskin uppers; filled with grass

Yew long bow (unfinished)

Hazel and larchwood frame for a fur backpack

Bearskin cap

Deerskin quiver with 14 arrows (only 2 finished) of viburnum and dogwood, an antler point and 2 fragments, coiled string, and 2 bundles of animal sinews

Cape of woven grass or reeds

Sewn birchbark containers (1 with evidence of fire)

right ankle, and a blue cross on his inner right knee. These marks may be therapeutic, aimed at relieving the arthritis that he had in his neck, lower back, and right hip.

His nails had dropped off, but one fingernail was recovered. Its analysis revealed not only that he undertook manual labor, but also that he experienced periods of reduced nail growth corresponding to episodes of serious illness – 4, 3, and 2 months before he died. The fact that he was prone to periodic crippling disease supported the view that he fell prey to adverse weather and froze to death. However, recent work has revealed what appears to be an arrowhead lodged in the Iceman's left shoulder, cuts on his hands, wrists, and ribcage, and a blow to the head – either from being struck or from falling – which is probably what killed him.

The items found with him constitute a unique "time-capsule" of everyday life. A great variety of woods and a range of sophisticated techniques of working with leather and grasses were used to create the collection of 70 objects, which add a new dimension to our knowledge of the period.

COLD PRESERVATION 2: MOUNTAIN "MUMMIES"

Since the 1950s, sporadic discoveries have been made of frozen bodies high in the Andes mountains of South America – these finds have become known as mummies, even though they were preserved only by the cold, not by any process of artificial mummification. The Incas of the 15th–16th centuries AD built more than 100 ceremonial centers on many of the highest peaks in their empire, since they worshipped the snowcapped mountains, believing that they provided the water for irrigating their fields, and hence controlled fertility of crops and animals.

Among the offerings left for the mountain gods were food, alcoholic drinks, textiles, pottery and figurines – but also human sacrifices, often young children. In the 1990s, American archaeologist Johan Reinhard carried out a series of expeditions to high peaks in the Andes, and discovered some of the best-preserved ancient bodies ever found, thanks to this "extreme archaeology."

On the Ampato volcano, at 6312 m (20,708 ft), he found a bundle lying on the ice which contained an Inca girl – dubbed the "Ice Maiden" or "Juanita" – who had been ritually sacrificed (by a blow to the head) at the age of about 14, and buried with figurines, food, textiles, and pottery. The buried bodies of a boy and girl were later excavated at 5850 m (19,193 ft).

In 1999, on the peak of Llullaillaco – at 6739 m (22,109 ft) – he encountered a 7-year-old boy, and two girls of 15 and 6, all with figurines and textiles. So perfect is the preservation of all these bodies that detailed analyses can be carried out on their internal organs, their DNA, and their hair. For example, isotopes in the hair suggest that they chewed coca leaves, a common practice in the region even today.

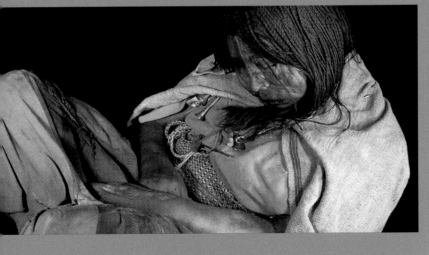

The older, better-preserved Llullaillaco girl had neatly braided hair and wore a selection of ornaments.

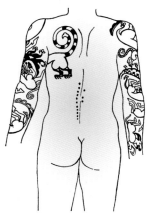

Frozen conditions in southern Siberia helped to preserve many remarkable finds from the burial mounds of steppe nomads at Pazyryk dating from about 400 BC, including this tattoo pattern on the torso and arms of a chieftain.

The most famous frozen archaeological remains are those from the burial mounds of steppe nomads at Pazyryk in the Altai, southern Siberia, dating to the Iron Age, about 400 BC. They comprise pits dug deep into the ground, lined with logs, and covered with a low cairn of stones. They could only have been dug in the warm season, before the ground froze solid. Any warm air in the graves rose and deposited its moisture on the stones of the cairn; moisture also gradually infiltrated down into the burial chambers, and froze so hard there during the harsh winter that it never thawed during subsequent summers, since the cairns were poor conductors of heat and shielded the pits from the warming and drying effects of wind and sun. Consequently, even the most fragile materials have survived intact – despite the boiling water that had to be used by excavators to recover them.

The Pazyryk bodies had been placed inside log coffins, with wooden pillows, and survived so well that their spectacular tattoos can still be seen. Clothing included linen shirts, decorated caftans, aprons, stockings, and headdresses of felt and leather. There were also rugs, wall-coverings, tables laden with food, and horse carcasses complete with elaborate bridles, saddles, and other trappings. A further well-preserved burial has been found in the region, containing a female accompanied by six horses and grave-goods including a silver mirror and various wooden objects.

Similar standards of preservation have also been encountered in other regions such as Greenland and Alaska. More southerly regions can produce the same effect at high altitude, for instance the Inca-period "mummies" found at a number of high-altitude sites in the Andes; or the 5300-year-old Iceman found preserved in the ice in the Alps near the border between Italy and Austria (see box on previous pages).

Waterlogged Environments.   A useful distinction in land archaeology (as opposed to archaeology beneath the sea) can be drawn between dryland and wetland sites. The great majority of sites are "dry" in the sense that moisture content is low and preservation of organic remains is poor. Wetland sites include all those found in lakes, swamps, marshes, fens, and peat bogs. In these situations organic materials are effectively sealed in a wet and airless environment which favors their preservation, as long as the waterlogging is more or less permanent up to the time of **excavation**. (If a wet site dries out, even only seasonally, decomposition of the organic materials can occur.)

It has been estimated that on a wet site often 75–90 percent, sometimes 100 percent, of the finds are organic. Little or none of this material, such as wood, leather, textiles, basketry, and plant remains of all kinds, would survive on most dryland sites. It is for this reason that archaeologists are turning their attention more and more to the rich sources of evidence about past human activities to be found on wet sites. Growing threats from drainage and peatcutting in the wetlands, which form only about 6 percent of the world's total land area, give this work an added urgency.

Wetlands vary a great deal in their preservative qualities. Acidic peat bogs preserve wood and plant remains, but may destroy bone, iron, and even pottery. The famous lake sites of the Alpine regions of Switzerland, Italy, France, and southern Germany on the other hand preserve most materials well. Sometimes other forces can help to preserve waterlogged remains, such as the mudslide that buried the Ozette site in Washington State (see box overleaf).

Peat bogs, nearly all of which occur in northern latitudes, are some of the most important environments for wetland archaeology. The Somerset Levels in southern England, for example, have been the scene not only of excavations in the early 20th century to recover the well-preserved Iron Age lake villages of Glastonbury and Meare, but of a much wider campaign in the last few decades that has unearthed numerous wooden trackways (including the world's "oldest road," a 6000-year-old 1.6-km (1-mile) stretch of track), and many details about early woodworking skills, and the ancient environment. On the continent of Europe, and in Ireland, peat bogs have likewise preserved many trackways – sometimes with evidence for the wooden carts that ran along them – and other fragile remains. Other types of European wetlands, such as coastal marshes, have yielded dugout logboats, paddles, even fish-nets and fish-weirs.

Bog bodies, however, are undoubtedly the best-known finds from the peat bogs of northwest Europe. Most of them date from the Iron Age. The degree of preservation varies widely, and depends on the particular conditions in which the corpses were deposited. Most individuals met a violent death and were probably either executed as criminals or killed as a sacrifice before being thrown into the bog. For example, in 2003 two partial Iron Age bodies were recovered from peat bogs in Ireland: Clonycavan Man had been killed with axe blows to the head and chest, and possibly disembowelled, while the huge (1.91 m (6 ft 3½ in) tall) Oldcroghan Man was stabbed, decapitated, and tied down to the bottom of a bog pool.

The surviving parts of Oldcroghan Man's body are superbly preserved, particularly his hands: the well-kept fingernails and absence of calluses suggest that he may have been an individual of relatively high status. Analysis of his stomach contents revealed a final meal of cereals and buttermilk.

A special kind of waterlogging occurred at the Ozette site, Washington, on the U.S. Northwest Coast. About AD 1750, a huge mudslide buried part of a whale-hunting settlement. The village lay protected for two centuries – but not forgotten, for the descendants of the village kept the memory of their ancestors' home alive. Then the sea began to strip away the mud, and it seemed as if the site would fall prey to looters. Local people called on the government to excavate the site and to protect the remains. Richard Daugherty was appointed to organize the excavation. As the mud was cleared with high-pressure hoses, a wealth of organic material came to view.

Several cedarwood long houses, up to 21 m (68 ft 3 in) in length and 14 m (45 ft 6 in) wide, were found, with adzed and carved panels (painted with black designs including wolves and thunderbirds), roof-support posts, and low partition walls. These houses contained hearths, cooking platforms, sleeping benches, and mats.

Over 50,000 artifacts were recovered in a fine state of preservation – almost half in wood or other plant material. The most spectacular was a block of red cedar, a meter high, carved in the form of a whale's dorsal fin. Even ferns and cedar leaves had survived, together with an abundance of whale bones.

The project was an excellent example of cooperation between archaeologists and indigenous peoples. The Makah Native Americans value the contribution made by archaeologists to the understanding of their past, and have built a museum to display the finds.

Pieces of preserved wood in one of the Ozette houses.

Richard Daugherty with the carved cedar representation of the dorsal fin of a whale. It was inlaid with over 700 sea-otter teeth arranged in the shape of a thunderbird holding a serpent in its claws.

A Makah Native American crew member cleans a basket found on the site.

The best-preserved specimens, such as Denmark's Tollund Man, were in a truly remarkable state, with only the staining caused by bogwater and tannic acid as an indication that they were ancient rather than modern. Within the skin, the bones have often disappeared, as have most of the internal organs, although the stomach and its contents may survive. In Florida, prehistoric human brains have even been recovered.

Occasionally, waterlogged conditions can occur inside burial mounds. The oak-coffin burials of Bronze Age northern Europe, and most notably those of Denmark dating to about 1000 BC, had an inner core of stones packed round the tree-trunk coffin, with a round barrow built above. Water infiltrated the inside of the mound and by combining with tannin from the tree trunks, set up acidic conditions which destroyed the skeleton but preserved the skin (discolored like the bog bodies), hair, and ligaments of the bodies inside the coffins, as well as their clothing and objects such as birch-bark pails.

A somewhat similar phenomenon occurred with the ships that the Vikings used as coffins. The Oseberg ship in Norway, for example, held the body of a Viking queen of about AD 800, and was buried in clay, covered by a packing of stones and a layer of peat that sealed it in and ensured its preservation.

Lake-dwellings have rivaled bog bodies in popular interest ever since the discovery of wooden piles or house supports in Swiss lakes well over a century ago. The range of preserved material is astonishing, not simply wooden structures, artifacts, and textiles but, at Neolithic Charavines in France for example, even nuts, berries, and other fruits.

Perhaps the greatest contribution to archaeology that lake-dwellings and other European wetland sites have made in recent years, however, is to provide abundant well-preserved timber for the study of tree-rings, the annual growth rings in trees, for dating purposes. In Chapter 4 we explore the breakthrough this has brought about in the establishment of an accurate tree-ring chronology for parts of northern Europe stretching back thousands of years.

Another rich source of waterlogged and preserved timbers in land archaeology can be found in the old waterfronts of towns and cities. Archaeologists have been particularly successful in uncovering parts of London's Roman and medieval waterfront, but such discoveries are not restricted to Europe. In the early 1980s New York archaeologists excavated a well-preserved 18th-century ship that had been sunk to support the East River waterfront there. Underwater archaeology itself, in rivers and lakes and especially beneath the sea, is not surprisingly the richest source of all for waterlogged finds (see pp. 97–99).

The major archaeological problem with waterlogged finds, and particularly wood, is that they deteriorate rapidly when they are uncovered, beginning to dry and crack almost at once. They therefore need to be kept wet until they can be treated or freeze-dried at a laboratory. Conservation measures of this kind help to explain the enormous cost of both wetland and underwater archaeology. It has been estimated that "wet archaeology" costs four times as much as "dry archaeology." But the rewards, as we have seen above, are enormous.

The rewards in the future, too, will be very great. Florida, for example, has about 1.2 million ha (3 million acres) of peat deposits, and on present evidence these probably contain more organic artifacts than anywhere else in the world. So far the wetlands here have yielded the largest number of prehistoric watercraft from any one region, together with totems, masks, and figurines dating as far back as 5000 BC. In the Okeechobee Basin, for instance, a 1st-millennium BC burial platform has been found, decorated with a series of large carved wooden totem posts, representing an array of animals and birds. After a fire, the platform had collapsed into its pond. Yet it is only recently that wet finds in Florida have come to us from careful excavation rather than through the drainage that is destroying large areas of peat deposits and, with them, untold quantities of the richest kinds of archaeological evidence.

STUDY QUESTIONS

• What is the difference between an artifact and an ecofact?
• Why is it important for archaeologists to distinguish between cultural and natural formation processes?
• Why is the context of an artifact so very important to archaeologists?
• Why do inorganic materials survive better than organic materials?
• Why are archaeologists particularly interested in wet or waterlogged sites?
• What is experimental archaeology?

SUMMARY

- The archaeological evidence available to us depends on a number of important factors:

  - What people, past and present, have done to it (cultural formation processes).

  - What natural conditions such as soil and climate have preserved or destroyed (natural formation processes). Inorganic materials usually survive far better than organics, but the latter can be well preserved in a range of special environments – the dry, the cold and the waterlogged.

  - Our ability to find, recognize, recover, and conserve it.

- We can do nothing about the first two factors, being at the mercy of the elements and previous human behavior. But the third factor, which is the subject of this book, is constantly improving, as we understand better the processes of decay and destruction, and design research strategies and technical aids to make the most of what archaeological evidence actually survives.

FURTHER READING

Good introductions to the problems of differential preservation of archaeological materials can be found in:

Binford, L.R. 2002. *In Pursuit of the Past: Decoding the Archaeological Record*. University of California Press: Berkeley & London.

Coles, B. & J. 1989. *People of the Wetlands: Bogs, Bodies and Lake-Dwellers*. Thames & Hudson: London & New York.

Lillie, M.C. & Ellis, S. (eds.). 2007. *Wetland Archaeology and Environments: Regional Issues, Global Perspectives*. Oxbow Books: Oxford.

Schiffer, M.B. 2002. *Formation Processes of the Archaeological Record*. University of Utah Press: Salt Lake City.

Sheets, P.D. 2006. *The Ceren Site: An Ancient Village Buried by Volcanic Ash in Central America*. (2nd ed.) Wadsworth: Stamford.

Where?
Survey and excavation of sites and features

Traditionally, archaeologists are known for finding and excavating **sites**, but today, while sites and their **excavation** do remain of paramount importance, the focus has broadened. Archaeologists have become aware that there is a great range of "off-site" or "non-site" evidence, from scatters of **artifacts** to **features** such as plowmarks and field boundaries, that provides important information about the past. The study of entire landscapes by regional survey, for example, is now a major part of archaeological fieldwork.

It should also not be forgotten that suitable evidence for study often comes from new work at sites already the subject of fieldwork. Much potentially rich and rewarding material also lies locked away in museum and institution vaults, waiting to be analyzed by imaginative modern techniques. It is only recently, for example, that the plant remains discovered in Tutankhamun's tomb in the 1920s have received thorough analysis. Yet it remains true that the great majority of archaeological research is still dependent on the collection of new material by fresh fieldwork. The main way that archaeologists find this new material – in other words new sites and features – is by **reconnaissance survey**, either on the ground or from the air.

In the early days of **archaeology** the next step would have been to excavate. But when archaeologists excavate a site, digging through the layers of evidence, uncovering features and removing artifacts that may have been lying undisturbed for thousands of years, it is important to remember that this is essentially a destructive act – there is just one chance to record exactly what is found and the "experiment" can never be repeated. Excavation is also very expensive and after the digging the excavators must be prepared to put considerable time, effort, and money into the conservation and storage of their finds, and into the interpretation and publication of their results. Non-destructive means of assessing the layout of sites and features, using, for example, site **surface survey** or **remote sensing** devices, have therefore taken on a new importance, often providing enough information for archaeologists to interpret features at a site,

KEY CONCEPTS

Research Design

1 *Formulation of a research strategy* to resolve a particular question or test a hypothesis or idea

2 *Collecting and recording of evidence* against which to test that idea, usually by the organization of a team of specialists and conducting of fieldwork – whether survey or excavation or both

3 *Processing and analysis* of that evidence and its interpretation in the light of the original idea to be tested

4 *Publication* of the results in articles, books, etc.

and making large-scale excavation unnecessary. Although excavation does remain a very important aspect of archaeology, archaeologists are becoming increasingly aware that it should not be undertaken lightly, and that it is only absolutely vital where sites would otherwise be destroyed by modern development or natural erosion.

Before any archaeological fieldwork begins, archaeologists try to make explicit what their objectives are and what their plan of campaign will be. This procedure is commonly called devising a **research design**, which broadly has four stages (listed in the box above). There is seldom if ever a straightforward progression through these stages. In real life the research strategy will constantly be refined as evidence is collected and analyzed. All too often, and inexcusably, publication may be neglected. But in the best planned research the overall objective – the broad question or questions to be answered – will stand even if the strategy for achieving it alters.

In this chapter we are focusing on stage 2 of the research process – on the methods and techniques archaeologists use to obtain evidence against which to test their ideas. We will distinguish between *methods used in the discovery* of archaeological sites and non-site features or artifact scatters, which include a variety of ground-based and aerial survey techniques, and those employed *once those sites and features have been identified*, which include detailed survey and selective excavation at individual sites.

LOCATING ARCHAEOLOGICAL SITES AND FEATURES

One major task of the archaeologist is to locate and record the whereabouts of sites and features. In this section we will be reviewing some of the principal techniques used to locate sites. But we should not forget that many monuments have never been lost to posterity: the massive pyramids of Egypt have always been known to succeeding generations, as has the Great Wall of China. Their exact function or purpose may indeed have aroused controversy down the centuries, but their presence, the fact of their existence, was never in doubt.

And not all those sites that were once lost were discovered by archaeologists. No one has ever made a precise count, but a significant number of sites known today were found by accident, from the decorated French cave of Lascaux, and more recently Cosquer, the underwater entrance to which was discovered by a deep-sea diver in 1985, to the amazing terracotta army of China's first emperor, unearthed in 1974 by farmers digging for a well, as well as the countless underwater wrecks first spotted by fishermen, sponge-gatherers, and sport-divers. Construction workers building new roads, subways, dams, and office blocks have made their fair share of discoveries too.

Nevertheless, it is archaeologists who have systematically attempted to record these sites, and it is archaeologists who seek out the full range of sites and features, large or small, that make up the great diversity of past landscapes. How do they achieve this?

A practical distinction can be drawn between site identification conducted at ground level (**ground reconnaissance**) and identification from the air or from space (**aerial reconnaissance**), although any one field project will usually employ both types of reconnaissance.

The Great Wall of China, over 2000 km (1250 miles) long, was begun in the 3rd century BC. Like the pyramids of Egypt, it has never been lost to posterity.

Ground Reconnaissance

Methods for identifying individual sites include consultation of documentary sources and place-name evidence, but primarily actual fieldwork, whether the monitoring of building developers' progress in applied or compliance archaeology, or reconnaissance survey in circumstances where the archaeologist is more of a free agent.

Documentary Sources.   In the nineteenth century, Homer's account of the Trojan Wars in his narrative poem the *Iliad* fired the imagination of German banker Heinrich Schliemann, sending him on a quest for the city of Troy; with remarkable luck and good judgment he successfully identified it in western Turkey. A more recent success story of the same kind was the location and excavation by Helge and Anne Stine Ingstad of the Viking settlement of L'Anse aux Meadows in Newfoundland, thanks in large part to clues contained in the medieval Viking sagas. Much of modern biblical archaeology concerns itself with the search in the Near East for evidence of the places – as well as the people and events – described in the Old and New Testaments. Treated objectively as one possible source of information about Near Eastern sites, the Bible can be a rich source of documentary material, but there is certainly the danger that belief in the absolute religious truth of the texts can cloud an impartial assessment of their archaeological validity.

Much research in biblical archaeology involves attempting to link named biblical sites with archaeologically known ones. Place-name evidence, however, can also lead to actual discoveries of new archaeological sites. In southwest Europe, for example, many prehistoric stone tombs have been found thanks to old names printed on maps that incorporate local words for "stone" or "tomb."

Cultural Resource Management and Applied or Compliance Archaeology. In this specialized work – discussed more fully in Chapter 12 – the role of the archaeologist is to locate and record sites, in some cases before they are destroyed by new roads, buildings, or dams, or by peatcutting and drainage in wetlands. In the USA a large number of sites are located and recorded in inventories every year under **Cultural Resource Management** (CRM) laws which were considerably broadened and strengthened in the 1970s. Proper liaison with a developer should allow archaeological survey to take place in advance along the projected line of road or in the path of development. Important sites thus discovered may require excavation, and in some cases can even cause construction plans to be altered. Certain archaeological remains unearthed during the digging of subways in Rome and Mexico City, for instance, were incorporated into the final station architecture.

Reconnaissance Survey.   How does the archaeologist set about locating sites, other than through documentary sources and salvage work? A conventional and still valid method is to look for the most prominent remains in a landscape, particularly surviving remnants of walled buildings, and burial mounds such as those in eastern North America or Wessex in southern Britain. But many sites are visible on the surface only as a scatter of artifacts and thus require more thorough survey – what we may call reconnaissance survey – to be detected.

Furthermore in recent years, as archaeologists have become more interested in reconstructing the full human use of the landscape, they have begun to realize that there are very faint scatters of artifacts that might not qualify as sites, but which nevertheless represent significant human activity. Some scholars have therefore suggested that these "off-site" or "non-site" areas (that is, areas with a low density of artifacts) should be located and recorded, which can only be done by **systematic survey** work involving careful sampling procedures (see below). This approach is particularly useful in areas where people leading a mobile way of life have left only a sparse archaeological record, as in much of Africa.

Reconnaissance survey has become important for another major reason: the growth of regional studies. Thanks to the pioneering researches of scholars such as Gordon Willey in the Virú Valley, Peru, and William T. Sanders in the Basin of Mexico, archaeologists increasingly seek to study settlement patterns – the distribution of sites across the landscape within a given region. The significance of this work for the understanding of past societies is discussed further in Chapter 5. Here we may note its impact on archaeological fieldwork: it is rarely enough now simply to locate an individual site and then to survey it and/or excavate it in isolation from other sites. Whole regions need to be explored, involving a program of reconnaissance survey.

In the last few decades, reconnaissance survey has developed from being simply a preliminary stage in fieldwork (looking for appropriate sites to excavate) to a more or less independent kind of inquiry, an area of research in its own right which can produce information quite different from that achieved by digging. In some cases excavation may not take place at all, perhaps because permission to dig was not forthcoming, or because of a lack of time or funds – modern excavation is slow and costly, whereas survey is cheap, quick, relatively non-destructive, and requires only maps, compasses, and tapes. Usually, however, archaeologists deliberately choose a surface approach as a source of regional data in order to investigate specific questions that interest them and that excavation could not answer.

Reconnaissance survey encompasses a broad range of techniques: no longer just the identification of sites and the recording or collection of surface artifacts, but sometimes also the sampling of natural and mineral resources such as stone and clay. Much survey today is aimed at studying the spatial distribution of human activities, variations between regions, changes in population through time, and relationships between people, land, and resources.

Reconnaissance Survey in Practice.   For questions formulated in regional terms, it is necessary to collect data on a regional scale, but in a way which provides a maximum of information for a minimum of cost and effort. First, the region to be surveyed needs to be defined: its boundaries may be either natural (such as a valley or island), cultural (such as the extent of an artifact **style**), or purely arbitrary, though natural boundaries are the easiest to establish.

The area's history of development needs to be examined, not only to familiarize oneself with previous archaeological work and with the local materials but also to assess the extent to which surface material may have been covered or removed by natural processes. There is little point, for example, in searching for prehistoric material in sediments only recently laid down by river action. Other factors may have affected surface evidence as well. In much of Africa, for example, great animal herds or burrowing animals will often have disturbed surface material, so that the archaeologist may be able to examine only very broad distribution patterns. Geologists and environmental specialists can generally provide useful advice.

This background information will help determine the intensity of surface coverage of the survey. Other factors to take into consideration are the time and resources available, and how easy it is actually to reach and record an area. Arid (dry) and semi-arid environments with little vegetation are among the best for this type of work, whereas in equatorial rainforest survey may be limited to soil exposures along river banks, unless time and labor permit the cutting of trails. Many regions, of course, contain a variety of landscapes, and more than one strategy for survey is often needed. Moreover, it must be remembered that some archaeological phases (with easily distinguishable artifacts or pottery styles, for example) are more "visible" than others, and that mobile **hunter-gatherer** or pastoral communities leave a very different – and generally sparser – imprint on the landscape than do agricultural or urban communities. All these factors must be taken into account when planning the search patterns and recovery techniques.

There are two basic kinds of reconnaissance survey: the *unsystematic* and the *systematic*. The former is the simpler, involving walking across each part of the area (for example, each plowed field), scanning a strip of ground, collecting or examining artifacts on the surface, and recording their location together with that of any surface features. It is generally felt, however, that the results may be biased and misleading. Walkers have an inherent desire to find material, and will therefore tend to concentrate on those areas that seem richer, rather than obtaining a sample representative of the whole area that would enable the archaeologist to assess the varying distribution of material of different periods or **types**. On the other hand, the method is flexible, enabling the team to focus greater efforts on the areas that have proved most likely to contain sites or finds.

Much modern survey is done in a *systematic* way, employing either a grid system or a series of equally spaced transects (straight paths) across the area. The area to be searched is divided into sectors, and these are walked systematically. Because of the constraints of time and money, it is often not possible to survey the entirety of an area in this way, so archaeologists have to employ a *sampling strategy* (see box opposite) where only certain sectors or transects are picked to be searched. Systematic survey also makes it easier to plot the location of finds since an exact position is always known.

For example, from 1992 to 1998 the Sydney Cyprus Survey Project, led by Bernard Knapp and Michael Given of the University of Glasgow, undertook an intensive archaeological survey in a 65-sq. km (25-sq. mile) area in the northern Troodos Mountains of Cyprus. This is an area famed for its copper sulphide ore deposits, exploited as early as the Bronze Age. The project examined the human transformation of the landscape over a period of 5000 years and placed it in its regional context. A first requirement for the systematic intensive survey strategy was good maps. Enlarged aerial photographs were used to create a base map of the entire survey region. The main survey approach was a transect survey with the aim of obtaining a broad systematic sample of the area; areas with extensive evidence of early industrial, agricultural, or settlement activities and locales with high densities of artifacts were investigated more closely. It took the team around 6 years to survey just 10 percent of the area. The survey identified 11 Special

Archaeologists cannot usually afford the time and money necessary to investigate the whole of a large site or all sites in a given region, so they need to sample the area being researched. In a ground reconnaissance survey this will involve using one of the methods described below to choose a number of smaller areas to be searched, with the objective being to draw reliable conclusions about the whole area.

The way archaeologists use sampling is similar to the way it is employed in public opinion polls, which make generalizations about the opinions of millions of people using samples of just a few thousand. Surprisingly often the polls are more or less right. This is because the structure of sampled populations is well known – for example, we know their ages and occupations. We have much less background information to work with in archaeology, so must be more careful when we extrapolate generalizations from a sample. But as with opinion polls, in archaeological work the larger and better designed the sample, the more likely the results are to be valid.

Some sites in a given region, however, may be more accessible than others, or more prominent in the landscape, which may prompt a more informal sampling strategy. Long years of experience in the field will also give some archaeologists an intuitive "feel" for the right places to undertake work.

Types of Sampling

The simplest form is a **simple random sample**, where the areas to be sampled are chosen using a table of random numbers. However, the nature of random numbers results in some areas being allotted clusters of squares, while others remain untouched – the sample is, therefore, inherently biased.

One answer is the **stratified random sample**, where the region or site is divided into its natural zones (strata, hence the technique's name), such as cultivated land

and forest, and squares are then chosen by the same random-number procedure, except that each zone has the number of squares proportional to its area. Thus, if forest comprises 85 percent of the area, it must be allotted 85 percent of the squares.

Another solution, **systematic sampling**, entails the selection of a grid of equally spaced locations – e.g. choosing every other square. By adopting such a regular spacing one runs the risk of missing (or hitting) every single example in an equally regular pattern of distribution – this is another source of potential bias.

A more satisfactory method is to use a stratified unaligned systematic sample, which combines the main elements from all three techniques just described. In collecting artifacts from the surface of a large tell or mound site at Girik-i-Haciyan in Turkey, Charles Redman and Patty Jo Watson used a grid of 5-m squares, but orientated it along the site's main N-S/E-W axes, and the samples were selected with reference to these axes. The strata chosen were blocks of 9 squares (3 x 3), and one square in each block was picked for excavation by selecting its N-S/E-W coordinates from a table of random numbers. This method ensures an unbiased set of samples, more evenly distributed over the whole site.

Transects vs Squares

In large-scale surveys, transects (straight paths) are sometimes preferable to squares. This is particularly true in areas of dense vegetation such as tropical rainforest. It is far easier to walk along a series of paths than to locate accurately and investigate a large number of randomly distributed squares. In addition, transects can easily be segmented into units, whereas it may be difficult to locate or describe a specific part of a square; and transects are useful not merely for finding sites but also for recording artifact densities across the landscape. On the other

hand, squares have the advantage of exposing more area to the survey, thus increasing the probability of intersecting sites. A combination of the two methods is often best: using transects to cover long distances, but squares when larger concentrations of material are encountered.

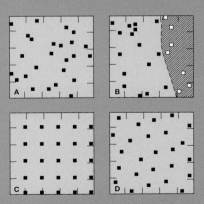

Types of sampling: (A) simple random; (B) stratified random; (C) systematic; (D) stratified unaligned systematic.

KEY CONCEPTS

Locating Sites Using Ground Reconnaissance

- *Documentary Sources*: mainly of use in locating Classical, biblical, and relatively recent sites

- *Cultural Resource Management*: sites in areas that may be under threat from development are located, recorded, and sometimes excavated prior to their destruction

- *Reconnaissance Survey*: surveys can be either *unsystematic* (where archaeologists randomly search an area on foot for artifacts or evidence of features) or, more commonly, *systematic* (where archaeologists walk an area using carefully laid out grid systems or transects). A *sampling strategy*, where only a representative part of an area is actually searched, is often used to save time and money. Small-scale excavations can be undertaken to check survey results

Interest Areas and 142 Places of Special Interest, which were investigated. The count in the field totalled 87,600 sherds of pottery, 8111 tile fragments, and 3092 lithics. About one third of these were collected and analyzed and entered into the project's database.

Results tend to be more reliable from long-term projects that cover a region repeatedly, since the visibility of sites and artifacts can vary widely from year to year or even with the seasons, thanks to vegetation and changing land-use. In addition, members of field crews inevitably differ in the accuracy of their observations, and in their ability to recognize and describe sites (the more carefully we look, and the more experience we have, the more we see); this factor can never be totally eliminated, but repeated coverage can help to counter its effects. The use of standardized recording forms makes it easy to put the data into a computer at a later stage.

Finally, it may be necessary or desirable to carry out small excavations to supplement or check the surface data (particularly for questions of chronology, contemporaneity, or site function), or to test hypotheses which have arisen from the survey. The two types of investigation are complementary, not mutually exclusive. Their major difference can be summarized as follows: excavation tells us a lot about a little of a site, and can only be done once, whereas survey tells us a little about a lot of sites, and can be repeated.

Extensive and Intensive Survey. Surveys can be made more extensive by combining results from a series of individual projects in neighboring regions to produce very large-scale views of change in landscape, land-use, and settlement through time – though, as with individual members of a field crew, the accuracy and quality of different survey projects may vary widely. Alternatively survey can be made more intensive by aiming at total coverage of a single large site or site-cluster. It is a paradox that some of the world's greatest and most famous archaeological sites have never, or only recently, been studied in this way, since attention has traditionally focused on the grand monuments themselves rather than on any attempt to place them within even a local context. At Teotihuacán, near Mexico City, a major mapping project initiated in the 1960s has added hugely to our knowledge of the area around the great pyramid-temples (the work is described on pp. 83–84).

Ground reconnaissance survey has a vital place in archaeological work, and one that continues to grow in importance. In modern projects, however, it is usually supplemented (and often preceded) by reconnaissance from the air, one of the most important advances made by archaeology in the 20th century. In fact, the availability of air photographs can be an important factor in selecting and delineating an area for ground reconnaissance.

Aerial Reconnaissance

It must be stressed that aerial reconnaissance, particularly aerial photography, is not merely or even mainly used for the discovery of sites, being more crucial to their recording and interpretation, and to monitoring changes in them through time. Nevertheless, aerial survey – together with remote sensing from space – has been responsible for a large number of discoveries, and continues to find more sites every year.

Aerial Photography. The first major archaeological applications of this technique occurred at the start of the 20th century with photographs of the Roman town of Ostia taken from a balloon. World War I gave the technique a great impetus when archaeologists in England discovered the clarity that air photographs taken from aircraft and balloons could provide in their plan view of prehistoric monuments. From these beginnings aerial photography developed into one of the archaeologist's most valued aids, able to detect sites, roads, field-systems, and even underwater sites such as ancient harbors.

Archaeologists use aircraft to search the ground for traces of former sites and past landscapes. Photographs are usually oblique and taken by handheld cameras. Such oblique photography is a selective process, involving archaeological judgment, in contrast to the unselective view obtained by vertical survey. Single-frame shots of a site or feature are usual, although stereoscopic pairs of oblique photographs considerably assist subsequent interpretation. Oblique aerial photographs show sites in the context of the landscape and can also be used for preparing archaeological maps.

(Below) Aerial photographs are of two types: oblique and vertical. Obliques are easier to view and understand than verticals but may present more difficulty to the interpreter who must transform the information to plan views.

(Bottom) Oblique aerial photograph taken in 1922 of the vicinity of Monk's Mound, Cahokia (center right), revealing other features in the vicinity of the mound.

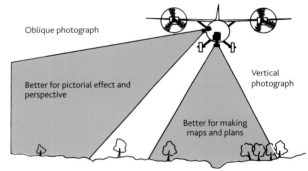

Oblique photograph

Better for pictorial effect and perspective

Vertical photograph

Better for making maps and plans

Earthworks seen from the air: the Iron Age hillfort of Maiden Castle, southern England, whose complex ramparts are thrown into relief by shadows cast by massive earthen banks. The air photograph also highlights an interesting earlier feature: a shallow Neolithic ditch running across the middle of the fort.

Winter plowing has scraped the chalk foundations of this Gallo-Roman villa in France. This process of destruction has in fact revealed the plan of its main structures against the dark soil.

How Sites Show from the Air.   Those who take and use aerial photographs must understand the means by which the evidence is made visible in order to determine the type of feature that has been recorded. Conventionally, features photographed from the air are often described according to the way they are revealed, rather than by the archaeological reality they represent, thus "earthworks," "soil-marks," or "crop-marks."

Earthworks is a term used to describe banks and associated ditches, or stone-walled features – in fact, any feature that can be seen in relief. These features are usually revealed from the air as shadow marks – an effect that is dependent on the lighting and weather conditions at the time of photography. They also show in relief when viewed as a stereoscopic pair. Such features may also be seen by the differences in vegetation supported by banks and ditches, by differential melting or drifting of snow, or by retention of water in ditches in times of flood. Time of day and time of year are thus important in the discovery and recording of such sites.

Soil-marks reveal the presence of buried ditches, banks, or foundations by the changes in subsoil color caused when a plowshare catches and turns over part of the buried feature, bringing it to the surface. Most soil-marked sites are being destroyed by modern cultivation. They are mostly visible in photographs

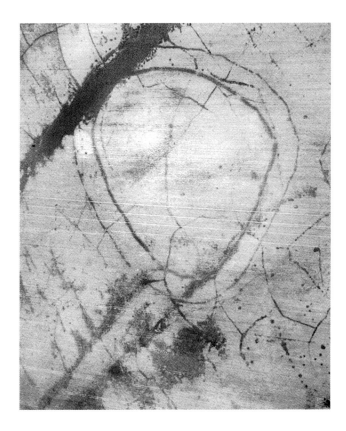

Crop-marks clearly reveal two concentric rings of ditches defining an enclosure at Merzien, Sachsen-Anhalt, Germany. Both ditch circuits are interrupted and may therefore be of Neolithic date. Note also the crop-marked pits and polygons caused by periglacial action in the gravel subsoil.

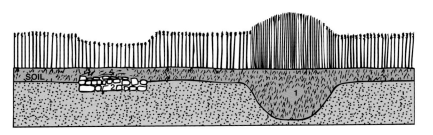

How crop-marks are formed: crops grow taller and more thickly over sunken features such as ditches (1), and show stunted growth over buried walls (2). Such variations may not be obvious at ground level, but are often visible from the air, as different colored bands of vegetation.

taken in winter months. Bare soil will sometimes also reveal features through differential moisture retention – damp marks – or by differences in thermal properties that affect the melting of snow and frost.

Crop-marks develop when a buried wall or ditch either stunts or boosts crop growth by affecting the availability of moisture and nutrients through changing the depth of soil. Suitable crops, such as wheat, barley, and some root vegetables, provide a perfect medium for revealing features in the underlying soil. This response to buried features is very delicate and dependent on variables such as the type and condition of soil, weather during the growing season, crop type, and agricultural practices. Thus features can stand out strongly in one year and be invisible the next. Knowledge of recent and past land-use in an area can be particularly valuable when assessing the potential of apparently blank modern fields. Some features simply do not produce crop-marked evidence.

Photo Interpretation and Mapping.   Interpretation is the process by which features photographed from the air, such as soil-marks, are analyzed in order to deduce the types of archaeological structures causing them. Given that the visibility of features varies from year to year, photos taken over several years need to be studied to compile an accurate plan. Such plans may guide excavation to key points in a structure, place field-collected data in context, or themselves be used as the starting point for new research.

Aerial photos can also be employed to produce a map of known features within a region. In Britain, Rog Palmer used thousands of individual photographs of a 450-sq. km (175-sq. mile) territory around the Iron Age hillfort of Danebury to produce accurate maps. These show that the site lay within very complex agricultural landscapes, with at least eight other hillforts in the area. Crop- and soil-marks revealed the presence of 120 ditched farming enclosures, hundreds of acres of small fields, regularly arranged, and 240 km (150 miles) of linear ditches and boundary works, many of which were roughly contemporaneous with Danebury to judge from their forms and/or surface finds. Many such records are drawn on to transparent sheets that are overlaid on to maps showing topographical or other information, but more up-to-date systems have converted such information as part of computerized **Geographic Information Systems** (GIS, see pp. 78–82).

Map of the area around Danebury, an Iron Age hillfort in southern England (6th–2nd centuries BC), created from aerial survey, with details of ancient fields, tracks, and enclosures.

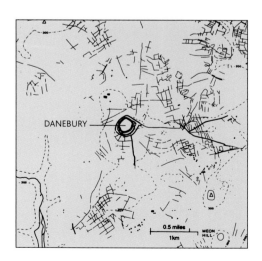

Recent Developments in Aerial and Satellite Photography.
New technology is having an impact on aerial photography in different ways. Computer enhancement of pictures can improve their sharpness and contrast. Digital manipulation of images has also been developed and enables a single image, from an oblique or vertical photograph, to be transformed to match the map of the area. Computer programs also exist which allow several images to be transformed and then combined. This is especially useful in cases where a site may lie in two modern fields from which crop-marked information has been recorded in different years. Such plan-form images may help subsequent photo interpretation and mapping. Use of aerial data as a GIS layer may lead to fruitful results from analyses in conjunction with topographic and other archaeological information.

Although the majority of existing photographs have been taken on film – black and white (panchromatic), color, or false color infrared – in the last few years digital sensors have become sufficiently good to be used in precision vertical cameras and the handheld cameras used by airborne archaeologists. For the latter, cameras taking images of sizes greater than 10 megapixels provide more than adequate resolution for most archaeological purposes. Modern flying, be this to capture a series of parallel overlapping strips of vertical photographs or to examine a chosen area by an archaeologist, is usually planned and recorded to take advantage of GPS (Global Positioning System) navigation. The track of an archaeological flight is likely to be recorded at preset intervals to provide a continuous record that shows the ground that has been overflown and searched. In addition, top-of-the-range Nikon cameras can be linked to GPS so that coordinates are recorded on an Exif file when each photograph is taken. This eases the occasional problem of locating shots when the archaeologist is back on the ground.

One current trend is to georeference and mosaic vertical photographs and satellite images so that they can be layered in a GIS. This provides useful comparative data but is not ideal for interpretation of the photographs, which is best done using overlapping stereoscopic prints or images, and it is usual to view on-screen images of the northern hemisphere with north to the top rather than the ideal of having shadows falling toward the viewer. Photo interpretation and photogrammetry have long histories that have been developed to aid reading aerial photographs and it would help many GIS users if they were aware of some of the "tricks" of this slightly earlier age.

Digital images can be manipulated using readily available computer programs to enhance their archaeological content to the viewer's satisfaction. It is wise to devise a storage system that allows rapid retrieval of images, is adequately backed up, and takes account of the possible short-term life of

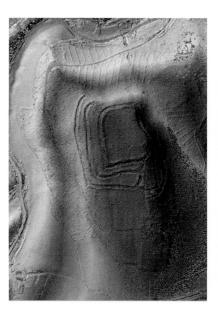

LIDAR in operation: the Iron Age hillfort of Welshbury in the Forest of Dean, England, is almost invisible in conventional aerial photographs (left). The initial LIDAR image shows little improvement (center) but once reflections from leaves and trees (the "first return") have been filtered out using a software algorithm the earthworks are clearly visible (right).

digital formats so as to provide good archival storage of what may be unique and irretrievable data.

Use of LIDAR (Light Detection and Ranging) has proved extremely valuable in the past few years. The aircraft, whose exact position is known through use of a differential GPS, carries a laser scanner that rapidly pulses a series of beams to the ground. By measuring the time taken for these to return to the aircraft an accurate picture of the ground in the form of a digital elevation model (or digital surface model) is created. Software used with LIDAR provides archaeologists with two great advantages over conventional aerial photography. Tree canopies can be eliminated by switching off the "first return" and so the sensor can see into woodland; and the angle and azimuth of the sun can be moved to enable ground features to be viewed under optimal (and sometimes naturally impossible) lighting. Both facilities have been used to advantage in England where new sites – mostly enlargements to field systems – have been found, and locational corrections made to the existing record of the landscape around Stonehenge.

High altitude mapping has also helped reveal a hitherto undocumented people in Costa Rica. In 1984–85, Thomas Sever of NASA flew over the area around the volcano of Arenal, which was of interest to archaeologists because local people had found potsherds and tools when roads were cut through the terrain of ash. Sever scanned the area using radar, infrared photographic film, and LIDAR. The resulting images showed roadways radiating from a central graveyard. Subsequent excavation of 62 sites by Payson Sheets revealed that a wandering people had lived in the volcano's shadow from about 11,000 BC, and had settled permanently on the shore of Lake Arenal in 2000 BC. Their campsites, graves, and houses had been buried and protected by a volcanic eruption.

New World archaeological projects now routinely use the commercially available and cost-effective black-and-white aerial photographs. The 9 x 9 in negatives can be enlarged considerably before showing grain and thus quite small features such as walls, pits, etc. can be clearly seen. Digital cameras may be used to advantage to acquire images of larger-scale structures and systems, more common in arid and jungle zones. It is also routine to access Google Earth and use the high resolution air photos and satellite cover there, or to buy copies of them. The high-resolution images available from the Ikonos (about 1 m resolution) and QuickBird (60 cm) satellites offer data comparable with aerial photographs, while Google Earth has basic world cover from NASA's LANDSAT series (28.5 m) but includes blocks of QuickBird images and some conventional aerial photographs. Ikonos and QuickBird provide both multispectral (MS) and panchromatic (PAN) high-resolution imagery in which details like buildings are easily visible. The imagery can be imported into remote sensing image-processing software, as well as into GIS packages for analysis.

The introduction of Google Earth has been a true "aerial revolution" since it offers every archaeologist the opportunity to examine the ground and look for archaeological sites, but the same "rules" of visibility apply to those images as they do to conventional aerial photos, and absence of evidence on one particular date is not evidence of absence. NASA's World Wind and Microsoft's Live Search also offer worldwide cover but at lower resolutions or using aerial photographs available elsewhere. It is important to note, however, that most users have never been trained to interpret such photos and many expect sites to be visible at all times.

QuickBird and Ikonos images can also be taken to order, although the minimum cost may be high for some archaeological projects. In parts of the world where maps are still regarded as secret or do not exist, an up-to-date satellite image may be the only way to provide a "base map" for archaeological investigations. Both satellite "owners" maintain libraries of old images that are lower in price. Much use has also been made of the Cold War CORONA satellite photographs (at best about 2 m resolution), and these too provide a useful base map and allow provisional interpretation of sites that can later be checked by fieldwork – for example, CORONA images have led to the detection and detailed mapping of numerous kinds of archaeological remains such as ancient roads, ruins, irrigation networks and so forth. Since CORONA takes two images of the

Two satellite images of the Urartian citadel of Erebuni, near Yerevan, Armenia, founded in 782 BC: on the left, with resolution of about 2 m (10 ft) is an image from the American CORONA series taken in 1971; on the right is a higher resolution screen shot from Google Earth of a QuickBird image taken in 2006. Both images are displayed with south to the top so that shadows assist photo-reading of topography and structures.

same spot (forward and afterward), these can be processed to produce a stereoscopic view and a 3-D Digital Surface Model.

Other recent additions to the archaeologist's arsenal include SAR (Synthetic Aperture Radar) in which multiple radar images are processed to yield extremely detailed high-resolution results which can provide data for maps, databases, land-use studies and so forth. One of its many advantages is that, unlike conventional aerial photography, it provides results day or night and regardless of weather conditions. It can be used with multispectral data from satellites to make inventories of archaeological sites in a survey area – a rapid, non-destructive alternative to surface survey which does not involve the collection of artifacts and can thus save a great deal of time and effort in some circumstances.

As their resolution increases, photographs and images taken from satellites are increasingly being used in archaeological surveys. Some useful early work was done using images from the LANDSAT (Earth Resources Technology). Scanners record the intensity of reflected light and the infrared radiation from the earth's surface, and convert these electronically into photographic images. LANDSAT images have been used to trace large-scale features such as ancient levee systems in Mesopotamia and an ancient riverbed running from the deserts of Saudi Arabia to Kuwait, as well as sediments around Ethiopia's Rift Valley that are likely to contain hominin fossil beds. Space Imaging Radar (which can reveal features beneath 5 m (16 ft) of sand) has been used from the space shuttle to locate ancient riverbeds beneath the deserts of Egypt and hundreds of kilometers of long-abandoned caravan routes in Arabia, many of which converged on a spot in Oman, that may be the lost city of Ubar.

A pioneering archaeological application was carried out in Mesoamerica. Using false-color LANDSAT imagery, in which natural colors are converted into more sharply contrasting hues, NASA scientists working with archaeologists in 1983 found an extensive network of Maya farmed fields and settlements in the Yucatán peninsula of Mexico. In this expensive experiment, costing $250,000, Maya ruins showed up in false color as tiny dots of blue, pink, and light red – blue for ancient reservoirs cut out of the limestone surface, pink and light red for vegetation on and adjacent to the sites. By looking for examples of blue dots next to pink and light red ones, archaeologists were able to pinpoint 112 sites. They visited 20 by helicopter in order to verify their conclusions.

The project also found an unknown city with twin pyramids, dating to the Classic Maya phase of AD 600–900; and relocated the major city of Oxpemul which had been discovered in the early 1930s but was then lost again in the thick jungle.

The international Greater Angkor Project has found that the vast ruins of the 1000-year-old temple complex of Angkor in northern Cambodia may cover an area of up to 3000 sq. km (11,500 sq. miles). The ruins, shrouded in dense jungle and surrounded by land-mines, have been the subject of studies using high-resolution radar imagery obtained from NASA satellites. The resulting dark squares and rectangles on the images are stone moats and reflecting pools around the temples. At least 74 new temples and more than 1000 man-made

A satellite image of the huge ancient site of Angkor in Cambodia.

Locating Sites Using Aerial Reconnaissance

- *Aerial Photography*: aerial photographs can be either oblique (better for pictorial effect and perspective) or vertical (better for maps and plans). Features visible from the air are classed as either earthworks, soil-marks, or crop-marks

- *LIDAR*: a new laser scanning technique which can accurately map whole landscapes, even beneath tree cover. Resulting digital plans can be manipulated to reveal subtle features such as the remains of ancient field systems

- *Satellite Photography*: useful primarily at the largest scales, for example mapping very large sites or tracing ancient irrigation systems

ponds have been detected. The main temple complex of Angkor Wat is readily visible as a small square bounded with black. The most important discovery for archaeologists so far has been the network of ancient canals surrounding the city (visible as light lines) which irrigated rice fields and fed the pools and moats. They were probably also used to transport the massive stones needed for constructing the complex.

ASTER (Advanced Spaceborne Thermal Emission and Reflection Radiometer) is an imaging instrument that flies on Terra, a satellite launched in 1999 as part of NASA's Earth Observing System (EOS), and which is used to obtain detailed maps of land surface temperature, reflectance, and elevation. It goes beyond LANDSAT since it captures high spatial resolution data in 14 bands, from the visible to the thermal infrared wavelengths, and also provides a stereo viewing capability for the creation of digital elevation models.

The application of these new techniques to archaeology is a recent phenomenon and is constantly evolving along with the satellites and what they can offer. And as the methods become cheaper they will be adopted ever more widely.

Geographic Information Systems

The standard approach to archaeological mapping is now the use of GIS (Geographic Information Systems), described in one official report as "the biggest step forward in the handling of geographic information since the invention of the map." GIS is a collection of computer hardware and software and of geographic data, designed to obtain, store, manage, manipulate, analyze and display a wide range of spatial information. A GIS combines a database with powerful digital mapping tools. GIS developed out of computer-aided design and computer-aided mapping (CAD/CAM) programs during the 1970s. Some CAD programs, such as AutoCAD, can be linked to commercial databases and have proved valuable in allowing the automatic mapping of archaeological sites held in a computer database. A true GIS, however, also incorporates the ability to carry out a statistical analysis of site distribution, and to generate new information.

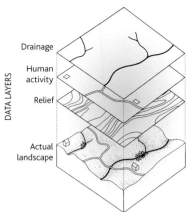

Diagram showing some possible GIS data layers.

A GIS may include an enormous amount of topographical and environmental data on relief, communications, hydrology etc. To make all this information easier to handle, it is normal to divide it into different map layers, each representing a single variable (see the illustration at right). Archaeological data may themselves be split into several layers, most often so that each layer represents a discrete time slice. As long as they can be spatially located, many different types of data can be integrated in a GIS. These can include site plans, satellite images, aerial photographs, geophysical survey, as well as maps. A good example of a many different types of data being incorporated into a GIS is the Giza Plateau Mapping Project in Egypt (see box overleaf).

The ability to incorporate satellite and aerial photographs can be particularly valuable for site reconnaissance as they can provide detailed and current land-use information. Many topographic data already exist in the form of digital maps which can be taken directly into a GIS. Knowing exact ground coordinates is essential in archaeological practice for mapping purposes, and learning about distribution patterns of archaeological **material culture**. This is done by means of a handheld GPS (Global Positioning System), which allows archaeologists to map their ground position (in some cases within as little as 3 cm) by connecting to a global satellite system. A minimum of four satellites has to be communicating with the GPS to provide close X and Y data, which can display the received information in longitude/latitude (degrees minutes seconds), or to a UTM (Universal Transverse Mercator) coordinate system that provides data in eastings and northings. These data are extremely useful where a region is unmapped, or where the maps are old or inaccurate.

Once the basic outlines of a site have been mapped with reasonable accuracy by means of the GPS, and control points placed around the site, standard practice is to use a **total station** to record its more detailed features to a greater degree of accuracy. This instrument is an electronic theodolite integrated with an electronic distance meter, used to read distances to a particular point. Angles and distances are measured from the total station to points under survey and the coordinates (X, Y, Z, or northing, easting, and elevation) of the surveyed points relative to the total station positions are calculated. These data can then be downloaded from

For the past 17 years American Egyptologist Mark Lehner has been systematically exploring Egypt's Giza Plateau in an effort to find the settlements which housed the workforce that built the pyramids. To the south of the Great Sphinx, 4500-year-old paved streets have been uncovered, as well as various buildings from barracks to bakeries.

The Giza Plateau Mapping Project (GPMP) has so far exposed about 10.5 ha (26 acres) of what seems to be a vast urban center attached to the pyramids, sometimes known as "The Lost City of the Pyramid Builders."

Directed by Farrah Brown LaPan, GIS is being used to integrate all the project's drawings, thousands of digital photographs, notebooks, forms, and artifacts into a single organized data store. This enables the team to map patterns of architecture, burials, artifacts and other materials such as foodstuffs: for example, it has been found that the people in the bigger houses ate the best meat (beef) and fish (perch), while the others ate more pig and goat. Color-coded graphs and charts can be produced, representing the densities and distributions of various artifact types in different areas, buildings, rooms, or even features.

(Left) The Giza Plateau Mapping Project began with an extremely accurate survey of the cultural and natural features of the entire area. The survey grid is centered on the Great Pyramid.

(Below left) Using digitized 1-meter contours of the plateau and CAD data depicting the architectural components of the pyramid complex, the GPMP GIS team created a nearly three-dimensional surface called a TIN, or triangulated irregular network, over which they can lay other data layers, such as maps. Here, the GPMP survey grid is draped over the surface of the plateau. The Lost City of the Pyramid Builders is the dark area on the right.

DATA COLLECTED OVER 15 YEARS
all being incorporated in the GIS:

- over 2600 field drawings
- over 11,900 digital photographs
- over 12,200 non-burial features
- over 1000 burial features
- over 190 supervisors' notebooks
- survey and remote sensing data
- artifact/ecofact content and distribution information for every feature

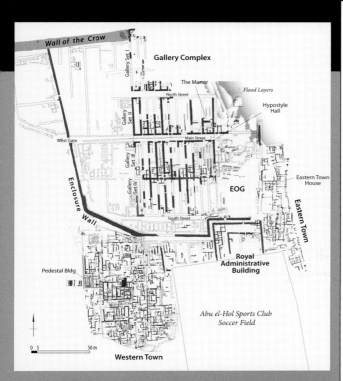

(Above) Since 1988 survey and excavations have been concentrated on the area known as "The Lost City of the Pyramid Builders," some 400 m (1300 ft) south of the Sphinx. This detailed plan (above) of the settlement, which was abandoned at the end of the 4th Dynasty (2575–2465 BC), the period of Giza pyramid building, now forms part of the GIS.

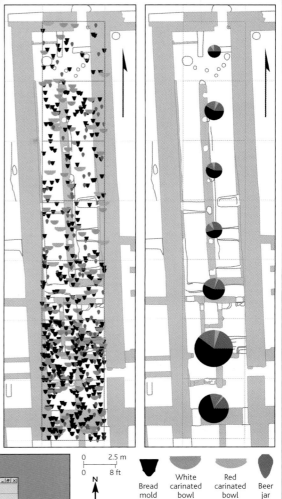

0   2.5 m
0   8 ft

N

Bread mold   White carinated bowl   Red carinated bowl   Beer jar

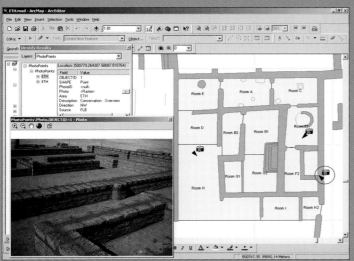

The spatial distribution of artifacts is easy to represent within the GIS (above). The distribution of common pottery types in one of the structures in the "Gallery Complex" is shown here. On the left, distribution within excavated squares is shown with dot density pots (with each "pot" representing 10 potsherds); on the right, it is shown with proportional pie charts. This structure may have served as a barracks for workmen: the concentrations at the southern end of the building suggest that bread may have been baked there for the long open barracks rooms to the north, where pot distribution is relatively even.

This ArcGIS 9 interface (left) shows a plan of the "Eastern Town House" linked to a photo of the reconstructed building. The circled camera icon indicates where the shot was taken, with further icons indicating other available images.

the total station to a computer to generate a map of the surveyed area. All the information is recorded and then submitted as GIS data to the client or sponsoring organization of the work as a matter of course.

Once data are stored within a GIS it is relatively straightforward to generate maps on demand, and to query the database to select particular categories of site to be displayed. Individual map layers, or combinations of layers, can be selected according to the subject under investigation.

One of the earliest, and most widespread, uses of GIS within archaeology has been the construction of *predictive models* of site locations. Most of the development of these techniques has taken place within North American archaeology, where the enormous spatial extent of some archaeological landscapes means that it is not always possible to survey them comprehensively. The underlying premise of all predictive models is that particular kinds of archaeological sites tend to occur in the same kinds of place. For example, certain settlement sites tend to occur close to sources of fresh water and on southerly aspects because these provide ideal conditions in which humans can live (not too cold, and within easy walking distance of a water source). Using this information it is possible to model how likely a given location is to contain an archaeological site from the known environmental characteristics of that location. In a GIS environment this operation can be done for an entire landscape producing a predictive model map for the whole area.

An example was developed by the Illinois State Museum for the Shawnee National Forest in southern Illinois. It predicts the likelihood of finding a prehistoric site anywhere within the 91 sq. km (35 sq. miles) of the forest by using the observed characteristics of the 68 sites which are known from the 12 sq. km (4.6 sq. miles) which have been surveyed. A GIS database was constructed for the entire area and the characteristics of the known sites were compared with the characteristics of the locations known not to contain sites. This resulted in a model which can be used to predict the likelihood that any location with known environmental characteristics will contain a prehistoric site.

ASSESSING THE LAYOUT OF SITES AND FEATURES

Finding and recording sites and features is the first stage in fieldwork, but the next stage is to make some assessment of site size, type, and layout. These are crucial factors for archaeologists, not only for those who are trying to decide whether, where, and how to excavate, but also for those whose main focus may be the study of settlement patterns, site systems, and **landscape archaeology** without planning to carry out any excavation.

We have already seen how aerial photographs may be used to plot the layout of sites as well as helping to locate them in the first place. What are the other main methods for investigating sites without excavating them?

Site Surface Survey

The simplest way to gain some idea of a site's extent and layout is through a site surface survey – by studying the distribution of surviving features, and recording and possibly collecting artifacts from the surface.

The Teotihuacán Mapping Project, for instance, used site surface survey to investigate the layout and orientation of the city, which had been the largest and

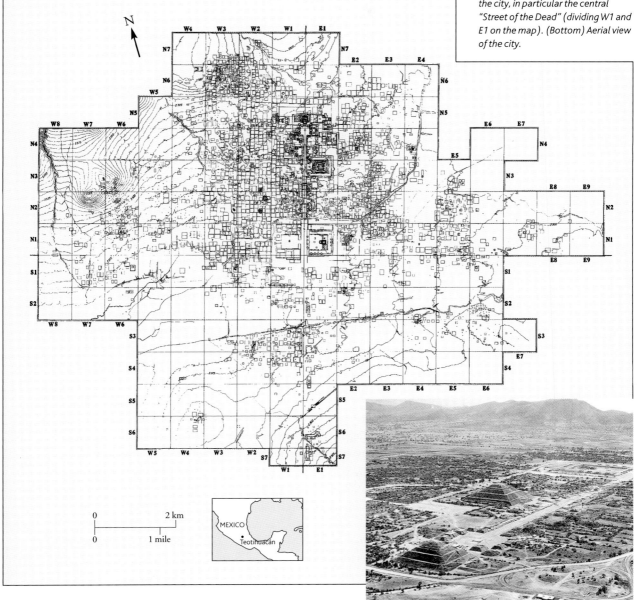

Archaeological and topographic map of Teotihuacán produced by the Teotihuacán Mapping Project. The survey grid system of 500-m squares is oriented to the north–south axis of the city, in particular the central "Street of the Dead" (dividing W1 and E1 on the map). (Bottom) Aerial view of the city.

most powerful urban center in Mesoamerica in its heyday from AD 200 to 650. The layout and orientation of the city had intrigued scholars for decades; however, they considered the grandiose pyramid-temples, plazas, and the major avenue – an area now known as the ceremonial center – to be the entire extent of the metropolis. It was not until the survey conducted by the Teotihuacán Mapping Project that the outer limits, the great east–west axis, and the grid plan of the city were discovered and defined.

Fortunately, structural remains lay just beneath the surface, so that the team were able to undertake the mapping from a combination of aerial and surface survey, with only small-scale excavation to test the survey results. Millions of potsherds were collected, and over 5000 structures and activity areas recorded. Teotihuacán had been laid out on a regular plan, with four quadrants orientated on the great north–south "Street of the Dead" and another major avenue running east–west across it. Construction had occurred over several centuries, but always following the master plan.

For artifacts and other objects collected or observed during site surface survey, it may not be worth mapping their individual locations if they appear to come from badly disturbed secondary contexts. Or there may simply be too many artifacts realistically to record all their individual proveniences. In this latter instance the archaeologist will probably use sampling procedures for the selective recording of surface finds. However, where time and funds are sufficient and the site is small enough, collection and recording of artifacts from the total site area may prove possible.

For example, a site surface survey was conducted at the Bronze Age city of Mohenjodaro in Pakistan. Here, a team of archaeologists from Pakistan, Germany, and Italy investigated the distribution of craft-working debris and found, to their surprise, that craft activities were not confined to a specific manufacturing zone within the city, but were scattered throughout the site, representing assorted small-scale workshops.

Reliability of Surface Finds. Archaeologists have always used limited surface collection of artifacts as one way of trying to assess the date and layout of a site prior to excavation. However, now that surface survey has become not merely a preliminary to excavation but in some instances a substitute for it – for cost and time reasons – a vigorous debate is taking place in archaeology about how far surface traces do in fact reflect distributions below ground.

We would logically expect single-period or shallow sites to show the most reliable surface evidence of what lies beneath. Equally one might predict that multi-period, deep sites such as Near Eastern village mounds would show few if any traces on the surface of the earliest and deepest levels. However, this is by no means always true – for example, at Tell Halula in northern Syria, a survey was

CORONA satellite image of the Halula district, showing the location of the tell and the boundary of the sampling area.

Plan of Tell Halula showing the layout of collection squares, plus outline plans of the tell showing the changing location and size of settlement during 5 of the 10 occupation phases.

carried out by an Australian team in 1986, involving the collection of artifacts such as potsherds and stone tools from the surface using stratified random sampling procedures based on a grid system. Forty-six squares in this grid were sampled, amounting to 4 percent of the 12.5-ha (31-acre) site area. Typological analysis of the artifacts made it possible to identify 10 major occupation phases, representing 15 different cultural periods.

Those who support the validity of surface survey, while agreeing that there is bound to be a quantitative bias in favor of the most recent periods on the surface, nevertheless point out that one of the surprises for most survey archaeologists is how many of their sites, if collected with care, are truly multi-period, reflecting many phases of a site's use, not just the latest one. The reasons for this are not yet entirely clear, but they certainly have something to do with the kind of **formation processes** discussed in Chapter 2 – from erosion and animal disturbance to human activity such as plowing.

The relationship between surface and subsurface evidence is undoubtedly complex and varies from site to site. It is therefore wise wherever possible to try to determine what really does lie beneath the ground, perhaps by digging test pits (usually meter squares) to assess a site's horizontal extent, ultimately by more thorough excavation (see below). There are, however, a whole

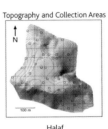

Topography and Collection Areas

Pre-Pottery Neolithic B

8.0 ha

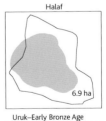

Halaf

6.9 ha

Ubaid–Late Chalcolithic

2.3 ha

Uruk–Early Bronze Age

1.9 ha

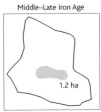

Middle–Late Iron Age

1.2 ha

battery of **subsurface detection** devices that can be used before – or indeed sometimes instead of – excavation, which of course is destructive as well as expensive.

Subsurface Detection

Probes. The most traditional technique is that of probing the soil with rods or borers (augers), and noting the positions where they strike solids or hollows. Metal rods with a T-shaped handle are the most common, but augers – large corkscrews with a similar handle – are also used, and have the advantage of bringing samples of soil to the surface, clinging to the screw. Many archaeologists routinely use hand-held probes that yield small, solid cores. Probing of this type was used, for example, by Chinese archaeologists to plot the 300 pits remaining to be investigated near the first emperor's buried terracotta army. However, there is always a risk of damaging fragile artifacts or features.

One notable advance in this technique was developed by Carlo Lerici in Italy in the 1950s for Etruscan tombs of the 6th century BC. Having detected the precise location of a tomb through aerial photography and **soil resistivity** (see below), he would bore down into it a hole 8 cm (3 in) in diameter, and insert a long tube with a periscope head and a light, and also a tiny camera attached if needed. Lerici examined some 3500 Etruscan tombs in this way, and found that almost all were completely empty, thus saving future excavators a great deal of wasted effort. He also discovered over 20 with painted walls, thus doubling the known heritage of Etruscan painted tombs at a stroke.

Shovel-Test Pits (STPs). To gain a preliminary idea of what lies beneath the surface, small pits may often be dug into the ground at consistent distances from each other; in Europe these are usually in the form of meter-squares, but in some parts of North America small round holes are dug, about the diameter of a dinner-plate and less than a meter deep. These pits help show what an area has to offer, and help identify the extent of a possible site, while analysis and plotting of the material retrieved from them by sieving of the soil can produce maps showing areas with high concentrations of different kinds of artifacts. This method is commonly employed as part of site surveys for CRM projects in areas of the USA with poor surface visibility, such as forested areas of the east coast.

Probing the Pyramids. Modern technology has taken this kind of work even further, with the development of the endoscope and miniature TV cameras. In a project reminiscent of Lerici's, a probe was carried out in 1987 of a boat pit beside the Great Pyramid of Cheops (Khufu), in Egypt. This lies adjacent to another pit, excavated in 1954, that contained the perfectly preserved and disassembled parts of a 43-m (141-ft) long royal cedarwood boat of the 3rd millennium BC. The $250,000 probe revealed that the unopened pit does indeed contain all the dismantled timbers of a second boat but that the pit was not airtight – thus dashing hopes of analyzing the "ancient" air to see whether carbon dioxide in the atmosphere had increased over the millennia, and which component of the air preserves antiquities so efficiently.

Projects of this kind are beyond the resources of most archaeologists. But in future, funds permitting, probes of this type could equally well be applied to other Egyptian sites, to cavities in Maya structures, or to the many unexcavated tombs in China. The Great Pyramid itself has been the subject of probes by French and Japanese teams who believe it may contain as yet undiscovered chambers or corridors. Using ultrasensitive microgravimetric equipment – which is normally employed to search for deficiencies in dam walls, and can tell if a stone has a hollow behind it – they detected what they think is a cavity some 3 m (10 ft) beyond one of the passage walls. However, test drilling to support this claim has not been completed and all tests are carefully monitored by the Egyptian authorities until their potential contribution to Egyptology has been established.

Ground-Based Remote Sensing

Probing techniques are useful, but inevitably involve some disturbance of the site. There are, however, a wide range of non-destructive techniques ideal for the archaeologist seeking to learn more about a site before – or without – excavation. These are geophysical sensing devices which can be either active (i.e. they pass energy of various kinds through the soil and measure the response in order to "read" what lies below the surface); or passive (i.e. they measure physical properties such as magnetism and gravity without the need to inject energy to obtain a response).

Electromagnetic Methods.   A method which employs radio pulses is called ground-penetrating (or probing) radar (GPR). An emitter sends short pulses through the soil, and the echoes not only reflect back any changes in the soil and sediment conditions encountered, such as filled ditches, graves, walls, etc., but also measure the depth at which the changes occur on the basis of the travel time of the pulses. Three-dimensional maps of buried archaeological remains can then be produced from data processing and image-generation programs (see "time-slices" below).

In the field, the technique usually employs a single surface radar antenna which transmits very short pulses of electromagnetic energy (radar waves) down into the ground. A receiver records reflections from the discontinuities encountered, whether these are natural changes in soil horizons or properties, or buried archaeological features. The time it takes radar waves to travel from the surface source to the discontinuity and back to the receiver is measured in nanoseconds (i.e. billionths of a second), and since the wave velocity can be estimated, this indicates the distance involved.

In archaeological exploration and mapping, the radar antenna is generally dragged along the ground at walking speed in transects, sending out and receiving many pulses per second. In the early years of this method, the reflections were printed on paper and interpreted visually, and thus relied heavily on the experience and ability of the operator who had to guess what the buried feature might be from often indecipherable images. Inevitably this led to uncertainties and inconclusive results, with some notable successes and failures. Now, however, the method has greatly improved, and the reflection data can be stored digitally, which enables sophisticated data processing and analysis to be carried out, producing records which are easier to interpret. Powerful computers and software programs make it possible to store and process large three-dimensional sets of GPR data, and computer advances now permit automated data and image processing which can help to interpret complicated reflection profiles.

One such advance is the use of "time-slices" or "slice-maps." Thousands of individual reflections are combined into a single three-dimensional dataset which can then be "sliced" horizontally, each slice corresponding to a specific estimated depth in the ground, and revealing the general shape and location of buried features at successive depths. A variety of colors (or shades of gray) are used to make a visual image that the brain can interpret more easily – e.g. areas with little

Amplitude slice-maps from the Forum Novum site, Italy. The top slice, at 0–10 ns (nanosecond, equivalent to 0–50 cm) reveals a Y-shaped anomaly, reflecting two gravel roads. As the slices go deeper, the Roman walls begin to emerge very clearly, showing a well-organized plan of rooms, doors, and corridors. The deepest slice shows the actual floor levels of the rooms and the objects preserved on them.

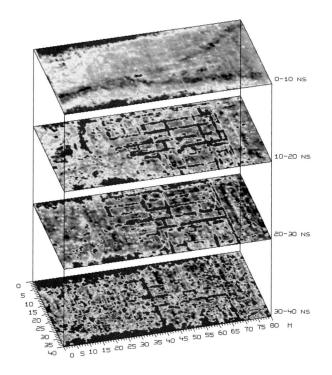

or no subsurface reflection may be colored blue, those with high reflection may be red. Each slice therefore becomes like a horizontal surface, and can illustrate the buried components of the site.

For example, in the Forum Novum, an ancient Roman marketplace located about 100 km (62 miles) north of Rome, British archaeologists from the University of Birmingham and the British School of Archaeology in Rome needed a fuller picture of an unexcavated area than they had been able to obtain from aerial photographs and other techniques such as resistivity (see below). A series of GPR slices of the area revealed a whole series of walls, individual rooms, doorways, courtyards – in short, produced an architectural layout of the site which means that future excavation can be concentrated on a representative sample of the structures, thus avoiding a costly and time-consuming uncovering of the whole area.

Earth Resistance Survey.   A commonly used method that has been employed on archaeological sites for several decades, particularly in Europe, is ***electrical resistivity***. The technique derives from the principle that the damper the soil the more easily it will conduct electricity, i.e. the less resistance it will show to an electric current. A **resistivity meter** attached to electrodes in the ground can thus measure varying degrees of subsurface resistance to a current passed between the electrodes. Silted up ditches or filled-in pits retain more moisture than stone walls or roads and will therefore display lower resistivity than stone structures.

The technique works particularly well for ditches and pits in chalk and gravel, and masonry in clay. It usually involves first placing two "remote" probes, which remain stationary, in the ground. Two "mobile" probes, fixed to a frame that also supports the meter, are then inserted into the earth for each reading. A variation of the method is "resistivity profiling," which involves the measurement of earth resistance at increasing depths by widening the probe spacings and thus building up a vertical "pseudosection" across a site.

Magnetic Survey Methods.   These are among the most widely used methods of survey, being particularly helpful in locating fired clay structures such as hearths and pottery kilns; iron objects; and pits and ditches. Such buried features all produce slight but measurable distortions in the earth's magnetic field. The reasons for this vary according to the type of feature, but are based on the presence of iron, even if only in minute amounts. For example, grains of iron oxide in clay, their magnetism randomly orientated if the clay is unbaked, will line up and become permanently fixed in the direction of the earth's magnetic field when heated to about 700°C (1292°F) or more. The baked clay thus becomes a weak permanent magnet, creating an anomaly in the surrounding magnetic field. Anomalies caused by pits and ditches, on the other hand, occur because the so-called magnetic susceptibility of their contents is greater than that of the surrounding subsoil.

MEASURING MAGNETISM

Most terrestrial magnetometer surveys are undertaken either with fluxgate or with alkali metal vapor magnetometers.

Fluxgate instruments usually comprise two sensors fixed rigidly at either end of a vertically-held tube and measure only the vertical component of the local magnetic field strength. The magnetometer is carried along a succession of traverses, usually 1.0 m apart, tied in to an overall pre-surveyed grid, until the entire site is covered. The signal is logged automatically and stored in the instrument's memory, to be downloaded and processed later. To speed up the coverage of large areas, two or more fluxgate instruments can be moved across the site at once – either on a frame carried by the operator, or sometimes on a wheeled cart. In this way, many hectares of ground can be covered quite quickly, revealing features such as pits, ditches, hearths, kilns, or entire settlement complexes and their associated roads, trackways and cemeteries.

An alternative and sometimes more effective magnetometer is the alkali-metal vapor type, typically a caesium magnetometer. Although more expensive and quite difficult to operate, an advantage these magnetometers have over fluxgate types is that they are more sensitive and can therefore detect features which are only very weakly magnetic, or more deeply buried than usual. Such instruments have been used for many years with great success in continental Europe and are finding favor elsewhere. Unlike a fluxgate gradiometer they measure the total magnetic field (but can be operated as a total-field gradiometer if configured with two vertically mounted sensors). It is also usual for two or more of these sensors to be used at once – often mounted on a non-magnetic wheeled cart. Surveys with such systems can cover up to about 5 hectares each day at a high resolution sampling interval (0.5 m × 0.25 m). Arrays of fluxgate sensors are now also being introduced, but

many surveys are conducted with a dual sensor system with a sample interval of *c*. 0.1 m × 0.25 m. Fluxgates are often favored for their lower cost, versatility, and ability to detect a similar range of features to caesium systems.

Metal detectors are also helpful in detecting buried remains – and not just metal ones. An alternating magnetic field is generated by passing an electrical current through a transmitter coil. Buried metal objects distort this field and are detected as a result of an electrical signal picked up by a receiver coil. These electromagnetic devices can be of great value to archaeologists, particularly as they can provide general results and are able to locate modern metal objects that may lie near the surface. They are also very widely used by non-archaeologists, most of whom are responsible enthusiasts; some of whom, however, vandalize sites mindlessly and often illegally dig holes without recording or reporting the finds they make, which are therefore without context. There are now 30,000 metal detector users in Britain alone.

The Bartington Grad 601/1 single vertical component high stability fluxgate gradiometer, capable of 10 readings per second with a resolution of 0.1nT/m.

Results of a magnetometer survey of the site of Stanton Drew in Somerset. This revealed the existence of a wooden henge structure consisting of nine concentric rings of timbers that had completely disappeared above ground.

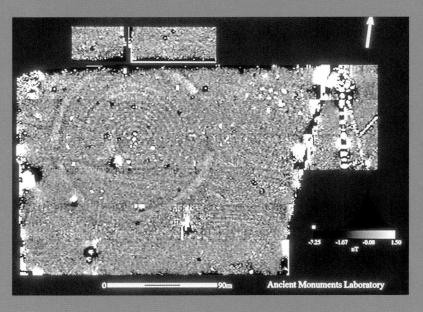

KEY CONCEPTS

Assessing the Layout of Sites and Features

- *Site Surface Survey*: the study of the distribution of surviving features at a site (such as earthworks or traces of structures), and the recording and sometimes collecting of artifacts (often pottery or stone tools) from the surface

- *Subsurface Detection*: the use of probes and shovel-test pits (and sometimes miniature TV cameras and endoscopes) to find and map subsurface features

- *Ground-Based Remote Sensing*: the use of non-destructive techniques, such as ground-penetrating radar and magnetometry, to find and map subsurface features

All the magnetic instruments (see box opposite) can produce informative site plans which help to delimit archaeological potential. Common means of presentation are contour, dot density, and color and gray-scale maps, all also used to display **earth resistance survey** results. In the case of magnetic survey, the contour map has contour lines that join all points of the same value of the magnetic field intensity – this successfully reveals separate anomalies, such as tombs in a cemetery. In dot-density mapping, individual magnetometer readings are plotted as dots on a plan, with shading dependent on the magnetic intensity, the blacker areas therefore represent the highest anomalies in the local magnetic field. This makes it easier for the eye to distinguish patterns, even where changes may be slight.

So far, we have discovered sites and mapped as many of their surface and subsurface features as possible. But, despite the growing importance of survey, the only way to check the reliability of surface data, confirm the accuracy of the remote sensing techniques, and actually see what remains of these sites is to excavate them. Furthermore, survey can tell us a little about a large area, but only excavation can tell us a great deal about a relatively small area.

EXCAVATION

Excavation retains its central role in fieldwork because it yields the most reliable evidence for the two main kinds of information archaeologists are interested in: (1) human activities at a particular period in the past; and (2) changes in those activities from period to period. Very broadly we can say that contemporary activities take place *horizontally in space*, whereas changes in those activities occur *vertically through time*. It is this distinction between horizontal "slices of time" and vertical sequences through time that forms the basis of most excavation methodology.

In the horizontal dimension archaeologists demonstrate that activities occurred at the same time by proving through excavation that artifacts and features are found in association in an undisturbed **context**. Of course, as we saw in Chapter 2, there are many formation processes that may disturb this primary context. One of the main purposes of the survey and remote sensing procedures outlined in the earlier sections is to select for excavation sites, or areas within sites, that are reasonably undisturbed. On a single-period site such as an East African early human camp site this is vital if human behavior at the camp is to be reconstructed at all accurately. But on a multi-period site, such as a long-lived European town or Near Eastern village mound, finding large areas of undisturbed deposits will be almost impossible. Here archaeologists have to try to reconstruct during and after excavation just what disturbance there has been and then decide how to interpret it. Clearly, adequate records must be made as excavation progresses if the task of interpretation is to be undertaken with any chance of success. In the vertical dimension archaeologists analyze changes through time by the study of **stratigraphy**.

Stratigraphy

As we saw in Chapter 1, one of the first steps in understanding the great antiquity of humankind was the recognition by geologists of the process of **stratification** – that layers or strata are laid down, one on top of the other, according to processes that still continue. Archaeological strata (the layers of cultural or natural debris visible in the side of any excavation) accumulate over much shorter periods of time than geological ones, but nevertheless conform to the same *law of superposition*. Put simply, this states that where one layer overlies another, the lower was deposited first. Hence, an excavated vertical profile showing a series of layers constitutes a sequence that has accumulated through time.

Chapter 4 explores the significance of this for dating purposes. Here we should note that the law of superposition refers only to the sequence of deposition, not to the age of the material in the different strata. The contents of lower layers are indeed usually older than those of upper layers, but the archaeologist must not simply assume this. Pits dug down from a higher layer or burrowing animals (even earthworms) may introduce later materials into lower levels. Moreover, occasionally strata can become inverted, as when they are eroded all the way from the top of a bank to the bottom of a ditch.

In recent years, archaeologists have developed an ingenious and effective method of checking that artifacts – so far mostly of stone or bone – discovered in a particular deposit are contemporaneous and not intrusive. They have found that in a surprising number of cases flakes of stone or bone can be fitted back together again: reassembled in the shape of the original stone block or pieces of bone from which they came. At the British **Mesolithic** (Middle Stone Age) site of Hengistbury Head, for example, reanalysis of an old excavation showed that two groups of flint flakes, found in two different layers, could be **refitted**. This cast doubt on the stratigraphic separation of the two layers, and demolished the original excavator's argument that the flints had been made by two different groups of people. As well as clarifying questions of stratification, these refitting or **conjoining** exercises are transforming archaeological studies of early technology (Chapter 7).

Stratigraphy, then, is the study and validating of stratification – the analysis in the vertical, time dimension of a series of layers in the horizontal, space dimension (although in practice few layers are precisely horizontal).

What are the best excavation methods for retrieving this information?

The complexity of stratification varies with the type of site. This hypothetical section through an urban deposit indicates the kind of complicated stratigraphy, in both vertical and horizontal dimensions, that the archaeologist can encounter. There may be few undisturbed stratified layers. The chances of finding preserved organic material increase as one approaches the water table, near which deposits may be waterlogged.

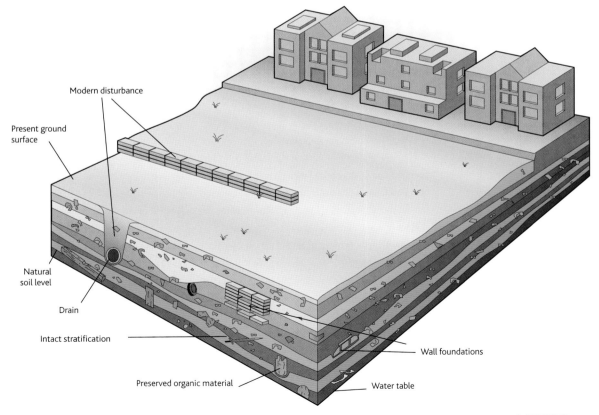

Modern disturbance

Present ground surface

Natural soil level

Drain

Intact stratification

Preserved organic material

Wall foundations

Water table

Methods of Excavation

Excavation is both costly and destructive, and therefore never to be undertaken lightly. Wherever possible non-destructive approaches outlined earlier should be used to meet research objectives in preference to excavation. But assuming excavation is to proceed, and the necessary funding and permission to dig have been obtained, what are the best methods to adopt?

It goes without saying that all excavation methods need to be adapted to the research question in hand and the nature of the site. It is no good digging a deeply stratified urban site, with hundreds of complex structures, thousands of intercutting pits, and tens of thousands of artifacts, as if it were the same as a shallow **Paleolithic** open site, where only one or two structures and a few hundred artifacts may survive. On the Paleolithic site, for example, it may be possible to uncover all the structures and record the exact position, vertically horizontally – i.e. the *provenience* – of each and every artifact. On the urban site there is no chance of doing this, given time and funding constraints. Instead, we have to adopt a sampling strategy, and only key artifacts such as coins (important for dating purposes: see Chapter 4) will have their provenience recorded with three-dimensional precision, the remainder being allocated simply to the layer and perhaps the grid-square in which they were found (sites are usually divided up into grid-squares, just like maps are, in order to aid in accurate recording; naturally, the size and number of the grid squares will depend on the type, size and likely depth of the site).

It should be noted, however, that we have already reintroduced the idea of the vertical and horizontal dimensions. These are as crucial to the methods of excavation as they are to the principles behind excavation. Broadly speaking we can divide excavation techniques into:

1 those that emphasize the vertical dimension, by cutting into deep deposits to reveal stratification;
2 those that emphasize the horizontal dimension, by opening up large areas of a particular layer to reveal the spatial relationships between artifacts and features in that layer.

Most excavators employ a combination of both strategies, but there are different ways of achieving this. All presuppose that the site has first been surveyed and a grid of squares laid down over it. A site grid is laid out from a datum, which is simply a selected location that serves as a reference point for all horizontal and vertical measurements taken at the site, so that the site can be accurately mapped and the exact location of any artifact or feature can be recorded in three dimensions if that is necessary or feasible.

The **Wheeler box-grid** – developed from the work of Pitt-Rivers, as noted in Chapter 1 – seeks to satisfy both vertical and horizontal requirements by retaining intact balks of earth between the squares of the grid, as can be clearly seen in the picture at right, so that different layers can be traced and correlated across the site in vertical profiles. Once the general extent and layout of the site have been ascertained, some of the balks can be removed and the squares joined into an open excavation to expose any features (such as a mosaic floor) that are of special interest.

Advocates of **open-area excavation** criticize this method, arguing that the balks are invariably in the wrong place or wrongly orientated to illustrate the relationships required from sections, and that they prevent the distinguishing of spatial patterning over large areas. It is far better, these critics say, not to have such permanent or semi-permanent balks, but to open up large areas and only to cut vertical sections (at whatever angle is necessary to the main site grid) where they are needed to elucidate particularly complex stratigraphic relationships. Apart from these "running sections," the vertical dimension is recorded by accurate three-dimensional measurements as the dig proceeds and reconstructed on paper after the end of the excavation. The introduction since Wheeler's day of more advanced recording methods, including field computers, makes this more demanding open-area method feasible, and it has become the norm, for instance, in much of British archaeology. The open-area method is particularly effective where single-period deposits lie near the surface, as for instance with remains of Native American or European **Neolithic** long houses. Here the time dimension may be represented by lateral movement (a settlement rebuilt adjacent to, not on top of, an earlier one) and it is essential to expose large horizontal areas in order to understand the complex pattern of rebuilding. Large open-area excavations are often undertaken in salvage or rescue operations when

Box-grid excavation trenches at Anuradhapura's Abhayagiri Buddhist monastery, Sri Lanka.

Open-area excavation at Sutton Hoo, eastern England. A large area, 32 x 64 m, was uncovered to establish the perimeters of two burial mounds. Detailed stratigraphy was then studied in smaller squares. Immediately below the topsoil lay early medieval features, recorded using overhead color photographs to emphasize soil variations, and plotted on site plans at scales of 1:10 and 1:100.

The Native American site of Koster, in the Illinois River Valley: large horizontal areas were uncovered to locate living floors and activity zones. However, so that the vertical dimension could be analyzed at this deep site, vertical sections were cut as steps as the excavation descended. At this complex site 14 occupation levels were identified, dating from c. 7500 BC to AD 1200.

land is going to be destroyed – otherwise farmers are naturally opposed to stripping large areas of plow-disturbed soil. The box-grid method is still widely used in parts of South Asia where it was introduced by Wheeler in the 1940s. It remains popular as it enables large numbers of untrained workers in individual boxes to be easily supervised by small numbers of staff.

No single method, however, is ever going to be universally applicable. The rigid box-grid, for instance, has rarely been employed to excavate very deep sites, such as Near Eastern **tells**, because the trench squares rapidly become uncomfortable and dangerous as the dig proceeds downward. One solution

KEY CONCEPTS

Excavation

- Excavation yields evidence of contemporary activities (which are found horizontally through space) and changes through time (which are found vertically in sequences)

- Stratigraphy is the study of archaeological layers found during excavations. The law of superposition states that where one layer overlies another, the lower was deposited first. This forms the basis of the way archaeologists investigate changes through time

- Excavation methods should be adapted to the site and particular questions that need to be answered. The two main strategies are the Wheeler box-grid and open-area excavation; a combination of both is often used. A sampling strategy of some kind can be required to save time and money

commonly adopted is **step-trenching**, with a large area opened at the top which gradually narrows as the dig descends in a series of large steps. This technique was used effectively at the Koster site, Illinois.

Each site is different and one needs to adapt to its conditions – for example, in some cases by following the natural geological strata or the cultural layers instead of using arbitrary spits or imposing a false regularity where it does not exist. Whatever the method of excavation, a dig is only as good as its methods of recovery and recording. Since excavation involves destruction of much of the evidence, it is an unrepeatable exercise. Well-thought-out recovery methods are essential, and careful records must be kept of every stage of the dig.

Underwater Archaeology

One special category of both survey and excavation is constituted by *underwater archaeology*, which is generally considered to have been given its first major impetus during the winter of 1853–54, when a particularly low water level in the Swiss lakes laid bare enormous quantities of wooden posts, pottery, and other artifacts. From the earliest investigations, using crude diving-bells, it has developed into a valuable complement to work on land. It encompasses a wide variety of sites, including wells, sink holes, and springs (e.g. the great sacrificial well at Chichén Itzá, Mexico); submerged lakeside settlements; and marine sites ranging from shipwrecks to sunken harbors and drowned cities.

The invention in recent times of miniature submarines, other submersible craft, and above all of scuba diving gear has been of enormous value, enabling divers to stay underwater for much longer, and to reach sites at previously impossible depths. As a result, the pace and scale of discovery have greatly increased. More than 1000 shipwrecks are known in shallow Mediterranean waters, but recent explorations using deep-sea submersibles, such as miniature unmanned submarines (remotely operated vehicles – ROV) with sonar, high-powered lighting, and video cameras, have begun to find Roman wrecks at depths of up to 850 m (2790 ft), and two Phoenician wrecks packed with amphorae discovered off the coast of Israel are the oldest vessels ever found in the deep sea.

Underwater Reconnaissance. Geophysical methods are as useful for finding sites underwater as they are for locating land sites. For example, in 1979 it was magnetometry combined with **side-scan sonar** that discovered the *Hamilton* and the *Scourge*, two armed schooners sunk during the War of 1812 at a depth of 90 m (295 ft) in Lake Ontario, Canada. The latest multibeam side-scan sonar gives brilliantly clear images and allows accurate measurements to be taken of shipwrecks on the sea bed. Nevertheless, in regions such as the Mediterranean the majority of finds have resulted from methods as simple as talking to local sponge-divers, who collectively have spent thousands of hours scouring the seabed.

Three methods of geophysical underwater survey. (1) The proton magnetometer is towed well behind the survey boat, detecting iron and steel objects (e.g. cannons, steel hulls) that distort the earth's magnetic field. (2) Side-scan sonar transmits sound waves in a fan-shaped beam to produce a graphic image of surface (but not sub-surface) features on the seafloor. (3) The sub-bottom profiler emits sound pulses that bounce back from features and objects buried beneath the seafloor.

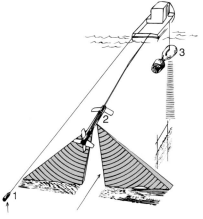

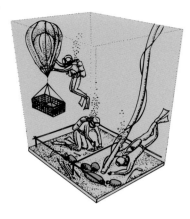

Underwater excavation techniques: at left, the lift bag for raising objects; center, measuring and recording finds in situ; right, the air lift for removing sediment.

Model, at a scale of 1:10, to show how the San Juan's surviving timbers may have fitted together.

Structural plan of the wreck on the harbor bottom (2-m grid squares).

Underwater Excavation. Excavation underwater is complex and expensive (not to mention the highly demanding post-excavation conservation and analytical work that is also required). Once underway, the excavation may involve shifting vast quantities of sediment, and recording and removing bulky objects as diverse as storage jars (amphorae), metal ingots, and cannons. George Bass, founder of the Institute of Nautical Archaeology in Texas, and others have developed many helpful devices, such as baskets attached to balloons to raise objects, and air lifts (suction hoses) to remove sediment. If the vessel's hull survives at all, detailed drawings must be made so that specialists can later reconstruct the overall form and lines, either on paper or in three dimensions as a model or full-size replica. In some rare cases, like that of England's *Mary Rose* (a 16th-century AD warship that sank off Portsmouth), preservation is sufficiently good for the remains of the hull to be raised – funds permitting.

Nautical archaeologists have now excavated more than 100 sunken vessels, revealing not only how they were constructed but also many insights into shipboard life, cargoes, trade routes, early metallurgy, and glassmaking. For example, a Basque whaling ship, the *San Juan*, which had sunk in Red Bay, Labrador, in 1565, was excavated in the 1980s from a specially equipped barge, anchored above the site, that contained a workshop, storage baths for artifacts, a crane for lifting timbers, and a compressor able to run 12 air lifts for removing silt. Salt water was heated on board and pumped down through hoses direct to the divers' suits to maintain body warmth in the near-freezing conditions. An important technique devised during the project was the use of latex rubber to mold large sections of the ship's timbers in position underwater, thereby reproducing accurately the hull shape and details such as toolmarks and wood

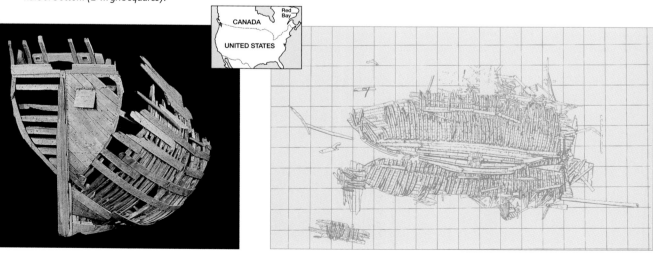

grain. The remains of the vessel were also raised in pieces to the surface for precise recording, but the latex molds eliminated the need for costly conservation of the original timbers, which were reburied on-site.

Recovery and Recording of the Evidence

As we saw above, different sites have different requirements. We should aim to recover and plot the three-dimensional provenience of every artifact from a shallow single-period Paleolithic or Neolithic site, an objective that is simply not feasible for the urban archaeologist. On both types of site, a decision may be made to save time by using mechanical diggers to remove topsoil, but thereafter the Paleolithic or Neolithic specialist will usually want to screen or sieve as much excavated soil as possible in order to recover tiny artifacts, animal bones, and plant remains. The urban archaeologist on the other hand will only be able to adopt sieving much more selectively, as part of a sampling strategy, for instance where plant remains can be expected to survive, as in a latrine or garbage pit. Decisions need to be made about the type of sieving to be undertaken, the size of the screen and its mesh, and whether dry or wet sieving will yield the best results. Naturally all these factors will depend on the resources of the excavation project, the period and scale of the site, whether it is dry or waterlogged, and what kind of material can be expected to have survived and to be retrievable.

Once an artifact has been recovered, and its provenience recorded, it must be given a number which is entered in a catalog book or field computer and on the bag in which it is to be stored. Day-to-day progress of the dig is recorded in site notebooks, or on data sheets preprinted with specific questions to be answered (which helps produce uniform data suitable for later analysis by computer).

Unlike artifacts, which can be removed for later analysis, features and structures usually have to be left where they were found (or *in situ*), or destroyed as the excavation proceeds to another layer. It is thus imperative to record them, not simply by written description in site notebooks, but by accurately scaled drawings and photography. The same applies to vertical profiles (sections), and for each horizontally exposed layer good overhead photographs taken from a stand or tethered balloon are also essential.

It is the site notebooks, scaled drawings, photographs and computer data – in addition to recovered artifacts, animal bones, and plant remains – that form the total record of the excavation, on the basis of which all interpretations of the site will be made. This post-excavation analysis will take many months, perhaps years, often much longer than the excavation itself. However, some preliminary analysis, particularly sorting and **classification** of the artifacts, will be made in the field during the course of the excavation.

The Roman baths at Huggin Hill in London. A Museum of London archaeologist uses a theodolite (a surveying instrument) to measure the accurate position of a column base on which another archaeologist holds a survey rod (range pole). Their measurements will later form the basis for a detailed plan.

Processing and Classification

Like excavation itself, the processing of excavated materials in the field laboratory is a specialized activity that demands careful planning and organization. For example, an archaeologist excavating a wet site will need experts in the conservation of waterlogged wood, and facilities for coping with such material.

Two important aspects of field laboratory procedure are cleaning of artifacts and sorting and classifying them. In both cases the archaeologist always needs to consider in advance what kinds of questions the newly excavated material might be able to answer. Thorough cleaning of artifacts, for example, is a traditional part of excavations worldwide. But many of the new scientific techniques discussed later in this book make it quite evident that artifacts should *not* necessarily be cleaned thoroughly before a specialist has had a chance to study them. For instance, we now know that food residues are often preserved in pots and possible blood residues on stone tools. The chances of such preservation need to be assessed before evidence is destroyed.

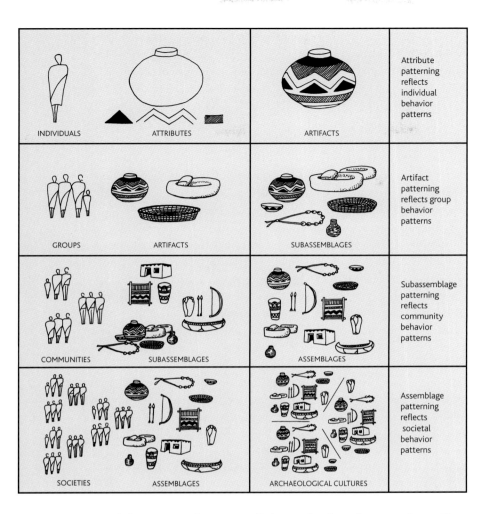

Terms used in archaeological classification, from attributes (shape, decoration) of a pot to the complete archaeological culture: a diagram developed by the American archaeologist James Deetz. The columns at left and right give the inferred human meaning of the terms.

Nevertheless most artifacts eventually have to be cleaned to some degree if they are to be sorted and classified. Initial sorting is into broad categories such as stone tools, pottery, and metal objects. These categories are then subdivided or classified, so as to create more manageable groups that can later be analyzed. Classification is commonly done on the basis of three kinds of characteristics or **attributes**:

1 surface attributes (including decoration and color);
2 shape attributes (dimensions as well as shape itself);
3 technological attributes (primarily raw material).

Artifacts found to share similar attributes are grouped together into artifact types – hence the term **typology**, which simply refers to the creation of such types.

Typology dominated archaeological thinking until the 1950s, and still plays an important role. The reason for this is straightforward. Artifacts make up a large part of the archaeological record, and typology helps archaeologists create order in this mass of evidence. As we saw in Chapter 1, C. J. Thomsen demonstrated early on that artifacts could be ordered in a **Three Age System** or sequence of stone, bronze, and iron. This discovery underlies the continuing use of typology as a method of dating (Chapter 4). Typology has also been used as a means of defining archaeological entities at a particular moment in time: groups of artifact (and building) types at a particular time and place are termed *assemblages*, and groups of assemblages have been taken to define *archaeological cultures*. These definitions are also long established, but, as we shall see later, the difficulty comes when one tries to translate this terminology into human terms and to relate an archaeological "culture" with an actual group of people in the past.

This brings us back to the purpose of classification. Types, assemblages, and **cultures** are all concepts designed to put order into disordered evidence – they are artificial. The trap that former generations of scholars fell into was to allow these concepts to determine the way they thought about the past, rather than using them merely as one means of giving shape to the evidence. We now recognize more clearly that different classifications are needed for the different kinds of questions we want to ask. A student of ceramic technology would base a classification on variations in raw material and methods of manufacture, whereas a scholar studying the various functions of pottery for storage, cooking etc. might classify the vessels according to shape and size. Our ability to construct and make good use of new classifications has been immeasurably enhanced by computers, which allow archaeologists to compare the association of different attributes on hundreds of objects at once. However, post-excavation work in the laboratory or store does not cease with cleaning, labeling and classification. Curation is also of immense importance, and the conservation of objects and materials plays a major role, not only for the arrangement of long-term storage but also for collections management in general. The material needs to be preserved and readily available for future research, re-interpretation and, in some cases, display to the public, whether permanently or in temporary exhibitions.

In conclusion, it cannot be stressed too strongly that all the effort put into survey, excavation, and post-excavation analysis will have been largely wasted unless the results are published.

STUDY QUESTIONS
- What are the pros and cons of unsystematic and systematic survey methods?
- What types of archaeological sites can be identified through aerial photography?
- What is GIS and how can archaeologists use it?
- How is archaeological excavation different from archaeological survey?
- What are the benefits and drawbacks of the Wheeler box-grid method of excavation?
- What are some of the ways in which artifacts can be classified?

SUMMARY

- Although many sites are found either by accident or during modern development, the archaeologist has a barrage of ground and aerial reconnaissance techniques available with which to find new sites.

- Until the present century, individual sites were the main focus of archaeological attention, but today archaeologists study whole regions, often employing sampling techniques to bring ground reconnaissance survey within the scope of individual research teams. Having located sites within those regions, and mapped them (usually using GIS), archaeologists can then turn to a whole battery of remote sensing site survey devices able to detect buried features without excavation.

- Remote sensing methods almost all involve either passing energy into the ground and locating buried features from their effect on that energy or measuring the intensity of the earth's magnetic field. In either case, they depend on contrast between the buried features and their surroundings. Many of the techniques are costly in both equipment and time, but they are often cheaper and certainly less destructive than random trial trenches. They allow archaeologists to be more selective in deciding which parts of a site, if any, should be fully excavated.

- Excavation itself relies on methods designed to elucidate the horizontal extent of a site in space, and the vertical stratification representing changes through time. Good recording methods are essential, together with a well-equipped field laboratory for processing and classifying the finds. Classification based on selected attributes (decoration, shape, material) of each artifact is the fundamental means of organizing the excavated material, usually into types – hence typology. But classification is only a means to an end, and different schemes are needed for the different questions archaeologists want to address.

- However, little of the material retrieved during survey and excavation will be of much use unless it can be dated in some way. In the next chapter we turn to this crucial aspect of archaeology.

FURTHER READING

Useful introductions to methods of survey and excavation can be found in the following:

Collis, J. 2004. *Digging up the Past: An Introduction to Archaeological Excavation*. Sutton: Stroud.

Gaffney, V. & Gater, J. 2003. *Revealing the Buried Past. Geophysics for Archaeologists*. Tempus: Stroud.

Hester, T.N., Shafer, H.J., & Feder, K.L. 2008. *Field Methods in Archaeology*. (7th ed.). Left Coast Press: Walnut Creek.

McIntosh, J. 1999. *The Practical Archaeologist: How We Know What We Know About the Past*. (2nd ed.). Facts on File: New York; Thames & Hudson: London.

Oswin, J. 2009. *A Field Guide to Geophysics in Archaeology*. Springer: Berlin.

Wheatley, D. & Gillings, M. 2002. *Spatial Technology and Archaeology. The Archaeological Applications of GIS*. Routledge: London.

Wiseman, J.R. & El-Baz, F. (eds.). 2007. *Remote sensing in Archaeology* (with CD-Rom). Springer: Berlin.

Zimmerman, L.J. & Green, W. (eds.). 2003. *The Archaeologist's Toolkit* (7 vols.). AltaMira Press: Walnut Creek.

When?
Dating methods and chronology

RELATIVE DATING
STRATIGRAPHY: ORDERING ARCHAEOLOGICAL LAYERS

TYPOLOGICAL SEQUENCES: COMPARING OBJECTS
Seriation: Comparing Assemblages of Objects

ENVIRONMENTAL SEQUENCES

ABSOLUTE DATING
CALENDARS & HISTORICAL CHRONOLOGIES
Using a Historical Chronology

ANNUAL CYCLES
Tree-Ring Dating

RADIOACTIVE CLOCKS
Radiocarbon Dating
Other Radiometric Methods

OTHER ABSOLUTE DATING METHODS

WORLD CHRONOLOGY

Study Questions
Summary
Further Reading

All human beings experience time. An individual
experiences a lifetime of perhaps 70 years or so. That person, through the
memories of his or her parents and grandparents, may also indirectly experience
earlier periods of time, back over more than 100 years. The study of history gives
us access to hundreds more years of recorded time. But it is only **archaeology**
that opens up the almost unimaginable vistas of thousands and even a few
millions of years of past human existence. This chapter will examine the various
ways in which we, as archaeologists, date past events within this great expanse
of time.

Relative and Absolute Dating.   It might seem surprising that in order to study
the past it is not always essential to know precisely how long ago (in years) a
particular period or event occurred. It is often very helpful simply to know
whether one event happened before or after another. By ordering **artifacts**,
deposits, societies, and events into sequences, earlier before later, we can study
developments in the past without knowing how long each stage lasted or how
many years ago such changes took place. This idea that something is older (or
younger) relative to something else is the basis of **relative dating**.

Ultimately, however, we want to know the full or absolute age in years
before the present of different events or parts of a sequence – we need methods
of **absolute dating**. Absolute dates help us find out how quickly changes such
as the introduction of agriculture occurred, and whether they occurred
simultaneously or at different times in different regions of the world. Only
in the last 50 years or so have independent means of absolute dating become
available, transforming archaeology in the process. Before then, virtually the
only reliable absolute dates were historical ones, such as the date of the reign
of the ancient Egyptian pharaoh Tutankhamun.

Measuring Time.   How do we detect the passage of time? We can all observe its
passing through the alternating darkness and light of nights and days, and then
through the annual cycle of the seasons. In fact, for most of human history these

were the only ways of measuring time, other than by the human lifespan. As we shall see, some dating methods still rely on the annual passage of the seasons. Increasingly, however, dating methods in archaeology have come to rely on other physical processes, many of them not observable to the human eye. The most significant of these is the use of radioactive clocks.

Some degree of error, usually expressed as an age-bracket which can stretch over several centuries or even millennia, is inevitable when using any dating technique. But while the science behind dating methods is being ever more refined, the main source of errors remains the archaeologist – by poor choice of samples to be dated, by contaminating those samples, or by misinterpreting results.

Dating Conventions. To be meaningful, our timescale in years must relate to a fixed point in time. In the Christian world, this is by convention taken as the birth of Christ, supposedly in the year AD 1 (there is no year 0), with years counted back before Christ (BC) and forward after Christ (AD or *Anno Domini*, which is Latin for "In the Year of Our Lord"). However, this is by no means the only system. In the Muslim world, for example, the basic fixed point is the date of the Prophet's departure from Mecca (AD 622 in the Christian calendar). As a result of these differences some scholars prefer to use the terms "Before the Common Era" (BCE) and "in the Common Era" (CE) instead of BC and AD.

Scientists who derive dates from radioactive methods want a neutral international system, and have chosen to count years back from the present (BP). But since scientists too require a firm fixed point to count from, they take BP to mean "before 1950" (the approximate year of the establishment of the first radioactive method, radiocarbon). This may be convenient for scientists, but can be confusing for everyone else (a date of 400 BP is not 400 years ago but AD 1550, currently over 450 years ago). It is therefore clearest to convert any BP date for the last few thousand years into the BC/AD system.

For the **Paleolithic** period, however (stretching back two or three million years before 10,000 BC), archaeologists use the terms "BP" and "years ago" interchangeably, since a difference of 50 years or so between them is irrelevant. For this remote epoch we are dating **sites** or events at best only to within several thousand years of their "true" date. If even the most precise dates for the Paleolithic give us glimpses of that epoch only at intervals of several thousand years, clearly archaeologists can never hope to reconstruct a conventional history of Paleolithic events. On the other hand, Paleolithic archaeologists can gain insights into some of the broad long-term changes that shaped the way modern humans evolved – insights that are denied archaeologists working with shorter periods of time, where in any case there may be too much "detail" for the broader pattern to be apparent.

The way in which archaeologists carry out their research therefore depends very much on the precision of dating obtainable for the period of time in question.

RELATIVE DATING

The first, and in some ways the most important, step in much archaeological research involves ordering things into sequences. The things to be put into sequence can be archaeological deposits in a stratigraphic **excavation**. Or they can be artifacts as in a typological sequence. Changes in the Earth's climate also give rise to local, regional, and global environmental sequences – the most notable being the sequence of global fluctuations during the Ice Age. All these sequences can be used for relative dating.

STRATIGRAPHY: ORDERING ARCHAEOLOGICAL LAYERS

Stratigraphy, as we saw in Chapter 3, is the study of **stratification** – the laying down or depositing of strata or layers (also called deposits) one above the other. From the point of view of relative dating, the important principle is that the underlying layer was deposited first and therefore earlier than the overlying layer. A succession of layers provides a relative chronological sequence, from earliest (bottom) to latest (top).

Good stratigraphic excavation at an archaeological site is designed to obtain such a sequence. Part of this work involves detecting whether there has been any human or natural disturbance of the layers since they were originally deposited (such as garbage pits dug down by later occupants of a site into earlier layers, or animals burrowing holes). Armed with carefully observed stratigraphic information, the archaeologist can hope to construct a reliable relative chronological sequence for the deposition of the different layers.

But of course what we mostly want to date are not so much the layers or deposits themselves as the materials that humans have left within them – artifacts, structures, organic remains – which ultimately reveal past human activities at the site. Here the idea of **association** is important. When we say that two objects were found in association within the same archaeological deposit, we generally mean that they became buried at the same time. Provided that the deposit is a sealed one, without stratigraphic intrusions from another deposit, the associated objects can be said to be no more recent than the deposit itself. A sequence of sealed deposits thus gives a sequence – and relative chronology – for the time of burial of the objects found associated in those deposits.

This is a crucial concept to grasp, because if one of those objects can later be given an absolute date – say a datable coin or a piece of charcoal that can be dated by radiocarbon in the laboratory – then it is possible to assign that absolute date not only to the charcoal but to the sealed deposit and the other objects associated

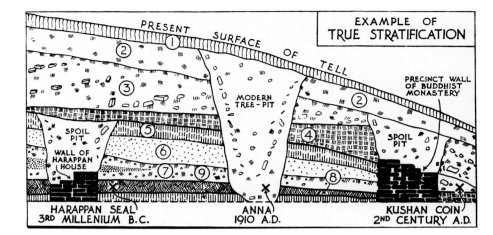

EXAMPLE OF TRUE STRATIFICATION

PRESENT SURFACE OF TELL

MODERN TREE-PIT

PRECINCT WALL OF BUDDHIST MONASTERY

SPOIL PIT

WALL OF HARAPPAN HOUSE

SPOIL PIT

HARAPPAN SEAL
3RD MILLENIUM B.C.

ANNA
1910 A.D.

KUSHAN COIN
2ND CENTURY A.D.

Stratigraphy in action: a section across a mound or tell in the Indus Valley. Attention to stratigraphy is crucial because, as with the coins and the seal here, not everything found at the same level is always equally old.

with it as well. A series of such dates from different deposits will give an absolute chronology for the whole sequence. It is this interconnecting of stratigraphic sequences with absolute dating methods that provides the most reliable basis for dating archaeological sites and their contents. The example shown above is Sir Mortimer Wheeler's drawing of a section across an ancient mound in the Indus Valley (modern Pakistan). The site has been disturbed by more recent pits, but the sequence of layers is still visible, and the Harappan seal, of known age and found in an undisturbed **context** in layer 8, helps to date that layer and the wall next to it.

But there is another important point to consider. So far we have dated, relatively and with luck absolutely, the time of burial of the deposits and their associated material. As we have observed, however, what we want ultimately to reconstruct and date are the past human activities and behavior that those deposits and materials represent. If a deposit is a garbage pit with pottery in it, the deposit itself is of interest as an example of human activity, and the date for it is the date of human use of the pit. This will also be the date of final burial of the pottery – but it will *not* be the date of human use of that pottery, which could have been in circulation tens or hundreds of years earlier, before being discarded with other garbage in the pit. It is necessary therefore always to be clear about which activity we are trying to date, or can reliably date in the circumstances.

TYPOLOGICAL SEQUENCES: COMPARING OBJECTS

When we look at the artifacts, buildings, or any of the human creations around us, most of us can mentally arrange them into a rough chronological sequence. One kind of aircraft looks older than another, one set of clothes looks more "old-fashioned" than the next. How do archaeologists exploit this ability for relative dating?

Archaeologists define the form of an artifact such as a pot by its specific **attributes** of material, shape, and decoration. Several pots with the same attributes constitute a pot **type**, and **typology** groups artifacts into such types. Underlying the notion of relative dating through typology are two other ideas.

The first is that the products of a given period and place have a recognizable **style**: through their distinctive shape and decoration they are in some sense characteristic of the society that produced them. The archaeologist or anthropologist can often recognize and classify individual artifacts by their style, and hence assign them to a particular place in a typological sequence.

The second idea is that the change in style (shape and decoration) of artifacts is often quite gradual, or evolutionary. This idea came from the Darwinian theory of the **evolution** of species, and was used by 19th-century archaeologists who applied a very convenient rule, that "like goes with like." In other words, particular artifacts (e.g. bronze daggers) produced at about the same time are often alike, but those produced several centuries apart will be different as a result of centuries of change. It follows, then, that when studying a series of daggers of unknown date, it is logical first to arrange them in a sequence in such a way that the most closely similar are located beside each other. This is then likely to be the true chronological sequence, because it best reflects the principle that "like goes with like." In the diagram below, designs of automobiles and prehistoric European axes have been arranged in a relative chronological sequence; however, the rate of change (a century for the automobile, millennia for the axe) has to be deduced from absolute dating methods.

For many purposes, the best way to assign a relative date to an artifact is to match it with an artifact already recognized within a well-established typological

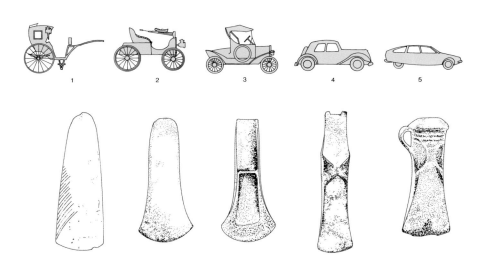

Gradual changes in design are evident in the history of the automobile and of the prehistoric European axe – (1) stone; (2–5) bronze.

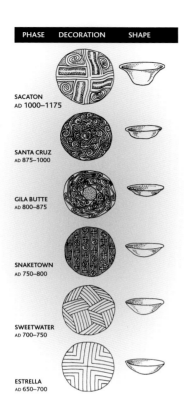

PHASE	DECORATION	SHAPE

SACATON
AD 1000–1175

SANTA CRUZ
AD 875–1000

GILA BUTTE
AD 800–875

SNAKETOWN
AD 750–800

SWEETWATER
AD 700–750

ESTRELLA
AD 650–700

Pottery typology, as exemplified by this 500-year sequence of Hohokam bowl styles from the American Southwest.

system. Pottery typologies usually form the backbone of the chronological system, and nearly every area has its own well-established ceramic sequence. One example is the very extensive ceramic sequence for the ancient societies of the American Southwest, a part of which is shown in the diagram, left. If such a typology is tied into a stratigraphic sequence of deposits that can be dated by radiocarbon or other absolute means, then the artifacts in the typological sequence can themselves be assigned absolute dates in years.

Different types of artifact change in style (decoration and shape) at different rates, and therefore vary in the chronological distinctions that they indicate. Usually, with pottery, surface decoration changes most rapidly (often over periods of just a few decades) and is therefore the best attribute to use for a typological sequence. On the other hand, the shape of a vessel or container may be most strongly influenced by a practical requirement, such as water storage, which need not alter for hundreds of years.

Other artifacts, such as metal weapons or tools, can change in style quite rapidly, and so may be useful chronological indicators. By contrast stone tools, such as **hand-axes**, are often very slow to change in form and therefore rarely make useful indicators of the passage of time (and are more useful in making general distinctions between much longer periods).

Seriation: Comparing Assemblages of Objects

The insights of the principle that "like goes with like" have been developed further to deal with associations of finds (**assemblages**) rather than with the forms of single objects taken in isolation. The technique of **seriation** allows assemblages of artifacts to be arranged in a succession or serial order, which is then taken to indicate their ordering in time, or their relative chronology.

The great pioneer of Egyptian archaeology, Sir William Flinders Petrie, was one of the first to develop a technique for arranging the graves of a cemetery in relative order by considering carefully and systematically the associations of the various pottery forms found within them. His lead in the late 19th century was taken up half a century later by American scholars who realized that the frequency of a particular ceramic style, as documented in the successive layers of a settlement, is usually small to start with, rises to a peak as the style gains popularity, and then declines again (which diagrammatically produces a shape like a battleship viewed from above, known as a "battleship curve"). Using this insight they were able to compare the pottery assemblages from different sites in the same area, each with a limited stratigraphic sequence, and arrange these sites into chronological order so that the ceramic frequencies would conform to the pattern of rising to a maximum and then declining.

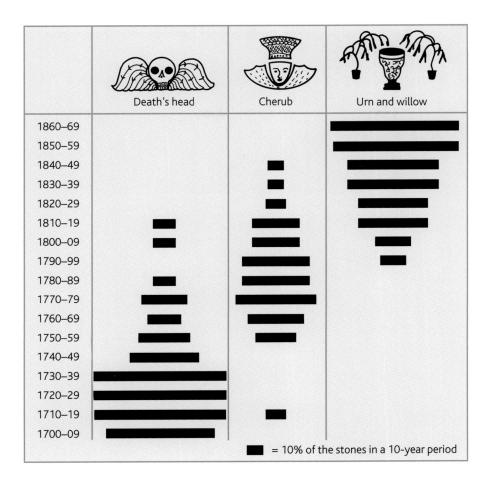

	Death's head	Cherub	Urn and willow
1860–69			████████████
1850–59			████████████
1840–49		██	████████
1830–39		█	████████
1820–29		██	██████
1810–19	██	█████	██████
1800–09	██	█████	███
1790–99		███████	███
1780–89	██	███████	
1770–79	████	████████	
1760–69	███	████████	
1750–59	████	████	
1740–49	██████		
1730–39	██████████		
1720–29	██████████		
1710–19	██████████	██	
1700–09	████████		

■ = 10% of the stones in a 10-year period

Seriation: changes in the popularity of central Connecticut tombstone designs.

The diagram above shows how this technique has been applied to changes in the popularity of three tombstone designs found in central Connecticut cemeteries dating from 1700 to 1860. The fluctuating fortunes of each design produce characteristic and successive battleship curves – as elsewhere in New England, the Death's head design (peak popularity 1710–1739) was gradually replaced by the Cherub (peak 1760–1789) which in turn was replaced by the Urn and willow tree (peak 1840–1859).

Seriation has been used in an archaeological context by the American archaeologist Frank Hole in his excavations in the Deh Luran Plain in Iran. The **Neolithic** ceramic assemblages he was studying were derived from stratigraphic excavations, so it was possible to compare the sequences obtained through **frequency seriation** with the true stratigraphic sequences discovered in their excavations. There were no serious contradictions, again proving the validity of the method.

KEY CONCEPTS

ENVIRONMENTAL SEQUENCES

So far in this chapter we have been discussing sequences that can be established either stratigraphically for individual sites, or typologically for artifacts. In addition, there is a major class of sequences, based on changes in the earth's climate, that has proved useful for relative dating on a local, regional, and even global scale. Some of these environmental sequences can also be dated by various absolute methods.

The Ice Age (or Pleistocene epoch, dating from 1.7 million years ago to 10,000 years ago), when world temperatures were usually much lower and ice covered large parts of the earth's surface, was not one long unbroken spell of cold. A complex sequence of cold periods (called *glacials*) were separated by warmer interludes (called *interglacials*). The interglacial period we now live in, known as the Holocene, covers the last 10,000 years. These climatic fluctuations are recorded in **deep-sea cores**, **ice cores**, and sediments containing pollen.

Deep-Sea Cores and Ice Cores. The most coherent record of climatic changes on a worldwide scale is provided by deep-sea cores. These cores contain shells of microscopic marine organisms known as foraminifera, laid down on the ocean floor through the slow continuous process of sedimentation. Variations in the chemical structure of these shells are a good indicator of the sea temperature at the time the organisms were alive. Cold episodes in the deep-sea cores relate to glacial periods of ice advance, and the warm episodes to interglacial periods of ice retreat. Radiocarbon and uranium-series dating (see below) can also be applied to the foraminiferan shells to provide absolute dates for the sequence, which now stretches back 2.3 million years.

As with deep-sea cores, cores extracted from the polar ice of the Arctic and Antarctic have yielded impressive sequences revealing past climatic changes. The layers of compacted ice represent annual deposits for the last 2000–3000 years that can be counted – thus giving an absolute chronology for this part of the sequence. For earlier time periods – at greater depths – the annual stratification is no longer visible, and dating of the ice cores is much less certain. Good correlations have been made with climatic variations deduced from the study of the deep-sea cores.

Evidence of major volcanic eruptions can also be preserved in the ice cores, theoretically meaning that particular eruptions, such as the huge Thera eruption in the Aegean roughly 3500 years ago (associated by some scholars with the destruction of Minoan palaces on Crete), can be given a precise absolute date. In practice, though, it is hard to be certain that a volcanic event preserved in the ice actually relates to a particular historically documented eruption – it could relate to an unknown eruption that happened somewhere else in the world.

Pollen Dating. All flowering plants produce grains called pollen, and these are almost indestructible, surviving for many thousands (and even millions) of years in all types of conditions. Its preservation in bogs and lake sediments has allowed pollen experts (palynologists) to construct detailed sequences of past vegetation and climate. These sequences are an immense help in understanding ancient environments, but they have also been – and to some extent still are – important as a method of relative dating.

The best-known pollen sequences are those developed for the Holocene of northern Europe, where an elaborate succession of so-called *pollen zones* covers the last 10,000 years. By studying pollen samples from a particular site, that site can often be fitted into a broader pollen zone sequence and thus assigned a relative date. Isolated artifacts and finds such as bog bodies discovered in contexts where pollen is preserved can also be dated in the same way. However, it is important to remember that the pollen zones are not uniform across large areas. Regional pollen zone sequences must first be established, and then the sites and finds in the area can be linked to it. If tree-ring or radiocarbon dates are available for all or part of the sequence, we can work out an absolute chronology for the region.

KEY CONCEPTS

Environmental Dating Methods

- *Deep-sea cores*: analysis of the chemical structure of microscopic marine organisms in datable layers of sediment can be used to reconstruct climate and provide a relative chronology

- *Ice cores*: similarly, layers of annual ice deposits can produce a chronology of world climate

- *Pollen dating*: pollen produced by past vegetation in a given area can reveal the climate of particular pollen zones and help to produce a relative chronology

Thanks to the durability of pollen grains, they can yield environmental evidence even as far back as 3 million years ago for sites in East Africa. Different interglacial periods in areas such as northern Europe have also been shown to have characteristic pollen sequences, which means that the pollen evidence at an individual site in the area can sometimes be matched to a particular interglacial – a useful dating mechanism since radiocarbon cannot be used for these early time periods.

ABSOLUTE DATING

Although relative dating methods can be extremely useful, archaeologists ultimately want to know how old sequences, sites, and artifacts are in calendar years. To achieve this they need to use the methods of absolute dating described in the following sections. The three most commonly used and most important to the archaeologist are calendars and historical chronologies, **tree-ring dating**, and **radiocarbon dating**. **DNA** dating is also now beginning to be used to date population events.

CALENDARS AND HISTORICAL CHRONOLOGIES

Until the development of the first scientific dating techniques around the beginning of the 20th century, dating in archaeology depended almost entirely on historical methods. That is to say, it relied on archaeological connections with chronologies and calendars that people in ancient times had themselves established. Such dating methods are still of immense value today.

In the ancient world, literate societies recorded their own history in written documents. In Egypt, the Near East, and ancient China, for example, history was recorded in terms of the successive kings, who were organized in groups of "dynasties." As we shall see, there were also very precise calendrical systems in Mesoamerica.

Archaeologists have to bear in mind three main points when working with early historical chronologies. First, the chronological system requires careful reconstruction, and any list of rulers or kings needs to be reasonably complete. Second, the list, although it may reliably record the number of years in each reign, has still to be linked with our own calendar. Third, the artifacts, **features**, or structures to be dated at a particular site have somehow to be related to the historical chronology, for example by their association with an inscription referring to the ruler of the time.

These points can be well illustrated by the Egyptian and Maya chronologies. Egyptian history is arranged in terms of 31 dynasties, themselves organized into the Old, Middle, and New Kingdoms. The modern view is a synthesis based on several documents including the so-called Turin Royal Canon. This synthesis gives an estimate of the number of years in each reign, right down to the conquest

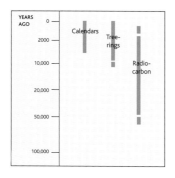

The spans of time for which the main three absolute dating methods are applicable.

of Egypt by Alexander the Great in the year 332 BC (a date recorded by Greek historians). So the Egyptian dynasties can be dated by working backward from there, although the exact length of every reign is not known. This system can be confirmed and refined using astronomy: Egyptian historical records describe observations of certain astronomical events that can be independently dated using current astronomical knowledge and knowledge of where in Egypt the ancient observations were carried out. Egyptian dates are generally considered to be quite reliable after about 1500 BC, with a margin of error of perhaps one or two decades at most, but by the time we go back to the beginning of the dynastic period, around 3100 BC, the accumulated errors might amount to some 200 years or so.

Of the calendrical systems of Mesoamerica, the Maya calendar was the most elaborate and precise. It was used for recording exact dates of historical (and mythical) events in inscriptions on stone columns or **stelae** erected at Maya sites during the so-called Classic period (AD 300–900). The Maya had glyphs or signs for the days and the months, and a straightforward system of numerals, with a dot representing "one" and a bar "five." The Maya actually had two concurrent calendrical systems, the first of which, the Calendar Round, was used for everyday purposes. Any day in the Calendar Round was identified by the conjunction of two different cycles: a Sacred Round of 260 days, and a solar year of 365 days. Thus a specific day would only reoccur once every 52 years. The second system, the Long Count, recorded days past since a mythical zero or starting point – 13 August 3113 BC in terms of our own calendar – and was used to refer to historical (or future) dates. The understanding of the Maya calendar, and the more recent decipherment of the Maya glyphs, mean that a well-dated Maya history is now emerging in a way which seemed impossible a few decades ago.

Using a Historical Chronology

It is relatively easy for the archaeologist to use a historical chronology when abundant artifacts are found that can be related closely to it. Thus, at major Maya sites such as Tikal or Copán there are numerous stelae with calendrical inscriptions that can often be used to date the buildings with which they are associated. The artifacts associated with the buildings can in turn be dated: for instance, if a pottery typology has been worked out, the finding of known types of pottery in such historically dated contexts allows the pottery typology itself to be dated. Contexts and buildings on other sites lacking inscriptions can be dated approximately through the occurrence of similar pot types.

Sometimes artifacts themselves carry dates, or the names of rulers that can be dated. This is the case with many Maya ceramics that bear hieroglyphic inscriptions. For the Roman and medieval periods of Europe, coins normally carry the name of the issuing ruler, and inscriptions or records elsewhere usually allow the ruler to be dated. But it is crucial to remember that to date a coin or an artifact is not the same thing as to date the context in which it is found. The date of the coin indicates the year in which it was made. Its inclusion within a sealed archaeological deposit establishes simply a *terminus post quem* (Latin for "date after which"): in other words, the deposit can be no earlier than the date on the coin – but it could be later (perhaps much later) than that date.

A well-established historical chronology in one country may be used to date events in neighboring and more far-flung lands that lack their own historical records but are mentioned in the histories of the literate homeland. Similarly, archaeologists can use exports and imports of objects to extend chronological linkages by means of *cross-dating* with other regions. For instance, the presence of foreign pottery in well-dated ancient Egyptian contexts establishes a *terminus ante quem* ("date before which") for the manufacture of that pottery: it cannot be more recent than the Egyptian context. In addition, Egyptian objects, some with inscriptions allowing them to be accurately dated in Egyptian terms, occur at various sites outside Egypt, thereby helping to date the contexts in which they are found.

Dating by historical methods remains the most important procedure for the archaeologist in countries with a reliable calendar supported by a significant degree of literacy. Where there are serious uncertainties over the calendar, or over its correlation with the modern calendrical system, the correlations can often be checked using other absolute dating methods, to be described below.

Outside the historic and literate lands, however, cross-dating and broad typological comparisons have been almost entirely superseded by the various scientifically based dating methods described below. So that now, all the world's **cultures** can be assigned absolute dates.

ANNUAL CYCLES

Any absolute dating method depends on the existence of a regular, time-dependent process. The most obvious of these is the system by which we order our modern calendar: the rotation of the earth around the sun once each year. Because this yearly cycle produces regular annual fluctuations in climate, it has an impact on features of the environment which can in certain cases be measured to create a chronology. For absolute dating purposes the sequence needs to be a long one (with no gaps), linked somehow to the present day, and capable of being related to the structures or artifacts we actually want to date.

Evidence of these annual fluctuations in climate is widespread. For example, the changes in temperature in polar regions result in annual variations in the thickness of polar ice, which scientists can study from cores drilled through the ice (see section above, Environmental Sequences). Similarly, in lands bordering the polar regions, the melting of the ice sheets each year when temperatures rise leads to the formation of annual deposits of sediment in lake beds, called **varves**, which can be counted. Considerable deposits of varves were found in Scandinavia, representing thousands of years, stretching (when linked together) from the present back to the beginning of the retreat of the glacial ice sheets in Scandinavia some 13,000 years ago. The method allowed, for the first time, a fairly reliable estimate for the date of the end of the last Ice Age, and hence made a contribution to archaeological chronology not only in Scandinavia but in many other parts of the world as well.

But today, while varves remain of restricted use, another annual cycle, that of *tree-rings,* has come to rival radiocarbon as the main method of dating for the last few thousand years in many parts of Europe, North America, and Japan.

Tree-Ring Dating

The modern technique of tree-ring dating (**dendrochronology**) was developed by an American astronomer, A.E. Douglass, in the early decades of the last century – although many of the principles had been understood long before that. Working on well-preserved timbers in the arid American Southwest, by 1930 Douglass could assign absolute dates to many of the major sites there, such as Mesa Verde and Pueblo Bonito. But it was not until the end of the 1930s that the technique was introduced to Europe, and only in the 1960s that the use of statistical procedures and computers laid the foundations for the establishment of the long tree-ring chronologies now so fundamental to modern archaeology. Today dendrochronology has two distinct archaeological uses: (1) as a successful means of calibrating or correcting radiocarbon dates (see below); and (2) as an independent method of absolute dating in its own right.

Basis of Method.   Most trees produce a ring of new wood each year and these circles of growth can easily be seen in a cross-section of the trunk of a felled tree. These rings are not of uniform thickness. In an individual tree, they will vary for two reasons. First, the rings become narrower with the increasing age of the tree. Second, the amount a tree grows each year is affected by fluctuations in climate. In arid regions, rainfall above the average one year will produce a particularly thick annual ring. In more temperate regions, sunlight and temperature may be more critical than rainfall in affecting a tree's growth. Here, a sharp cold spell in spring may produce a narrow growth ring.

Dendrochronologists measure and plot these rings and produce a diagram indicating the thickness of successive rings in an individual tree. Trees of the same species growing in the same area will generally show the same pattern of rings so that the growth sequence can be matched between successively older timbers to build up a chronology for an area. (It is not necessary to fell trees in order to study the ring sequence: a usable sample can be extracted by boring without harming

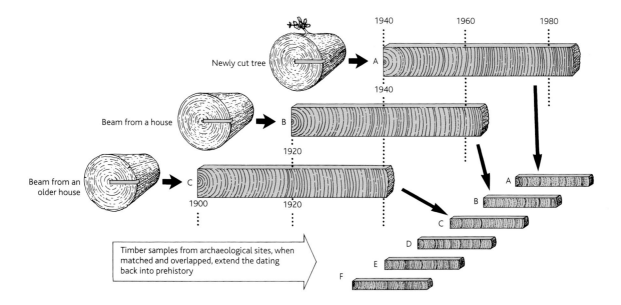

Tree-ring dating: annual growth rings can be counted, matched, and overlapped, to build up a master sequence for a particular region.

the tree.) By matching sequences of rings from living trees of different ages as well as from old timber, dendrochronologists can produce a long, continuous sequence, such as that in the diagram above, extending back hundreds, even thousands, of years from the present. Thus, when an ancient timber of the same species (e.g. Douglas fir in the American Southwest or oak in Europe) is found, it should be possible to match its tree-ring sequence of, say, 100 years with the appropriate 100-year length of the master sequence or chronology. In this way, the felling date for that piece of timber can usually be dated to within a year.

Applications. One of the most important uses of tree-ring dating has been the development of long tree-ring sequences, against which it is possible to check radiocarbon dates. The pioneering research was done in Arizona on a remarkable species, the Californian bristlecone pine which can live up to 4900 years. By matching samples from dead trees also, an unbroken sequence was built up back from the present as far as 6700 BC. The importance of this for the calibration of radiocarbon dates is discussed below. The research in the American Southwest has been complemented by studies in Europe of tree-rings of oak, often well preserved in waterlogged deposits. The oak sequence in Northern Ireland stretches back unbroken to *c.* 5300 BC, and the master sequence in western Germany to *c.* 8500 BC.

Direct tree-ring dating of preserved timber found in archaeological contexts has itself been important in several areas, but results are particularly impressive in the American Southwest, where the technique is longest established and wood is

Tree-Ring Dating

- *Method*: based on the annual cycle of tree-ring growth

- *Date range*: 0–11,500 years ago

- *Applications*: direct dating of wood; calibration of radiocarbon dates

- *Limitations*: restricted to regions outside the tropics and to certain species of tree (although calibration is thought to work on a worldwide scale); care must be taken when interpreting results

well preserved in the arid conditions. For instance, Betatakin, a cliff dwelling in Arizona, has been precision dated using dendrochronology, so that not only do we know that the settlement was founded in AD 1267, but we also can track the expansion of the site room by room, year by year until it reached a peak in the mid-1280s, before being abandoned shortly thereafter.

Limiting Factors.   Unlike radiocarbon, dendrochronology is not a worldwide dating method because of two basic limitations:

1 it applies only to trees in regions outside the tropics where pronounced differences between the seasons produce clearly defined annual rings;

2 for a direct tree-ring date it is restricted to wood from those species that (a) have yielded a master sequence back from the present and (b) people actually used in the past, and where (c) the sample affords a sufficiently long record to give a unique match.

In addition, there are important questions of interpretation to consider. A tree-ring date refers to the date of felling of the tree. This is determined by matching the tree-ring sample ending with the outermost rings (the sapwood) to a regional sequence. Where most or all of the sapwood is missing, the felling date cannot be identified. But even with an accurate felling date, the archaeologist has to make a judgment – based on context and **formation processes** – about how soon after felling the timber entered the archaeological deposit. Timbers may be older or younger than the structures into which they were finally incorporated, depending on whether they were reused from somewhere else, or used to make a repair in a long-established structure. The best solution is to take multiple samples, and to check the evidence carefully on-site. Despite these qualifications, dendrochronology looks set to become the major dating technique alongside radiocarbon for the last 8000 years in temperate and arid lands.

RADIOACTIVE CLOCKS

Many of the most important developments in absolute dating have come from the use of what might be called "radioactive clocks," based on that widespread and regular feature in the natural world, **radioactive decay**. The best known of these methods is radiocarbon, today the main dating tool for the last 50,000 years or so.

Radiocarbon Dating

Radiocarbon is the single most useful method of dating for the archaeologist. As we shall see, it has its limitations, both in terms of accuracy, and for the time range where it is useful. Archaeologists themselves are also the cause of major errors, thanks to poor sampling procedures and careless interpretation. Nevertheless, radiocarbon has transformed our understanding of the past, helping archaeologists to establish for the first time a reliable chronology of world cultures.

History and Basis of Method. In 1949, the American chemist Willard Libby published the first radiocarbon dates. During World War II he had been studying cosmic radiation, the sub-atomic particles that constantly bombard the earth. These produce high-energy neutrons which in turn react with nitrogen atoms in the atmosphere to produce atoms of carbon-14 (^{14}C), or radiocarbon, which are unstable because they have eight neutrons in the nucleus instead of the usual six as for ordinary carbon (see box on the principles of radioactive decay below).

THE PRINCIPLES OF RADIOACTIVE DECAY

Like most elements occurring in nature, carbon exists in more than one isotopic form. It has three isotopes: ^{12}C, ^{13}C, and ^{14}C – the numbers correspond to the atomic weights of these isotopes. In any sample of carbon 98.9 percent of atoms are of ^{12}C type and have six protons and six neutrons in the nucleus, and 1.1 percent are of the ^{13}C type with six protons and seven neutrons. Only one atom in a million millions of atoms of carbon will be that of the isotope ^{14}C with eight neutrons in the nucleus. This isotope of carbon is produced in the upper atmosphere by cosmic rays bombarding nitrogen (^{14}N) and it contains an excess of neutrons, making it unstable. It decays by the emission of weak beta radiation back to its precursor isotope of nitrogen – ^{14}N –

with seven protons and seven neutrons in a nucleus. Like all types of radioactive decay the process takes place at a constant rate, independent of all environmental conditions.

The time taken for half of the atoms of a radioactive isotope to decay is called its half-life. In other words, after one half-life, there will be half of the atoms left; after two half-lives, one-quarter of the original quantity of isotope remains, and so on. In the case of ^{14}C, the half-life is now agreed to be 5730 years.

Half-lives of radioactive isotopes of other elements can range from thousands of millions of years to a minute fraction of a second. But in every case, there is a regular pattern to the decay.

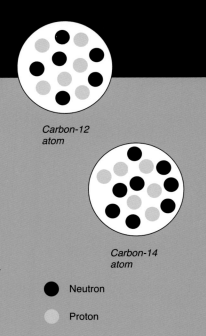

Carbon-12 atom

Carbon-14 atom

● Neutron

○ Proton

This instability leads to radioactive decay of ^{14}C at a regular rate. Libby estimated that it took 5568 years for half the ^{14}C in any sample to decay – its **half-life** (see diagram below) – although modern research indicates that the more accurate figure is 5730 years.

Libby realized that the decay of radiocarbon at a constant rate should be balanced by its constant production through cosmic radiation, and that therefore the proportion of ^{14}C in the atmosphere should remain the same throughout time. Furthermore, this steady atmospheric concentration of radiocarbon is passed on uniformly to all living things through carbon dioxide, as part of what is known as the "carbon cycle." Plants take up carbon dioxide during photosynthesis, they are eaten by herbivorous animals, which in turn are eaten by carnivores. When a plant or animal dies the uptake of ^{14}C ceases, and the steady concentration of ^{14}C begins to decline through radioactive decay. Thus, knowing the decay rate or half-life of ^{14}C, Libby recognized that the age of dead plant or animal tissue could be calculated by measuring the amount of radiocarbon left in a sample. Samples usually consist of organic materials found on archaeological sites, such as charcoal, wood, seeds, and other plant remains, and human or animal bone. Inorganic materials, like stone, are not part of the carbon cycle and so cannot be radiocarbon dated.

Libby's great practical achievement was to devise an accurate means of measurement. He discovered that each atom of ^{14}C decays by releasing a beta particle, and he succeeded in counting these emissions using a Geiger counter, still the basis of the conventional method employed by many radiocarbon laboratories today. Advances were made in the late 1970s and early 1980s with the introduction of special gas counters capable of taking measurements from very small samples.

(Below left) Radiocarbon is produced in the atmosphere and absorbed by plants through carbon dioxide, and by animals through feeding off plants or other animals. Uptake of ^{14}C ceases when the plant or animal dies. (Below) After death, the amount of ^{14}C decays at a known rate (50 percent after 5730 years, etc.). Measurement of the amount left in a sample gives the date.

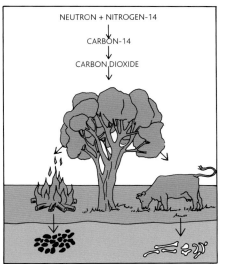

NEUTRON + NITROGEN-14
↓
CARBON-14
↓
CARBON DIOXIDE

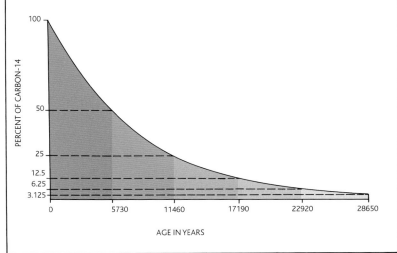

AGE IN YEARS

PERCENT OF CARBON-14

In the conventional method some 5 g of pure carbon after purification were needed, which means an original sample of some 10–20 g of wood or charcoal, or 100–200 g of bone. The special gas-counting equipment required only a few hundred milligrams (mg) of charcoal.

Increasingly, the accelerator mass spectrometry (AMS) method is becoming the dominant technique used in radiocarbon dating. This requires smaller samples still. Disregarding their radioactivity, AMS counts the atoms of ^{14}C directly. The minimum sample size is reduced to as little as 5–10 mg – thus enabling precious organic materials, such as the Turin Shroud (see below), to be sampled and directly dated, and making feasible the direct dating of pollen. Initially it was hoped that the datable timespan for radiocarbon using AMS could be pushed back from 50,000 to 80,000 years, although this is proving difficult to achieve, in part because of sample contamination.

Radiocarbon dates are usually quoted in years BP (before the present, currently taken to be AD 1950), but because the accurate measurement of the ^{14}C activity of a sample is affected by counting errors, background cosmic radiation, and other intrinsic factors, there is always an element of uncertainty to the measurements. Thus there is always a statistical error or "standard deviation" attached to a radiocarbon date, expressed as a plus/minus term. A radiocarbon date quoted as 3700 ±100 BP, for example, implies that there is a 68 percent probability, or two chances in three, that the correct estimate in radiocarbon years lies between 3800 and 3600 BP. Double the standard deviation, and there is a 95 percent chance (19 chances in 20) that the radiocarbon age of the sample lies between 3900 and 3500 BP. But there is a complication: these dates still do not, unfortunately, equate with true calendar years. To convert radiocarbon years into calendar years requires *calibration*.

Calibration of Radiocarbon Dates.   One of the basic assumptions of the radiocarbon method has turned out to be not quite correct. Libby assumed that the concentration of ^{14}C in the atmosphere has been constant through time, but we now know that it has varied. The method that demonstrated the inaccuracy – tree-ring dating – has also provided the means of correcting or calibrating radiocarbon dates.

Radiocarbon dates obtained from tree-rings show that before about 1000 BC dates expressed in radiocarbon years are increasingly too young in relation to true calendar years. In other words, before 1000 BC trees (and all other living things) were exposed to greater concentrations of atmospheric ^{14}C than they are today. By obtaining radiocarbon dates systematically from the long tree-ring master sequences of bristlecone pine and oak (see above), scientists have been able to plot radiocarbon ages against tree-ring ages (in calendar years) to produce calibration curves, such as the one shown overleaf. Very broadly, these curves show that radiocarbon ages diverge increasingly from true ages before 1000 BC, so that by

Radiocarbon laboratories will generally supply calibrated dates of their samples, but archaeologists may need to calibrate raw radiocarbon dates themselves, usually from a calibration graph.

The section of tree-ring calibration curve shown in the diagram (below) illustrates the relationship between radiocarbon years (BP) and tree-ring samples dated in actual calendar years (Calibrated or "Cal" BC/AD).

The so-called wiggles in the curve can have a big impact on calibration: occasionally, sections of the curve run so flat that two samples with the same age

in radiocarbon years might in reality be 400 years apart in calendar years. This particularly affects the period 800–400 BC in calendar years.

In order to find the calibrated age range of a radiocarbon sample dated 2200 ±100 BP using this curve, the simplest method is to draw two horizontal lines (A1 and A2) from the appropriate dates on the radiocarbon years axis to the calibration curve, and drop lines (B1 and B2) from these intercept points to the calendar axis. The calibrated date is then quoted as the range enclosed between the vertical lines. In this instance the result would be an

approximately 68 percent chance that the date of the sample falls between c. 395 Cal BC and 110 Cal BC. Doubling the standard deviation (to 200 years either side of 2200 BP in this case) results in a 95 percent chance that the date of the sample falls between c. 405 Cal BC and Cal AD 5.

Unfortunately, though, this method does not reflect the true complexity of the probability information stored in the radiocarbon result. A specialized form of statistical analysis, necessitating the use of a computer program, is required for a fully accurate calibration.

A calibrated age range of 405 Cal BC to Cal AD 5 is too broad to be useful for most archaeological purposes. There are two ways of narrowing the age range: high-precision dates and multiple dates. High-precision dates, obtainable so far from only a handful of the world's radiocarbon laboratories, can offer dates quoted with a realistic error of ±20 years, which, after calibration, generally allows the sample to be dated within a century or less (at the 95 percent probability level). Otherwise archaeologists use multiple dates of the same sample to produce mean dates with a smaller standard deviation.

Calibration programs and curves can be obtained directly from the *Radiocarbon* website at www.radiocarbon.org.

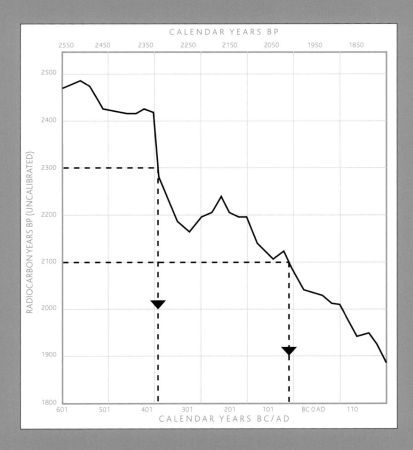

A section of calibration curve to show the simple intercept method to obtain calibrated dates.

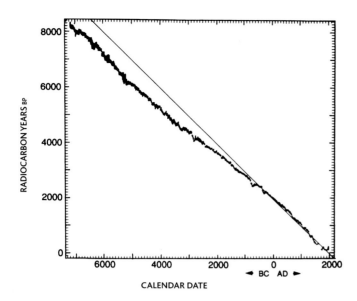

A calibrated radiocarbon timescale based on Irish oak. The straight line indicates the ideal 1:1 radiocarbon/ calendar age timescale.

5000 BC in calendar years the radiocarbon age is 900 years too young. Thus an age estimate in radiocarbon years of 6050 BP might well in fact when calibrated be somewhere near 5000 BC. For dates beyond the scope of tree-ring dating, scientists have been able to use data from uranium-thorium dated corals and varve-counted marine sediments to produce a calibration curve going back some 24,000 years. The box on p.123 gives a more detailed explanation of the calibration process.

Contamination and Interpretation of Radiocarbon Samples. Although radiocarbon dates have certain inescapable levels of error associated with them, inaccurate results are as likely to derive from poor sampling and incorrect interpretation by the archaeologist as from inadequate laboratory procedures. The major sources of error in the field are summed up below:

- *Contamination before sampling.* Problems of contamination of the sample within the ground can be serious. For instance, groundwater on waterlogged sites can dissolve organic materials and also deposit them, thus changing the amount of ^{14}C in a sample. These matters can usually be tackled in the laboratory.
- *Contamination during or after sampling.* Any modern organic material coming into contact with a sample can contaminate it, but some, such as roots and

KEY CONCEPTS

Radiocarbon Dating

- *Method*: based on the regular decay of a radioactive isotope of carbon

- *Date range*: 400–50,000 years ago

- *Applications*: dating of any organic matter; new techniques allow very small sample sizes, meaning grain, seeds, and very precious objects can be dated

- *Calibration*: radiocarbon dates must be calibrated to arrive at a calendar date

- *Limitations*: samples must be carefully chosen; samples can easily be contaminated with more recent (or older) material; results can be difficult to interpret correctly and require statistical treatment

earth, cannot always be avoided. However, such sources of contamination can be eliminated in the laboratory.

- *Context of deposition.* Most errors in radiocarbon dating arise because the excavator has not fully understood the formation processes of the context in question. Unless it is appreciated how the organic material found its way to the position where it was found, and how and when (in terms of the site) it came to be buried, then precise interpretation is impossible.
- *Date of context.* Too often, it is assumed that a radiocarbon determination, e.g. on charcoal, will give a straightforward estimate for the date of the charcoal's burial context. However, if that charcoal derives from roof timbers that might themselves have been several centuries old when destroyed by fire, then some early construction is being dated, not the fire. For this reason, samples with a short life are often preferred, such as twigs of brushwood, or charred cereal grains that are not likely to be old at the time of burial.

A strategy for sampling should be based on the wise saying that "one date is no date": several are needed. The best procedure is to work toward an internal relative sequence of dates – for instance, in the stratigraphic succession on a well-stratified site such as the Gatecliff Shelter, Monitor Valley, Nevada, shown right. If the samples can be arranged in relative sequence in this way with the lowest unit having the earliest date and so on, then there is an internal check on the coherence of the laboratory determinations and on the quality of field sampling. Some of the dates from such a sequence may come out older than expected. This is quite reasonable as some of the material may have been "old" at the time of burial. But if they come out younger (i.e. more recent) than expected, then there is something wrong. Either some contamination has affected the samples, or the laboratory has made a serious error, or the stratigraphic interpretation is wrong.

The Impact of Radiocarbon Dating.
Radiocarbon has undoubtedly offered the most generally useful way of answering the question "When?" in archaeology. The greatest advantage is that the method can be used anywhere, whatever the climate, as long as there is material of organic (i.e. living) origin. Thus the method works as well

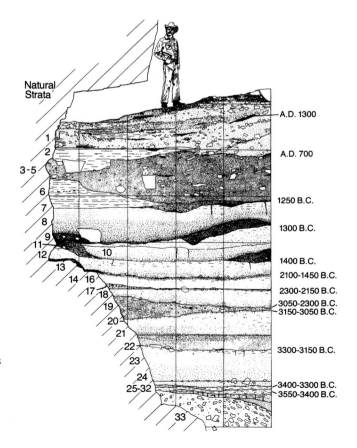

Master profile for Gatecliff Shelter, Nevada, showing how dates derived from radiocarbon determinations are consistent with the stratigraphic succession.

in South America or Polynesia as it does in Egypt or Mesopotamia. And it can take us back 50,000 years – although at the other end of the timescale it is too imprecise to be of much use for the 400 years of the most recent past. Radiocarbon has been incredibly important in establishing for the first time broad chronologies for the world's cultures that previously lacked timescales (such as calendars) of their own. Calibration of radiocarbon has increased, not diminished, this success.

Radiocarbon dating by the AMS technique is opening up new possibilities. Precious objects and works of art can now be dated because minute samples are all that is required. In 1988 AMS dating resolved the longstanding controversy over the age of the Turin Shroud, a piece of cloth with the image of a man's body on it that many genuinely believed to be the actual imprint of the body of Christ. Laboratories at Tucson, Oxford, and Zurich all placed it in the 14th century AD, not from the time of Christ at all, although this remains a matter of controversy.

Other Radiometric Methods

Radiocarbon is likely to maintain its position as the main dating tool back to 50,000 years ago for organic materials, but the half-life of radiocarbon is such that, for particularly old samples, there is hardly any radioactivity left to measure. So, for inorganic or very ancient materials, other methods have to be used. The most important of them are also radiometric – they depend upon the measurement of natural radioactivity. But they use elements whose radioactive isotopes have very much longer half-lives than the 5730 years of carbon-14. They have two drawbacks. In the first place, they depend upon elements less frequently found in archaeological contexts than is carbon. And secondly, the long half-lives generally mean that the datings are less precise.

Potassium-Argon Dating   The **potassium-argon** (K-Ar) method is used by geologists to date volcanic rocks hundreds or even thousands of millions of years old, but no more recent than around 100,000 years old.

K-Ar dating is based on the steady but very slow decay of the radioactive isotope potassium-40 (^{40}K) to the inert gas argon-40 (^{40}Ar) in volcanic rock. Knowing the decay rate of ^{40}K – its half life is around 1.3 billion years – a measure of the quantity of ^{40}Ar trapped within a 10g rock sample gives an estimate of the date of the rock's formation. The principal limitation of the technique is that it can only be used to date sites buried by volcanic rock.

The dates produced are effectively geological dates for the date of eruption leading to the formation of volcanic strata. Fortunately, some of the most important areas for the study of the Lower Paleolithic, notably the Rift Valley in East Africa, are areas of volcanic activity. The chronology of Olduvai Gorge, for example, which has provided important fossil remains of ***Australopithecus***, *Homo habilis*, and *Homo erectus*, has been well established by K-Ar dating (see

KEY CONCEPTS

Potassium-Argon Dating

- Based on the decay of radioactive potassium-40 into argon-40

- Dates volcanic rocks, and the archaeological remains associated with them

Uranium Series Dating

- Based on the decay of radioactive isotopes of uranium

- Dates travertine (calcium carbonate), and associated archaeological remains

- Useful in areas where there is no volcanic activity

Fission-Track Dating

- Dates a variety of rocks and minerals which contain radioactive uranium-238

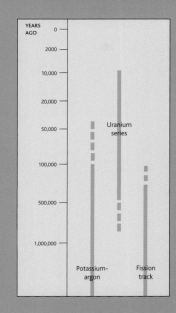

box overleaf). At this and other similar sites, archaeological remains frequently lie on volcanic strata, which are suitable for K-Ar dating, and moreover they are often overlain by comparable volcanic rock, so that dates for these two geological strata provide a time range for the material we are trying to date.

Uranium-Series Dating   This dating method is based on the radioactive decay of isotopes of uranium. It has proved particularly useful for the period 500,000 to 50,000 years ago, which again lies outside the time range of radiocarbon dating. In Europe, where there are relatively few volcanic rocks suitable for dating by the potassium-argon technique, **uranium series** (U-series) **dating** may be the method of first choice for early human sites – it has been used effectively, for example, on the skulls and other skeletal remains of very early *Homo sapiens* found at Qafzeh and Skhul caves in Israel.

The method dates the time of formation of travertine (calcium carbonate) which is often deposited on cave walls and floors, and hence can be used to date any material, such as an artifact or bone, embedded in a layer of travertine or in another type of sediment between two layers of it. The method is also applicable

Thanks to the discoveries of early hominin fossils in Olduvai Gorge by Louis and Mary Leakey, Olduvai is one of the most crucial sites for the study of human evolution. It has proved possible to establish a chronology for the site, particularly on the basis of K-Ar dating of deposits of hardened volcanic ash (tuff), between which the fossil remains lie. For example, the age of the important Tuff IB in Bed I was estimated as 1.79 ±0.03 my (million years).

As with all archaeological dating, for a reliable result one should cross-check age estimates derived from one method with those from another. A fission-track reading gave a date of 2.03 ±0.28 my, which is within the statistically acceptable confidence limits for the K-Ar estimate. A further radioactive method produced a result of 1.8–1.75 my.

Another means of checking the K-Ar sequence proved to be geomagnetic dating (see p. 131). It transpired that Beds I–III and part of IV at Olduvai lay within the so-called Matuyama epoch of reversed polarity, with a significant period of normal polarity 1.87–1.67 my ago now known, appropriately, as the "Olduvai event." The discovery of the same sequence of reversals at other East African sites (e.g. East Turkana) has helped correlate their deposits with those at Olduvai.

Nowhere has the need for extreme care in dating fossil human remains been more evident than in the case of the *Homo habilis* skull, "1470," unearthed by Richard Leakey at East Turkana, Kenya, some 500 miles to the north of Olduvai Gorge, in 1972. Early K-Ar results on the so-called KBS tuff above the skull deposit gave a date of c. 2.6 my, at least 0.8 my earlier than *H. habilis* finds elsewhere. Could the

K-Ar date be right? At first, cross-checking by fission-track and **geomagnetic reversals** seemed to support it. But in 1974 an American laboratory produced K-Ar readings of c. 1.8 my for the tuff.

The controversy dragged on for several years. Eventually one of the scientists who had originally published fission-track dates

supporting the older K-Ar readings re-ran fission-track tests and confirmed the younger estimate of c. 1.8 my. Finally, to resolve the issue, Leakey commissioned an Australian laboratory to obtain new K-Ar dates. The result was a now generally accepted age for the KBS tuff of 1.88 ±0.02 my.

Olduvai Gorge schematic stratigraphy, together with hominins and tool industries from the site, and magnetic reversals.

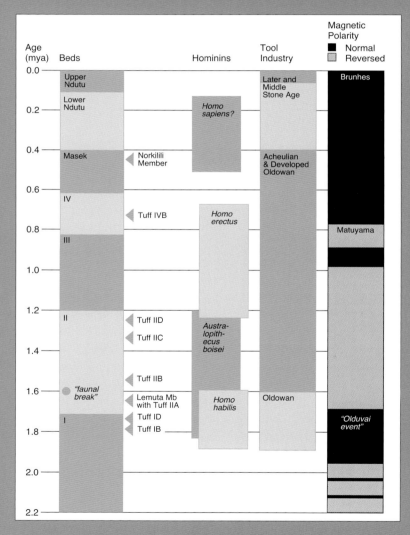

to teeth, since these absorb water-soluble uranium when buried. High-precision measurement can give an error margin of less than 1000 years for a 100,000 year-old sample, and the method can also be cross-checked with **electron spin resonance** dates using the same materials (see below).

Fission-Track Dating   **Fission-track dating** depends upon the spontaneous fission (or division) of radioactive uranium atoms (^{238}U), present in a wide range of rocks and minerals, which causes damage to the structures of the minerals involved. In materials where ^{238}U is present, such as volcanic and manufactured glasses, and minerals like zircon and apatite found within rock formations, the damage is recorded in pathways called fission tracks. The tracks can be counted in the laboratory under an optical microscope. Since we know the rate of fission of ^{238}U, this allows the date of formation of the rock or glass to be determined.

In this case, the radioactive clock is set at zero by the formation of the mineral or glass, either in nature (as with **obsidian**) or at the time of manufacture (as with manufactured glass). The method produces useful dates from suitable rocks that contain or are adjacent to those containing archaeological evidence, and has been used with success at early Paleolithic sites such as Olduvai Gorge, Tanzania, providing independent confirmation of potassium-argon and other results.

OTHER ABSOLUTE DATING METHODS

There are several more dating methods which can be used in special circumstances, but none is as important in practice to archaeologists as those already described. Some are of relevance to the solution of specific problems, such as the dating of Paleolithic rock art. Several of the most significant are mentioned below, so that the overview given in this chapter is reasonably complete. But the discussion here is deliberately kept brief, to give a flavour of a field which can easily become rather complicated, yet which is not directly relevant to much mainstream archaeology. The rather special case of DNA dating is of particular interest.

Thermoluminescence Dating   **Thermoluminescence** (TL) dating can be used to date crystalline materials (minerals) buried in the ground which have been fired – usually pottery, but also baked clay, burnt stone, and in some circumstances burnt soil. But unfortunately it is a method which is difficult to make precise, and so it is generally used when other methods, such as radiocarbon dating, are not available.

Like many other methods it depends upon radioactive decay, but in this case it is the amount of radioactivity received by the specimen since the start date which is of interest, not the radiation emitted by the specimen itself. When atoms located within the structure of a mineral are exposed to radiation from the decay of radioactive elements in the nearby environment, some of that energy is "trapped." If the amount of radiation remains constant over time, then this energy will accumulate at a uniform rate and the total amount of energy will depend upon the total time of exposure. When a sample is heated to 500°C or more, the trapped energy is released as thermoluminescence, and the "radioactive clock" is set back to zero.

This means that archaeological artifacts, such as pottery, will have had their clocks reset when they were originally fired, and that by reheating samples from these objects, we can measure the thermoluminescence released and hence date the material. The main complication of the method is that the level of background radiation that a sample might have been exposed to is not uniform – it must be measured for every sample by burying a small capsule containing a radiation-sensitive material, or by using a radiation counter, at the exact spot the sample was found. In general, the difficulties of making these measurements mean that TL dates rarely have a precision of better than ±10 percent of the age of the sample.

A good example of the archaeological application of TL is the dating of the terracotta head known as the Jemaa head, from the alluvium of a tin mine near the Jos Plateau of Nigeria. The head and similar examples belong to the Nok culture, but such sculptures could not be dated reliably at the site of Nok itself

KEY CONCEPTS

Thermoluminescence Dating

- Dates minerals that have been sufficiently heated and then buried
- Can be applied to pottery, other baked clay, and burnt stone
- Methodological complications and limited accuracy

Optical Dating

- Similar to TL dating, but dates minerals that have been exposed to light and then buried

Electron Spin Resonance Dating

- Dates tooth enamel, bone and shell

Archaeomagnetism and Geomagnetic Reversals

- Changes in the Earth's magnetic field over time can be tracked in the archaeological record

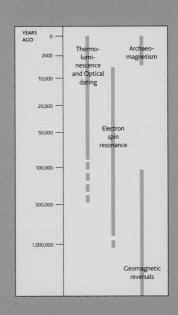

because of the lack of any plausible radiocarbon dates. A TL reading on the head gave an age of 1520 ±260 BC, allowing this and similar heads from the Nok region to be given a firm chronological position for the first time.

Optical Dating   This method is similar in principle to TL, but it is used to date minerals that have been exposed to light, rather than heat. Most minerals contain some trapped energy that will be released by several minutes' exposure to sunlight. Such exposure is in effect the start point. Once buried they begin to accumulate electrons once more as a result of radioactive radiation experienced in the soil. In the laboratory, optically stimulated luminescence (OSL) is produced by directing light of a visible wavelength onto the sample, and the resultant luminescence is measured. And once again the background radiation at the place of burial has to be measured, so optical dating suffers from many of the same complications as TL.

Electron Spin Resonance Dating   Electron spin resonance (ESR) is a technique similar to but less sensitive than TL, but it can be used for materials which decompose when heated and thus where TL is not applicable. Its most successful application so far has been for the dating of tooth enamel. Newly formed tooth enamel contains no trapped energy, but it begins to accumulate once the tooth is buried and exposed to natural background radiation. The precision of the method when used to date tooth enamel is in the order of 10–20 percent, but it is still very useful for the study of early humans and the cross-checking of other dating methods.

Archaeomagnetic Dating and Geomagnetic Reversals   **Archaeomagnetic** (or Paleomagnetic) **dating** has so far been of limited use in archaeology. It is based on the constant change, both in direction and intensity, of the earth's magnetic field. The direction of that magnetic field at a particular time is recorded in any baked clay structure (oven, kiln, hearth etc.) that has been heated to a temperature of 650 to 700°C. At that temperature the iron particles in the clay permanently take up the earth's magnetic direction and intensity at the time of firing. This principle is called *thermoremanent magnetism* (TRM). Charts can be built up of the variation through time which can be used to date baked clay structures of unknown age, whose TRM is measured and then matched to a particular point on the master sequence.

Another aspect of Archaeomagnetism, relevant for the dating of the Lower Paleolithic, is the phenomenon of complete reversals in the earth's magnetic field (magnetic north becomes magnetic south, and vice versa). The most recent major reversal occurred about 780,000 years ago, and a sequence of such reversals stretching back several millions of years has been built up with the aid of potassium-argon and other dating techniques. The finding of part of this sequence of reversals in the rock strata of African early hominin sites has proved a helpful check on the other dating methods that have been used at those sites.

DNA Dating   The methods now being used by molecular geneticists present rather a special case. They use DNA samples from living human populations to date population events, notably migrations. Using assumptions about genetic mutation rates they can date approximately the appearance of new genetic categories and so give a date to such important processes such as the 'out-of-Africa' dispersal of our species (around 60,000–55,000 years ago). It is the information within living humans that provides the data, not ancient excavated samples: our past within us!

WORLD CHRONOLOGY

As a result of the application of the various dating techniques discussed above, it is possible to summarize the world archaeological chronology, from the evolution of human ancestors millions of years ago in Africa, to the spread of our own species around the world, and the eventual development of agriculture and complex societies.

The human story as understood at present begins in East Africa, with the emergence there of the earliest **hominins** of the genus *Australopithecus*, such as *A. afarensis*, around 4 million years ago, and the possibly earlier *Ardipithecus*. By around 2 million years ago, there is clear fossil evidence for the first known representative of our own genus, *Homo habilis*, from such sites as Koobi Fora (Kenya) and Olduvai Gorge (Tanzania). The earliest stone tools (from Hadar, Ethiopia) date from about 2.5 million years ago, but it is not known which hominin made them because *Homo habilis* fossils of this age have not yet been found. It is possible that australopithecines also had a tool culture before or during *Homo habilis*'s time. The early toolkits, comprising flake and pebble tools, are called the **Oldowan industry**, after Olduvai Gorge where they are particularly well represented.

Paleoanthropologists hold strongly differing views on how the fossil remains for human evolution should be interpreted. This family tree presents the evidence as four adaptive radiations: the australopithecines, paranthropines, early Homo, *and later* Homo *(including modern humans).*

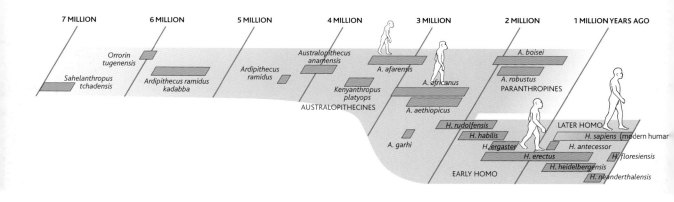

By more than 1.6 million years ago, the next stage in human evolution, *Homo erectus*, had emerged in East Africa. These hominins had larger brains than *Homo habilis*, their probable ancestor, and were makers of the characteristic teardrop-shaped stone tools flaked on both sides called Acheulian hand-axes. These artifacts are the dominant tool form of the Lower Paleolithic. By the time *Homo erectus* became extinct (400,000–200,000 years ago), the species had colonized the rest of Africa, southern, eastern, and western Asia, and central and western Europe. Their remote descendents (now designated *Homo floresiensis*) seem to have survived in Indonesia to the remarkably recent date of 18,000 years ago, as new discoveries on the island of Flores suggest.

The Middle Paleolithic period – from about 200,000 to 40,000 years ago – saw the emergence of *Homo sapiens*. Neanderthals, who used to be classified as a subspecies of *Homo sapiens* (*H. sapiens neanderthalensis*) lived in Europe and

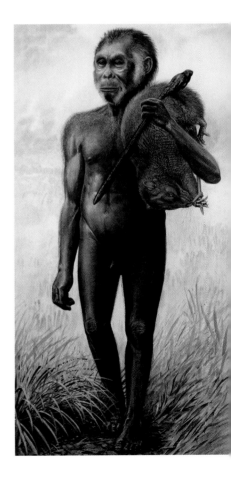

This skull (left) was discovered along with other skeletal remains and stone tools in a cave on the island of Flores in Indonesia in 2004. The remains have been designated as a new species of human, Homo floresiensis, probably descended from Homo erectus – adults (as reconstructed at right) were just 1 m (3 ¼ ft) tall, and brain volume was about the same as a chimpanzee. They lived on the island from roughly 80,000 to 18,000 years ago.

WORLD CHRONOLOGY

Key Events

• Earliest stone tools	2.5 million years ago
• Acheulian hand-axes	1.6 million years ago
• *Homo sapiens*	at least 100,000 years ago
• First Australians	50,000 years ago
• First Americans	14,000 years ago or more
• First farmers	at least 10,000 years ago in the Near East
	9000 years ago in China
	9000 years ago in the Americas
	8500 years ago in Europe
• First state societies	5500 years ago in the Near East
	3500 years ago in China
	3500 years ago in the Americas

western and central Asia from about 130,000 to 30,000 years ago. But as a result of analysis of ancient Neanderthal DNA they are now seen as more distant cousins, and again regarded as a different species, *Homo neanderthalensis*. As a result of DNA work it seems clear that *Homo sapiens* evolved in Africa, and that there was a major "Out of Africa" expansion between 60,000 and 50,000 years ago of humans ancestral to all present-day humans. Australia was colonized by humans some 50,000 years ago (the dates are still debated) and Europe and Asia by at least 40,000 years ago. There may have been an earlier dispersal of archaic modern humans who reached the eastern Mediterranean some 100,000 to 90,000 years ago but they probably have no surviving descendants.

It is uncertain when humans initially crossed from northeastern Asia into North America across the Bering Strait, and south to Central and South America. The earliest secure dates for the first Americans are around 14,000 years ago, but there is controversial evidence that the continent was populated before then.

By 10,000 BC, most of the land areas of the world, except the deserts and Antarctica, were populated. The most conspicuous exception is the Pacific, where Western Polynesia does not seem to have been colonized until the 1st millennium

BC, and Eastern Polynesia progressively from *c.* AD 300. By around AD 1000 the colonization of Oceania was complete. The spread of humans around the world is summarized in the map overleaf.

Nearly all the groups of humans so far mentioned may be regarded as **hunter-gatherer** societies, made up of relatively small groups of people.

One of the most significant occurrences in world history or **prehistory** at a global level is the development of food production, based on domesticated plant species and also (although in some areas to a lesser extent) of domesticated animal species. One of the most striking facts of world prehistory is that the transition from hunting and gathering to food production seems to have occurred independently in several areas, in each case after the end of the Ice Age, i.e. after *c.* 10,000 years ago.

In the Near East, we can recognize the origins of this transition even before this time, for the process may have been gradual, the consequence (as well as the cause) of restructuring of the social organization of human societies. At any rate, well-established farming, dependent on wheat and barley as well as sheep and goats (and later cattle), was underway there by about 8000 BC. Farming had spread to Europe by 6500 BC, and is documented in South Asia at Mehrgarh in Baluchistan at about the same time.

A separate development, based at first on the cultivation of millet, seems to have taken place in China, in the valley of the Huang Ho by 5000 BC or even earlier. Rice cultivation began at about the same time in the Yangzi Valley in China and spread to Southeast Asia. The position in Africa south of the Sahara is more complicated due to the diversity of environments, but millet and sorghum wheat were cultivated by the 3rd millennium BC. The Western Pacific (Melanesian) complex of root and tree crops had certainly developed by that time: indeed, there are indications of field drainage for root crops very much earlier.

In the Americas, a different range of crops was available. Cultivation of beans, squash, peppers, and some grasses may have begun by 7000 or even 8000 BC in Peru, and was certainly underway there and in Mesoamerica by the 7th millennium BC. Other South American species, including manioc and potato, were soon added, but the plant with the greatest impact on American agriculture was maize, believed to have been brought into cultivation in Mexico by 5600 years ago, though possibly earlier in northwest Argentina.

These agricultural innovations were rapidly adopted in some areas (e.g. in Europe), but in others, such as North America, their impact was less immediate. Certainly, by the time of Christ, hunter-gatherer economies were very much in the minority.

The urban revolution, the next major transformation that we recognize widely, is not simply a change in settlement type: it reflects profound social

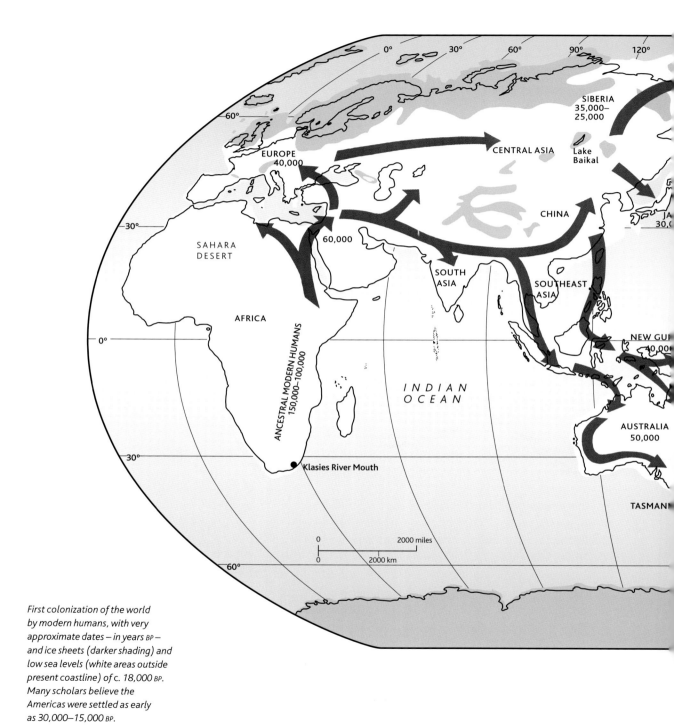

First colonization of the world
by modern humans, with very
approximate dates – in years BP –
and ice sheets (darker shading) and
low sea levels (white areas outside
present coastline) of c. 18,000 BP.
Many scholars believe the
Americas were settled as early
as 30,000–15,000 BP.

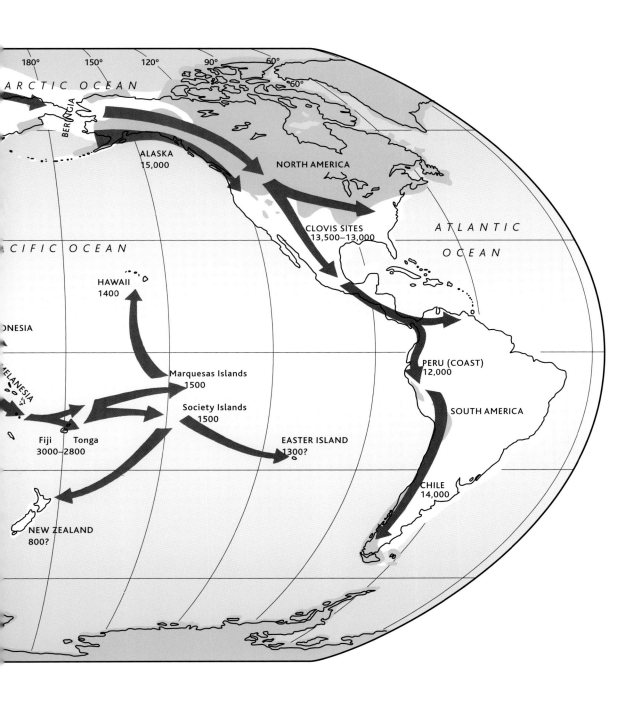

changes. Foremost among these is the development of **state** societies displaying more clearly differentiated institutions of government than do **chiefdoms**. Many state societies had writing. We see the first state societies in the Near East by about 3500 BC, in Egypt only a little later, and in the Indus Valley by 2500 BC. In the Near East, the period of the early Mesopotamian city-states was marked by the rise of famous sites such as Ur, Uruk, and later Babylon, and was followed in the 1st millennium BC by an age of great empires, notably those of Assyria and Achaemenid Persia. In Egypt, it is possible to trace the continuous development of cultural and political traditions over more than 2000 years, through the pyramid age of the Old Kingdom and the imperial power of New Kingdom Egypt.

On the western edge of the Near East, further civilizations developed: Minoans and Mycenaeans in Greece and the Aegean during the 2nd millennium BC, Etruscans and Romans in the 1st millennium BC. At the opposite end of Asia, state societies with urban centers appear in China before 1500 BC, marking the beginnings of the Shang civilization. At about the same time, Mesoamerica saw the rise of the Olmec, the first in a long sequence of Central American civilizations including Maya, Zapotec, Toltec, and Aztec. On the Pacific coast of South America, the Chavín (from 900 BC), Moche, and Chimú civilizations laid the foundations for the rise of the vast and powerful Inca empire that flourished in the 15th century AD.

The further pattern is the more familiar one of literate history, with the rise of the Classical world of Greece and Rome as well as of China, and then of the world of Islam, the Renaissance of Europe and the development of the colonial powers. From the 18th century to the present there followed the independence of the former colonies, first in the Americas, then in Asia and in Africa. We are talking now not simply of state societies but of nation states and, especially in colonial times, of empires.

STUDY QUESTIONS

- How are absolute dating methods different from relative dating methods?
- Why is an understanding of stratigraphy vital to most relative dating methods?
- Why is tree-ring dating considered to be an absolute dating method?
- Why is it necessary to calibrate radiocarbon dates?
- What types of artifacts cannot be radiocarbon dated? Why?
- What are some of the main sources of errors in the field of radiocarbon dating?

SUMMARY

- The answer to the question "When?" in archaeology has two main components. Relative dating methods allow us to determine that something is *relatively* older or younger than something else. Absolute methods make it possible to give a date in years. Archaeological dating is at its most reliable when the two methods are used together, e.g. when the relative order assigned to layers in an excavation can be confirmed by absolute dates for each layer. Wherever possible, results from one absolute method should be cross-checked by those from another.

- In areas where ancient calendars and historical chronologies are available, such as Mesoamerica, these remain one of the most important methods of dating. Elsewhere, the two methods most useful to the archaeologist are radiocarbon dating and tree-ring dating. Although many other absolute dating techniques exist, these tend to be reserved either for very specific applications or for sites that are beyond the range of radiocarbon back in the Paleolithic period.

- Ultimately the precision of dating attainable for each period helps determine the kinds of questions we ask about the past – for the Paleolithic, questions are about long-term change; for later periods, the questions are more usually concerned with the shorter-term variations in worldwide human development.

FURTHER READING

The following provide a good introduction to the principal dating techniques used by archaeologists:

Aitken, M.J. 1990. *Science-based Dating in Archaeology*. Longman: London & New York.

Biers, W.R. 1992. *Art, Artefacts and Chronology in Classical Archaeology*. Routledge: London.

Bowman, S.G.E. 1990. *Radiocarbon Dating*. British Museum Publications: London; University of Texas Press: Austin.

Brothwell, D.R. & Pollard, A.M. (eds.). 2005. *Handbook of Archaeological Sciences*. Wiley: Chichester & New York.

Pollard, A.M., Batt, C.M., Stern, B., & Young S.M.M. 2007. *Analytical Chemistry in Archaeology*. Cambridge University Press: Cambridge.

Speer, J.H. 2010. *Fundamentals of Tree-Ring Research*. University of Arizona Press: Tucson.

Taylor, R.E. & Aitken, M.J. (eds.). 1997. *Chronometric Dating in Archaeology*. Plenum: New York.

Wintle, A.G. 1996. Archaeologically relevant dating techniques for the next century. *Journal of Archaeological Science* 23, 123–38.

How Were Societies Organized?

Social archaeology

Some of the most interesting questions we can ask about early societies are social. They are about people and about relations between people, about the exercise of power, and about the nature and scale of organization. But the answers are not directly visible in the archaeological record: we have to ask the right questions of the data, and devise the means of answering them.

In this respect **archaeology** is very different from cultural or social **anthropology**, where the observer can actually visit the living society and rapidly form conclusions about its social and power structures before moving on to other more complex matters, such as the details of the kinship system or the minutiae of ritual behavior. The archaeologist has to work hard to gain even basic details of these kinds, but the prize is a rich one: an understanding of the social organization not just of societies in the present or very recent past (like **cultural anthropology**) but of societies at many different points in time, with all the scope that that offers for studying change. Only the archaeologist can obtain that perspective, and hence seek some understanding of the processes of long-term change.

Different kinds of society need different kinds of questions and the techniques of investigation will need to vary radically with the nature of the evidence. We cannot tackle a **Paleolithic hunter-gatherer** camp in the same way as the capital city of an early **state**. Thus, the questions we put, and the methods for answering them, must be tailored to the sort of community we are dealing with. So it is all the more necessary to be clear at the outset about the general nature of that community, which is why the most basic social questions are always the first ones to ask.

We must first address the size or *scale* of the society. The archaeologist will often be excavating a single **site**. But was that an independent political unit, like a Maya or Greek city-state, or a simpler unit, like the base camp of a hunter-gatherer group? Or was it, on the other hand, a small cog in a very big wheel, a subordinate settlement in some far-flung empire, like that of the Incas of Peru?

Any site we consider will have its own hinterland, or catchment area, for the feeding of its population. But one of our interests is to go beyond that local area, and to understand how that site interacts with others. From the standpoint of the individual site – which is often a convenient perspective to adopt – that raises questions of *dominance*. Was the site politically independent, autonomous? Or, if it was part of a larger social system, did it take a dominant part (like the capital city of a kingdom) or a subordinate one?

If the scale of the society is a natural first question, the next is certainly its internal organization. What kind of society was it? Were the people forming it on a more-or-less equal social footing? Or were there instead prominent differences in status, rank, and prestige within the society – perhaps different social classes? And what of the professions: were there people who specialized in particular crafts? And if so, were they controlled within a centralized system, as in some of the palace economies of the Near East and Egypt? Or was this a freer economy, with a flourishing free exchange, where merchants could operate at will in their own interest?

These questions, however, may all be seen as "top-down" questions, looking at the society from above and investigating its organization. But increasingly an alternative perspective is being followed, looking first at the individual, and at the way the identity of the individual in the society in question is defined – a "bottom-up" perspective. Archaeologists are coming to realize that the way such important social aspects as gender, status, and even age are constituted in a society are not "givens," but are specific to each different society. These insights are leading to new fields: the archaeology of the individual and the archaeology of identity.

ESTABLISHING THE NATURE AND SCALE OF THE SOCIETY

The first step in social archaeology is so obvious that it is often overlooked. It is to ask, what was the scale of the largest social unit, and what kind of society, in a very broad sense, was it? The largest social unit could be anything from a small and completely independent hunter-gatherer **band** to a great empire. In the case of a complex society it can comprise many lesser units.

In terms of research in the field, the question is often best answered from a study of settlement: both in terms of the scale and nature of *individual sites* and in relationships between them, through the analysis of *settlement pattern*. But we should not forget that *written records*, where a society is literate and uses writing, *oral tradition*, and **ethnoarchaeology** – the study from an archaeological point of view of present-day societies – can be equally valuable in assessing the nature and scale of the society under review.

First, however, we need a frame of reference, a hypothetical **classification** of societies against which to test our ideas.

The Classification of Societies

	MOBILE HUNTER-GATHERER GROUPS	SEGMENTARY SOCIETY	CHIEFDOM	STATE
	San hunters, South Africa	*Man plowing, Valcamonica, Italy*	*Horseman, Gundestrup caldron*	*Terracotta army, tomb of first emperor of China*
TOTAL NUMBERS	Less than 100	Up to few 1000	5000–20,000+	Generally 20,000+
SOCIAL ORGANIZATION	Egalitarian Informal leadership	Segmentary society Pan-tribal associations Raids by small groups	Kinship-based ranking under hereditary leader High-ranking warriors	Class-based hierarchy under king or emperor Armies
ECONOMIC ORGANIZATION	Mobile hunter-gatherers	Settled farmers Pastoralist herders	Central accumulation and redistribution Some craft specialization	Centralized bureaucracy Tribute-based Taxation Laws
SETTLEMENT PATTERN	Temporary camps	Permanent villages	Fortified centers Ritual centers	Urban: cities, towns Frontier defenses Roads
RELIGIOUS ORGANIZATION	Shamans	Religious elders Calendrical rituals	Hereditary chief with religious duties	Priestly class Pantheistic or monotheistic religion
ARCHITECTURE	Temporary shelters	Permanent huts Burial mounds Shrines	Large-scale monuments	Palaces, temples, and other public buildings
	Paleolithic skin tents, Siberia	*Neolithic shrine, Çatalhöyük, Turkey*	*Stonehenge, England – final form*	*Pyramids at Giza* *Castillo, Chichén Itzá, Mexico*
ARCHAEOLOGICAL EXAMPLES	All Paleolithic societies, including Paleo-Indians	All early farmers (Neolithic/Archaic)	Many early metalworking and Formative societies	All ancient civilizations, e.g. in Mesoamerica, Peru, Near East, India and China; Greece and Rome
MODERN EXAMPLES	Inuit San, southern Africa Australian Aborigines	Pueblos, Southwest USA New Guinea Highlanders Nuer and Dinka, E. Africa	Northwest Coast Native Americans, USA 18th-century Polynesian chiefdoms in Tonga, Tahiti, Hawaii	All modern states

Classification of Societies

The American anthropologist Elman Service developed a four-fold classification of societies that many archaeologists have found useful, though his terminology has since been amended. Particular kinds of site and settlement pattern are associated with each of the societies. Some archaeologists question the value of broad classifications such as "**chiefdom**," but at a preliminary stage of analysis they are useful, especially if they are not taken too seriously. The classification is summarized in the box on p. 143.

Mobile hunter-gatherer groups. These are small-scale societies of hunters and gatherers (sometimes called "bands"), generally of fewer than 100 people, who move seasonally to exploit wild food resources. Most surviving hunter-gatherer groups today are of this kind, such as the San of southern Africa. Band members are generally kinsfolk, related by descent or marriage, and bands do not have formal leaders, so there are no marked economic differences or disparities in status among their members.

Because bands are mobile groups, their sites consist mainly of seasonally occupied camps, and other smaller and more specialized sites. These include kill or butchery sites – locations where large mammals are killed and sometimes butchered – and work sites, where tools are made or other specific activities carried out. Camps may show evidence of insubstantial dwellings or temporary shelters, along with the debris of residential occupation.

During the Paleolithic period (before 12,000 years ago) most archaeological sites seem to conform to one or other of these categories – camp sites, kill sites, work sites – and archaeologists usually operate on the assumption that most Paleolithic societies were organized into bands.

Segmentary societies. These are generally larger than mobile hunter-gatherer groups, but their population rarely numbers more than a few thousand, and their diet or subsistence is based largely on cultivated plants and domesticated animals. They are sometimes referred to as **tribes**. Typically, they are settled farmers, but they may be nomad pastoralists with a mobile economy based on the intensive exploitation of livestock. **Segmentary societies** generally consist of many individual communities integrated into the larger society through kinship ties. Although some have officials and even a "capital" or seat of government, such officials lack the economic base necessary for effective use of power.

The typical settlement pattern for segmentary societies is one of settled agricultural homesteads or villages. Characteristically, no one settlement dominates any of the others in the region. Instead, the archaeologist finds evidence for isolated, permanently occupied houses (a *dispersed* settlement pattern) or for permanent villages (a *nucleated* pattern). Such villages may be made up of a collection of free-standing houses, like those of the first farmers of the Danube valley in Europe, *c.* 4500 BC. Or they may be clusters of buildings grouped together – so-called *agglomerate* structures, for example, the pueblos of the American Southwest.

Chiefdoms. These societies are characterized by ranking – differences in social status between people. Different **lineages** (a lineage is a group claiming descent from a common ancestor) are graded on a scale of prestige, and the senior lineage, and hence the society as a whole, is governed by a chief. Prestige and rank are determined by closeness of relationship to the chief. There is no true stratification into classes, and the role of the chief is crucial. Chiefdoms vary greatly in size, but the range is generally between about 5000 and 20,000 persons.

Often, there is local specialization in craft production, and surpluses of these and of foodstuffs are periodically paid as obligations to the chief. He uses these to maintain his close personal followers, and may use them for **redistribution** to his subjects.

The chiefdom generally has a center of power, often with temples, residences of the chief and his retainers, and craft specialists. It is a permanent ritual and ceremonial center that acts as a central focus for the entire group. However, this is not a permanent urban center (such as a city) with an established bureaucracy, as we find in state societies. But chiefdoms do give indications that some sites were more important than others (or in other words, that there was a site hierarchy). An example is Moundville in Alabama, USA, which flourished *c.* AD 1000–1500 (see box on pp. 154–55).

The personal ranking characteristic of chiefdom societies is also visible in the very rich grave-goods that often accompany the burials of deceased chiefs.

Early States. These share many of the features of chiefdoms, but the ruler (perhaps a king or sometimes a queen) has explicit authority to establish laws and also to enforce them by the use of a standing army. Society no longer depends totally upon kin relationships: it is now stratified into different classes. Agricultural workers or serfs and the poorer urban dwellers form the lowest classes, with the craft specialists above, and the priests and kinsfolk of the ruler higher still. The functions of the ruler are often separated from those of the priest: palace is distinguished from temple. The territory is "owned" by the ruling lineage and populated by tenants who have an obligation to pay taxes. Taxes and other revenues are collected by officials based in the central capital, and then distributed to government, army, and craft specialists. Many early states developed complex redistributive systems to support these essential services.

Early state societies generally show a characteristic urban settlement pattern in which *cities* play a prominent part. The city is typically a large population center (often of more than 5000 inhabitants) with major public buildings, including temples and work places for the administrative bureaucracy. Often, there is a pronounced settlement hierarchy, with the capital city as the major center, and with subsidiary or regional centers as well as local villages.

This rather simple social typology should not be used unthinkingly. For instance, there is some difference between the rather vague idea of the "tribe" and the more modern concept of the "segmentary society." The term "tribe," implying a larger grouping of smaller units, carries with it the assumption that these communities share a common ethnic identity and self-awareness, which is now known not generally to be the case. The term "segmentary society" refers to a relatively small and autonomous group, usually of agriculturalists, who regulate their own affairs: in some cases, they may join together with other comparable segmentary societies to form a larger ethnic unit or "tribe"; in other cases, they do not. For the remainder of this chapter, we shall therefore refer to *segmentary societies* in preference to the term "tribe." And what in Service's typology were called "bands" are now more generally referred to as "mobile hunter-gatherer groups."

Certainly, it would be wrong to overemphasize the importance of the four types of society given above, or to spend too long trying to decide whether a specific group should be classed in one category rather than another. It would also be wrong to assume that somehow societies inevitably evolve from hunter-gatherer groups to segmentary societies, or from chiefdoms to states. One of the challenges of archaeology is to attempt to explain why some societies become more complex and others do not.

Nevertheless, Service's categories provide a good framework to help organize our thoughts. They should not, however, deflect us from focusing on what we are really looking for: changes over time in the different institutions of a society – whether in the social sphere, the organization of the food quest, technology, contact and exchange, or spiritual life. Archaeology has the unique advantage of being able to study processes of change over thousands of years, and it is these processes we are seeking to isolate. Fortunately there are sufficiently marked differences between simple and more complex societies for us to find ways of doing this.

As we saw above in the description of Service's four types of society, complex societies show in particular an increased specialization in, or separation between, different aspects of their **culture**. In complex societies people no longer combine, say, the tasks of obtaining food, making tools, or performing religious rites but become specialists at one or other of these tasks, either as full-time farmers, craftspeople, or priests. As technology develops, for example, groups of individuals may acquire particular expertise in pottery-making or metallurgy, and will become full-time *craft specialists*, occupying distinct areas of a town or city and thus leaving traces for the archaeologist to discover. Likewise, as farming develops and population grows, more food will be obtained from a given piece of land (food production will *intensify*) through the introduction of the plow or irrigation. As this specialization and intensification take place, so too does the tendency for some people to become wealthier and wield more authority than others – differences in social status and *ranking* develop.

It is the methods for looking at these processes of increasing specialization, intensification, and social ranking that help us identify the presence of more complex societies in the archaeological record. For simpler groups like hunter-gatherers, other methods are needed if we are to identify them archaeologically, as will become apparent.

METHODS OF SOCIAL ANALYSIS

Different methods are suitable for investigating the social interactions and social structures of different kinds of societies. The principal source of data about early societies comes from settlement analysis and **excavation**. The study of burials with their associated **artifacts** is often a very good way of assessing the dress, possessions and status of deceased individuals in a society. For some societies, the study of the monuments which they have built can also be very informative.

The data available from a hunter-gatherer camp are naturally very different from those from a city. For one thing, state societies are often literate societies, and written records may be available. For societies for which no written testimony is available, archaeologists have often relied upon ethnographic analogy, drawing upon what anthropologists have observed in more recent

KEY CONCEPTS
Methods of Social Analysis

- *Settlement Analysis*: the main method of investigating past social organization. Data are collected by survey and excavation, but the specific methods used can vary greatly depending on the society in question

- *Burial Analysis*: rank and social status are best revealed by the analysis of grave-goods within individual burials

- *Monuments and Public Works*: the scale of monuments and public works, as well as their distribution, can be a good indicator of social organization

- *Written Records*: an excellent source of information about the organization of early state societies

- *Ethnoarchaeology*: the study of living societies in order to help interpret the past, with a specific emphasis on the use and significance of artifacts, buildings and structures, and how these material things might become incorporated into the archaeological record

non-urban societies so as to suggest interpretations for what is found in the archaeological record. Ethnoarchaeology, as this field is known, seeks to use the experience derived from living societies to suggest interpretive and explanatory approaches to archaeological data.

Settlement Analysis and Site Hierarchy

One of the principal ways of answering the basic question "what is the scale of the society" is through an understanding of *settlement pattern*, and this can only come from survey. Whatever the period in question, we should be interested in finding the major center or centers of settlement along with any smaller sites. We can use many of the survey, sampling, and **remote sensing** techniques described in Chapter 3 to do this, but the exact nature of the work will depend on the society in question – it is much harder to find the scanty traces that are left by mobile hunter-gatherers than it is to find an ancient city, so more intensive survey is needed.

Any survey will result in a map and a catalog of the sites discovered, together with details of each site including size, chronological range (as may be determined from surface remains such as pottery), architectural features, and possibly an approximate estimate of population. The aim is then to reach some classification of the sites on the basis of their relative importance – a *site hierarchy*. Possible categories for the different types of site encountered might include, for instance, Regional Center, Local Center, Nucleated Village, Dispersed Village, and Hamlet.

Various techniques can be used to establish the site hierarchy of a region, but the simplest is based solely on site size. Sites are arranged in rank order by size and then displayed as a histogram, which will usually show that the small sites are the most frequent. Such histograms allow comparisons to be made between the site hierarchies of different regions, different periods, and different types of society. In band societies, for example, there will usually be only a narrow range of variation in site size and all the sites will be relatively small. State societies, on the other hand, will have both hamlets and farmsteads and large towns and cities. The degree to which a single site is dominant within a settlement system will also be evident from this type of analysis, and the organization of the settlement system will often be a direct reflection of the organization of the society which created it. In a general way, the more hierarchical the settlement pattern, the more hierarchical the society.

Work by Gregory Johnson on the Early Dynastic (*c.* 2800 BC) settlement sites in a region of Mesopotamia showed this very clearly, as can be seen in the graph opposite. The sites ranged in size from 25 ha (60 acres) to just over one tenth of a hectare (0.25 acres), and could be divided into five categories based on their size: Johnson called these large towns, towns, large villages, small villages, and hamlets.

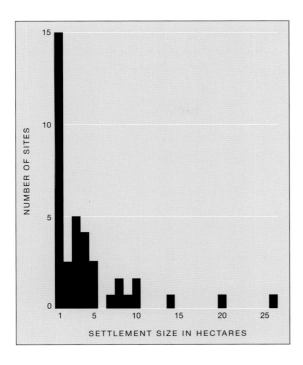

Site hierarchy for Early Dynastic settlements in a region of Mesopotamia.

The existence of a settlement hierarchy of this kind has been used by some archaeologists as an indicator of a state society.

However, the excavation of settlement remains is the major source of information about social relations within a society. This applies for any level of complexity, but the methods used can vary greatly, the main distinction being between mobile and sedentary societies.

Mobile Hunter-Gatherer Societies. In mobile hunter-gatherer societies organization is exclusively at a local level, with no permanent administrative centers. So having identified various sites, the first approach is to concentrate on the sites themselves, with the aim being to understand the nature of the activities that took place there, and of the social group that used them.

Among mobile communities of hunter-gatherers archaeologists draw a distinction between *cave sites* and *open sites*. Occupation deposits in cave sites tend to be deep, usually indicating intermittent human activity over thousands or tens of thousands of years, and meticulous excavation and recording are required to interpret the **stratigraphy** of the site accurately. Open sites may have been occupied for shorter periods of time, but the deposits, without the protection provided by a cave, may have suffered greater erosion.

If it proves possible to distinguish single short phases of human occupation at a hunter-gatherer site, we can then look at the distribution of artifacts and bone fragments within and around **features** and structures (hut foundations, remains of hearths) to see whether any coherent patterns can be observed. However, it is not always clear whether the distribution is the result of human activity on the spot (or *in situ*) or whether the materials have been transported by flowing water and redeposited. In some cases, too, especially with bone debris, distribution may be the result of the action of predatory animals, not of humans.

The study of such questions requires sophisticated sampling strategies and very thorough analysis. The work of Glynn Isaac's team at the Early Paleolithic site of Koobi Fora on the eastern shore of Lake Turkana, Kenya, gives an indication of the recovery and analytical techniques involved. The excavation procedure was highly controlled, with exact recording of the coordinates of every piece of bone or stone recovered, and careful analysis of the degree of post-depositional disturbance. Isaac's team was able to fit some fragments of bone and stone back together again. They interpreted the network of joins (see diagram below) as showing areas where **hominins** broke open bones to extract marrow, and where stone tools were knapped – so called activity areas.

Glynn Isaac's research at the Early Paleolithic site of Koobi Fora, Kenya, East Africa. (Top row) Location of bones and stone artifacts. (Second row) Lines joining bones and stones that could be fitted back together, perhaps indicating activity areas.

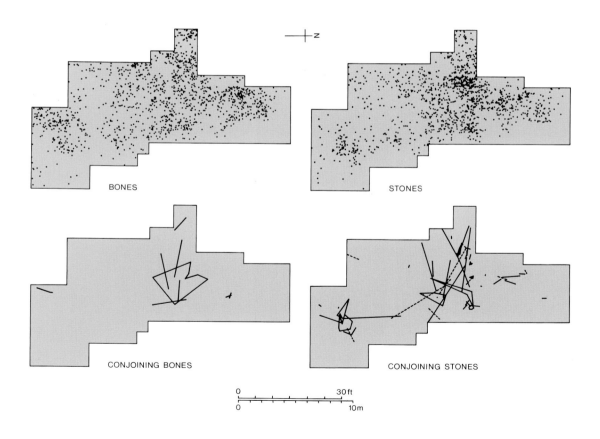

BONES

STONES

CONJOINING BONES

CONJOINING STONES

For a wider perspective, we need to consider the entire territory in which the group or band operated, and the relationship between sites. Ethnoarchaeology (see pp. 162–64) has helped to establish a framework of analysis, so that we may think in terms of an annual home range (i.e. the whole territory covered by the group in the course of a year) and specific types of site within it, such as a home base camp (for a particular season), transitory camps, hunting blinds, butchery or kill sites, storage caches, and so on. These issues are basic to hunter-gatherer archaeology, and a regional perspective is essential to understand the annual life cycle of the group and its behavior. This means that, in addition to conventional sites (with a high concentration of artifacts), we need to look for sparse scatters of artifacts, consisting of perhaps just one or two objects in every 10-m survey square. One must also study the whole regional environment and the likely human use of it by hunter-gatherers.

A good example is provided by the work of the British anthropologist Robert Foley in the Amboseli region of southern Kenya. He collected and recorded some 8531 stone tools from 257 sample locations within a study area covering 600 sq.

Robert Foley's model (below left) of activities within the annual home range of a hunter-gatherer band, and the artifact scatters (below) resulting from such activities.

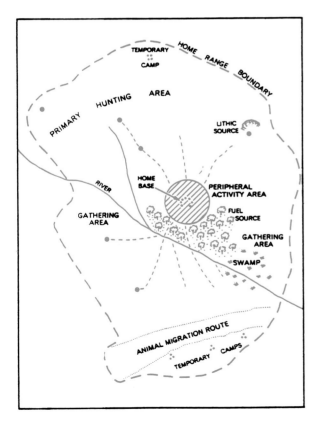

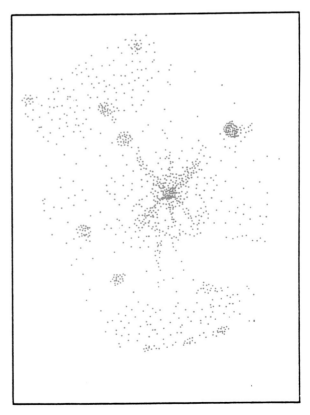

km (232 sq. miles). From this evidence he was able to calculate the rate of discard of stone tools within different environmental and vegetation zones, and interpret the distribution patterns in terms of the strategies and movements of hunter-gatherer groups. In a later study, he developed a general model of stone tool distribution based on a number of studies of hunter-gatherer bands in different parts of the world. One conclusion was that a single band of some 25 people might be expected to discard as many as 163,000 artifacts within their annual territory in the course of a single year. These artifacts would be scattered across the territory, but with significant concentrations at home base camps and temporary camps. According to Foley's study, however, only a very small proportion of the artifacts discarded would be found by archaeologists working at a single site, and it is vitally important that individual site **assemblages** are interpreted as parts of a broader pattern.

Sedentary Societies.   Investigation of the social organization of sedentary communities, which include segmentary societies, chiefdoms, and states, is best approached with an investigation of settlement (although, as we shall see below, cemeteries and public monuments evident in these societies also form useful areas of study).

Although much can be learned from survey, for effective analysis of the community as a whole some structures need to be excavated completely and the remainder sampled intensively enough to obtain an idea of the variety of different structures. The careful excavation of individual houses and of complete villages is a standard procedure when dealing with smaller sedentary communities. This opens the way to the study of households, and of community structure, as well as to well-founded estimates of population.

A good example is offered by Kent Flannery's excavation of Early Formative houses at Tierras Largas in Oaxaca, Mexico. He was able to establish the first map showing the layout of a Formative village in Oaxaca. Evidence for differences in social status emerged. Residences, deduced to be of relatively high status, had not only a house platform built of higher-quality adobe and stone, but a greater quantity of animal bone, imported **obsidian**, and imported marine shell than the area of wattle-and-daub houses deduced to be of lower status. Significantly, locally available (and therefore less prestigious) chert formed a higher proportion of the tools in the lower-status area.

Most of the techniques of analysis appropriate to less developed societies remain valid for the study of centralized chiefdoms and states, which incorporate within themselves most of the social forms and patterns of interaction seen in the simpler societies. Additional techniques are needed because of the centralization of society, the hierarchy of sites, and the organizational and communicational devices that characterize chiefdom and state societies. A good example is provided by the work at the Mississippian site of Moundville, described in the box overleaf.

Plan of a house at Tierras Largas, c. 900 BC, with certain artifacts plotted in position.

One of the first steps when looking at a complex society is to identify one or more primary centers, and this is done by considering the size of a site, either in absolute terms, or in terms of the distances between major centers, so as to determine which are dominant and which subordinate. With this information a map can be created identifying the principal independent centers and the approximate extent of the territories surrounding them.

The reliance on size alone, however, can be misleading, and it is necessary to seek other indications of which are the primary centers. The best way is to try to find out how the society in question viewed itself and its territories. This might seem an impossible task until one remembers that, for most state societies at any rate, written records exist. These may name various sites, identifying their place within the hierarchy. The archaeologist's task is then to find those named sites, usually by the discovery of an actual inscription including the name of the relevant site – one might for example hope to find such an inscription in any substantial town of the Roman empire. In recent years, the decipherment of Maya hieroglyphs has opened up a whole new source of evidence of this sort.

During its heyday in the 14th and 15th centuries AD, Moundville was one of the greatest ceremonial centers of the Mississippian culture in North America. The site takes its name from an impressive group of 20 mounds constructed within a palisaded area, 150 ha (370 acres) in extent, on the banks of the Black Warrior river in west-central Alabama. Moundville was first dug into as long ago as 1840, but major excavations did not take place until the 20th century. Recently, Christopher Peebles and his colleagues have combined **systematic survey** with limited excavation and reanalysis of earlier work to produce a convincing social study of the site.

Peebles and his team first needed a reliable chronology. This was achieved through an analysis of the pottery. The resultant relative chronology was then cross-checked with excavated ceramics from radiocarbon dated contexts to produce an absolute chronology.

This chronology enabled the team to study the development of the site through several phases. Preliminary survey of neighboring sites also established the regional settlement pattern for each phase, summarized in the maps below. Over 3000 burials have been excavated at Moundville, and Peebles used statistical techniques to group 2053 of them according to social rank. Peebles observed that the small number of people of highest rank (Segment A: classes IA, IB and II in the pyramid diagram below) were buried in

Pyramid-shaped social hierarchy at Moundville, based on the analysis of 2053 burials. Artifacts listed against each rank (Classes I–X) are grave-goods.

IA: Copper axes **IA** 7 burials in central mounds

IB: Copper earspools, bear teeth, stone discs **IB** 43 mound and non-mound burials

A

II: Shell beads, copper gorgets, galena **II** 67 mound and non-mound burials

III: Effigy vessels, animal bone, shell gorgets
IV: Discoidals, bone awls, projectile points **III** **IV** Non-mound burials **III:** 221 **IV:** 50

B

V & VIII: Bowls **VI, VII & IX:** Water bottles **V** **VI** **VII** **VIII** **IX** **X** Non-mound burials **V:** 55 **VI:** 45 **VII:** 55 **VIII:** 70 **IX** 46 **X:** 70

C

No grave goods   1256 burials

Changing settlement patterns in the Moundville region. In Phase I (AD 1050–1250) Moundville was simply a site with a single mound, like other similar sites in the area. By Phase II, however, it had grown larger, establishing itself as the major regional center. After its heyday in Phase III, Moundville disappeared as a significant site in Phase IV (after 1550), when the region no longer had a dominant center.

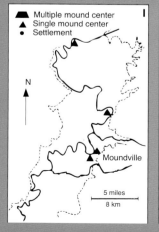

- ▲ Multiple mound center
- ▲ Single mound center
- • Settlement

I

N

5 miles
8 km

Moundville

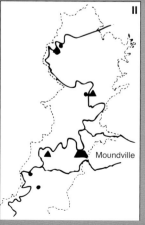

II

Moundville

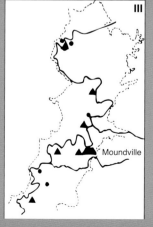

III

Moundville

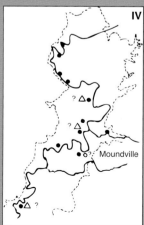

IV

Moundville

UNITED STATES
Moundville

or near the mounds with artifacts exclusive to them, such as copper axes and earspools. Lower-ranking individuals of Segment B (Classes III and IV) had non-mound burials with some grave-goods but no copper artifacts, while those of Segment C, buried on the periphery, had few or no grave-goods.

Peebles found interesting differences according to age and sex. The seven individuals in Class IA, the top of the social pyramid, were all adults, probably males. Those of Class IB were adult males and children, while Class II comprised individuals of all ages and both sexes. It seems clear that adult males had the

highest status. The presence of children in Class IB suggests that their high status was inherited at birth.

Peebles's study suggests a regional organization with a well-marked hierarchy of sites, controlled by a highly ranked community at Moundville itself – what Peebles terms a chiefdom society.

Usually, however, site hierarchy must be deduced by more directly archaeological means, without relying on the written word. A "highest-order" center, such as the capital city of an independent state, can best be identified from direct indications of central organization, on a scale not exceeded elsewhere, and comparable with that of other highest-order centers of equivalent states.

One indication is the existence of an archive (even without understanding anything of what it says) or of other symbolic indications of centralized organization. For instance, many controlled economies used seals to make impressions in clay as indications of ownership, source, or destination. The finding of a quantity of such materials can indicate organizational activity. Indeed, the whole practice of literacy and of symbolic expression is so central to organization that such indications are valuable evidence.

A further indication of central status is the presence of buildings of standardized form known to be associated with central functions of high order. Examples of such buildings include palaces, such as those found in Minoan Crete; buildings of ritual function (since in most early societies the control of administration and control of religious practice were closely linked), for example a Maya temple complex; fortifications; and mints for producing coinage.

In a hierarchically organized society, it always makes sense to study closely the functions of the center, considering such possible factors as kinship, bureaucratic organization, redistribution and storage of goods, organization of ritual, craft specialization, and external trade. All of these offer insights into how the society worked.

Burial Analysis: The Study of Ranking from Individual Burials

In archaeology, the individual is seen all too rarely. One of the most informative insights into the individual and his or her social status is offered by the discovery of human physical remains – the skeleton or the ashes – accompanied by artifacts deposited in the grave. Examination of the skeletal remains by a physical anthropologist will often reveal the sex and age at death of each individual, and possibly any dietary deficiency or other pathological condition. Communal or collective burials (burials of more than one individual) may be difficult to interpret, because it will not always be clear which grave-goods go with which deceased person. It is, therefore, from single burials that we can hope to learn most.

In segmentary societies, and others with relatively limited differentiation in terms of rank, a close analysis of grave-goods can reveal much about disparities in social status. However, it is important to remember that what is buried with a deceased person is not simply the exact equivalent either of status or of material goods owned or used during life. Burials are made by living individuals, and are used by them to express and influence their relationships with others still alive as much as to symbolize or serve the dead. But there is nevertheless often a relationship between the role and rank of the deceased during life and the manner in which the remains are disposed of and accompanied by artifacts.

The analysis will seek to determine differences between male and female burials, and to assess whether these differences carry with them distinctions in terms of wealth or higher status. The other common factor involved with rank or status is age, and age differences may be systematically reflected in the treatment of the deceased. In relatively egalitarian societies, high status won through the individual's own achievements (e.g. in hunting) in his or her own lifetime is something commonly encountered, and often reflected in funerary practice. But the archaeologist must ask, from the evidence available, whether such a burial really reflects status achieved by the individual or instead hereditary status through birth. To distinguish between the two is not easy. One useful criterion is to investigate whether children are in some cases given rich burial goods and other indications of preferential attention. If so, there may have been a system of hereditary ranking, because at so early an age the child is unlikely to have reached such a status through personal distinction.

Once the graves in the cemetery have been dated, the first step in most cases is simply to produce a frequency distribution (a histogram) of the number of different artifact **types** in each grave. For further analysis, however, it is more interesting to seek some better indication of wealth and status so that greater weight can be given to valuable objects, and less weight to commonplace ones. This at once raises the problem of the recognition of value (for we cannot assume that past societies had the same ideas of value as we do). One answer might be to assume that valuable objects were those that took a long time to make, or were made of materials brought from a distance or difficult to obtain. We must also remember that ranking is not expressed solely in the grave-goods, but in the entire manner of burial.

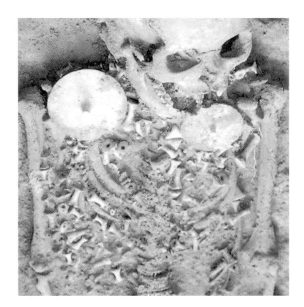

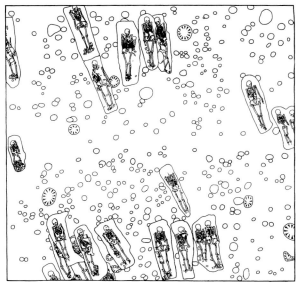

A good example of the analysis of an entire cemetery is offered by the excavations of Charles Higham and Rachanie Thosarat at the site of Khok Phanom Di, a large mound inland from the Gulf of Siam in central Thailand. The settlement had been occupied for about 500 years from *c.* 2000 BC, and left a cemetery containing 154 human burials with bone and shell ornaments intact. The graves occurred in clusters with spaces between them. A very detailed burial sequence was worked out which provided insights into the community's kinship system over about 20 generations. The ability to trace families down the generations like this is extremely rare in **prehistory**. In the later phases there was a predominance of women, some of them buried with considerable wealth, such as the so-called "Princess." Also there was a clear link between the wealth of children and the adults with whom they were buried – poor children accompanied poor adults. The analysis of a complete cemetery in this way can yield many insights which are not available even from the very careful examination of a single grave.

Khok Phanom Di. (Above left) The "Princess," who was accompanied by a set of shell jewelry, with over 120,000 beads, a headdress, and a bracelet, as well as fine pottery vessels. (Above) The dead were buried individually, in neat, clustered rows.

Monuments and Public Works

Some societies invest a great deal of labor and considerable resources in the construction of monuments and public works. Such monuments were generally built with the intention of being conspicuous and in some cases – like the pyramids of Egypt – they remain conspicuous today. Many early state societies had at their center a major ceremonial site, and the monuments at such sites are informative not only about the religious beliefs of the society in question but also about aspects of their social organization.

View south across the central plaza at Monte Albán, with the restored ruins of several temples visible. The site was founded on a mountain top in 500 BC.

The great plazas at the ceremonial centers of Mesoamerica are a good example. Monte Albán in Oaxaca, Mexico, became the principal center of the Zapotec state around 200 BC. Its wonderfully situated central plaza, shown above, dominated the surrounding countryside. From this time on Monte Albán was the home of some 10,000 to 20,000 people, and the primary center of Oaxaca. Its monuments celebrate and reflect the power of the state and the city's central authority.

In some segmentary societies the surviving monuments, frequently burial monuments, were much more conspicuous than the often not very substantial settlements. In some cases the settlements are rarely recovered, sometimes obliterated by erosion, while clear traces of the monuments still remain. This is the case for the **Neolithic** period in the Wessex area of southern England where earthen burial mounds, called "long barrows" are the most evident trace of the early farmers who lived there from *c.* 4000 BC.

Each mound in this part of Neolithic Wessex was the territorial focus for a small group of farmers. This was a segmentary society, where no one group was dominant.

There are reasons for thinking that each mound was the focal point in the landscape for a single community. If we draw lines between each mound, as shown in the diagram left, we can see how the landscape might have been divided territorially into units of approximately equal size, each serving as the homeland of the farming community associated with a single burial monument.

The spatial analysis of monuments undertaken in this way can be supplemented by a consideration of the labor input needed to construct them. It is estimated that each Wessex long barrow required 10,000

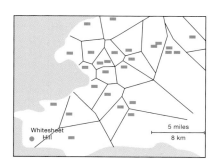

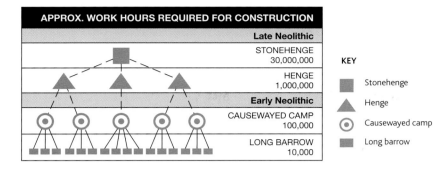

APPROX. WORK HOURS REQUIRED FOR CONSTRUCTION	
Late Neolithic	
	STONEHENGE 30,000,000
	HENGE 1,000,000
Early Neolithic	
	CAUSEWAYED CAMP 100,000
	LONG BARROW 10,000

KEY

- Stonehenge
- Henge
- Causewayed camp
- Long barrow

Analysis of the scale of the Wessex monuments in terms of labor hours needed for their construction suggests the emergence of a hierarchy in the later phase that may mirror a development in social relations and the emergence of a ranked society. Stonehenge, built at this time, is the greatest of the Wessex monuments. In the earlier Neolithic the scale of monuments is commensurate with an egalitarian, segmentary society.

work hours to construct. A class of larger monuments contemporary with the long barrows, known as "causewayed camps" and formed essentially of a circular ditch, may have each taken 100,000 work hours to construct. The long barrow/causewayed camp phase was succeeded around 2500 BC by a phase in which still larger bank-and-ditch monuments, termed "henges" were built. The great henges have approximately the same distribution as the earlier causewayed camps, but to construct each required an estimated 1,000,000 work hours. Toward the end of this phase, around 2100 BC, the great stone structure at Stonehenge was built, requiring some 30,000,000 hours of work. So great a construction may suggest some centralizing organization at this time for the whole Wessex area.

Although the calculations are very approximate they do show how some notion of the changing social organization can be formed through the study of the monuments, even at a time when the traces of domestic settlement are very scanty indeed.

The structures built at this early time can be very impressive. Stonehenge is certainly one of the largest, but it is not the oldest. Indeed over much of northwestern Europe there are stone monuments of the Neolithic period, mainly collective tombs, which are often termed "megalithic" (from the Greek *megas* (great) and *lithos* (stone)).

Some of these go back as far as 4000 BC, a millennium before the pyramids of Egypt. In the Orkney Islands, beyond the northern tip of Scotland, the local sandstone could readily be worked, already before the use of metal tools, and the remaining monuments, some of them well preserved, are sophisticated works of stone architecture.

For instance, in the chambered tomb at Quanterness in the Orkney Islands, off the north coast of Scotland, dating to *c.* 3300 BC, remains of a large number of individuals were found, perhaps as many as 390. Males and females were about equally represented, and the age distribution could represent the pattern of deaths in the population at large; that is to say, that the age at death of the people buried in the tomb (46 percent below 20 years, 47 percent aged 20–30 years, and only 7 percent over the age of 30 years) could in proportional terms be the same as that of the whole population. The excavators concluded that this was a tomb equally available to most sectors of the community, and representative of a segmentary society rather than a hierarchical one, which the sophistication of its architecture might at first have suggested.

Written Records

For literate societies – those that use writing, for instance all the great civilizations in Mesoamerica, China, Egypt, and the Near East – historical records can answer many of the social questions set out at the beginning of this chapter. One of the main goals of the archaeologist dealing with these societies is therefore to find appropriate texts. Many of the early excavations of the great sites of the Near East, for example, concentrated on the recovery of archives of clay writing tablets. Major finds of this kind are still made today – for example, at the ancient city of Ebla (Tell Mardikh) in Syria in the 1970s, where an archive of 5000 clay tablets written in an early, probably provincial, dialect of Akkadian (Babylonian) was discovered.

Some of the 5000 clay tablets discovered in the royal palace at Ebla (Tell Mardikh in modern Syria), dating from the late 3rd millennium BC. The tablets formed part of the state archives, recording over 140 years of Ebla's history. Originally they were stored on wooden shelving, which collapsed when the palace was sacked.

In each early literate society, writing had its own functions and purposes. For instance, the clay tablets of Mycenaean Greece, dating from *c.* 1200 BC, are almost without exception records of commercial transactions (goods coming in or going out) at the Mycenaean palaces. This gives us an impression of many aspects of the Mycenaean economy, and a glimpse into craft organization (through the names for the different kinds of craftspeople), as well as introducing the names of the offices of state. But here, as in other cases, accidents of preservation may be important. It could be that the Mycenaeans wrote on clay only for their commercial records, and used other, perishable materials for literary or historical texts now lost to us. It is certainly true that for the Classical Greek and Roman civilizations, it is mainly official decrees inscribed on marble that have survived. Fragile rolls of papyrus – the predecessor of modern paper – with literary texts on them, have usually only remained intact in the dry air of Egypt, or, for example, buried in the volcanic ash covering Pompeii. Coinage is also an important written source. The findspots of coins give interesting economic evidence about trade. But the inscriptions themselves are informative about the issuing authority

– whether city-state (as in ancient Greece) or sole ruler (as in Imperial Rome, or the kings of medieval Europe).

The decipherment of an ancient language transforms our knowledge of the society that used it. In recent years one of the most significant advances has been the decipherment of Maya inscriptions, the inscribed symbols (glyphs) often found on stone **stelae** at the largest centers. It had been widely assumed that Maya inscriptions were exclusively of a calendrical nature, or that they dealt with purely religious matters, notably the deeds of deities. But the inscriptions can now in many cases be interpreted as relating to real historical events, mainly the deeds of the Maya kings. We can also now begin to deduce the likely territories belonging to individual Maya centers. Maya history has thus taken on a new dimension.

A more detailed example of the value of written sources for reconstructing social archaeology is Mesopotamia, where a huge number of records of Sumer and Babylon (*c.* 3000–1600 BC), mainly in the form of clay tablets, have been preserved. The uses of writing in Mesopotamia may be summarized as follows:

Recording information for future use	- Administrative purposes
	- Codification of law
	- Formulation of a sacred tradition
	- Annals
	- Scholarly purposes
Communicating current information	- Letters
	- Royal edicts
	- Public announcements
	- Texts for training scribes
Communicating with the gods	- Sacred texts, amulets, etc.

The famous law code of the Babylonian king Hammurabi, c. 1750 BC.

Perhaps most evocative of all are the law codes, of which the most impressive example is the law code of Hammurabi of Babylon, written in the Akkadian language (and in cuneiform script) around 1750 BC. The ruler is seen at the top of the stone, standing before Shamash, the god of justice. The laws were promulgated, as Hammurabi states, "so that the strong may not oppress the weak, and to protect the rights of the orphan and widow." These laws cover many aspects of life – agriculture, business transactions, family law, inheritance, terms of employment for different craftspeople, and penalties for crimes such as adultery and homicide.

Impressive and informative as it is, Hammurabi's law code is not straightforward to interpret, and emphasizes the need for the archaeologist to reconstruct the full social context that led to the drafting of a text. As the British scholar Nicholas Postgate has pointed out, the code is by no means complete, and seems to cover only those areas of the law that had proved troublesome. Moreover, Hammurabi had recently conquered several rival city states, and the law code was therefore probably designed to help integrate the new territories within his empire.

Ethnoarchaeology

Ethnoarchaeology is a fundamental method of approach for the social archaeologist. It involves the study of both the present-day use and significance of artifacts, buildings, and structures within living societies, and the way these material things become incorporated into the archaeological record – what happens to them when they are thrown away or (in the case of buildings and structures) torn down or abandoned. It is therefore an *indirect* approach to the understanding of any past society.

There is nothing new in the idea of looking at living societies to help interpret the past. In the 19th and early 20th centuries European archaeologists frequently turned for inspiration to researches done by ethnographers among societies in Africa or Australia. But the so-called "ethnographic parallels" that resulted often simply and crudely likened past societies to present ones, stifling new thought rather than promoting it. In the United States archaeologists were confronted from the beginning with the living reality of complex Native American societies, which taught them to think rather more deeply about how **ethnography** might be used to aid archaeological interpretation. Nevertheless, fully-fledged ethnoarchaeology is a development really of only the last 35 years. The key difference is that now it is archaeologists themselves, rather than ethnographers or anthropologists, who carry out the research among living societies.

A good example is the work of Lewis Binford among the Nunamiut Eskimo, a hunter-gatherer group of Alaska. In the 1960s Binford was attempting to interpret archaeological sites of the Middle Paleolithic of France (the Mousterian period, 180,000–40,000 years ago). He realized that only by studying how *modern* hunter-gatherers used and discarded bones and tools, or moved from site to site, could he begin to understand the mechanisms that had created the Mousterian archaeological record – itself almost certainly the product of a mobile hunter-gatherer economy. Between 1969 and 1973 he lived intermittently among the Nunamiut and observed their behavior. For instance, he studied the way bone debris was produced and discarded by men at a seasonal hunting camp (the Mask site, Anaktuvuk Pass, Alaska). He saw that, when sitting round a hearth and processing bone for marrow, there was a "drop zone" where small fragments of

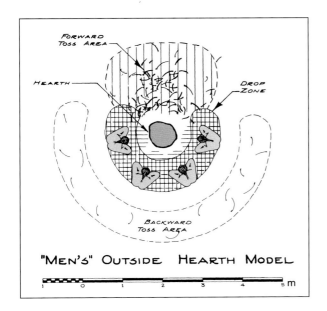

BONE DISTRIBUTION
RELATIVE TO "MEN'S" OUTSIDE HEARTH MODEL
PINCEVENT No. 1

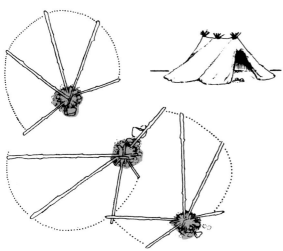

Ethnoarchaeology: the work of Lewis Binford.
(Above) The "drop zone" and "toss zones" model derived
from observations of the Nunamiut. (Left) At the site of
Pincevent, France, the excavator Leroi-Gourhan interpreted
three hearths as being evidence for a complex skin tent (plan
and reconstruction shown). (Above left) Binford applied his
"outside hearth model" to the three Pincevent hearths, and
deduced from the distribution of bones that his model fitted
the evidence better than that of Leroi-Gourhan: i.e. that the
hearths lay outside, and not within a tent.

bone fell as they were broken. The larger pieces, which were thrown away by the
men, formed a "toss zone," both in front and behind them.

The Nunamiut might not provide an exact "ethnographic parallel" for
Mousterian societies, but Binford recognized that there are certain actions or
functions likely to be common to all hunter-gatherers because – as in the case
of the processing of bone – the actions are dictated by the most convenient
procedure when seated round a camp fire. The discarded fragments of bone then
leave a characteristic pattern round the hearth for the archaeologist to find and
interpret – indeed, Binford went on to use his model to reinterpret data from a

Paleolithic camp site. From such analysis, it also proved possible to infer roughly how many people were in the group, and over what period of time the camp site was used. These are questions very relevant to our understanding of the social organization (including the size) of hunter-gatherer groups.

Ethnoarchaeology is not restricted to observations at the local scale. The British archaeologist Ian Hodder, in his study of the female ear decorations used by different tribes in the Lake Baringo area of Kenya, undertook a regional study to investigate the extent to which **material culture** (in this case personal decoration) was being used to express differences between the tribes. Partly as a result of such work, archaeologists no longer assume that it is an easy task to take archaeological assemblages and group them into regional "cultures," and then to assume that each "culture" so formed represents a social unit. Such a procedure might, in fact, work quite well for the ear decorations Hodder studied, because the people in question chose to use this feature to assert their tribal distinctiveness. But, as Hodder showed, if we were to take other features of the material culture, such as pots or tools, the same pattern would not necessarily be followed. His example documents the important lesson that material culture cannot be used by the archaeologist in a simple or unthinking manner in the reconstruction of supposed ethnic groups.

THE ARCHAEOLOGY OF THE INDIVIDUAL AND OF IDENTITY

The discussion so far in this chapter has as its starting point the concept of the society and its organization. This is a deliberate feature of the structure of this book: before questions are asked about the variety of human experience it is necessary first to form some view about the scale of a society and its complexity. But at the same time this might be criticized as a "top-down" approach, beginning with questions of organization and of hierarchy, of power and of centralization, and only then turning to the individual who actually lives in society, to that person's role, gender, and status and to what it was really *like* to live there at that time and in that social context.

It would be equally valid to start with the individual and with social relationships, including kinship relations, and to work outward from there: what one might term a "bottom-up" approach. This involves the consideration of issues such as social inequality, **ethnicity**, and gender.

One important aspect of the individual to remember is that most sides of our "humanness" and many of the concepts that we enshrine as "human," including our schemes of perception, thought, gender, and sense of morals, our ways of moving our bodies around and communicating (such as standing, sitting, looking, speaking, and walking), and even the way we respond to our senses (such as our sense of smell and taste), are not natural "givens" but are in fact culturally specific: they are developed and adopted by humans within a society and vary

- Many aspects of individual human behavior are not a cross-cultural "given" but are learned, and differ widely across both ancient and modern cultures

- The existence of ethnic groups is difficult to recognize from the archaeological record: an affiliation to a particular style of material culture, for example, does not necessarily equate to ethnicity

- It is important to recognize gender in the archaeological record (particularly the roles of women which have traditionally been overlooked). There is also a distinction between sex and gender: sex is biologically determined whereas gender roles in different societies vary greatly

through time and space. If we are to really know what it was like to live in a past society, we must be careful not to make assumptions based on our own experience of what it is to be "human."

Social Inequality

The theme of the archaeology of social inequality has perhaps not been very comprehensively addressed yet, but in the field of historical archaeology there have been systematic studies of the material culture of some underprivileged groups, including some interesting studies of town areas known from documentary accounts to be considered poor.

The infamous Five Points slum area of lower Manhattan, New York, described by early 19th-century writers including Charles Dickens, has been investigated through rescue excavations at the site of a new federal courthouse at Foley Square, providing some graphic insights. For instance, the excavated area included the site of a cellar brothel at 12 Baxter Street, historically documented (in the 1843 indictment of its keeper) as a "disorderly house – a nest for prostitutes and others of ill fame and name, where great numbers of characters are in the nightly practice of revelling until late and improper hours of the night." The excavations revealed further insights based upon the material culture:

> The quality of the household goods found in the privy behind 12 Baxter far exceeded that of goods found anywhere else on the block. The prostitutes lived well, at least when they were at work. One attraction was the opportunity to live in a style that seamstresses, laundresses, and maids could not afford. Afternoon tea at the brothel was served on a set of

A view of the rescue excavation of the 19th-century slum area of Five Points in lower Manhattan, New York. The cellar of a brothel was investigated and yielded much information concerning the daily lives of inhabitants. While of a low social rank, the prostitutes at least enjoyed the use of a set of Chinese porcelain (inset) for afternoon tea.

Chinese porcelain that included matching teacups and coffee cups, saucers and plates, a slop bowl and a tea caddie. Meals consisted of steak, veal, ham, soft-shell clams and many kinds of fish. There was a greater variety of artifacts from the brothel than from other excavated areas of the courthouse block.... Other personal items suggested the occupational hazards of prostitution. Two glass urinals, designed especially for women, were probably used when venereal disease confined a prostitute to bed.

Not far from Foley Square another excavation, that of the African Burial Ground, formerly known as the Negros Burial Ground, which was recorded on a plan of 1755, has proved highly informative and has had wide repercussions.

The rescue excavation of skeletons there in 1991 provoked outrage in the African-American community of today, which felt it had not been adequately consulted, and ultimately led to the establishment of a Museum of African and African-American History in New York City. There were no grave markers, and other than wood, coffin nails, and shroud pins, few artifacts were found. Studies of the skeletons have combined **DNA** analysis with cranial metrics, morphology, and historical data, to discover where the people came from. The large size of the

A Yoruba priestess and a Khamite priest perform a libation ceremony for the ancestors over the grave of a person buried in the African Burial Ground in lower Manhattan, New York.

sample will allow study of nutrition and pathology. The remains of 419 individuals disinterred during the excavations were ceremonially reburied in October 2003, after being taken in a procession up Broadway.

Certainly the controversy and the excavation have proved a stimulus toward the development of African-American archaeology, already well-defined through the investigation of plantation sites.

Ethnicity and Conflict

Ethnicity (i.e. the existence of ethnic groups, including tribal groups) is difficult to recognize from the archaeological record. For example, the idea that such features as pottery decoration are automatically a sign of ethnic affiliation has been questioned. This is a field where ethnoarchaeology is only now beginning to make some progress.

The theme of ethnicity is a difficult one to approach archaeologically, unless with the help of written records, since ethnicity is based largely upon self-awareness. There is frequently a correlation between ethnic groups and language groups, which can offer further avenues for study. Questions of group self-identity, which is often much the same as ethnicity, often underlie conflict and warfare.

The role of *warfare* in early societies is one topic that merits further investigation. It has long been agreed that warfare is a recurrent feature of early state societies, but for prehistoric times it has been more common to think in terms of peace-loving "noble savages." There is, however, an increasing amount of evidence to suggest that warfare in prehistory was not so much the exception

Skeletons found in a pit at Talheim, Germany, dating to c. 5000 BC, indicative of mass killing.

as the norm. A good example is provided by the Neolithic ditched enclosures (*c.* 5000 to 2000 BC) of Talheim, Germany. Fieldwork suggested that they were not simply of symbolic significance, as many archaeologists had thought, but genuine fortifications. One pit contained the bodies of 18 adults and 16 children, all killed by blows from at least six different axes, contradicting the notion of a peaceful early farming society.

War need not be undertaken with the objective of permanently occupying the lands of the vanquished in a process of territorial expansion. The American archaeologist David Freidel made this point in his study of Maya warfare, based on the wall paintings at the site of Bonampak and also early written sources. According to his analysis, the function of Maya warfare was not to conquer, and thus enlarge the frontiers of the state in question, but instead to give Maya rulers the opportunity to capturing kings and princes from neighboring states, many of whom were then later offered as sacrifices to the gods. Warfare thus allowed the Maya rulers to reaffirm their royal status: it had a central role in upholding the system of government, but that role was not one of territorial expansion.

Investigating Gender

An important aspect of the study of social archaeology is the investigation of gender. Initially this was felt to overlap with feminist archaeology, which often had the explicit objective of exposing and correcting the male bias (androcentrism) of archaeology. There is no doubt that in the modern world the role of women professionals, including archaeologists, has often been a difficult one. For instance, Dorothy Garrod, the first female professor of archaeology in Britain, was appointed in 1937, at a time when women at her university (Cambridge) were not allowed to take a degree at the end of their course, as male undergraduates did, but only a diploma. There was – and still is – an imbalance to be rectified in the academic world, and that was one of the early objectives of feminist archaeology. A second was to illuminate the roles of women in the past more clearly, where often they had been overlooked.

But the study of gender is much more than simply the study of women. An important central idea soon became the distinction between sex and gender. It was argued that sex – female or male – may be regarded as biologically determined and can be established archaeologically from skeletal remains. But gender – at its simplest woman or man – is a social construct, involving the sex-related roles of individuals in society. Gender roles in different societies vary greatly both from place to place and through time. Systems of kinship, of marriage, inheritance, and the division of labor are all related to biological sex but not determined by it. These perspectives permitted a good deal of profitable work in this second phase of gender studies in archaeology, but they have now in their turn been criticized by a new "third wave" feminism, as emphasizing supposedly "inherent" differences between women and men, and emphasizing women's links to the natural world through reproduction.

The work of Marija Gimbutas on the prehistory of southeast Europe, for example, is now criticized. She argued that the predominantly female figurines seen in the Neolithic and Copper Age of southeast Europe and in Anatolia demonstrate the important status of women at that time. She had a vision of an Old Europe influenced by feminine values which was to disappear with the succeeding Bronze Age with the dominance of a warlike male hierarchy, supposedly introduced by Indo-European warrior nomads from the east.

Marija Gimbutas became something of a cult figure in her own right, and her support for the concept of a great "Mother Goddess" representing a fertility principle has been embraced by modern "ecofeminist" and New Age enthusiasts. The current excavations by Ian Hodder at the early Neolithic site of Çatalhöyük in Turkey, where female figurines of baked clay have been found, are now visited regularly by devotees of the "Goddess" whose views are treated respectfully by the excavators, even though they do not share them. Hodder has argued instead that the figurines may represent the subordination of women as objects of ownership and male desires. Comparable figurines from the Aegean can often be shown to lack definite features diagnostic of sex or gender, and studies of rather similar baked clay figurines from Oaxaca, Mexico, have suggested that they were made by women for use in rituals relating to ancestors rather than deities. The notion that they represented a "Mother Goddess" lacks supporting evidence.

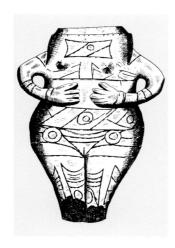

Different images symbolizing female power? (Top) A Neolithic vase from Romania. (Above) A Zapotec figurine from Oaxaca, Mexico.

The third phase in the development of gender archaeology, in tune with the "third wave" of feminists of the 1990s, takes a different view of gender in two senses. First, in the narrower sense, and, as Lynn Meskell puts it, "led by women of color, lesbian feminists, queer theorists and postcolonial feminists," it recognizes that the field of gender and gender difference is more complex than a simple polarity between male and female, and that other kinds of difference have to be recognized. Indeed the very recognition of a simple structural opposition between male and female is itself, even in our own society, an over-simplification. In many societies children are not regarded as socially male or female until they reach the age of puberty – in the modern Greek language, for instance, while men and women are grammatically male and female in gender, the words for children generally belong to the third, neuter gender.

This leads on to the second point, that gender is part of a broader social framework, part of the social process – in Margaret Conkey's words "a way in which social categories, roles, ideologies and practices are defined and played out." While gender is, in any society, a system of classification, it is part of a larger system of social differences, including age, wealth, **religion**, ethnicity and so forth. Moreover these are not static constructs but fluid and flexible, constructed and re-constructed in the practice of daily life.

The complexities in analyzing burial data with respect to gender are indicated by the study by Bettina Arnold of the so-called "Princess of Vix" burial from east-central France. The grave contained skeletal remains which analysis indicated were female, but the grave-goods consisted of various prestige items normally thought to be indicative of males. This exceptionally rich 5th-century BC burial was initially interpreted as a transvestite priest because it was considered inconceivable that a woman could be honored in such a way. Arnold's careful reanalysis of the grave-goods supported the interpretation of the burial as an elite female. This may lead to a fresh assessment of the potentially powerful, occasionally paramount role that women played in Iron Age Europe. But this work may yet lead on to a wider consideration of gender distinctions in the Iron Age in a context which may reassess whether in individuals of very high status the traditional bipolar concept of gender is appropriate.

STUDY QUESTIONS

- Societies are typically classified into what four main groups?
- Why is the analysis of burials important to the study of segmentary societies?
- How can the ethnoarchaeology of modern societies inform us about the past?
- What are the key methods through which the structure of societies is analyzed?
- Why is it hard to study ethnicity in the archaeological record?
- What is the difference between sex and gender? Why is this difference important to archaeologists?

SUMMARY

- This chapter has shown that a formidable battery of techniques is now available to archaeologists who wish to investigate the social organization of early societies. Only the main themes have been touched on, but these will have made it clear that the potential for understanding the more complex and highly organized societies represented by states and chiefdoms is especially great. Written records, when they exist (only in state societies) can be an important resource.

- We can investigate ranked societies through their site hierarchies and, in the case of state societies, through their urban centers. It should in this way be possible to identify the ruling center using archaeological methods alone, and the extent of the area over which it held jurisdiction.

- For ranked or stratified societies (chiefdoms and states), the study of the buildings and other evidence of administration at the center gives valuable information about the social, political, and economic organization of society, as well as a picture of the life of the ruling elite. We can identify and analyze their palaces and tombs, and studies of lower-order administrative centers give further information about the social and political structure. The study of the differences in the treatment accorded to different individuals at death, in both the size and wealth of grave offerings, can reveal the complete range of status distinctions in a society.

- Similar approaches may be applied to segmentary societies: the study of individual settlements, the evidence for social ranking revealed by burials, and the existence of cooperative communal mechanisms for the construction of major monuments.

- On a smaller scale (and particularly important for the Paleolithic period), the camps of mobile hunter-gatherer societies and the seasonal movement between different sites may also be studied using the methods outlined in this chapter, especially when the insights provided by ethnoarchaeological research on living societies are used in conjunction with direct study of the archaeological record.

- In recent studies a "bottom-up" perspective in social archaeologies has become important: the archaeology of individuals and of identity. Gender studies in particular are now adding new insight into the structure of society.

FURTHER READING

The following works illustrate some of the ways in which social organization can be reconstructed:

Binford, L.R. 2002. *In Pursuit of the Past*. University of California Press: Berkeley & London.

Hodder, I. 2009. *Symbols in Action*. Cambridge University Press: Cambridge & New York.

Janusek, J.W. 2004. *Identity and Power in the Ancient Andes*. Routledge: London & New York.

Journal of Social Archaeology (since 2001).

Meskell, L. 2006. *A Companion to Social Archaeology*. Wiley-Blackwell: Oxford.

Pyburn, K.A. (ed.). 2004. *Ungendering Civilization*. Routledge: London & New York.

What Was the Environment and What Did They Eat?

Environment, subsistence, and diet

Environment and diet

Environment and diet constitute two of the most fundamental and crucial factors of human life which the archaeologist needs to assess. The *environment* governs human life: latitude and altitude, landforms and climate determine the vegetation, which in turn determines animal life, and both of these determine diet. And all these things taken together determine how and where humans have lived – or at least they did until very recently.

The reconstruction of the environment first requires an answer to very general questions of global climate change. What was the global climate like when the human activities under study took place? Does a **context** belong to a glacial or interglacial phase? These broad questions can be answered by relating the date of a context to evidence of long-term climatic fluctuations obtained from sea and **ice cores**, as well as from tree-rings.

More specific questions about past environments will follow, and these are particularly relevant for all postglacial contexts, after about 10,000 years ago. There are two main sources of evidence: plant and animal remains. Analysis of these will not only reveal the range of flora and fauna that people would have encountered at a particular time and place, but since many plants and animals are quite sensitive to climate change, we can also find out what the regional and local environment would have been like.

Unfortunately, owing to the poor preservation of many forms of organic evidence, and to the distorted samples we recover, we can never be certain about our conclusions. We simply have to aim for the best approximation available. No single method will give a full and accurate picture – all are distorted in one way or another – and so as many methods as data and funds will allow need to be applied to build up a composite image.

Once we know what the environment might have been like, as well as the kinds of plants and animals present, we can try to find out how people exploited those conditions and resources and what they might have been eating. *Subsistence*, the quest for food, is one of the most basic of all necessities and there is a variety of evidence for it to be found in the archaeological record. Plant and animal remains and the residues found on **artifacts** such as pots or stone tools can give indirect clues to what peoples' *diet* might have consisted of, but the only direct evidence we have is from the study of actual human remains: stomach contents, fecal material, teeth, and bones.

INVESTIGATING ENVIRONMENTS ON A GLOBAL SCALE

The first step in assessing previous environmental conditions is to look at them globally. Local changes make little sense unless seen against this broader climatic background. Tree-rings are a good source of information for the last 10,000 years or so, but since water covers almost three-quarters of the Earth, we should begin by examining evidence about past climates that can be obtained from this area, including data within glaciers and ice caps. We will then go on to look at what can be learned about past environments at a more local level from plant and animal remains.

Evidence from Water and Ice

The sediments of the ocean floor accumulate very slowly, just a few centimeters every thousand years, but they can contain evidence of thousands or even millions of years of climate history. In some areas ocean sediments consist primarily of an ooze made up of microfossils such as the shells of foraminifera – tiny one-celled marine organisms that live in the surface water of the oceans and sink to the bottom when they die. As in an archaeological **stratigraphy**, we can trace changes in environmental conditions through time by studying cores extracted from the seabed and fluctuations in the species represented and the physical form of single species through the sequence. *Oxygen isotope analysis* of foraminifera can also reveal changes in the environment (see box opposite).

Thousands of **deep-sea cores** have now been extracted and studied, but cores can also be obtained from stratified ice sheets (some containing hundreds of thousands of annual growth layers), and here the oxygen isotopic composition also gives some guide to climatic oscillations. Results from cores in Greenland and the Antarctic, and Andean and Tibetan glaciers are consistent with, and add detail to, those from deep-sea cores. It is also possible to analyze bubbles of ancient methane gas trapped in the ice (resulting from plant decomposition, which is sensitive to temperature and moisture variations).

Ancient Winds. Isotopes can be used not merely for temperature studies but also for data on precipitation. And since it is the temperature differences between the equatorial and polar regions that largely determine the storminess of our weather, isotope studies can even tell us something about winds in different periods.

As air moves from low latitudes to colder regions, the water it loses as rain or snow is enriched in the stable isotope oxygen 18, while the remaining vapour

SEA AND ICE CORES AND GLOBAL WARMING

The stratigraphy of sediment on the ocean floor is obtained from cores taken out of the seabed. Ships use a "piston-corer" to extract a thin column of sediment, usually about 10–30 m (33–98 ft) in length. The core can then be analyzed in the laboratory.

Dates for the different layers in the core are obtained by radiocarbon, **paleomagnetism**, or the uranium-series method (Chapter 4). Changing environmental conditions in the past are then deduced by two kinds of tests on microscopic fossils of tiny one-celled organisms called foraminifera found in

Microscopic fossils of the foraminiferan species Globorotalia truncatulinoides, *which coils to the left during cold periods and to the right during warm ones.*

the sediment. First, scientists study the simple presence, absence, and fluctuations of different foraminiferan species. Second, they analyze, by mass spectrometer, fluctuations in the ratio of the stable oxygen isotopes 18 and 16 in the calcium carbonate of the foraminiferan shells. Variations discernible by these two tests reflect not simply changes in temperature, but also oscillations in the continental glaciers. For example, as the glaciers grew, water was drawn up into them, reducing sea levels and increasing the density and salinity of the oceans, and thus causing changes in the depths at which certain foraminiferan species lived. At the same time the proportion of oxygen 18 in

seawater increased. When the glaciers melted during periods of warmer climate, the proportion of oxygen 18 decreased. A similar technique can be used to extract cores from present-day ice sheets in Greenland and Antarctica. Here too, variations in oxygen and also hydrogen isotopic composition at different depths of the cores reveal the temperature when the ice formed, and thus provide some indication of past changes in climate; these results coincide well with those from the deep-sea cores. In addition, high carbon and methane levels (the so-called "greenhouse gases") indicate periods of global warming.

The ice cores suggest that the next ice age should be about 15,000 years in the future; however, the stability of our climate has been overturned by the effects of human activity, and the ice shows that today's greenhouse gas concentrations in the atmosphere are the highest for at least

440,000 years. In the cores, even much smaller rises in the gas level have been followed by significant rises in global temperatures, but the current rate of increase in greenhouse gases is over 100 times faster than anything so far detected in ice cores dating back half a million years. During that period, levels of carbon dioxide varied between 200 parts per million in ice ages, and 280 ppm in interglacials – but since the industrial revolution, the levels have risen to 375 ppm, which alarms scientists.

Three climate records compared. Left to right: proportions of different shell species in a deep-sea core; ratio of oxygen 18 to oxygen 16 in shells from a deep-sea core; and oxygen ratios from an ice core. The resemblance of the three records is good evidence that long-term climatic variation has been worldwide.

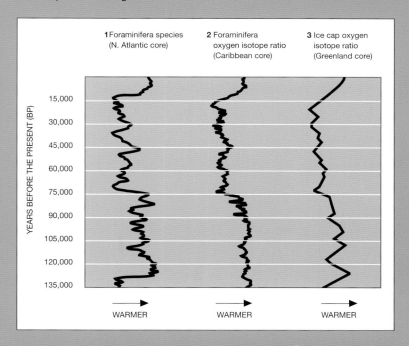

becomes correspondingly richer in the other stable isotope of oxygen, oxygen 16. Thus from the ratio between the two isotopes in precipitation at a particular place, we can calculate the temperature difference between that place and the equatorial region.

Using this technique, the changing ratios found over the last 100,000 years in ice cores from Greenland and the Antarctic have been studied. The results show that during glacial periods the temperature difference between equatorial and polar regions increased by 20–25 percent, and thus wind circulation must have been far more violent. Confirmation has come from a deep-sea core off the coast of West Africa, analysis of which led to estimates of wind strength over the last 700,000 years. Apparently wind "vigor" was greater by a factor of two during each glacial episode than at the present; and wind speeds were 50 percent greater during glacial than interglacial phases. In future, analysis of the minute plant debris in these cores may also add to the history of wind patterns.

It has also been found that raindrops in hurricanes have more oxygen 16 than normal rain, and this leaves traces in layers of stalagmites – for example in caves in Belize – as well as in tree-rings. This method has pinpointed hurricane events of the past 200 years, and so it should also be possible to use older stalagmites to establish a record of hurricanes stretching back tens of thousands of years, thus revealing any changes in their patterns, locations and intensity. So data from the past may clarify the possible linkage of modern global warming with such extreme weather.

Why should archaeologists be interested in ancient winds? The answer is that winds can have a great impact on human activity. For example, it is thought that increased storminess may have caused the Vikings to abandon their North Atlantic sea route at the onset of a cold period. Similarly, some of the great Polynesian migrations in the southwestern Pacific during the 12th and 13th centuries AD seem to have coincided with the onset of a short period of slightly

KEY CONCEPTS

Reconstructing the Environment on a Global Scale

- Evidence from sea and ice cores: analysis of isotopic ratios within dateable layers of ocean sediment and ice can give an accurate idea of climate. Studies from all over the world are all in broad agreement about what global climate was like over the past few million years

- Evidence from tree-rings: Similar analysis of tree-rings gives a finer-scale idea of what the environment was like in different areas up to about 10,000 years ago

warmer weather, when violent storms would have been rare. These migrations were brought to an end a few centuries later by the Little Ice Age, which may have caused a sharp increase in the frequency of storms. Had the Polynesians been able to continue, they might conceivably have gone on from New Zealand to reach Tasmania and Australia.

Tree-Rings and Climate

Tree-rings have a growth that varies with the climate, being strong in the spring and then declining to nothing in the winter; the more moisture available, the wider the annual ring. As we saw in Chapter 4, these variations in ring width have formed the basis of a major dating technique. However, study of a particular set of rings can also reveal important environmental data, for example whether growth was slow (implying dense local forest cover) or fast (implying light forest). Tree growth is complex, and many other factors may affect it, but temperature and soil moisture do tend to be dominant.

Annual and decade-to-decade variations show up far more clearly in tree-rings than in ice cores, and tree-rings can also record sudden and dramatic shocks to the climate. For example, data from Virginia indicate that the alarming mortality and near abandonment of Jamestown Colony, the first permanent white settlement in the United States, occurred during an extraordinary drought, the driest 7-year episode in 770 years (AD 1606–12).

The study of tree-rings and climate (dendroclimatology) has also progressed by using X-ray measurements of cell-size and density as an indication of environmental productivity. More recently, ancient temperatures have been derived from tree-rings by means of the carbon isotope ratios preserved in their cellulose. Isotopic evidence preserved in the cellulose of timbers of the tamarisk tree, contained in the ramp which the Romans used to overcome the besieged Jewish citadel of Masada in AD 73, have revealed to Israeli archaeologists that the climate at that time was wetter and more amenable to agriculture than it is today.

The role of tree-rings makes it clear that it is organic remains above all that provide the richest source of evidence for environmental reconstruction. We now take a look at the surviving traces of plants and animals and what these can tell us about ancient environments.

RECONSTRUCTING THE PLANT ENVIRONMENT

The prime goal in archaeological plant studies is to try to reconstruct what the vegetation was like in the past at any particular time or place. But we should not forget that plants lie at the base of the food chain. The plant communities of a given area and period will therefore provide clues to local animal and human life, and will also reflect soil conditions and climate. Some types of vegetation react relatively quickly to changes in climate (though less quickly than insects, for

All hay fever sufferers will be aware of the pollen "rain" that can afflict them in the spring and summer. Pollen grains – the tiny male reproductive bodies of flowering plants – have an almost indestructible outer shell (exine) that can survive in certain sediments for tens of thousands of years. In pollen analysis the exines are extracted from the soil, studied under the microscope, and identified according to the distinctive exine shape and surface ornamentation of different families and genera of plants. Once quantified, these identifications are plotted as curves on a pollen diagram. Fluctuations in the curve for each plant category may then be studied for signs of climatic fluctuation, or forest clearance and crop-planting by humans.

Preservation

The most favorable sediments for preservation of pollen are acidic and poorly aerated peat bogs and lake beds, where biological decay is impeded and grains undergo rapid burial. Cave sediments are also usually suitable because of their humidity and constant temperature. Other contexts, such as sandy sediments or open sites exposed to weathering, preserve pollen poorly.

In wet sites, or unexcavated areas, samples are extracted in long cores, but in dry sites a series of separate samples can be removed from the sections. On an archaeological excavation, small samples are usually extracted at regular stratified intervals. Great care must be taken to avoid contamination from the tools used or from the atmosphere. Pollen can also be found in mud bricks, vessels, tombs, mummy wrappings, the guts of preserved bodies, ancient feces, and many other contexts.

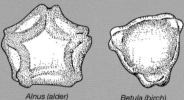

Alnus (alder)

Betula (birch)

Corylus (hazel)

Hedera helix (ivy)

Quercus (oak)

Salix (willow)

Tilia (lime)

Ulmus (elm)

A selection of pollen grains, as seen under the microscope.

Pollen data from Northern Ireland reveal the impact of the first farmers in the region.

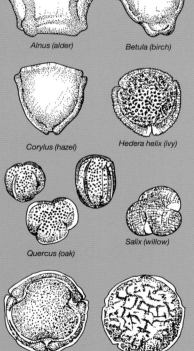

2.15 m depth							Clearance
3280BC							Forest cover
3695BC							Regeneration
4105BC							Farming
							Clearance
4200BC							Natural forest cover
3.15 m depth	Pine, alder, birch	Elm	Oak	Hazel	Sorrel & ribwort plantain	Nettles & grass	

instance), and the shifts of plant communities in both latitude and altitude are the most direct link between climatic change and the terrestrial human environment, for example in the Ice Age.

Plant studies in **archaeology** have always been overshadowed by faunal analysis, simply because bones are more conspicuous than plant remains in **excavation**. Bones may sometimes survive better, but usually plant remains are present in greater numbers than bones. Thanks to the discovery that some of the constituent parts of a plant are much more resistant to decomposition than was believed, and that a huge amount of data survives which can tell us something about long-dead vegetation, plant studies have become very important. As with so many of the specializations on which archaeology can call, these analyses require a great deal of time and funds.

Some of the most informative techniques for making an overall assessment of plant communities in a particular period involve analysis not of the biggest remains but of the tiniest, microbotanical remains, especially pollen.

Microbotanical Remains

Pollen Analysis. **Palynology**, or the study of pollen grains (see box), was developed by a Norwegian geologist, Lennart von Post, at the beginning of the 20th century. It has proved invaluable to archaeology, since it can be applied to a wide range of **sites** and provides information on chronology as well as environment and forest clearance.

While palynology cannot produce an exact picture of past environments, it does give some idea of fluctuations in vegetation through time, whatever their causes

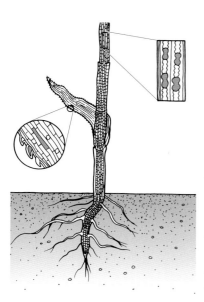

Phytoliths are minute particles of silica in plant cells which survive after the rest of the plant has decomposed. Some are specific to certain parts of the plant (e.g. stem or leaf).

may be (whether climatic or human) which can be compared with results from other methods. Pollen studies can also supply much-needed information for environments as ancient as those of the Hadar sediments and the Omo valley in Ethiopia around 3 million years ago. It is usually assumed that these regions were always as dry as they are now, but pollen analysis has shown that they were much wetter and greener between 3.5 and 2.5 million years ago, with even some tropical plants present. The Hadar, which is now semi-desert with scattered trees and shrubs, was rich, open grassland, with dense woodland by lakes and along rivers. The change to drier conditions, around 2.5 million years ago, can be seen in the reduction of tree pollen in favor of more grasses.

Phytoliths. A better-known and fast-developing branch of microbotanical studies concerns phytoliths, which were first recognized as components in archaeological contexts as long ago as 1908, but have only been studied systematically in the last few decades. These are minute particles of silica (plant opal) derived from the cells of plants, and they survive after the rest of the organism has decomposed or been burned. They are common in hearths and ash layers, but are also found inside pottery, plaster, and even on stone tools and the teeth of animals: grass phytoliths have been found adhering to herbivorous animal teeth from Bronze Age, Iron Age, and medieval sites in Europe.

These crystals are useful because, like pollen grains, they are produced in large numbers, they survive well in ancient sediments, and they have myriad distinctive shapes and sizes that vary according to type. They inform us primarily about the use people made of particular plants, but their simple presence adds to the picture of the environment built up from other sources.

In particular, a combination of phytolith and pollen analysis can be a powerful tool for environmental reconstruction, since the two methods have complementary strengths and weaknesses. The American scholar Dolores Piperno has studied cores from the Gatun Basin, Panama, whose pollen content had already revealed a sequence of vegetation change from 11,300 years ago to the present. She found that the phytoliths in the cores confirmed the pollen sequence, with the exception that evidence for agriculture and forest clearance (i.e. the appearance of maize, and an increase in grass at the expense of trees) appeared around 4850 years ago in the phytoliths, about 1000 years earlier than in the pollen. This early evidence is probably attributable to small clearings which do not show up in pollen diagrams because grains from the surrounding forest overwhelm the samples.

Moreover, phytoliths often survive in sediments that are hostile to the preservation of fossil pollen (because of oxidation or microbial activity), and may thus provide the only available evidence for paleoenvironment or vegetational change. Another advantage is that, while all grass pollen looks the same, grass phytoliths can be assigned to ecologically different groups. It has recently been discovered that aluminum ions in phytoliths can be used to distinguish between forested and herbaceous vegetations, while oxygen and hydrogen isotope signatures in phytoliths will also provide important environmental data.

Diatom Analysis. Another method of environmental reconstruction using plant microfossils is **diatom analysis**. Diatoms are single-cell algae that have cell walls of silica instead of cellulose, and these silica cell walls survive after the algae die. They accumulate in great numbers at the bottom of any body of water in which the algae live; a few are found in peat, but most come from lake and shore sediments.

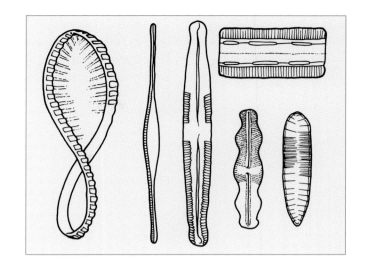

A variety of diatoms, the microscopic single-cell algae, whose silica cell walls survive in many sediments after death. Study of the changing species in a deposit can help scientists reconstruct fluctuations in past environments.

Diatoms have been recorded, identified, and classified for over 200 years. The process of identifying and counting them is much like that used in palynology, as is the collection of samples in the field. Their well-defined shapes and ornamentations permit identification to a high level, and their assemblages directly reflect the types of algae present and their diatom productivity, and, indirectly, the water's salinity, alkalinity, and nutrient content. From the environmental requirements of different species (in terms of habitat, salinity, and nutrients), one can determine what their immediate environment was at different periods.

Since diatom assemblages can indicate whether water was fresh, brackish, or salt, they have been used to identify, for example, the period when lakes became isolated from the sea in areas of tectonic uplift, to locate the positions of past shorelines, and to reveal water pollution. For instance, the diatom sequence in sediments at the site of the former Lake Wevershoof, Medemblick (the Netherlands) suggests that in around AD 800 seawater entered and overcame what had been a freshwater lake, causing a hiatus in human occupation of the immediate area.

All these microbotanical techniques mentioned – studies of pollen, phytoliths, and diatoms – can only be carried out by specialists. For archaeologists, however, a far more direct contact with environmental evidence comes from the larger plant remains that they can actually see and conserve in the course of excavation.

Macrobotanical Remains

A variety of bigger types of plant remains are potentially retrievable, and provide important information about which plants grew near sites, which were used or consumed by people, and so on. Here we shall focus on the valuable clues that macrobotanical remains can provide to local environmental conditions.

Retrieval of vegetation from sediments has been made easier by the development of screening (sieving) and **flotation** techniques able to separate organic material from soil. In flotation, samples of soil from an excavation are poured into an overflowing tank, the lighter organic material floating to the top and spilling over the lip to be caught in sieves of different grades. This material is then dried and identified.

Sediments are by no means the only source of plant remains, which have also been found in the stomachs of frozen mammoths and preserved bog bodies; in ancient feces; on teeth; on stone tools; and in residues inside vessels. The remains themselves are varied:

Seeds and Fruits. Ancient seeds and fruits can usually be identified to species, despite changes in their shape caused by charring or waterlogging. In some cases, the remains have disintegrated but have left their imprint behind – grain impressions are fairly common on pottery, leaf impressions are also known, and imprints exist on materials ranging from plaster to leather and corroded bronze. Identification, of course, depends on type and quality of the traces. Not all such finds necessarily mean that a plant grew locally: grape pips, for example, may come from imported fruit, while impressions on potsherds may mislead since pottery can travel far from its place of manufacture.

Plant Residues. Chemical analysis of plant residues in vessels will be dealt with below in the context of human diet, but the results can give some idea of what species were available. Pottery vessels themselves may incorporate plant fibers (not to mention shell, feathers, or blood) as a tempering material, and microscopic analysis can sometimes identify these remains – for example, study of early pots from South Carolina and Georgia in the United States revealed the presence of shredded stems of Spanish Moss, a member of the pineapple family.

Remains of Wood. Study of *charcoal* (burnt wood) is making a growing contribution to archaeological reconstruction of environments and of human use of timber. A very durable material, charcoal is commonly found by the archaeologist during excavation. Fragments can be examined by the specialist under the microscope, and identified (thanks to the anatomy of the wood) normally at the genus level, and sometimes to species. Charcoal and charred seeds have also proved the most reliable material from which to take samples for **radiocarbon dating** (Chapter 4).

Many charcoal samples are the remains of firewood, but others may come from wooden structures, furniture, and implements burnt at some point in a site's history. Samples therefore inevitably tend to reflect human selection of wood rather than the full range of species growing around the site. Nevertheless, the totals for each species provide some idea of one part of the vegetation at a given time.

Occasionally, charcoal analysis can be combined with other evidence to reveal something not only of local environment but also of human adaptation

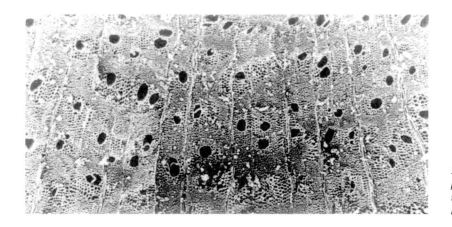

Scanning electron microscope photograph of charcoal from the thorn tree Acacia karroo *found at Boomplaas Cave.*

to it. At Boomplaas Cave, in southern Cape Province (South Africa), excavation has uncovered traces of human occupation stretching back 70,000 years. There is a clear difference between Ice Age and post-Ice Age charcoals: at times of extreme cold when conditions were also drier, between 22,000 and *c.* 14,000 years ago, the species diversity both in the charcoals and the pollen was low, whereas at times of higher rainfall and/or temperature the species diversity increased. A similar pattern of species diversity is seen also in the small mammals.

The vegetation around Boomplaas Cave at the time of maximum cold and drought was composed mainly of shrubs and grass with few plant resources that could be used by people; the larger mammal fauna was dominated by grazers that included "giant" species of buffalo, horse, and hartebeest, which became extinct by about 10,000 years ago.

The Boomplaas charcoal directly reflects the gradual change in climate and vegetation which led to the disappearance of the large grazers, and to a corresponding shift in subsistence practices by the cave's occupants. The charcoal analysis also highlights more subtle changes that reflect a shift in the season of maximum rainfall. The woody vegetation in the Cango Valley today is dominated by the thorn tree, *Acacia karroo*, characteristic of large areas in southern Africa where it is relatively dry and rain falls mostly in summer. Thorn tree charcoal is absent in the Ice Age samples at Boomplaas but it appears from about 5000 years ago and by 2000 years ago is the dominant species, indicating a shift to hot, relatively moist summers. As the number of species that enjoy summer rainfall increased, the inhabitants of the cave were able to make more use of a new range of fruits, the seeds of which can be found preserved at the site.

By no means all wood subjected to this kind of analysis is charred. Increasing quantities of *waterlogged wood* are recovered from wet sites in many parts of the world. And in some conditions, such as extreme cold or dryness, *desiccated wood* may survive without either burning or waterlogging.

KEY CONCEPTS

Reconstructing the Plant Environment

Microbotanical remains:

- **Pollen**: most useful for the study of minor fluctuations in climate over the last 12,000 years, although pollen can be preserved for millions of years in some contexts

- **Phytoliths**: survive very well in most archaeological sediments and can add to the picture of the environment built up from other sources

- **Diatoms**: found in lake and shore sediments and thus useful for the analysis of past marine environments

Macrobotanical remains:

- **Seeds and fruits**: can usually be identified to species, but interpretation can be difficult since they can be brought in to a site from elsewhere

- **Plant residues**: can give some idea of what species were available

- **Wood**: charcoal survives well in the archaeological record, and can be identified to species, but what is found tends to reflect human selection of wood rather than the full range of species growing around a site

Other Sources of Evidence. A great deal of information on vegetation in the less remote periods studied by archaeologists can be obtained from art, from texts (e.g. the writings of Pliny the Elder, Roman farming texts, accounts and illustrations by early explorers such as Captain Cook), and even from early photographs.

No single category of evidence can provide us with a total picture of local or regional vegetation, of small-scale trends or long-term changes: each produces a partial version of past realities. Input is needed from every source available, and, as will be seen below, these must be combined with results from the other forms of data studied in this chapter in order to reconstruct the best approximation of a past environment.

In this section we have seen how we can use a variety of archaeological data to try to reconstruct the plant environment at any particular place or time in the past. But what evidence of animal life is there and what can this tell us about past environments?

RECONSTRUCTING THE ANIMAL ENVIRONMENT

Animal remains were the first evidence used by 19th-century archaeologists to characterize the climate of the prehistoric periods that they encountered in their excavations. It was realized that different species were absent, present, or particularly abundant in certain layers, and hence also in certain periods, and the assumption was that this reflected changing climatic conditions.

Today, in order to use faunal remains as a guide to environment, we need to look more critically at the evidence than did those 19th-century pioneers. For instance, we need to understand the complex relationship that exists between modern animals and their environment. We also need to investigate how the animal remains we are studying arrived at a site – either naturally, or through the activities of carnivores or people, and thus how representative they may be of the variety of animals in their period.

Microfauna

Small animals (microfauna) tend to be better indicators of climate and environmental change than are large species, because they are much more sensitive to small variations in climate and adapt to them relatively quickly. In addition, since microfauna tend to accumulate naturally on a site, they reflect the immediate environment more accurately than the larger animals whose remains are often accumulated through human or animal predation. As with pollen, small animals, and especially insects, are also usually found in far greater numbers than larger ones, which improves the statistical significance of their analysis.

The remains of a wide variety of insectivores, rodents, and bats are found on archaeological sites, but it is necessary to ensure as far as possible that the bones were deposited at the same time as the layer in question, and that burrowing has not occurred. Certain small species can be indicative of fairly specific environmental conditions, but it should be remembered that, even if the remains are not intrusive, they will not always indicate the immediate environment – if they come from owl pellets, for example, they may have been caught up to a few kilometers from the site (the contents of bird pellets can nevertheless be of great value in assessing local environments).

Bones of birds and fish are particularly fragile, but are well worth studying. They can for example be used to determine the seasons in which particular sites were occupied. Birds are sensitive to climatic change, and the alternation of "cold" and "warm" species in the last Ice Age has been of great help in assessing environment. One problem is that it is sometimes difficult to decide whether a bird is present naturally or has been brought in by a human or animal predator.

The calcium carbonate shells of land molluscs (such as snails) are preserved in many types of sediment. They reflect local conditions, and can be responsive to changes in microclimate, particularly to changes in temperature and rainfall. But we need to take into account that many species have a very broad tolerance, and their reaction to change is relatively slow, so that they "hang on" in adverse areas, and disperse slowly into newly acceptable areas. The changing percentages of marine mollusc species through time can reveal something of the nature of the coastal micro-environment – such as whether it was sandy or rocky – through study of the modern preferences of the species represented. The climatic change suggested by these alterations in the presence or abundance of different species can be matched with the results of oxygen isotope analysis of the shells.

A wide range of insects may also be found, in the form of adults, larvae, and (in the case of flies) puparia. The study of insects (**paleoentomology**) was rather neglected in archaeology until about 30 years ago, since when a great deal of pioneering work has been done. Insect exoskeletons can be quite resistant to decomposition, and some assemblages comprise thousands of individuals. Since we know the distribution and environmental requirements of their modern descendants, it is often possible to use insect remains as accurate indicators of the likely climatic conditions (and to some extent of the vegetation) prevailing in particular periods and local areas. Some species have very precise requirements in terms of where they like to breed and the kinds of food their larvae need. However, rather than use single "indicator species" to reconstruct a micro-environment, it is safer to consider a number of species (the ancient climate lying within the area of overlap of their tolerance ranges).

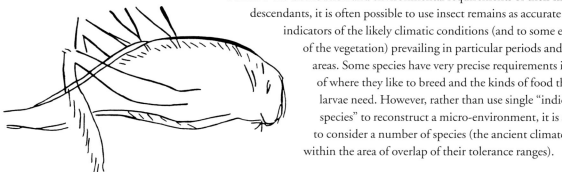

Grasshopper engraved on a bone fragment from the late Ice Age (Magdalenian) site of Enlène, Ariège, France. Insects respond rapidly to climatic change, and are sensitive indicators of the timing and scale of environmental variations.

Macrofauna

Remains of large animals found on archaeological sites mainly help us build up a picture of past human diet (see below). As environmental indicators they have proved less reliable than was once assumed, primarily because they are not so sensitive to environmental changes as small animals, but also because their remains will very likely have been deposited in an archaeological context through human or animal action. Bones from animals killed by people or by carnivores have been selected, and so cannot accurately reflect the full range of fauna present in the environment. The ideal is therefore to find accumulations of animal remains brought about by natural accident or catastrophe – animals caught in a flash flood perhaps, or buried by volcanic eruption, or which became frozen in permafrost. But such discoveries are rare – very different from the usual accumulations of animal bones encountered by archaeologists.

Assuming a suitable bone assemblage has been found and identified to species, what can the results tell us about the ancient environment?

The anatomy and especially the teeth of large animals tell us something about their diet and hence, in the case of herbivores, of the type of vegetation they prefer. However, most information about range and habitat comes from studies of modern species, on the assumption that behavior has not changed substantially since the period in question. These studies also show that large animals will tolerate – that is, have the potential to withstand or exploit – a much wider range of temperatures and environments than was once thought. So the presence of a species such as a woolly rhinoceros in an Ice Age deposit should be regarded merely as proof of the ability of that species to tolerate low temperatures, rather than as evidence of a cold climate.

Large mammals are also not generally good indicators of *vegetation*, since herbivores can thrive in a wide range of environments and eat a variety of plants. Thus, individual species cannot usually be regarded as characteristic of one particular habitat, but there are exceptions. For example, reindeer reached northern Spain in the last Ice Age, as is shown not only by discoveries of their bones but also by cave art. Such major shifts clearly reflect environmental change. In the rock art of the Sahara, too, one can see clear evidence for the presence of species such as giraffe and elephant that could not survive in the area today, and thus for dramatic environmental modification.

As will be seen below, fauna can also be used to determine in which seasons of the year a site was occupied. In coastal sites, marine resources and herbivore remains may come and go through the archaeological sequence as changes in sea level extended or drowned the coastal plain, thus changing the sites' proximity to the shore and the availability of grazing.

We always have to bear in mind that faunal fluctuations can have causes other than climate or people; additional factors may include competition, epidemics, or fluctuations in numbers of predators. Moreover, small-scale local variations in climate and weather can have enormous effects on the numbers and distribution of wild animals, so that despite its high powers of resistance a species may decline from extreme abundance to virtual extinction within a few years.

KEY CONCEPTS

Reconstructing the Animal Environment

- Microfauna are better indicators of climate and environmental change than macrofauna because they are much more sensitive to small variations in climate and adapt to them relatively quickly

- Microfauna tend to accumulate naturally on a site and reflect the immediate environment more accurately than the larger animals whose remains are often accumulated through human or animal predation

SUBSISTENCE AND DIET

Having discussed methods for reconstructing the environment, we now turn to how we find out about what people extracted from it, in other words, how they subsisted. When reconstructing early subsistence, it is useful to make a distinction between *meals*, direct evidence of various kinds as to what people were eating at a particular time, and *diet*, which implies the pattern of consumption over a long period of time.

So far as meals are concerned, the sources of information are varied. Written records, when they survive, indicate some of the things people were eating, and so do representations in art. Even modern **ethnoarchaeology** helps indicate what they *might* have been eating by broadening our understanding of their range of options. And the actual remains of the foodstuffs eaten can be highly informative.

These millet noodles, the earliest known (dating from around 4000 years ago) were found preserved in an overturned bowl at the Lajia site in northwestern China. Discovered in 2005, the remains indicate that routine millet-milling, including the repeated stretching of dough by hand to form a strand and its cooking in boiling water, was practiced in Late Neolithic China.

For the much more difficult question of diet, there are several helpful techniques of investigation. Some methods focus on human bones. Isotopic analyses of the skeletal remains of a human population can indicate, for example, the balance of marine and terrestrial foods in the diet, and even show differences in nutrition between the more and less advantaged members of the same society.

Most of our information about early subsistence, however, comes directly from the remains of what was eaten. Zooarchaeology (or **archaeozoology**), the study of past human use of animals, is now big business in archaeology. There can be few excavations anywhere that do not have a specialist to study the animal bones found. The Paleo-Indian rockshelter of Meadowcroft, Pennsylvania, for example, yielded about a million animal bones (and almost 1.5 million plant specimens). On medieval and recent sites, the quantities of material recovered can be even more formidable. **Paleo-ethnobotany** (or archaeobotany), the study of past human use of plants, is likewise a growing discipline, with a number of techniques for determining the plant species recovered. In both areas, a detailed understanding of the conditions of preservation on a site is a first prerequisite to ensure that the most efficient extraction technique is adopted. In both areas, too, the focus of interest has developed to include not just the species eaten, but the way these were managed. The process of domestication for both plants and animals is now a major research topic.

Interpretation of food remains can be problematic and requires quite sophisticated procedures. We can initially reconstruct the range of food available in the surrounding environment (see above), but the only incontrovertible proof that a particular plant or animal species was actually consumed is the presence of its traces in stomach contents or in desiccated ancient fecal matter. If such evidence is not available, the archaeologist must try to determine whether a foodstuff was actually eaten from the context or condition of the finds. For instance, if bones are cut or burned they may have been butchered and cooked.

Plants that were staples in the diet may be under-represented thanks to the generally poor preservation of vegetable remains; fish bones likewise may not survive well. The archaeologist therefore has to consider how far a site's food remains are representative of total diet. Here we need to assess a site's function, and whether it was inhabited once or frequently, for short or long periods, irregularly or seasonally (season of occupation can sometimes be deduced from plant and animal evidence as well). A long-term settlement is likely to provide more representative food remains than a specialized camp or kill site. Ideally, however, archaeologists should sample remains from a variety of contexts or sites before making judgments about diet.

We will now look at some of the main forms of evidence for human subsistence, as well as some of the different types of interpretations that can be made.

WHAT CAN PLANT FOODS TELL US ABOUT DIET?

We can learn something of diet from the study of microbotanical remains, particularly through the study of phytoliths, which can, for example, help in differentiating between wild and domestic species of plant. But the vast majority of plant evidence that reaches the archaeologist is in the form of macrobotanical remains, and these are much more useful when trying to reconstruct diet.

Macrobotanical Remains

Macrobotanical remains may be desiccated (only in absolutely dry environments such as deserts or high mountains), waterlogged (only in environments that have been permanently wet since the date of deposition), or preserved by charring. In exceptional circumstances, volcanic eruption can preserve botanical remains, such as Cerén in El Salvador where a wide variety have been found carbonized, or as impressions, in numerous vessels. Plant remains preserved in several different ways can sometimes be encountered within the same site, but in most parts of the world charring is the principal or only cause of preservation on habitation sites.

Occasionally, a single sample on a site will yield very large amounts of material. Over 27 kg (60 lb) of charred barley, wheat, and other plants came from one storage pit on a Bronze Age farm at Black Patch, southern England, for example. This can sometimes give clues to the relative importance of different cereals and legumes and weed flora, but the sample nevertheless simply reflects a moment in time. What the archaeologist really needs is a larger number of samples (each of preferably more than 100 grains) from a single period on the site, and, if possible, from a range of types of deposit, in order to obtain reliable information about what species were exploited, their importance, and their uses during the period of time in question.

When we have obtained enough samples we need to quantify the plant remains: for example by weight or by number of remains. Some archaeologists simply arrange samples in order of abundance. But this can be misleading, as was shown by the British archaeobotanist Jane Renfrew in her study of the material from the **Neolithic** settlement of Sitagroi, Greece. She noted that the most abundant plant may have been preserved by chance (such as an accident in the course of baking). Similarly, species that produce large quantities of seeds or grains may appear more important in the archaeological record than they actually were: at Sitagroi 19,000 seeds of knotgrass barely filled a thimble.

Interpreting the Context and the Remains. It is crucial for the archaeologist or specialist to try to understand the archaeological context of a plant sample, as this can reveal more about exactly how the plant was being used. In the past attention used to be focused primarily on the botanical history of the plants themselves, their morphology, place of origin, and **evolution**. Now, however, archaeologists also want to know more about the human use of plants in hunting and gathering economies, and in agriculture – which plants were important in the diet, and how they were gathered or grown, processed, stored, and cooked. This means understanding the different stages of traditional plant processing; recognizing the effect different processes have on the remains; and identifying the different contexts in the archaeological record. In many cases it is the plant remains that reveal the function of the location where they are found, and thus the nature of the context, rather than vice versa.

In a farming economy, for instance, there are many different stages of plant processing, summed up in the illustration below: cereals have to be threshed, winnowed, and cleaned before consumption, in order to separate the grain from the chaff, straw, and weeds; but seed corn also has to be stored for the next year's crop; and food grain might also be stored unthreshed in order to get the harvested crop out of the rain, and would then be threshed only when needed. From ethnoarchaeological and experimental observations it is known that certain of these activities leave characteristic residues with which archaeological samples can be compared, whether they are from ovens, living floors, latrines, or storage pits.

Cereal crop processing: waste products from many of these stages may survive as charred or waterlogged remains.

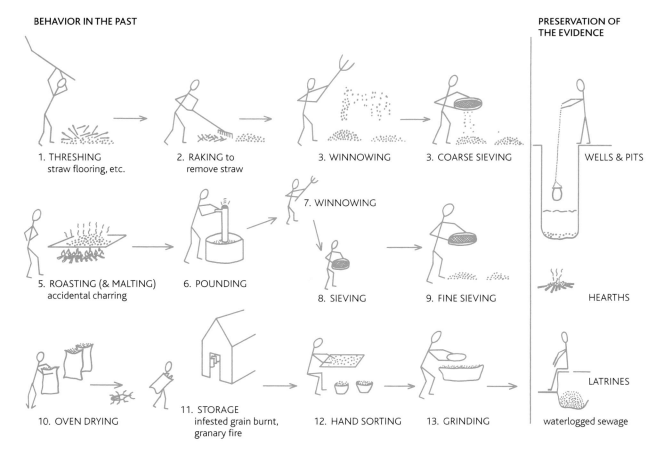

BEHAVIOR IN THE PAST

PRESERVATION OF THE EVIDENCE

1. THRESHING
straw flooring, etc.

2. RAKING to remove straw

3. WINNOWING

3. COARSE SIEVING

WELLS & PITS

5. ROASTING (& MALTING)
accidental charring

6. POUNDING

7. WINNOWING

8. SIEVING

9. FINE SIEVING

HEARTHS

10. OVEN DRYING

11. STORAGE
infested grain burnt,
granary fire

12. HAND SORTING

13. GRINDING

LATRINES

waterlogged sewage

Chemical Residues in Plant Remains. Various chemicals survive in plant remains themselves which provide an alternative basis for their identification. These compounds include proteins, fatty lipids, and even **DNA**. The analysis of lipids has so far proved the most useful method for distinguishing different cereal and legume species, but always in combination with other non-chemical identification techniques. DNA offers the prospect of eventually resolving identification at an even more detailed level and of perhaps tracing family trees of the plants and patterns of trade in plant products.

Plant Impressions. Impressions of plant remains are quite common in fired clay, and do at least prove that the species in question was present at the spot where the clay was worked. Such impressions, however, do not necessarily prove that the plant was important in the economy or diet, since they constitute a very skewed sample and only seeds or grains of medium size tend to leave imprints. One has to be particularly careful with impressions on potsherds, because pottery can be discarded far from its point of manufacture, and in any case many pots were deliberately decorated with grain impressions, thus perhaps overemphasizing the importance of a species.

Analysis of Plant Residues on Artifacts

As we shall see in Chapter 7, **microwear analysis** of a tool edge can identify broadly whether the tool was used to cut meat, wood, or some other material. Discovery of phytoliths can show what type of grasses were cut by a tool. Microscopic study can also reveal and identify plant fibers. Another method is chemical analysis of residues on tool edges: certain chemical reagents can provide a means of proving whether plant residues are present on tools or in vessels – thus, potassium iodide turns blue if starch grains are present, and yellow-brown for other plant materials. Starch grains can also be detected by microscope and, for example, have been extracted with a needle from crevices in the surfaces of prehistoric grinding stones from Aguadulce Shelter in the humid tropics of Panama. The species of the grains can be identified, and show that tubers such as manioc and arrowroot – which do not usually leave recoverable fossilized remains – were being cultivated here *c.* 5000 BC, the earliest recorded occurrence of manioc in the Americas.

The site also yielded maize starch, and this technique is thus important for proving the presence of maize in structures or sites without charred remains: for example, at the Early Formative village of Real Alto (Ecuador), maize starch grains and phytoliths from maize cobs have been retrieved from stone tools and sediments dating to 2800–2400 BC. Recently, starch grains have even been recovered from a large flat piece of basalt in a hut at Ohalo II, Israel, dating to about 23,000 years ago. This was clearly a grindstone, and the grains from barley, and perhaps wheat, show that wild cereals were already being processed at this early date.

Chemical investigation of fats preserved in vessels is also making progress, because it has been found that fatty acids, amino acids (the constituents of protein), and similar substances are very stable and preserve well. Samples are extracted from residues, purified, concentrated in a centrifuge, dried, and then analyzed by means of a spectrometer, and by a technique known as chromatography, which separates the major constituent components of the fats. Interpretation of the results is made by comparison with a reference collection of "chromatograms" (read-outs) from different substances.

For example, the German chemist Rolf Rottländer has identified mustard, olive oil, seed oils, butter, and other substances on potsherds, including specimens from Neolithic lake dwellings. In work on sherds from the German Iron Age hillfort of the Heuneburg, he has been able to prove that some amphorae – storage vessels usually associated with liquids – did indeed contain olive oil and wine, whereas in the case of a Roman amphora the charcoal-like black residue proved to be not liquid but wheat flour. This important technique not only provides dietary evidence, but also helps to define the function of the vessels with which the fats are associated. Ever more refined techniques are currently being developed for identifying food species from protein, lipid, and DNA biochemical analysis of small fragments of plant material.

The Domestication of Wild Plant Species

One of the major areas of debate in modern archaeology concerns the question of human management of plants, and particularly whether some species that we find were *wild* or *domesticated*, since this sheds light on one of the most crucial aspects of human history: the transition from a mobile (**hunter-gatherer**) to a settled (agricultural) way of life. It can often be difficult, impossible, or irrelevant to try to distinguish between wild and domesticated varieties since many types of cultivation do not change the form of the plant, and even in cases where such change occurs we do not know how long it took to appear. Experimental evidence suggests that the transition from wild to domestic could have been complete within only 20 to 200 years – without conscious intervention on the farmers' part. Any line drawn between wild and domestic plants does not necessarily correspond to a distinction between gathering and agriculture.

There are nevertheless cases where a clear distinction can be made between wild and fully domestic forms. Macrobotanical remains are of most use here. For example, the American archaeologist Bruce Smith found that 50,000 charred seeds of *Chenopodium* (goosefoot), nearly 2000 years old from Russell Cave, Alabama, exhibited a set of interrelated characteristics reflecting domestication. He was thus able to add this starchy-seed species to the brief list of cultivated plants – including bottle gourd, squash, marsh elder, sunflower, and tobacco – available in the garden plots of the Eastern Woodlands before the introduction of maize by about AD 200.

Wild and domestic cereals. Left to right: wild and domestic einkorn, domestic maize, extinct wild maize. The wild einkorn is sheds its grain easily. But the tougher domestic form does so only when threshed: a real advantage for the early farmer, since if grains fall off before threshing, they are lost.

There has been some debate in recent years about whether wild and domestic legumes can be differentiated by their structure, but archaeobotanical work by the British scholar Ann Butler suggests that there is no foolproof way to do this, even in a scanning electron microscope. Cereals, on the other hand, where well preserved, are more straightforward, and domestication can be identified by clues such as the loss of anatomical features like the brittle rachis that facilitate the dispersal of seed by natural agents. In other words, once people began to cultivate cereals, they gradually developed varieties that retained their seeds until they could be harvested.

Plant Evidence from Literate Societies

Archaeologists studying the beginnings of plant cultivation, or plant use among hunter-gatherers, have to rely on the kind of scientific evidence outlined above, coupled with the judicious use of ethnoarchaeological research and modern experiments. For the student of diet among literate societies, however, particularly the great civilizations, there is a wealth of evidence for domestication of plants, as well as for farming practices, cookery, and many other aspects of diet to be found written in documents and in art.

The Greek writer Herodotus, for example, gives us plenty of information about eating habits in the 5th century BC, notably in Egypt, a civilization for which there is extensive evidence about food and diet. Much of the evidence for

KEY CONCEPTS

What Can Plant Foods Tell Us About Diet?

- *Macrobotanical Remains*: these can give us a good idea of what plants were present at a site, but there are problems of quantification and interpretation. It's important to understand how a plant might have been processed and used

- *Plant Residues on Artifacts*: chemical traces of plants can be found on some artifacts (often pots and tools) and these can be tested and compared against a reference collection in order to identify a species

- *Domestication of Wild Plant Species*: various techniques can help to answer the crucial question of whether plant remains found in the archaeological record are from wild or domesticated species

Harvesting and processing a cereal crop: scenes depicted on the walls of a New Kingdom tomb at Thebes in Egypt.

the pharaonic period comes from paintings and foodstuffs in tombs, so it has a certain upper-class bias, but there is also information to be found about the diet of humbler folk from plant remains in workers' villages such as that at Tell el-Amarna, and from hieroglyphic texts. In the later Ptolemaic period there are records of corn allowances for workers, such as the 3rd-century BC accounts concerning grain allotted to workers on a Faiyum agricultural estate. Models are also instructive about food preparation: the tomb of Meketre, a nobleman of the 12th dynasty (2000–1790 BC), contained a set of wooden models, including women kneading flour into loaves, and others brewing beer. Three newly deciphered Babylonian clay tablets from Iraq, 3750 years old, present cuneiform texts containing 35 recipes for a wide variety of rich meat stews, and thus constitute the world's oldest cookbook.

In the New World, we owe much of our knowledge of Aztec food crops, fishing practices, and natural history to the invaluable writings of the 16th-century Franciscan scholar Bernardino de Sahagún, based on his own observations and on the testimony of his Native American informants.

It should be remembered, however, that written evidence and art tend to give a very short-term view of subsistence. Only archaeology can look at human diet with a long-term perspective.

INVESTIGATING DIET, SEASONALITY, AND DOMESTICATION FROM ANIMAL REMAINS

Although plant foods may always have constituted the greater part of the diet – except in special circumstances or high latitudes like the Arctic – meat may well have been considered more important, either as food or as a reflection of the prowess of the hunter or the status of the herder. Animal remains are usually better preserved on archaeological sites too so that, unlike plant remains, they have been studied since the very beginnings of archaeology.

The first question the archaeologist must face when interpreting animal remains is to decide whether they are present through human actions rather than through natural causes or other predators (as in the case of carnivore debris, owl pellets, burrowing animals, etc.). Animals may also have been exploited at a site for non-dietary purposes (skins for clothing, bone and antler for tools).

As with plant remains, therefore, one must be particularly careful to examine the context and content of faunal samples. This is usually straightforward in sites of recent periods, but in the **Paleolithic**, especially the Lower Paleolithic, the question is crucial.

Proving Human Exploitation of Animals in the Paleolithic. In the past, association of animal bones and stone tools was often taken as proof that humans were responsible for the presence of the faunal remains, or at least exploited them. We now know, however, that this is not always a fair assumption, and since in any case many used bones are not associated with tools, archaeologists have sought more definite proof from the marks of stone tools on the bones themselves. A great deal of work is currently aimed at proving the existence of such marks, and finding ways of differentiating them from other traces such as scratches and punctures made by animal teeth, etching by plant roots, abrasion by sedimentary particles or post-depositional weathering, and damage by excavation tools. This is also part of the search for reliable evidence in the current major debate in Paleolithic studies as to whether early humans were genuine hunters, or merely scavenged meat from carcasses of animals killed by other predators.

Much attention has been directed to bones from the famous Lower Paleolithic sites of Olduvai Gorge and Koobi Fora, in East Africa, that are over 1.5 million years old. Archaeologists used a scanning electron microscope to examine suspected toolmarks on the bones, comparing their results with marks produced by known processes on modern bones. The diagnostic feature of a toolmark produced by a slicing action, for example, was a V-shaped groove with a series of longitudinal parallel lines at the bottom; marks made by carnivores were much more rounded (see illustration opposite). They found that many bones had both toolmarks and carnivore scratches, suggesting some competition for the carcass. In some cases, the carnivore marks were clearly superimposed on the toolmarks, but in most cases the carnivores seem to have got there first!

However, recent work suggests that very similar marks can be produced by other causes, such as when bones are damaged by trampling. Thus microscopic features alone are not sufficient evidence to prove human intervention. The context of the find and the position of the marks need to be studied too.

More work still needs to be done before we can be sure of proving early human activity in this way, and also of identifying episodes where our early ancestors were hunters rather than scavengers. However, there are other

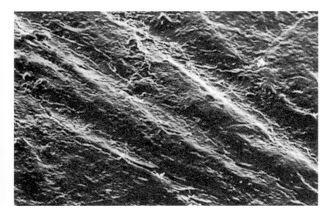

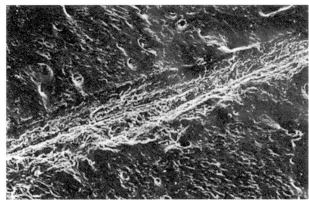

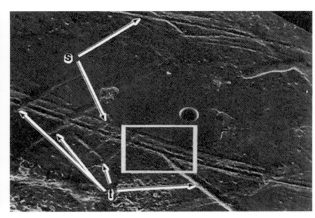

Carnivore marks or toolmarks? Bone surfaces analyzed in the scanning electron microscope. (Above left) Round-bottomed groove made on a modern bone by a hyena. (Above right) V-shaped groove made on a modern bone by a sharp stone flake. (Left) Fossil bone from Olduvai Gorge that may show two slicing marks (s) made by a stone flake, and carnivore tooth marks (t) made later.

types of evidence that can provide proof of human processing of bones. These include artificial concentrations of bones in particular places, such as the use of mammoth bones for the construction of huts in the Paleolithic of central and eastern Europe. Burning of bones is another clear indication of human processing.

Having demonstrated so far as possible that animal remains were indeed produced by human action, the archaeologist then can move on to try to answer the interesting questions such as what did people eat, in which seasons did they eat particular foods, how did they hunt and butcher the animals, and were the animals domesticated?

The most abundant and informative residues of animals are the macroremains – bones, teeth, antlers, shells, etc. Numerous techniques are now available to help extract information from data of this type.

In analyzing an assemblage of bones, we have first to identify them and then quantify them, both in terms of numbers of animals and of meat weight. The amount of meat represented by a bone will depend on the sex and age of the animal, the season of death, and geographical variation in body size and in nutrition. But if factors of age, sex, and season of death need to be allowed for, how are they established?

Strategies of Use: Deducing Age, Sex, and Seasonality from Large Fauna

Sexing is easy in cases where only the male has antlers (most deer), or large canines (pig), or where a penis bone is present (e.g. dog), or where the female has a different pelvic structure. Measurements of certain bones, such as the foot bones of some animals, can sometimes provide two distinct clusters of results, interpreted as male (large) and female (small).

The *age* of an animal can be assessed from features such as the degree of closure of sutures in the skull, or, to a certain extent, from the stage of development of limb bones. Age is then estimated by comparison with information on these features in modern populations. However, estimates of the age at which mammals were killed are usually based on the eruption and wear patterns of the teeth.

The season of death is also a crucial factor. There are many ways of studying *seasonality* from animal remains – for example, the identification of species only available at certain times of year, or which shed their antlers in specific seasons. If it is known at what time of year the young of a species were born, then remains of fetuses, or bones of the newly born, can pinpoint a season of occupation (see box overleaf).

The Question of Animal Domestication

An entirely different set of methods is required to assess the status of the animals – i.e. whether they were wild or domesticated. Like the study of plant domestication described above, this is a crucial question about one of the most important developments in human history: the transition from a mobile to a settled, agricultural way of life. In some cases the answer can be obvious, such as where non-indigenous animals have been introduced on to islands by humans – for example, the appearance of cattle, sheep, goat, dog, and cat on Cyprus.

One criterion of animal domestication is human interference with the natural breeding habits of certain species, which has led to changes in the physical characteristics of those species from the wild state. But there are other definitions, and specialists disagree about which physical changes in animals are diagnostic of domestication. Too much emphasis on the wild/domestic dichotomy may also mask a whole spectrum of human-animal relationships, such as herd management without selective breeding. Nevertheless, domestication, by any definition, clearly occurred separately in many parts of the world, and archaeologists therefore need to differentiate fully wild from fully domestic animals, and to investigate the process of domestication.

Information from animal resources

- Animal remains are often well-preserved on archaeological sites

- It's important to establish whether animal remains are present on a site through human agency or through other causes

- We can sex and age animal bones, study their seasonality, and deduce whether the animals were wild or domesticated, all of which helps us to understand how humans were exploiting the animal environment

Amongst a number of other possible lines of evidence, certain tools may indicate the presence of domesticated animals – for example, plows, yokes, and horse trappings. Deformities and disease can also provide convincing evidence for domestication. When used for traction, horses, cattle, and camels all sometimes suffer osteoarthritis or strain-deformities on their lower limbs. Work is also progressing on tracing the history of domestication through DNA.

Remains of Individual Meals

One of the most direct kinds of evidence of what people ate comes from occasional finds of actual meals. At Pompeii, for example, meals of fish, eggs, bread, and nuts were found intact on tables, as well as food in shops. Food is often preserved in funerary contexts, as in the desiccated corncobs and other items in Peruvian graves, or at Saqqara, Egypt, where the 2nd-dynasty tomb of a noblewoman contained a huge variety of foodstuffs, constituting a rich and elaborate meal – cereals, fish, fowl,

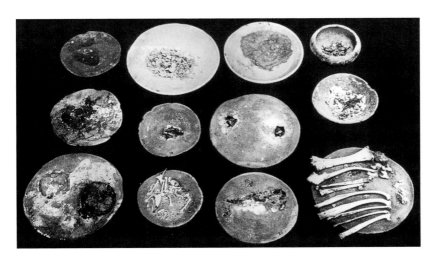

A meal as a funerary offering: the rich and elaborate food remains found in the 2nd-dynasty tomb of a noblewoman at Saqqara, Egypt. These include a triangular loaf of bread; nabk berries (similar in appearance to cherries); cut ribs of beef; a cooked quail; two cooked kidneys; stewed fruit, probably figs; cakes; pigeon stew; a cooked fish. Impressive as such remains are, they are unlikely to be representative of the everyday diet of the ancient Egyptians.

BISON DRIVE SITES

The driving of bison over bluff or cliff edges was an important periodic hunting method for thousands of years in North America. Much was known from accounts by Native American informants recorded in the first decades of this century, but the picture needed filling out through archaeological investigation of actual drive sites.

The Boarding School Site

One of the first of such excavations was undertaken by Thomas Kehoe in the 1950s at the Boarding School site, Montana. The work was carried out with the help of the local Blackfoot Tribe. Boarding School was not a cliff, but one of the more common, lower but abrupt drops that led to a natural enclosure. In a deep stratigraphy, three main bone layers were found, with well-preserved bison remains that gave insights into the size and composition of the herd, and hence into the seasons of the drives. Bison numbers were assessed using the "minimum number of individuals" technique. Ages of the animals came from the eruption sequence and degree of wear on the teeth, and from bone-fusion, while sex was established on the basis of size and pelvic shape.

The site proved to have been used intermittently for a long period as a temporary camp. Then c. AD 1600 (according to radiocarbon dating of charred bone) a herd of about 100 bison was driven over the bluff. Their remains formed the "3rd bone layer," which included a fetal bone but no mature bulls, implying a late fall or winter drive of a herd composed of cows, calves, and young bulls. A season or two later, another herd of 150 were driven in, forming the "2nd bone layer." This had remains of mature bulls, and together with the lack of fetal or newborn calves it indicated a drive of a

Gull Lake bison drive.

Excavation of a group of bison skulls at Gull Lake.

SASKATCH-
EWAN
Gull Lake
CANADA
USA
Boarding School
MONTANA

Mapping bones at the Boarding School site.

poles were found and the total of 440 projectile points suggested an average of four or five arrows used on each animal.

The Gull Lake Site

In the early 1960s Kehoe carried out a similar excavation at the Gull Lake site, over the border in southwest Saskatchewan. Here, too, bison had been driven over a bluff into a depression serving as a corral. Five bone layers were encountered, one of them (c. AD 1300) perhaps representing the remains of as many as 900 bison.

The drives began in the late 2nd century AD, and show little processing of bone: many limb bones and even spinal columns are intact. In the later drives, however, processing was far more thorough, with few articulated bones, and extensive scattering and burning of scrap, indicating a utilization for grease and pemmican.

"cow-and-bull" herd in the rutting season, between July and September, when pemmican (dried meat) had to be prepared for the winter.

A much later drive (probably just before historic contact), produced the "1st bone layer." Here the remains of 30 bison were subjected to light butchering, probably for transport to a distant camp: much of what was left behind was in articulated units. In the earlier two layers, butchery techniques were similar but far more of each animal was utilized, and much was processed on the spot. Clearly, the distance to the home base was shorter than in the case of the later drive. The lack of pottery at the site emphasized its role as strictly a kill and meat-processing station. Traces of corral

beef, fruit, cakes, honey, cheese, and wine – which, to judge by the tomb paintings, was not unusual. The Han period in China (206 BC–AD 220) has tombs stocked with food: that of the wife of the Marquis of Dai has a unique collection of provisions, herbal medicines, and prepared dishes in containers of lacquer, ceramic, and bamboo, with labels attached, and even inventory slips giving the composition of the dishes! However, it is unlikely that such magnificent remains are representative of everyday diet. Even the meals found so wonderfully preserved at Pompeii are merely a tiny sample from a single day. The only way in which we can really study what people ate habitually is to examine actual human remains.

ASSESSING DIET FROM HUMAN REMAINS

The only incontrovertible evidence that something was actually consumed by humans is its presence in either stomachs or feces. Both kinds of evidence give us invaluable information about individual meals and short-term diet. The study of human teeth also helps us to reconstruct diet, but the real breakthrough in recent years in understanding long-term diet has come from the analysis of bone collagen. What human bones can reveal about general health will be examined in Chapter 8.

Individual Meals

Stomach Contents.   Stomachs survive only rarely in archaeological contexts, except in bog bodies. Some mummies also provide dietary evidence: the overweight wife of the Marquis of Dai from 2nd-century BC China, mentioned above, seems to have died of a heart attack caused by acute pain from her gallstones an hour or so after enjoying a generous helping of watermelon (138 melon seeds were discovered in her stomach and intestines).

When stomachs survive in bog bodies, the dietary evidence they provide can be of the greatest interest. Pioneering studies of the stomach contents of Danish Iron Age bogmen showed that Grauballe Man, for instance, had consumed over 60 species of wild seeds, together with one or two cereals and a little meat (as shown by some small bone splinters), while Tollund Man had eaten only plants. But we should keep in mind that these results, while fascinating, do not necessarily indicate everyday diet, since these victims were possibly executed or sacrificed, and thus their last meal may have been out of the ordinary.

Fecal Material.   Experiments have been done to assess the survival properties of different foodstuffs relevant to the study of ancient diet, and it has been found that many organic remains can survive surprisingly well after their journey through the human digestive tract. Feces themselves survive only rarely, in very dry sites such as caves in the western United States and Mexico, or very wet sites (these feces are often wrongly called "**coprolites**," which means fossilized/petrified excrement). But, where they are preserved, they have proved to be a highly important source of information about what individuals ate in the past.

Macroremains can be extremely varied in human excrement, in fact this variety is an indication of human origin. Bone fragments, plant fibers, bits of charcoal, seeds, and the remains of fish, birds, and even insects are known. Shell fragments – from molluscs, eggs, and nuts – can also be identified. Hair can be assigned to certain classes of animals by means of its scale pattern, visible under the microscope, and thus help us to know which animals were eaten.

Exceptional conditions in Lovelock Cave, Nevada, have preserved 5000 feces dating from 2500 to 150 years ago, and Robert Heizer's study of their contents yielded remarkable evidence about diet, which seems to have comprised seeds, fish, and birds. Feather fragments were identified from waterfowl such as the heron and grebe; fish and reptile scales, which pass through the alimentary canal unaltered, also led to identification of several species. Fish remains were abundant in some of the feces; one, for example, from 1000 years ago, contained 5.8 g (0.2 oz) of fish bone which, it was calculated, came from 101 small chubs, representing a total live weight of 208 g (7.3 oz) – the fish component of a meal for a single person.

Excrement and fecal residues represent single meals, and therefore provide short-term data on diet, unless they are found in great quantities, as at Lovelock Cave, and even there the feces represent only a couple of meals a year. For human diet over whole lifetimes, we need to turn to the human skeleton itself.

Human Teeth as Evidence for Diet

Teeth survive in extremely good condition, made as they are of the two hardest tissues in the body, and microscopic examination of the abrasions on certain dental surfaces can provide evidence for the sort of food that their owners enjoyed. Abrasive particles in food leave striations on the enamel whose orientation and length are directly related to the meat or vegetation in the diet and its process of cooking. Modern meat-eating Greenland Eskimos, for instance, have almost exclusively vertical striations on their lateral tooth surfaces, while largely vegetarian Melanesians have both vertical and horizontal striations, with a shorter average length.

When these results are compared with data from fossil teeth hundreds of thousands of years old, it has been found that there is an increase in horizontal and a decrease in vertical striations, and a decrease in average striation length over time. In other words, less and less effort was needed to chew food, and meat may have decreased in importance as the diet became more mixed: early people crushed and broke down their food with their teeth, but less chewing was required as cooking techniques developed and improved.

Tooth decay as well as wear will sometimes provide us with dietary information. Remains of the California Native Americans display very marked tooth decay, attributed to their habit of leaching the tannin out of acorns, their staple food, through a bed of sand which caused excessive tooth abrasion. Decay and loss of teeth can also set in thanks to starchy and sugary foods. Dental caries became abundant on the coast of Georgia (USA) in the 12th century AD, particularly among the female population. It was in this period that the transition occurred from hunting, fishing, and gathering to maize agriculture. Anthropologist Clark Larsen believes that the rise in tooth decay over this period, revealed by a study of hundreds of skeletons, was caused by the carbohydrates in maize. Since the women of the group were more subject to the caries than were the men, it is probable that they were growing, harvesting, preparing, and cooking the corn, while the men ate more protein and less carbohydrate.

KEY CONCEPTS

Assessing Diet From Human Remains

- *Individual Meals*: we can find direct evidence of what humans in the past ate from the examination of preserved stomach contents and fecal material

- *Teeth*: evidence of wear on human teeth, which survive well in many archaeological sediments, can tell us about the relative importance of meat and plants in past diets

- *Isotopic Evidence*: can be used as evidence for long-term human diet, but needs to be combined with other evidence for a finer picture

Isotopic Methods: Diet Over a Lifetime

Recently, a revolution has taken place in dietary studies through the realization that **isotopic analysis** of human tooth enamel and bone collagen can reveal a great deal about long-term food intake. The method relies on reading the chemical signatures left in the body by different foods – we are what we eat.

Plants can be divided into three groups based on their differing ratios of two carbon isotopes: temperate, tropical, and marine plants. As animals eat plants, these different chemical signatures are passed along the food chain and are eventually fixed in human and animal bone tissue. They can show whether diet was based on land or marine plants. Only archaeological evidence, however, can provide more detail about precisely which species of plants or animals contributed to the diet. Recently, for example, isotopic analysis of tooth enamel from four *Australopithecus africanus* individuals from Makapansgat, South Africa, revealed that they ate not only fruits and leaves, as had been thought, but also large quantities of grasses or sedges, or the animals which ate those plants, or both. In other words, they regularly exploited fairly open environments (woodlands or grasslands) for food; and since their tooth wear lacks the characteristic scratches of grass-eaters, it is possible that they were indeed already consuming meat, by hunting small animals or scavenging larger ones.

STUDY QUESTIONS

- What techniques do scientists use to study the environment on a global scale?
- How are plant remains used to reconstruct past environments?
- Why is the question of plant and animal domestication important to archaeologists?
- What is the difference between meals and diet?
- What are some of the complications in determining if humans have processed animal bones?
- How can human teeth aid in the study of diet?

SUMMARY

- Humankind has developed from being an inconsequential species at the mercy of the environment and the food resources it provided to one with a huge influence over its surroundings. The environment is of crucial importance to archaeology. During every period of the past it has played a vital role in determining where and how people could live, and on what. Archaeologists now have a battery of techniques, largely based on the analysis of plant and animal remains, to help reconstruct such past environments.

- Where food is concerned, the evidence available varies from botanical and animal remains, large and microscopic, to tools and vessels, plant and animal residues, and art and texts. We can discover what was eaten, in which seasons, and sometimes how it was prepared. We need to assess whether the evidence arrived in the archaeological record naturally or through human actions, and whether the resources were wild or under human control. Occasionally we encounter the remains of individual meals left as funerary offerings or the contents of stomachs or feces. Finally, the human body itself contains a record of diet in its toothwear and in the chemical signatures left in bones by different foods.

- Many of the techniques must be carried out by the specialist, particularly the biochemist, but archaeologists should know how to interpret the results, because the rewards are enormous for our knowledge of what the environment was like, what people ate, how they exploited their resources, and in what proportions.

FURTHER READING

General introductions to environmental archaeology and the subject of diet can be found in the following:

Barker, G. 2006. *The Agricultural Revolution in Prehistory*. Oxford University Press: Oxford.

Bellwood, P. 2004. *First Farmers: The Origins of Agricultural Societies*. Blackwell: Oxford.

Brothwell, D. & P. 1997. *Food in Antiquity: A Survey of the Diet of Early Peoples*. Johns Hopkins Univ. Press: Baltimore, MD.

Dincauze, D.F. 2000. *Environmental Archaeology*. Cambridge University Press: Cambridge.

Gilbert, R.I. & Mielke, J.H. (eds.). 1985. *The Analysis of Prehistoric Diets*. Academic Press: New York & London.

O'Connor, T. 2000. *The Archaeology of Animal Bones*. Sutton: Stroud.

Pearsall, D.M. 2009. *Paleoethnobotany: A Handbook of Procedures* (2nd ed.). Left Coast Press: Walnut Creek.

Reitz, E.J. & Wing, E.S. 2008. *Zooarchaeology* (2nd ed.). Cambridge University Press: Cambridge.

Smith, B.D. 1998. *The Emergence of Agriculture* (2nd ed.). Scientific American Library: New York.

How Were Artifacts Made, Used, and Distributed?

Technology, trade, and exchange

7

It is the physical remains of humanly made **artifacts** down the ages that form the bulk of the archaeological record. We have seen how archaeologists can find and date artifacts, but in this chapter we will start by addressing two questions of fundamental importance: how were artifacts made, and what were they used for? There are several approaches to these two questions – the purely archaeological, the scientific analysis of objects, the ethnographic, and the experimental.

When assessing ancient technologies, the archaeologist always needs to bear in mind that the sample preserved may well be biased. During the long **Paleolithic** period, for instance, implements of wood and bone must surely have rivaled those of stone in importance – as they do in hunting and gathering societies today – but stone tools dominate the archaeological record.

Once made, artifacts usually move around as they are acquired or passed on between individuals or groups – a phenomenon which can tell us a great deal about the frequency and extent of contacts between different groups, as well as about transportation, economics, and so forth. By analyzing where the materials used to make an artifact came from, as well as the distribution of artifacts as found by archaeologists, we can reconstruct something of these trading relationships: who was exchanging goods with whom, and by what method?

When an archaeologist investigates an object, it must first be decided whether it was actually made or used by people in the past. For most periods the answer will be obvious (although we have to beware of fakes and forgeries), but for the Paleolithic, and especially the Lower Paleolithic, judgment can be more difficult. Where the very earliest tools are concerned, on which we would expect the traces of human work to be minimal, the question is not easy to resolve, since the crudest human working may be indistinguishable from the damage caused by nature.

We will make a convenient distinction in the next section on ancient technology between two classes of raw material used in creating objects –

between those that are largely unaltered, such as flint, and those that are synthetic, the product of human activities, such as pottery or metal. Of course even supposedly unaltered materials have often been treated by heat or by chemical reactions in order to assist the manufacturing process. But synthetic materials have undergone an actual change in state, usually through heat treatment. The human use of fire – **pyrotechnology** – is a crucial factor here.

UNALTERED MATERIALS
Stone

From the first recognizable tools, dating back about 2.5 million years, up to the adoption of pottery-making, dated to 14,000 BC in Japan, the archaeological record is dominated by stone. How were stone artifacts, from the smallest stone tools to the greatest stone monuments, extracted, manufactured, and used?

Much of the stone for early tools was probably picked up from streambeds or other parts of the landscape; but the sources most visible archaeologically are the mines and quarries. The best-known *mines* are the **Neolithic** and later flint mines in various parts of northern Europe, such as Grimes Graves in England where multiple 15-m (50-ft) deep shafts were sunk into the chalk to reach the best quality flint layers; rough estimates suggest that the **site** could have produced 28 million flint axes. *Quarries* were a common source of larger stones for building or monuments. The job of the archaeologist is sometimes made easier by the discovery of unfinished or abandoned stones within or near to ancient quarry sites. One of the most impressive examples is the statue-quarry on Easter Island, where many statues lie in various stages of manufacture.

A combination of archaeological investigation and modern experimentation can give us valuable insights into how stones were worked. Here we will concentrate on stone tool manufacture, although much archaeological and experimental work is also done on larger stones and how they were moved, dressed, and fitted.

Stone Tool Manufacture and Function. Most stone tools are made by removing material from a pebble or "**core**" until the desired shape of the core has been attained. The first flakes struck off (primary flakes) bear traces of the outer surface (cortex). Trimming flakes are then struck off to achieve the final shape, and certain edges may then be "retouched" by further removal of tiny secondary flakes.

Stone quarry on Easter Island: one of the giant statues lies flat on its back, unfinished but at an advanced stage of manufacture – yielding clues as to how it was made.

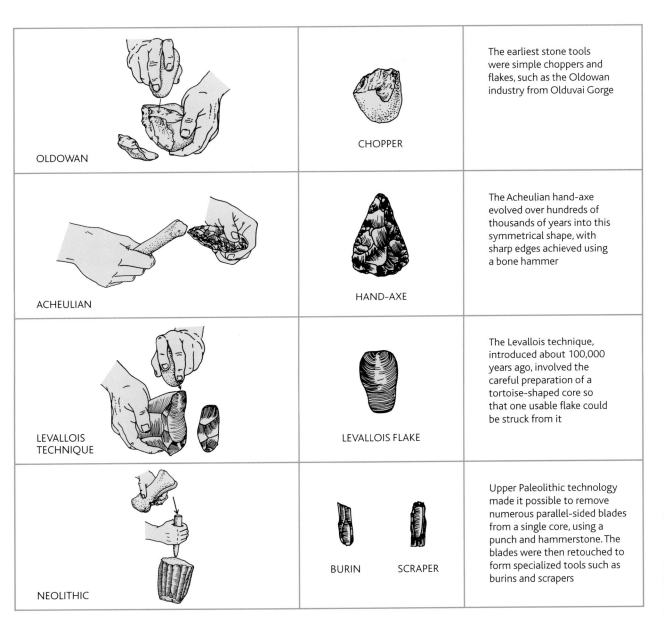

OLDOWAN	**CHOPPER**	The earliest stone tools were simple choppers and flakes, such as the Oldowan industry from Olduvai Gorge
ACHEULIAN	**HAND-AXE**	The Acheulian hand-axe evolved over hundreds of thousands of years into this symmetrical shape, with sharp edges achieved using a bone hammer
LEVALLOIS TECHNIQUE	**LEVALLOIS FLAKE**	The Levallois technique, introduced about 100,000 years ago, involved the careful preparation of a tortoise-shaped core so that one usable flake could be struck from it
NEOLITHIC	**BURIN** **SCRAPER**	Upper Paleolithic technology made it possible to remove numerous parallel-sided blades from a single core, using a punch and hammerstone. The blades were then retouched to form specialized tools such as burins and scrapers

The evolution of stone tools, from the earliest, Oldowan technology to the refined methods of the Upper Paleolithic.

Although the core is the main implement thus produced, the flakes themselves may well be used as knives, scrapers etc. The toolmaker's work will have varied in accordance with the type and amount of raw material available.

The history of stone tool technology (illustrated above) shows a sporadically increasing degree of refinement. The first recognizable tools are simple choppers and flakes made by knocking pieces off pebbles to obtain sharp edges. The best-known examples are the so-called Oldowan tools from Olduvai Gorge, Tanzania, the earliest of which date back some 2.5 million years. After hundreds of thousands of years, people progressed to flaking both surfaces of the tool, eventually producing the symmetrical Acheulian **hand-axe** shape. The next improvement, dating to around 100,000 years ago, came with the introduction of the "Levallois technique" – named after a site in a Paris suburb where it was first identified – where the core was knapped in such a way that large flakes of predetermined size and shape could be removed.

Around 35,000 years ago, with the Upper Paleolithic period, blade technology became dominant in some parts of the world. Long, parallel-sided blades were systematically removed with a punch and hammerstone from a cylindrical core. This was a great advance, not only because it produced large numbers of blanks that could be further trimmed and retouched into a wide range of specialized tools (scrapers, burins, borers), but also because it was far less wasteful of the raw material, obtaining a much greater total length of working edges than ever before from a given amount of stone. This trend toward greater economy reached its peak around 10,000 years ago, with the rise to dominance of microliths, tiny stone tools many of which were probably used as barbs on composite implements.

To find out how a stone tool was made we must try to reconstruct the sequence of manufacturing steps, and there are two principal approaches to doing this: replication and **refitting**. Stone tool replication is a type of **experimental archaeology** that involves making exact copies of different types of stone tool – using only the technology available to the original makers – in order to assess the processes entailed, and the amount of time and effort required. Many years of patient practice are required to become proficient at tool replication.

One specific problem that expert knapper Donald Crabtree was able to solve through trial and error was how the Paleo-Indians of North America had made their fluted stone tools known as Folsom points, dating to some 11,000–10,000 years ago. In particular, how had they removed the "flute" or channel flake? This had remained a mystery and experiments with a variety of techniques met with disappointing results, until the decisive clue was found in a 17th-century text by a Spanish priest who had seen Aztecs make long knife-blades from **obsidian**. The method, as experiments proved, involves pressing the flake out, downward, by means of a T-shaped crutch placed against the chest; the crutch's tip is forced down against a precise point on the core which is clamped firm.

Replication cannot usually prove conclusively which techniques were used in the past, but it does narrow the possibilities and often points to the most likely method, as in the Folsom example above. *Refitting*, on the other hand, involves working with the original tools and demonstrates clearly the precise chain of actions of the knapper. This entails attempting to put tools and flakes back together again, like a 3-D jigsaw puzzle. The work is tedious and time-

How were Paleo-Indian Folsom points made? Experiments by Donald Crabtree showed that the flakes were pressed from the core using a T-shaped crutch (above). Flintknappers have produced almost perfect replica points (below).

consuming, but when successful can allow us to follow the stages of the knapper's craft.

But how can we discover the function of a stone tool? Ethnographic observation of the use of similar tools in living societies often gives valuable clues, as do the minute traces of organic residues that can sometimes be found on tool surfaces; and experimentation can determine which uses are feasible or most probable. However, a single tool can be used for many different purposes – an Acheulian hand-axe could be used for hacking wood from a tree, for butchering, smashing, scraping, and cutting – and conversely the same task can be done by many different tools. The only direct *proof* of function is to study the minute traces, or microwear patterns, that remain on the original tools. These minute polishes and marks, only properly visible using a scanning electron microscope, can be compared against evidence from modern experiments, and we can deduce the type of material a tool was used to work (such as wood, bone, hide, or meat) and the type of action used (such as piercing, cutting, or scraping).

Wood

Wood is one of the most important organic materials, and must have been used to make tools for as long as stone and bone. Indeed, many prehistoric stone tools were employed to obtain and work timber. If wood survives in good condition, it may preserve toolmarks to show how it was worked. A wide range of wooden tools can survive under special conditions. In the dry environment of ancient Egypt, for instance, numerous wooden implements for farming (rakes, hoes, grain-scoops, sickles), furniture, weapons and toys, carpentry tools such as mallets and chisels, and even whole ships have come down to us. Egyptian paintings such as those in the tomb of the nobleman Rekhmire at Thebes sometimes depict carpenters using drills and saws. But it has been waterlogged wood (including the remains of ships and boats) that has yielded the richest information about woodworking skills.

Plant and Animal Fibers

The making of containers, fabrics, and cords from skins, bark, and woven fibers probably dates back to the very earliest archaeological periods, but these fragile materials rarely survive. However, as we saw in Chapter 2, they do survive in very dry or wet conditions. In arid regions, such as Egypt or parts of the New World, such perishables have come down to us in some quantity, and the study of basketry and cordage there reveals complex and sophisticated designs and techniques that display complete mastery of these organic materials. Waterlogged conditions can also yield a great deal of fragile evidence.

Where textiles are concerned, the most crucial question is how they were made, and of what. In the New World, information on pre-Columbian weaving methods

KEY CONCEPTS

Artifacts Made From Unaltered Materials

- *Stone*: the archaeological record is dominated by stone artifacts. A combination of archaeological investigation, modern experimentation, and ethnographic observation can tell us a great deal about how stone artifacts were made and used

- *Wood*: wood does not survive well, apart from in very dry or waterlogged conditions, but was almost certainly as important a resource as stone

- *Plant and animal fibers*: containers, fabrics, and cords made from plant and animal fibers would also have been common objects in the past, but, again, they rarely survive in the archaeological record

- *Other materials*: bone, antler, shell, and leather are also often found by archaeologists, but, along with most other artifacts made from unaltered materials, we must be careful to establish whether an object is actually humanly made, or whether it has been created by natural processes

is available from ethnographic observation, as well as from Colonial accounts and illustrations, from depictions on Moche pottery, and from actual finds of ancient looms and other objects found preserved in the Peruvian desert. The richest New World evidence, however, comes from Peruvian textiles themselves, which have survived well in the dry conditions. The Andean **cultures** mastered almost every method of textile weaving or decoration now known, and their products were often finer than those of today – indeed, were some of the best ever made.

Other Unaltered Materials

Artifacts made from bone, antler, shell, and leather are also commonly found on archaeological sites. **Microwear analysis** combined with experimental archaeology are the most successful means of determining firstly whether the find really is humanly made (sharp bone points or pierced shells, for instance, can easily be created by natural processes), as well as reconstructing manufacturing techniques and deducing function.

SYNTHETIC MATERIALS

It is possible to consider the whole development of technology, as far as it relates to synthetic materials, in terms of the control of fire: pyrotechnology. Until very recent times, nearly all synthetic materials depended upon the control of heat; and the development of new technologies has often been largely dependent upon achieving higher and higher temperatures under controlled conditions.

Clearly the first step along this path was the mastery of fire, possible evidence for which already occurs in the Swartkrans Cave, South Africa, in layers dating to 1.5 million years ago. Cooked food and preserved meat then became a possibility, as did the use of heat in working flint, and in hardening wooden implements such as the yew spear from the Middle Paleolithic site of Lehringen, Germany.

A significant development of the Early Neolithic period in the Near East, around 8000 BC, was the construction of special ovens used both to parch cereal grains (to facilitate the threshing process) and to bake bread. These ovens consisted of a single chamber in which the fuel was burnt. When the oven was hot the fuel was raked out and the grain or unbaked bread placed inside. This represents the first construction of a deliberate facility to control the conditions under which the temperature was raised. We may hypothesize that it was through these early experiences in pyrotechnology that the possibility of making pottery by firing clay was discovered. Initially pottery was made by firing in an open fire, but the introduction of the potter's kiln meant higher temperatures could be achieved, which also spurred on the development of metallurgy.

Pottery

Throughout the earlier periods of **prehistory** containers made of light, organic materials were probably used. This does not mean, as has often been assumed, that Paleolithic people did not know how to make pottery: every fire lit on a cave floor will have hardened the clay around it, and terracotta figurines were sometimes produced. The lack of pottery vessels before the Neolithic period is mainly a consequence of the mobile way of life of Paleolithic **hunter-gatherers**, for whom heavy containers of fired clay would have been of limited usefulness.

Evidence for pot-making using a wheel. An Egyptian potter shapes a vessel on the turntable type of wheel in this limestone portrait of c. 2400 BC.

The introduction of pottery generally seems to coincide with the adoption of a more sedentary way of life, for which vessels and containers that are durable and strong are a necessity. The almost indestructible potsherd is as common in later periods as the stone tool is in earlier ones – and just as some sites yield thousands of stone tools, others contain literally tons of pottery fragments.

How Were Pots Made?   The making or "throwing" of pots on a wheel or turntable was only introduced after 3400 BC at the earliest (in Mesopotamia), but in the New World only after European contact. The previous method, still used in some parts of the world, was to build the vessel up by hand in a series of coils or slabs of clay. A simple examination of the interior and exterior surfaces of a pot usually allows us to identify the method of manufacture. Wheelthrown pots generally have a telltale spiral of ridges and marks that is absent from handmade wares. These marks are left by the fingertips as the potter draws the vessel up on the turntable.

The firing technique can be inferred from certain characteristics of the finished product. For example, if the surfaces are vitrified or glazed (i.e. have a glassy appearance), the pot was fired at over 900°C (1652°F) and probably in an enclosed kiln. The extent of oxidization in a pot (the process by which organic substances in the clay are burnt off) is also indicative of firing methods. Complete oxidization produces a uniform color throughout the paste. If the core of a sherd is dark (gray or black), the firing temperature was too low to oxidize the clay fully, or the duration of the firing was insufficient, factors which often point to the use of an open kiln. Experimental firing of different pastes at different temperatures and in various types of kiln provides a guide to the colors and effects that can be expected.

Unlike the making of stone tools, the production of pottery by traditional methods is still widespread in the world, so a good deal can be learned from ethnoarchaeological studies not only about the technological aspects but also about the use and trade of pottery.

Metals

The study of ancient metal artifacts and manufacturing processes is known as archaeometallurgy. Many of the advances in metalworking techniques made in the past were dependent on the ability to achieve and control ever higher temperatures.

Non-Ferrous Metals. The most important non-ferrous metal – that is, one not containing iron – used in early times was copper. In due course it was learned that a harder, tougher product could be made by **alloying** the copper with tin to produce bronze. Other elements, notably arsenic and antimony, were sometimes used in the alloying process; and in the later Bronze Age of Europe it was realized that a small amount of lead would improve the casting qualities. Gold and silver were also important, as was lead itself.

The techniques of manufacture of artifacts made from these materials can be investigated in several ways. The first point to establish is composition. Traditional laboratory methods readily allow the identification of major constituents. For instance, the alloys present in bronze may be identified in this way. However, in practice it is now more usual to utilize the techniques of **trace element analysis** (see below). The other essential approach is that of **metallographic examination**, when the structure of the material is examined microscopically. This will determine whether an artifact has been formed by cold-hammering, **annealing**, casting, or a combination of these methods.

Iron. Iron was not used in the New World during pre-Columbian times, and makes its appearance in quantity in the Old World with the beginning in the Near East of the Iron Age around 1000 BC. Once the technique of smelting iron was well understood, it became very important, since iron is more widely found in nature than is copper. But it is much more difficult to reduce – i.e. to separate

KEY CONCEPTS

Artifacts Made From Synthetic Materials

- Many of the developments in pottery and metalworking technology can be linked to developments in pyrotechnology – the ability to control fire and attain and maintain ever higher temperatures

- *Pottery*: pottery is very hard-wearing and potsherds are a common find on archaeological sites. We can learn through simple observation how pottery was made (either by hand or on a wheel) and through experiment and ethnographic studies how it was fired

- *Metals*: we can identify what metal or combination of metals an artifact is made from with simple laboratory techniques. The examination of the microscopic structure of the metal can give clues as to how an artifact was manufactured

from oxygen with which it is found combined in nature in the form of iron oxides – requiring temperatures of about 800°C (1472°F).

It is clearly important and interesting to identify what an artifact is made of, how it was made, and what it was used for. But once an artifact has been created, it takes on a life of its own – not only in terms of being used, broken or discarded, but also in terms of being transported, bought, or exchanged. The study of these processes teaches us a great deal about past human societies and how they operated. In the next section we will discuss what can be learned from the study of trade and exchange, and examine some methods for investigating the movements of different kinds of materials.

TRADE AND EXCHANGE

Societies and economies depend upon exchanges – on exchange of information and of actual goods – between individuals and between organizations. Every social transaction implies some interaction between people, and the study of the movement and flow of goods in the course of such exchange transactions is often the most direct way for the archaeologist to monitor such interactions.

In many exchanges the relationship is more important than what is exchanged. In the Christian tradition, for instance, when presents are exchanged within a family at Christmas, the giving of presents between relatives is generally more important than the actual objects: "it's the thought that counts." There are also different kinds of exchange relationship: some where generosity is the order of the day (as in the family Christmas); others where the aim is profit, and the personal relationship is not emphasized. Moreover, there are different kinds of goods: everyday commodities that are bought and sold, and special goods, valuables (see box overleaf), that are suitable for gifts.

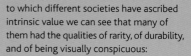

Nearly all cultures have valuables. Although some of these are useful (e.g. pigs in Melanesia, which can be eaten) most of them have no use at all, other than display. They are simply prestige objects.

Valuables tend to be in a limited range of materials to which a particular society ascribes a high value. For instance, in our own society gold is so highly valued as to be a standard against which all other values are measured.

We tend to forget that this valuation is an entirely arbitrary one, and we speak of gold's intrinsic value, as if in some way it were inherent. But gold is not a very useful material (although it is bright, and does not tarnish), nor is it the product of any special skills of the craftsperson. Intrinsic value is a misnomer: the Aztecs valued feathers more highly, unlike the Conquistadors who craved gold; both were following subjective systems of value. When we survey the range of materials to which different societies have ascribed intrinsic value we can see that many of them had the qualities of rarity, of durability, and of being visually conspicuous:

• The bright *feathers* favored by the Aztecs and by **tribes** of New Guinea fulfill two of these qualities.

• *Ivory:* elephant and walrus tusks have been valued since Upper Paleolithic times.

• *Shell,* especially of large marine molluscs, has been highly prized in many cultures for millennia.

• That very special organic material *amber* was valued in Upper Paleolithic times in northern Europe.

• *Jade* is a favored material in many cultures, from China to Mesoamerica, and was valued as long ago as 4000 BC in Neolithic Europe.

• Other naturally hard and *colorful stones* (e.g. rock crystal, lapis lazuli, obsidian, quartz, and onyx) have always been valued.

• *Gemstones* have taken on a special value in recent centuries, when the technique of cutting them to a faceted, light-catching shape was developed.

• *Gold* has perhaps pride of place (certainly in European eyes) among "intrinsically" valuable commodities, followed by silver.

• *Copper* and other metals have taken a comparable role: in North America copper objects had a special value.

• With the development of pyrotechnology, artificial materials such as *faience* and *glass* came into full prominence.

• The finest *textiles* and other clothing materials (e.g. tapa, bark-cloth, in Polynesia) have also always been highly valued, for prestige often means personal display.

A jade mask from Palenque, Mexico, found in Lord Pakal's tomb.

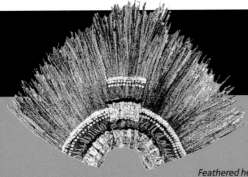

Feathered headdress (above) of the Aztec emperor Motecuhzoma II (Moctezuma).

The Portland vase (left), a superb example of 1st-century AD Roman glassworking.

Gold mask (above) thought by Schliemann to represent King Agamemnon, from a shaft grave at Mycenae, late 16th century BC.

Prestige objects of North America's Mississippian culture (c. AD 900–1450). (Left) Shell pendant (c. 14 cm) from Texas, showing a panther and bird of prey. (Below) Embossed copper face, with typical forked eye motif.

Mammoth ivory carving (below) of a lion-human figure from Hohlenstein-Stadel in southern Germany, c. 30,000 years old.

Woven silk robe (below) from the reign of the Chinese emperor Yung Cheng (1723–35), bearing the Imperial dragon.

Fifty years ago, when "diffusionist" explanations were popular in archaeology, the presence of objects of foreign type or material at an archaeological site was often thought to indicate significant "influence" from other, perhaps more advanced cultures. Today, however, we are more interested in finding out what those objects can tell us about social and economic interactions between distant groups. But the mere resemblance in the form of an artifact with those found elsewhere is not usually enough to be sure an exchange has occurred or that there is a definite link between two groups. We must show that the actual material the artifact is made from *must* have come from a distant source, and we can do this by **characterization**.

Discovering the Sources of Traded Goods: Characterization

The discovery of an artifact at a particular location does not mean that it originated in that place: it may, in fact, have been brought over hundreds or even thousands of miles. The study of where artifacts originated is not simple: artifact forms can be imitated, or can resemble each other by chance. So it is not always safe to recognize an import in an archaeological **context** just because it resembles objects that are known to have been made elsewhere. Much more reliable evidence for trade can be provided if the raw material of which the object is made can be reliably shown to have originated elsewhere. Characterization, or sourcing, refers to those techniques of examination by which characteristic properties of the constituent material may be identified, and so allow the source of that material to be determined. Some of the main methods for sourcing of materials by characterization are described below.

For characterization to work, there must obviously be something about the source of the material that distinguishes its products from those coming from other sources. Of course, sometimes a material is so unusual and distinctive in itself that it can at once be recognized as deriving from a given source. But in practice, there are very few materials for which the different sources can be distinguished by eye. Usually, it is necessary to use scientific techniques which allow a much more precise description of the material. During the past 40 years there have been striking advances in the ability to analyze very small samples with accuracy. A successful characterization, however, does not just depend on analytical precision: sources of some materials (e.g. flint, or some metals) are often very similar and so cannot be distinguished whatever the precision of the testing. For other materials (e.g. obsidian), the sources are all quite different and can be distinguished relatively easily.

An important point to note is that the sourcing of materials by characterization studies depends crucially on our knowledge of the distribution of the raw materials in nature. This comes mainly from the fieldwork of such specialists as geologists. For example, we might have a good knowledge of the exact kinds of rock a whole range of stone axes were made from, but this would not help us unless we could match those particular kinds of rock with their specific occurrences in nature (i.e. the quarries). Thus, good geological mapping is a necessary basis for a sound sourcing study.

Microscopic Examination of Thin Section. Since the middle of the 19th century techniques have existed for cutting a thin section of a sample taken from a stone object or a potsherd to determine the source of the material. It is made thin enough to transmit light and then, by means of petrological examination (studying the rock or mineral structure) with a light microscope, it is usually possible to recognize specific minerals that may be characteristic of a specific source. This part of the work has to be done by someone with petrological training.

This method has been applied to *stone* objects in different parts of the world – to pinpoint the sources of building stones (e.g. the special colored stones used by the ancient Greeks and Romans), monuments (e.g. Olmec heads, Stonehenge), and portable artifacts, such as stone axes (e.g. in Australia and New Guinea). One of the success stories of characterization studies is the analysis of the patterns of trade in stone axes in Neolithic times in Britain, which started before 3000 BC.

With *pottery*, the clay itself may be distinctive, but more often it is the inclusions – particles of minerals or rock fragments – that are characteristic. Sometimes the inclusions are naturally present in the clay. In other cases, the inclusions are deliberately added as "**temper**" to improve drying and firing qualities, and this can complicate characterization studies, since the pottery fabric may then consist of material from two or more separate sources. Fossil constituents, such as diatoms (see Chapter 6) can also be an aid to identification of the source of the raw materials.

The picture of the prehistoric trade in pottery in Britain that such analyses have documented is quite surprising. Until the **thin-section** work of David Peacock and his associates it was simply not realized that pottery bowls and other vessels might be traded over quite long distances (of the order of 100 km (62 miles)) in Neolithic times, before 3000 BC. Now that we know the extent of this exchange of pottery, and that of stone axes discussed above, it is clear that many individuals and settlements were linked by quite far-flung exchange systems.

Trace-Element Analysis. The basic composition of many materials is very consistent. Obsidian, a volcanic glass used in the manufacture of chipped stone tools in the same manner as flint, is a good example of this. The concentration of the main elements of which obsidian is formed (silicon, oxygen, calcium, etc.) is broadly similar whatever the source of the material. However, the *trace elements* (elements present only in very small quantities, measured in just a few parts per million) do vary according to the source, and there are a variety of useful methods for measuring their concentration.

When obsidian from New Britain and the Admiralty Islands in the Pacific was examined using trace-element analysis, it was found that obsidian from one source in New Britain (Talasea) was being traded as far as Fiji to the east and Sabah (northern Borneo) to the west, a distance of 6500 km (4000 miles), at about 3000 years ago. This is surely the widest distribution of any commodity in the global Neolithic record.

Isotopic Analysis. Atoms of the same element, but with different numbers of neutrons in the nucleus, are called isotopes. Most elements occurring in nature consist of a number of isotopes. Particularly when we are investigating metal sources, we can analyze the sources (as well as the artifacts we are investigating) for the presence of different proportions of lead isotopes in order to characterize them. Sometimes more than one source can have the same isotope ratios, but this can usually be resolved by consideration of trace-element data.

Lead isotope analysis is of direct use not only for lead artifacts, but also for those of silver, in which lead is usually present as an impurity. Copper sources also contain at least a trace of lead, and it has been shown by experimentation that a large proportion of that lead passes into the copper metal produced during smelting. Here, then, is a characterization method applicable to lead, silver, and copper artifacts. It has been used successfully for the determination of mineral sources of Classical and medieval silver coins, Bronze Age copper and bronze tools, lead weights, as well as lead in pigments of glasses and glazes, and lead-based white paint.

Oxygen isotope ratios have also proved useful for the characterization of marine shell. The shell of *Spondylus gaederopus* was widely traded in the form of bracelets and decorations during the Neolithic in southeast Europe. Archaeologists needed to know whether it came from the Aegean, or possibly from the Black Sea. As discussed in the section on **deep-sea cores** in Chapter 6, the oxygen isotopic composition of marine shell is dependent on the temperature of the sea where the organism lives. The Black Sea is much colder than the Mediterranean, and analysis confirmed that the shells in question came from the Aegean.

KEY CONCEPTS

Characterization

- Characterization allows archaeologists to discover the source of the material from which an artifact was made

- Successful characterization depends on all the sources of a material being sufficiently different so as to be distinguishable through scientific analysis

- The main methods for sourcing materials by characterization are microscopic thin-section analysis, trace-element analysis, and isotopic analysis

The Study of Distribution

The study of the traded goods themselves, and the identification of their sources by means of characterization, are the most important procedures in the investigation of exchange. But it is the study of distribution, or the movement of goods, that allows us to get to the heart of the matter – how societies operated and how they interrelated socially and economically.

In the absence of written records it is not easy to determine what were the mechanisms of distribution, or what was the nature of the exchange relationship. However, where such records exist, they can be most informative.

Earlier evidence from pre-literate societies – societies without written records – can, however, give some clear idea of ownership and of the managed distribution of goods. For example, clay sealings, used to stopper jars, to secure boxes, and to seal the doors of storehouses, and distinguished by the impression of a carved seal, are widely found in the pre-literate phases in the Near East, and in the Aegean Bronze Age.

In some cases, however, the traded goods themselves were marked by their owner or producer. For instance, the potters who produced storage containers (amphorae) in Roman times used to stamp their name on the rim. The general pattern of export can be made clear by the production of a distribution map.

But a distribution map must be interpreted if we are to understand the processes that lay behind it: and at this point it is useful to consider how the spatial distribution of finds may depend on the exchange mechanism – or in

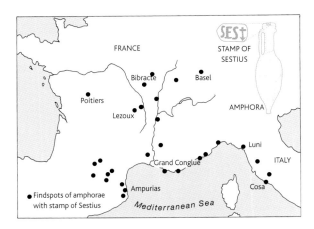

A distribution study. Roman storage containers (amphorae) bearing the stamp of the potter Sestius have been found in northern Italy and widely throughout central and southern France. They and their contents (no doubt wine) were probably made on an estate near Cosa. The distribution map thus indicates the general pattern of the export from the Cosa area of this commodity.

other words, what can the pattern of distribution of finds tell us about the type of exchange that was occurring? The different mechanisms can be summarized as follows:

- "Direct access": the user goes directly to the source of the material, without the intervention of any exchange mechanism
- "Down-the-line" exchange: repeated exchanges of a **reciprocal** nature, so that a commodity travels across successive territories through successive exchanges
- "Freelance (middleman)" trading: traders operate independently and for gain: usually the traders work by bargaining but instead of a fixed marketplace they are travelers who take the goods to the consumer
- "Emissary" trading: the "trader" is a representative of a central organization based in the home country

Not all of these types of transaction can be expected to leave clear and unmistakable indications in the archaeological record, although, as we shall see, down-the-line trading apparently does. And a former port of trade ought to be recognizable if the materials found there come from a wide range of sources, and it is clear that the site was not principally an administrative center, but was specialized in trading activities.

Spatial Analysis of Distribution

Several formal techniques are available for the study of distribution. The first and most obvious technique is naturally that of plotting the distribution map for finds, as in the case of the stamped Roman amphorae mentioned above. Quantitative studies of distributions are also helpful; the size of the dot or some other feature can be used as a simple device to indicate the number of finds on the map. This kind of map can give a good indication of important centers of consumption and of **redistribution**. Direct use of distribution maps, even when aided by quantitative plotting, may not, however, be the best way of studying the data, and more thorough analysis may be useful.

Recently, there has been a considerable focus of interest in "**fall-off analysis**." The quantity of a traded material usually declines as the distance from the source increases. This is not really very surprising, but in some cases (such as when a particular type of trade is happening) there are regularities in the way in which the decrease occurs. If the quantities of material are plotted against the distance from source on a graph, a *fall-off curve* is created. Although different mechanisms of distribution sometimes produce comparable end-results, down-the-line trading, for instance, produces a quite distinctive exponential curve (which on a logarithmic scale is represented by a straight line, as in the example below). *Distribution Studies of Obsidian.*   A good example is the obsidian found at Early Neolithic sites in the Near East. Characterization studies pinpointed two sources in central Anatolia and two in eastern Anatolia. Samples were obtained

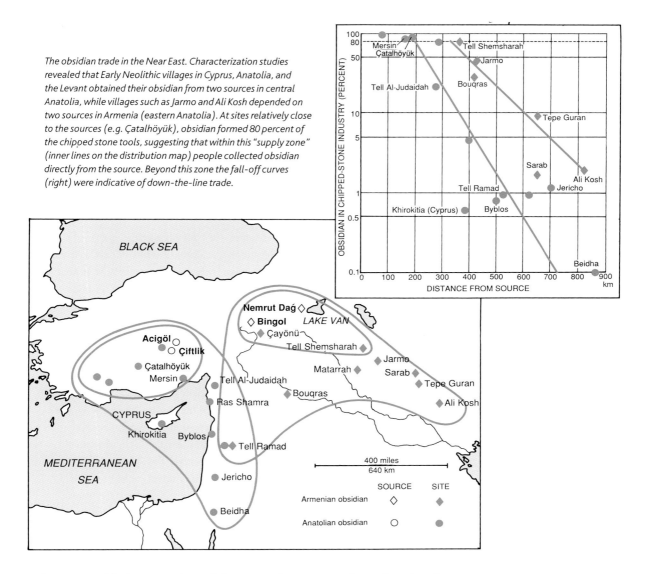

The obsidian trade in the Near East. Characterization studies revealed that Early Neolithic villages in Cyprus, Anatolia, and the Levant obtained their obsidian from two sources in central Anatolia, while villages such as Jarmo and Ali Kosh depended on two sources in Armenia (eastern Anatolia). At sites relatively close to the sources (e.g. Çatalhöyük), obsidian formed 80 percent of the chipped stone tools, suggesting that within this "supply zone" (inner lines on the distribution map) people collected obsidian directly from the source. Beyond this zone the fall-off curves (right) were indicative of down-the-line trade.

from most of the known Early Neolithic sites in the Near East, dating from the 7th and 6th millennia BC. A rather clear picture emerged with the central Anatolian obsidians being traded in the Levant area (down to Palestine), while those of eastern Anatolia were mostly traded down the Zagros Mountain range to sites in Iran such as Ali Kosh.

A quantitative distributional study revealed a pattern of fall-off which indicated down-the-line trade. It could therefore be concluded that obsidian was being handed on down from village settlement to village settlement. Only in the area close to the sources (within 320 km (200 miles) of the sources) – termed the supply zone – was there evidence that people were going direct to the source to

KEY CONCEPTS

Distribution

- Analysis of the spatial distribution of finds can help us to understand the exchange mechanisms that were operating in the past

- The main different exchange mechanisms can be summarized as: direct access; down-the-line; freelance; and emissary trading

- Quantitative studies, for example fall-off analysis, can give a statistical indication of which method was in use

collect their own obsidian. Outside that area – within what has been termed the contact zone – the exponential fall-off indicates a down-the-line system. There is no indication of specialist middleman traders at this time, nor does it seem that there were central places which had a dominant role in the supply of obsidian.

Shipwrecks and Hoards: Trade by Sea and Land.   A different approach to distribution questions is provided by the study of transport. Travel by water was often much safer, quicker, and less expensive than travel by land. The best source of information, both for questions of transport and for the crucial question of what commodity was traded against what, and on which scale, is offered by shipwrecks. From earlier times, for instance, complete cargoes of the Roman amphorae referred to above have been recovered. Our knowledge of marine trade has been greatly extended by George Bass's investigations of two important Bronze Age shipwrecks off the south coast of Turkey, at Cape Gelidonya and Uluburun (see box overleaf).

The terrestrial equivalent of the shipwreck is the trader's cache or **hoard**. When substantial **assemblages** of goods are found in archaeological deposits, it is not easy to be clear about the intentions of those who left them there: some hoards evidently had a votive character, left perhaps as offerings to deities, but those with materials for recycling, such as scrap metal, may well have been buried by itinerant smiths who intended to return and retrieve them.

In such cases, particularly with a well-preserved shipwreck, we come as close as we shall ever do to understanding the nature of distribution.

Exchange and Interaction: The Complete System

The archaeological evidence is rarely sufficient to permit the reconstruction of a complete exchange system. It is extremely difficult, for example, to establish without written records what was traded against what, and which particular values were ascribed to each commodity. Furthermore, exchange in perishable materials will have left little or no trace in the archaeological record. In most cases, all we can hope to do is to fit together the evidence about sources and distribution that can be established archaeologically. A good example of such a project is the work of Jane Pires-Ferreira in Oaxaca, Mexico.

An Exchange System in Ancient Mexico.   Pires-Ferreira studied five materials used in Oaxaca during the Early and Middle Formative periods (1450–500 BC). The first was obsidian, of which some nine sources were identified. These were characterized and the relevant networks were established. Pires-Ferreira then proceeded to consider exchange networks for another material, mother-of-pearl shell, and concluded that two different networks were in operation here, one bringing marine material from the Pacific Coast, the other material from freshwater sources in the rivers draining into the Atlantic.

For her next study she considered the iron ore (magnetite) used to manufacture mirrors in the Formative period. Finally, she was able to bring into consideration two classes of pottery whose area of manufacture (in Oaxaca and in Veracruz, respectively) could be determined stylistically. These results were then fitted together onto a single map, showing some of the commodities that linked regions of Mesoamerica in the Early Formative period into several exchange networks. The picture is evidently incomplete, and it does not offer any notion of

The complete system: Pires-Ferreira's map which shows some of the commodities that linked regions of Early Formative Mesoamerica from the study of five different materials.

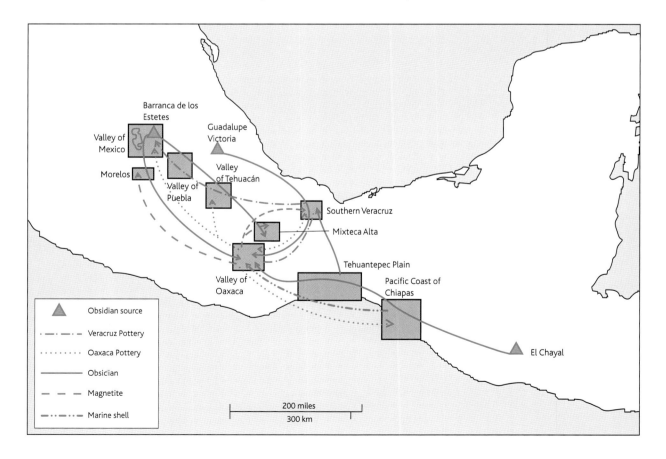

It is difficult for the archaeologist to learn what commodity was traded against what other commodity, and to understand the mechanics of trade. The discovery of the shipwreck of a trading vessel, complete with cargo, is thus of particular value.

In 1982, just such a wreck, dating from close to 1300 BC, was found at Uluburun, near Kas, off the south Turkish coast in 43 m (141 ft) to 60 m (198 ft) of water. It was excavated between 1984 and 1994 by George Bass and Cemal Pulak of the Institute of Nautical Archaeology in Texas.

The ship's cargo contained about 10 tons of copper in the form of over 350 of the so-called "oxhide" ingots (i.e. shaped like an oxhide) already known from wall paintings in Egypt and from finds in Cyprus, Crete, and elsewhere. The copper for these ingots was almost certainly mined on the island of Cyprus (as suggested by lead-isotope analysis, and trace-element analysis). Also of particular importance are nearly a ton of ingots and other objects of tin found on the

seafloor in the remains of the cargo. The source of the tin used in the Mediterranean at this time is not yet clear. It seems evident that at the time of the shipwreck, the vessel was sailing westwards from the east Mediterranean coast, and taking with it tin, from some eastern source, as well as copper from Cyprus.

The pottery included jars of the type known as Canaanite amphorae, because they were made in Palestine or Syria (the Land of Canaan). Most held turpentine-like resin from the terebinth tree, but several contained olives, and another glass beads.

Similar jars have been found in Greece, Egypt, and especially along the Levantine coast.

The exotic goods in the wreck included lengths of a wood resembling ebony, which grew in Africa south of Egypt. Then there were Baltic amber beads, which came originally from northern Europe (and which probably reached the Mediterranean overland). There was also ivory in the form

of elephant and hippopotamus tusks, possibly from the eastern Mediterranean, and ostrich eggshells that probably came from North Africa or Syria. Bronze tools and weapons from the wreck show a mixture of types that include Egyptian, Levantine, and Mycenaean forms. Among other important

(Above) Three striking objects from the wreck: (clockwise, from top) impression of a hematite seal, cut in Mesopotamia c. 1750 BC, with a new scene carved over it some 400 years later; a gold scarab, the first ever found bearing the name of the famous Egyptian queen Nefertiti, who reigned with her consort Akhenaten during the 14th century BC; and gold pendant showing an unknown goddess with a gazelle in each upraised hand.

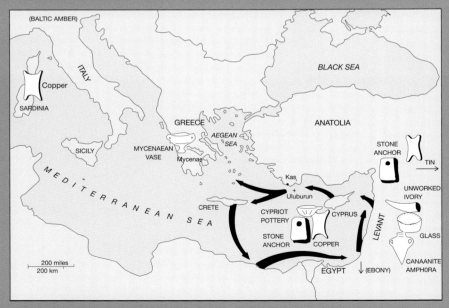

(Left) The map shows the probable route of the ill-fated ship found at Uluburun. Also indicated are likely sources of materials for the various artifacts found on board the wreck.

finds were several cylinder seals of Syrian and Mesopotamian types, ingots of glass (at that time a special and costly material), and a chalice of gold.

This staggering treasure from the seabed gives a glimpse into Bronze Age trade in the Mediterranean. Bass and Pulak consider it likely that the trader started his final voyage on the Levantine coast. His usual circuit probably involved sailing across to Cyprus, then along the Turkish coast, past Kaş and west to Crete, or, more likely, to one of the major Mycenaean sites on the Greek mainland, or even further north, as hinted by the discovery on the wreck of spears and a ceremonial scepter/mace from the Danube region of the Black Sea. Then, profiting from seasonal winds, he would head south across the open sea to the coast of North Africa, east to the mouth of the Nile and Egypt, and, finally, home again to Phoenicia. On this occasion, however, he lost his ship, his cargo, and possibly his life at Uluburun.

Divers working on the oxhide ingots.

the relative values of the traded goods. But it does make excellent use of the available characterization data, and undertakes a preliminary synthesis of the area's exchange networks that is securely based on the archaeological evidence.

Symbolic Exchange and Interaction. Interaction involves the exchange not only of material goods but also of information, which includes ideas, symbols, inventions, aspirations, and values. Modern archaeology has been able to learn quite a lot about material exchanges, using characterization studies and spatial analyses, but it has been more difficult to identify and explain the more symbolic aspects of interaction.

While similar innovations separated by long distances should not be used as indicators of contact in the absence of other evidence, the development of a striking new technology, making its appearance at a number of locations over a limited area, is usually an indication of the flow of information and hence of contact.

In the past archaeologists talked of "diffusion" when they discussed interactions between neighboring areas. The term implied that one area was dominant over the other, and that new technologies passed down to the subordinate area. The opposite approach would be to consider different areas as completely autonomous and independent. But it seems unrealistic to exclude the possibility of significant interactions between different groups.

The solution is to seek ways of analyzing interactions, including their symbolic components, that do not make assumptions about dominance and subordination, core and periphery, but consider different areas as on a more or less equal footing. When discussing such interactions between independent societies of equal status, it has been found useful to speak of **interaction spheres**.

One major interaction sphere is competition. Neighboring areas compete with one another in various ways, judging their own success against that of their neighbors. This often takes a symbolic form in periodic meetings at some major ceremonial centers where representatives of the various areas meet, celebrate ritual, and sometimes compete in games and other enterprises.

Such behavior is seen among hunter-gatherer **bands**, which meet periodically in larger units (at what in Australia are called corroborees). It is seen also in the pilgrimages and rituals of **state** societies, most conspicuously in ancient Greece at the Olympic Games and at other Panhellenic assemblies, when representatives of all the city states would meet.

At such gatherings there is a tendency for one society to try to outdo its neighbors in conspicuous consumption, such as in the expensive public feasts of the Northwest Coast Native Americans, the institution of the potlatch. Very similar in some ways is the erection of magnificent monuments at regional ceremonial centers, each outdoing its neighbor in scale and grandeur. Something similar may have occurred in the ceremonial centers of Maya cities, and the same phenomenon is seen in the magnificent cathedrals in the capital cities of medieval Europe.

Warfare is, of course, an obvious form of competition. But the object of the competition is not necessarily to gain territory – for example, it might also be used to capture prisoners for sacrifice. It operated under well-understood rules, and was as much a form of interaction as the others listed here.

Innovations can also be transmitted – naturally a technical advance made in one area will soon spread to other areas. And there may also be a ceremonial exchange of valuables: although we have emphasized non-material (i.e. symbolic) interactions here, it is certainly the case that between the elites of different societies there may also be a series of material exchanges – the transfer of marriage partners and of valuable gifts. At the same time, large-scale exchanges between participating societies of everyday commodities should not, of course, be overlooked. Economies in some cases became linked together.

Such concepts, where as much emphasis is laid on symbolic aspects as on the physical exchange of material goods, can profitably be used to analyze interactions in most early societies and cultures. Systematic analysis of this kind has, however, so far been rare in archaeology.

STUDY QUESTIONS
• What are some of the differences between unaltered and synthetic materials?
• How is experimental archaeology used in the study of stone tools?
• What is characterization and how does it aid in the study of ancient trade?
• What are the four main types of exchange mechanisms and how do they differ?
• What are some of the common qualities of valuables?
• What is fall-off analysis and how does it relate to the study of distribution?

SUMMARY

- In this chapter we have highlighted some basic questions about early technology, and considered how to find answers to them. First, one must assess whether an object is indeed an artifact, and then of what material – unaltered (primarily stone, wood, fibers) or synthetic (pottery, metals). Ethnography and archaeological context may suggest the function of a tool; but only analysis of its microwear or residues can demonstrate its likely use. Nevertheless, ethnoarchaeology is proving extremely valuable.

- Studies of characterization – i.e. the sources of the raw materials that make up artifacts – have been of enormous importance in archaeology, by shedding light on technological processes, and contact and trade between different regions and cultures. Thin-sections, as well as trace-element analysis and isotopic analysis, have played a major role in these investigations.

- Once an understanding of the whole process of making and using the artifacts has been attained, we can turn to their distribution – the spatial analysis of their places of manufacture and discovery, and hence the exchange and transportation systems which have caused these distribution patterns to come about.

FURTHER READING

Broad surveys of ancient technology, trade, and exchange include:

Cuomo, S. 2007. *Technology and Culture in Greek and Roman Antiquity*, Cambridge University Press: Cambridge.

Earle, T.K. & Ericson, J.E. (eds.). 1977. *Exchange Systems in Prehistory*. Academic Press: New York & London.

Ericson, J.E. & Earle, T.K. (eds.). 1982. *Contexts for Prehistoric Exchange*. Academic Press: New York & London.

Fagan, B.M. (ed.). 2004. *The Seventy Great Inventions of the Ancient World*. Thames & Hudson: London & New York.

Forbes, R.J. (series) *Studies in Ancient Technology*. E.J. Brill: Leiden.

Lambert, J.B. 1997. *Traces of the Past: Unraveling the Secrets of Archaeology through Chemistry*. Helix Books/Addison-Wesley Longman: Reading, Mass.

Nicholson, P. & Shaw, I. (eds.). 2009. *Ancient Egyptian Materials and Technology.* Cambridge University Press: Cambridge.

Scarre, C. & Healy, F. (eds.). 1993. *Trade and Exchange in Prehistoric Europe*. Oxbow Monograph 33: Oxford.

Torrence, R. 2009. *Production and Exchange of Stone Tools: Prehistoric Obsidian in the Aegean*. Cambridge University Press: Cambridge.

What Were They Like?

The bioarchaeology of people

One of archaeology's principal aims is to recreate the lives of the people who produced the archaeological record, and what more direct evidence can there be than the physical remains of past humanity? In the next chapter we will see how **archaeology** can help us to understand the ways in which ancient people thought, but the archaeological record also provides us with much more tangible evidence – complete skeletons, bones, and bone fragments, and sometimes corpses that have been preserved in special circumstances – that enables us to reconstruct the physical attributes of past individuals and groups. If sufficient evidence has survived, archaeologists can determine, for example, the sex and age of an individual, perhaps how that person died, and even their physical appearance. The word "**bioarchaeology**" means the study of human remains from archaeological **sites**.

The Variety of Human Remains

How does the archaeologist know that human remains are present? This is relatively easy where intact bodies, complete skeletons, or skulls are found. Archaeologists can usually reliably identify individual bones and large fragments as human. Even small fragments may include diagnostic features by which human beings can be recognized. In some recent, careful **excavations**, individual hairs have been recovered which can be identified under the microscope as human.

Even where the physical remains of the body have disappeared, evidence may sometimes survive. The best-known examples are the hollows left by the bodies of the people of Pompeii as they disintegrated inside their hardened casing of volcanic ash. Modern plaster casts of these bodies show not only the general physical appearance, hairstyles, clothing, and posture, but even such fine and moving detail as the facial expression at the moment of death.

Nevertheless the vast majority of human remains are in the form of actual skeletons and bone fragments, which yield a wide range of information, as we shall see. Indirect physical evidence about people also comes from ancient art, and provides important evidence about what people looked like.

IDENTIFYING PHYSICAL ATTRIBUTES

Once the presence and abundance of human remains have been established, how can we attempt to reconstruct physical characteristics – sex, age at death, build, appearance, and relationships? A good example of what we can learn from human remains is provided by the Lindow Man bog body (see box overleaf). The techniques for assessing each different physical characteristic are described below.

Bones of the human skeleton, with salient differences between the sexes.

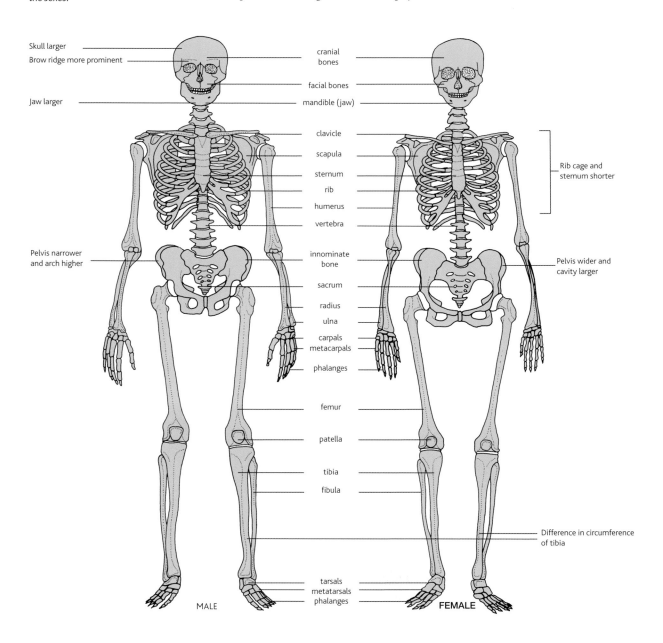

Skull larger

Brow ridge more prominent

Jaw larger

Pelvis narrower and arch higher

cranial bones

facial bones

mandible (jaw)

clavicle

scapula

sternum

rib

humerus

vertebra

innominate bone

sacrum

radius

ulna

carpals

metacarpals

phalanges

femur

patella

tibia

fibula

tarsals
metatarsals
phalanges

Rib cage and sternum shorter

Pelvis wider and cavity larger

Difference in circumference of tibia

MALE

FEMALE

Which Sex?

Where *intact bodies* and *artistic depictions* are concerned, sexing is usually straightforward from the genitalia. If these are not present, secondary characteristics such as breasts and beards and moustaches provide fairly reliable indicators. Where *human skeletons* and *bone remains* without soft tissue are concerned, however, there are lots more sources of evidence. The best indicator of sex is the shape of the pelvis, since this is visibly different in males and females (see diagram, opposite).

Other parts of the skeleton can also be used in sex differentiation. Male bones are generally bigger, longer, more robust, and have more developed muscle markings than those of females, which are slighter.

For *children* it is worth noting that, with the exception of preserved bodies and artistic depictions showing genitalia, their remains cannot be sexed with the same degree of reliability as adults, although analysis of teeth can provide some evidence. When we examine subadult skeletal remains we can often only guess – though the odds of being right are 50:50.

How Long Did They Live?

However confidently some scholars may indicate the exact age at death of particular deceased human beings, it should be stressed that what we can usually establish with any certainty is biological age at death – young, adult, old – rather than any accurate measurement in years and months. The best indicators of age, as with animals, are the *teeth*. We can study the eruption and replacement of the milk teeth; the sequence of eruption of the permanent dentition; and finally the degree of wear, allowing as best one can for the effects of diet and method of food preparation.

A timescale for age at death derived from this kind of dental information in modern people works reasonably well for recent periods, despite much individual variation. But can it be applied to the dentition of our remote ancestors? New work on the microstructure of teeth suggests that old assumptions may not be correct. Tooth enamel grows at a regular, measurable rate, and its microscopic growth lines form ridges that can be counted from epoxy resin replicas of the tooth placed in a scanning electron microscope. In modern populations a new ridge grows approximately each week, and analysis of molar-structure in Neanderthals has shown that they had a very similar rate of growth to that of modern humans.

By measuring tooth growth ridges in fossil specimens, Tim Bromage and Christopher Dean have concluded that previous investigators overestimated the age at death of many early **hominins**. The famous 1–2 million-year-old australopithecine skull from Taung, South Africa, for example, belonged to a child who probably died at just over 3 years of age, not at 5 or 6 as had been believed. This suggests that our earliest ancestors grew up more quickly than we

In 1984, part of a human leg was found by workers at a peat-shredding mill in northwest England. Subsequent investigation of the site at Lindow Moss, Cheshire, where the peat had been cut, revealed the top half of a human body still embedded in the ground. This complete section of peat was removed and later "excavated" in the laboratory by a multi-disciplinary team of scientists. The various studies made of the body have yielded remarkable insights into the life and death of this ancient individual, now dated to the late Iron Age or Roman period – perhaps the 1st century AD.

Despite the missing lower half, it was obvious from the beard, sideburns, and moustache that this was the body of a male. The age of Lindow Man (as he is now called) has been estimated at around the mid-20s. He appears to have been well-built, and probably weighed around 60 kg (132 lb). His height, calculated from the length of his humerus (upper arm bone), was estimated to be between 1.68 and 1.73 m (5 ft 6 in to 5 ft 8 in) – average today, but fairly tall for the period.

Lindow Man wore no clothing apart from an armband of fox fur. His brown/ginger hair and whiskers were cut, and analysis by scanning electron microscopy indicated that their ends had a stepped surface, implying that they had probably been cut by scissors or shears. His manicured fingernails indicate that he did not do any heavy or rough work – he was clearly not a laborer.

The bog acid had removed the enamel from his teeth, but what survived seemed normal and quite healthy – there were no visible cavities.

Lindow Man appears to have had very slight osteoarthritis; and a CAT-scan revealed changes in some vertebrae caused by stresses and strains. Parasite eggs show that he had a relatively high infestation of whipworm and maw worm, but these would have caused him little inconvenience. Overall, therefore, he was fairly healthy.

His blood group was found to be O, like the majority of modern Britons. The food residues in the part of his upper alimentary tract that survived revealed that his last meal had consisted of a griddle cake.

X-rays confirmed that his head had been fractured from behind – they revealed splinters of bone in the vault of the skull. A forensic scientist deduced from

Cleaning the back of Lindow Man in the laboratory. Distilled water is being sprayed to keep the skin moist.

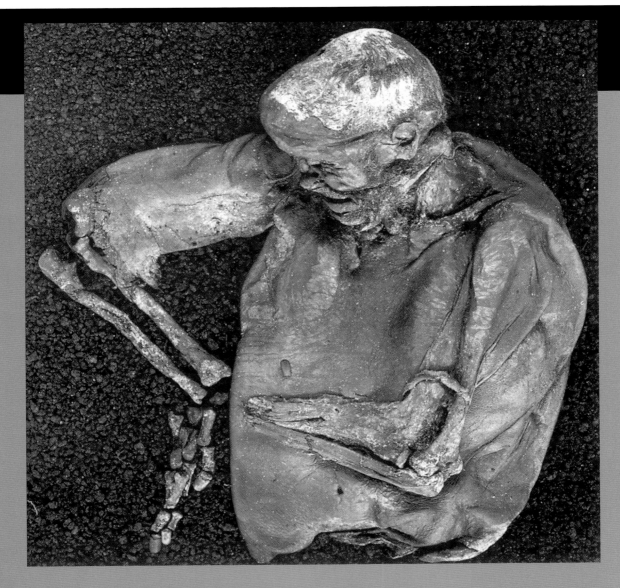

the two lacerated wounds joined together that the skull had been driven in twice by a narrow-bladed weapon. There may also have been a blow (from a knee?) to his back, because X-rays showed a broken rib.

The blows to the head would have rendered him unconscious, if not killed him outright, so that he cannot have felt the subsequent garotting or the knife in his throat. A knotted thong of sinew, 1.5 mm thick, around his throat had broken his neck and strangled him, and his throat had been slit with a short, deep cut at the side of the neck that severed the jugular. Once he had been bled in this way, he was dropped face-down into a pool in the bog.

We do not know why he died – perhaps as a sacrifice, or as an executed criminal – but we have been able to learn a great deal about the life and death of Lindow Man.

Fully conserved remains of Lindow Man photographed in ultraviolet light to enhance the details.

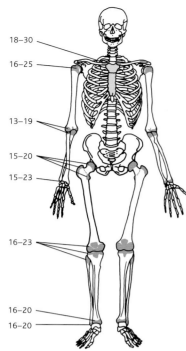

18–30

16–25

13–19

15–20

15–23

16–23

16–20
16–20

Assessing age: the years at which bone ends fuse.

Assessing age: changes in bone structure are visible under the microscope as humans grow older. The circular osteons become more numerous and extend to the edge of the bone.

do, and that their development into maturity was more like that of the modern great apes.

Bones are also used in assessing age. The sequence in which the articulating ends of bones become fused to the shafts gives a timescale that can be applied to the remains of young people. One of the last bones to fuse is the inner end of the clavicle (collar bone) at about 26; after that age, different criteria are needed to age bones.

Skull thickness in immature individuals bears a rough relationship to age – the thicker the skull the older the specimen – and in old age all bones usually get thinner and lighter, although skull bones actually get thicker in about 10 percent of elderly people.

But what if the bone remains are small fragments? The answer lies under the microscope, in *bone microstructure*. As we get older, the architecture of our bones changes in a distinct and measurable way. A young longbone, at about 20, has rings around its circumference, and a relatively small number of circular structures called osteons. With age the rings disappear, and more and smaller osteons appear. By this method, even a fragment can provide an age. Putting a thin section of a femur (thigh bone) under the microscope and studying the stage of development is a technique which, in tests with modern specimens, has achieved accuracy to within 5 years.

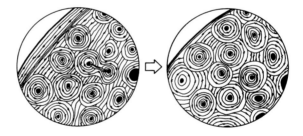

What Did They Look Like?

Once again, it is preserved bodies that provide us with our clearest glimpses of faces. Tollund Man, one of the remarkable Iron Age bog bodies from Denmark, is the best-known prehistoric example. Discoveries at Thebes in Egypt in 1881 and 1898 of two royal burial caches have given us a veritable gallery of mummified pharaohs, their faces still vivid, even if some shrinkage and distortion has taken place.

Thanks to artists from the Upper **Paleolithic** onward, we also have a huge array of portraits. Some of them, such as images painted on mummy cases, are directly associated with the remains of their subject. Others, such as Greek and Roman busts, are accurate likenesses of well-known figures whose remains may be

Faces from the past. (Left) An old man with a wrinkled face is portrayed (with an accompanying duck) on this 1000-year-old Tiwanaku period (AD 500–1100) vase from the island of Pariti in Lake Titicaca, Bolivia. (Below left) Bronze head of the Roman emperor Hadrian (reigned AD 117–138), from the Thames river. (Below right) Head of Tollund Man, the Iron Age bog body from Denmark.

lost for ever. The extraordinary life-size terracotta army found near Xi'an, China, is made up of thousands of different models of soldiers of the 3rd century BC. Even though only the general features of each are represented, they constitute an unprecedented "library" of individuals, as well as providing invaluable information on hairstyles, armor, and weaponry. From later periods we have many life- or death-masks, sometimes used as the basis for life-size funerary effigies or tomb-figures, such as those of European royalty and other notables from medieval times onward.

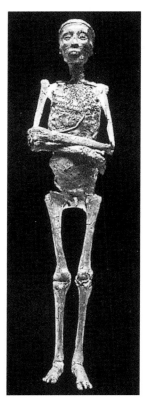

Tutankhamun's mummy was unwrapped in 1923, revealing within the bandages a shrunken body. The young king's original height was estimated by measuring the longbones. Tutankhamun's facial features have recently been reconstructed using CAT-scans of his skull as a base – three teams separately produced very similar reconstructions, one of which is shown here.

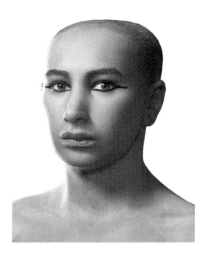

Attempts to reconstruct faces were already being carried out in the 19th century by German anatomists in order to produce likenesses from the skulls of celebrities such as Schiller, Kant, and Bach. But the best-known exponent of the technique in the 20th century was the Russian Mikhail Gerasimov, who worked on specimens ranging from fossil humans to Ivan the Terrible. It is now felt that much of his work represented "inspired interpretation," rather than factual reconstruction. Currently, the process has reached a higher degree of accuracy.

One of the most intriguing recent facial reconstructions has been of the best-preserved Etruscan skeleton known today, that of a noblewoman called Seianti Hanunia Tlesnasa, who died about 2200 years ago in central Italy. Since 1887 her remains have been housed in the British Museum inside a splendid painted terracotta sarcophagus which bears her name engraved on it. The lid of this sarcophagus features a life-size image of the dead woman, reclining on a soft pillow, with a bronze mirror in her jeweled hand. This is perhaps the earliest identifiable portrait in western art, but is it really Seianti?

Anthropologists deduced from the skeleton that the woman was about 1.5 m (4 ft 11 in) tall, and middle-aged at death. Damage and wear on her bones, and the fact that she was almost toothless, had at first suggested old age, but in fact she had incurred severe injuries, most likely a riding accident which had crushed

The terracotta sarcophagus of Seianti Hanunia Tlesnasa, which contained her bones; the lid takes the form of a life-size image of the dead woman – but how accurately did it represent her appearance?

her right hip and knocked out the teeth of her right lower jaw. The bone was damaged where the jaw joins the skull, and opening her mouth wide would have been painful. This prevented her from eating anything but soups and gruels, and from keeping her remaining teeth clean – most of them subsequently fell out. Seianti would also have had painful arthritis and increasing disabilities.

Two of the surviving teeth confirmed, from analysis of the dentine, that she was about 50 when she died. And **radiocarbon dating** of the bones produced a result of 250–150 BC, which proved that the skeleton was genuinely ancient and of the right period. The facial reconstruction showed a middle-aged woman who had grown rather obese. How did it compare with the coffin image?

From the side, there were differences, since the artist had given Seianti a prettier nose, but from the front the resemblances were clearer. The final confirmation came from a computerized technique for matching facial proportions and features – the computer photocomparison of the reconstruction and the portrait left no doubt that this was the same person. The sarcophagus image showed her as some years younger, with fewer chins, and a smaller, more girlish mouth. In other words, the sculptor had made flattering improvements to the portrait of this short, portly, middle-aged woman, but also captured Seianti's likeness extremely well.

The reconstruction made from the skull found in the sarcophagus.

KEY CONCEPTS

Assessing Human Physical Attributes

- *Sex*: intact bodies can be sexed from the genitalia; skeletons and bone remains, much more common in the archaeological record, are sexed from size and form differences between male and female bones. Children are difficult to sex

- *Age*: the main methods of establishing the age of a skeleton are by examinations of the growth patterns of bones and teeth and of bone microstructure

- *Appearance*: it is now possible to make accurate facial reconstructions of ancient individuals, as long as their skull or fragments of it survive

- *Relationships*: examinations of skull shape, hair type, teeth, and blood group can help to establish whether two individuals were related

How Were They Related?

In certain cases it is possible to assess the relationship between two individuals by comparing skull shape or analyzing the hair. There are other methods of achieving the same result, primarily by study of dental morphology. Some dental anomalies (such as enlarged or extra teeth, and especially missing wisdom teeth) run in families.

Blood groups can be determined from soft tissue, bone, and even from tooth dentine up to more than 30,000 years old. Since blood groups are inherited in a simple fashion from parents, different systems – of which the best known is the A-B-O system in which people are divided into those with blood types A, B, O, AB etc. – can sometimes help clarify physical relationships between different bodies. For example, it was suspected that Tutankhamun was somehow related to the unidentified body discovered in Tomb 55 at Thebes in 1907. The shape and diameter of the skulls were very similar, and when X-rays of the two crania were superimposed there was almost complete conformity. Robert Connolly and his colleagues therefore analyzed tissue from the two mummies, which showed that both had blood of group A, subgroup 2 with antigens M and N, a type relatively rare in ancient Egypt. This fact, together with the skeletal similarities, makes it almost certain that the two were closely related. The exact identity of the mysterious Tomb 55 body is still unresolved, however, some scholars holding that it is Tutankhamun's father, Akhenaten, others that it is his possible brother, Smenkhkare.

STUDY QUESTIONS

• What physical attributes can be determined from human remains?
• How can archaeologists determine if two individuals are related?
• How are teeth used to assess how old an individual was at death?
• What are some of the methods archaeologists use to determine what people in the past looked like?

SUMMARY

- The physical remains of past peoples provide direct evidence about their lives. Bioarchaeology is the study of human remains from archaeological sites. Though whole human bodies can be preserved in a variety of ways, including mummification and freezing, the vast majority of human remains recovered by archaeologists are in the form of skeletons and bone fragments.

- An important part of the analysis of human remains is the identification of physical attributes. The gender of skeletal remains, for example, can be determined through observing the shape of the pelvis as well as other bones. Teeth and bones can help establish an individual's relative age at death, namely whether they were young, adult or old. It is even possible to reconstruct what an individual looked like through careful analysis of skull features, or to assess the relationship between two individuals.

FURTHER READING

The following provide an introduction to the study of the physical remains of humans:

Aufderheide, A. C. 2003. *The Scientific Study of Mummies*. Cambridge University Press: Cambridge.

Blau, S. & Ubelaker, D.H. 2008. *Handbook of Forensic Archaeology and Anthropology*. World Archaeological Congress Research Handbooks in Archaeology. Left Coast Press: Walnut Creek.

Brothwell, D. 1986. *The Bog Man and the Archaeology of People*. Harvard University Press: Cambridge, Mass.

Chamberlain, A.T. & Parker Pearson, M. 2004. *Earthly Remains. The History and Science of Preserved Human Bodies*. Oxford University Press: New York.

Donnan, C.B. 2003. *Moche Portrait Vessels from Ancient Peru*. University of Texas Press: Austin.

Larsen, C.S. 2002. *Skeletons in our Closet: Revealing our Past through Bioarchaeology*. Princeton University Press: New York.

Mays, S. 2010. *The Archaeology of Human Bones*. Routledge: London.

Waldron, T. 2001. *Shadows in the Soil: Human Bones and Archaeology*. Tempus: Stroud.

What Did They Think?
Cognitive archaeology

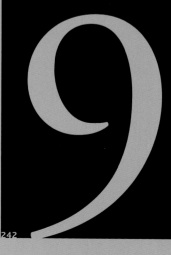

This chapter is about the attributes – both mental and physical – of our ancestors. Strangely, introductory books on **archaeology** generally say little or nothing about the archaeology of people themselves – about their physical characteristics and **evolution**. Yet one of archaeology's principal aims is to recreate the lives of the people who produced the archaeological record, and what more direct evidence can there be than the physical remains of past humanity? In some cases we can tell the age and sex of a person, what they looked like, and how they died; and we can deduce more general facts about groups of people rather than individuals. And, of course, the lives of ancient people were not just about the physical aspects of existence: they had mental abilities, thoughts, and spiritual lives just as we do today.

We will begin this chapter by looking at **cognitive archaeology** – the study of past ways of thought from material remains – which is in many respects one of the newer branches of modern archaeology. Rather than simply "imagining" what people in the past must have thought or believed, it is possible to use the more disciplined techniques of cognitive archaeology to gain insights into these important aspects of the past: we can analyze the concepts people had and the way they thought.

We can, for example, investigate how people went about describing and measuring their world: as we shall see, the system of weights used in the Indus Valley civilization can be understood very well today. We can investigate which material goods people valued most highly, and perhaps viewed as symbols of authority or power. And we can investigate the manner in which people conceived of the supernatural, and how they responded to these conceptions in their ritual practice.

Having examined the ways in which we can try to discover what people were thinking, we will move on to investigate how we can tell what people looked like – what were their physical attributes?

COGNITIVE ARCHAEOLOGY

It is generally agreed today that what most clearly distinguishes the human species from other life forms is our ability to use *symbols*. All intelligent thought and indeed all coherent speech are based on symbols, for words are themselves symbols, where the sound or the written letters stand for and thus represent (or symbolize) an aspect of the real world. Usually, however, meaning is attributed to a particular symbol in an arbitrary way. And that meaning is specific to a particular cultural tradition. It is usually impossible to infer the meaning of a symbol within a given **culture** from the symbolic form of the image or object alone. We have to see how that form is used, and to try to understand its meaning from the context in which it is used. Cognitive archaeology has thus to be very careful about specific contexts of discovery. There are very few symbols that have a universal meaning cross-culturally. It is the **assemblage** that matters, not the individual object in isolation.

Investigating How Human Symbolizing Faculties Evolved

The field of cognitive archaeology is concerned primarily with the cognitive behavior or our own species, *Homo sapiens*. Modern genetic studies suggest that we are all closely related, and that the innate cognitive abilities within any one regional group of our species, along with other behavioral attributes, are much like those in another. For instance all human groups today have the capacity of complex speech, and that is a capacity which in all probability we share with our ancestors of 80,000 to 60,000 years ago, the time of the first human dispersals out of Africa. Clearly, however, as we go back much further in time and consider earlier **hominin** species, whether *Homo habilis* or *Homo erectus*, we are dealing with creatures of more limited cognitive abilities. Their study represents an important subdivision of cognitive archaeology – the development of hominin cognitive abilities up to the emergence of our own species. It presents special problems, since for these earlier ancestors we cannot make the assumption that they had innate cognitive facilities much like our own. That is something which has to be investigated.

Language and Self-Consciousness. Most physical anthropologists agree that modern human abilities have been present since the emergence of *Homo sapiens* some 100,000–40,000 years ago. But as we look earlier, scholars are less united. Some archaeologists and physical anthropologists consider that an effective language may have been developed by *Homo habilis* around 2 million years ago, along with the first chopper tools, but others think that a full language capability developed very much more recently, with the emergence of *Homo sapiens*. This would imply that the tools made by hominins in the Lower and Middle **Paleolithic** periods were produced by beings without true linguistic capacities.

The origins of self-consciousness have been debated by scientists and philosophers, but with few definite conclusions. There is little evidence available to clarify the matter, but one philosopher, John Searle, has argued that there is no sudden transition, but rather a gradual development: he asserted, for example, that his dog Ludwig has a significant degree of self-consciousness.

There are several lines of approach into other aspects of early human abilities. One way that we can try to assess early human cognitive ability is by examining the way stone tools and other **artifacts** were made.

Design in Tool Manufacture.   Whereas the production of simple pebble tools – for instance by *Homo habilis* – may perhaps be considered a simple, habitual act, not unlike a chimpanzee breaking off a stick to poke at an ant hill, the fashioning by *Homo erectus* of so beautiful an object as an Acheulian **hand-axe** seems more advanced.

So far, however, that is just a subjective impression. How do we investigate it further? One way is to measure, by experiment, the amount of time taken in the manufacturing process. A more rigorous quantitative approach, as developed by Glynn Isaac, is to study the range of variation in an assemblage of artifacts. For if the toolmaker has, within his or her **cognitive map**, some enduring notion of what the end-product should be, one finished tool should be much like another. Isaac distinguished a tendency through time to produce an increasingly well-defined variety or assemblage of tool **types**. This implies that each person making tools had a notion of different tool forms, no doubt destined for different functions. Planning and design in tool manufacture thus become relevant to our consideration of the cognitive abilities of early hominins, abilities that moreover distinguish them from higher apes such as the chimpanzee.

The production of a stone tool, a pot, a bronze artifact, or any product of a well-defined manufacturing process involves a complicated and often highly standardized sequence of events. For early periods, such as the Paleolithic, the study of the processes involved in making artifacts offers one of the few insights available into the way cognitive structures underlay complex aspects of human behavior. French prehistorians Claudine Karlin and Michèle Julien analyzed the sequence of events necessary for the production of blades in the Magdalenian period of the French Upper Paleolithic; many other production processes can be investigated along similar lines.

Procurement of Materials and Planning Time.   Another way of investigating the cognitive behavior of early hominins is to consider planning time, defined as the time between the planning of an act and its execution. For instance, if the raw material used to manufacture a stone tool comes from a specific rock outcrop, but the tool itself is produced some distance away (as documented by waste flakes produced in its manufacture), that would seem to indicate some enduring intention or foresight by the person who transported the raw material. Similarly, the transport of natural or finished objects, whether tools, seashells, or attractive fossils, as has been documented, indicates at least a continuing interest in them,

Deliberate burial of the dead: an elderly man buried at Sungir, near Moscow, c. 25,000 years ago, with thousands of ivory beads across his chest and a cap sewn with fox canines.

or the intention of using them, or a sense of "possession." The study of such objects, by the techniques of **characterization** discussed in Chapter 7 and other methods, has now been undertaken in a systematic way.

Deliberate Burial of Human Remains. From the Upper Paleolithic period there are many well-established cases of human burial, where the body or bodies have been deliberately laid to rest within a dug grave, sometimes accompanied by ornaments of personal adornment. Evidence is emerging, however, from even earlier periods. The act of burial itself implies some kind of respect or feeling for the deceased individual, and perhaps some notion of an afterlife (although that point is less easy to demonstrate). The adornment seems to imply the existence of the idea that objects of decoration can enhance the individual's appearance, whether in terms of beauty or prestige or whatever. A good Upper Paleolithic example is the discovery made at Sungir, some 200 km (125 miles) northeast of Moscow and dating from *c.* 25,000 years ago: burials of a man and two children together with mammoth ivory spears, stone tools, ivory daggers, small animal carvings, and thousands of ivory beads.

In assessing such finds, we must be sure to understand the **formation processes** – in particular what may have happened to the burial after it was made. For example, animal skeletons have been discovered alongside human remains in graves. Traditionally this would have been taken as proof that animals were deliberately buried with the humans as part of some ritual act. Now, however, it is thought possible that in certain cases animals scavenging for food found their way into these burials and died accidentally – thus leaving false clues to mislead archaeologists.

Representations. Any object, and any drawing or painting on a surface that can be unhesitatingly recognized as a depiction – that is, a representation of an object in the real world (and not simply a mechanical reproduction of one, as a fossil is) – is a symbol. General questions about representations and depictions for

KEY CONCEPTS

Early Human Symbolizing Faculties

- The development of language and self-consciousness

- Evidence of design in tool manufacture

- Evidence of the procurement of materials and planning

- The deliberate burial of human remains

- Representations and "art"

Piece of red ocher with abstract engravings, from Blombos Cave, South Africa, dating to c. 77,000 years ago.

all time periods are discussed in a later section. For the Paleolithic period, there are two issues of prime importance: evaluating the date (and hence in some cases the authenticity), and confirming the status as a depiction. Although it has long been believed that the earliest depictions are of Upper Paleolithic date and produced by *Homo sapiens*, increasing numbers of earlier examples are forcing us to re-examine this supposition.

So far the earliest well-dated product which might securely be described as "art", or at least as "graphic design" (of however modest a kind) is a piece of red ocher with an incised network pattern, from the Blombos Cave, South Africa, dating to 77,000 years ago. It is believed to be the work of our own species *Homo sapiens*.

We should, however, note the enormous cognitive significance of the act of depiction itself, in all the vividness seen in the art of Chauvet or Lascaux in France, or Altamira in Spain. We do not yet understand very well, however, why such representation was rare in the Pleistocene (Ice Age) period, or what the significance to their creators of the remarkable depiction of animals in the painted caves of France and Spain may have been (see box overleaf).

WORKING WITH SYMBOLS

We are interested in studying *how symbols were used*. Perhaps we cannot fully understand their meaning, if that implies the full meaning they had for the original users. Without going into a profound analysis, we can define "meaning" as "the relationship between symbols." As researchers today we can hope to establish some, but by no means all, of the original relationships between the symbols observed.

In the pages that follow we shall consider cognitive archaeology in terms of five different uses to which symbols are put.

Cave Art

Much has been written about the Ice Age caves of western Europe, decorated with images of animals and with abstract markings. Clustered in specific regions – most notably the Périgord and Pyrenees in southwest France and Cantabria in northern Spain – they span the whole of the Upper Paleolithic, from about 30,000 BC onward. The majority of the art, however, dates to the latter part of the Ice Age, to the Solutrean and especially the Magdalenian period, ending around 10,000 BC.

The cave artists used a great range of techniques, from simple finger tracings and modeling in clay to engravings and bas-relief sculpture, and from hand stencils to paintings using two or three colors. Much of the art is unintelligible – and therefore classified by scholars as "signs" or abstract marks – but of the figures that can be identified, most are animals. Very few humans and virtually no objects were drawn on cave walls. Figures vary greatly

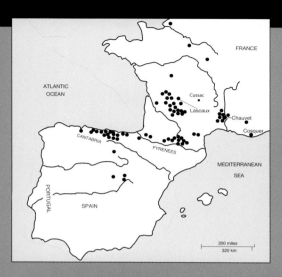

Principal locations of Paleolithic cave art in western Europe.

in size, from tiny to over 5 m (16.5 ft) in length. Some are easily visible and accessible, while others are carefully hidden in recesses of the caves.

The first systematic approach to the study of cave art ("parietal art") was that of the French archaeologist André Leroi-Gourhan, working in the 1960s. Following the lead of Annette Laming-Emperaire, Leroi-Gourhan argued that the pictures formed compositions. Previously they had been seen as random accumulations of

The spectacular paintings of Chauvet Cave (left), southern France, discovered in 1994, depict over 440 animals.

An engraving of a mammoth (above) from Cussac Cave in the Dordogne, France.

individual images, representing simple "hunting magic" or "fertility magic." Leroi-Gourhan studied the positions and associations of the animal figures in each cave. He established that horse and bison are by far the most commonly depicted animals, accounting for about 60 percent of the total, and that they are concentrated on what seem to be the central panels of caves. Other species (e.g. ibex, mammoth, and deer) are located in more peripheral positions, while less commonly drawn animals (e.g. rhinoceroses, felines, and bears) often cluster in the cave depths. Leroi-Gourhan therefore felt sure he had found the "blueprint" for the way each cave had been decorated.

We now know that this scheme is too generalized. Every cave is different, and some have only one figure whereas others (e.g. Lascaux in southwest France) have hundreds. Nevertheless, Leroi-Gourhan's work established that there is a basic thematic unity – profiles of a limited range of animals – and a clearly intentional layout of figures on the walls. Currently, research is exploring how each cave's decoration was adapted to the shape of its walls, and even to the areas in the cave where the human voice resonates most effectively.

New finds continue to be made – an average of one cave per year, including major discoveries in France, such as Cosquer Cave (1991) near Marseilles, whose Ice Age entrance is now drowned beneath the sea, and the spectacular Chauvet Cave (1994) in the Ardèche, with its unique profusion of depictions of rhinoceroses and big cats.

However, in the 1980s and 1990s a series of discoveries also revealed that "cave art" was produced in the open air. Indeed this was probably the most common form of art production in the Ice Age, but the vast majority of it has succumbed to the weathering of many millennia, leaving us with the heavily skewed sample of figures that survived more readily inside caves. Only a dozen sites are known so far, in Spain, Portugal, and France, but they comprise hundreds of figures, mostly pecked into rocks, which by their style and content are clearly Ice Age in date.

Portable Art

Ice Age portable ("mobiliary") art comprises thousands of engravings and carvings on small objects of stone, bone, antler, and ivory. The great majority of identifiable figures are animals, but perhaps the most famous pieces are the so-called "Venus figurines," such as the limestone Venus of Willendorf, from Austria. These depict females of a wide span of ages and types, and are by no means limited to the handful of obese specimens that are often claimed to be characteristic.

Portable art: three bone carvings from the cave of La Garma, northern Spain.

1 A basic step is the *establishment of place* by marking and delimiting territory and the territory of the community, often with the use of symbolic markers and monuments, thereby constructing a perceived landscape, generally with a sacred as well as a secular dimension, a land of memories.

2 A fundamental cognitive step was the development of symbols of *measurement* – as in units of time, length, and weight – which help us organize our relationships with the natural world.

3 Symbols allow us to cope with the future world, as instruments of *planning*. They help us define our intentions more clearly, by making models for some future intended action, for example plans of towns or cities.

4 Symbols are used to regulate and organize *relations between human beings*. Money is a good example of this, and with it the whole notion that some material objects have a higher value than others. Beyond this is a broader category of symbols, such as the badges of rank in an army, that have to do with the exercise of power in a society.

5 Symbols are used to represent and to try to regulate *human relations with the Other World*, the world of the supernatural or the transcendental – which leads on to the archaeology of **religion** and cult.

No doubt there are other kinds of uses for symbols, but this rather simplistic listing will help us in our discussion of how we should set about analyzing them.

Establishing Place: The Location of Memory

One of the fundamental aspects of the cognition of the individual is the establishment of place, often through the establishment of a center, which in a permanent settlement is likely to be the hearth of the home. For a community another significant place is likely to be the burial place of the ancestral dead, whether within the house or at some collective tomb or shrine. For a larger community, whether sedentary or mobile, there may be some communal meeting place, a sacred center for periodic gatherings.

These various **features**, some of them deliberate symbolic constructions, others more functional works which nonetheless are seen to have meaning – the home, the tilled agricultural land, the pasture – together constitute a constructed landscape in which the individual lives. As some archaeologists have pointed out, this landscape structures the experience and the world view of that individual. These observations are just as relevant to small-scale societies as to **state** societies. Many great cities from China to Cambodia and from Sri Lanka to the Maya Lowlands and Peru are laid out on cosmological principles, allowing the ruler to ensure harmony between his subjects and the prevailing sacred and supernatural forces. But the sacred center can be important in smaller societies also, and many of those which appear to have had a corporate structure rather than a powerful central leader, were capable of major public works – the temples of Malta and the megalithic centers of Carnac

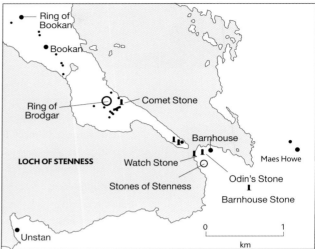

The ceremonial center of Orkney, a ritual landscape in which individuals lived and which in turn shaped their experience and world view. The Ring of Brodgar (left) was one element of a complex and rich sacred landscape (right) which demonstrates that not only large, organized state societies were capable of creating major public works.

and of Orkney are good examples, as well as Stonehenge and Chaco Canyon. Such monuments can also be used to structure time and can operate to facilitate access to the other, sacred world.

But these things operate also at a local level, not only at great centers. So the entire countryside becomes a complex of constructed landscapes, with meaning as well as of practical use. The landscape is composed of places bringing memories, and the history of the community is told with reference to its significant places.

Landscape archaeology thus has a cognitive dimension, which takes it far beyond the preoccupation with productive land-use characteristic of a purely materialist approach: the landscape has social and spiritual meaning as well as utility.

Measuring the World

One aspect of an individual's cognition we can readily reconstruct is the way in which it copes with measurement or quantitative description. The development of units was a fundamental cognitive step. In many cases, they can be recovered archaeologically, especially in the case of units of time, length, and weight.

The measurement of time is implied whenever a calendrical system can be documented. It is implied also when alignment, preserving the direction of the sun (or moon) at one of the major turning points can be documented. That is well known to be the case for the major axis of Stonehenge, the great **Neolithic** monument in England, which is oriented toward the midsummer sunrise. Such

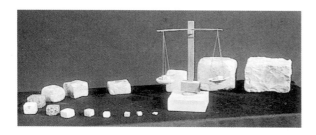

Units of weight: stone cubes from Mohenjodaro, Pakistan, were produced in multiples of 0.836 g (0.03 oz). Scale pans indicate the practical use to which the cubes were put.

is also the case for the stone tomb of Newgrange in Ireland, dating from 3200 BC, whose entrance passage is oriented toward the midwinter sunrise.

The existence of measurements of weight can be demonstrated by the discovery of objects of standard form that prove to be multiples of a recurrent quantity (by weight), which we can assume to be a standard unit. Such finds are made in many early civilizations. Sometimes the observations are reinforced by the discovery of markings on the objects themselves, that accurately record how many times the standard the piece in question weighs. Systems of coinage are invariably graded using measurement by weight, as well as by material (gold, silver etc.), although their purpose is to measure differences in value, discussed in a later section. More directly relevant here are discoveries of actual weights.

An excellent example comes from the **site** of Mohenjodaro, a major city of the Indus Valley civilization around 2500–2000 BC. Attractive and carefully worked cubes of colored stone were found there. They proved to be multiples of what we may recognize as a constant unit of mass (namely 0.836 g, or 0.03 oz), multiplied by integers such as 1 or 4 or 8 up to 64, then 320 and 1600.

It can be argued that this simple discovery indicates:

1 that the society in question had developed a concept equivalent to our own notion of weight or mass;

2 that the use of this concept involved the operation of units of measure;

3 that there was a system of numbering, involving hierarchical numerical categories (e.g. tens and units), in this case apparently based on the fixed ratio of 16:1;

4 that the weight system was used for practical purposes (as the finding of scale pans indicates);

5 that there probably existed a notion of equivalence, on the basis of weight among different materials, and hence, it may follow, a ratio of value between them;

6 that this inferred concept of value may have entailed some form of constant rate of exchange between commodities

Items 5 and 6 are more hypothetical than the others in the list. But it seems a good example of the way that superficially simple discoveries can, when subjected to analysis, yield important information about the concepts and procedures of the communities in question.

Symbols of Organization and Power

Symbols are used for regulating and organizing people as well as the material world. They may simply convey information from one person to another, as with language or, as in the case of archival records, from one point in time to another.

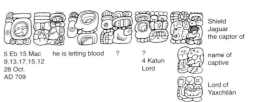

5 Eb 15 Mac
9.13.17.15.12
28 Oct.
AD 709

he is letting blood

?

?
4 Katun
Lord

Shield
Jaguar
the captor of

name of
captive

Lord of
Yaxchilán

she is
letting
blood

name
or titles

Lady
K'abal Xoc

Lady
Batab

Lintel 24 from Yaxchilán showing Shield Jaguar and his wife, Lady K'abal Xoc, during a bloodletting ritual. The glyphs which frame their images give details of their names, the calendar date, and a description of the rite.

But sometimes they are symbols of power, commanding obedience and conformity, for example the giant statues of rulers found in many civilizations.

Power relations are sometimes documented graphically, as in the great statues of the Egyptian pharaohs, or on the splendid **stelae** and reliefs of the Maya. For example Lintel 24 from Yaxchilán shows the ruler ("Shield Jaguar") and his wife during a blood-letting ritual. The glyphs which frame their images give details of their names, the calendar date, and a description of the rite. The images do of course have religious significance, but they also emphasize the role of the ruler and his family in subjecting themselves to this painful ritual for the good of the community. Shield Jaguar holds aloft a flaming torch. He has a magnificent headdress, with feathers at the rear and the shrunken head of a past sacrificial victim tied to the top of his head by a headband. The inscription indicates a date in the Maya Long Count calendar equivalent to October 28, AD 709.

More often, however, power relations are not documented pictorially but have to be inferred from the **association** of prestigious artifacts made, often with beautiful craftsmanship, from exotic materials.

Deducing scales of value: the great worth of the gold from Varna, Bulgaria, is suggested by, among other things, its use to decorate significant parts of the body.

Archaeological evidence on its own can in fact yield evidence of scales of value, as work on the analysis of finds from the late Neolithic cemetery at Varna in Bulgaria, dating from *c.* 4000 BC, has shown. Numerous golden artifacts were discovered in the cemetery, constituting what is the earliest known major find of gold anywhere in the world. But it cannot simply be assumed that the gold is of high value (its relative abundance in the cemetery might imply the opposite).

Three arguments, however, can be used to support the conclusion that the gold here was indeed of great worth:

1 Its use for artifacts with evidently symbolic status: e.g. to decorate the haft of a perforated stone axe which, through its fine work and delicate nature, was clearly not intended for use.

2 Its use for ornaments at particularly significant parts of the body: e.g. for face decorations, for a penis sheath.

3 Its use in simulation: sheet gold was used to cover a stone axe to give the impression of solid gold; such a procedure normally indicates that the material hidden is less valuable than the covering material.

The demonstration that gold objects were highly valued by society at this time in ancient Bulgaria also implies that the individuals with whom the gold finds were associated had a high social status. The importance of burials as sources of evidence for social status and ranking was discussed in Chapter 5. Here we are more interested in the use of grave-goods like the Varna gold-covered axes, and other discoveries, as *symbols of authority and power*. The display of such authority is not very pronounced in a society like that excavated at Varna, but it becomes more blatant the more hierarchical and stratified the society becomes.

The Archaeology of Religion

One leading English dictionary defines religion as: "Action or conduct indicating a belief in, or reverence for, and desire to please, a divine ruling power." Religion thus involves a framework of beliefs, and these relate to supernatural or superhuman beings or forces that go beyond the everyday material world. In other words superhuman beings are conceptualized by humans, and have a place in the shared cognitive map of the world.

One problem that archaeologists face is that these belief systems are not always given expression in **material culture**. And when they are – in what can be termed the **archaeology of cult** – there is the problem that such actions are not always clearly separated from the other actions of everyday life: cult can be embedded within everyday functional activity, and thus difficult to distinguish from it archaeologically.

The first task of the archaeologist is to recognize the evidence of cult for what it is, and not make the old mistake of classifying as religious activity every action in the past that we do not understand.

Recognition of Cult   If we are to distinguish cult from other activities, such as the largely secular ceremonial that may attend a head of state (which can also have very elaborate symbolism), it is important not to lose sight of the transcendent or supernatural object of the cult activity. Religious ritual involves the performance of expressive acts of worship toward the deity or transcendent being. In this there are generally at least four main components (we will see below how these may then help us draw up a list of aspects that are identifiable archaeologically):

• *Focusing of attention* The act of worship both demands and induces a state of heightened awareness or religious excitement in the human celebrant. In communal acts of worship, this invariably requires a range of attention-focusing devices, including the use of a sacred location, architecture (e.g. temples), light, sounds, and smell to ensure that all eyes are directed to the crucial ritual acts.

• *Boundary zone between this world and the next* The focus of ritual activity is the boundary area between this world and the Other World. It is a special and mysterious region with hidden dangers. There are risks of pollution and of failing to comply with the appropriate procedures: ritual washing and cleanliness are therefore emphasized.

• *Presence of the deity* For ritual to be effective, the deity or supernatural force must in some sense be present. It is the divine as well as human attention that needs to be heightened. In most societies, the deity is symbolized by some material form or image: this need be no more than a very simple symbol – for

KEY CONCEPTS
Working With Symbols

The human species is distinguished from other life forms by its use of symbols

Symbols are used by humans for a variety of purposes, some of which can be recognized in the archaeological record:

- The marking of place and the definition of territory

- The construction of systems of measurement

- Design, mapping, and the planning of future actions

- Shaping and reflecting social realities, including identity and power relationships

- Communicating with supernatural powers in the Other World

instance, the outline of a sign or container whose contents are not seen – or it may be a three-dimensional cult image such as a statue.

• *Participation and offering* Worship makes demands on the celebrant. These include not only words and gestures of prayer and respect, but often active participation involving movement, perhaps eating and drinking. Frequently, it involves also the offering of material things to the deity, both by sacrifice and gift.

An excellent example of cult activity visible in the archaeological record is offered by the site of Göbekli Tepe in Turkey (see box overleaf). Another is the great ceremonial center at Chavín de Huantar in north-central Peru, which flourished from 850 to 200 BC. The most immediately obvious feature of the site is its imposing architecture, comprising a complex of stone-faced platforms built in the earliest phase on a U-shaped plan and set apart from living areas at the site. Ritual involving both conspicuous public display and hidden mysteries is implied by the presence of an open circular sunken plaza that could hold 300 participants, and hidden underground passageways, the most important of which led to a narrow chamber dominated by a 4.5 m (14 ft 9 in) high granite shaft know as the Lanzón (Great Image).

The carving on this shaft of a fanged anthropomorphic being, its location in a central chamber facing east along the temple's main axis, and its size and workmanship all suggest that this was the principal cult image of the site.

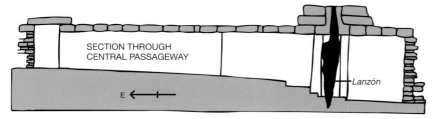

SECTION THROUGH
CENTRAL PASSAGEWAY

E ←

Lanzón

(Left) Perspective and plan views of the early U-shaped platforms at the site, with a section through the central passageway showing the narrow chamber dominated by the Lanzón or Great Image.

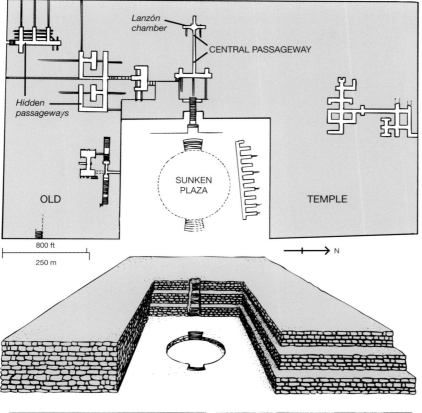

Lanzón
chamber

CENTRAL PASSAGEWAY

Hidden
passageways

OLD

SUNKEN
PLAZA

TEMPLE

800 ft

250 m

N

(Below) Two views of the Lanzón or Great Image (a side view, left, and a rollout drawing, right), depicting a fanged anthropomorphic being.

SOUTH AMERICA
• Chavín de Huantar

Transformation of a masked shaman (far left) into a jaguar (left). These sculptures were displayed on the outer wall of the temple, and hint at drug-induced rituals.

THE WORLD'S OLDEST SANCTUARY

The site of Göbekli Tepe, near the town of Urfa in southeast Turkey, can lay claim to be the world's oldest sanctuary. Dating from between 9000 and 8000 BC, it is a large mound 300 m (1,000 ft) in diameter, containing a series of enclosures, perhaps as many as 20, of which four are under **excavation** by Klaus Schmidt of the German Archaeological Institute in Istanbul. Although radiocarbon dates set it contemporary with the very earliest Neolithic of the Levant, Pre-Pottery Neolithic A, there are no traces of cultivated plants at the site, and the fauna includes only wild species, such as gazelle, wild cattle, wild ass, red deer, and wild pig. The society that built and used the site was effectively one of **hunter-gatherers**. But this was not a settlement site.

The most characteristic feature of Göbekli Tepe are the pillars, arranged to create oval structures including up to 12 such pillars, interconnected by stone benches. Each is a T-shaped monolith of limestone standing several meters high and weighing up to 12 tons. The largest, not yet fully excavated, seems to be 5 m (16 ft) high.

Upon these pillars are carvings in relief of animals — lions, foxes, gazelle, wild boar, wild asses, aurochs, snakes, birds, insects, and spiders. The excavator suggests that the pillars themselves represent stylized humans, the horizontal and vertical elements representing the head and body, for the pillars sometimes show arms and hands in low relief. There are also three-dimensional sculptures of animals, mainly boar, that seem to have been placed on the tops of walls.

These enclosures certainly suggest the practice of ritual, with their special architectural forms, meeting the "focusing of attention" criteria discussed in this chapter. Moreover they are rich in animal symbolism. Klaus Schmidt suggests that funerary rituals were practiced there, which he suggests would account for the very considerable labor involved in the construction of each of the enclosures. But no burials have yet been found: Schmidt predicts that they will be discovered beneath the benches or behind the walls of the enclosures when those areas are excavated. But so far there is no direct evidence. Certainly it seems reasonable to suggest that Göbekli Tepe was a special central place, a ritual focus for the regional population. Contemporary villages are known nearby: Nevali Çori, also excavated by Schmidt, was one such. In it was a small enclosure, likewise containing T-shaped megalithic pillars and life-sized limestone sculptures of humans and animals, which may be regarded as a small sanctuary.

But Göbekli Tepe was much larger and more specialized, lacking the residential

A view from above of one of the enclosures at Göbekli Tepe. Large T-shaped stone pillars are connected by walls and benches.

accommodation of the village. Ritual practice at this special site seems highly likely. As we have seen, funerary ritual is possible, but not yet documented. Nor is there yet evidence of "deities" (in the sense of beings with transcendent powers) – no iconography to suggest supernatural beings. It is possible, of course, that the rituals at the site involved veneration for the ancestors. So it might be premature to speak of "cult" if that is taken to imply the worship of deities.

What is remarkable, however, is that the use of Göbekli Tepe seems to precede the development of farming in this area – although the site lies close to the region where einkorn wheat was first domesticated. It may have been visited seasonally and need not document a sedentary population. But for the archaeologist interested in the origins of farming in this very area, it is a notable and intriguing site.

A wild boar and other animals carved in relief on one of the pillars at Göbekli Tepe.

Moreover, some 200 other finely carved stone sculptures were discovered in and around the temple, the **iconography** of which was dominated by images of caymans, jaguars, eagles, and snakes. A cache of over 500 broken high-quality pots containing food found in an underground gallery may have been offerings (though the excavator believes they were used for storage). There is some evidence for drug-induced rituals and the possibility that canals beneath the site were used for ritual washing and to create roaring sounds to heighten the impact of ceremonies.

The study of Chavín thus demonstrates that a careful archaeological and art historical analysis of different kinds of evidence can produce sound proof of cult activity – even for a site and society concerning which there are no written records whatsoever.

THE IMPACT OF LITERACY

Symbols of depiction provide us with perhaps our most direct insight into the cognition of an individual or a society for pre-literate periods. Among literate communities, however, written words – those deceptively direct symbols used to describe the world – inevitably dominate the evidence. The locations and dates of the world's earliest writing systems are summarized on the map below.

Ancient literature in all its variety, from poems and plays to political statements and early historical writings, provides rich insights into the cognitive world of the great civilizations. But, to use such evidence accurately and effectively, we need to understand something of the social context of the use of writing in different societies.

The very existence of writing implies a major extension of human cognitive processes. Written symbols have proved the most effective system ever devised by humans not only to describe the world around them, but to communicate with and control people, to organize society as a whole, and to pass on to posterity the accumulated knowledge of a society.

Map to show locations of the world's earliest writing systems.

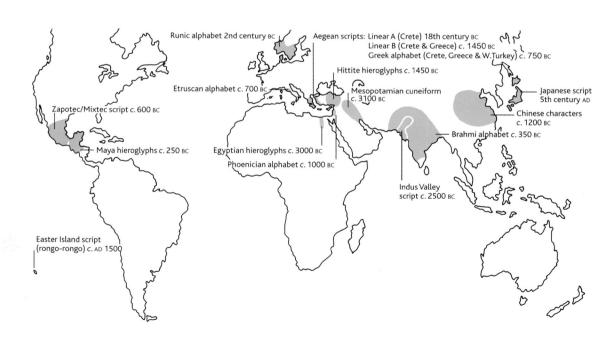

Runic alphabet 2nd century BC

Aegean scripts: Linear A (Crete) 18th century BC
Linear B (Crete & Greece) c. 1450 BC
Greek alphabet (Crete, Greece & W. Turkey) c. 750 BC

Hittite hieroglyphs c. 1450 BC

Etruscan alphabet c. 700 BC

Mesopotamian cuneiform c. 3100 BC

Japanese script 5th century AD

Zapotec/Mixtec script c. 600 BC

Chinese characters c. 1200 BC

Brahmi alphabet c. 350 BC

Maya hieroglyphs c. 250 BC

Egyptian hieroglyphs c. 3000 BC

Phoenician alphabet c. 1000 BC

Indus Valley script c. 2500 BC

Easter Island script (rongo-rongo) c. AD 1500

Literacy in Classical Greece

The importance of literacy is well illustrated by the case of Classical Greece, where literacy was widespread among the population. In several ancient civilizations writing was practiced only by a small segment of the population, notably scribes – for instance in Ancient Egypt or Mesopotamia, and the same was probably true in Mesoamerica. In Greece, however, it is likely that many of the people who had the status of citizens were able to read.

For extended texts, whether works of literature or accounts, the Greeks wrote on papyrus. Examples of such texts have been found at Pompeii and in the very dry conditions of the Faiyum depression in Egypt. For public inscriptions, the Greeks used stone or bronze, although notices that were not of permanent interest were put on display on whitened boards (the simple alphabetic script of the Greeks favored such relatively casual use).

Among the functions of Greek inscriptions carved on stone or bronze were:
- Public decree by the ruling body (council or assembly)
- Award of honors by the ruling body to an individual or group
- Treaty between states
- Letters from a monarch to a city
- List of taxes imposed on tributary states
- Inventories of property and dedications belonging to a deity
- Rules for divination (understanding omens), e.g. from the flight of birds
- Building accounts, records of specifications, contracts, and payments
- Public notices: e.g. list for military service
- Boundary stones and mortgage stones
- Epitaph
- Curse laid on whoever might disturb a particular tomb.

It is clear from this list what an important role writing had within the democratic government of the Greek states.

A better indication of literacy and of the role of writing in Greek daily life is given by the various objects bearing inscriptions, and by comments scrawled on walls (graffiti). One type of object, the *ostrakon*, was a voting ticket in the form of a fragment of pottery with the name of the individual – for (or against) whom the vote was being cast – incised on it. Many have been found in Athens where (by the system of "ostracism") public men could, by a vote of the assembly, be driven into exile.

Other Greek uses of writing on a variety of objects were:
- On coins, to show the issuing authority (city)
- To label individuals shown in scenes on wall paintings and painted vases
- To label prizes awarded in competitions
- To label dedications made to a deity
- To indicate the price of goods

Potsherds (ostraka) inscribed with two famous Greek names: above, Themistokles; below, Perikles.

- To give the signature of the artist or craftsperson
- To indicate jury membership (on a jury ticket)

Many of these simple inscriptions enable us to glimpse aspects of everyday life in Ancient Greece, and even to identify and learn things about individuals. The British Museum has a black-figure drinking cup of *c.* 530 BC, made in Athens and imported to Taranto, Italy, bearing the inscription: "I am Melousa's prize: she won the maiden's carding contest."

It can be seen from this brief summary that writing touched nearly every aspect of Classical Greek life, private as well as public. The cognitive archaeology of ancient Greece thus inevitably draws to a great extent on the insights provided by such literary evidence – as will become apparent, for example, in our discussion of procedures for identifying supernatural beings in art and individual artists. But we should not imagine that cognitive archaeology is thus necessarily dependent on literary sources to generate or test its theories.

Textual evidence is indeed of paramount importance in helping us understand ways of thought among literate societies but, as we saw above for the Paleolithic period, there are in addition purely archaeological sources that may be used to create theories about the thought processes of ancient individuals and peoples, and purely archaeological criteria to judge their validity. Moreover, literary sources may themselves be biased in ways which need to be fully assessed before any attempt can be made to match such sources with evidence from the archaeological record.

STUDY QUESTIONS

- What are symbols and how do they relate to cognitive archaeology?
- What are some of the ways in which humans use symbols?
- How do archaeologists and anthropologists investigate the cognitive abilities of our hominin ancestors?
- What are some of the ways in which the people of the past measured their world?
- How do archaeologists recognize religion or cult in the archaeological record?
- What was the role of writing in Classical Greek daily life?

SUMMARY

- In this chapter we have shown how archaeological evidence can be used to provide insights into the way of thinking of cultures and civilizations long dead.

- Whether it be evidence for measurement, means of organization and power, or cult activity – there are good archaeological procedures for analyzing and testing cognitive hypotheses about the past. An archaeological project may focus on one aspect of the way ancient people thought (for example, in the search for a possible standard unit of measurement), or it may be much broader (for example, the work at Chavín). While textual evidence may be of crucial importance in supporting or helping to assess cognitive claims – as in Mesoamerica or Mesopotamia – cognitive archaeology does not depend on literary sources for its validity.

FURTHER READING

The following provide an introduction to the study of the attitudes and beliefs of ancient humans:

Arsuaga, J.L. 2003. *The Neanderthal's Necklace: In Search of the First Thinkers*. Four Walls Eight Windows: New York.

Aveni, A.F. (ed.). 2008. *People and the Sky: Our Ancestors and the Cosmos*. Thames & Hudson: London & New York.

Bahn, P. & Vertut, J. 1997. *Journey Through the Ice Age*. University of California Press: Berkeley.

Johnson, M. 2010. *Archaeological Theory*. Blackwell: Oxford.

Marshack, A. 1991. *The Roots of Civilization* (2nd ed.). Moyer Bell: New York.

Renfrew, C. & Zubrow E.B.W. (eds.). 1994. *The Ancient Mind: Elements of Cognitive Archaeology*. Cambridge University Press: Cambridge & New York.

Renfrew, C. 2009. *Prehistory: Making of the Human Mind*. Modern Library: New York.

Why Did Things Change?

Explanation in archaeology

To answer the question "why?" is the most difficult task in **archaeology**. We must go beyond simply describing the appearance of things and try to *understand* the pattern of events.

This is the goal motivating many who take up the study of the human past. There is a desire to learn something from a study of what is dead and gone that is relevant for the conduct of our own lives and our societies today. Archaeology, which allows us to study early and remote prehistoric periods as well as the more recent historical ones, is unique among the human sciences in offering a considerable time depth. Thus, if there are patterns to be found among human affairs, the archaeological timescale may reveal them.

There is no agreed and accepted way of setting out to understand the human past. A chapter such as this is therefore bound to be inconclusive, and certain to be controversial. But it is a chapter worth writing and worth thinking about, for it is in this area of inquiry that archaeological research is now most active. The main debates have developed over the past 40 years or so.

Traditional explanations of change in the past focused on the concepts of diffusion and migration – they assumed that changes in one group must have been caused either by the influence or influx of a neighboring and superior group. But in the 1960s the development of the **processual** approach of the New Archaeology exposed the shortcomings of the earlier explanations. It was realized that there was no well-established body of theory to underpin archaeological inquiry (to a large extent this is still true, although there have been many attempts).

The early New Archaeology involved the explicit use of theory and of models, and above all of generalization. However, it was criticized as being too much concerned with ecological aspects of adaptation and with efficiency, and with the purely utilitarian and functional aspects of living (in other words, it was too "functionalist"). Meanwhile, an alternative perspective, inspired by Marxism, was laying more stress on social relations and the exercise of power.

- *Migrationist and Diffusionist*: explanations rely on rather simple ideas of the supposed migrations of peoples, or the often ill-defined spread of ideas

- *Processual*: attempts to provide more general explanations (using, for instance, evolutionary theory), sometimes using law-like formulations, and (more successfully) framing hypotheses and testing deductions from these against the data

- *Postprocessual or Interpretive*: emphasizes the specific context, drawing sometimes on structuralist or neo-Marxist ideas, stressing often the role ("agency") of the individual, and avoiding the generalizations of the processual approach

From the 1970s, in reaction to the processual "functionalists," some archaeologists favored a **structuralist** archaeology, then a post-structuralist, and, finally, a **postprocessual** one. These approaches stressed that the ideas and beliefs of past societies should not be overlooked in archaeological explanation.

Since that time archaeologists have given more systematic attention to the way humans think, how they make and use symbols, and to what may be described as cognitive issues. One approach, today termed "**cognitive archaeology**," seeks to work in the tradition of processual archaeology while stressing social and cognitive aspects.

So far there is no single, widely agreed approach.

MIGRATIONIST AND DIFFUSIONIST EXPLANATIONS

The New Archaeology made the shortcomings of traditional archaeological explanations much more apparent. These shortcomings can be made clearer in an example of the traditional method – the appearance of a new kind of pottery in a given area and period, the pottery being distinguished by shapes not previously recognized and by new decorative motifs. The traditional approach will very properly require a closer definition of this pottery **style** in space and time. The archaeologist will be expected to draw a distribution map of its occurrence, and also to establish its place in the stratigraphic sequence at the **sites** where it occurs. The next step is to assign it to its place within an archaeological **culture**.

Using the traditional approach, it was argued that each archaeological culture is the manifestation in material terms of a specific *people* – that is, a well-defined ethnic group, detectable by the archaeologist by the method just outlined. This is an ethnic classification, but of course the "people," being prehistoric, were given an arbitrary name. Usually, they were named after the place where the pottery was first recognized (e.g. the Mimbres people in the American Southwest), or sometimes after the pottery itself (e.g. the Beaker Folk).

Next it was usual to see if it is possible to think in terms of a folk *migration* to explain the changes observed. Could a convenient homeland for this group of people be located? Careful study of the ceramic **assemblages** in adjoining lands might suggest such a homeland, and perhaps even a migration route.

Alternatively, if the migration argument did not seem to work, a fourth approach was to look for specific features of the cultural assemblage that have *parallels* in more distant lands. If the whole assemblage cannot be attributed to an external source, there may be specific features of it that can. Links may be found with more civilized lands. If such "parallels" can be discovered, the traditionalist would argue that these were the points of origin for the features in our assemblage, and were transmitted to it by a process of cultural *diffusion*. Indeed, before the advent of **radiocarbon dating**, these parallels could also be used to date the pottery finds in our hypothetical example, because the features and traits lying closer to the heartlands of civilization would almost certainly already be dated through comparison with the historical chronology of that civilization.

It would be easy to find many actual examples of such explanations. For instance, in the New World, the very striking developments in architecture and other crafts in Chaco Canyon in New Mexico have been explained by comparisons of precisely this kind with the more "advanced" civilizations of Mexico to the south.

Traditional explanations rest, however, on assumptions that are easily challenged today. First, there is the notion among traditionalists that archaeological "cultures" can somehow represent real entities rather than merely the classificatory terms devised for the convenience of the scholar. Second is the view that ethnic units or "peoples" can be recognized from the archaeological record by equation with these notional cultures. It is in fact clear that ethnic groups do not always stand out clearly in archaeological remains. Third, it is assumed that when resemblances are noted between the cultural assemblages of one area and another, this can be most readily explained as the result of a migration of people. Of course, migrations did indeed occur (see below), but they are not so easy to document archaeologically as has often been supposed.

Finally, there is the principle of explanation through the diffusion of culture. Today, it is felt that this explanation has sometimes been overplayed, and nearly always oversimplified. For although contact between areas, not least through trade, can be of great significance for the developments in each area, the effects of this contact have to be considered in detail: explanation simply in terms of diffusion is not enough.

Nevertheless it is worth emphasizing that migrations did take place in the past, and on rare occasions this can be documented archaeologically. The colonization of the Polynesian islands in the Pacific offers one example. A complex of finds – especially pottery with incised decoration – known as the Lapita culture provides a record of the rapid movement of islanders eastward across a vast uninhabited area, from the northern New Guinea region to as far as Samoa, between 1600 and 1000 BC (see overleaf). Also, innovations are frequently made in one place and adopted in neighboring areas, and it is still perfectly proper to speak of the mechanism as one of diffusion (see illustration of the origins of the Roman alphabet overleaf). A good example of what was first a migrationist explanation, and then became a diffusionist explanation, until it was subsequently rejected, is offered by the case of Great Zimbabwe (see box on p. 271).

THE PROCESSUAL APPROACH

The processual approach attempts to isolate and study the different processes at work within a society, and between societies, placing emphasis on relations with the environment, on subsistence and the economy, on social relations within the society, on the impact which the prevailing ideology and belief system have on these things, and on the effects of the interactions taking place between the different social units.

It is a characteristic of processual explanations that they have usually focused on ecological and social factors whose operation can be analyzed in some detail. Sometimes a systems model is used, looking at the interaction of what may be defined as the subsystems of the culture system. A good early example of a processual explanation, even though today it is regarded as incomplete, is offered by Lewis Binford's explanation for the origins of sedentary society and of a farming economy.

In 1968, Binford published an influential paper, "Post-Pleistocene Adaptations," in which he set out to explain the origins of farming, or food production. Attempts to do this had been made by earlier scholars. But Binford's explanation had one important feature that distinguished it from earlier explanations and made it very much a product of the New Archaeology: its generality. For he was setting out to explain the origins of farming not just in the Near East or the Mediterranean – although he focused on these areas – but worldwide. He drew attention to global events at the end of the last Ice Age (i.e. at the end of the Pleistocene epoch, hence the title of his paper).

Binford centered his explanation on demography: he was concerned with population dynamics within small communities, stressing that once a formerly mobile group becomes sedentary – ceases to move around – its population size will increase markedly. For in a settled village the constraints no longer operate that, in a mobile group, severely limit the number of small children a mother can rear. There is no longer the difficulty, for instance, of carrying small children from place to place. Crucial to the question was the fact that in the Near East some communities (of the Natufian culture around 9000 BC) did indeed become sedentary before they were food-producing. He could see that, once settled, there would be considerable population pressure, in view of the greater number of surviving children. This would lead to increasing use of locally available plant foods such as wild cereals that had hitherto been considered marginal and of little value. From the intensive use of cereals, and the introduction of ways of processing them, would develop the regular cycle of sowing and harvesting, and thus the course of plant-human involvement leading to domestication would be well underway.

But why did these pre-agricultural groups become sedentary in the first place? Binford's view was that rising sea levels at the end of the Pleistocene (caused by the melting of polar ice) had two significant effects. First, they reduced the extent of the coastal plains available to the **hunter-gatherers**. And second, the new habitats created by the rise in sea level offered to human groups much greater access to migratory fish and to migrant fowl. Using these rich resources, rather as the inhabitants of the Northwest Coast of North America have done in more recent times, the hunter-gatherer groups found it possible for the first time to lead a sedentary existence. They were no longer obliged to move.

In some respects Binford's explanation is seen today as rather too simple. Nevertheless, it has many strengths. Although the focus was on the Near East, the same arguments can equally be applied to other parts of the world. Binford avoided migration or diffusion, and analyzed the origins of farming in processual terms.

Marxist Archaeology

Following the upsurge in theoretical discussion that followed the initial impact of the New Archaeology, there has been a reawakening of interest in applying to archaeology some of the implications of the earlier work of Karl Marx. Marx was an extremely influential 19th-century philosopher and political economist. Although his work covered a wide range of issues, he is most famous for his analysis of history in terms of conflicts between social classes.

The key feature of "**Marxist archaeology**," then, is that change within a past society was caused mainly by the *contradictions* that arise between the forces of production and social organization. Characteristically these contradictions emerge as a struggle between classes (if this is a society where distinct social classes have already developed). Emphasis on class struggle and internal differences is a feature of most Marxist explanations: this is a view of the world where change comes about through the resolution of internal dissent. It may be contrasted with the "functionalist" view favored by the early New Archaeology where selective pressures toward greater efficiency are seen to operate, and changes are often viewed as mutually beneficial.

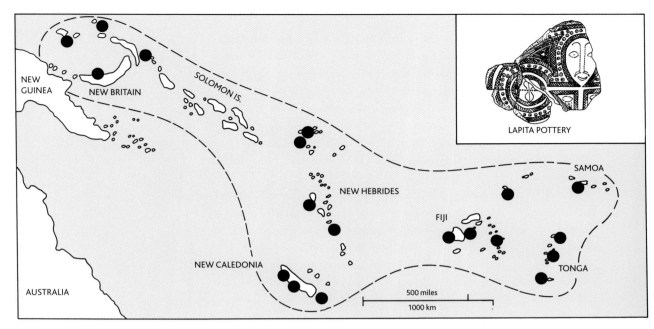

LAPITA POTTERY

Migration: a positive example. The question of first settlement of the Polynesian islands has apparently been resolved by the discovery of the Lapita culture, which is characterized in particular by pottery with incised decoration. Lapita sites providea record of the rapid movement of islanders by boat, eastwards from the northern New Guinea region to as far as Samoa in western Polynesia, between 1600 and 1000 BC.

Diffusion: a positive example. One instance where an innovation in one place is known to have spread widely elsewhere through diffusion is that of the alphabet. Around the 12th century BC, on the Levantine coast, the Phoenicians developed a simplified phonetic script to write their Semitic language. By the early 1st millennium BC, the script had been adapted by the Greeks to write their language. Then the Greek alphabet was modified in Italy, to write Etruscan and Latin, the Roman language. It was through Latin that our own alphabet (known as the Roman alphabet) came to much of Europe, and later the rest of the world.

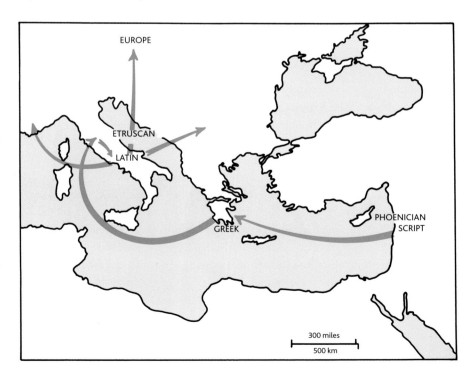

AFRICA

Great
Zimbabwe

The remarkable monument of Great Zimbabwe, near Masvingo in modern Zimbabwe, has been the object of intense speculation ever since this region of Africa was first explored by Europeans in the 19th century. For here was an impressive structure of great sophistication, with beautifully finished stonework.

Early scholars followed the traditional pattern of explanation in ascribing Great Zimbabwe to architects and builders from "more civilized" lands to the north. On a visit to the site by the British explorer Cecil Rhodes, the local Karange chiefs were told that "the Great Master" had come "to see the ancient temple which once upon a time belonged to white men."

This was thus a migrationist view.

Systematic **excavations** were undertaken by Gertrude Caton-Thompson (p. 32), and she concluded her report in 1931: "Examination of all the existing evidence, gathered from every quarter, still can produce not one single item that is not in accordance with the claim of Bantu origin

and medieval date." Despite her carefully documented conclusions, however, other archaeologists continued to follow the typical pattern of diffusionist explanation in speaking of "influences" from "higher centers of culture." Portuguese traders were one favored source of inspiration.

Subsequent research has backed up the conclusions of Gertrude Caton-Thompson. Great Zimbabwe is now seen as the most notable of a larger class of monuments in this area.

Although the site has an earlier history, the construction of a monumental building probably began there in the 13th century AD, and the site reached its climax in the 15th century. Various archaeologists have now been able to give a coherent picture of the economic and social conditions in the area that made this great achievement possible. Significant influence – diffusion – from more "advanced" areas is no longer part of that picture. Today a processual framework of explanation has replaced the diffusionist one.

Carved soapstone bird found in the Great Zimbabwe Eastern Enclosure in 1889, and later sold to Cecil Rhodes.

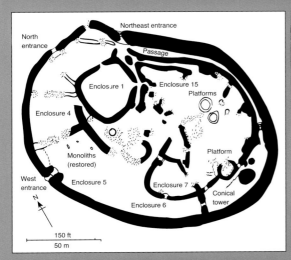

Site plan: Great Zimbabwe, with its series of enclosed areas, platforms, and impressive conical tower.

An aerial view of Great Zimbabwe.

In traditional Marxism the ideology of a society – the whole system of knowledge and belief – is seen as largely determined by the nature of the economic base. This point is disputed by the "neo-Marxists" who regard ideology and economics as interrelated and mutually influential, rather than one as dominant and the other subordinate.

There are many positive features that Marxist analyses share with processual archaeology, but, in comparison with the processual studies of the New Archaeologists, many such Marxist analyses seem rather short on the handling of concrete archaeological data. The gap between theoretical archaeology and field archaeology is not always effectively bridged, and the critics of Marxist archaeology sometimes observe that since Karl Marx laid down the basic principles more than a century ago, all that remains for the Marxist archaeologists to do is to elaborate them: research in the field is superfluous. Despite these differences, processual archaeology and Marxist archaeology have much in common.

Evolutionary Archaeology

Evolutionary archaeology explores the notion that the processes responsible for biological **evolution** (as set out by Charles Darwin) also drive culture change.

Some evolutionary anthropologists see the modern mind as the product of biological evolution, and argue that the only way so complex an entity can have arisen is by natural selection. In particular they argue that the human mind evolved under the selective pressures faced by hunter-gatherers during the Pleistocene (Ice Age) period, and that our minds remain adapted to that way of life.

Evolutionary archaeologists in the United States advocate the application of Darwinian evolutionary theory to the archaeological record. They can justifiably point to long-standing cultural traditions in different parts of the world which reflect the inheritance of cultural traits from generation to generation. It could be argued that they have shown how the transmission of human culture can validly be seen in Darwinian evolutionary terms. However, it is less clear that to analyze culture change in those terms offers fresh insights not already available to archaeologists. Evolutionary archaeology has not yet produced case studies of culture change which explain its processes more coherently or persuasively than other approaches: that is the challenge which it currently faces.

THE FORM OF EXPLANATION: SPECIFIC OR GENERAL

To understand these debates within archaeology it is useful to consider what exactly we mean by "explanation." The different things we try to explain might require different kinds of explanation.

There are two completely opposite forms of explanation. The first approach is specific: it seeks to know more and more of the details surrounding an event. It assumes that if we can establish enough of what led up to the event we hope to explain, then that event itself will become much clearer for us. Such explanation has sometimes been called "historical."

Some historical explanations lay great stress on any insights we can gain into the ideas of the historical people in question, and for that reason are sometimes termed *idealist*. If you want to know why an action was taken it is necessary to get inside the mind of the decision-maker, and thus to know as many of the surrounding details, and as much about their life, as possible.

The second form of explanation, that of the New Archaeology, lays much more stress on generalization. The early New Archaeologists sought for "regularities," for patterns in the data, and turned to the philosophy of science (of the time) for help. Unluckily, perhaps, they turned to the American philosopher Carl Hempel, who argued that all explanations should be framed in terms of *natural laws*. A lawlike statement is a universal statement, meaning that in certain circumstances (and other things being equal) X always implies Y, or that Y varies with X according to a certain definite relationship. Hempel argued that the events we might be seeking to explain could be accounted for by bringing together two things: the detailed circumstances leading up to the event, and the "law" which would allow us to forecast what actually happened.

A few New Archaeologists tried to write archaeology in the form of universal laws. Most, however, saw that it is very difficult to make universal laws about human behavior that are not either very trivial, or untrue. Some archaeologists, such as Kent Flannery, saw that when Hempel's approach was applied to archaeology, it produced only "Mickey Mouse laws" of little conceivable value. Flannery's favorite example was: "as the population of a site increases, the number of storage pits will go up."

One of the positive contributions of the New Archaeology, however, was in fact to follow the scientific convention of making specific and explicit, as far as is possible, the assumptions on which an argument rests. It makes very good sense to formulate a hypothesis, establish by **deduction** what would follow from it if it were true, and then to see if these consequences are in fact found in the archaeological record by testing the hypothesis against fresh data. Processual archaeologists argued that it is this willingness to test our beliefs and assumptions against real data that separates a scientific approach from mere uncontrolled speculation.

EXPLANATION: ONE CAUSE OR SEVERAL?

As soon as we start to address the really big questions in archaeology, explanation becomes a very complicated matter: many of the big questions refer not to a single event, but to a class of events.

One of the biggest questions, for example, is the development of urbanization and the emergence of **state** societies. This process apparently happened in different parts of the world independently. Each case was, in a sense, no doubt unique. But each was also a specific instance of a more general process. In just the same way, a biologist can discuss (as Darwin did) the process by which the different species emerged without denying the uniqueness of each species, or the uniqueness of each individual within a species.

If we focus now on the origins of urbanization and the state as an example, we shall see that this is a field where many different explanations have been offered. Broadly speaking, we can distinguish between explanations that concentrate largely on one cause (**monocausal explanations**) and those that consider a number of factors (**multivariate explanations**).

Monocausal Explanations: The Origins of the State

If we look at different monocausal explanations in turn, we shall find that some of them are in their way very plausible. Often, however, one explanation works more effectively than another when applied to a particular area – to the emergence of the state in Mesopotamia, for instance, or in Egypt, but not necessarily in Mexico or in the Indus Valley. Each of the following examples today seems incomplete. Yet each makes a point that remains valid.

The Hydraulic Hypothesis.   The historian Karl Wittfogel, writing in the 1950s, explained the origin of the great civilizations in terms of the large-scale irrigation of the alluvial plains of the great rivers. It was, he suggested, this alone that brought about the fertility and the high yields, which led to the considerable density of population in the early civilizations, and hence to the possibility of urbanism. At the same time, however, irrigation required effective management – a group of people in authority who would control and organize the labor needed to dig and maintain irrigation ditches, etc. So irrigation and "hydraulic organization" had to go together, and from these, Wittfogel concluded, emerged a system of differentiated leadership, greater productivity and wealth, and so on.

Wittfogel categorized the system of government characteristic of those civilizations founded on irrigation agriculture as one of "oriental despotism." Among the civilizations to which this line of thinking has been applied are:
- Mesopotamia: the Sumerian civilization from *c.* 3000 BC and its successors
- Ancient Egypt: the Valley of the Nile from *c.* 3000 BC
- India/Pakistan: the Indus Valley civilization from *c.* 2500 BC
- China: the Shang civilization, *c.* 1500 BC, and its successors

Internal Conflict.   In the late 1960s the Russian historian Igor Diakonoff developed a different explanation for state origins. In his model, the state is seen as an organization that imposes order on class conflict, which itself arises from increased wealth. Internal differentiation within the society is here seen as a major causative element, from which other consequences follow.

Warfare.   Warfare between adjacent groups is increasingly seen as an agent of change. While in some cases there were cyclical conflicts with little long-term effect, in others the result was conquest and the formation of larger, inclusive state societies. Kent Flannery has recently emphasized the historically documented role of individual military leaders in the initial formation of state societies (an example of the "agency" of the individual, see below).

Population Growth.   An explanation much favored by many archaeologists focuses on the question of population growth. The 18th-century English scholar Thomas Malthus argued that human population tends to grow to the limit permitted by the food supply. When the limit or "carrying capacity" is reached, further population increase leads to food shortage, and this in turn leads to increased death rate and lower fertility (and in some cases to armed conflict). That sets a firm ceiling on population.

population growth → food shortage → increased death rate & lower fertility

Esther Boserup, in her influential book *The Conditions of Agricultural Growth* (1965), effectively reversed the position of Malthus. He had viewed food supply as essentially limited. She argued that agriculture will intensify – farmers will produce more food from the same area of land – if population increases. In other words, by shortening the periods during which land is left to lie fallow, or by introducing the plow, or irrigation, farmers can increase their productivity. Population growth can then be sustained to new levels.

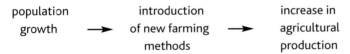

population growth → introduction of new farming methods → increase in agricultural production

So increase of population leads to intensification of agriculture, and to the need for greater administrative efficiencies and economies of scale, including the development of craft specialization. People work harder because they have to, and the society is more productive. There are larger units of population, and consequent changes in the settlement pattern. As numbers increase, any decision-making machinery will need to develop a hierarchy. Centralization ensues, and a centralized state is the logical outcome.

Environmental Circumscription.   A different approach, although one that uses some of the variables already indicated, is offered by Robert Carneiro. Taking as his example the formation of state society in Peru, he developed an explanation that laid stress on the constraints ("circumscription") imposed by the environment, and on the role of warfare. Population increase is again an important component of his model, but the model is put together in a different way, and the development of strong leadership in time of war is one of the key factors.

External Trade. The importance of trading links with communities outside the homeland area has been stressed by several archaeologists seeking explanations for the formation of the state. One of the most elaborate of these is the model put forward by the American archaeologist William Rathje for the emergence of state societies in the Maya Lowlands. He argued that in lowland areas lacking basic raw materials there will be pressure for the development of more integrated and highly organized communities able to ensure the regular supply of those materials. He used this hypothesis to explain the rise of the Classic Maya civilization in the lowland rainforest.

Multivariate Explanations: The Classic Maya Collapse

All the preceding explanations for the origins of the state primarily emphasize one chief variable, a principal strand in the explanation, even though there are several strands involved. In reality, when there are so many factors at work, there is something rather too simplified about such monocausal explanations. It is necessary somehow to be able to deal with several factors at once: that is why such explanations are termed multivariate. Of course, none of the explanations summarized above is so naive as to be truly monocausal: each involves a number of factors. But these factors are not systematically integrated. Several scholars have therefore sought for ways of coping with a large number of variables that simultaneously vary.

One example of a multivariate explanation has been developed for the collapse of Classic Maya society in the 9th century AD (see box overleaf).

POSTPROCESSUAL OR INTERPRETIVE EXPLANATION

After the mid-1970s, the early New Archaeology we have termed here functional-processual archaeology came under criticism from several quarters. For example, early on it was criticized by Bruce Trigger in his book *Time and Tradition* (1978), who found the approach which sought to formulate explanatory laws too constraining. He preferred the broadly descriptive approach of the traditional historian. It was also criticized by Kent Flannery, who was scornful of the trivial nature of some of the so-called laws proposed and felt that more attention should be focused on the ideological and symbolic aspects of societies. Ian Hodder, likewise, felt that archaeology's closest links were with history, and wanted to see the role of the individual in history more fully recognized.

Hodder also very validly stressed what he called "the active role of material culture," emphasizing that the **artifacts** and the material world we construct are not simply the reflections of our social reality that become embodied in the material record. On the contrary, material culture and actual objects are a large part of what makes society work: wealth, for instance, is what spurs many to work in a modern society. Hodder goes on to assert that material culture is "meaningfully constituted," or in other words that it is the result of deliberate actions by individuals whose thoughts and actions should not be overlooked.

Discussions of these issues led some archaeologists in Britain and in the United States to create the postprocessual archaeology of the 1990s, overcoming some of what they saw as the limitations of processual archaeology (and indeed much of traditional Marxist archaeology also). These debates are now largely over, but the result is a series of interesting approaches which together will shape the interpretive archaeologies of the early 21st century, operating alongside the continuing processual or **cognitive-processual** tradition.

Structuralist Approaches

Several archaeologists have been influenced by the structuralist ideas of the French anthropologist Claude Lévi-Strauss, and by the advances in linguistics of the American Noam Chomsky. Structuralist archaeologists stress that human actions are guided by beliefs and symbolic concepts, and that the proper object of study is the structures of thought – the ideas – in the minds of human actors who made the artifacts and created the archaeological record. These archaeologists argue that there are recurrent patterns in human thought in different cultures, many of which can be seen in such polar opposites as: cooked/raw; left/right; dirty/clean; man/woman, etc. Moreover, they argue that thought categories seen in one sphere of life will be seen also in other spheres, so that, for example, a preoccupation with boundaries in the field of social relations is likely to be detectable in other areas such as "boundaries" visible in pottery decoration.

Critical Theory

Critical Theory is the term given to the approach developed by the so-called "Frankfurt School" of German social thinkers, which came to prominence in the 1970s. This stresses that any claims to seek "objective" knowledge are illusory. By their interpretive approach these scholars seek a more enlightened view, which will break out of the limitations of existing systems of thought. They see research workers (including archaeologists) who claim to be dealing in a scientific way with social matters as tacitly supporting the "ideology of control" by which domination is exercised in modern society.

This overtly political critique has serious implications for archaeology. For the philosophers of this school stress that there is no such thing as an objective fact. Facts only have meaning in relation to a view of the world, and in relation to theory. Followers of this school are critical of the criterion of testing as used by processual archaeologists, seeing this procedure as merely the importing

THE CLASSIC MAYA COLLAPSE

Chichén Itzá
MEXICO
Southern
Maya Lowlands

Contrary to widespread belief, Maya civilization did not suffer a single, sudden, and total collapse. When the Spaniards reached northern Yucatán in the early 16th century they found dense populations of Maya-speaking people living in hundreds of local polities. Some paramount rulers boasted as many as 60,000 subjects. Temples and palaces dominated substantial towns. Priests consulted books of prophecy and divination which, along with complex calendars, regulated a cycle of annual rituals.

Preclassic to Classic Maya

Archaeologists now know that cycles of collapse and recovery were commonplace in Maya society for 1500 years. The earliest "big" collapse occurred in the Mirador Basin of northern Guatemala, where Nakbé, El Mirador, Tintal, and other huge centers thrived in the Middle and Late Preclassic. By around AD 150 this region was largely abandoned (and never repopulated) and there is evidence that ecosystems there and elsewhere were increasingly degraded. The Classic period (AD 250–900) Southern Maya Lowlands also saw many local collapses, as Maya capitals and their dynastic lines waxed and waned, and a final collapse in the 10th century.

Collapse in the Southern Lowlands

The final collapse of Classic Maya society in the Southern Lowlands has long been the most difficult to explain because of its scale and because there was no recovery in that region. In AD 750 this vast area supported a population of at least several million people divided among 40–50 major kingdoms. But eight centuries later, when Europeans first traversed the region, it was almost deserted. Explorers in the 19th century reported a landscape with imposing ruins overgrown by forest, creating romanticized impressions of a catastrophic collapse. By the beginning of the 20th century scholars could decipher dates carved on Maya monuments. These suggested a steady growth of dynasties and kingdoms beginning in the 3rd century AD, peak activity around AD 790, and then a precipitous decline in monument building over the next 120 years that signaled the collapse of centralized rulership.

In the absence of a systematic archaeological record and independent chronological information it was presumed that each Classic political system and population suffered a catastrophic collapse in one or two generations.

We now know that the collapse process was more complicated and protracted than this old model suggests. Most scholars agree that the decline began at least as early as AD 760, when centers such as Dos Pilas and Aguateca in the western Petexbatún region were abandoned during well-documented cycles of destructive warfare. Centers elsewhere continued to erect monuments for some time, but by about AD 909 the old epigraphic traditions had disappeared. Royal building projects ceased – sometimes very suddenly – and no more royal burials were interred. Although some polities and capitals collapsed abruptly and with clear signs of violence, others were abandoned more gradually (and apparently peacefully). If our perspective is the whole Southern Lowlands, the disintegration of centralized political institutions thus occurred over a period of roughly 150 years (some imposing centers, such as Lamanai and Cobá, somehow survived these troubles). What happened to the people is a more complex and controversial issue. Many regions do appear to have suffered abrupt demographic declines, but others did not. At Copán, for example, elite activity continued until about AD 1000, and the population dwindled away over some four centuries. So protracted and varied was the demise of the southern Classic Maya tradition that some archaeologists reject the word "collapse" to describe it.

Temple I at Tikal, Guatemala, built around AD 740–750. Tikal was one of the great Maya centers, but was almost completely deserted after AD 950.

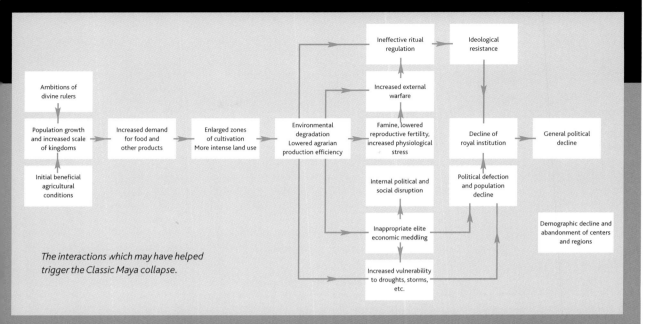

The interactions which may have helped trigger the Classic Maya collapse.

Explaining the Collapse

Any explanation of the collapse must account for all this complexity, and the best approach is to determine what happened to particular capitals or polities before making broad generalizations. Our efforts to explain the Classic collapse are also hindered by our ignorance (or disagreements) concerning Maya agricultural strategies, how people asserted claims to resources, and the details of social, political, and economic institutions. Nevertheless, archaeologists have discarded or demoted some influential earlier explanations, such as the idea that oppressive demands for labor caused peasants to rebel against their rulers.

Most archaeologists do agree that no single cause can explain what happened. Instead, a set of interlocked stresses such as overpopulation, deterioration of the agricultural landscape, famine, disease, warfare, internal social unrest, climate change, and ideological fatigue increasingly afflicted the Late Classic Maya (see diagram). None of these stresses was new, and earlier Maya kingdoms had survived them. The Late Classic Maya, however, were more

numerous and contentious than ever, and had inherited an unusually fragile ecosystem shaped and degraded by centuries of human use. Populations peaked in the 8th century, and over-shot the capacity of the agricultural landscape. The whole shaky edifice of Classic society came down, although it was more of a slump than a crash.

Some causes were certainly more important than others. Most recently, paleoclimatologists have postulated a "megadrought" that afflicted much of the northern hemisphere between c. AD 800 and 1000. Some believe this episode was the single most important trigger of the collapse. Others disagree because the paleoclimatic data are inconsistent, and because the northern Maya, who lived in the driest part of the Lowlands, thrived during this interval – especially at Chichén Itzá. Episodes of drought affected the southern Maya throughout their history, and protracted droughts in the 8th and 9th centuries might have affected food production on an increasingly damaged and vulnerable landscape.

Although materialist stresses were probably most important, there were also

social and ideological components to the collapse. Warfare intensified, and there are signs at some centers of internal unrest. Evidence from Cancuén and other centers reveals the violent elimination of whole royal families, although it is not always clear who the perpetrators were. The ancient Maya were also adaptively constrained by their own ideology, particularly their obsessive focus on maize not just as a food, but as an almost mystical substance. Kingship, the central institution of Maya political life, stressed the supernatural potency of rulers. Kings projected themselves as the great guarantors of prosperity and stability, and manifestly were unable to deliver on these promises during the critical 8th and 9th centuries. Many things about the collapse were gradual, but the rejection of kingship and its symbolic correlates – royal monuments, art, burials, palaces, inscriptions – appears to have been everywhere abrupt. Even where Maya populations survived for centuries they did not revive the old royal ways of Classic times. The Postclassic rulers of the northern Maya adopted different strategies of dynastic presentation.

into archaeology and history of "positivistic" approaches from the sciences. They call into question most of the procedures of reasoning by which archaeology has operated.

The processualists' response to these ideas is to point out that to follow them seems to imply that one person's view of the past is as good as another's (so-called "relativism"), without any hope of choosing systematically between them. This would open the way to the "fringe" or "alternative" archaeologies discussed in Chapter 11, where explanations can be offered in terms of flying saucers, or extraterrestrial forces or any fantasies which the human mind may conjure up. It is not entirely clear how the Critical Theorists can answer this criticism.

Neo-Marxist Thought

Neo-Marxist thought places a much greater emphasis on the significance of ideology in shaping change in societies than does traditional Marxism (which treats ideology as subordinate to economy).

One example of a neo-Marxist approach is offered by the work of Mark Leone at Annapolis in Maryland, as part of a research project concerned with establishing a deeper historical identity for the area. His example is the 18th-century garden of William Paca, a wealthy landowner: the garden has been studied archaeologically and has now been reconstructed.

Leone examines the Annapolis garden in detail, and emphasizes the contradiction represented between a slave-owning society and one proclaiming independence in order to promote individual liberty, a contradiction seen also in Paca's life. "To mask this contradiction," Leone writes, "his position of power was placed in law and in nature. This was done both in practicing law and in gardening."

This neo-Marxist outlook has its echo in the emerging local archaeologies of some countries in the developing world, where there is an understandable desire to construct a history (and an archaeology) that lays stress on the local population and its achievements before the colonial era.

COGNITIVE ARCHAEOLOGY

During the 1980s and 1990s a new perspective emerged, which transcends some of the limitations of functional-processual archaeology of the 1970s. This new synthesis, known as **cognitive archaeology** (or "cognitive-processual" archaeology), while willingly learning from any suitable developments in postprocessual archaeology, remains in the mainstream of processual archaeology. It still wishes to explain rather than merely describe. It also still emphasizes the role of generalization within its theoretical structure, and stresses the importance not only of formulating hypotheses but of testing them against the data. It rejects the total relativism that seems to be the end point of Critical Theory, and it is suspicious of structuralist (and other) archaeologists who claim privileged insight into "meaning" in ancient societies, or proclaim "universal principles of meaning."

Cognitive-processual archaeology differs from its functional-processual predecessor in several ways:

1 It seeks actively to incorporate information about the cognitive and symbolic aspects of early societies into its formulations (see below).

2 It recognizes that ideology is an active force within societies and must be given a role in many explanations, as neo-Marxist archaeologists have argued, and that ideology acts on the minds of individuals.

3 Material culture is seen as an active factor in constituting the world in which we live. Individuals and societies construct their own social reality, and material culture has an integral place within that construction, as effectively argued by Ian Hodder and his colleagues.

4 The role of internal conflict within societies is a matter to be more fully considered, as Marxist archaeologists have always emphasized.

5 The rather limited view of historical explanation being entirely related to the human individual should be revised.

6 It can take account of the creative role of the individual without relying on intuition or becoming extremely subjective.

7 "Facts" can no longer be viewed as having an objective existence independent of theory.

This last point needs further discussion. Philosophers of science have long contrasted two approaches to the evaluation of the truth of a statement. One approach evaluates the statement by comparing it with relevant facts, to which, if true, it should correspond. The other approach evaluates the statement by judging whether or not it is consistent with the other statements that we believe to be true within our framework of beliefs. Although it might be expected that the scientist would follow the first of these two procedures, in practice any assessment is based on a combination of the two. For it is accepted that facts have to be based on observations, and observations themselves cannot be made without using some framework of inference, which itself depends on theories about the world. It is more appropriate to think of facts modifying theory, yet of theory being used in the determination of facts.

Cognitive-processual archaeologists, like their functional-processual predecessors, believe that theories must be tested against facts. They reject the relativism of the Critical Theory and postprocessual archaeology of the 1990s. They do, however, accept that the relationship between fact and theory is more complicated than some philosophers of science 40 years ago recognized. Cognitive-processual archaeology at present appears to be exploring two main directions: investigation of the role of symbols within processes of change, and exploration of the structure of transformations.

Symbol and Interaction

The point has already been made that the early New Archaeology aspired to investigate social structures. But it was slow to explore symbolic aspects of culture, which is why cognitive-processual archaeology is a recent development.

The role of religious ritual within society has been investigated in a new way over the past 30 years by the cultural anthropologist Roy Rappaport. Instead of seeking to immerse himself in the agricultural society in New Guinea under study, becoming totally familiar with the meanings of its symbolic forms, he followed instead a strategy of distancing himself – of looking at the society from the outside, at what it actually does (not what it says it does) in its ritual behavior. This position is a convenient one for the archaeologist who is always outside the society under study, and unable to discuss issues of meaning with its participants. Rappaport has studied the way ritual is used within society and his focus is on the functioning of symbols rather than on their original meaning.

His work influenced Kent Flannery, one of the few of the original generation of New Archaeologists to concern himself in detail with symbolic questions. The book written by Joyce Marcus and Kent Flannery, *Zapotec Civilization* (1996), is one of those rare archaeological studies where symbolic and cognitive questions are integrated with subsistence, economic, and social ones to form an integrated view of society.

Quite clearly **religion** and other ideologies such as modern Communism have brought about great changes, not just in the way societies think but in the way they act and behave – and this will leave its mark in the archaeological record. The whole field of official symbolism, and of religious symbolism within it, is now the focus of archaeological research in several parts of the world.

Postprocessual archaeology has not shown itself adept at explaining classes of events or general processes, since the focus in postprocessual thought is upon the specific conditions of the context in question, and the validity of wider or cross-cultural generalizations is not accepted. Cognitive-processual archaeology on the other hand is very willing to generalize, and indeed to integrate the individual into the analysis as an active agent.

Two recent works in the mainstream processual tradition exemplify well the emphasis that is now placed upon the cognitive dimension. Timothy Earle in *How Chiefs Come to Power* devotes successive chapters to economic power, military power, and ideology as a source of power, utilizing three widely separated case studies situated in Denmark, Hawaii, and the Andes.

And, likewise treating the subject within a comparative perspective, Richard Blanton has examined the sources of power in early states, contrasting the "cognitive-symbolic base of power" with what he terms the "objective base of power." The study fully integrates the cognitive dimension into the analysis, alongside economic issues. In such works the limitations of the earlier processual

Cognitive Archaeology

Cognitive archaeology is the study of the ways of thought and structures of belief of past societies on the basis of their material remains. It:

- attempts to use the more rigorous and explicit methods of the processual approach

- applies these to symbolic and ideological issues many of which were first addressed by postprocessual or interpretive approaches (e.g. questions of identity, gender, and religious belief in the past)

- shows willingness to address the symbolizing and reasoning abilities of hominins before the emergence of *Homo sapiens*, sometimes within an evolutionary framework

- accepts the postprocessual emphasis on the active role of material culture

- recognizes that cognitive developments are also social developments

archaeology have been transcended and the roots of change are investigated with full weight being given to the cognitive and the symbolic dimensions.

AGENCY AND MATERIAL ENGAGEMENT

In the past decade or so archaeologists working in different conceptual traditions have sought in various ways to reconcile the cognitive and symbolic on the one hand with the practical and productive on the other. One aim is to reconcile the short-term intentions or agency of the individual with the long-term and often unintended consequences of cumulative actions. Archaeologists who take this approach hope to combine a broad outline of processes of change with the finer texture of specific culture histories.

The concept of agency has been introduced to permit discussion of the role of the individual in promoting change, but the scope of the term is not always clear, particularly when used, as by some anthropologists, as a quality which can be assigned to artifacts as well as to people. The various discussions of agency attempt to illuminate the role of the individual, but it is very difficult to determine clearly how the actions of one individual had a wider and longer-term impact.

A related notion, that change arises from conscious and often purposeful human activities, is associated with the recently developed concepts of material engagement or materialization. They seek, as others have, to overcome the duality in discussions of human affairs between the practical and the cognitive, the material and the conceptual. Indeed most innovations and long-term changes in human societies, even technical ones, have a symbolic dimension as well as a material one, involving what the philosopher John Searle terms "institutional facts," which are themselves social creations.

There is still a tension also between those using archaeology to write culture history (usually of a single society) and those using evolutionary thinking to analyze long-term change. Each perspective has clear coherence and validity, but the two rarely seem to mesh together.

In these different approaches to the explanation of change there is some commonality of aspiration and this may yet lead to interesting new developments. But there is no single theoretical perspective which commands universal or even widespread respect.

STUDY QUESTIONS
- Why is archaeology unique among the human sciences?
- What are the key differences between Processual and Postprocessual archaeology?
- What is Marxist archaeology and how is it different from the New Archaeology?
- What are some monocausal explanations for the origins of the state?
- What is Critical Theory and what are its implications for archaeology?
- Is there a correct way to explain change in the past?

SUMMARY

- It is difficult to explain *why* things happened in the past, yet this must be one of the key tasks of archaeology.

- Explanations in terms of the migrations of people or using the rather vague idea of the "diffusion" of culture used to be very popular: today they are less frequent.

- The processual approach has consistently tried to see broader patterns and general explanations. In general multivariate (several factor) explanations work better than monocausal (single factor) explanations for complex outcomes such as the origins of state societies.

- Interpretive explanations, on the other hand, usually emphasize the specific context. Both approaches converge toward a cognitive archaeology which acknowledges the role of human intelligence, creativity, and initiative.

- Yet there remain several different approaches to the difficult task of explanation. Some scholars advocate the notion of human agency, others analyze the knowledgeable engagement between humans and the material world. This remains an under-developed area of archaeological theory. Watch this space!

FURTHER READING

The broad topics covered in this chapter are explored in:

DeMarrais, E., Gosden, C. & Renfrew, C. (eds.). 2004. *Rethinking Materiality, the Engagement of Mind with the Material World*. McDonald Institute: Cambridge.

Earle, T. 1997. *How Chiefs Come to Power, the Political Economy in Prehistory*. Stanford University Press.

Gamble, C. 2007. *Origins and Revolutions: Human Identity in Earliest Prehistory*. Cambridge University Press: Cambridge & New York.

Hodder, I. 2004. *Reading the Past* (3rd ed.). Cambridge University Press: Cambridge & New York.

Mithen, S. 1999. *The Prehistory of the Mind*. Thames & Hudson: London & New York.

Renfrew, C. 2003. *Figuring It Out – the Parallel Visions of Artists and Archaeologists*. Thames & Hudson: London & New York.

Renfrew C. 2007. *Prehistory: Making of the Human Mind*. Weidenfeld & Nicolson: London; Modern Library: New York.

Shennan, S. 2002. *Genes, Memes and Human History*. Thames & Hudson: London & New York.

Webster, D.L. 2002. *The Fall of the Ancient Maya*. Thames & Hudson: London & New York.

Whose Past?
Archaeology and the public

This book is concerned with the way that archaeologists investigate the past, with the questions we can ask, and our means of answering them. But the time has come to address much wider questions: Why, beyond reasons of scientific curiosity, do we want to know about the past? What does the past mean to us? What does it mean to others who have different viewpoints? And whose past is it anyway?

These issues lead us to questions of responsibility, public as well as private. For surely a national monument, such as the Parthenon in Athens, means something special to the modern descendants of its builders? Does it not also mean something to all humankind? If so, should it not be protected from destruction, in the same way as endangered plant and animal species? If the looting of ancient **sites** is to be deplored, should it not be stopped, even if the sites are on privately owned land? Who owns, or should own, the past?

These very soon become ethical questions – of right and wrong, of appropriate action and reprehensible action. The archaeologist has a special responsibility because **excavation** itself entails destruction. Future workers' understanding of a site can never be much more than our own, because we will have destroyed the evidence and recorded only those parts of it we considered important and had the energy to publish properly.

The past is big business – in tourism and in the auction rooms. But by their numbers tourists threaten the sites they seek to enjoy; and the plunder of looters and illegal excavators finds its way into private collections and public museums. The past is politically highly charged, ideologically powerful, and significant. And the past, as we shall see in the next chapter, is subject to increasing destruction through unprecedented commercial, industrial, and agricultural exploitation of the earth's surface and through damage in war.

THE MEANING OF THE PAST: THE ARCHAEOLOGY OF IDENTITY

When we ask what the past means, we are asking what the past means for *us*, for it means different things to different people. An Australian Aborigine, for example, may attach a very different significance to fossil human remains from an early site like Lake Mungo or to paintings in the Kakadu National Park, than a white Australian. Different communities have very different conceptions about the past which often draw on sources well beyond **archaeology**.

At this point we go beyond the question of what actually happened in the past, and of the explanation of why it happened, to issues of meaning, significance, and interpretation. And it is at this point, therefore, that many of the concerns which have become explicit in archaeology over the past couple of decades become entirely relevant. How we interpret the past, how we present it (for instance in museum displays), and what lessons we choose to draw from it, are to a considerable extent matters for subjective decision, often involving ideological and political issues.

For in a very broad sense the past is where we came from. Individually we each have our personal, genealogical past – our parents, grandparents, and earlier kinsfolk from whom we are descended. Increasingly in the western world there is an interest in this personal past, reflected in the enthusiasm for family trees and for "roots" generally. Our personal identity, and generally our name, are in part defined for us in the relatively recent past, even though those elements with which we choose to identify are largely a matter of personal choice. Nor is this inheritance purely a spiritual one. Most land tenure in the world is determined by inheritance, and much other wealth is inherited: the material world in this sense comes to us from the past, and is certainly, when the time comes, relinquished by us to the future.

Either Philip II of Macedon, father of Alexander the Great, or Philip III, Alexander's half-brother, was buried in a gold casket decorated with an impressive star. This was adopted as the national symbol of the former Yugoslav republic of Macedonia, as seen on one of their stamps.

Nationalism and its Symbols

Collectively our cultural inheritance is rooted in a deeper past: the origins of our language, our faith, our customs. Increasingly archaeology plays an important role in the definition of national identity. This is particularly the case for those nations that do not have a very long written history, though many consider oral histories of equal value to written ones. The national emblems of many recently emerged nations are taken from **artifacts** seen as typical of some special and early local golden age: even the name of the state of Zimbabwe comes from the name of an archaeological site.

Yet sometimes the use of archaeology and of images recovered from the past to focus and enhance national identity can lead to conflict. A major crisis related to the name and national emblems adopted by the then newly independent Former Yugoslav Republic of Macedonia. For in Greece, immediately to the south, the name Macedon refers not only to contemporaneous provinces within

Greece, but to the ancient kingdom of that famous Greek leader, Alexander the Great. The affront which the name caused in Greece was compounded by the use by the FYR Macedonia of a star as a national symbol, using the image on a gold casket found among the splendid objects in a tomb from the 4th century BC at Vergina, a tomb located well within modern Greek territory, thought to have belonged to either to Philip II of Macedon, the father of Alexander, or Philip III, Alexander's brother. Territorial claims can sometimes be based on contentious histories, and some Greeks thought that the FYR Macedonia was seeking not only to appropriate the glorious history of Macedonia but perhaps also to incorporate Greece's second city, Thessaloniki, within its territorial boundaries. Riots ensued, based, however, more on inflamed ethnic feelings than upon political reality.

Archaeology and Ideology

The legacy of the past goes beyond sentiments of nationalism and **ethnicity**. Sectarian sentiments often find expression in major monuments, and many Christian churches were built on the site of deliberately destroyed "pagan" temples. In just a few cases they actually utilized such temples – the Parthenon in Athens is one example – and one of the best preserved Greek temples is now the Cathedral in Syracuse in Sicily.

Religious extremism is responsible for many acts of destruction. The senseless destruction in March 2001 by the Taliban of the two giant Buddhas carved into the sandstone cliffs at Bamiyan, in the Hindu Kush, perhaps in the 3rd century AD, shocked the world. The only motivation seems to have been that these were religious images not in accordance with the faith of the Taliban. Despite a

The larger of the colossal Buddhas of Bamiyan, carved from the cliff face in perhaps the 3rd century AD, and now destroyed.

The shocking sequence of images recording the destruction of the colossal Buddha statue. Such historical monuments have now become targets in politics and war.

delegation from the Islamic Conference, at which 55 Islamic nations were represented, the destruction went ahead. Standing 53 and 36 m high (174 and 118 ft), these were the tallest standing Buddhas in the world; explosive charges destroyed them almost totally.

These are cases of religious ideology leading to the destruction of important symbols which are part of the world's archaeological heritage. In war the sentiments are sometimes national or ethnic, rather than religious. Such was the case in the civil war in Yugoslavia, although it also had religious overtones. The bridge at Mostar in Bosnia, built by the Ottoman Turks in 1566 and a symbol of Bosnian identity, was destroyed by Croatian forces in 1993. Although it has now been rebuilt, the loss of the original structure was one of the most tragic acts in Europe since World War II: the deliberate destruction of the cultural heritage on purely ethnic grounds.

The bridge at Mostar, in Bosnia, dating from the 16th century, was destroyed in fighting in 1993 but has now been rebuilt.

ARCHAEOLOGICAL ETHICS

Ethics is the science of morals – i.e. what it is right or wrong to do – and increasingly most branches of archaeology are seen to have an ethical (or sometimes unethical) dimension. Precisely because archaeology relates to identity (as reviewed in the last section), and to the existence of communities and of nations and indeed of humankind itself, it touches upon urgent practical problems of an ethical nature. These are often difficult problems because they deal in conflicting principles.

The Latin author Terence is quoted as saying: "Homo sum: nihil humanum mihi alienum est" – "I am a human being, so nothing human is alien to me." Such thinking is central to the Universal Declaration of Human Rights. Many anthropologists feel that "the proper study of (hu)mankind is (hu)man(ity)," to update the 17th-century English poet Alexander Pope. The implication is that the entire field of human experience should be our study. Such sentiments encourage the study of fossil **hominins**, for instance, and clearly make the study of Australian aboriginal remains (pp. 298–99) or those of Kennewick Man

(p. 298) a necessary part of the work of the biological anthropologist. So there is one principle. But, on the other hand, it is usual to have a decent respect for the earthly remains of our own relatives and ancestors. In many tribal societies such respect imposes obligations, which often find recognition in the law, for instance in the Native American Graves Protection and Repatriation Act (NAGPRA: see p. 298). This then is a second principle, which has led to the reburial (and consequent destruction) of ancient human remains whose further study could have been of benefit to science. Which of the two principles is right? That is what one may term an ethical dilemma. It is one which is difficult to resolve, and which underlies several of the sections in this chapter and the next.

The right to property is another such principle. But the legitimate rights of the individual property owner (including the collector) can come into conflict with the very evident rights of wider communities. So it is that the commercial property developer can disagree with the conservationist. The ethical tensions between conservation and development are dealt with in the next chapter. Similar difficulties arise when the purchasing power of the private collector of antiquities leads to the destruction of archaeological sites through illicit excavation (looting). Increasingly the importance of **material culture** as something with significant social meaning is appreciated in our society. There are problems here which will not go away, because they are the product of the conflict of principles. That is why archaeological ethics is now a growth subject.

POPULAR ARCHAEOLOGY VERSUS PSEUDOARCHAEOLOGY

The purpose of archaeology is to learn more about the past, and archaeologists believe that it is important that everyone should have some knowledge of the human past – of where we have come from, and how we have come to be where we are. Archaeology is not just for archaeologists. For that reason it is crucially important that we communicate effectively with the wider public. But there are several ways in which this important mission can be subverted. The first is the development of **pseudoarchaeology**, often for commercial purposes – that is to say the formulation of extravagant but ill-founded stories about the past. Sometimes those telling these stories may actually believe them, but often, as with Dan Brown's popular novel *The Da Vinci Code*, it is suspected that the primary motive of the author is just to make money. Archaeology can be subverted, also, when people actually manufacture false evidence, and perpetrate archaeological fraud.

Archaeology at the Fringe.   In the later years of the 20th century "Other Archaeologies" grew up at the fringe of the discipline, offering alternative interpretations of the past. To the scientist these seem fanciful and extravagant – manifestations of a postmodern age in which horoscopes are widely read, New Age prophets preach alternative lifestyles, and when many members of the public are

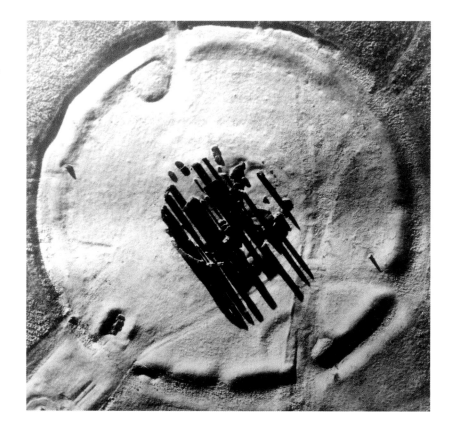

willing to believe that "corn circles" and megalithic monuments are the work of aliens. Many archaeologists label such populist approaches as "pseudoarchaeology," and place them on a par with archaeological frauds such as Piltdown Man, where deliberate deception can be demonstrated or inferred.

But how does an archaeologist persuade the self-styled Druids who perform their rituals at Stonehenge at the summer solstice (if the governing authority, English Heritage, allows them access) that their beliefs are not supported by archaeological evidence? This brings us back to the central question of this chapter: "Whose Past?" It is not clear that we should question the reality of the Dreamtime of the Australian Aborigines, even if aspects of their belief effectively clash with current scientific interpretations. Where do we distinguish between respect for deeply held beliefs and the role of the archaeologist to inform the public and to dismiss credulous nonsense?

One of the most popular and durable myths concerns a "lost Atlantis," a story narrated by the Greek philosopher Plato in the 5th century BC, and attributed by him to the Greek sage Solon, who had visited Egypt and consulted with priests, the heirs to a long religious and historical tradition. They told him of a legend of the lost continent beyond the Pillars of Hercules (the modern Straits of

Gibraltar), hence in the Atlantic Ocean, with its advanced civilization, which vanished centuries earlier "in a night and a day." In 1882 Ignatius Donnelly published *Atlantis, the Antediluvian World*, elaborating this legend. His work was one of the first to seek a simple explanation of all ancient civilizations of the world by a single marvellous means. Such theories often share characteristics:

1   They celebrate a remarkable lost world whose people possessed many skills surpassing those of the present.
2   They account for most of the early accomplishments of prehistoric and early **state** societies with a single explanation: all were the work of the skilled inhabitants of that lost world.
3   That world vanished in a catastrophe of cosmic proportions.
4   Nothing of that original homeland is available for scientific examination, nor are any artifacts surviving.

The basic structure of Donnelly's argument was repeated with variants by Immanuel Velikovsky (meteors and astronomical events) and recently by Graham Hancock (who sites his lost continent in Antarctica). A popular alternative, elaborated with great financial profit by Erich von Däniken, is that the source of progress is outer space, and that the advances of early civilizations are the work of aliens visiting earth. Ultimately, however, all such theories trivialize the much more remarkable story which archaeology reveals – the history of humankind.

Fraud in Archaeology.   Fraud in archaeology is nothing new and takes many forms – from the manipulation of evidence by Heinrich Schliemann to the infamous cases of fakery such as Britain's Piltdown Man. It has been suggested that more than 1200 fake antiquities are displayed in some of the world's leading museums. A particularly serious example came to light as recently as 2000 when a leading Japanese archaeologist admitted planting artifacts at excavations. Shinichi Fujimura – nicknamed "God's hands" for his uncanny ability to uncover ancient objects – had been videotaped burying his "discoveries" before digging them up again as new finds. He admitted having buried dozens of artifacts in secret,

A cluster of hand-axes at Kamitakamori faked by Japanese archaeologist Shinichi Fujimura.

claiming that it was the pressure of having to discover older sites which forced him to fake them by using artifacts from his own collections.

Of 65 pieces unearthed at the Kamitakamori site north of Tokyo, Fujimura admitted to having faked 61, together with all 29 pieces found in 2000 at the Soshinfudozaka site in northern Japan. He later admitted having tampered with evidence at 42 sites; but in 2004 the Japanese Archaeological Association declared that all of the 168 sites he dug had been faked. Japanese archaeological authorities are understandably worried about the potential impact on evidence for the Early **Paleolithic** period in Japan unearthed since the mid-1970s.

It seems that this phenomenon may currently be on the rise. Some of this can be blamed on the increased "mediatization" of the field, where, as in Japan, it can be important to generate publicity to further one's career and scientific publication often takes a back seat to press conferences where the latest finds are trumpeted. Spectacular discoveries are now sometimes seen as more important than scholarly debate or critical review. Nevertheless, the actual fabrication or planting of fake objects is an extreme form of fraud. Japanese archaeologists are worried that there may be other fraudulent artifacts, yet to be unearthed, a situation which has been likened to "archaeological landmines," ready to wreak havoc on future generations of scholars.

The Wider Audience.   Although the immediate aim of most research is to answer specific questions, the fundamental purpose of archaeology must be to provide people with a better understanding of the human past. Skillful popularization – site and museum exhibits, books, television, and increasingly

One of the most fanciful fringe claims involves this hill above the Bosnian town of Visoko: the "Bosnian Pyramid." Regularly fissured (and entirely natural) rocks are seemingly the best evidence offered that this hill is a man-made structure allegedly linked to Maya temples and with a supposedly common root in "Atlantean" architecture – but the media campaign waged by those involved still managed to attract attention around the world. Since 2005, uncontrolled "excavations" on the hill have almost certainly damaged genuine archaeological sites.

the Internet – is therefore required, but not all archaeologists are prepared to devote time to it, and few are capable of doing it well.

Excavators often regard members of the public as a hindrance to work on-site. More enlightened archaeologists, however, realize the financial and other support to be gained from encouraging public interest, and they organize information sheets, open days, and on long-term projects even fee-paying daily tours, as at the Bronze Age site of Flag Fen in eastern England. In Japan, on-the-spot presentations of excavation results are given as soon as a dig is completed. Details are released to the press the previous day, so that the public can obtain information from the morning edition of the local paper before coming to the site itself.

Clearly, there is an avid popular appetite for archaeology. In a sense, the past has been a form of entertainment since the early digging of burial mounds and the public unwrapping of mummies in the 19th century. The entertainment may now take a more scientific and educational form, but it still needs to compete with rival popular attractions if archaeology is to thrive.

WHO OWNS THE PAST?

Until recent decades, archaeologists gave little thought to the question of the ownership of past sites and antiquities. Most archaeologists themselves came from western, industrialized societies whose economic and political domination seemed to give an almost automatic right to acquire antiquities and excavate sites around the world. Since World War II, however, former colonies have grown into independent nation states eager to uncover their own past and assert control over their own heritage. Difficult questions have therefore arisen. Should antiquities acquired for western museums during the colonial era be returned to their lands of origin? And should archaeologists be free to excavate the burials of groups whose modern descendants may object on religious or other grounds?

Museums and the Return of Cultural Property

At the beginning of the 19th century Lord Elgin, a Scottish diplomat, removed many of the marble sculptures that adorned the Parthenon, the great 5th-century BC temple that crowns the Acropolis in Athens. Elgin did so with the permission of the then Turkish overlords of Greece, and later sold the sculptures to the British Museum, where they still reside, displayed in a special gallery. The Greeks now want the "Elgin Marbles" back. That in essence is the story so far of perhaps the best-known case where an internationally famous museum is under pressure to return cultural property to the country of origin.

But there are numerous other claims directed at European and North American museums. The Berlin Museum, for example, holds the famous bust of the Egyptian queen Nefertiti, which was shipped out of Egypt illegally. The

Part of the "Elgin Marbles" in the British Museum: a horse-man from the frieze of the Parthenon in Athens, c. 440 BC.

Greek government has officially asked France for the return of the Venus de Milo, one of the masterworks of the Louvre, bought from Greece's Ottoman rulers. And Turkey has recently been successful in recovering art treasures, including the "Lydian Hoard," from New York's Metropolitan Museum of Art (which has also agreed to return the now infamous "Euphronios Vase" to Italy, see below), and may now pursue Turkish statuary and objects in European countries, including the British Museum.

Excavating Burials: Should We Disturb the Dead?

The question of excavating burials can be equally complex. For prehistoric burials the problem is not so great, because we have no direct written knowledge of the relevant **culture**'s beliefs and wishes. For burials dating from historic times, however, religious beliefs are known to us in detail. We know, for example, that the ancient Egyptians and Chinese, the Greeks, Etruscans, and Romans, and the early Christians all feared disturbance of the dead. Yet it has to be recognized that tombs were falling prey to the activities of robbers long before archaeology began. Egyptian pharaohs in the 12th century BC had to appoint a commission to inquire into the wholesale plundering of tombs at Thebes. Not a single Egyptian royal tomb, including that of Tutankhamun, escaped the robbers completely. Similarly, Roman carved gravestones became building material in cities and forts; and at Ostia, the port of ancient Rome, tomb inscriptions have even been found serving as seats in a public latrine!

The Native Americans.   For some Native Americans in North America, archaeology has become a focal point for complaints about wrongdoings of the past. They have expressed their grievances strongly in recent years, and their political influence has resulted in legal mechanisms that sometimes restrict or prevent archaeological excavations, or provide for the return to Native American peoples of some collections now in museums. Apart from the question of returning and/or reburying material, sometimes there have been vehement objections to new excavations. The Chumash, for example, refused permission for scientists to remove what may be the oldest human remains in California, even though an offer was made to return and rebury the bones after a year's study. The bones, thought to be about 9000 years old, were eroding out of a cliff on Santa Rosa Island, 100 km (62 miles) west of Los Angeles. Under California's state laws the fate of the bones lay with their most likely descendants – and the Chumash were understandably angry about past treatment of their ancestors' skeletons, with hundreds of remains scattered in various universities and museums. Like many Maori, they preferred to see the bones destroyed "in accordance with nature's law" than to have other people interfere with them. In other cases, however, Native American communities have provided for the systematic curation of such remains once they have been returned to them.

As in Australia (see overleaf), there is no single, unified indigenous tradition. Native Americans have wide-ranging attitudes toward the dead and the soul. Nonetheless demands for reburial of ancestral remains are common. The solution to the problem has been found to lie in acquiescence, compromise, and collaboration. Often archaeologists have supported or acquiesced in the return of remains of fairly close ancestors of living people. Material has also been returned that had no archaeological **context** and was thus of minimal value to science.

Seminole Native American bones from Florida are reburied in 1989 by archaeologists and Native Americans at Wounded Knee.

Repatriation of older and more important material is a difficult issue. The longstanding position of the Society for American Archaeology is that scientific and traditional interests in archaeological materials must be balanced, weighted by the closeness of relationship to the modern group making a claim and the scientific value of the remains or objects requested. With the Society's support, in 1990 the Native American Graves Protection and Repatriation Act (NAGPRA) was passed. It requires some 5000 federally funded institutions and government agencies to inventory their collections and assess the "cultural affiliation" of Native American skeletons, funerary and sacred objects, and items of cultural patrimony. If cultural affiliation can be shown, the human remains and objects must, on request, be returned to the affiliated Native American **tribe** or Native Hawaiian organization. Difficult problems lie in interpreting key terms in the law, such as "cultural affiliation," and in weighing diverse forms of evidence in the context of prehistoric material. In addition to archaeological and historical information, the law explicitly recognizes the validity of oral traditions. This has led to broad expectations by tribes that prehistoric remains can be claimed if their oral traditions say that its people were created in the same region where the remains were found. However, when these expectations were tested in court it was found that the law requires a balanced consideration of oral tradition with scientific evidence.

Controversy and a legal battle dogged the bones of "Kennewick Man," found in 1996 in Washington State, and radiocarbon dated to 9300 BP. Eight prominent anthropologists sued the Army Corps of Engineers, which has jurisdiction over the site, for permission to study the bones, but the Corps wanted to hand the skeleton to the local Native American Umatilla Tribe for reburial, in accordance with NAGPRA. The scientists were extremely anxious to run tests, since preliminary examination had suggested that Kennewick Man was a 19th-century settler, so that its early date raises complex, important and fascinating questions about the peopling of the Americas. The Umatilla, on the other hand, were adamantly against any investigation, insisting that their oral tradition says their tribe has been part of this land since the beginning of time, and so all bones recovered from here are necessarily their ancestors – and must not be damaged for dating or genetic analysis. In 2002 a magistrate affirmed the right of the scientists to study the bones and, despite subsequent legal appeals, in June 2005 the battle (which cost millions of dollars in legal fees) was finally won, and analysis began in earnest.

An archaeologist and a sculptor work on the reconstruction of the head of Kennewick Man (with the aid of a cast of the original skull).

The Australian Aborigines.   In Australia, the present climate of Aboriginal emancipation and increased political power has focused attention on wrongdoings during the colonial period, when anthropologists had little respect for Aboriginal feelings and beliefs. Sacred sites were investigated and published, burial sites desecrated, and cultural and skeletal material exhumed, to be stored or displayed in museums. The Aborigines were thus, by implication, seen as laboratory specimens. Inevitably, the fate of all this material, and particularly of the bones, has assumed great symbolic significance. Unfortunately, here as in other countries, archaeologists are being blamed for the misdemeanors of the non-archaeologists who obtained most of the human remains in question.

The view of Aborigines in some parts of Australia is that all human skeletal material (and occasionally cultural material too) must be returned to them, and then its fate will be decided. In some cases they themselves wish the remains to be curated in conditions that anthropologists would consider to be satisfactory, usually under Aboriginal control. Since the Aborigines have an unassailable moral case, the Australian Archaeological Association (AAA) is willing to return remains which are either quite modern or of "known individuals where specific descendants can be traced," and for these to be reburied. However, such remains are somewhat the exception. The University of Melbourne's Murray Black Collection consists of skeletal remains from over 800 Aborigines ranging in date from several hundred years to at least 14,000 years old. They were dug up in the 1940s without any consultation with local Aborigines. Owing to a lack of specialists the collection has still by no means been exhaustively studied – but nevertheless it has been returned to the relevant Aboriginal communities. In 1990 the unique series of burials from Kow Swamp, 19,000 to 22,000 years old, were handed back to the Aboriginal community and reburied; more recently the first skeleton found at Lake Mungo, the world's oldest known cremation (26,000 years BP), was returned to the custody of the Aborigines of the Mungo area; and Aboriginal elders have announced they may rebury all the skeletal material (up to 30,000 years old) from Mungo.

Archaeologists are understandably alarmed at the prospect of having to hand over material many thousands of years old. Some also point out that the Aborigines – like indigenous peoples elsewhere – tend to forget that not all of their recent forebears took pious care of the dead. But, not least in the light of Aboriginal sufferings at European hands, their views are entitled to respect.

THE RESPONSIBILITY OF COLLECTORS AND MUSEUMS

It has become clear in recent years that private collectors and even public museums, for centuries regarded as guardians and conservators of the past, have become (in some cases) major causative agents of destruction. The market in illegal antiquities – excavated illegally and clandestinely with no published record – has become a major incentive for the looting of archaeological sites. The looting is funded, whether directly or indirectly, by unscrupulous private collectors and by unethical museums. All over the world looters are continuing their destructive work. Several languages have a word for them: in Greece they are *archaiokapiloi*, in Latin America *huaqueros*. Italy has two special words: *clandestini* and *tombaroli*. They unearth beautiful, saleable objects. But deprived of their archaeological context, these objects no longer have the power to tell us much that is new about the past. Many of them end up on display in some of the less scrupulous museums of the world. When a museum fails to indicate the context of discovery, including the site the exhibit came from, it is often a sign that the object displayed has come via the illicit market.

One such *clandestino*, Luigi Perticarari, a robber in Tarquinia, Italy, published his memoirs in 1986 and makes no apology for his trade. He has more first-hand knowledge of Etruscan tombs than any archaeologist, but his activity destroys the chance of anyone sharing that knowledge. He claims to have emptied some 4000 tombs dating from the 8th to the 3rd centuries BC in 30 years. So it is that, while the world's store of Etruscan antiquities in museums and private collections grows larger, our knowledge of Etruscan burial customs and social organization does not.

The same is true for the remarkable marble sculptures of the Cycladic islands of Greece, dating to around 2500 BC. We admire the breathtaking elegance of these works in the world's museums, but we have little idea of how they were produced or of the social and religious life of the Cycladic communities that made them. Again, the contexts have been lost.

In the American Southwest, 90 percent of the Classic Mimbres sites (*c.* AD 1000) have now been looted or destroyed (see box opposite). In southwestern Colorado, 60 percent of prehistoric Ancestral Pueblo sites have been vandalized. Pothunters work at night, equipped with two-way radios, scanners, and lookouts. It is very difficult to prosecute them under the present legislation unless they are caught red-handed, which is almost impossible.

The *huaqueros* of Central and South America, too, are interested only in the richest finds, in this case gold – whole cemeteries are turned into fields of craters, with bones, potsherds, mummy wrappings, and other objects smashed and scattered. The remarkable tombs excavated between 1987 and 1990 at Sipán, northwest Peru, of the Moche civilization, were rescued from the plunderers only by the persistence and courage of the local Peruvian archaeologist, Walter Alva.

So far as illicit antiquities are concerned, the spotlight has indeed turned upon museums and private collectors. Many of the world's great museums, following the lead of the University Museum of Pennsylvania in 1970, now decline to purchase or receive by gift any antiquities which cannot be shown to have been exported legally from their country of origin. But others, such as the Metropolitan Museum of Art, New York, have in the past had no such scruples: Thomas Hoving, at that time Director of the museum stated: "We are no more illegal in anything we have done than Napoleon was when he brought

The Mimbres potters of the American Southwest created a unique art tradition in the prehistoric period, painting the inside of hemispherical bowls with vigorous animal and human forms. These bowls are now much admired by archaeologists and art lovers. But this fascination has led to the systematic looting of Mimbres sites on a scale unequaled in the United States, or indeed anywhere in the world.

The Mimbres people lived along a small river, the Rio Mimbres, in mud-built villages, similar in some respects to those of the later Puebloans. Painted pottery began, as we now know, around AD 550, and reached its apogee in the Classic Mimbres period, from about AD 1000 to 1130.

Systematic archaeological work on Mimbres sites began in the 1920s, but it was not in general well published. Looters soon found, however, that with pick and shovel they could unearth Mimbres pots to sell on the market for primitive art. Nor was this activity necessarily illegal. In United States law there is nothing to prevent excavation of any kind by the owner on private land, and nothing to prevent the owner permitting others to destroy archaeological sites in this way (although some state laws, in New Mexico and Arizona, for example, now protect human burials on both private and state land).

In the early 1960s, a method of bulldozing Mimbres sites was developed which did not destroy all the pottery. The operators found that by controlled bulldozing they could remove a relatively small depth of soil at a time and extract many of the pots unbroken. In the process sites were of course completely destroyed, and all hope of establishing an archaeological context for the material was lost.

Since 1973 there has at last been a concerted archaeological response. The Mimbres Foundation, under the direction of Steven LeBlanc, was able to secure funding from private sources to undertake excavations in the remains of some of the looted sites. They also made good progress in explaining to the owners of those sites how destructive this looting process was to any hope of learning about the Mimbres past. From 1975 to 1978 a series of field seasons at several partially looted sites succeeded in establishing at least the outlines of Mimbres archaeology, and in putting the chronology upon a sure footing.

A masked coyote dancer is the subject of this fine Mimbres bowl, dating from AD 1100–1250.

The Mimbres Foundation also reached the conclusion that archaeological excavation is an expensive form of conservation, and decided to purchase a number of surviving (or partially surviving) Mimbres sites in order to protect them. Moreover, this is a lesson that has been learned more widely. Members of the Mimbres Foundation have joined forces with other archaeologists and benefactors to form a national organization, the Archaeological Conservancy. Several sites in the United States have now been purchased and conserved in this way. The story thus has, in some sense, a happy ending. But nothing can bring back the possibility of really understanding Mimbres culture and Mimbres art, a possibility which did exist at the beginning of the 20th century before the wholesale and devastating looting.

Unfortunately, in other parts of the world there are similar stories to tell.

Funerary bowl of the 10th century AD. The figures may be male and female, or life or death. The "kill" hole at the base allowed the object's spirit to be released.

all the treasures to the Louvre." The Getty Museum, with its great wealth, has a heavy responsibility in this, and has recently adopted a much more rigorous acquisition policy.

Museums like the Metropolitan Museum of Art, which in 1990 put on display the collection of Shelby White and the late Leon Levy, and the J. Paul Getty Museum which in 1994 exhibited (and then acquired) that of Barbara Fleischman and the late Lawrence Fleischman – both collections with a high proportion of antiquities of unknown provenience – must share some responsibility for the prevalence of collecting in circumstances where much of the money paid inevitably goes to reward dealers who are part of the ongoing cycles of destruction, and thus ultimately the looters. And the responsibility borne by collectors who, in buying such works, indirectly fund the looting process, is now being recognized. It has been argued that "Collectors are the real looters." Peter Watson in his revealing survey *The Medici Conspiracy* (2006) has outlined the surprising events which led the Italian government to bring criminal charges against the former curator of antiquities at the Getty, and to recover from the Metropolitan Museum of Art one of their most celebrated antiquities, the "Euphronios Vase," for which they had in 1972 paid a million dollars, but without obtaining secure evidence of its provenience. As the Romans had it: "caveat emptor" ("buyer beware").

The exhibition of the George Ortiz collection of antiquities at the Royal Academy in London in 1994 excited controversy and was felt by many archaeologists to have brought no credit to the Royal Academy. The art critic Robert Hughes has correctly observed that "Part of the story is the renewed cult of the collector as celebrity and of the museum as spectacle, as much concerned with show business as with scholarship."

It remains a real paradox that collectors, who often have a real feeling for the antiquities which they amass, are ultimately funding the looting which is the main threat to the world's archaeological heritage.

However, there are signs that things may be improving. The Dealing in Cultural Objects (Offences) Act was approved by the United Kingdom Parliament in 2003. For the first time it is now a criminal offence in UK knowingly to deal in illicitly excavated antiquities, whether from Britain or overseas. And in New York in June 2003 the United States Court of Appeals upheld the conviction of the antiquities dealer Frederick Schultz for conspiring to deal in antiquities stolen from Egypt. Frederick Schultz is a former president of the National Association of Dealers in Ancient, Oriental, and Primitive Art and has in the past sold antiquities to some leading museums in the United States. A jail term for so prominent a dealer will send a clear message to some conspicuous collectors and museum directors that they should be more attentive in future in the exercise of "due diligence" when acquiring unprovenienced antiquities.

Recent cases include:

The "Weary Herakles." Two parts of a Roman marble statue of the 2nd century AD are now separate. The lower part was excavated at Perge in Turkey in 1980 and is in the Antalya Museum, while the joining upper part was purchased by the late Leon Levy shortly afterwards, and is currently on view at the Boston Museum of Fine Arts, to which Levy gave a half share. The Museum and Levy's family decline to return the piece to Turkey.

The Sevso Treasure. A splendid late Roman assemblage of silver vessels was acquired as an investment by the Marquess of Northampton, but was subsequently claimed in a New York court action by Hungary, Croatia, and Lebanon. Possession was awarded to Lord Northampton, who then found the treasure unsaleable and sued his former legal advisors in London for their poor advice at the time of purchase; an out-of-court settlement, reportedly in excess of £15 million, was agreed on confidential terms in 1999. Hungary is now seeking to obtain this material, and perhaps Lord Northampton will sell his treasure after all.

The "Weary Herakles": the lower part, excavated in Turkey in 1980, is now in the Antalya Museum while the upper part is in the Boston Museum of Fine Arts, which has so far failed to return it to Turkey.

A splendid silver dish from the looted Sevso Treasure, one of the major scandals in the recent story of illicit antiquities.

The Getty Affair. The J. Paul Getty Museum in Los Angeles found itself in the spotlight of publicity in 2005 when its Curator of Antiquities, Marion True (subsequently fired), went on trial in Italy on charges relating to the purchase by the Getty of antiquities allegedly illegally excavated in Italy.

The UCL Aramaic Incantation Bowls. In 2005 University College London established a Committee of Inquiry into the provenience of 654 Aramaic

Incantation bowl from Mesopotamia (i.e. Iraq) dating from the 6th to 7th century AD with a text, written in black ink in the Aramaic language, intended to bind demons, deities and other hostile forces who might harm the owner.

incantation bowls (dating to the 6th to 7th centuries AD, and believed to come from Iraq) which had been lent for purposes of study by a prominent Norwegian collector, Martin Schøyen. It did so following claims that the bowls had been illegally exported from their country of origin. UCL received the Report of the Committee in July 2006, but subsequently returned the bowls to Schøyen with whom it had concluded a confidential out-of-court settlement preventing publication of the Report, and agreeing to pay an undisclosed sum to Schøyen. This episode highlights the need for "due diligence" when antiquities are accepted, on loan as well as through gift or purchase, by public institutions. The full story of the UCL Aramaic incantation bowls remains to be told.

It is ironic that a love and respect for the past and for the antiquities which have come down to us should lead to such destructive and acquisitive behaviour. "Who owns the past?" is indeed the key issue if the work of archaeology is to continue, and to provide us with new information about our shared heritage and about the processes by which we have become what we are. In that sense we may well ask "Does the past have a future?" That is the theme addressed in our final chapter.

STUDY QUESTIONS

• Who owns the past?
• What are some ways in which symbols from the past have led to conflict?
• What are ethics? What sorts of ethical issues do archaeologists encounter?
• Why are many archaeologists critical of "pseudoarchaeology"?
• What are illicit antiquities?

SUMMARY

- The past has different meanings for different people, and often personal identity is defined by the past. Increasingly archaeology is playing a role in the definition of national identity where the past is used to legitimize the present by reinforcing a sense of national greatness. Ethnicity, which is just as strong a force today as in earlier times, relies upon the past for legitimization as well, sometimes with destructive consequences.

- Ethics is the science of what is right and wrong, or morality, and most branches of archaeology are seen to have an ethical dimension. Until recent decades archaeologists gave little thought to such questions as "who owns the past." Now every archaeological decision should take ethical concerns into account.

- We cannot simply dismiss the alternative theories of fringe archaeology as farcical, because they have been so widely believed. Anyone who has read this book, and who understands how archaeology proceeds, will already see why such writings are a delusion. The real antidote is a kind of healthy skepticism: to ask "where is the evidence?" Knowledge advances by asking questions – that is the central theme of this book, and there is no better way to disperse the lunatic fringe than by asking difficult questions, and looking skeptically at the answers.

- The archaeology of every land has its own contribution to make to the understanding of human diversity and hence of the human condition. Although earlier scholars behaved with flagrant disregard for the feelings and beliefs of native peoples, interest in these matters today is not an attempt further to appropriate the native past.

- Perhaps the saddest type of archaeological destruction comes from the looting of sites. Through this act, all information is destroyed in the search for highly saleable artifacts. Museums and collectors bear some of the responsibility for this. Museums are also under increasing pressure to return antiquities to their lands of origin.

FURTHER READING

General introductions to the topics covered in this chapter include:

Brodie, N., Kersel, M., Luke, C. & Tubb, K.W. (eds.). 2008. *Archaeology, Cultural Heritage, and the Antiquities Trade*. University Press of Florida: Gainsville.

Burke, H., Smith, C., Lippert, D., Watkins, J.E. & Zimmerman, L. 2008. *Kennewick Man: Perspectives on the Ancient One*. Left Coast Press: Walnut Creek.

Feder, K. 2008. *Frauds, Myths, and Mysteries: Science and Pseudoscience in Archaeology*. McGraw-Hill: New York.

Greenfield, J. 2007. *The Return of Cultural Treasures* (3rd ed.). Cambridge University Press: Cambridge & New York.

Lynott, M.J. & Wylie, A., 2002. *Ethics in American Archaeology* (2nd ed.). Society for American Archaeology: Washington D.C.

Renfrew, C. 2009. *Loot, Legitimacy and Ownership: The Ethical Crisis in Archaeology*. Duckworth: London.

Watson, P. 2006. *The Medici Conspiracy*. PublicAffairs: New York.

The Future of the Past
Managing our heritage

What is the future of archaeology? Can our discipline continue to produce new information about the human past, the **evolution** of our species, and the achievements of humankind? This is one of the dilemmas which currently confront all archaeologists, and indeed all those concerned to understand the human past. For just as global warming and increasing pollution threaten the future ecology of our planet, so the record of the past is today faced by forces of destruction that demand a coherent and energetic response.

Some of those forces of destruction have been discussed earlier, and others are confronted here. The big question continues to be: what can be done? That is the problem that faces us, whose solution will determine the future both of our discipline and of the material record which it seeks to understand. Here we review two parallel approaches: conservation (protection) and mitigation. The two, working together, have generated in recent years new attitudes toward the practice of **archaeology**, which may yet offer viable solutions.

THE DESTRUCTION OF THE PAST

There are two main agencies of destruction, both of them human. One is the construction of roads, quarries, dams, office blocks, etc. These are conspicuous and the threat is at least easily recognizable. A different kind of destruction – agricultural intensification – is slower but much wider in its extent, thus in the long term much more destructive. Elsewhere, reclamation schemes are transforming the nature of the environment, so that arid lands are being flooded and wetlands, such as those in Florida, are being reclaimed through drainage. The result is destruction of remarkable archaeological evidence. A third agent of destruction is conflict, the most obvious current threat being in the war zones of the Middle East.

There are two further human agencies of destruction, which should not be overlooked. The first is tourism, which, while economically having important effects on archaeology, makes the effective conservation of archaeological **sites** more difficult. The second, as we have seen in Chapter 11, is not new, but has grown dramatically in scale: the looting of archaeological sites by those who dig for monetary gain, seeking only saleable objects and destroying everything else in their search. More ancient remains have been lost in the last two decades than ever before in the history of the world.

Agricultural Damage.   Ever increasing areas of the earth, once uncultivated or cultivated by traditional non-intensive methods, are being opened up to mechanized farming. The tractor and the deep plow have replaced the digging stick and the ard. In other areas, forest plantations now cover what was formerly open land, and tree roots are destroying settlement sites and field monuments.

Although most countries keep some control over the activities of developers and builders, the damage to archaeological sites from farming is much more difficult to assess. The few published studies make sober reading. One shows that in Britain even those sites that are notionally protected – by being listed on the national Schedule of Ancient Monuments – are not, in reality, altogether safe. The position may be much better in Denmark and in certain other countries, but elsewhere only the most conspicuous sites are protected. The more modest field monuments and open settlements are not, and these are the sites that are suffering from mechanized agriculture.

Damage in War.   Among the most distressing outrages of recent years has been the continuing destruction, sometimes deliberate, of monuments and of archaeological materials in the course of armed conflict. Already, during World War II, historic buildings in England were deliberately targeted in German bombing raids.

The failure of Coalition forces in the 2003 invasion of Iraq to secure the Iraqi National Museum in Baghdad allowed the looting of the collections, including the celebrated Warka Vase, one of the most notable finds from the early Sumerian civilization – although, like many other important antiquities, this was later returned to the Museum. The failure was all the more shocking since archaeologists

The Warka Vase was looted from the Iraqi National Museum, Baghdad, during the 2003 invasion of Iraq. Fortunately it was recovered (right) and, though in pieces, these were probably ancient breaks.

in the United States had met with representatives of the Defense Department some months prior to the war to warn of the risk of looting in museums and at sites, and archaeologists in Britain had similarly indicated the dangers to the Prime Minister's office and the Foreign Office months before the war began. Only parts of the collection were taken, and it seems that it was the work both of looters from the street, who smashed cases, decapitated statues, and trashed offices, but also perhaps some well-informed individuals who knew what they were looking for and who had access to keys to the storerooms. It is these who are likely to have taken the Museum's collection of Mesopotamian cylinder seals, the finest in the world, for sale to collectors overseas.

It seems all the more extraordinary that the United States and the United Kingdom have still not ratified the 1954 Hague Convention for the Protection of Cultural Property in the Event of Armed Conflict, or its protocols. The British Government has announced its intention of doing so, but claims – some 50 years after the initial drafting of the Convention – that "to do so will require extensive consultation on legal, operational, and policy issues relating to the implementation of the Protocol."

THE RESPONSE: SURVEY, CONSERVATION, AND MITIGATION

In many countries of the world where the material remains of the past are valued as an important component of the national heritage, the response has been the development of a public archaeology: the acceptance that the public and therefore both national and regional government have a responsibility to avoid unnecessary destruction of that heritage. And of course there is an international dimension also.

This acceptance implies that steps should be taken to conserve what remains, often with the support of protective legislation. And when development is undertaken, which is often necessary and inescapable – to build freeways for instance, or to undertake commercial development, or to bring land into cultivation – steps need to be taken to research and record any archaeological remains which in the process are likely to be destroyed. In this way the effects of development can be mitigated.

These approaches have highlighted the need, in advance of any potential development, of reliable information concerning whatever archaeological remains may be located in the areas to be developed. This puts crucial emphasis on one of the key developments in the archaeological methodology of the late 20th century: site location and survey. The actions undertaken in response to the threat to the heritage need have a logical and natural order: survey, conservation, mitigation.

Within the United States, what are termed "preservation" laws to protect heritage resources do not guarantee that archaeological remains will be preserved.

The laws mandate a weighing of options and dictate the process by which the value of the resource is assessed against the value of the development project. In rare cases, the value of a site is so great that it will be preserved and a project canceled or re-routed. In most cases, though, important archaeological remains that can't be avoided are destroyed through scientific **excavation**. This is a compromise between development needs and heritage values. The vast majority of archaeological sites that are found during survey, though, do not meet the criteria for significance and are simply recorded and destroyed in the course of construction.

Survey

It has been widely realized that before major developments are undertaken, a key part of the planning phase must be a survey or assessment of the likely effects of such development upon what may be termed the archaeological resource. In the terminology employed in the USA this requires an "environmental assessment" (which will often lead to an "environmental impact statement"). Such an assessment extends beyond archaeology to more recent history and other aspects of the environment, including threatened plant and animal species. The cultural heritage, and especially its material remains, needs to be carefully assessed.

Such assessment today will often involve the use of satellite imagery as well as aerial photography. It requires mapping with the aid of GIS. And it also needs to involve field survey, using on-the-ground evaluation through field walking (sometimes called "ground truthing") so that unknown archaeological sites – and extant historical buildings and infrastructure, historic landscapes, and traditional cultural properties – can be located and evaluated before development begins.

Conservation and Mitigation

Most nations today ensure a degree of protection for their major monuments and archaeological sites. In England, as early as 1882, the first Ancient Monuments Act was passed and the first Inspector of Ancient Monuments appointed: the energetic archaeologist and pioneer excavator Lieutenant-General Augustus Lane-Fox Pitt-Rivers. A "schedule" of ancient monuments was drawn up, which were to be protected by law. Several of the most important monuments were taken into "guardianship," whereby they were conserved and opened to the public under the supervision of the Ancient Monuments Inspectorate.

In the United States, the first major federal legislation for archaeological protection, the American Antiquities Act, was signed into law in 1906 by Theodore Roosevelt. The act set out three provisions: that the damage, destruction, or excavation of historic or prehistoric ruins or monuments on federal land without permission would be prohibited; that the president would have the authority to establish national landmarks and associated reserves on federal land; and that permits could be granted for the excavation or collection of archaeological materials on federal land to qualified institutions that pursued such excavations for the purpose of increasing knowledge of the past and preserving the materials.

The American Antiquities Act set the foundation and fundamental principles for archaeology in the United States. These include that federal protection is limited to federal land (although some individual states and local governments have their own laws), that excavation is a permitted activity for those seeking to learn and conduct research in the public interest, that unpermitted archaeological activities and vandalism are criminally punishable, and that archaeological resources are important enough that the president may create reserves for protection independent of the other branches of government. These principles continue through the many other federal laws that followed. Today, the principal laws that practicing archaeologists must know and follow include the National Historic Preservation Act of 1966, the National Environmental Policy Act of 1969, the Archaeological Resources Protection Act of 1979, the Abandoned Shipwrecks Act of 1987, and the Native American Graves Protection and Repatriation Act of 1990. These laws, and a host of others, updated and expanded the basic principles and practices of protecting, preserving, and managing archaeological resources on federal lands in the United States (see the following section on **Cultural Resource Management** and "applied archaeology").

Similar provisions hold for the major monuments of many nations. But in the field of heritage management it is with the less obvious, perhaps less important sites that problems arise. Above all, it is difficult or impossible for sites to be protected if their existence is not known or recognized. That is where the crucial role of survey is obvious.

The conservation of the archaeological record is a fundamental principle of heritage management. It can be brought about by partnership agreement with the landowner – for instance to avoid plowing for agricultural purposes on recognized sites. Measures can be taken to mitigate the effects of coastal erosion (although this can be very difficult) or inappropriate land use. And above all, effective planning legislation can be used to avoid commercial development in sensitive archaeological areas. Indeed increasingly the approach is to think of entire landscapes and their conservation, rather than focusing upon isolated archaeological sites.

When considering the impact of commercial or industrial development, one aspect of mitigation is the carefully planned avoidance of damage to the archaeological record. A well-considered strategy in advance of development will usually favour this approach. In some cases, however, the development necessarily involves damage to the archaeological record. It is at this point that salvage or **rescue archaeology** becomes appropriate. Rarely, when particularly important

When the Spanish Conquistadors under Hernán Cortés occupied the Aztec capital, Tenochtitlán, in 1521, they destroyed its buildings and established their own capital, Mexico City, on the same site.

In 1790 the now-famous statue of the Aztec mother goddess Coatlicue was found, and also the great Calendar Stone, but it was not until the 20th century that more systematic archaeological work took place.

Various relatively small-scale excavations were carried out on remains within the city as they came to light in the course of building work. But in 1975 a more coherent initiative was taken: the institution by the Department of Pre-Hispanic Monuments of the Basin of Mexico Project. Its aim is to halt the destruction of archaeological remains during the continuing growth of the city. In 1977, a Museum of Tenochtitlán Project was begun, with the aim of excavating the area where remains of what appeared to be the Great Temple of the Aztecs had been found in 1948. The project was radically transformed early in 1978 when electricity workers discovered a large stone carved with a series of reliefs. The Department of Salvage Archaeology of the National Institute of Anthropology and History took charge. Within days, a huge monolith, 3.25 m (10 ft 7 in) in diameter, was revealed depicting the dismembered body of the Aztec goddess Coyolxauhqui who, according to myth, had been killed by her brother, the war god Huitzilopochtli.

The Museum of Tenochtitlán Project, under the direction of Eduardo Matos Moctezuma, became the Great Temple Project, which over the next few years brought to light one of the most remarkable archaeological sites in Mexico.

No one had realized how much would be preserved of the Great Temple. Although the Spaniards had razed the standing structure to the ground in 1521, this pyramid was the last of a series of re-buildings. Beneath the ruins of the last temple the excavations revealed those of earlier temples.

In addition to these architectural remains was a wonderful series of offerings to the temple's two gods, Huitzilopochtli and the rain god Tlaloc – objects of **obsidian** and jade, terracotta and stone sculptures, and

The Great Stone (above), found in 1978, provided the catalyst for the Great Temple excavations. The goddess Coyolxauhqui is shown decapitated (left, a detail of her head) and dismembered – killed by her brother, the war god Huitzilopochtli.

MEXICO

Mexico City •

other special dedications, including rare coral and the remains of a jaguar buried with a ball of greenstone in its mouth.

A major area of Mexico City has now been turned into a permanent museum and national monument. Mexico has regained one of its greatest pre-Columbian buildings, and the Great Temple of the Aztecs is once again one of the marvels of Tenochtitlán.

(Above) The skeleton of a jaguar from a chamber in the fourth of seven building stages of the Great Temple. The greenstone ball in its mouth may have been placed there as a substitute for the spirit of the deceased.

(Below) A recent discovery: this massive stone slab depicting the god Tlaltecuhtli ("Lord of the Earth") was found at the site in 2006. It may cover a chamber entrance.

(Above) The Great Temple excavation site, with stairways visible of successive phases of the monument. The building was originally pyramidal in form, surmounted by twin temples to the war god Huitzilopochtli and the rain god Tlaloc. Conservation work is in progress here on the Coyolxauhqui stone, visible under scaffolding (left of center).

archaeological remains are unexpectedly uncovered, development may be halted entirely (for an example, see box on previous pages).

It is inevitable in the case of some major developments, for instance the construction of a freeway, that in the course of the undertaking many archaeological sites, major as well as minor, will be encountered. In the survey stage of the planning process, most of these will have been located, observed, noted, and evaluated. A mitigation plan would address what steps are required to protect the archaeological record or recover significant information if it cannot be protected by avoidance. In some cases it may be possible to alter the route of the highway so as to avoid damage to important sites: that is one aspect of mitigation. But usually, if the project is to go ahead, the "preventive" archaeology will involve the investigation of the site by appropriate means of sampling, including excavation.

In Britain, for example, the important **Neolithic** site of Durrington Walls was first located and then systematically excavated in the course of road construction. It turned out to be a major "henge" monument – a very large ditched enclosure – and was the first of its class to give clear indications of a series of major circular timber buildings.

In many countries a significant proportion of the budget available for archaeological research is now deliberately assigned to these projects, where damage to the archaeological record seems inevitable and where it can be mitigated in this way. There is a growing presumption that sites which are not threatened should not be excavated when there is a potentially informative site which can provide comparable excavation whose future is in any case threatened by damage through development. It is increasingly realized that important research questions can be answered in the course of such mitigation procedures.

The Practice of CRM in the United States

Over the past four decades North American archaeology has become embedded in Cultural Resource Management (CRM), a complex of laws, regulations, and professional practice designed to manage historic buildings and sites, cultural landscapes, and other cultural and historic places. The practice of CRM is often known as "applied archaeology."

The National Historic Preservation Act and the National Environmental Policy Act are the major legal bases for CRM in the United States. These laws require agencies of the US government to consider the environmental impacts of their actions (through an "environmental assessment," which may lead to an "environmental impact statement"), including effects on historical, archaeological, and cultural values. The role of "State Historic Preservation Officer" (SHPO) was created in each US state. Each agency runs its own compliance program.

Construction and land use projects in which US government agencies are involved – whether on federal land or on other lands but federally funded or requiring a federal permit – must be reviewed to determine their effects on environmental, cultural, and historical resources. CRM programs in state and local governments, federal agencies, academic institutions, and private consulting firms have grown out of this requirement. The SHPOs coordinate many CRM activities, and keep files on historic and prehistoric sites, structures, buildings, districts, and landscapes.

Section 106 of the National Historic Preservation Act requires federal agencies to identify historic places of all kinds (archaeological sites, historic buildings, Native American tribal sacred sites, etc.) that may be affected by their actions, in consultation with SHPOs, tribes, and others. They are then required to determine what to do about project effects – all in consultation with SHPOs and other interested parties. Identification often requires archaeological surveys both to find and evaluate archaeological sites. Evaluation involves applying published criteria to determine eligibility for the National Register of Historic

KEY CONCEPTS
CRM in the USA

- CRM (Cultural Resource Management) or "applied archaeology" accounts for over 90 percent of the field archaeology carried out in the USA today

- *Legal Basis*: under Section 106 of the National Historic Preservation Act (NHPA), archaeological investigation is often carried out in advance of projects on federal land, using federal funds, or requiring a federal permit

- *Funding*: generally speaking, the proponent of the construction or land use project pays for the work, whether that party is a federal, state, or local agency, or a private developer

- *Compliance*: project proponents fund legally required compliance work that includes inventory (survey), evaluation of a resource's importance, assessment of impacts to important resources, and mitigation (which may include avoidance, excavation, and conservation)

- *Outcome*: the fieldwork typically results in at least a report filed with the SHPO and data entered in government and other databases. Many CRM projects also result in published journal articles, monographs, and books

UNITED STATES

Lubbub
Creek ●

At the time the largest earth-moving project ever undertaken, the Tennessee-Tombigbee Waterway connects those two rivers with a 234-mile-long series of canals running through Mississippi and Alabama. A CRM survey of the huge area of land involved identified 682 sites; it was determined that 27 would be affected by waterway construction. Of these, 17 had good research potential, and another 24 sites were selected for data recovery. Twelve sites could be preserved by altering the construction program.

Excavation was designed to investigate the evolution of cultures in the area, with emphasis on sampling a good range of sites. The largest site was Lubbub Creek, the only major settlement in the threatened

area belonging to the Mississippian culture (AD 900–1450). It includes a major ceremonial mound surrounded by a fortified village. The work undertaken in mitigation of environmental impact gave an excellent opportunity for systematic excavation of both settlement and cemeteries.

An aerial view of the Lubbub Creek site on the Tombigbee River, Alabama. The smaller photograph shows two of the salvage archaeologists carefully cleaning a large urn.

Places – the US schedule of significant historic and cultural land areas, sites, structures, neighborhoods, and communities.

If the agency and its consulting partners find that significant sites are present and will be adversely affected, they seek ways to mitigate the effect. Often this involves redesigning the project to reduce, minimize, or even avoid the damage. Sometimes, where archaeological sites are concerned, the decision is to conduct excavations to recover significant data before they are destroyed. If the parties cannot agree on what to do, an independent body known as the Advisory Council on Historic Preservation makes a recommendation and then the responsible federal agency makes its final decision.

Most surveys and data recovery projects in the USA are carried out by private firms – sometimes companies that specialize in CRM work, but otherwise by branches of large engineering, planning, or environmental impact assessment companies. Some academic institutions, museums, and non-profit organizations also carry out CRM work. CRM-based surveys and excavations now comprise at least 90 percent of the field archaeology carried out in the USA.

The review system under Section 106 can produce excellent archaeological research, but research interests must be balanced with other public interests, especially the concerns of Native American tribes and other communities. The quality of work depends largely on the integrity and skill of the participants – agency employees, SHPOs, tribal and community representatives, and private-sector archaeologists. Among the recurring problems are quality control in fieldwork, applying the results of fieldwork to important research topics, publication and other dissemination of results, and the long-term preservation and management of recovered **artifacts**.

One good example of this process is the vast Tennessee-Tombigbee Waterway project (see box opposite), although not all CRM projects are so well or responsibly managed. Particularly in the case of small projects, which are carried out by the thousands, it is easy for very shoddy work to be done and little useful data to be produced. The Society for American Archaeology has helped to fund a Register of Professional Archaeologists in an attempt to improve standards. Professional requirements and qualifications have been established by the Department of the Interior, various land-managing agencies, and even some local governments. Permits to undertake archaeological work are designed to require credentials, experience, and acceptable past performance.

International Protection

Since world government is currently based upon the effective autonomy of the nation states of the United Nations, measures of conservation and mitigation likewise operate at the level of the nation states. Only in a few cases does some broader perspective prevail, often through the agency of UNESCO (The United

Nations Educational, Scientific and Cultural Organization) whose headquarters are located in Paris, France.

The World Heritage List.   One effective initiative arises from the World Heritage Convention of 1972, under which the World Heritage Committee can place major sites on the World Heritage List. At the time of writing there are 689 cultural sites on the List, along with 176 natural sites and 25 classified as mixed. Although election to the list does not in itself afford protection, and certainly does not in reality bring additional international resources to assist in conservation, it does act as an incentive for the responsible nation state to ensure that recognized standards are met.

There is in addition a World Heritage in Danger List which highlights the needs of specific threatened sites. The ancient city of Bam in Iran, seriously damaged by an earthquake in December 2003, is a case in point, as is the Bamiyan Valley in Afghanistan which has suffered sadly through war and unrest. The walled city of Baku in Azerbaijan is another major site, damaged by earthquake in November 2000 and now receiving support.

Countering the Traffic in Illicit Antiquities.   The principal international measure against the traffic in illicit antiquities is the 1970 UNESCO Convention on the Means of Preventing the Illicit Import, Export and Transfer of Ownership of Cultural Property. But its principles are not directly enforced by international law, and depend rather on national legislation and on bilateral agreements between nations. The responsibilities of collectors and museums were reviewed in Chapter 11. There are signs that it is becoming more difficult to sell recently looted antiquities on the open market, at any rate in some countries, but the problem remains a massive one.

Protecting the Cultural Heritage in Times of War.   The 1954 Hague Convention for the Protection of Cultural Property in the Event of Armed Conflict and its protocols in principle offer a degree of protection. In practice, however, they have not been effective and, as noted earlier, have not yet been ratified by the United Kingdom or by the United States of America. Both nations were criticized for their shortcomings during the invasion of Iraq in 2003.

These international initiatives are all important, and potentially significant. But at present they are very limited in their effectiveness. In the future they may be better supported, but most of the effective measures safeguarding the future of the past still work primarily at a national level.

PUBLICATION, ARCHIVES, AND RESOURCES: SERVING THE PUBLIC

The pace of discovery through the surveys conducted to assess environmental impact and the excavation procedures undertaken in mitigation is remarkable. But the results are often not well published or otherwise made available either to specialists or to the public. In the United States there is an obligation that environmental impact statements and a summary of any measures taken in mitigation should be lodged with the state archive, but not that they should be published. In Greece the government has for some years failed to fund publication of the Archaiologikon Deltion, the official record of nationally funded excavations. The record is better in France and to some extent in Germany. But few countries can boast effective publication of the quite considerable activities undertaken, generally with a measure of state funding.

In some countries this has led to a division between the practice of academic archaeologists (working in universities and museums) and of those undertaking **contract archaeology**, whether funded by the developer or by the state, but in both cases working to mitigate the impact of development. The work of the former is supposed to be problem-oriented and often does indeed lead to publication in national or international archaeological journals and in detailed monographs. The work of the contract archaeologist is sometimes carefully coordinated, leading to informative regional and national surveys. But in too many instances its publication is not well coordinated at all.

The solution to these problems is not yet clear. But one possibility is certainly emerging: online publication. In this respect some of the major museums have led the way, making the catalogs of their collections available online. Few contract archaeologists currently make their environmental impact statements or mitigation reports available in that way, but this may one day become a requirement: a condition for funding in the first place. In the United Kingdom an important initiative has been taken by the national archaeological Find Reporting Scheme. There the practice of metal detecting in the search for archaeological artifacts is not prohibited by law, as it is in many countries, and this has been a concern to professional archaeologists. But at least state funding has been established for a scheme whereby metal detectorists can voluntarily report their finds to a reporting officer, and many in fact do so. In particular the results are being made available online, with a significant increase in information about the distributions of particular classes of artifact. The new dimension here is that the data are available online to the public, and that some of the traditional barriers between professional researchers and the wider public are breaking down. It is likely that in the future excavation data will also become available online and thus more rapidly accessible than is often currently the case. The obligation to inform the public, who ultimately provide the resources for much of the research, is being met.

WHAT USE IS THE PAST?

The popularity of archaeology has markedly increased in recent years, if television programs and magazine articles are used as a measure. Certainly the number of archaeology students in university courses has increased greatly in many countries. And the world's great museums have ever-increasing visitor numbers. As we have seen, in many countries public resources are invested in conservation, and developers are obliged to ensure that proper measures are undertaken in mitigation of their impact upon the cultural environment. But are these resources expended simply to satisfy the idle curiosity of the world's citizens? Is their main purpose simply to create agreeable historic sites to visit?

We think that there is more at work than this. It can be argued that there is today a growing awareness that humankind needs to feel and to know that it has a past – a past which can be documented securely by concrete material evidence which we can all access, examine, and assess. For without our roots we are lost. Over recent generations those roots are well represented by our friends, by our families, and by our existing communities. But in a deeper sense, and in a deeper past, we are all in this together. The different **religions** of the world provide meaning for the lives of many people. But they do not all agree, or so it might seem, about some of the questions of human origins and early history that we have been discussing here. Some offer creation stories that are profound and illuminating. Each of these can be enriched by knowledge of the material evidence for early human development. The finds are there, in every part of the world. And more finds continue to be made.

It is abundantly clear, from the pace of archaeological discovery, that there is more to learn. That is one reason why the subject is so interesting. And it always will be. So long as the practices of conservation and mitigation are maintained we shall continue to learn more about the human past, and in that sense about what it means to be human. We hope that such will be the future of the past. And we do not doubt that it will be useful.

STUDY QUESTIONS
• What are some of the ways that humans damage or destroy archaeological sites?
• In the United States, what are the key pieces of legislation that relate to archaeological protection, conservation, and mitigation?
• What is Cultural Resource Management (CRM)? What percentage of archaeological work in the USA can be considered CRM?
• Why is the publication of archaeological information so important?
• How is archaeology relevant to today's world?

SUMMARY

- Many nations believe that it is the duty of the government to have policies with regard to conservation, and these conservation laws often apply to archaeology. Construction, agricultural intensification, tourism, and looting are all human activities that damage or destroy sites.

- Built on a strong legal foundation, CRM or "applied archaeology" plays a major role in American archaeology. When a project is on federal land, uses federal money, or needs a federal permit, the law requires that cultural resources are identified, evaluated, and if they cannot be avoided, addressed accordingly in an approved mitigation plan. A large number of private contract archaeology firms employ the majority of archaeologists in the US. These firms are responsible for meeting mitigation requirements, overseen by a lead agency and an SHPO. Publication of final reports is required, but the variable quality and usually limited dissemination of these reports remain a problem.

- Archaeologists have a duty to report what they find. Since excavation is, to a certain extent, destructive, published material is often the only record of what was found at a site. Perhaps up to 60 percent of modern excavations remain unpublished after 10 years. Governments and professional organizations are taking a harsher stance against archaeologists who do not publish and often will not grant digging permits to those who have unpublished work. The Internet and the popular media can help to fulfil one of the fundamental purposes of archaeology: to provide the public with a better understanding of the past.

FURTHER READING

The following books are useful introductions to heritage management:

Carman, J. 2002. *Archaeology and Heritage, an Introduction*. Continuum: London.

King, T.F. 2008. *Cultural Resource Laws and Practice, an Introductory Guide* (3rd ed.). Altamira Press: Walnut Creek.

King, T.F. 2005. *Doing Archaeology: A Cultural Resource Management Perspective.* Left Coast Press: Walnut Creek.

Sabloff, J.A. 2008. *Archaeology Matters: Action Archaeology in the Modern World.* Left Coast Press: Walnut Creek.

Smith, L. & Waterton, E. 2009. *Heritage, Communities and Archaeology*. Duckworth: London.

Sørensen, M.L.S. & Carman, J. 2009. *Heritage Studies: Methods and Approaches*. Routledge. London.

Tyler, N., Ligibel, T.J. & Tyler, I. 2009. *Historic Preservation: An Introduction to its History, Principles and Practice* (2nd ed.). W.W. Norton & Company: New York.

Glossary

(Terms in *italics* are defined elsewhere in the glossary)

absolute dating The determination of age with reference to a specific time scale, such as a fixed calendrical system; also referred to as chronometric dating.

aerial reconnaissance An important survey technique in the discovery and recording of archaeological sites (see also *reconnaissance survey*).

alloying Technique involving the mixing of two or more metals to create a new material, e.g. the fusion of copper and tin to make bronze.

annealing In copper and bronze metallurgy, this refers to the repeated process of heating and hammering the material to produce the desired shape.

anthropology The study of humanity – our physical characteristics as animals, and our unique non-biological characteristics we call *culture*. The subject is generally broken down into three subdisciplines: *biological (physical) anthropology, cultural (social) anthropology*, and *archaeology*.

archaeobotany See *paleoethnobotany*.

archaeological culture A constantly recurring *assemblage* of artifacts assumed to be representative of a particular set of behavioral activities carried out at a particular time and place (*cf. culture*).

archaeology A subdiscipline of anthropology involving the study of the human past through its material remains.

archaeology of cult The study of the material indications of patterned actions undertaken in response to religious beliefs.

archaeomagnetic dating Sometimes referred to as paleomagnetic dating, it is based on the fact that changes in the earth's magnetic field over time can be recorded as remanent magnetism in materials such as baked clay structures (ovens, kilns, and hearths).

archaeozoology Sometimes referred to as zooarchaeology, this involves the identification and analysis of faunal species from archaeological sites, as an aid to the reconstruction of human diets and to an understanding of the contemporary environment at the time of deposition.

artifact Any portable object used, modified, or made by humans; e.g. stone tools, pottery, and metal weapons.

assemblage A group of artifacts recurring together at a particular time and place, and representing the sum of human activities.

association The co-occurrence of an artifact with other archaeological remains, usually in the same *matrix*.

attribute A minimal characteristic of an artifact such that it cannot be further subdivided; attributes commonly studied include aspects of form, style, decoration, color, and raw material.

Australopithecus A collective name for the earliest known hominids emerging about 5 million years ago in East Africa.

band A term used to describe small-scale societies of hunters and gatherers, generally less than 100 people, who move seasonally to exploit wild (undomesticated) food resources. Kinship ties play an important part in social organization.

bioarchaeology The study of human remains (but in the Old World it is sometimes applied to other kinds of organic remains such as animal bones).

biological anthropology A subdiscipline of anthropology dealing with the study of human biological or physical characteristics and their evolution.

characterization (sourcing) The application of techniques of examination by which characteristic properties of the constituent material of traded goods can be identified, and thus their source of origin; e.g. petrographic *thin-section analysis*.

chiefdom A term used to describe a society that operates on the principle of ranking, i.e. differential social status. Different *lineages* are graded on a scale of prestige, calculated by how closely related one is to the chief. The chiefdom generally has a permanent ritual and ceremonial center, as well as being characterized by local specialization in crafts.

chronometric dating See *absolute dating*.

classification The ordering of phenomena into groups or other classificatory schemes on the basis of shared attributes (see also *type* and *typology*).

cognitive archaeology The study of past ways of thought and symbolic structures from material remains.

cognitive map An interpretive framework of the world which, it is argued, exists in the human mind and affects actions and decisions as well as knowledge structures.

cognitive-processual approach An alternative to the materialist orientation of the functional-processual approach, it is concerned with (1) the integration of the cognitive and symbolic with other aspects of early societies; (2) the role of ideology as an active organizational force.

computerized (computed) axial tomography (CAT or CT scanner) The method by which scanners allow detailed internal views of bodies such as mummies. The body is passed into the machine and images of cross-sectional "slices" through the body are produced.

conjoining See *refitting*.

context An artifact's context usually consists of its immediate *matrix* (the material around it e.g. gravel, clay, or sand), its provenience (horizontal and vertical position in the matrix), and its *association* with other artifacts (with other archaeological remains, usually in the same matrix).

contract archaeology Archaeological research conducted under the aegis of federal or state legislation, often in advance of highway construction or urban development, where the archaeologist is contracted to undertake the necessary research.

coprolites Fossilized feces; these contain food residues that can be used to reconstruct diet and subsistence activities.

core A lithic artifact used as a blank from which other tools or flakes are made.

Critical Theory A theoretical approach developed by the so-called "Frankfurt School" of German social thinkers, which stresses that all knowledge is historical, and in a sense biassed communication; thus, all claims to "objective" knowledge are illusory.

cultural anthropology A subdiscipline of anthropology concerned with the non-biological, behavioral aspects of society; i.e. the social, linguistic, and technological components underlying human behavior. Two important branches of cultural anthropology are *ethnography* (the study of living cultures) and *ethnology* (which attempts to compare cultures using ethnographic evidence). In Europe, it is referred to as *social anthropology*.

cultural ecology A term devised by Julian Steward to account for the dynamic relationship between human society and its environment, in which *culture* is viewed as the primary adaptive mechanism.

cultural resource management (CRM) The safeguarding of the archaeological heritage through the protection of sites and through salvage archaeology (rescue archaeology), generally within the framework of legislation designed to safeguard the past.

culture A term used by anthropologists when referring to the non-biological characteristics unique to a particular society (*cf. archaeological culture*).

culture-historical approach An approach to archaeological interpretation which uses the procedure of the traditional historian (including emphasis on specific circumstances elaborated with rich detail, and processes of *inductive* reasoning).

deduction A process of reasoning by which more specific consequences are inferred by rigorous argument from more general propositions (*cf. induction*).

deep-sea cores Cores drilled from the sea bed that provide the most coherent record of climate changes on a worldwide scale. The cores contain shells of microscopic marine organisms (foraminifera) laid down on the ocean floor through the continuous process of sedimentation. Variations in the ratio of two oxygen isotopes in the calcium carbonate of these shells give a sensitive indicator of sea temperature at the time the organisms were alive.

dendrochronology The study of tree-ring patterns; annual variations in climatic conditions which produce differential growth can be used both as a measure of environmental change, and as the basis for a chronology.

diatom analysis A method of environmental reconstruction based on plant microfossils. Diatoms are unicellular algae, whose silica cell walls survive after the algae die, and they accumulate in large numbers at the bottom of rivers and lakes. Assemblages directly reflect the floristic composition of the water's extinct communities, as well as the water's salinity, alkalinity, and nutrient status.

diffusionist approach The theory popularized by V.G. Childe that all the attributes of civilization from architecture to metalworking had diffused from the Near East to Europe.

DNA (Deoxyribonucleic acid) The material which carries the hereditary instructions (the "blueprint") which determine the formation of all living organisms.

earth resistance survey A method of *subsurface detection* which measures changes in conductivity by passing electrical current through ground soils. This is generally a consequence of moisture content, and in this way, buried features can be detected by differential retention of groundwater.

ecofacts Non-artifactual organic and environmental remains which have cultural relevance, e.g. faunal and floral material as well as soils and sediments.

electrical resistivity See *earth resistance survey*.

electrolysis A standard cleaning process in archaeological conservation. Artifacts are placed in a chemical solution, and by passing a weak current between them and a surrounding metal grill, the corrosive salts move from the cathode (object) to the anode (grill), removing any accumulated deposit and leaving the artifact clean.

electron spin resonance (ESR) Enables trapped electrons within bone and shell to be measured without the heating that *thermoluminescence* requires. As with TL, the number of trapped electrons indicates the age of the specimen.

environmental archaeology A field of inter-disciplinary research – archaeology and natural science – which is directed at the reconstruction of human use of plants and animals, and how past societies adapted to changing environmental conditions.

environmental circumscription An explanation for the origins of the state propounded by Robert Carneiro that emphasizes the fundamental role exerted by environmental constraints and by territorial limitations.

ethnicity The existence of ethnic groups, including tribal groups. Though these are difficult to recognize from the archaeological record, the study of language and linguistic boundaries shows that ethnic groups are often correlated with language areas.

ethnoarchaeology The study of contemporary cultures with a view to understanding the behavioral relationships which underlie the production of material culture.

ethnography A subset of *cultural anthropology* concerned with the study of contemporary cultures through first-hand observation.

ethnology A subset of *cultural anthropology* concerned with the comparative study of contemporary cultures, with a view to deriving general principles about human society.

evolution The process of growth and development generally accompanied by increasing complexity. In biology, this change is tied to Darwin's concept of natural selection as the basis of species survival. Darwin's work laid the foundations for the study of artifact *typology*, pioneered by such scholars as Pitt-Rivers and Montelius.

evolutionary archaeology The idea that the processes responsible for biological evolution also drive culture change, i.e. the application of Darwinian evolutionary theory to the archaeological record.

excavation The principal method of data acquisition in archaeology, involving the systematic uncovering of archaeological remains through the removal of the deposits of soil and the other material covering them and accompanying them.

experimental archaeology The study of past behavioral processes through experimental reconstruction under carefully controlled scientific conditions.

fall-off analysis The study of regularities in the way in which quantities of traded items found in the archaeological record decline as the distance from the source increases. This may be plotted as a fall-off curve, with the quantities of material (Y-axis) plotted against distance from source (X-axis).

feature A non-portable *artifact*; e.g. hearths, architectural elements, or soil stains.

fission-track dating A dating method based on the operation of a radioactive clock, the spontaneous fission of an isotope of uranium present in a wide range of rocks and minerals. As with *potassium-argon dating*, with whose time range it overlaps, the method gives useful dates from rocks adjacent to archaeological material.

flotation A method of screening (sieving) excavated *matrix* in water so as to separate and recover small *ecofacts* and *artifacts*.

fluxgate magnetometer A type of magnetometer used in *subsurface detection*, producing a continuous reading.

forensic anthropology The scientific study of human remains in order to build up a biological profile of the deceased.

formation processes Those processes affecting the way in which archaeological materials came to be buried, and their subsequent history afterwards. Cultural formation processes include the deliberate or accidental activities of humans; natural formation processes refer to natural or environmental events which govern the burial and survival of the archaeological record.

frequency seriation A *relative dating* method which relies principally on measuring changes in the proportional abundance, or frequency, observed among finds (e.g. counts of tool types, or of ceramic fabrics).

functional-processual approach See *processual archaeology*.

Geographic Information Systems/GIS GIS are software-based systems designed for the collection, organizing, storage, retrieval, analysis, and displaying of spatial/digital geographical data held in different "layers." A GIS can also include other digital data.

geomagnetic reversals An aspect of archaeomagnetism relevant to the dating of the Lower Paleolithic, involving complete reversals in the earth's magnetic field.

gift exchange See *reciprocity*.

ground reconnaissance A collective name for a wide variety of methods for identifying individual archaeological sites, including consultation of documentary sources, place-name evidence, local folklore, and legend, but primarily actual fieldwork.

half-life The time taken for half the quantity of a radioactive isotope in a sample to decay (see also *radioactive decay*).

hand-axe A Paleolithic stone tool usually made by modifying (chipping or flaking) a natural pebble.

hoards Deliberately buried groups of valuables or prized possessions, often in times of conflict or war, and which, for one reason or another, have not been reclaimed. Metal hoards are a primary source of evidence for the European Bronze Age.

hominins The subfamily to which humans belong, as opposed to the "hominids" which incude not only humans but also gorillas and chimps, and "hominoids" which group these with gibbons and orang-utans.

hunter-gatherers A collective term for the members of small-scale mobile or semi-sedentary societies, whose subsistence is mainly focused on hunting game and gathering wild plants and fruits; organizational structure is based on *bands* with strong kinship ties.

hypothetico-deductive explanation A form of explanation based on the formulation of hypotheses and the establishment from them by *deduction* of consequences which can then be tested against the archaeological data.

ice cores Borings taken from the Arctic and Antarctic polar ice caps, containing layers of compacted ice useful for reconstructing paleoenvironments and as a method of *absolute dating*.

iconography An important component of *cognitive archaeology*, this involves the study of artistic representations which usually have an overt religious or ceremonial significance; e.g. individual deities may be distinguished, each with a special characteristic, such as corn with the corn god, or the sun with a sun goddess etc.

induction A method of reasoning in which one proceeds by generalization from a series of specific observations so as to derive general conclusions (*cf. deduction*).

interaction sphere A regional or inter-regional exchange system, e.g. the Hopewell interaction sphere.

isotopic analysis An important source of information on the reconstruction of prehistoric diets, this technique analyzes the ratios of the principal isotopes preserved in human bone; in effect the method reads the chemical signatures left in the body by different foods. Isotopic analysis is also used in *characterization* studies.

landscape archaeology The study of individual features including settlements seen as single components within the broader perspective of the patterning of human activity over a wide area.

lineage A group claiming descent from a common ancestor.

market exchange A mode of exchange which implies both a specific location for transactions and the sort of social relations where bargaining can occur. It usually involves a system of price-making through negotiation.

Marxist archaeology Based principally on the writings of Karl Marx and Friedrich Engels, this posits a materialist model of societal change. Change within a society is seen as the result of contradictions arising between the forces of production (technology) and the relations of production (social organization). Such contradictions are seen to emerge as a struggle between distinct social classes.

material culture The buildings, tools, and other artifacts that constitute the material remains of former societies.

matrix The physical material within which artifacts are embedded or supported.

Mesolithic An Old World chronological period beginning around 10,000 years ago, between the *Paleolithic* and the *Neolithic*.

metallographic examination A technique used in the study of early metallurgy involving the microscopic examination of a polished section cut from an artifact, which has been etched so as to reveal the metal structure.

microwear analysis The study of the patterns of wear or damage on the edge of stone tools, which provides valuable information on the way in which the tool was used.

Midwestern taxonomic system A framework devised by McKern (1939) to systematize sequences in the Great Plains area of the United States, using the general principle of similarities between artifact *assemblages*.

monocausal explanation Explanations of culture change (e.g. for *state* origins) which lays stress on a single dominant explanatory factor or "prime mover."

multivariate explanation Explanation of culture change, e.g. the origin of the state, which, in contrast to monocausal approaches, stresses the interaction of several factors operating simultaneously.

Neolithic An Old World chronological period characterized by the development of agriculture and, hence, an increasing emphasis on sedentism.

Neolithic Revolution A term coined by V.G. Childe in 1941 to describe the origin and consequences of farming (i.e. the development of stock raising and agriculture), allowing the widespread development of settled village life.

New Archaeology A new approach advocated in the 1960s which argued for an explicitly scientific framework of archaeological method and theory, with hypotheses rigorously tested, as the proper basis for explanation rather than simply description (see also *processual archaeology*).

non-probabilistic sampling A non-statistical sampling strategy (in contrast to *probabilistic sampling*) which concentrates on sampling areas on the basis of intuition,

historical documentation, or long field experience in the area.

obsidian A volcanic glass whose ease of working and characteristically hard flint-like edges allowed it to be used for the making of tools.

off-site data Evidence from a range of information, including scatters of artifacts and features such as plowmarks and field boundaries, that provides important evidence about human exploitation of the environment.

Oldowan industry The earliest toolkits, comprising flake and pebble tools, used by hominids in the Olduvai Gorge, East Africa.

open-area excavation The opening up of large horizontal areas for *excavation*, used especially where single period deposits lie close to the surface as, for example, with the remains of American Indian or European Neolithic long houses.

paleoentomology The study of insects from archaeological contexts. The survival of insect exoskeletons, which are quite resistant to decomposition, is important in the reconstruction of paleo-environments.

paleoethnobotany (archaeobotany) The recovery and identification of plant remains from archaeological *contexts*, used in reconstructing past environments and economies.

Paleolithic The archaeological period before *c.* 10,000 BC, characterized by the earliest known stone tool manufacture.

paleomagnetism See *archaeomagnetic dating*.

palynology The study and analysis of fossil pollen as an aid to the reconstruction of past vegetation and climates.

physical anthropology See *biological anthropology*.

plating A method of bonding metals together, for instance silver with copper or copper with gold.

polity A politically independent or autonomous social unit, whether simple or complex, which may in the case of a complex society (such as a state) comprise many lesser dependent components.

pollen analysis See *palynology*.

postprocessual explanation Explanation formulated in reaction to the perceived

limitations of functional-processual archaeology. It eschews generalization in favor of an "individualizing" approach that is influenced by *structuralism, Critical Theory,* and neo-Marxist thought.

potassium-argon dating A method used to date rocks up to thousands of millions of years old, though it is restricted to volcanic material no more recent than *c.* 100,000 years old. One of the most widely used methods in the dating of early hominid sites in Africa.

prehistory The period of human history before the advent of writing.

prestige goods A term used to designate a limited range of exchange goods to which a society ascribes high status or value.

probabilistic sampling Sampling method, using probability theory, designed to draw reliable general conclusions about a site or region, based on small sample areas; 4 types of sampling strategies are recognized: (1) *simple random sampling*; (2) *stratified random sampling*; (3) *systematic sampling*; (4) *stratified systematic sampling*.

processual archaeology An approach that stresses the dynamic relationship between social and economic aspects of culture and the environment as the basis for understanding the processes of culture change. Uses the scientific methodology of problem statement, hypothesis formulation, and subsequent testing. The earlier functional-processual archaeology has been contrasted with *cognitive-processual archaeology*, where emphasis is on integrating ideological and symbolic aspects.

pseudoarchaeology The use of selective archaeological evidence to promulgate nonscientific, fictional accounts of the past.

pyrotechnology The intentional use and control of fire by humans.

radioactive decay The regular process by which radioactive isotopes break down into their decay products with a half-life which is specific to the isotope in question (see also *radiocarbon dating*).

radiocarbon dating An absolute dating method that measures the decay of the radioactive isotope of carbon (^{14}C) in organic material (see *half-life*).

ranked societies Societies in which there is unequal access to prestige and status e.g. *chiefdoms* and *states*.

reciprocity A mode of exchange in which transactions take place between individuals who are symmetrically placed, i.e. they are exchanging as equals, neither being in a dominant position.

reconnaissance survey A broad range of techniques involved in the location of archaeological sites, e.g. the recording of surface artifacts and features, and the sampling of natural and mineral resources.

redistribution A mode of exchange which implies the operation of some central organizing authority. Goods are received or appropriated by the central authority, and subsequently some of them are sent by that authority to other locations.

refitting Sometimes referred to as conjoining, this entails attempting to put stone tools and flakes back together again, and provides important information on the processes involved in the knapper's craft.

relative dating The determination of chronological sequence without recourse to a fixed time scale; e.g. the arrangement of artifacts in a typological sequence, or *seriation (cf. absolute dating)*.

religion A framework of beliefs relating to supernatural or superhuman beings or forces that transcend the everyday material world.

remote sensing The imaging of phenomena from a distance, primarily through airborne and satellite imaging. "Ground-based remote sensing" links geophysical methods such as radar with remote sensing methods applied at ground level, such as thermography.

rescue archaeology See *salvage archaeology*.

research design Systematic planning of archaeological research, usually including (1) the formulation of a strategy to resolve a particular question; (2) the collection and recording of the evidence; (3) the processing and analysis of these data and their interpretation; and (4) the publication of results.

resistivity meter See *soil resistivity*.

salvage archaeology The location and recording (usually through excavation) of archaeological sites in advance of highway construction, drainage projects, or urban development.

segmentary societies Relatively small and autonomous groups, usually of agriculturalists, who regulate their own affairs; in some cases, they may join together with other comparable segmentary societies to form a larger ethnic unit.

seriation A relative dating technique based on the chronological ordering of a group of artifacts or assemblages, where the most similar are placed adjacent to each other in the series. See *frequency seriation*.

side-scan sonar A survey method used in underwater archaeology which provides the broadest view of the sea-floor. An acoustic emitter is towed behind a vessel and sends out sound waves in a fan-shaped beam. These pulses of sonic energy are reflected back to a transducer – return time depending on distance traveled – and recorded on a rotating drum.

simple random sampling A type of *probabilistic sampling* where the areas to be sampled are chosen using a table of random numbers. Drawbacks include (1) defining the site's boundaries initially; (2) the nature of random number tables results in some areas being allotted clusters of sample squares, while others remain untouched.

simulation The formulation and computer implementation of dynamic models, i.e. models concerned with change through time.

site A distinct spatial clustering of *artifacts, features*, structures, and organic and environmental remains – the residue of human activity.

social anthropology See *cultural anthropology*.

soil resistivity See *earth resistance survey*.

state A term used to describe a social formation defined by distinct territorial boundedness, and characterized by strong central government in which the operation of political power is sanctioned by legitimate force. In cultural evolutionist

models, it ranks second only to the empire as the most complex societal development stage.

stela (pl. stelae) A free-standing carved stone monument.

step-trenching *Excavation* method used on very deep sites, such as Near Eastern *tell* sites, in which the excavation proceeds downwards in a series of gradually narrowing steps.

stratification The laying down or depositing of strata or layers (also called deposits) one above the other. A succession of layers should provide a relative chronological sequence, with the earliest at the bottom and the latest at the top.

stratified random sampling A form of *probabilistic sampling* in which the region or site is divided into natural zones or strata such as cultivated land and forest; units are then chosen by a random number procedure so as to give each zone a number of squares proportional to its area, thus overcoming the inherent bias in *simple random sampling*.

stratified systematic sampling A form of *probabilistic sampling* which combines elements of (1) *simple random sampling*, (2) *stratified random sampling*, and (3) *systematic sampling*, in an effort to reduce sampling bias.

stratigraphy The study and validation of *stratification*; the analysis in the vertical, time dimension, of a series of layers in the horizontal, space dimension. It is often used as a *relative dating* technique to assess the temporal sequence of artifact deposition.

structuralist approaches Interpretations which stress that human actions are guided by beliefs and symbolic concepts, and that underlying these are structures of thought which find expression in various forms. The proper object of study is therefore to uncover the structures of thought and to study their influence in shaping the ideas in the minds of the human actors who created the archaeological record.

style According to the art historian, Ernst Gombrich, style is "any distinctive and therefore recognizable way in which an act is performed and made." Archaeologists and anthropologists have defined "stylistic areas" as areal units representing shared ways of producing and decorating artifacts.

subsurface detection Collective name for a variety of remote sensing techniques operating at ground level, and including both invasive and non-invasive techniques.

surface survey Two basic kinds can be identified: (1) unsystematic and (2) systematic. The former involves field-walking, i.e. scanning the ground along one's path and recording the location of artifacts and surface features. Systematic survey by comparison is less subjective and involves a grid system, such that the survey area is divided into sectors and these are walked systematically, thus making the recording of finds more accurate.

systematic sampling A form of *probabilistic sampling* employing a grid of equally spaced locations; e.g. selecting every other square. This method of regular spacing runs the risk of missing (or hitting) every single example if the distribution itself is regularly spaced.

systematic survey See *surface survey*.

taphonomy The study of processes which have affected organic materials such as bone after death; it also involves the microscopic analysis of tooth-marks or cut marks to assess the effects of butchery or scavenging activities.

tectonic movements Displacements in the plates that make up the earth's crust.

tell A Near Eastern term that refers to a mound site formed through successive human occupation over a very long timespan.

temper Inclusions in pottery clay which act as a filler to give the clay added strength and workability and to counteract any cracking or shrinkage during firing.

thermoluminescence (TL) A dating technique that relies indirectly on radioactive decay, overlapping with radiocarbon in the time period for which it is useful, but also has the potential for dating earlier periods. It has much in common with *electron spin resonance* (ESR).

thin-section analysis A technique whereby microscopic thin sections are cut from a stone object or potsherd and examined with a petrological microscope to determine the source of the material.

Three Age System A *classification* system devised by C.J. Thomsen for the sequence of technological periods (stone, bronze, and iron) in Old World prehistory. It established the principle that by classifying artifacts, one could produce a chronological ordering.

total station An electronic/optical instrument used in surveying and to record excavations.

trace element analysis The use of chemical techniques for determining the incidence of trace elements in rocks. These methods are widely used in the identification of raw material sources for the production of stone tools.

tree-ring dating See *dendrochronology*.

tribes A term used to describe a social grouping generally larger than a *band*, but rarely numbering more than a few thousand; unlike bands tribes are usually settled farmers, though they also include nomadic pastoral groups whose economy is based on exploitation of livestock. Individual communities tend to be integrated into the larger society through kinship ties.

type A class of artifacts defined by the consistent clustering of *attributes*.

typology The systematic organization of artifacts into types on the basis of shared *attributes*.

underwater reconnaissance Geophysical methods of underwater survey include (1) a *proton magnetometer* towed behind a survey vessel, so as to detect iron and steel objects which distort the earth's magnetic field; (2) *side-scan sonar* that transmits sound waves in a fan-shaped beam to produce a graphic image of surface features on the sea-bed; (3) a sub-bottom profiler that emits sound pulses which bounce back from features and objects buried beneath the sea floor.

Uniformitarianism The principle that the stratification of rocks is due to processes still going on in seas, rivers, and lakes;

i.e. that geologically ancient conditions were in essence similar to or "uniform with" those of our own time.

uranium series dating A dating method based on the *radioactive decay* of isotopes of uranium. It has proved particularly useful for the period before 50,000 years ago, which lies outside the time range of *radiocarbon dating*.

varves Fine layers of alluvium sediment deposited in glacial lakes. Their annual deposition makes them a useful source of dating.

Wheeler box-grid An excavation technique developed by Mortimer Wheeler from the work of Pitt-Rivers, involving retaining intact baulks of earth between excavation grid squares, so that different layers can be correlated across the site in the vertical profiles.

zooarchaeology See *archaeozoology*.

Illustration Credits

15 Wiltshire Archaeological & Natural History Society; 16 *The London Sketchbook;* 18t F. Catherwood, *Views of Ancient Monuments in Central America, Chiapas and Yucatán,* London 1844; 19t The St. Louis Art Museum, Eliza McMillan Fund; 20a Courtesy the Peabody Museum, Harvard University; 20bl A. Pitt-Rivers, *Excavations in Cranborne Chase,* 1893–1898; 20br A. Pitt-Rivers, *Excavations in Cranborne Chase,* 1893–1898; 21a Petrie Museum of Egyptian Archaeology, University College London; 21bl Archaeological Survey of India; 22tl Courtesy the Peabody Museum, Harvard University; 23 The Royal Commission on the Ancient & Historical Monuments of Scotland; 32bl Courtesy of Mrs Mary Allsebrook, Oxford; 32br The Principal and Fellows of Newnham College, Cambridge; 33tl University of Colorado Museum; 33b Jen and Des Bartlett and Bruce Coleman Ltd.; 33tc P. Dorrell, Jericho Exploration Fund; 33tr Courtesy the Peabody Museum, Harvard University; 38–39 ML Design (after A. Sherratt (ed.) *Cambridge Encyclopedia of Archaeology,* 1980, fig. 20.5); 42a&b John Sibbick; 44 Annick Boothe (adapted from W. Rathje & M.Schiffer, *Archaeology* 1982, fig. 4.11); 50b Ian Bott; 50al, 50ar Griffith Institute, Oxford; 52 Tracy Wellman; 53 Johan Reinhard; 54 After Rudenko; 55 National Museum of Ireland, Dublin; 56 Richard D. Daugherty; 67 Annick Boothe (after Flannery (ed.) 1976, figs. 3.2, 5.2); 69b Cahokia Mounds State Historic Site; 70a Cambridge University Collection of Air Photos (photo J.K. St Joseph); 70b R. Agache, Service des Fouilles; 71b Annick Boothe (after Oxford Archaeological Unit); 72 Danebury Trust (from B. Cunliffe, *Danebury* 1983, fig. 64); 76l U.S. Geological Survey; 76r U.S. National Park Service; 77 Jet Propulsion Laboratory, National Aeronautics and Space Administration, California; 79 Tracy Wellman; 80 Mark Lehner; 81 Giza Plateau Mapping Project; 83 René Millon; 85 Courtesy Mandy Mottram; 85 Drazen Tomic adapted from information supplied by Mandy Mottram; 88 University of Miami, Japan Division; 90a Photo Oxford Archaeotechnics; 90b Andrew David, English Heritage; 93 Drazen Tomic (after M. Carver, *Underneath English Towns* 1987, fig. 2); 95a Courtesy Robin Coningham; 95b Sutton Hoo Research Trust, photos Nigel Macbeth; 96 Lewis Binford; 97 Annick Boothe (after *The Courier,* Unesco Nov. 1987, p. 16, drawing by M. Redknap); 98a Annick Boothe (after *National Geographic,*

supplement Jan. 1990); 98bl Canadian Parks Service (photo Rock Chan, Denis Pagé); 98br Canadian Parks Service (by P. Waddell & J. Farley); 100 Museum of London; 101 Annick Boothe (after J. Deetz, *Invitation to Archaeology,* Natural History Press/Doubleday & Co. 1967); 108 Wheeler, *Ancient India* 3 Jan. 1947; 109, 110 Annick Boothe (after Rathje & Schiffer, *Archaeology* 1982, fig. 4.17); 111 ML Design; 118 Simon S.S. Driver (information from Bannister & Smiley in *Geochronology,* Tucson 1955); 120 Annick Boothe; 121 Annick Boothe (121l after Hedges & Gowlett in *Scientific American* 254 (1), Jan. 1986, p. 84); 123 After Gordon Pearson; 124 After Gordon Pearson; 125 David Hurst Thomas & the American Museum of Natural History; 128 After R. Klein, *The Human Career* 1989, fig 3.9; 132 Drazen Tomic (adapted from R. Foley & R. Dunbar, *New Scientist* 14 Oct. 1989, p. 40, with addition by P. Winton); 133l Peter Brown; 133r Peter Schouten/National Geographic Society; 136–37 Simon S.S. Driver (with amendments by Drazen Tomic); 143 Igor Astrologo; 149 After C. Renfrew & E.V. Level in C. Renfrew & K.L. Cooke (eds.), *Transformations* 1979, figs. 6.11, 6.12; 150 Tracy Wellman (after Isaac); 153 From B. Fagan, *In the Beginning* (6th edn.)1988, fig. 16.4 (after Winter in Flannery (ed.) 1976, fig 2.17); 157 Charles Higham; 158a Mary Ellen Miller; 158b Simon S.S. Driver (after Renfrew); 160 Paolo Matthiae; 161 Hirmer Fotoarchiv; 163tl, tr Lewis Binford; 166 U.S. General Services Administration; 167 Chester Higgins; 168 Courtesy Landesdenkmalamt Baden-Württemberg-Archäologische Denkmalpflege; 170 Drazen Tomic after Lois Martin; 175l Lucy Maw; 178l Annick Boothe (after Shackley 1981, fig. 4.3); 178r Annick Boothe (after Scarre (ed.) 1988, p.107); 180 Philip Winton (after Piperno and Ciochon, *New Scientist* 10/11/90); 181 Philip Winton; 183 H.J. Deacon; 186 After A. Marshack, *The Roots of Civilization* 1972, fig. 78b; 188 Institute of Archaeology, Chinese Academy of Social Sciences, Beijing; 191 Annick Boothe (after J. Greig, Plant Foods in the Past, *J. of Plant Foods* 5 1983, 179–214); 194 After Mangelsdorf; 197 Pat Shipman & Richard Potts; 199 Netherlands Institute for the Near East, Leiden; 200–201 Thomas F. Kehoe; 208 Peter Bellwood; 209 Annick Boothe; 210a Simon S.S. Driver; 210b Brian Fagan; 213 Oriental Institute, University of Chicago; 216 Kenneth Garrett; 217al Museum für Völkerkunde,

Vienna; 217ar National Archaeological Museum, Athens; 217lc British Museum; 217bl Ulmer Museum, Ulm; 217c, br Werner Forman; 217bc By courtesy of the Board of Trustees of the Victoria & Albert Museum; 221 ML Design (after Peacock 1982, fig. 80); 223 ML Design (after Renfrew); 225 Annick Boothe (after Pires-Ferreira in Flannery (ed.) 1976, fig. 10.16); 226a George Bass/Cemal Pulak, Institute of Nautical Archaeology; 226b ML Design (after Bass); 227 George Bass/Cemal Pulak, Institute of Nautical Archaeology; 232 Annick Boothe; 234 British Museum; 235 British Museum; 236 Annick Boothe; 237a Antti Korpisari; 237lc British Museum; 237c Nationalmuseet, Copenhagen; 237bc Elisabeth Daynès/ National Geographic Image Collection; 237br British Museum; 238 British Museum; 239 John Prag; 246 British Museum; 247 Reproduced by permission of Chris Henshilwood, African Heritage Research Institute, Cape Town, South Africa; 248a ML Design; 248bl Eurelios/Ministère de la Culture, Paris (photo Jean Clottes); 249l Pablo Aries; 249c Sergey Lev; 249r Pedro Saura; 251l British Tourist Authority; 251r Philip Winton; 252 Colin Renfrew; 253 British Museum; 254 Musée des Antiquités Nationales, St-Germain-en-Laye; 257a Annick Boothe (after Burger); 257crl Annick Boothe (after Burger); 257crr Richard Burger; 257bl Richard Burger; 257br Wilfredo Loayzo L.; 258–59 D.A.I., Berlin; 261 Agora Excavations, American School of Classical Studies at Athens; 270a Annick Boothe (after Kirch); 270b Annick Boothe (after Gelb); 271cr R.D.K. Hadden; 271bl ML Design (after Garlake); 278 University of Pennsylvania Museum, Philadelphia [493]; 279 University of Pennsylvania Museum, Philadelphia [493]; 288a Tracy Wellman; 288b Photo Josephine Powell; 289 Karim Sahib/AFP; 290 Toni Schneiders; 292 Hiroshi Kasiwara; 293 Hiroko Koike; 294 © Fehim Demir/epa/Corbis; 296 Hirmer Fotoarchiv; 297 Paul Bahn; 298 Photo Katz Pictures; 301ar Colorado Springs Fine Art Center – Taylor Museum Collection; 301bl Werner Forman; 303tr Museum of Fine Arts, Boston; 303cr Antalya Museum; 303c By courtesy of the Trustee of the Marquess of Northampton 1987 Settlement; 304 British Museum; 308l Iraq Museum, Baghdad, Director General of Antiquities, Iraq; 308br Courtesy Dr John Curtis; 312, 313al&r Salvador Guillermo Arroyo, courtesy the Great Temple Project; 316 Christopher Peebles.

Index

Teach Yourself
VISUALLY™

Office 2013

Visual

Elaine Marmel

WILEY

John Wiley & Sons, Inc.

Teach Yourself VISUALLY™ Office 2013

Published by
John Wiley & Sons, Inc.
10475 Crosspoint Boulevard
Indianapolis, IN 46256

www.wiley.com

Published simultaneously in Canada

Wiley publishes in a variety of print and electronic formats and by print-on-demand. Some material included with standard print versions of this book may not be included in e-books or in print-on-demand. If this book refers to media such as a CD or DVD that is not included in the version you purchased, you may download this material at http://booksupport.wiley.com. For more information about Wiley products, visit www.wiley.com.

Library of Congress Control Number: 2012956423

ISBN: 978-1-118-51768-0

Manufactured in the United States of America

10   9   8   7   6   5   4   3

Trademark Acknowledgments

Wiley, the Wiley logo, Visual, the Visual logo, Teach Yourself VISUALLY, Read Less - Learn More and related trade dress are trademarks or registered trademarks of John Wiley & Sons, Inc. and/or its affiliates. Microsoft is a registered trademark of Microsoft Corporation. All other trademarks are the property of their respective owners. John Wiley & Sons, Inc. is not associated with any product or vendor mentioned in this book.

Contact Us

For general information on our other products and services please contact our Customer Care Department within the U.S. at 877-762-2974, outside the U.S. at 317-572-3993 or fax 317-572-4002.

For technical support please visit www.wiley.com/techsupport.

WILEY   **Sales** | Contact Wiley at (877) 762-2974 or fax (317) 572-4002.

Credits

Executive Editor
Jody Lefevere

Sr. Project Editor
Sarah Hellert

Technical Editor
Vince Averello

Copy Editor
Marylouise Wiack

Editorial Director
Robyn Siesky

Business Manager
Amy Knies

Sr. Marketing Manager
Sandy Smith

**Vice President and Executive
Group Publisher**
Richard Swadley

**Vice President and Executive
Publisher**
Barry Pruett

Project Coordinator
Sheree Montgomery

Graphics and Production Specialists
Noah Hart
Joyce Haughey
Jennifer Henry
Andrea Hornberger
Jennifer Mayberry

Quality Control Technician
Lauren Mandelbaum

Proofreader
Broccoli Information Mgt.

Indexer
Potomac Indexing, LLC

About the Author

Elaine Marmel is President of Marmel Enterprises, LLC, an organization that specializes in technical writing and software training. Elaine has an MBA from Cornell University and worked on projects to build financial management systems for New York City and Washington, D.C. This prior experience provided the foundation for Marmel Enterprises, LLC to help small businesses manage the project of implementing a computerized accounting system.

Elaine spends most of her time writing; she has authored and co-authored more than 65 books about Microsoft Excel, Microsoft Word, Microsoft Project, QuickBooks, Peachtree, Quicken for Windows, Quicken for DOS, Microsoft Word for the Mac, Microsoft Windows, 1-2-3 for Windows, and Lotus Notes. From 1994 to 2006, she also was the contributing editor to monthly publications *Inside Peachtree*, *Inside Timeslips*, and *Inside QuickBooks*.

Elaine left her native Chicago for the warmer climes of Arizona (by way of Cincinnati, OH; Jerusalem, Israel; Ithaca, NY; Washington, D.C., and Tampa, FL) where she basks in the sun with her PC, her cross stitch projects, and her dog, Jack.

Author's Acknowledgments

Because a book is not just the work of the author, I'd like to acknowledge and thank all the folks who made this book possible. Thanks to Jody Lefevere for the opportunity to write this book. Thank you, Vince Averello, for doing a great job to make sure that I "told no lies." Thank you, Marylouise Wiack, for making sure I was understandable. And, thank you, Sarah Hellert; your top-notch management of all the players and manuscript elements involved in this book made my life easy and writing the book a pleasure.

Dedication

To Buddy (1995-2012), my constant companion for 17 ½ years. You brought me nothing but joy and I will sorely miss you.

How to Use This Book

Who This Book Is For

This book is for the reader who has never used this particular technology or software application. It is also for readers who want to expand their knowledge.

The Conventions in This Book

① Steps

This book uses a step-by-step format to guide you easily through each task. **Numbered steps** are actions you must do; **bulleted steps** clarify a point, step, or optional feature; and **indented steps** give you the result.

② Notes

Notes give additional information — special conditions that may occur during an operation, a situation that you want to avoid, or a cross-reference to a related area of the book.

③ Icons and Buttons

Icons and buttons show you exactly what you need to click to perform a step.

④ Tips

Tips offer additional information, including warnings and shortcuts.

⑤ Bold

Bold type shows command names or options that you must click or text or numbers you must type.

⑥ Italics

Italic type introduces and defines a new term.

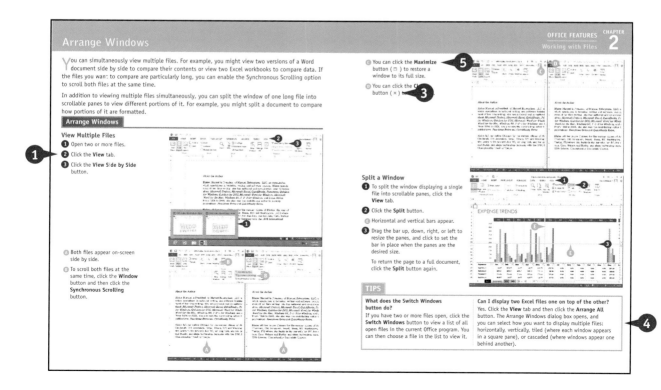

Table of Contents

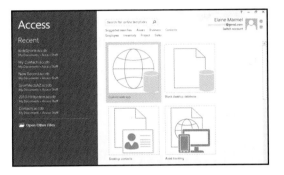

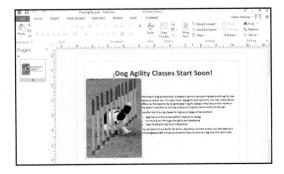

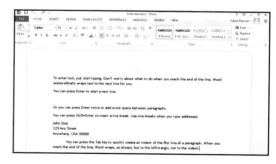

Part II Word

Chapter 5	Adding Text

Table of Contents

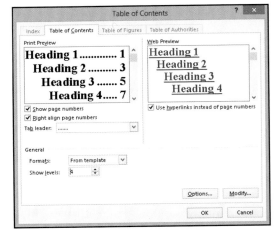

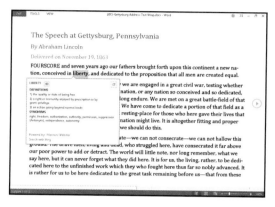

Part III   Excel

Table of Contents

Chapter 10 — Worksheet Basics

Chapter 11 — Working with Formulas and Functions

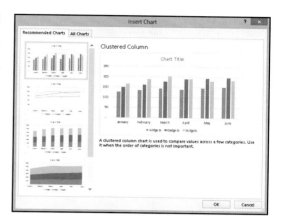

Part IV   PowerPoint

Table of Contents

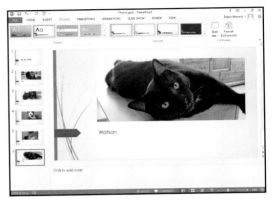

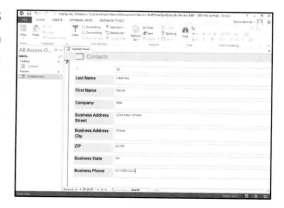

Table of Contents

Part VI Outlook

Chapter 18 Organizing with Outlook

Chapter 19 E-Mailing with Outlook

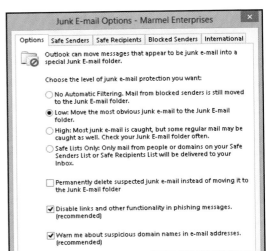

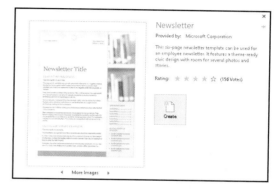

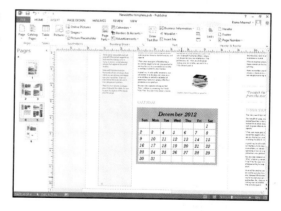

Table of Contents

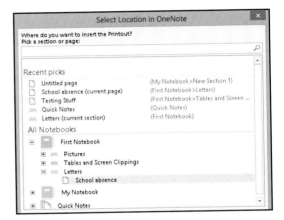

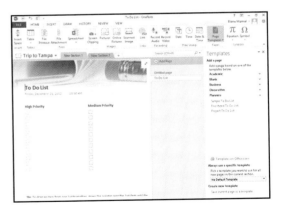

PART I

Office Features

The Office 2013 applications share a common look and feel. You can find many of the same features in each program, such as the Ribbon, Quick Access Toolbar, program window controls, and File tab. Many of the tasks you perform, such as creating and working with files, share the same processes and features throughout the Office suite. In this part, you learn how to navigate the common Office features and basic tasks.

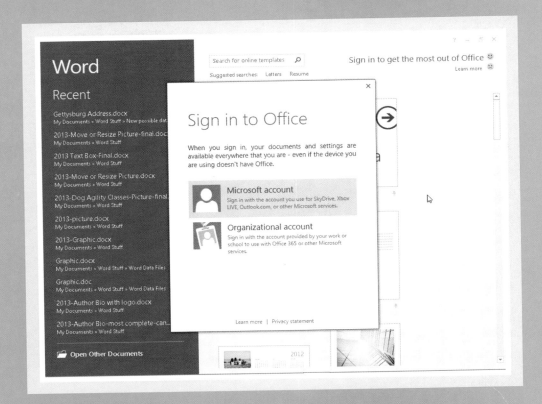

Start and Exit Office Applications

Office 2013 runs on a 1-gigahertz (GHz) or faster x86- or x64-bit processor with 1 or 2 gigabytes of RAM, based on your processor speed. Your system must be running Windows 7, Windows 8, Windows Server 2008 R2, or Windows Server 2012. For additional requirements, visit http://technet. microsoft.com/en-us/library/ee624351%28v=office.15%29.aspx.

This section uses Access to demonstrate how to open a program from the Windows 8 Start screen. Once an Office program opens, its Start screen appears, helping you to find a document on which you recently worked or to start a new document. For other ways to open or start a new document, see Chapter 2.

Start and Exit Office Applications

1 On the Windows Start screen, click ▬ to zoom.

Note: You can start typing the name of the program and then skip to Step **3**.

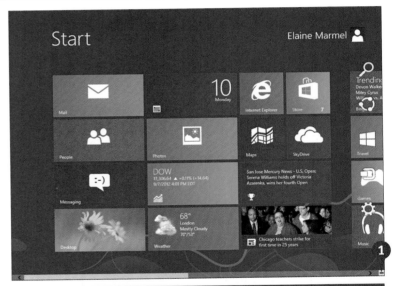

Windows zooms out so that you can see tiles for all installed programs.

2 Click any program tile on the right side of the Start screen.

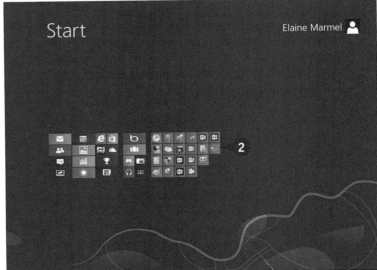

Windows zooms in and enlarges all tiles to their regular size.

3 Click the tile of the program you want to open.

Note: This example uses Access 2013.

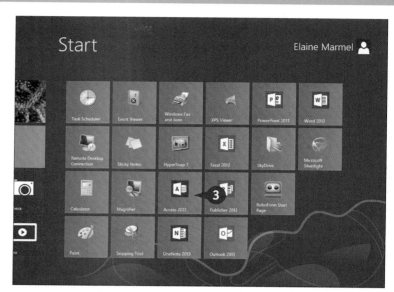

Windows switches to the Desktop and opens the program, displaying the program's Start screen, which helps you open new or existing documents; see Chapter 2 for other ways to open documents.

A You can use this panel to open an existing document.

B You can use this area to start a new document.

C This area indicates whether you have signed in to Office Online.

D To exit from the program, click the **Close** button (×) after closing all documents.

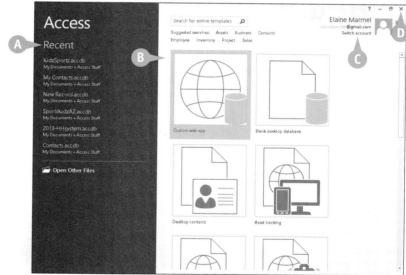

TIP

Can I create a shortcut to open an Office application?
Yes. You can create a shortcut icon that appears on the Windows Desktop; however, pinning the program to the Windows taskbar is easier and just as effective because you can then click the taskbar button to start the program. On the Windows Start screen, right-click the tile of the program that you want to pin to the Windows taskbar. The program's App bar appears; click **Pin to taskbar**. Windows 8 pins the program to the Windows taskbar. To open the program, display the Desktop and click the program's tile on the taskbar.

Navigate the Program Windows

All Office programs share a common appearance and many of the same features, and when you learn your way around one Office program, you can easily use the same skills to navigate the others. These common features include scroll bars, a Ribbon, and a Quick Access Toolbar (QAT). The Ribbon contains commands that Microsoft Office determines that users use most often, and the QAT contains frequently used commands; you can customize both of these elements.

Take a moment to familiarize yourself with each program's various on-screen elements so that you can learn to work quickly and efficiently while you create documents.

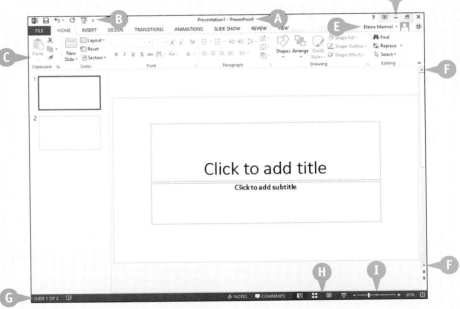

A Title Bar

Displays the name of the open file and the Office program.

B Quick Access Toolbar

Displays quick access buttons to the Save, Undo, and Redo commands.

C Ribbon

Displays groups of related commands in tabs. Each tab offers buttons for performing common tasks.

D Program Window Controls

These buttons enable you to view the program in a full screen, with only scroll bars but no other controls. They also allow you to minimize the program window, to maximize or restore the window including program controls, or to close the window.

E Office Online Indicator

If you see your name, you are signed in to Office Online. You can click ▼ to display a menu

that enables you to change your photo, manage your Microsoft account, or switch to a different Microsoft account. If you are not signed in, this area shows a Sign In link. See Chapter 4 for details.

F Scroll Bars

The vertical and, if available, horizontal scroll bars let you scroll through the item shown in the work area, such as a document or worksheet.

G Status Bar

Displays information about the current Office document.

H View Shortcuts

These shortcuts switch to a different view of your document.

I Zoom Controls

This feature changes the magnification of a document.

Work with Backstage View

You can click the File tab to display Backstage view, which resembles a menu. Backstage is the place to go when you need to manage documents or change program behavior. In Backstage view, you find a list of actions — you can think of them as commands — that you can use to, for example, open, save, print, remove sensitive information, and distribute documents as well as set Word program behavior options. You can also use Backstage to manage the places on your computer hard drive or in your network that you use to store documents and to manage your Office Online account.

Work with Backstage View

1 Click the **File** tab to display Backstage view.

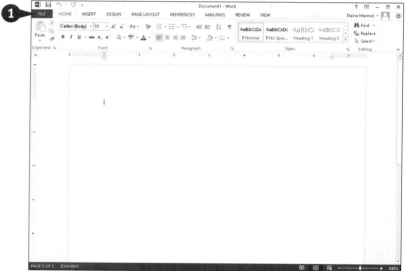

A Commonly used file and program management commands appear here.

B Buttons you can click appear here.

C Information related to the button you click appears here. Each time you click a button, the information shown to the right changes.

Note: The New, Close, and Options commands do not display buttons or information, but take other actions. See Chapter 2 for details.

2 Click here to return to the open document.

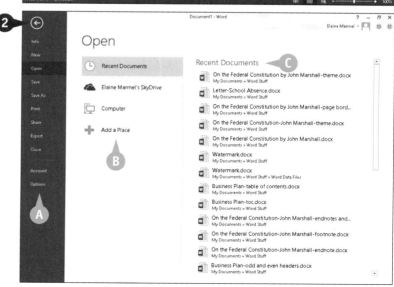

Work with the Ribbon

In Office 2013, you use the Ribbon to select commands. On each Ribbon tab, you find groups of related command buttons. Each button performs a common task. Some tabs appear only when needed. For example, if you select a picture, the Ribbon displays the Picture Tools tab.

In all Office programs, you can customize the Ribbon. You can create your own Ribbon tab that contains the buttons you use most often; that way, you do not need to switch tabs to use a particular command.

Work with the Ribbon

Using the Ribbon

1. Click the tab containing the command you want to use.

2. Click the command.

Ⓐ Buttons with arrows (▼) display additional commands.

Ⓑ You can click the dialog box launcher (⌐) to display a dialog box of additional settings.

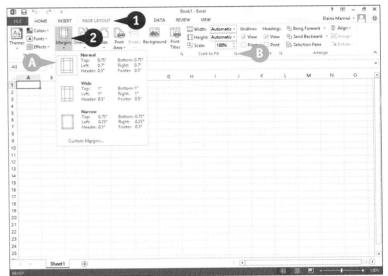

Create a Ribbon Tab

1. Click the **File** tab.

2. Click **Options** to display the Options dialog box.

3. Click **Customize Ribbon**.

4. Click the tab you want to appear to the left of the new tab.

5. Click **New Tab**.

Ⓒ Word creates a new tab and a new group on that tab. To reposition the tab, click it and click the arrows.

6. Click **New Tab (Custom)**.

7. Click **Rename** to display the Rename dialog box.

8. Type a name for your tab and click **OK**.

9. Click **New Group (Custom)** and repeat Steps **7** and **8** to rename the group.

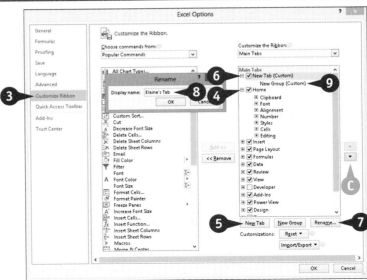

Add Buttons

1 Click the group on the tab you created.

2 Click a command.

D If the command you want does not appear in the list, click the list box arrow (⌄) and select **All Commands**.

3 Click **Add**.

E The command appears below the group you created.

4 Repeat Steps **2** and **3** for each button you want to add to the group.

5 Click **OK**.

F The new tab appears on the Ribbon. If you positioned your tab as the first tab, it will appear each time you open the program.

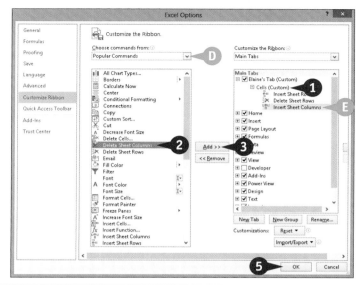

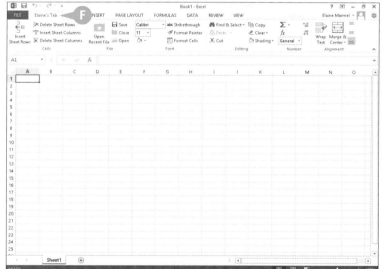

TIPS

How do I assign keyboard shortcuts to the buttons I add to my group?

You do not need to assign keyboard shortcuts; the program assigns them for you, based on the keys already assigned to commands appearing on the tab where you placed your group. Be aware that you can place the same button on two different tabs, and if you do, the program assigns different keyboard shortcuts to that button on each tab.

What can I do if I decide that I do not want a custom tab on the Ribbon?

Reopen the program's Options dialog box and deselect the check box beside the tab you created (☑ changes to ☐). Click **OK**. When the program redisplays the Ribbon, your tab will not appear.

9

Customize the Quick Access Toolbar

The Quick Access Toolbar, or QAT, is located in the top-left corner of the program window above the File and Home tabs. It offers quick access to the frequently used Save, Undo, and Redo commands. If you want, you can customize this toolbar to include other commands you use often, such as the Quick Print command or the Print Preview command, or any other command you want.

You can also reposition the QAT so that it appears below the Ribbon instead of above it; and, if you change your mind, you can put the QAT back above the Ribbon.

Customize the Quick Access Toolbar

1 Click ▾.

A You can click any of the common commands to add them to the toolbar.

B You can click **Show Below the Ribbon** if you want to display the toolbar below the Ribbon.

2 Click **More Commands**.

The Options dialog box appears.

3 Click the **Choose commands from** ▾.

4 Click a command group.

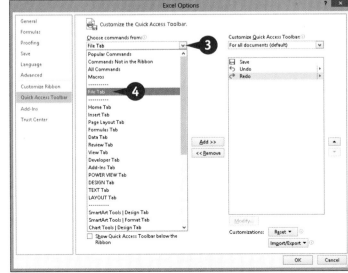

5 Click the command that you want to add to the toolbar.

6 Click **Add**.

C Office adds the command.

You can repeat Steps **3** to **6** to move additional buttons to the toolbar.

7 Click **OK**.

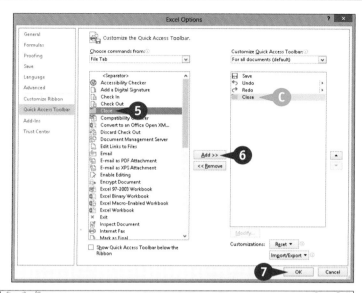

D The new command appears on the Quick Access Toolbar.

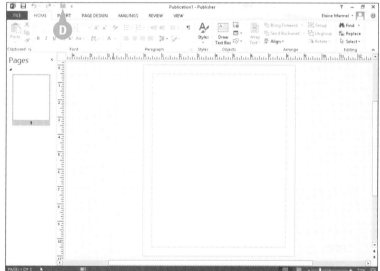

Using an Office Program on a Tablet PC

I f you are using Office 2013 with Windows 8 on a tablet PC, you need to know some basic touch gestures. Using a tablet PC is a different experience than using a computer with a keyboard and mouse, but Windows 8 was built with the tablet PC in mind, so the touch gestures are intuitive and easy to learn.

On a tablet PC, you use your fingers (or sometimes a stylus, if your tablet comes with one) to run applications, select items, and manipulate screen objects. This might seem awkward at first, but just a little practice of the gestures in this section will make your experience natural and easy.

Using an Office Program on a Tablet PC

Start a Program

Note: This section uses Word to demonstrate gestures.

1. Position your finger or the stylus over a blank spot toward the bottom of the Windows 8 Start screen.

2. Quickly move your finger or the stylus across the tablet screen — called *swiping* — from the right edge to the left edge of the tablet.

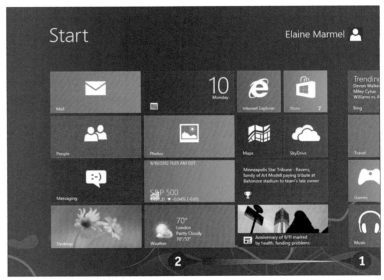

Windows 8 displays the tiles on the right side of the Start screen.

3. Tap the Word tile to switch to the Desktop and open Word to the Word Start screen.

Swipe the Screen

1 Click 📖 to switch to Word's Read Mode view.

Note: See Chapter 8 for details.

2 Swipe left from the right edge of the tablet to read the next page.

3 Swipe right from the left edge of the tablet to read the previous page.

Move an Object

1 Position your finger or the stylus over the item you want to move.

2 Tap and hold the item and begin moving your finger or the stylus.

A The object moves along with your finger or the stylus, and an alignment guide helps you find a position for the object.

3 When the object appears where you want it, lift your finger or the stylus off the screen to complete the move and hide the alignment guide.

TIPS

How do I close a program using gestures?

Position your finger or the stylus at the top edge of the tablet and then slide it down the screen. At first you see the Windows 8 application bar for the program, so keep sliding. When you get about halfway, the application becomes a small window. Keep dragging that small window to the very bottom of the screen, and then lift your finger or the stylus. Windows 8 shuts down the application.

After I tap the Desktop tile, how do I return to the Start screen?

You can do this in a couple of ways. Because the Desktop is an application, you can close it using the technique described in the preceding tip. Alternatively, swipe left from the right edge of the tablet to display the Charms bar, and then tap the **Start** icon.

Create a New File

When you open an Office program (except Outlook), the program's Start screen greets you; see Chapter 1 for details. If Word, Excel, PowerPoint, Access, or Publisher are already open and you want to create a new document, workbook, presentation, database, or publication, you create a new file using Backstage view. When you do, you have the option of creating a blank file or basing the file on a template. Outlook opens by default to the Inbox, and, to create a new item in Outlook, whether it is an e-mail message, a calendar appointment, a contact, or a task item, you use the Ribbon.

Create a New File

Create a New Word, Excel, PowerPoint, Access, or Publisher File

1 Click the **File** tab.

Backstage view appears.

2 Click **New**.

The New screen appears.

3 Click the type of file that you want to create.

If you click a template, a preview appears; if you like what you see, click **Create** and the new file opens.

If you click a blank document, no preview appears; instead, a new blank document appears.

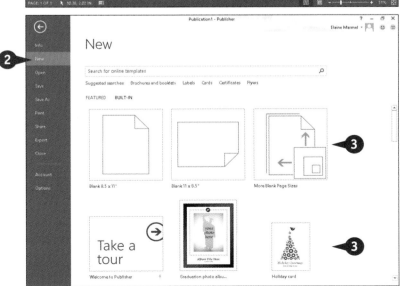

Create a New Outlook Item

1 In the Navigation bar at the bottom of the Outlook window, click the type of item you want to create — Mail, Calendar, People, or Tasks.

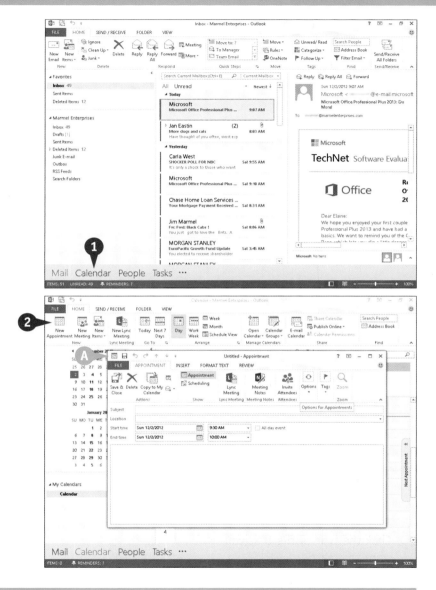

2 Click the appropriate **New** button. For example, if you are creating a Mail item, the button is labeled New Email. If you are creating a Calendar item, the button is labeled New Appointment, New Meeting, and so on.

A The new item opens.

What is a template?

A template is a file containing predefined settings that serve as the foundation for your document, saving you the effort of manually creating the settings. Word, Excel, PowerPoint, Access, and Publisher 2013 display a variety of templates on the program Start screen and also when you start a new document while working in the program.

Where can I find more templates to use with my Microsoft Office programs?

At Office Online. At the top of the program Start screen or on the New screen, click in the **Search online templates** box, describe the type of template you want, and click 🔍.

Save a File

You save files so that you can use them at another time in Office programs. When you save a file, you can give it a unique filename and store it in the folder or drive of your choice.

After you save a document for the first time, you can click the Save button on the Quick Access Toolbar (QAT) to save it again. The first time you save a document, the program prompts you for a document name. Subsequent times, when you use the Save button on the QAT, the program saves the document using its original name without prompting you.

Save a File

Ⓐ Before you save a document, the program displays a generic name in the title bar.

① Click the **File** tab.

Backstage view appears.

② Click **Save As**.

③ Click **Computer**.

Ⓑ If the folder in which you want to save the document appears here, click it and skip to Step **5**.

④ Click **Browse**.

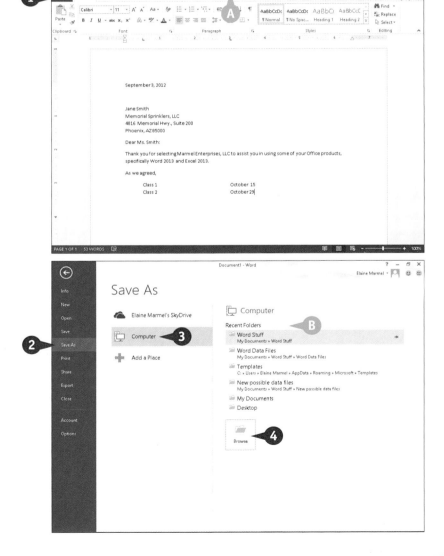

The Save As dialog box appears.

5 Type a name for the document here.

C You can click here to select a location on your computer in which to save the document.

D You can click the **New Folder** button to create a new folder in which to store the document.

6 Click **Save**.

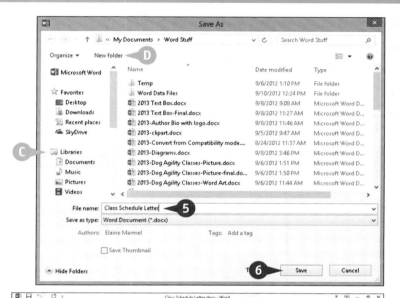

E Word saves the document and displays the name you supplied in the title bar.

F For subsequent saves, you can click the **Save** button (⊟) on the Quick Access Toolbar to quickly save the file.

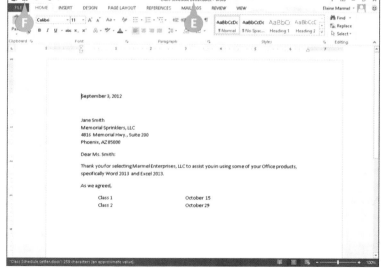

TIP

Can I save a file using a different file type?

Yes. Each Office program saves to a default file type. For example, a Word document uses the DOCX file format and Excel uses the XLSX file format. If you want to save the file in a format compatible with previous versions of Office, you must save it in the appropriate format, such as Word 97-2003 Document for previous versions of Word. To save a file in a different format, click the **Save as Type** ☑ in the Save As dialog box and choose the desired format from the list that appears.

Open a File

You can open documents that you have created and saved previously in order to continue adding data or to edit existing data, regardless of where you store the files. If you are not sure where you saved a file, you can use the Open dialog box's Search function to locate it.

New to Word 2013, you can open and edit PDF files. However, editing a PDF file in Word works best if you used Word to create the original PDF file. If you used a different program to create the PDF file, you will find that Word has difficulty maintaining the file's formatting.

Open a File

1 Click the **File** tab.

Backstage view appears.

2 Click **Open**.

A Recently opened documents appear here. If you see the file you want to open, you can click it to open it and skip the rest of these steps.

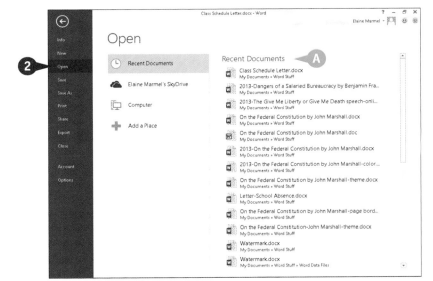

3 Click the place where you believe the document is stored. This example uses **Computer**.

Note: If you choose the wrong place, you can search for the file.

B If the folder containing the document appears here, click it and skip to Step **5**.

4 Click **Browse**.

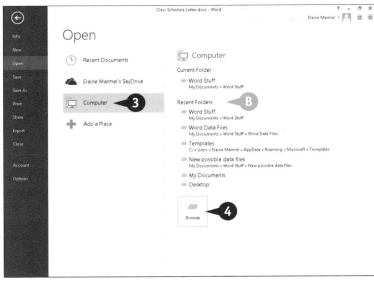

The Open dialog box appears.

5 Click here to navigate to the folder containing the document you want to open.

6 Click the document you want to open.

7 Click **Open**.

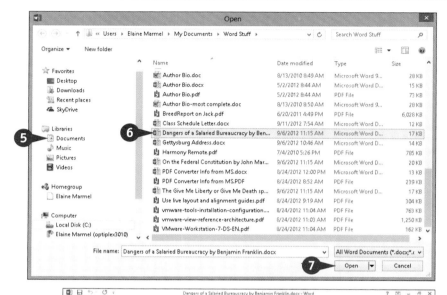

The file opens in the program window.

Note: To close a file, click ✕ in the upper-right corner. If you have not saved the file, the program prompts you to save it.

TIP

What if I cannot find my file?

You can use the Search box in the upper-right corner of the Open dialog box to locate files. Complete Steps **1** to **4** to display the Open dialog box. Locate and open the folder in which you believe the file was saved and type the file's name in the Search box. Files containing the search term appear highlighted along with files containing a close match.

Print a File

If a printer is connected to your computer, you can print your Office files. For example, you might distribute printouts of a file as handouts in a meeting.

When you print a file, you have two options: You can send a file directly to the printer using the default settings or you can open the Office application's Print screen to change these settings. For example, you might opt to print just a portion of the file, print using a different printer, print multiple copies of a file, collate the printouts, and so on. (Printer settings vary slightly among Office programs.)

Print a File

1 Click the **File** tab.

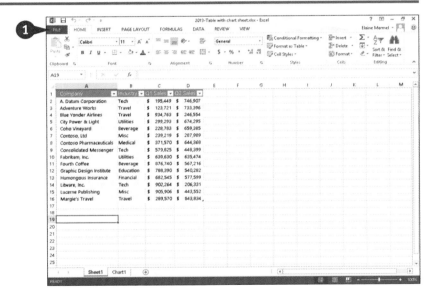

Backstage view appears.

2 Click **Print**.

Ⓐ You can specify the number of copies to print using the **Copies** spin box.

Ⓑ You can choose a printer from the **Printer** drop-down list.

Ⓒ You can choose to print a selection from the file or specific pages using the available settings in the Settings list.

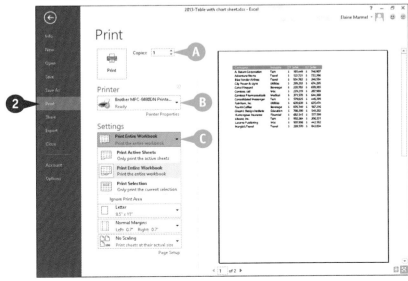

D You can select additional print options under Settings. For example, you can click here to choose from various paper sizes and to print in landscape or portrait orientation.

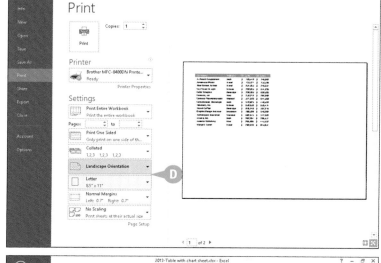

E You can page through a preview of your printed file by clicking here.

3 Click **Print**.

The Office program sends the file to the printer for printing.

How do I print using default settings?

If you do not need to change any of your default print settings, you can simply click the **Quick Print** button (🖨) on the Quick Access Toolbar. If the Quick Print button does not appear on your QAT, you can add it. To do so, click ⊡ to the right of the QAT and click **Quick Print** in the list of commands that appears. You can also add a Print Preview and Print button (🔍) to the QAT; clicking that button opens the Print screen.

Check Your File for Hidden or Personal Data

Y̶ou can remove any personal information that an Office program stores in a document. For issues of privacy, you may want to remove this information before you share a document with anyone.

Depending on the Office program, the Document Inspector searches your document for comments, revision marks, versions, and ink annotations. It searches document properties for hidden metadata and personal information. It inspects for task pane apps saved in the document as well as information like hidden rows, columns, or worksheets. If your document contains custom XML data, headers, footers, watermarks, or invisible content, the Document Inspector alerts you.

Check Your File for Hidden or Personal Data

1 In the document you want to check for sensitive information, click the **File** tab.

Backstage view appears.

2 Click **Info**.

3 Click **Check for Issues**.

4 Click **Inspect Document**.

Note: If you have unsaved changes, Word prompts you to save the document, which you do by clicking **Yes**.

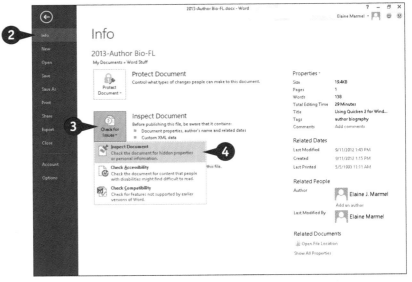

The Document Inspector
window appears.

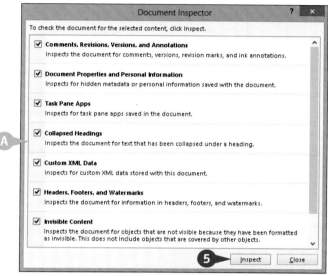

A You can deselect check marks
(☑ changes to ☐) to avoid
inspecting for these
elements.

5 Click **Inspect**.

The Document Inspector looks for
the information you specified and
displays the results.

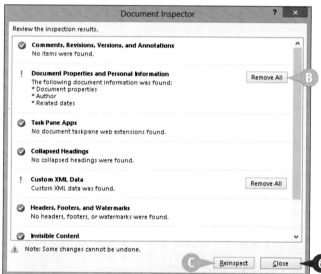

B You can remove any identified
information by clicking **Remove
All** beside that element.

C You can click **Reinspect** after
removing identifying information.

6 Click **Close**.

**Can I review the information that the Document
Inspector displays before I remove it?**
No. The only way to review the information before you
remove it is to close the Document Inspector *without*
removing information, use the appropriate Word
features to review the information, and then rerun the
Document Inspector as described in this section.

**What happens if I remove information and then
decide that I really want that information?**
You cannot undo the effects of removing the
information using the Document Inspector.
However, to restore removed information, you can
close the document *without* saving changes and
then reopen it.

E-Mail a File

You can share a file with others via e-mail. For example, suppose that you have a colleague who must present a project for approval at an upcoming meeting. Your colleague approaches you, asking for guidance concerning what to discuss. You put together a skeleton PowerPoint presentation and you want to e-mail it to your colleague.

You could create a new e-mail message in Outlook and add the file as an attachment, as discussed in Chapter 19. Or, you can send a file from the program you used to create the file, as described here. Note that, to open the file, recipients must have the appropriate software on their computer.

E-Mail a File

1 With the document you want to share via e-mail open, click the **File** tab.

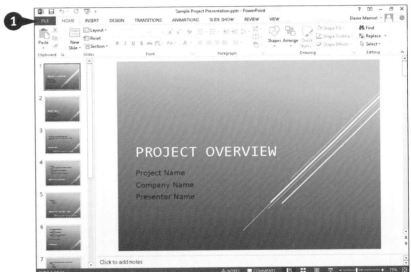

Backstage view appears.

2 Click **Share**.

3 Click **Email**.

Ⓐ Options for e-mailing the file appear here.

4 Click **Send as Attachment**.

Note: If you are sending a file that you do not want anyone to edit, click **Send as PDF** or **Send as XPS**.

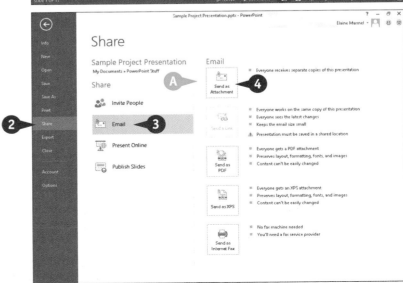

Office launches an Outlook New
Message window.

B The name of your file appears in
the New Message window's
Subject line.

C The file is attached to the
message.

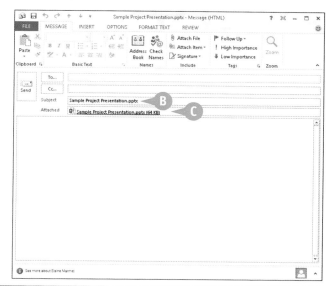

5 Type the message recipient's
e-mail address in the **To** field.

6 Type your text in the body of the
message.

7 Click **Send**.

Office places the message in your
e-mail program's outbox.

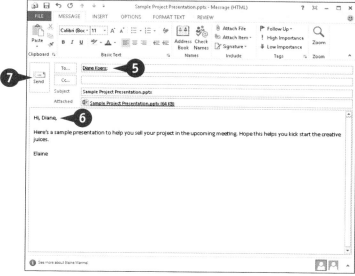

TIP

What if my recipient does not have the necessary software to open the file?
You can send the file in PDF or XPS format, which maintains the appearance of your file, but the file cannot
easily be changed — meaning your recipient cannot edit the file. Alternatively, you can suggest that the
recipient download an Office program viewer from http://office.microsoft.com; a viewer can, for example,
help an Office 2007 user open an Office 2013 file. Finally, you can suggest that the recipient use the
appropriate Office Web App, available in SkyDrive; see Chapter 4.

Select Data

You can select data in your file to perform different tasks, such as deleting it, changing its font or alignment, applying a border around it, or copying and pasting it. Selected data appears highlighted.

Depending on the program you are using, Office offers several different techniques for selecting data. For example, in Word, PowerPoint, Outlook, and Publisher, you can select a single character, a word, a sentence, a paragraph, or all the data in the file. In Excel and Access tables, you typically select cells. In One Note, use the technique appropriate to the type of data you want to select.

Select Data

Select Data in Word, PowerPoint, or Publisher

Note: You can use this technique to select characters, words, sentences, and paragraphs.

1 Click to one side of the word or character that you want to select.

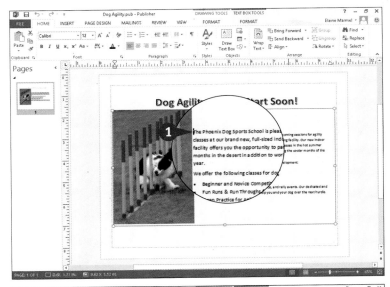

2 Drag the mouse pointer across the text that you want to select.

A The program highlights the characters to indicate that they are selected.

To cancel a selection, click anywhere outside the text or press any arrow key on your keyboard.

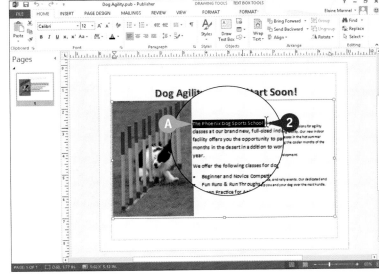

Select Cells in Excel or Access

1 Click the cell representing the upper-left corner of the cells you want to select.

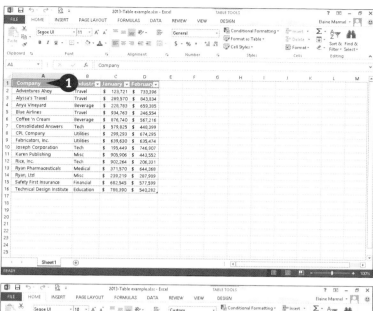

2 Drag the cell pointer across the cells you want to select.

B The program highlights the cells to indicate that they are selected.

To cancel a selection, click anywhere outside the text or press any arrow key on your keyboard.

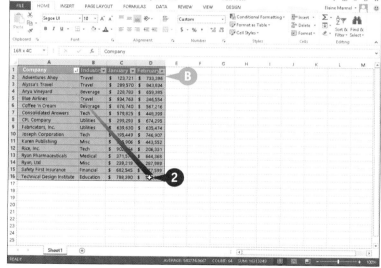

TIP

How can I use my keyboard to select text?

To select text or cells to the left or right of the insertion point or cell pointer, press `Ctrl`+`Shift`+`←` or `Ctrl`+`Shift`+`→`. To select a paragraph or cells above or below the insertion point or cell pointer, press `Ctrl`+`Shift`+`↑` or `Ctrl`+`Shift`+`↓`. To select all text or cells from the insertion point or cell pointer location onward, press `Ctrl`+`Shift`+`End`. To select all of the text or cells above the insertion point or cell pointer location, press `Ctrl`+`Shift`+`Home`. To select all the text or cells containing data in the file, press `Ctrl`+`A`.

Cut, Copy, and Paste Data

You can use the Cut, Copy, and Paste commands to move or copy data. For example, you might cut or copy text or a picture from a Word document and paste it elsewhere in the same Word document, in another Word document, or in a PowerPoint slide or a Publisher file.

When you cut data, it is removed from its original location; when you copy data, the selected data is duplicated, leaving it in its original location. You can move or copy data using two methods: drag-and-drop or buttons on the Ribbon. This section uses Word to drag-and-drop, and Excel to demonstrate Ribbon buttons.

Cut, Copy, and Paste Data

Cut or Copy in Word, PowerPoint, Publisher, or Outlook

1 Select the data that you want to cut or copy. This example cuts text.

2 Click and drag the data to a new location.

A As you drag, ⌖ changes to ⌖.

To copy the data, you can press and hold **Ctrl** as you drag, and ⌖ changes to ⌖.

B A bold insertion point marks where the text will appear as you drag.

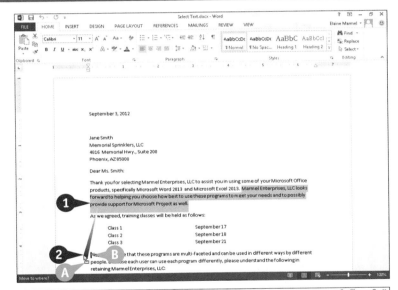

3 Release the mouse to drop the data in place.

C The data appears in the new location.

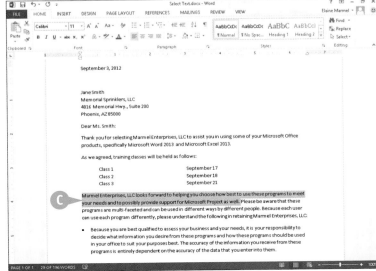

Cut or Copy in Excel or Access

1 Select the cell(s) that you want to cut or copy. This example copies a formula.

2 Click the **Home** tab.

3 Click the **Cut** button (✂) to move data or the **Copy** button (📋) to copy data.

Note: You can also press Ctrl+X to cut data or Ctrl+C to copy data.

The outline around the selected cell(s) changes to an animated dashed box and the data is stored in the Office Clipboard.

4 Select the cells where you want the cut or copied data to appear.

Note: You can also open another file into which you can paste the data.

5 On the Home tab, click the **Paste** button. Alternatively, to preview how the text will look before you paste it, click the down arrow below the Paste button and position your mouse pointer over each button that appears.

Note: You can also press Ctrl+V to paste data.

D The data appears in the new location.

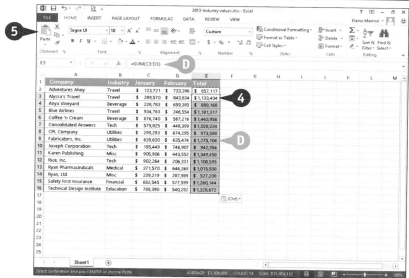

TIPS

When I paste cut or copied data, an icon appears. What is it?

This is the Paste Options button (📋(Ctrl)▾). You can use it to view Paste-formatting choices; the options that appear depend on the program you are using and the location where you want to paste. You can click one of these options or ignore 📋(Ctrl)▾ ; eventually, it disappears.

Can I cut or copy multiple selections?

Yes, you can, using the Office Clipboard, which holds up to 24 items that you can paste in any order you choose. To display the Office Clipboard, click the dialog box launcher (🗗) in the Clipboard group on the Ribbon's Home tab. Then select and cut or copy.

Arrange Windows

You can simultaneously view multiple files. For example, you might view two versions of a Word document side by side to compare their contents or view two Excel workbooks to compare data. If the files you want to compare are particularly long, you can enable the Synchronous Scrolling option to scroll both files at the same time.

In addition to viewing multiple files simultaneously, you can split the window of one long file into scrollable panes to view different portions of it. For example, you might split a document to compare how portions of it are formatted.

Arrange Windows

View Multiple Files

1 Open two or more files.

2 Click the **View** tab.

3 Click the **View Side by Side** button.

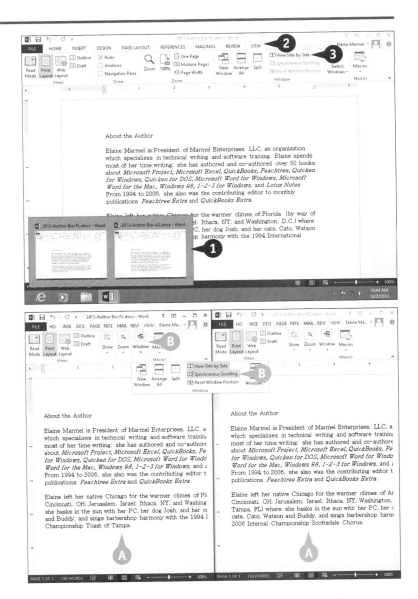

A Both files appear on-screen side by side.

B To scroll both files at the same time, click the **Window** button and then click the **Synchronous Scrolling** button.

C You can click the **Maximize** button (☐) to restore a window to its full size.

D You can click the **Close** button (×) to close a file.

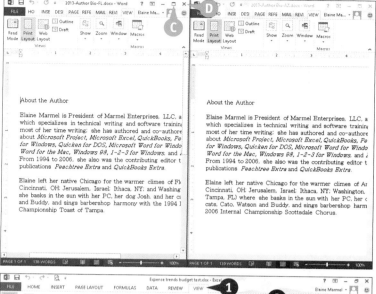

Split a Window

1 To split the window displaying a single file into scrollable panes, click the **View** tab.

2 Click the **Split** button.

E Horizontal and vertical bars appear.

3 Drag the bar up, down, right, or left to resize the panes, and click to set the bar in place when the panes are the desired size.

To return the page to a full document, click the **Split** button again.

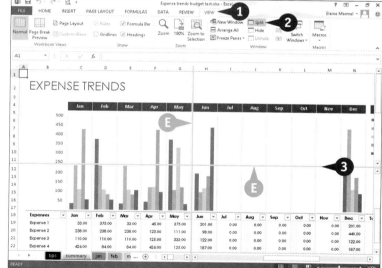

TIPS

What does the Switch Windows button do?

If you have two or more files open, click the **Switch Windows** button to view a list of all open files in the current Office program. You can then choose a file in the list to view it.

Can I display two Excel files one on top of the other?

Yes. Click the **View** tab and then click the **Arrange All** button. The Arrange Windows dialog box opens, and you can select how you want to display multiple files: horizontally, vertically, tiled (where each window appears in a square pane), or cascaded (where windows appear one behind another).

Insert a Picture

You can illustrate your Office files with images that you store on your computer. For example, if you have a photo or graphic file that relates to your Excel data, you can insert it onto the worksheet. If you have a photo or graphic file that relates to the subject matter in your document, you can insert it into the document to help the reader understand your subject. After you insert a picture, you can resize, move, or modify the graphic in a variety of ways, as described in the section "Understanding Graphic Object Modification Techniques" later in this chapter.

Insert a Picture

1 Click in your document where you want to add a picture.

Note: You can move the image to a different location after inserting it onto the page. See the section "Resize and Move Graphic Objects."

2 Click the **Insert** tab.

3 Click **Pictures**.

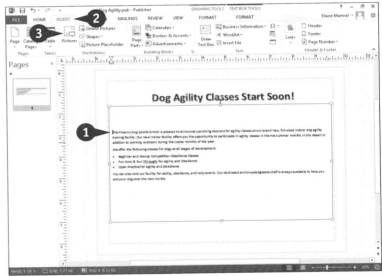

The Insert Picture dialog box appears.

Ⓐ The folder you are viewing appears here.

Note: Image files come in a variety of formats, including GIF, JPEG, and PNG.

Ⓑ To browse for a particular file type, you can click ⌄ and choose a file format.

Ⓒ You can click here to navigate to commonly used locations where pictures may be stored.

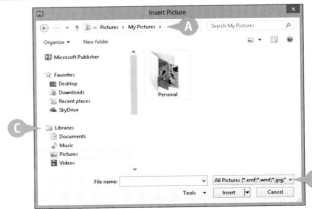

4 Navigate to the folder containing the picture you want to add to your document.

5 Click the picture you want to add.

6 Click **Insert**.

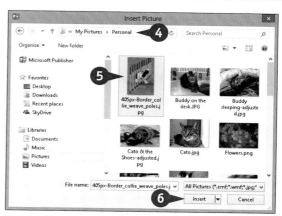

D The picture appears in your document, selected and surrounded by handles (▭ and ○).

E Drag ○ to rotate the picture (○ changes to ↻).

F On the Home tab, click **Wrap Text** to control text flow around the picture.

G Picture Tools appear on the Ribbon; you can use these tools to format pictures.

To remove a picture that you no longer want, you can click the picture and press Delete.

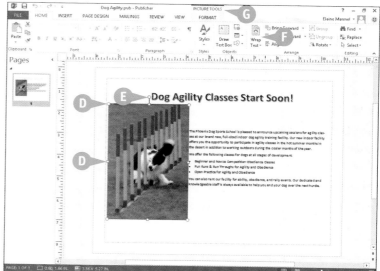

TIPS

If I am sharing my file with others, can I compress the pictures to save space?

Yes. You can compress image files that you add to any file. To do so, click the image, click the **Format** tab on the Ribbon, and click the **Compress Pictures** button (⬚) in the Adjust group. In the Compress Pictures dialog box, fine-tune settings as needed and click **OK** to compress the pictures.

I made changes to my picture, but I do not like the effect. How do I return the picture to the original settings?

You can click the **Reset Picture** button (🖼 ▾), located in the Adjust group on the Format tab, to restore a picture to its original state. This command removes any edits that you applied to the image. Activating this command does not restore the original size of the image.

Insert an Online Picture

In addition to pictures stored on your computer's hard drive, you can add interest to your Office files by inserting a picture or clip art image from an online source into a Word, Excel, PowerPoint, Publisher, Outlook, or OneNote document. Be careful when choosing online pictures and make sure that they fall into the public domain or that you have written permission to use the picture.

The pictures and clip art found at Office.com are all public domain art and you can freely use any of these images. None of the Office 2013 applications come with any preinstalled clip art as previous versions did.

Insert an Online Picture

Note: If you are working in Word or Excel, switch to Print Layout view.

1 Click in your document where you want to add a picture.

Note: You can move the graphic to a different location after you insert it. See the next section, "Resize and Move Graphic Objects."

2 Click the **Insert** tab.

3 Click **Online Pictures**.

Note: In some Office programs, Online Pictures does not appear directly on the Insert tab. In this case, click **Illustrations**.

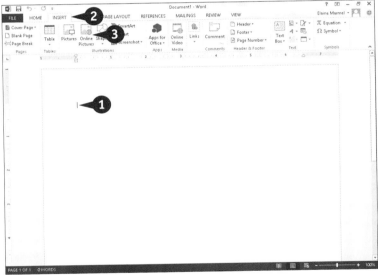

The Insert Pictures window appears.

4 Click here and type a description of the kind of image you want.

5 Click the **Search** button ($\mathcal{P}$).

The results of your search appear.

Ⓐ You can click here (⌃ and ⌄) to navigate through the search results.

Ⓑ You can click here to return to the Insert Picture window and search for a different image.

6 Click the picture you want to add to your document.

7 Click **Insert**.

Ⓒ The picture appears in your document, selected and surrounded by handles (⬚).

Ⓓ Drag 🔄 to rotate the picture.

Ⓔ You can click **Wrap Text** or 🖼 to control text flow around the picture.

Ⓕ Picture Tools appear on the Ribbon; you can use these tools to format the picture.

When you finish working with your online picture, click anywhere else in the work area.

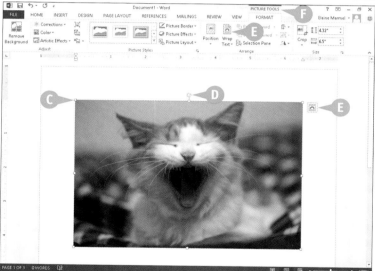

TIPS

Why must I make sure that the image I choose falls into the public domain?
Images that are privately owned are often available for use only if you agree to pay a fee and/or give credit to the owner of the image. To use a public domain image, you do not need to pay a royalty and you do not need permission from an image owner to use the image.

What happens when I search for images using Bing?
Like the results of a search of Office.com, the search results appear in a window. A message states that search results are licensed under Creative Commons and that you need to review the specific license for any image you want to use to ensure that you can comply with the license. Bing searches do not exclude pictures outside the public domain.

Resize and Move Graphic Objects

ictures and other types of images are also called *graphic objects*. If a graphic object is not positioned where you want it or if it is too large or too small, you can move or resize it. When you select a graphic object, handles appear on each side of the graphic object; you can use these handles to resize it. Alignment guides — green lines — appear as you move a graphic object to help you determine where to place it. Once you have picked the spot for the graphic, the alignment guides disappear.

Resize and Move Graphic Objects

Move a Graphic

1 Click a graphic object.

A Handles (▢) surround the graphic.

Note: In Publisher, ▢ and ◯ surround the graphic.

2 Position the mouse pointer over a graphic object or the edge of a text box ($I^=$, I, or ✛ changes to ↖).

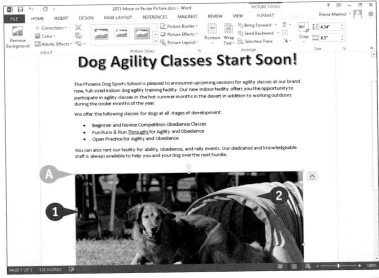

3 Drag the graphic object to a new location.

B In Word, green alignment guides help you position the graphic object.

4 Release the mouse button.

The graphic object appears in the new location and, in Word, the alignment guides disappear.

5 Click outside the graphic object to cancel its selection.

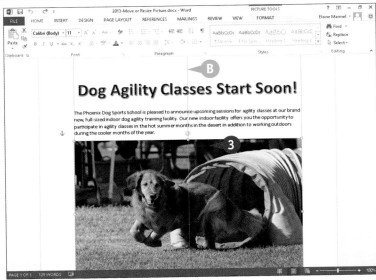

Resize a Graphic

1 Click a graphic object.

C Handles (⬜) surround the graphic.

Note: In Publisher, ⬜ and ◯ surround the graphic.

2 Position the mouse pointer over one of the handles (I꜔, I, or ✛ changes to ↖, ↕, ↙, or ⟺).

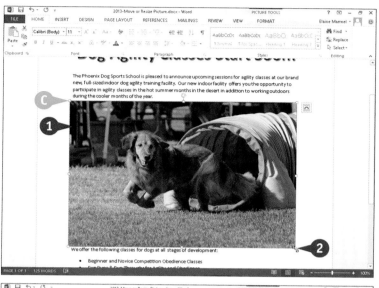

3 Drag the handle inward or outward until the graphic object is the appropriate size (↖, ↕, ↙, or ⟺ changes to +).

4 Release the mouse button.

The graphic object appears in the new size.

5 Click outside the graphic object to cancel its selection.

TIPS

Can I control how text wraps around an object?

Yes, if you insert the object into a Word or Publisher file. Click the object, click the **Wrap Text** button on the Format tab, and choose a wrap style. In Word, you also can click 🖼.

Does it matter which handle I use to resize a graphic?

Yes. If you click and drag any of the corner handles, you maintain the proportion of the graphic as you resize it. The handles on the sides, top, or bottom of the graphic only resize the width or the height of the graphic, so using one of them can make your graphic look distorted, especially if you resize a picture, video, or screenshot using any handle except a corner handle.

Understanding Graphic Object Modification Techniques

In addition to inserting, moving, and resizing pictures as described in this chapter, you can insert and modify other types of graphic objects — shapes, screenshots, SmartArt, WordArt, and charts — in all Office programs except Access. The available graphic objects vary from program to program; the specific types of available graphic objects appear on the Insert tab of the program. You insert these objects using basically the same techniques you use to insert pictures.

You can modify an object's appearance using a variety of Ribbon buttons that appear on a Tools tab specific to the type of graphic object you select.

Crop a Picture

You can use the Crop tool to create a better fit, to omit a portion of the image, or to focus the viewer on an important area of the image. You can crop a picture, screenshot, or clip art image. When you crop an object, you remove vertical and/or horizontal edges from the object. The Crop tool is located on the Format tab on the Ribbon, which appears when you click the object you want to crop.

Rotate or Flip a Graphic

After you insert an object such as a piece of clip art or a photo from your hard drive into a Word document, you may find that the object appears upside down or inverted. Fortunately, Word makes it easy to flip or rotate an object. For example, you might flip a clip art image to face another direction, or rotate an arrow object to point elsewhere on the page. Or, for dramatic effect, you can rotate or flip pictures, clip art images, and some shapes. Keep in mind that you cannot rotate text boxes.

Correct Images

You can change the brightness and contrast of a picture, clip art, or a screenshot to improve its appearance, and you can sharpen or soften an image. Suppose, for example, the image object you have inserted in your Word, Excel, or PowerPoint file is slightly blurry, or lacks contrast. You find the image-correction tools on the Picture Tools Format tab on the Ribbon, which appears when you click to select the object to which you want to apply the effect.

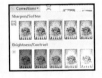

Make Color Adjustments

You can adjust the color of a picture, screenshot, or clip art image by increasing or decreasing color saturation or color tone. You can also recolor a picture, screenshot, or clip art image to create an interesting effect.

Color saturation controls the amount of red and green in a photo, while color tone controls the amount of blue and yellow.

Remove the Background of an Image

You can remove the background of a picture, screenshot, or clip art image. For example, suppose that you inserted a screenshot of an Excel chart in a Word document; the screenshot would, by default, include the Excel Ribbon. You can use the Remove Background tool in the Adjust group on the Picture Tools Format tab to remove the Excel Ribbon and focus the reader's attention on the chart.

Add an Effect

You can use tools to assign unique and interesting special effects to objects. For example, you can apply a shadow effect, create a mirrored reflection, apply a glow effect, soften the object's edges, make a bevel effect, or generate a 3D rotation effect. You can find these tools on the Format tab of the Ribbon, which appears when you click to select the object to which you want to apply the effect. (Note that the Picture Effects tool is not available in Publisher.)

Apply a Style to a Graphic

You can apply a predefined style to a shape, text box, WordArt graphic, picture, or clip art image. Styles contain predefined colors and effects and help you quickly add interest to a graphic. Applying a style removes other effects you may have applied, such as shadow or bevel effects. Sample styles appear on the Picture Tools Format or Drawing Tools Format tab when you click ⊡ in the Picture Styles or Shape Styles group.

Add a Picture Border or Drawing Outline

You can add a border to a picture, shape, text box, WordArt graphic, clip art image, or screenshot. Using the Picture Border or Shape Outline tool, which appears on the Picture Tools Format or Drawing Tools Format tab, you can control the thickness of the border, set a style for the border — a solid or dashed line — and change the color of the border.

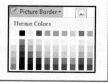

Apply Artistic Effects

You can apply artistic effects to pictures, screenshots, and clip art in order to liven them up. For example, you can make an image appear as though it was rendered in marker, pencil, chalk, or paint. Other artistic effects might remind you of mosaics, film grain, or glass. You find the Artistic Effects button on the Picture Tools Format tab, which appears when you click to select the object to which you want to apply the effect.

Office and the Cloud

Office 2013 offers a completely new experience when it comes to working in a mobile environment. Today, people are on the go but often want to take work with them to do while sitting in the waiting room of their doctor's office, at the airport, or in a hotel room. Office 2013 was designed to help you work from anywhere using almost any device available because, among other reasons, it works with SharePoint and SkyDrive, Microsoft's cloud space. From SkyDrive, you can log into cloud space and, using Office Web Apps — essentially, tools with which you are already familiar — get to work.

Sign In to Office Online

Office Online connects your Office programs to the world beyond your computer. When you sign in on any device and launch an Office program, the program Start screen and the program window show that you are signed in. Signing in gives you access to online pictures and clip art stored at Office.com and enables Office to synchronize files between your computer, SkyDrive, and SharePoint.

SkyDrive and Office 2013

The SkyDrive app is a cloud storage service from Microsoft that comes with Office 2013; 7GB are free, and you can rent additional space. Office 2013 saves all documents by default to your SkyDrive so that your documents are always available to you.

Using Office Web Apps

You can open and edit Word, Excel, OneNote, and PowerPoint documents from your SkyDrive using Office Web Apps, which are scaled-down editions of Office programs that you can use to easily review documents and make minor changes.

Take Your Personal Settings with You Everywhere

Office 2013 keeps track of personal settings like your recently used files and favorite templates and makes them available from any computer. Word and PowerPoint also remember the paragraph and slide you were viewing when you close a document, and they display that location when you open the document on another machine, making it easy for you to get back to work when you move from one work location to another.

Your Documents Are Always Up to Date

Office 2013 saves your Office documents by default in the SkyDrive folder that installs along with Office. As you work, Office synchronizes files with changes to your SkyDrive in the background. And, the technology does not slow down your work environment, because Office only uploads changes, not entire documents, saving bandwidth and battery life as you work from wireless devices.

Share Your Documents from Anywhere

You can share your documents both from within an Office program and from your SkyDrive. And, from either location, you can e-mail a document to recipients you choose, post a document at a social media site, or create a link to a document that you can provide to users so that they can view the document in a browser. You can also use Microsoft's free online presentation service to present Word and PowerPoint documents online.

Take Advantage of the Office Store

The Office Store contains add-in applications that work with Office programs. For example, the dictionary you use to look up words in Microsoft Word or Excel 2013 does not automatically install when you install the program. But, when you need an add-on for Word or Excel, you can download it from the Office Store. Click the **Office Store** button to open your browser to the Office Store web page.

Office 2013 on Demand

Office 2013 comes in three "traditional" editions, where you buy the program; you can install any traditional edition on one machine. Office 2013 also comes in two "subscription" editions; essentially, you pay an annual rental fee to use the software on five PCs or Macs.

Subscription editions include the Office on Demand feature; subscribers can run temporary instances of Word, Excel, PowerPoint, Access, Publisher, Visio, and Project on computers where they normally would not be able to install software. To keep the process fast, only parts of the application actually download as needed, and it runs locally. When a program closes, it uninstalls itself.

Subscribers must be online and logged in to validate their right to use Office on Demand.

Sign In to Office Online

You can use Office Online to work from anywhere. Sign in to Office Online using any of your devices and then, using one of the Office Web Apps, go to work. Office remembers some of your personal settings such as your Recent Documents list so that you always have access to them.

When you work offline, Office creates, saves, and opens your files from the local SkyDrive folder. Notifications appear periodically, reminding you that you are working offline. Occasionally, Office alerts you if changed files are pending upload to the cloud. Whenever you reconnect, Office automatically uploads your changes to the cloud.

Sign In to Office Online

1 Open an Office program.

The program's Start screen appears.

2 Click the Sign In link.

Note: If you are viewing a document, click the Sign In link in the upper-right corner of the screen.

The Sign In to Office window appears.

3 Click **Microsoft Account** or **Organizational Account**, depending on the user ID you use with Office.

The Microsoft account sign-in window appears.

4 Type your Microsoft account e-mail address.

5 Type your Microsoft account password.

A If you do not have a Microsoft account, you can click here to sign up for one. You can establish any existing e-mail address as your Microsoft account address.

6 Click **Sign in**.

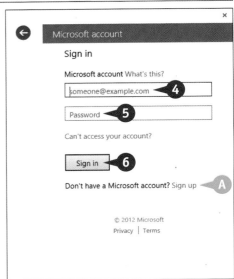

B This area indicates that you have signed in to Office Online.

How do I sign out of Office Online?

Sign in to Windows 8 using a local account and follow these steps:

1 Click the **File** tab.

2 Click **Account**.

Note: In Outlook, click **Office Account**.

3 Click **Sign Out**.

A The Remove Account dialog box appears to warn you that continuing removes all customizations and synchronization might stop.

Note: In most cases, it is perfectly safe to click **Yes**. If you are unsure, check with your system administrator.

4 Click **Yes**.

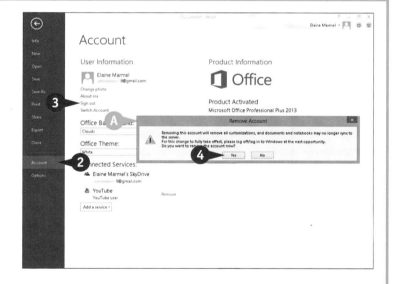

Share a Document from Office

You can easily share documents using Office Online. You can share an Office document by posting it using a social network or to a blog or sending a document as an e-mail attachment. You can also take advantage of a free presentation service Microsoft offers and share your document by presenting it online. Or, as shown in this section, you can send a link to your SkyDrive — as part of Office 2013, you receive free cloud space at SkyDrive — where the recipient can view and even work on only the shared document. When you finish, you can stop sharing the document.

Share a Document from Office

Share a Document

Note: The document you want to share must be stored in the cloud. See the tip at the end of this section for details.

1 With the document you want to share on-screen, click the **File** tab.

Backstage view appears.

2 Click **Share**.

3 Click **Invite People**.

4 Type e-mail addresses of people with whom you want to share here.

Note: If you type multiple addresses, Office separates them with a semicolon (;).

5 Specify whether these people can edit or simply view the document.

Ⓐ You can type a personal message to include with the invitation.

6 Click **Share**.

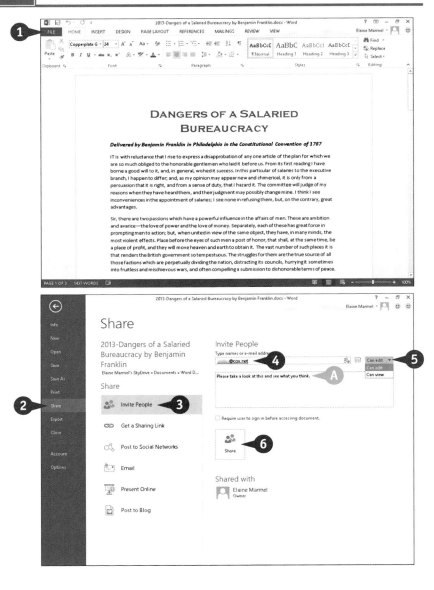

Office sends e-mails to the people you listed.

Ⓑ Recipients with whom you shared the document appear here.

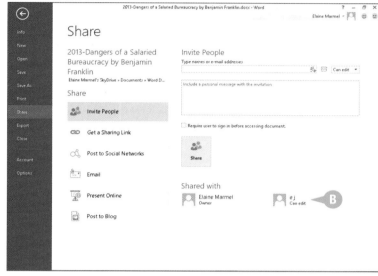

Stop Sharing

① Open the document you want to stop sharing and click the **File** tab.

② Click **Share**.

③ Click **Invite People**.

④ Right-click the recipient with whom you no longer want to share.

⑤ Click **Remove User**.

The program updates document permissions and removes the user from the screen.

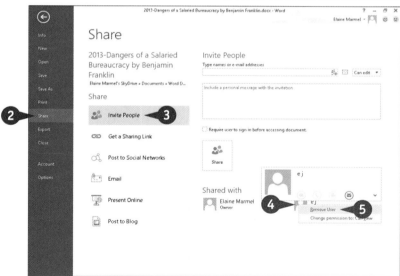

Why do I see a screen indicating I must save my document before sharing it?

If you have not previously saved your document to your SkyDrive, the Office program prompts you to do so before starting the Share process. By default, Office saves all your documents to your SkyDrive, but, if you changed that option, click the **Save to Cloud** button that appears. The program displays the Save As pane in Backstage view; click your SkyDrive and then click a folder in the Recent Folders list or click **Browse** to navigate to the SkyDrive folder where you want to place the document.

Download Apps from the Office Store

You can use the Office Store to download add-on applications, or *apps*, for Word, Outlook, or Excel. For example, the dictionary you use to look up words in Word 2013 does not automatically install when you install the program. But, when you need an add-on, you can download it from the Office Store.

The Office Store also contains apps created by developers outside of Microsoft — apps that work with Word and Excel. The developer can choose to charge for an app or make it available for free.

Download Apps from the Office Store

Install an App

1 Click the **Insert** tab.

2 Click **Apps for Office**.

The Apps for Office dialog box appears, displaying the My Apps tab of currently installed apps.

Ⓐ You can click **Featured Apps** to view apps you may find interesting. If you browse through featured apps and do not find what you need, click **More apps**.

3 Click **Office Store**.

The Office Store web page appears.

4 Search for apps using the search box at the top of the page or simply scroll down to find and click the app you want to add.

The web page describing the app appears.

Note: This section adds the Merriam-Webster Dictionary app to Word (and Excel) as an example.

Ⓑ You can read the information about the app.

Ⓒ The price of the app appears here.

5 Click **Add**.

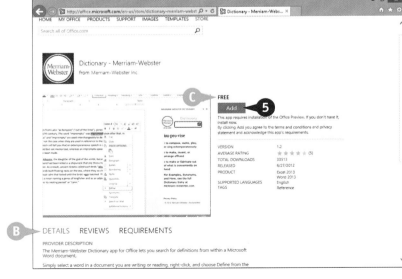

A web page appears, asking you to sign in to the Office Store using your Microsoft account.

6 Fill in the login information.

7 Click **Sign in**.

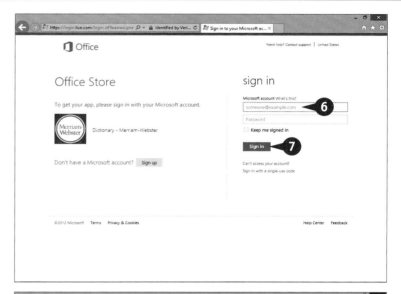

A web page appears, asking you to confirm that you want to add the app.

8 Click **Continue**.

TIP

What should I do for add-ins for other Office 2013 programs?
OneNote, PowerPoint, and Publisher use the Add-Ins pane of the Options dialog box, as they did in earlier editions of Office, to manage add-ins. For dictionary look-ups, these programs and Outlook use the same Research pane that appears in earlier editions of Office. To display the Research pane, click the **Review** tab (in Outlook, pop out a reply or a forward message window and the Review tab becomes visible), and then click **Research**. Available research sources appear in a list in the pane. Access manages its add-ins using the Add-In Manager, available from the Database Tools tab.

When you need an app for Microsoft Word or Excel, you go to the Office Store. You visit the Office Store from within the program to review available apps. You then choose, buy if necessary, download, and install apps that interest you.

After you finish installing an app that you download from the Office Store, you must, in most cases, activate the app so that you can use it in Microsoft Word or Excel. This section describes how to activate the Merriam-Webster Dictionary app and then use it in Word to look up definitions of words.

Download Apps from the Office Store (continued)

Another web page appears, providing directions to activate the app.

Activate the Dictionary App

1 In Word or Excel, click the **Insert** tab.

2 Click **Apps for Office**.

Note: If you click ▼ on the bottom of the Apps for Office button, click **See All**.

The Apps for Office dialog box appears, displaying the My Apps page, and the app you downloaded appears.

③ Click the app.

④ Click **Insert**.

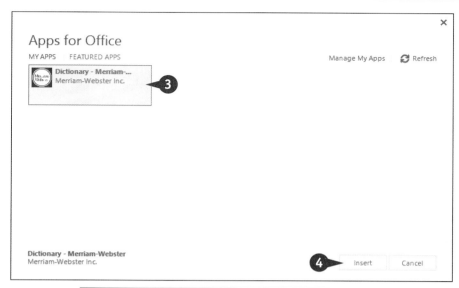

The app loads. For the Merriam-Webster Dictionary app, a pane opens on the right side of the Word screen, enabling you to type a word to look up.

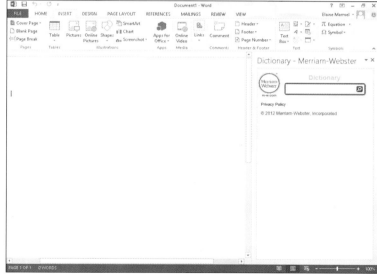

TIPS

Do I need to keep the Merriam-Webster Dictionary pane open all the time to use the dictionary?

No. Click ✕ in the pane to close it. See Chapter 8 to learn how to use the thesaurus and dictionary.

If I decide I no longer want an app that I previously downloaded, can I remove it?

Yes. Click the **Insert** tab and then click **Apps for Office**. In the dialog box that appears, click the **Manage My Apps** link in the upper-right corner. A web page opens, showing your installed apps; you can click **Hide** beside any app to remove it.

Sign In to SkyDrive

You can use your SkyDrive and Office 2013 programs to work from any location in the world on any trusted device. SkyDrive offers you online storage from Microsoft. With Office 2013, you automatically receive a small amount of storage space for free and you can rent additional storage space for a nominal fee.

You use a browser and a Microsoft Account to sign into SkyDrive. Once you have signed in to SkyDrive, you can use Office Web Apps to open and edit documents. Office 2013 technology synchronizes documents stored in your SkyDrive with documents stored on trusted devices.

Sign In to SkyDrive

1 Open your browser.

2 In the address bar, type **skydrive.com** and press **Enter**.

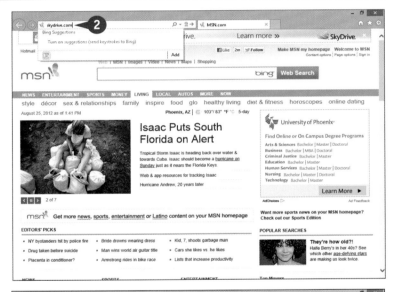

You are redirected to the SkyDrive sign-in page.

③ Type the e-mail address associated with your Microsoft Account.

④ Type your Microsoft Account password.

⑤ Click **Sign in**.

Your SkyDrive appears.

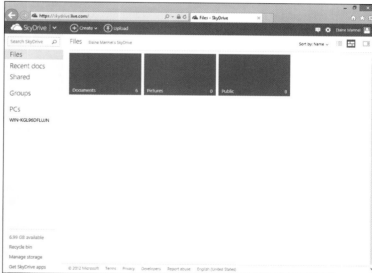

How do I sign out of SkyDrive?
Click your name (Ⓐ) and then click **Sign out** (Ⓑ).

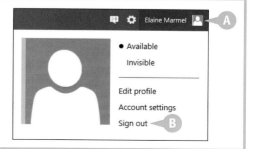

Using a Web App in SkyDrive

From SkyDrive, you can use Office Web Apps to open and edit Office documents with the same basic editing tools you use in the Office program.

While you cannot create or use macros, you can use these editing tools to perform basic functions in each Office program. For example, in the Word Web App, you can apply character and paragraph formatting, such as bold or italics, and you can align text. You can change margins, insert a table or a picture stored on the local drive, and add clip art available from Microsoft's Clip Art collection.

Using a Web App in SkyDrive

Open the Document

1 Sign in to SkyDrive at https://skydrive.live.com.

2 Open the folder containing the document you want to open.

3 Click the document.

The document appears for viewing only.

Edit in a Web App

① Perform Steps **1** to **3** in the previous subsection, "Open the Document."

② Click **Edit Document**.

③ Click **Edit in Word Web App**.

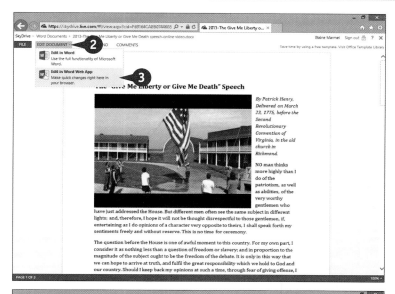

The document appears in the Word Web App, where you can perform basic edits.

Ⓐ The Ribbon contains only a few tabs.

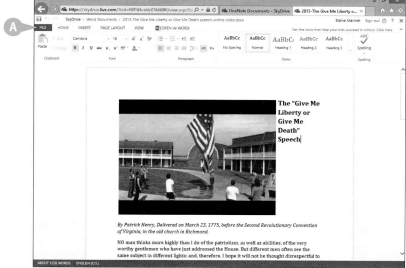

How do I save my work in a Web App?

The answer depends on the Web App. Excel, PowerPoint, and OneNote automatically save changes as you work. In the Word Web App, you click the **File** tab and then click **Save**. Publisher and Access do not have corresponding Web Apps; instead, the appropriate Office program opens when you open one of these file types from SkyDrive.

How do I close a document I opened in the cloud?

Click the **File** tab and then click **Exit**. Your browser reappears, showing the SkyDrive contents of the folder containing the document you opened.

Using an Office Program from SkyDrive

Using Office 2013, you can work from anywhere. For example, suppose you work on a document from your SkyDrive and discover that you need tools not available in the Web App. If Office 2013 is installed on the computer, you can use SkyDrive tools to open the file in the appropriate Office program.

If Office 2013 is *not* installed on the computer *and* you have a subscription to Office 2013, SkyDrive can open the Office program you need. In just a few seconds, SkyDrive installs it on the computer you currently use. When you close the program, SkyDrive uninstalls it.

Using an Office Program from SkyDrive

1 Open a document and edit it using a Web App.

Note: See the previous section, "Using a Web App in SkyDrive," for details.

Note: This section uses an Excel workbook as an example.

2 Click **Open In Excel**.

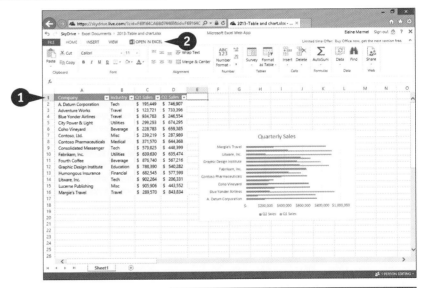

A security dialog box appears.

3 Click **Yes**.

The file opens in the appropriate Office program.

Note: As long as the file is open in the Office desktop application, you cannot edit it using the web app, but you can view it.

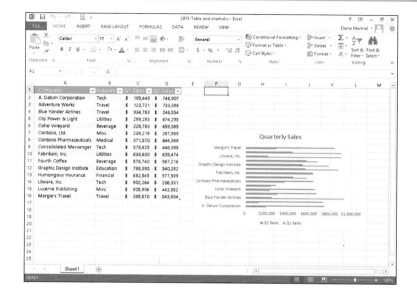

TIP

What happens when I close the Office program?

Save your document in the Office program as usual; the changes you made are automatically uploaded to your SkyDrive. In addition, if the program streamed to your computer using your Office 2013 subscription, SkyDrive uninstalls the program. When you return to your browser where SkyDrive is open, this message box appears. Click **My document opened successfully, close Excel Web App** (A) to dismiss it.

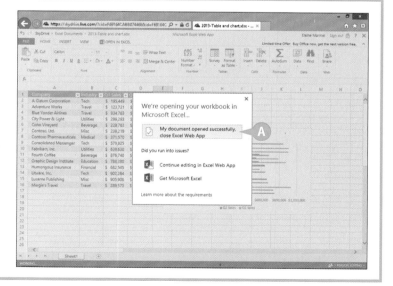

Upload a Document to SkyDrive

You can upload any document from your computer to your SkyDrive at any time. By default, Office 2013 saves all documents to the SkyDrive folder on your computer and then, in the background, synchronizes the contents of the SkyDrive folder with your SkyDrive.

But suppose that you sign out of Office Online and choose to save documents locally on your computer. For example, if you then find that you need a document on your SkyDrive to edit while you travel, you can place a document into your SkyDrive folder on your computer and then use the SkyDrive app to upload the document.

Upload a Document to SkyDrive

1 Sign in to SkyDrive using your browser.

Note: See the section "Sign In to SkyDrive" for details.

2 Click to display the folder where you want to place the document.

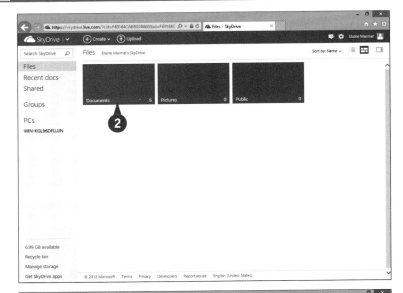

3 Click **Upload**.

The Choose File to Upload dialog box appears.

4 Navigate to the folder containing the file you want to upload.

5 Click the file.

6 Click **Open**.

Ⓐ The file appears in your SkyDrive.

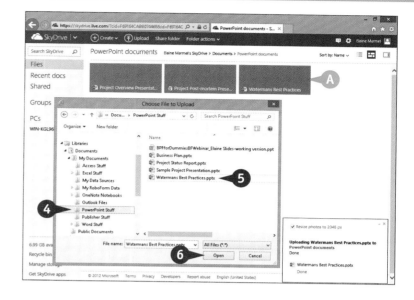

TIP

What can I do if I forgot to upload a file I need to use remotely?

You can access your PC remotely by downloading and installing SkyDrive for Windows. The SkyDrive app you get through Office 2013 is a scaled-down version of SkyDrive for Windows. To download SkyDrive for Windows, sign in to your SkyDrive account using your browser. In the SkyDrive Navigation pane, click **PCs** (Ⓐ) and follow the instructions.

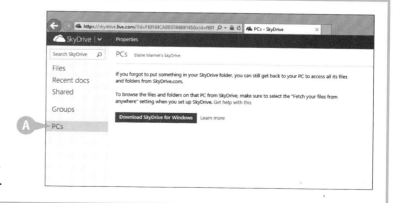

Share a Document Using SkyDrive

You can use the SkyDrive app to share a document stored on your SkyDrive. Suppose that you finish the work on a document from your SkyDrive and you are ready for others to review it. You do not need to use the Office program installed on your local computer to invite others to review the document; you can use commands available in SkyDrive.

SkyDrive offers three ways to share a document: you can send the document by e-mail, share it using a social media service of your choice, or send a link to the document on your SkyDrive.

Share a Document Using SkyDrive

Open a Document to Share

1 In SkyDrive, open the document you want to share.

2 Click **Share**.

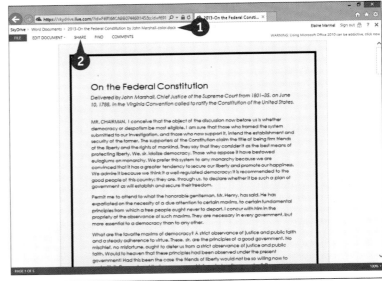

The Share dialog box appears, suggesting that you share by e-mail.

Note: Follow the steps in one of the following subsections to share the document.

Share via E-Mail

1 Fill in the e-mail address of the person with whom you want to share the document.

Ⓐ You can include a personal message here.

2 Click **Share**.

E-mail messages are sent to the recipients you supplied, providing a link that enables them to view the document in a Web App.

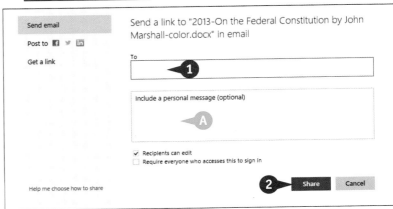

Share via Social Media

1 Click **Post to**.

2 Click here to add your social media services as needed.

3 Follow the on-screen directions.

4 Click **Post**.

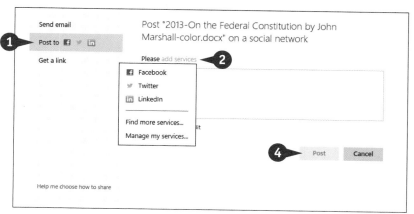

Share via a Link

1 Click **Get a link**.

2 Determine the type of link you want and click its associated button.

Note: This example shows a View Only link.

A link is generated; provide this link to anyone with whom you want to share the document.

3 Click **Done**.

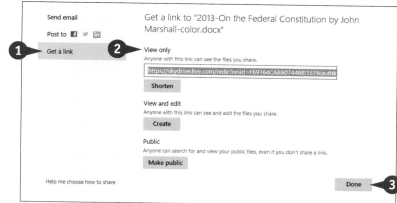

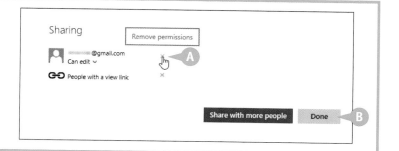

TIP

How do I stop sharing a document?
Open the document and click **Share**. A window like this one appears. Click ✕ beside each type of link you want to remove (Ⓐ). Then, click **Done** (Ⓑ).

PART II

Word

You can use Word to tackle any project involving text, such as correspondence, reports, and more. Word's versatile formatting features enable you to easily enhance your text documents and add elements such as tables or headers and footers. In this part, you learn how to build and format Word documents and tap into Word's tools to review and proofread your documents.

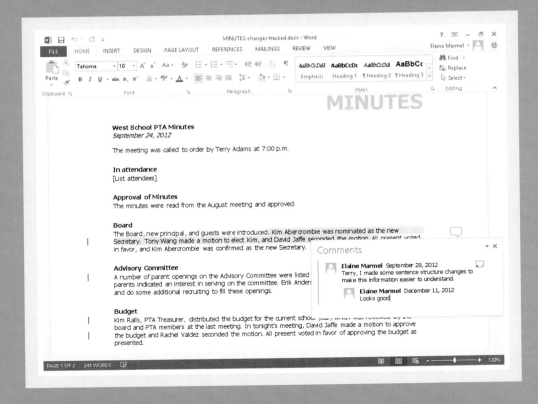

Change Word's Views

You can control how you view your Word document in several ways. For example, you can use the Zoom feature to control the magnification of your document with either the Zoom slider or the Zoom buttons. You can even zoom an image separately from your document.

You can also choose from five different views: Print Layout, which displays margins, headers, and footers; Outline, which shows the document's outline levels; Web Layout, which displays a web page preview of your document; Read Mode, which optimizes your document for easier reading; and Draft, which omits certain elements such as headers and footers.

Change Word's Views

Using the Zoom Tool

1 Drag the **Zoom** slider on the Zoom bar.

A You can also click a magnification button to zoom in or out.

B Click here to display the Zoom dialog box and precisely control zooming.

C Word magnifies the document, and the degree of magnification appears here.

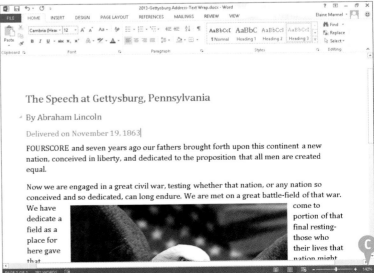

Switch Layout Views

1 Click the **View** tab on the Ribbon.

2 Click a layout view button.

Word displays a new view of the document.

In this example, Read Mode view helps you focus on reading a document. See Chapter 8 for details on Read Mode.

D You can also switch views using the View buttons at the bottom of the program window.

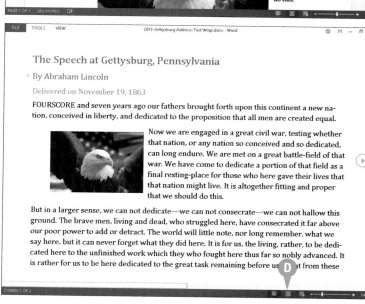

TIP

How can I zoom an image?

While in Read Mode view, double-click an image. Word enlarges the image and displays a zoom arrow (🔍) in the upper-right corner of the image. When you click the zoom arrow, the image enlarges to fill your screen. You can click the zoom arrow again to return to the first zoom level, or you can press `Esc` or click anywhere outside the image to return to Read Mode. See Chapter 8 for more on Read Mode.

Type and Edit Text

You can use Word to quickly type and edit text for a letter, memo, or report. By default, Word is set to Insert mode; when you start typing, any existing text moves over to accommodate the new text. If you have set up Word to toggle between Insert mode and Overtype mode, you can press `Insert` to switch to Overtype mode. In Overtype mode, the new text overwrites the existing text.

Word makes typing easy; you do not need to worry about when to start a new line within a paragraph and you can easily start new paragraphs and delete text.

Type and Edit Text

Type Text

1 Start typing your text.

A At the end of a line, Word automatically starts a new line, wrapping text to the next line for you.

B The insertion point marks your location in the document and moves to the right as you type. Text you type appears to the left of the insertion point.

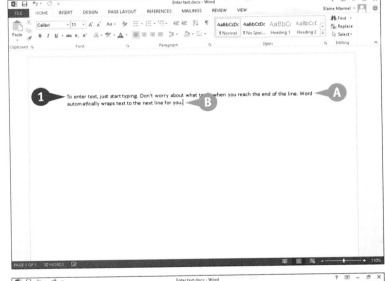

2 Press `Enter` to start a new paragraph.

C You can press `Enter` twice to add an extra space between paragraphs.

D You can press `Shift` + `Enter` to insert a line break and start a new line when your text does not fill the line. You often use line breaks when typing addresses.

E You can press `Tab` to quickly indent the first line of text in a paragraph.

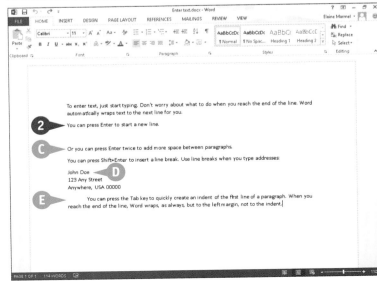

Edit Text

F If you make a spelling mistake, Word either corrects the mistake as you type or underlines it in red.

1 Click to the right of a mistake in a document.

2 Press **Backspace** to delete characters to the left of the insertion point.

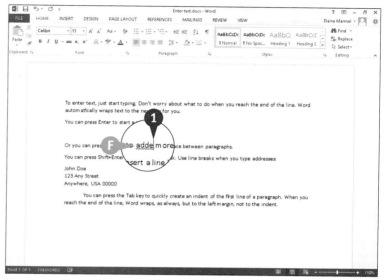

3 Click to the left of a mistake in a document.

4 Press **Delete** to delete characters to the right of the insertion point.

Note: You can delete larger quantities of text by selecting the text and pressing **Delete**.

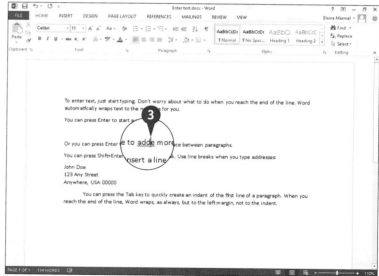

TIP

What is the difference between the Insert and Overtype modes?

By default, Word is set to Insert mode so that, when you click to place the insertion point and start typing, any existing text moves to the right to accommodate new text. In Overtype mode, new text overwrites existing text. To toggle between these modes, enable **Insert** and then press it. To enable **Insert**, click the **File** tab, click **Options**, and click the **Advanced** tab in the window that appears. Under Editing Options, select **Use the Insert key to control Overtype mode** (☐ changes to ☑) and then click **OK**.

Insert Quick Parts

Suppose you repeatedly type the same text in your documents — for example, your company name. You can add this text to the Quick Part Gallery in Word; then, the next time you need to add the text to a document, you can select it from the gallery instead of retyping it.

In addition to creating your own Quick Parts for use in your documents, you can use any of the wide variety of preset phrases included with Word. You access these preset Quick Parts from the Building Blocks Organizer window. (See the tip at the end of this section for more information.)

Insert Quick Parts

Create a Quick Parts Entry

1 Type the text that you want to store, including all formatting that should appear each time you insert the entry.

2 Select the text you typed.

3 Click the **Insert** tab.

4 Click the **Quick Parts** button (⊞ ▾).

5 Click **Save Selection to Quick Part Gallery**.

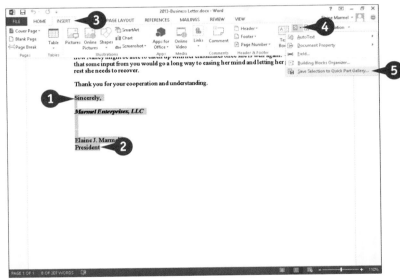

The Create New Building Block dialog box appears.

6 Type a name that you want to use as a shortcut for the entry.

Ⓐ You can also assign a gallery, a category, and a description for the entry.

7 Click **OK**.

Word stores the entry in the Quick Part Gallery.

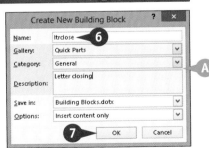

Insert a Quick Part Entry

1 Click in the text where you want to insert a Quick Part.

2 Click the **Insert** tab.

3 Click the **Quick Parts** button (▤ ▾).

All building blocks you define as Quick Parts appear in the Quick Part Gallery.

4 Click the entry that you want to insert.

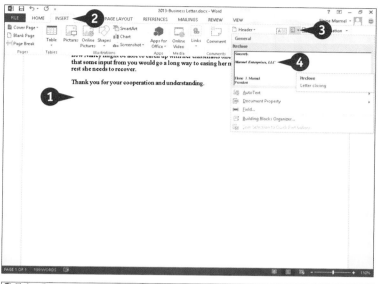

B Word inserts the entry into the document.

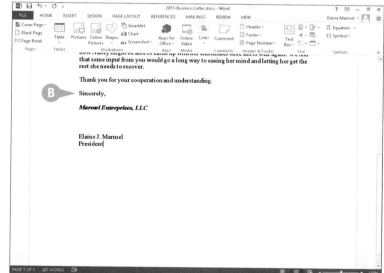

TIPS

How do I insert a preset Quick Part?
Click the **Insert** tab on the Ribbon, click the **Quick Parts** button (▤ ▾), and click **Building Blocks Organizer** to open the Building Blocks Organizer. Locate the Quick Part you want to insert (they are organized into galleries and categories), click it, and click **Insert**.

How do I remove a Quick Parts entry?
To remove a Quick Parts entry from the Building Blocks Organizer, open the Organizer (see the preceding tip for help), locate and select the entry you want to remove, click **Delete**, and click **Yes** in the dialog box that appears.

Insert Symbols

From time to time, you might need to insert a mathematical symbol or special character into your Word document. From the Symbol Gallery, you can insert many common symbols, including mathematical and Greek symbols, architectural symbols, and more.

If you do not find the symbol you need in the Symbol Gallery, you can use the Symbol dialog box. The Symbol dialog box displays a list of recently used symbols as well as hundreds of symbols in a variety of fonts. You can also use the Symbol dialog box to insert special characters.

Insert Symbols

1 Click the location in the document where you want the symbol to appear.

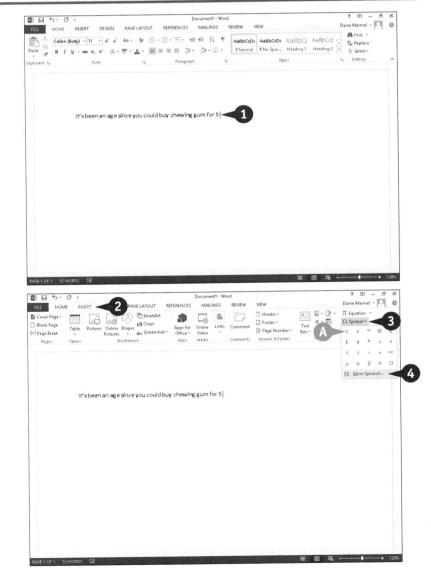

2 Click the **Insert** tab.

3 Click **Symbol**.

Ⓐ A gallery of commonly used symbols appears. If the symbol you need appears in the gallery, you can click it and skip the rest of these steps.

4 Click **More Symbols**.

The Symbol dialog box appears.

5 Click ▾ to select the symbol's font.

The available symbols change to match the font you selected.

B You can click ⋀ and ⋁ to scroll through available symbols.

6 Click a symbol.

7 Click **Insert**.

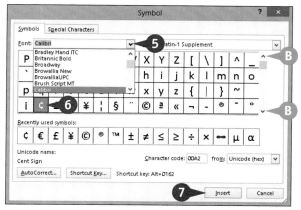

C The symbol appears at the current insertion point location in the document.

Note: You can control the size of the symbol the same way you control the size of text; see Chapter 6 for details on sizing text.

The dialog box remains open so that you can add more symbols to your document.

8 When finished, click **Close**.

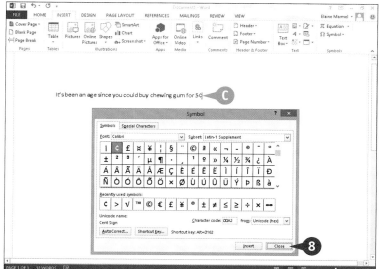

It's been an age since you could buy chewing gum for 5¢

How do I add a special character?
To add a special character, open the Symbol dialog box and click the **Special Characters** tab. Locate and click the character you want to add, and then click **Insert**. Click **Close** to close the dialog box.

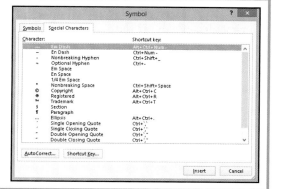

Create a Blog Post

If you keep an online blog, you can use Word to create a document to post on it. This enables you to take advantage of the many proofing and formatting tools that are available in Word. You can then post the blog entry directly from Word.

To post your blog entry, you must first set up Word to communicate with the Internet server that hosts your online blog; the first time you post a blog entry from Word, the program prompts you to register your blog account. Click **Register Now**, choose your blog provider in the dialog box that appears, and follow the on-screen prompts.

Create a Blog Post

Note: You must be connected to the Internet to complete this section.

1 Click the **File** tab.

2 Click **New**.

3 Click **Blog post**.

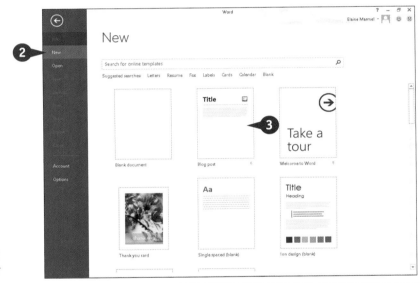

Word opens the blog post document.

Note: The first time you use the blog feature, Word prompts you to register your blog account. Click **Register Now**, choose your blog provider in the dialog box that appears, and follow the on-screen prompts.

Ⓐ You can use the buttons in the Blog group to manage blog entries. For example, you can click **Manage Accounts** to set up blog accounts.

Ⓑ You can use the tools in the other Ribbon groups to format text as you type.

4 Click the **Insert** tab.

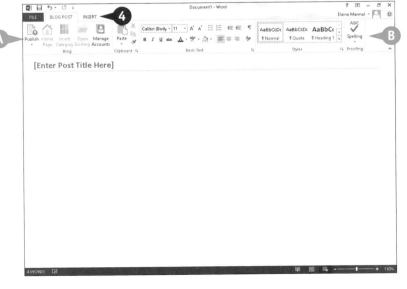

Ⓒ Use these buttons to incorporate tables, pictures, clip art, shapes, graphics, screenshots, WordArt, symbols, and hyperlinks in a blog entry.

⑤ Click here and type a title for your blog entry.

⑥ Click here and type your entry.

⑦ Click the **Blog Post** tab.

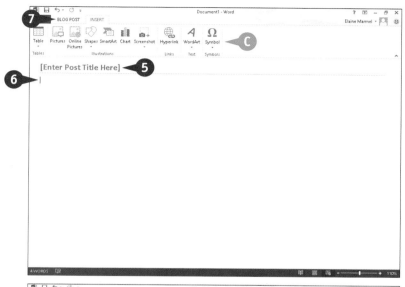

Note: You can save your blog entry on your hard drive the same way you save any document.

⑧ Click **Publish**.

Word connects to the Internet, prompts you for your blog username and password, and posts your entry.

A message appears above the blog entry title, identifying when the entry was posted.

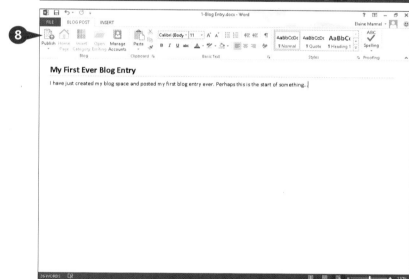

TIPS

Can I edit my blog accounts from within Word?
Yes. Click the **Manage Accounts** button on the Blog Post tab when viewing a blog page in Word to open the Blog Accounts dialog box. Here, you can edit an existing account, add a new account, or delete an account that you no longer use.

Can I post entries as drafts to review them before making them visible to the public?
Yes. Click ▼ on the bottom of the **Publish** button and click **Publish as Draft**. When you are ready to let the public view your entry, open it in Word and click **Publish**.

Change the Font, Size, and Color

By default, when you type text in a Word 2013 document, the program uses an 11-point Calibri font. You can change font — also called the *typeface* — text size, and color to alter the appearance of text in a document. For example, you might change the font, size, and color of your document's title text to emphasize it. In addition, you can use Word's basic formatting commands — Bold, Italic, Underline, Strikethrough, Subscript, and Superscript — to quickly add formatting to your text. And, you can change the font that Word 2013 applies by default for the body of a document.

Change the Font, Size, and Color

Change the Font

1 Select the text that you want to format.

A If you drag to select, the Mini toolbar appears faded in the background, and you can use it by moving ↳ toward the Mini toolbar.

2 To use the Ribbon, click the **Home** tab.

3 Click the **Font** ▼ to display the font.

Note: Word displays a sample of the selected text in any font at which you point the mouse.

4 Click the font you want to use.

B Word assigns the font to the selected text.

You can click anywhere outside the selection to continue working.

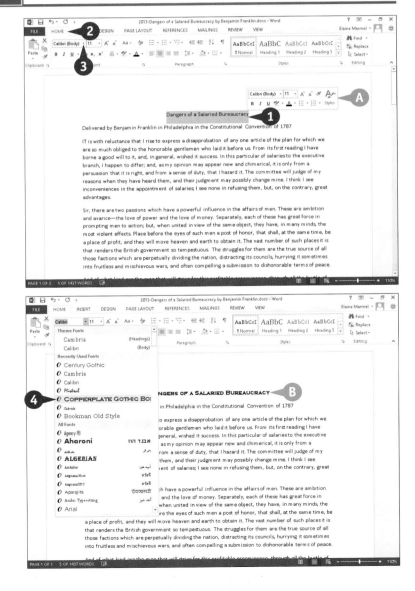

Change the Size

1 Select the text that you want to format.

C If you drag to select, the Mini toolbar appears faded in the background, and you can use it by moving ⌖ toward the Mini toolbar.

2 To use the Ribbon, click the **Home** tab.

3 Click the **Font Size** ▼ .

Note: Word displays a sample of the selected text in any font size at which you point the mouse.

4 Click a size.

D Word changes the size of the selected text.

This example applies a 24-point font size to the text.

Note: You also can change the font size using the **Grow Font** and **Shrink Font** buttons (A˄ and A˅) on the Home tab. Word increases or decreases the font size with each click of the button.

You can click anywhere outside the selection to continue working.

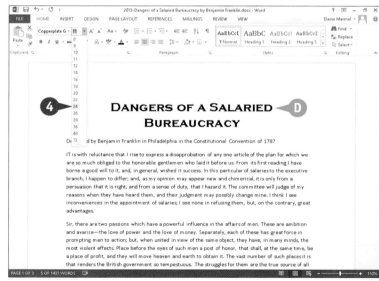

TIPS

How do I apply formatting to my text?
To apply formatting to your text, select the text you want to format, click the **Home** tab, and click the **Bold** (B), **Italic** (*I*), **Underline** (U ▾), **Strikethrough** (abc), **Subscript** (x₂), or **Superscript** (x²) button.

What is the toolbar that appears when I select text?
When you select text, the Mini toolbar appears, giving you quick access to common formatting commands. You can also right-click selected text to display the toolbar. To use any of the tools on the toolbar, simply click the desired tool; otherwise, continue working, and the toolbar disappears.

continued ▶

73

Changing the text color can go a long way toward emphasizing it on the page. For example, if you are creating an invitation, you might make the description of the event a different color to stand out from the other details. Likewise, if you are creating a report for work, you might make the title of the report a different color from the information contained in the report, or even color-code certain data in the report. Obviously, when selecting text colors, you should avoid choosing colors that make your text difficult to read.

Change the Font, Size, and Color (continued)

Change the Color

1 Select the text that you want to format.

A If you drag to select, the Mini toolbar appears faded in the background, and you can use it by moving ↖ toward the Mini toolbar.

2 To use the Ribbon, click the **Home** tab.

3 Click ▼ next to the **Font Color** button (**A** ▼) and point the mouse at a color.

B Word displays a sample of the selected text.

4 Click a color.

Word assigns the color to the text.

This example applies a blue color to the text.

You can click anywhere outside the selection to continue working.

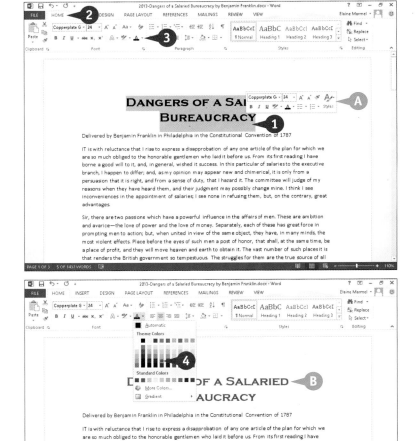

Using the Font Dialog Box

1 Select the text that you want to format.

2 Click the **Home** tab on the Ribbon.

3 Click the dialog box launcher (🔣) in the Font group.

The Font dialog box appears.

4 Click the font, style, size, color, underline style, or effect that you want to apply.

ⓒ A preview of your choices appears here.

5 Click **OK**.

ⓓ Word applies the font change.

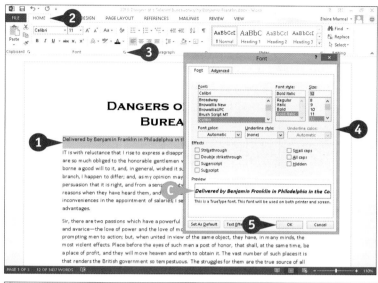

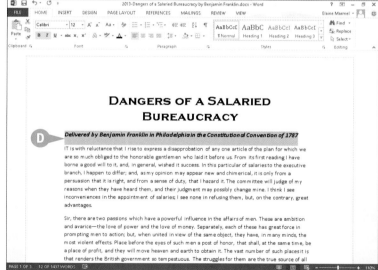

TIP

Can I change the default font and size?

Yes. To change the default font and size, follow these steps. Display the Font dialog box. Click the font and font size that you want to set as defaults. Click the **Set As Default** button. A new dialog box appears. Specify whether the change should apply to this document only or to all documents created with the current template. Click **OK**, and click **OK** again to close the Font dialog box. The next time you create a new document, Word applies the default font and size that you specified.

Align Text

You can use Word's alignment commands to change how text and objects are positioned horizontally on a page. By default, Word left-aligns text and objects. You can also choose to center text and objects on a page (using the Center command), align text and objects to the right side of the page (using the Right Align command), or justify text and objects so that they line up at both the left and right margins of the page (using the Justify command). You can change the alignment of all the text and objects in your document or change the alignment of individual paragraphs and objects.

Align Text

1 Click anywhere in the paragraph that you want to align or select the paragraphs and objects that you want to align.

2 Click the **Home** tab.

3 Click an alignment button.

The **Align Left** button (≡) aligns text with the left margin, the **Center** button (≡), centers text between the left and right margins, the **Align Right** button (≡) aligns text with the right margin, and the **Justify** button (≡) aligns text between the left and right margins.

Word aligns the text.

Ⓐ This text is aligned with the left margin.

Ⓑ This text is centered between both margins.

Ⓒ This text is aligned with the right margin.

Ⓓ This text is justified between both margins.

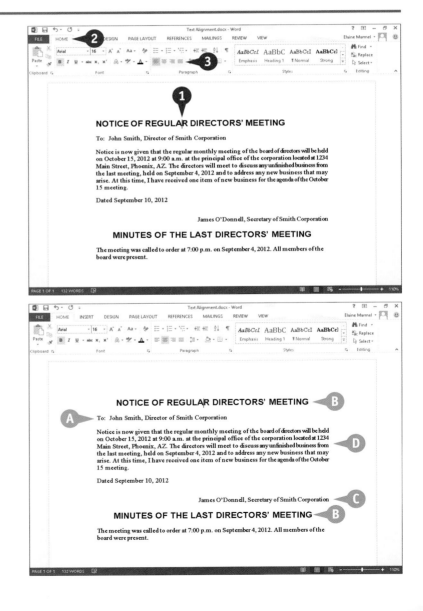

Set Line Spacing

You can adjust the amount of spacing that appears between lines of text in your paragraphs. You might set 2.5 spacing to allow for handwritten edits in your printed document, or 1.5 spacing to make paragraphs easier to read. By default, Word assigns 1.08 spacing for all new documents.

You can also control how much space appears before and after each paragraph in your document. For example, you might opt to single-space the text within a paragraph, but to add space before and after the paragraph to set it apart from the paragraphs that precede and follow it.

Set Line Spacing

1 Click anywhere in the paragraph that you want to format.

Note: To format multiple paragraphs, select them.

2 Click the **Home** tab.

3 Click the **Line Spacing** button (‡≡ ▾).

4 Click a line spacing option.

Ⓐ Word applies the new spacing.

This example applies 2.0 line spacing.

5 To control the spacing that surrounds a paragraph, click the dialog box launcher (▣) in the Paragraph group.

The Paragraph dialog box opens.

6 Use the **Before** spin arrow (⬍) to specify how much space should appear before the paragraph.

7 Use the **After** ⬍ to specify how much space should appear after the paragraph.

8 Click **OK** to apply the spacing settings.

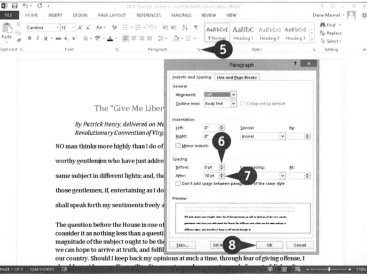

Indent Text

You can use indents as a way to control the horizontal positioning of text in a document. Indents are simply margins that affect individual lines or paragraphs. You might use an indent to distinguish a particular paragraph on a page — for example, a long quote.

You can indent paragraphs in your document from the left and right margins. You also can indent only the first line of a paragraph or all lines *except* the first line of the paragraph. You can set indents using buttons on the Ribbon, the Paragraph dialog box, and the Word ruler.

Indent Text

Set Quick Indents

1 Click anywhere in the paragraph you want to indent.

2 Click the **Home** tab on the Ribbon.

3 Click an indent button.

Ⓐ You can click the **Decrease Indent** button ( ) to decrease the indentation.

Ⓑ You can click the **Increase Indent** button ( ) to increase the indentation.

Ⓒ Word applies the indent change.

Set Precise Indents

1 Click anywhere in the paragraph you want to indent or select the text you want to indent.

2 Click the **Home** tab on the Ribbon.

3 Click the dialog box launcher (⌐) in the Paragraph group.

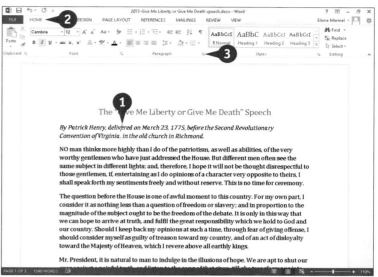

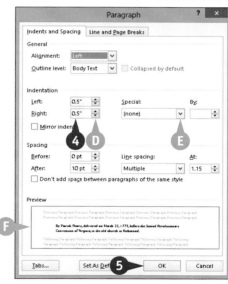

The Paragraph dialog box appears.

4 Type a specific indentation in the **Left** or **Right** indent text boxes.

D You can also click a spin arrow (⇕) to set an indent measurement.

E To set a specific kind of indent, you can click the **Special** ⌄ and then click an indent.

F The Preview area shows a sample of the indent.

5 Click **OK**.

Word applies the indent to the text.

TIP

How do I set indents using the Word ruler?

The ruler contains markers for changing the left indent, right indent, first-line indent, and hanging indent. Click the **View** tab and select **Ruler** (☐ changes to ☑) to display the ruler. On the left side of the ruler, drag the **Left Indent** button (☐) to indent all lines from the left margin, drag the **Hanging Indent** button (△) to create a hanging indent, or drag the **First Line Indent** button (▽) to indent the first line only. On the right side of the ruler, drag the **Right Indent** button (△) to indent all lines from the right margin.

Set Tabs

You can use tabs to create vertically aligned columns of text in your Word document. To insert a tab, simply press **Tab** on your keyboard; the insertion point moves to the next tab stop on the page.

By default, Word creates tab stops every 0.5 inches across the page and left-aligns the text on each tab stop. You can set your own tab stops using the ruler or the Tabs dialog box. You can also use the Tabs dialog box to change the tab alignment and specify an exact measurement between tab stops.

Set Tabs

Set Quick Tabs

1 Click the **View** tab.

2 Select **Ruler** (☐ changes to ☑) to display the ruler.

3 Click here until the type of tab marker that you want to set appears.

⌞ sets a left-aligned tab.

⊥ sets a center-aligned tab.

⌟ sets a right-aligned tab.

⊥ sets a decimal tab.

▯ sets a bar tab (displays a vertical bar at the tab location).

4 Select the lines to which you want to add the tab.

5 Click the ruler at the tab location you want.

On each selected line, Word adds a tab at the location you clicked.

6 Click at the end of the text after which you want to add a tab.

7 Press **Tab**.

8 Type the text that should appear in the next column.

Set Precise Tabs

1 Select the lines to which you want to add the tab.

2 Click the **Home** tab on the Ribbon.

3 Click the dialog box launcher (⟊) in the Paragraph group.

The Paragraph dialog box appears.

4 Click **Tabs** on the Indents and Spacing tab.

The Tabs dialog box appears.

5 Click here and type a new tab stop measurement.

6 Select a tab alignment (○ changes to ◉).

Ⓐ You can also select a tab leader character (○ changes to ◉).

7 Click **Set**.

Word saves the new tab stop.

8 Click **OK**.

Ⓑ Word closes the dialog box, and you can use the new tab stops.

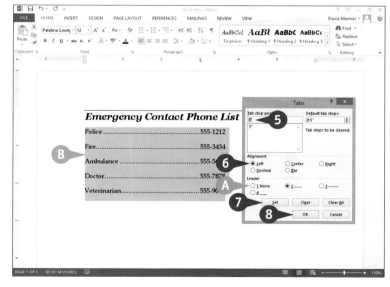

TIPS

Can I remove tab stops that I no longer need?

Yes. To remove a tab stop from the ruler, drag the tab stop off of the ruler. To remove a tab stop in the Tabs dialog box, select it, and then click **Clear**. To clear every tab stop that you saved in the Tabs dialog box, click **Clear All**.

What are leader tabs?

You can use leader tabs to separate tab columns with dots, dashes, or lines. Leader tabs help readers follow the information across tab columns. You can set leader tabs using the Tabs dialog box, as shown in this section.

Set Margins

By default, Word assigns a 1-inch margin all the way around the page in every new document that you create. However, you can change these margin settings. For example, you can set wider margins to fit less text on a page, or set smaller margins to fit more text on a page. You can apply your changes to the current document only, or make them the new default setting, to be applied to all new Word documents you create. When you adjust margins, Word sets the margins from the position of the insertion point to the end of the document.

Set Margins

Set Margins Using Page Layout Tools

1. Click anywhere in the document or section where you want to change margins.

2. Click the **Page Layout** tab on the Ribbon.

3. Click **Margins**.

   The Margins Gallery appears.

4. Click a margin setting.

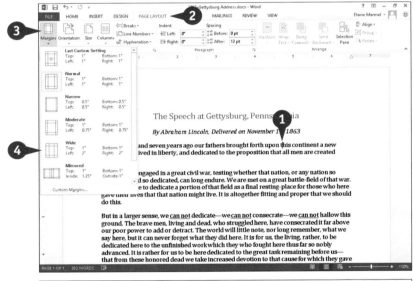

Ⓐ Word applies the new setting.

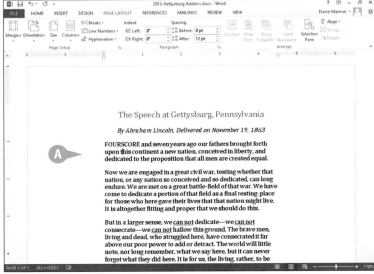

Set a Custom Margin

1 Click the **Page Layout** tab on the Ribbon.

2 Click **Margins**.

The Margins Gallery appears.

3 Click **Custom Margins**.

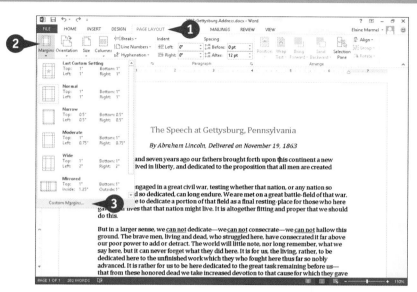

The Page Setup dialog box appears, displaying the Margins tab.

4 Type a specific margin in the **Top**, **Bottom**, **Left**, and **Right** boxes.

B You can also click a spin arrow ($\updownarrow$) to set a margin measurement.

5 Choose a page orientation.

C Preview the margin settings here.

6 Click $\vee$ and specify whether the margin should apply to the whole document or from this point forward.

7 Click **OK**.

Word immediately adjusts the margin in the document.

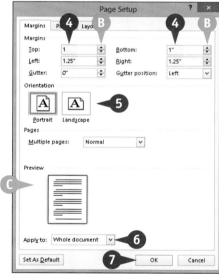

TIPS

How do I set new default margins?
To establish a different set of default margins for every new document that you create, make the desired changes to the Margins tab of the Page Setup dialog box, and click **Set As Default** before clicking **OK**.

Why is my printer ignoring my margin settings?
Some printers have a minimum margin setting and, in most cases, that minimum margin is .25 inches. If you set your margins smaller than your printer's minimum margin setting, you place text in an unprintable area. Be sure to test the margins, or check your printer documentation for more information.

Create Lists

You can draw attention to lists of information by using bullets or numbers. Bulleted and numbered lists can help you present your information in an organized way. A bulleted list adds dots or other similar symbols in front of each list item, whereas a numbered list adds sequential numbers or letters in front of each list item. As a general rule, use bullets when the items in your list do not follow any particular order and use numbers when the items in your list follow a particular order.

You can create a list as you type it or after you have typed list elements.

Create Lists

Create a List as You Type

1 Type **1.** to create a numbered list or * to create a bulleted list.

2 Press **Spacebar** or **Tab**.

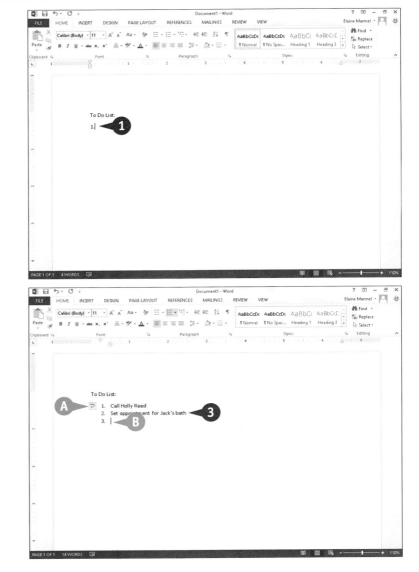

A Word automatically formats the entry as a list item and displays the AutoCorrect Options button (⚡) so that you can undo or stop automatic numbering.

3 Type a list item.

4 Press **Enter** to prepare to type another list item.

B Word automatically adds a bullet or number for the next item.

5 Repeat Steps **3** and **4** for each list item.

To stop entering items in the list, press **Enter** twice.

Create a List from Existing Text

1 Select the text to which you want to assign bullets or numbers.

2 Click the **Home** tab.

3 Click the **Numbering** button (⊟ ▾) or the **Bullets** button (⊟ ▾).

This example uses bullets.

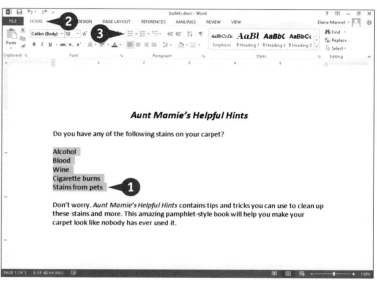

C Word applies numbers or bullets to the selection.

4 Click anywhere outside the selection to continue working.

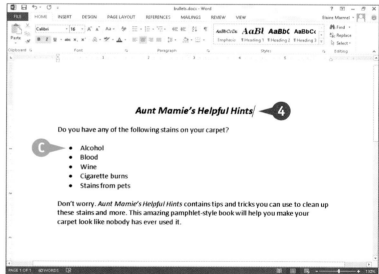

Can I create a bulleted or numbered list with more than one level, like the type of list you use when creating an outline?

Yes. Click the **Multilevel List** button (⋮▾). Click a format (**A**) from the menu that appears and then type your list. You can press **Enter** to enter a new list item at the same list level. Each time you press **Tab**, Word indents a level in the list. Each time you press **Shift** + **Tab**. Word outdents a level in the list.

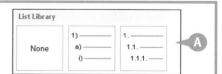

Copy Formatting

Suppose you have applied a variety of formatting options to a paragraph to create a certain look — for example, you changed the font, the size, the color, and the alignment. If you want to re-create the same look elsewhere in the document, you do not have to repeat the same steps as when you applied the original formatting, again changing the font, size, color, and alignment. Instead, you can use the Format Painter feature to "paint" the formatting to the other text in one swift action. With the Format Painter feature, copying formatting is as easy as clicking a button.

Copy Formatting

1 Select the text containing the formatting that you want to copy.

A If you drag to select, the Mini toolbar appears in the background, and you can use it by moving toward the Mini toolbar.

2 To use the Ribbon, click the **Home** tab.

3 Click the **Format Painter** button ( ).

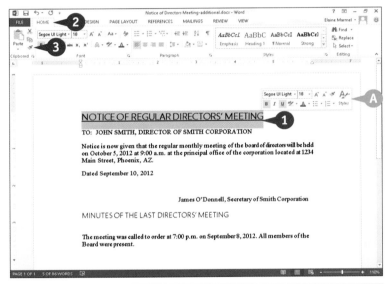

The mouse pointer changes to when you move the mouse over your document.

4 Click and drag over the text to which you want to apply the same formatting.

B Word copies the formatting from the original text to the new text.

To copy the same formatting multiple times, you can double-click .

You can press Esc to cancel the Format Painter feature at any time.

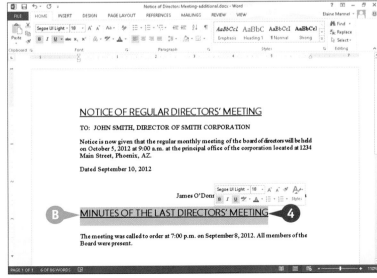

Clear Formatting

Sometimes, you may find that you have applied too much formatting to your text, making it difficult to read. Or perhaps you simply applied the wrong formatting to your text. In that case, instead of undoing all your formatting changes manually, you can use the Clear Formatting command to remove any formatting you have applied to the document text. When you apply the Clear Formatting command, which is located in the Home tab on the Ribbon, Word removes all formatting applied to the text, and restores the default settings.

Clear Formatting

1 Select the text from which you want to remove formatting.

Note: If you do not select text, Word removes text formatting from the entire document.

2 Click the **Clear Formatting** button ( ).

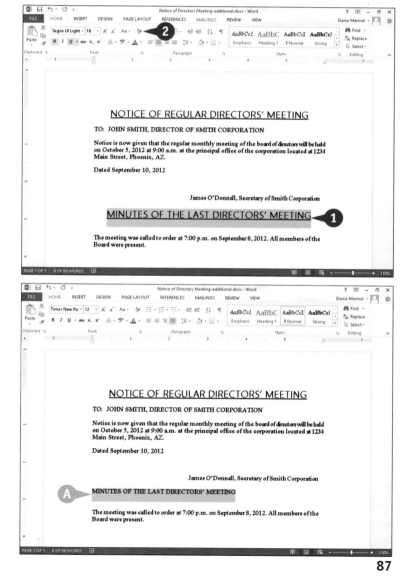

A Word removes all formatting from the selected text.

Format with Styles

Suppose you are writing a corporate report that requires specific formatting for every heading. Instead of assigning multiple formatting settings over and over again, you can create a style with the required formatting settings and apply it whenever you need it. A *style* is a set of text-formatting characteristics. These characteristics might include the text font, size, color, alignment, spacing, and more.

In addition to creating your own styles for use in your documents, you can apply any of the preset styles that Word supplies. These include styles for headings, normal text, quotes, and more.

Format with Styles

Create a New Quick Style

1. Format the text as desired and then select the text.

2. Click the **Home** tab on the Ribbon.

3. Click ⏷ in the Styles group.

4. Click **Create a Style**.

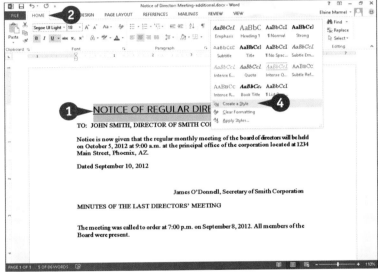

The Create New Style from Formatting dialog box appears.

5. Type a name for the style.

6. Click **OK**.

Word adds the style to the list of Quick Styles.

Apply a Quick Style

1 Select the text that you want to format.

2 Click the **Home** tab on the Ribbon.

3 Click a style from the Styles list.

Ⓐ You can click ⬛ to see the full palette of available styles.

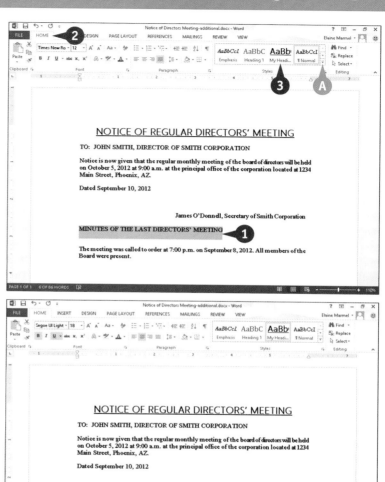

Ⓑ Word applies the style.

How do I remove a style that I no longer need?
From the Home tab, display the full Quick Styles palette, right-click the style that you want to remove, and click the **Remove from Style Gallery** command. Word immediately removes the style from the Quick Styles list.

How do I customize an existing style?
Apply the style to your text. Then, select the text, click the **Home** tab, click the **Change Styles** button, and click the type of change that you want to make. For example, to switch fonts, click the **Fonts** option and then select another font.

Apply a Template

A *template* is a special file that stores styles and other Word formatting tools. When you apply a template to a Word document, the styles and tools in that template become available for you to use with that document. Word comes with several templates preinstalled, and you can also create your own.

Of course, one way to apply a template to a document is to select it from the list of document types in the New screen that appears when you create a new Word document. Alternatively, you can attach a template to an existing document, as outlined here.

Apply a Template

1 With the document to which you want to apply a template open in Word, click the **File** tab.

2 Click **Options**.

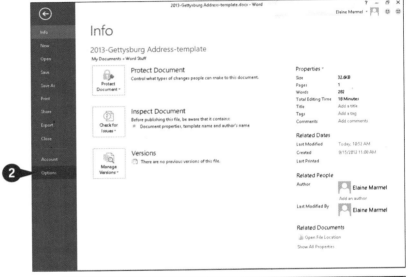

The Word Options window opens.

3 Click **Add-Ins**.

4 Click the **Manage** ⌄.

5 Click **Templates**.

6 Click **Go**.

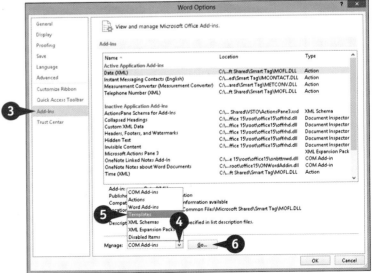

The Templates and Add-ins dialog box opens.

7 Select **Automatically update document styles** (☐ changes to ☑).

8 Click **Attach**.

The Attach Template dialog box opens.

9 Locate and select the template you want to apply.

10 Click **Open**.

11 Click **OK** in the Templates and Add-ins dialog box.

Word applies the template, and then updates the styles used in the document to reflect those appearing in the template.

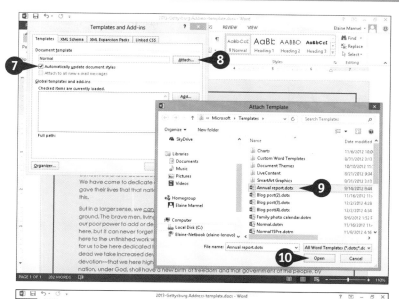

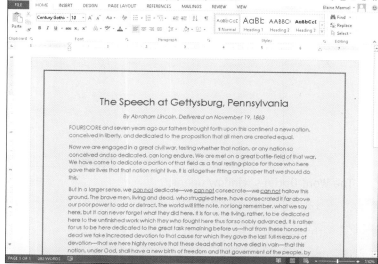

Can I create my own templates?

Yes. The easiest way to create a template is to base it on an existing Word document. Open the document on which you want to base your template, click the **File** tab, and click **Save As**. Select a place and click a folder, or click **Browse**. The Save As dialog box opens; locate and select the folder in which you want to save the template, type a name for it in the **File Name** field, click the **Save as Type** ☑, and choose **Word Template**. Click **Save** and Word saves the template in the folder you chose.

Insert an Online Video

Y ou can insert a video available on the Internet into a Word document. Once you have inserted the video, you can play it directly from the Word document.

You can insert videos you find using Bing Search or videos available on YouTube, or you can insert a video embed code — an HTML code that uses the `src` attribute to define the video file you want to embed. Most videos posted on the Internet are public domain, but, if you are unsure, do some research to determine whether you can use the video freely.

Insert an Online Video

1 Click where you want the video to appear.

2 Click the **Insert** tab.

3 Click **Online Video**.

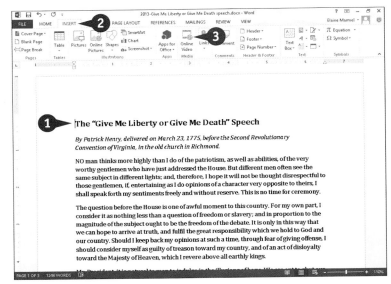

The Insert Video window appears.

4 In one of the search boxes, type a description of the video you want to insert.

Note: This example searches YouTube. Initially, YouTube appears as a button at the bottom of the Insert Video window. Click the **YouTube** button; Word redisplays the window with a search box as shown here.

5 Click the **Search** button (🔍).

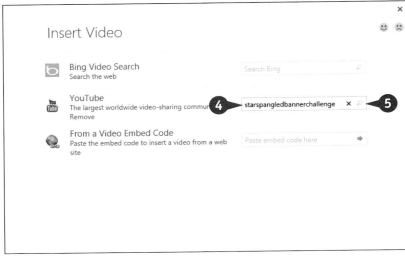

The results of your search appear.

A You can click here (∧ and ∨) to navigate through the search results.

B You can click here to return to the Insert Video window and search for a different video.

6 Click the video you want to add to your document.

7 Click **Insert**.

C The video appears in your document, selected and surrounded by handles (▱).

D Drag ↻ to rotate the video.

E ▣ controls text flow around the video as described in Chapter 3.

F Picture Tools appear on the Ribbon; you can use these tools to format the video.

TIP

How do I play an inserted video?
From Print Layout view or Read Mode view, click the video **Play** button (▶). The video appears in its own window. Click the **Play** button again to start the video. To stop the video and return to the document, click outside the video anywhere on the document.

Assign a Theme

A *theme* is a predesigned set of color schemes, fonts, and other visual attributes. Applying a theme to a document is a quick way to add polish to it. And, because themes are shared among the Office programs, you can use the same theme in your Word document that you have applied to worksheets in Excel or slides in PowerPoint.

Note that the effect of applying a theme is more obvious if you have assigned styles such as headings to your document. The effects of themes are even more pronounced when you assign a background color to a page.

Assign a Theme

Apply a Theme

1. Click the **Design** tab.

2. Click the **Themes** button.

Note: You can point the mouse at each theme to see its effect on your document.

3. Click a theme.

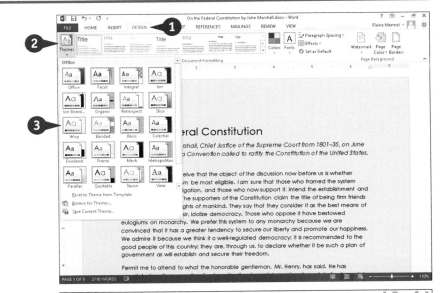

Ⓐ Word applies the theme to the current document.

Ⓑ You can use these tools to change the formatting of the theme's colors, fonts, paragraph spacing, and effects.

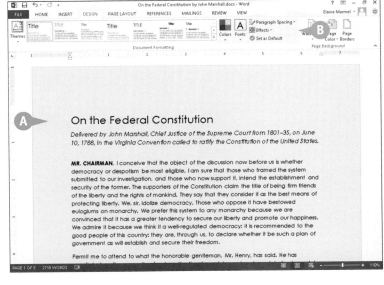

Create a Custom Theme

1 Apply a theme and edit the formatting to create the theme that you want to save.

2 Click the **Design** tab.

3 Click the **Themes** button.

4 Click **Save Current Theme**.

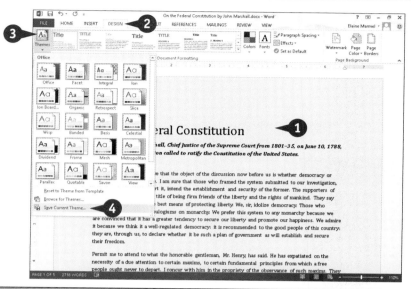

The Save Current Theme dialog box appears.

5 Type a unique name for the theme.

C By default, Word saves the theme to the Document Themes folder so that it is accessible in the Themes Gallery.

6 Click **Save**.

Word saves the theme and adds it to the list of available themes.

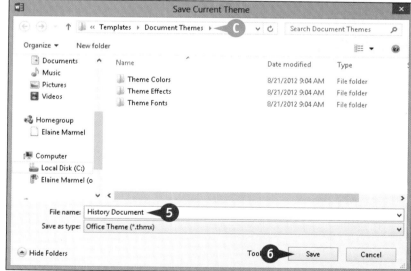

TIP

How can I make the effects of my theme more obvious?

As mentioned, the effects of your theme are more obvious if you have applied page styles such as headings and a background color to your document. To apply a background color, click the **Design** tab on the Ribbon, click the **Page Color** button in the Page Background group, and click a color in the palette; Word applies the color you selected to the background of the page. For help applying a heading style, see Chapter 6.

Add Borders

You can apply borders around your text to add emphasis or make the document aesthetically appealing. You can add borders around a single paragraph, multiple paragraphs, or each page in the document. (Be aware that you should not add too many effects, such as borders, to your document because it will become difficult to read.)

Word comes with several predesigned borders, which you can apply to your document. Alternatively, you can create your own custom borders — for example, making each border line a different color or thickness. Another option is to apply shading to your text to set it apart.

Add Borders

Add a Paragraph Border

① Select the text to which you want to add a border.

② Click the **Home** tab on the Ribbon.

③ Click the **Borders** button (⊞ ▾).

④ Click a border.

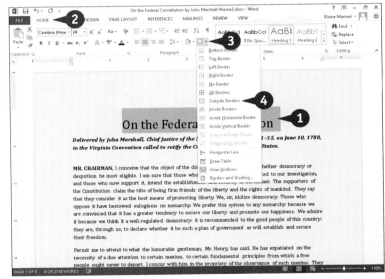

Ⓐ Word applies the border to the text.

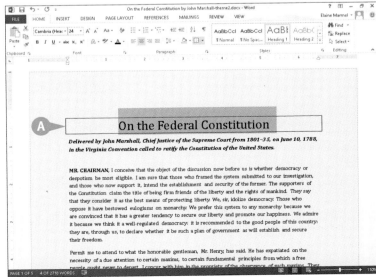

Add a Page Border

1 Click the **Design** tab.

2 Click the **Page Borders** button.

The Borders and Shading dialog box appears, and displays the Page Border tab.

3 Click the type of border that you want to add.

Ⓑ You can use these settings to select a different border line style, color, and width.

Ⓒ You can click 🔽 to specify whether to apply the border to each page of your entire document, a section, the first page of a section, or all pages of a section except the first.

Ⓓ The Preview area displays a sample of the selections.

4 Click **OK**.

Ⓔ Word applies the page border.

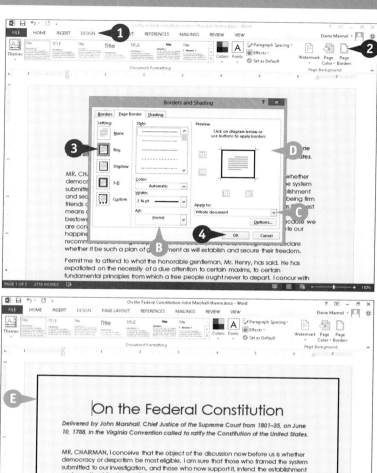

TIPS

How do I add shading to my text?
To add shading behind a block of text, select the text, click the **Home** tab on the Ribbon, click the **Shading** button (🎨 ▾) in the Paragraph group, and click a color to apply.

How do I create a custom border?
Select the text you want to add a border to, open the Borders and Shading dialog box, click the **Borders** tab, and click **Custom**. Choose the settings you want to apply to the first line of the border; then click in the **Preview** area where you want the line to appear. Repeat for each line you want to add, and then click **OK**.

Create Columns

You can create columns in Word to present your text in a format similar to a newspaper or magazine. For example, if you are creating a brochure or newsletter, you can use columns to make text flow from one block to the next.

If you simply want to create a document with two or three columns, you can use one of Word's preset columns. Alternatively, you can create custom columns, choosing the number of columns you want to create in your document, indicating the width of each column, specifying whether a line should appear between them, and more.

Create Columns

Create Quick Columns

1 Select the text that you want to place into columns.

Note: If you want to apply columns to all text in your document, skip Step **1**.

2 Click the **Page Layout** tab.

3 Click the **Columns** button.

4 Click the number of columns that you want to assign.

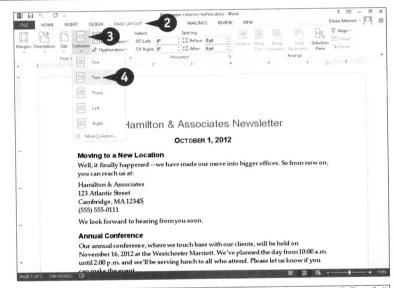

A Word displays the selected text, or your document if you skipped Step **1**, in the number of columns that you specify.

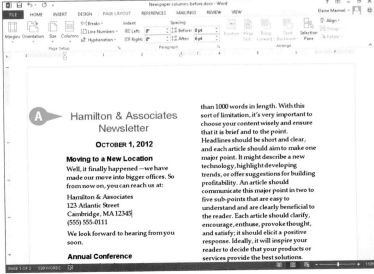

Create Custom Columns

1 Select the text that you want to place into columns.

Note: If you want to apply columns to all text in your document, skip Step **1**.

2 Click the **Page Layout** tab.

3 Click the **Columns** button.

4 Click **More Columns**.

The Columns dialog box appears.

5 Click a preset for the type of column style that you want to apply.

Ⓑ You can include a vertical line separating the columns (☐ changes to ☑).

6 Deselect this option to set exact widths for each column (☑ changes to ☐).

7 Set an exact column width and spacing here.

Ⓒ You can specify whether the columns apply to the selected text or the entire document.

8 Click **OK**.

Ⓓ Word applies the column format to the selected text, or to your document if you skipped Step **1**.

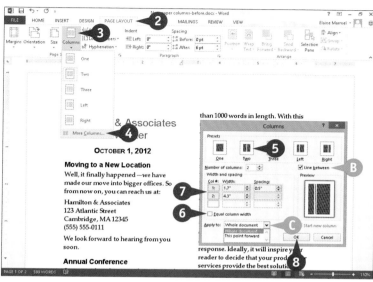

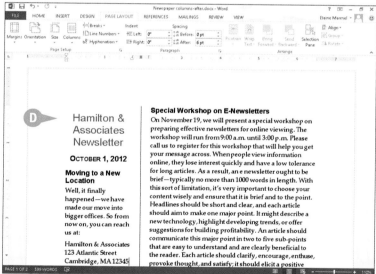

How do I wrap column text around a picture or other object?

Click the picture or other object that you want to wrap, click the **Format** tab, click the **Wrap Text** button, and then click the type of wrapping that you want to apply.

Can I create a break within a column?

Yes. To add a column break, click where you want the break to occur and then press `Ctrl`+`Shift`+`Enter`. To remove a break, select it and press `Delete`. To return to a one-column format, click the **Columns** button on the Page Layout tab, and then select the single-column format.

Insert a Table

You can use tables to present data in an organized fashion. For example, you might add a table to your document to display a list of items or a roster of classes. Tables contain columns and rows, which intersect to form cells. You can insert all types of data in cells, including text and graphics.

To enter text in a cell, click in the cell and then type your data. As you type, Word wraps the text to fit in the cell. Press **Tab** to move from one cell to another. You can select table cells, rows, and columns to perform editing tasks and apply formatting.

Insert a Table

Insert a Table

1 Click in the document where you want to insert a table.

2 Click the **Insert** tab.

3 Click the **Table** button.

Ⓐ Word displays a table grid.

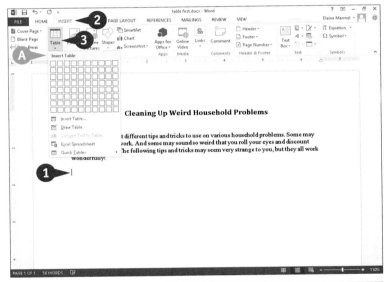

4 Slide the mouse pointer across the squares that represent the number of rows and columns you want in your table.

Ⓑ Word previews the table as you drag over cells.

5 Click the square representing the lower-right corner of your table.

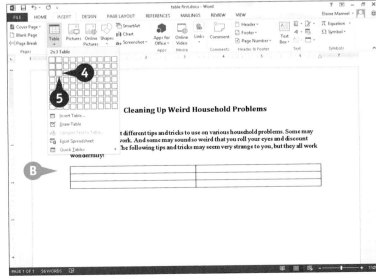

The table appears in your document.

C Table Tools appear on the Ribbon.

6 Click in a table cell and type information.

D If necessary, Word expands the row size to accommodate the text.

You can press **Tab** to move the insertion point to the next cell.

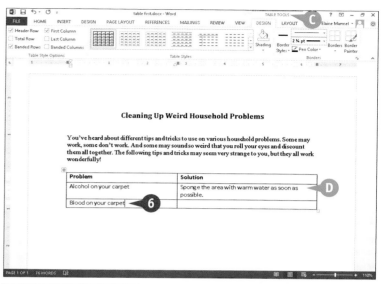

Delete a Table

1 Click anywhere in the table you want to delete.

2 Click the **Layout** tab.

3 Click **Delete**.

4 Click **Delete Table**.

Word removes the table and its contents from your document.

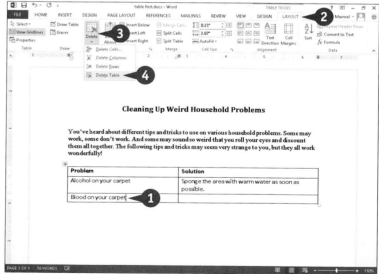

TIPS

Can I add rows to a table?

Yes. To add a row to the bottom of the table, place the insertion point in the last cell and press **Tab**. To add a row anywhere else, use the buttons in the Rows & Columns section of the Layout tab.

What, exactly, is a table cell?

A *cell* refers to the intersection of a row and column in a table. In spreadsheet programs, columns are named with letters, rows with numbers, and cells are named using the column letter and row number. For example, the cell at the intersection of column A and row 2 is called A2.

Apply Table Styles

When you click in a table you have added to your document, two new tabs appear on the Ribbon: Design and Layout. You can use the table styles found in the Design tab to add instant formatting to your Word tables. Word offers numerous predefined table styles, each with its own unique set of formatting characteristics, including shading, color, borders, and fonts.

The Design tab also includes settings for creating custom borders and applying custom shading. You can also use check boxes in the Table Style Options group to add a header row, emphasize the table's first column, and more.

Apply Table Styles

1 Click anywhere in the table that you want to format.

2 Click the **Table Tools Design** tab on the Ribbon.

3 Click a style from the Table Styles list.

Note: You can click ☑ in the lower-right corner of the Table Styles Gallery to display the entire palette of available styles.

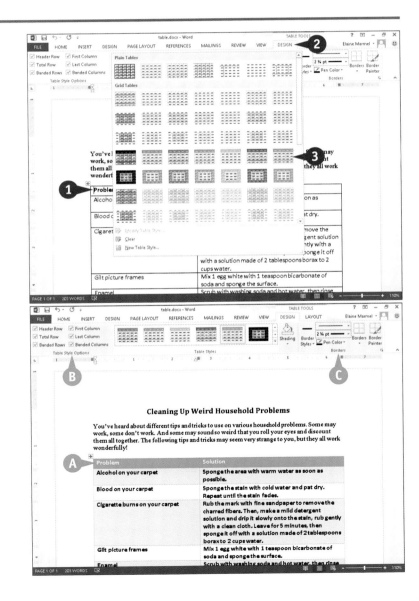

Ⓐ Word applies the style.

Ⓑ You can toggle table parts on or off using the Table Style Options check boxes.

Ⓒ You can click these options to change the shading and borders.

Insert an Excel Spreadsheet

I f Excel is installed on your computer, you can insert a new Excel spreadsheet into your Word document. You can then insert data such as text or graphics in the cells in the spreadsheet. To add text, click in a cell and begin typing; press **Tab** to move from one cell to another.

When you click in an Excel spreadsheet that you have inserted in your Word document, the Ribbon in Word changes to display various Excel tools and features. You can use these tools and features to work with any data you add to the spreadsheet.

Insert an Excel Spreadsheet

1 Click in the document where you want to insert a table.

2 Click the **Insert** tab on the Ribbon.

3 Click the **Table** button.

4 Click **Excel Spreadsheet**.

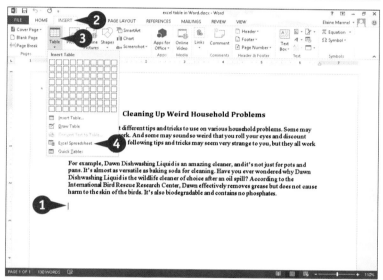

A An Excel spreadsheet appears, along with tools associated with Excel.

Note: Do not worry if the table seems misaligned; when you click outside the table, it will align properly.

5 Click in a cell and type the data that you want to add.

B The Home tab displays tools for formatting your cells and data.

C The Formulas tab offers tools for building Excel formulas.

You can click anywhere outside of the table to return to the Word tools and features.

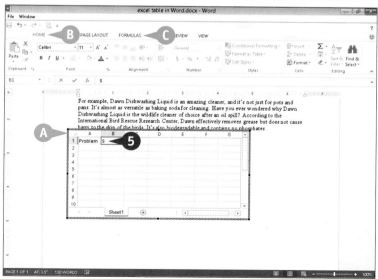

Add Headers and Footers

If you want to include text at the top or bottom of every page, such as the title of your document, your name, or the date, you can use headers and footers. Header text appears at the top of the page above the margin; footer text appears at the bottom of the page below the margin.

To view header or footer text, you must display the document in Print Layout view. To switch to this view, click the View tab and click the Print Layout button. Then double-click the top or bottom of the page, respectively, to view the header or footer.

Add Headers and Footers

1 Click the **Insert** tab.

2 Click the **Header** button to add a header, or click the **Footer** button to add a footer.

This example adds a footer.

A The header or footer gallery appears.

3 Click a header or footer style.

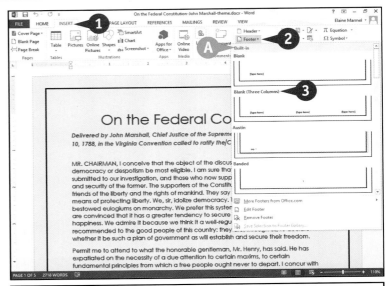

Word adds the header or footer and displays the Header & Footer Tools tab.

B The text in your document appears dimmed.

C The insertion point appears in the Footer area.

D Header & Footer Tools appear on the Ribbon.

E Some footers contain information prompts.

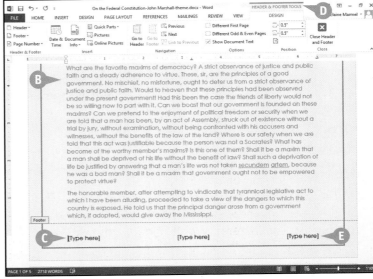

4 Click or select an information prompt.

5 Type footer information.

6 Click **Close Header and Footer**.

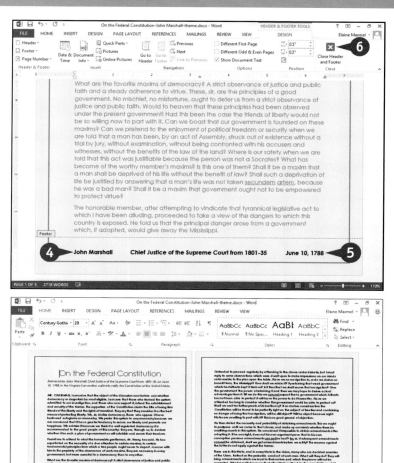

F Word closes the Header & Footer Tools tab and displays the header or footer on the document page.

G You can zoom out to view the header or footer on multiple pages of your document.

Note: To edit a header or footer, click the **Insert** tab on the Ribbon, click the **Header** or **Footer** button, and click **Edit Header** or **Edit Footer** to redisplay the Header & Footer Tools tab.

TIPS

Can I omit the header or footer from the first page?
Yes. Click the **Insert** tab, click the **Header** or **Footer** button, and click **Edit Header** or **Edit Footer**. Next, select the **Different First Page** check box in the Options group. If you want to remove the header or footer for odd or even pages, click to select the **Different Odd & Even Pages** check box.

How do I remove a header or footer?
Click the **Insert** tab, click the **Header** or **Footer** button, and click **Remove Header** or **Remove Footer**. Word removes the header or footer from your document.

Insert Footnotes and Endnotes

You can include footnotes or endnotes in your document to identify sources or references to other materials or to add explanatory information. When you add a footnote or endnote, a small numeral or other character appears alongside the associated text, with the actual footnote or endnote appearing at the bottom of a page or the end of the document, respectively.

When you insert footnotes or endnotes in a document, Word automatically numbers them for you. As you add, delete, and move text in your document, any associated footnotes or endnotes are likewise added, deleted, or moved, as well as renumbered.

Insert Footnotes and Endnotes

Insert a Footnote

1 Click where you want to insert the footnote reference.

2 Click the **References** tab.

3 Click **Insert Footnote**.

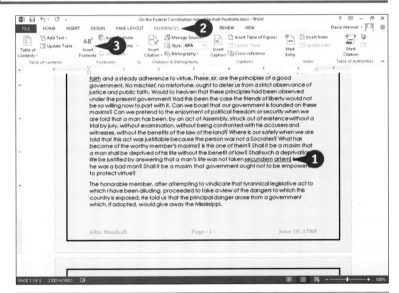

A Word displays the footnote number in the body of the document and in the note at the bottom of the current page.

4 Type the footnote text.

You can double-click the footnote number or press **Shift** + **F5** to return the insertion point to the place in your document where you inserted the footnote.

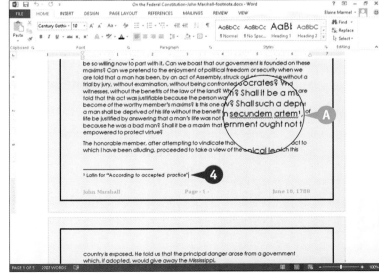

Insert an Endnote

1 Click where you want to insert the endnote reference.

B In this example, the endnote number appears on Page 1.

2 Click the **References** tab.

3 Click **Insert Endnote**.

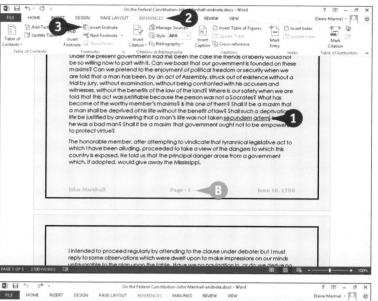

Word inserts the endnote number in the body of your document.

C Word inserts the endnote number at the end of your document and displays the insertion point in the endnote area at the bottom of the last page of the document.

4 Type your endnote text.

You can double-click the endnote number or press Shift + F5 to return the insertion point to the place in your document where you inserted the endnote.

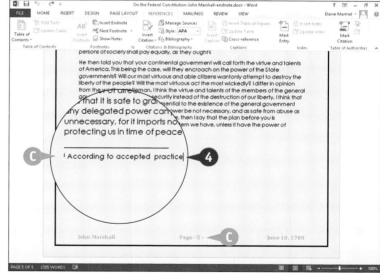

TIP

How can I change the starting number for footnotes or endnotes in my document?

If you need to change the starting footnote or endnote number in your document — for example, if you are working on a new chapter, but you want the numbering to continue from the previous one — click the **References** tab and click the dialog box launcher (⬚) in the Footnotes group. The Footnote and Endnote dialog box appears; click in the **Start at** text box and type a number or use the spin arrow (⬍) to set a new number. Click **Apply** to apply the changes to the document.

Insert Page Numbers and Page Breaks

You can add page numbers to make your documents more manageable. For example, adding page numbers to longer documents can help you keep the pages in order after printing. You can add page numbers to the top or bottom of a page or in the page margins or at the current location of the insertion point.

Adding page breaks can help you control where text appears. For example, add a page break at the end of one chapter to ensure that the next chapter starts on its own page. You can insert page breaks using the Ribbon or your keyboard.

Insert Page Numbers and Page Breaks

Insert Page Numbers

1 Click the **Insert** tab.

2 Click **Page Number**.

Page number placement options appear.

3 Click a placement option.

A gallery of page number alignment and formatting options appears.

4 Click an option.

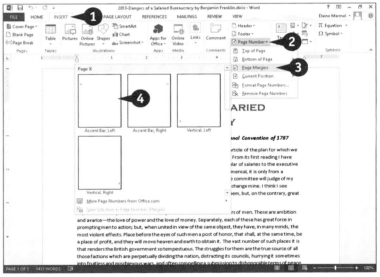

Ⓐ Word inserts the page number as part of the header or footer.

Ⓑ Header & Footer Tools appear on the Ribbon.

5 Click **Close Header and Footer** to exit the header or footer area.

Note: See the section "Add Headers and Footers" to learn more.

Insert Page Breaks

1 Click in the document where you want to insert a page break.

2 Click the **Insert** tab.

3 Click **Page Break**.

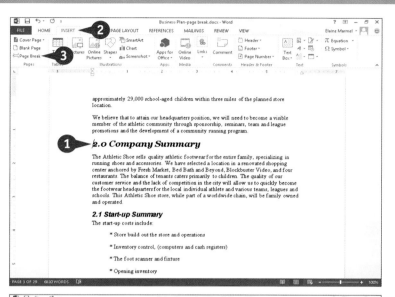

C Word inserts a page break and moves all text after the page break onto a new page.

TIPS

Is there a faster way to insert a page break?

Yes. You can use keyboard shortcuts to quickly insert a page break as you type in your document. You can insert a page break by pressing **Ctrl**+**Enter**. You can also insert a line break by pressing **Shift**+**Enter**.

Can I change the page number style?

Yes. Click the **Page Number** button on the Insert tab, and then click **Format Page Numbers**. The Page Number Format dialog box appears. You can change the number style to Roman numerals, alphabetical, and more. You can also include chapter numbers with your page numbers.

Mark Index Entries

If your document requires an index, you can use Word to build one. Indexes can contain main entries and subentries as well as cross-references (entries that refer to other entries).

Before you can build an index, you must mark any words or phrases in your document that should appear in the index. When you do, Word adds a special index field, called an XE field, to the document; this field includes the marked word or phrase, as well as any cross-reference information you might have added. After you mark index entries, you can generate the index (discussed in the next section).

Mark Index Entries

Mark a Word or Phrase

1 Select the text for which you want to create an index entry.

2 Click the **References** tab.

3 Click the **Mark Entry** button.

The Mark Index Entry dialog box appears.

A The text you selected appears in the Main Entry field.

Note: To create an entry for a person's name, type the name in the **Main Entry** field in this format: Last Name, First Name.

B Select **Current Page** (○ changes to ◉).

C If you want the index to include an entry for the word or phrase on this page only, click **Mark**.

D To mark all occurrences of the word or phrase in the document, click **Mark All**.

E Word adds an index entry field to your document.

Note: To view the field, click the Home tab's **Show/Hide** button (¶).

4 Click **Close**.

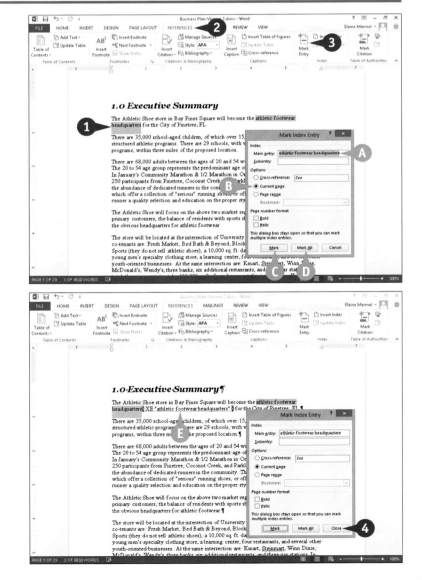

Mark a Word or Phrase that Spans a Range of Pages

1 Select the range of text to which the index entry should refer.

2 Click the **Insert** tab.

3 Click **Links**.

4 Click **Bookmark**.

5 In the Bookmark dialog box, type a bookmark name. Do not include spaces.

6 Click **Add**.

Note: The Cancel button becomes the Close button.

7 Click **Close**.

8 Click at the end of the text you selected.

9 Click the **References** tab.

10 Click **Mark Entry**.

11 In the Mark Index Entry dialog box, type the word or phrase that should appear in the index for this entry.

12 Select **Page range** (○ changes to ◉).

13 Click the **Bookmark** ⌄ and choose the bookmark you just created.

14 Click **Mark**.

G Word adds an XE field to your document.

15 Click **Close**.

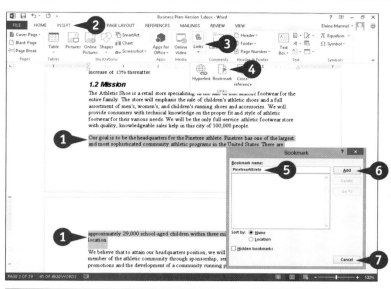

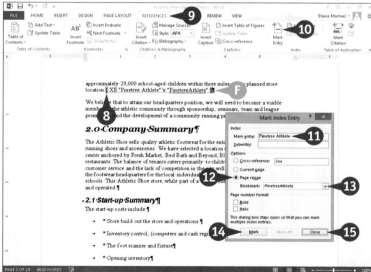

TIPS

Can I add a subentry?
Yes. Select the text and, in the Mark Index Entry dialog box, type the entry under which the text should appear in the **Main entry** field. Then type subentry text in the **Subentry** field. If the text should appear as a subentry *and* a main entry, add two XE fields — one for each entry.

Can I add index entry cross-references?
Yes. Click **Cross-reference** in the Mark Index Entry dialog box and type the index word or phrase to which the entry should refer.

Generate an Index

After you mark the words and phrases in your Word document that you want to appear as index entries, including main entries, subentries, and cross-references, you can generate the index. When you generate an index, Word searches for marked words and phrases, sorts them alphabetically, adds page-number references, and removes duplicate entries that cite the same page number.

If you do not care for the default appearance of the index, you can customize it to suit your taste. Also, if you make a change to your document after generating the index, you can update the index to reflect the change.

Generate an Index

Generate an Index

1 Click the spot in your document where you want to insert the index.

2 Click the **References** tab.

3 Click the **Insert Index** button.

The Index dialog box appears.

4 Click the **Formats** ☑ and select an index design.

A Preview the selected index design here.

5 Select **Indented** (○ changes to ◉).

6 Click the **Columns** ↕ to change the number of columns per page in the index.

7 Click **OK**.

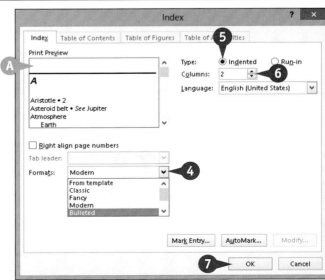

B Word generates the index and inserts it in your document where you placed the insertion point in Step **1**.

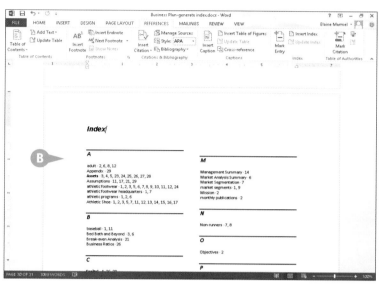

Update the Index

1 After making changes to your document, click anywhere in the index.

The index entries appear highlighted in gray, indicating that they are fields.

2 Click the **References** tab.

3 Click the **Update Index** button.

Word updates the index to reflect changes to the document that have occurred since the original index was generated.

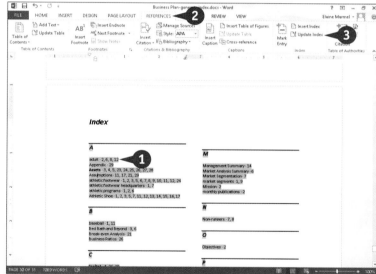

TIPS

Can I customize the layout of my index?
Yes. Open the Index dialog box, click the **Formats** ⌄, choose **From Template**, and click **Modify**. The Style dialog box opens; click the index style you want to change, and again click **Modify**. Finally, select the desired options in the Formatting section.

How do I edit index entries?
Click the **Home** tab, click the **Replace** button, type the contents of the XE field that you need to replace in the **Find What** field (for example, **XE "John Adams"**), type the replacement text in the **Replace With** field (for example, **XE "Adams, John"**), and click **Replace All**.

Generate a Table of Contents

You can use Word to generate a table of contents (TOC) for your document that automatically updates as you change your document. Word generates a TOC by searching for text that you format using one of Word's predefined heading styles — Heading 1, Heading 2, and Heading 3. It then copies this text and pastes it into the TOC. You can select from Word's gallery of TOC styles to establish the TOC's look and feel.

You can create a TOC at any time, continue working, and update the TOC automatically with new information whenever you want.

Generate a Table of Contents

Style Text as Headings

1 Click anywhere in the line that you want to style as a heading.

2 Click the **Home** tab.

3 In the Styles group, click the style you want to apply.

A If you do not see the style you want to apply, click ⊡ and choose the desired style from the Quick Style Gallery.

B If the style you want to apply does not appear in the Quick Style Gallery, click ▭ and choose the desired style from the Styles pane, as shown here.

C Word applies the style you chose to the selected text.

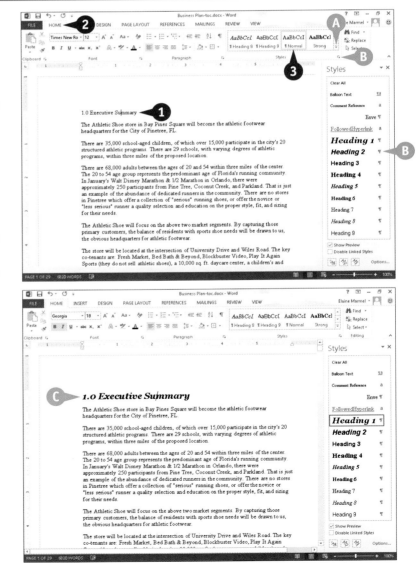

Generate a Table of Contents

1 Click the location in your document where you want to insert a TOC.

2 Click the **References** tab.

3 Click **Table of Contents**.

4 From the gallery that appears, click the TOC style you want to use.

D Word generates a TOC.

Note: To delete a TOC, click the **Table of Contents** button and choose **Remove Table of Contents**.

Note: If you edit your document, you can update your TOC to reflect the changes by clicking the **Update Table** button in the References tab's Table of Contents group; then specify whether to update page numbers only or the entire table, including heading names and levels.

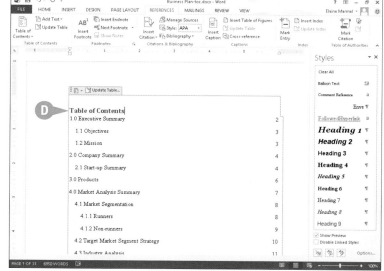

TIP

Can I include additional heading styles, such as Heading 4, in the table of contents?

Yes. Complete Steps **2** to **4** in the subsection "Generate a Table of Contents," selecting **Custom Table of Contents** in Step **4** to display the Table of Contents dialog box. Click the **Show levels** (**A**) to change the number of heading styles included in the TOC. Click **OK**. Word prompts you to replace the current TOC. Click **Yes** to update the TOC.

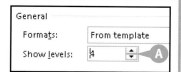

Create a Bibliography

You can use Word to generate a bibliography for your document, formatting the entries using the style of your choice: APA, The Chicago Manual of Style, GB7714, GOST – Name Sort, GOST – Title Sort, Harvard – Anglia, IEEE, ISO 690 – First Element and Date, ISO 690 – Numerical Reference, and so on.

For Word to determine what entries should appear in the bibliography, you must cite sources in your document as you work. Word then collects the information from these citations to generate the bibliography. (Note that when you add a source to a document, Word saves it for use in subsequent documents.)

Create a Bibliography

Add a Citation

1 Click at the end of the sentence or phrase that contains information you want to cite.

2 Click the **References** tab.

3 Click **Insert Citation**.

4 Click **Add New Source**.

The Create Source dialog box opens.

5 Click the **Type of Source** ⌄ and select the type of source you want to cite (here, **Journal Article**).

The fields in the Create Source dialog box change depending on the source you select.

6 Type the requested information.

7 Click **OK**.

A Word adds a citation to your document, and adds the source to the Insert Citation menu.

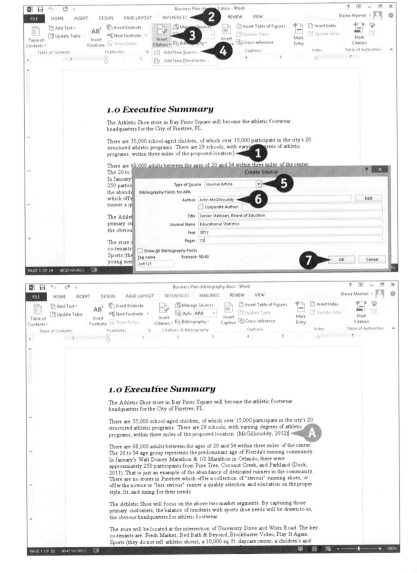

Generate the Bibliography

1 Click the location where the bibliography should appear (typically at the end of the document).

2 Click the **References** tab.

3 Click the **Bibliography** button.

4 Choose one of the predesigned bibliography gallery options.

B Word inserts the bibliography.

If you slide the mouse pointer over the bibliography, light gray shading appears, indicating a Word field.

Note: To specify which style guide you want to use, click the **References** tab, click the **Style** ▼ in the Citations & Bibliography group, and choose a style guide from the list that appears.

TIP

What can I do if I do not have all the information I need about a citation?

If you want to add a citation to your document but you are missing some of the required information, you can create a placeholder. To do so, click the **References** tab, click **Insert Citation**, and choose **Add New Placeholder**. The Placeholder Name dialog box opens; type a name for the placeholder. Later, add citation information by clicking the **Manage Sources** button in the **References** tab to open the Manage Sources dialog box, clicking the placeholder under Current List, clicking **Edit**, and typing the necessary information.

Work in Read Mode View

Read Mode view optimizes your document for easier reading and helps minimize eye strain when you read the document on-screen. This view removes most toolbars, and supports mouse, keyboard, and tablet motions. To move from page to page in a document using your mouse, you can click the arrows on the left and right sides of the pages or use the scroll wheel. To navigate using the keyboard, you can press the Page Up, Page Down, space bar, and Backspace keys on the keyboard, or press any arrow key. If you use a tablet or other touch pad device, swipe left or right with your finger.

Work in Read Mode View

Look Up Information Using Define

1 Click 📖 to display the document in Read Mode view.

2 Select the word you want to look up and right-click.

3 From the menu that appears, click **Define**.

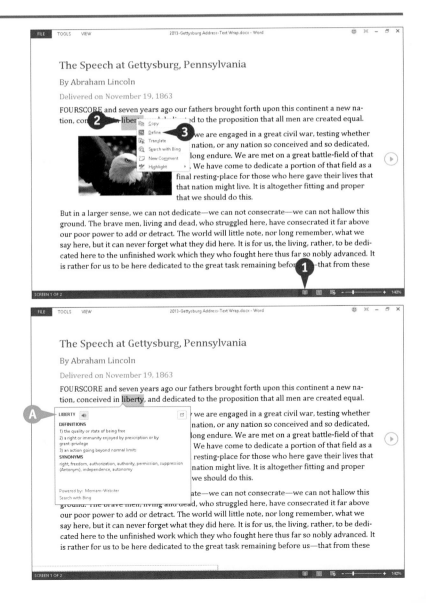

Note: If you have not yet installed a dictionary, a pane appears, giving you dictionary choices. See Chapter 4 for details on downloading and installing a dictionary.

Ⓐ Word displays a balloon containing definition information.

To close the balloon, click anywhere outside of it.

Search for Information Using Bing

1 Click 📖 to display the document in Read Mode view.

2 Select the word or phrase you want to look up and right-click.

3 From the menu that appears, click **Search with Bing**.

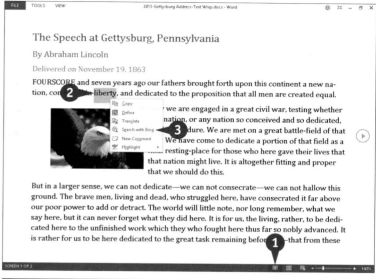

Your browser opens, displaying search results for the word you selected in Step **2**.

4 Close the browser window by clicking ✕ in the upper-right corner to redisplay your document in Word.

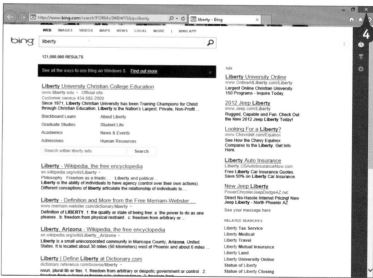

Can I change the color of the page?
Yes. Follow these steps:

1 Click **View**.

2 Click **Page Color**.

3 Choose a page color.

This example uses Sepia.

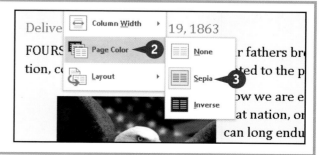

Work in Read Mode View (continued)

Read Mode view offers more than just minimized eye strain; while you work in Read Mode view, you can look up words in the dictionary, search the Internet for a word or phrase, highlight important text, and insert comments in documents you are reviewing. If you are viewing a long document in Read Mode view, you can also use the Navigation pane to move around the document. You can open the Navigation pane from the Tools menu in Read Mode view; for details on using the Navigation pane, see the section "Scan Document Content" later in this chapter.

Work in Read Mode View (continued)

Highlight Important Text

1 Click 📖 to display the document in Read Mode view.

2 Select the words you want to highlight and right-click.

3 From the menu that appears, click **Highlight**.

4 Click a highlight color.

Ⓐ Word highlights the selected text in the color you chose.

You can click anywhere outside the highlight to see its full effect and continue working.

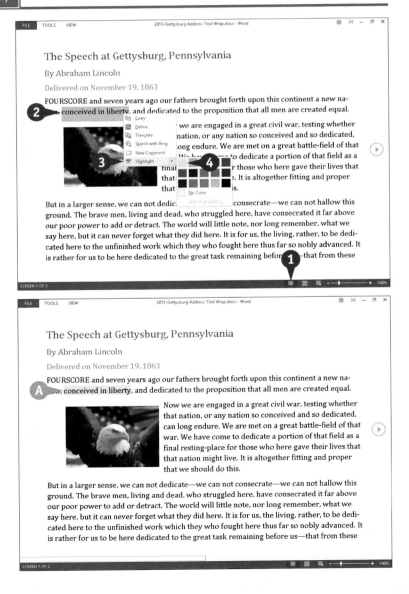

120

Insert a Comment

1 Click 📖 to display the document in Read Mode view.

2 Select the words about which you want to comment, and right-click.

3 From the menu that appears, click **New Comment**.

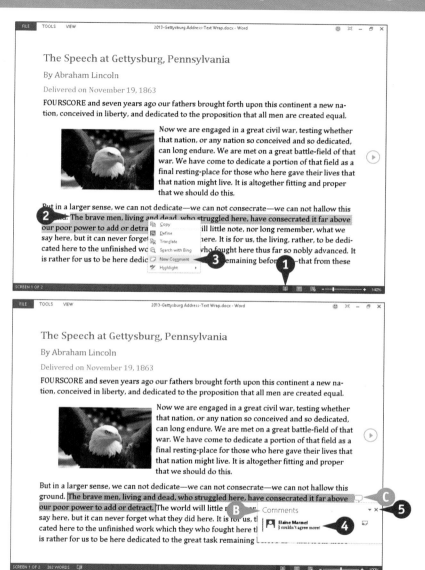

B Word changes the color used to select the text and displays a comment block containing the insertion point.

4 Type your comment.

5 Click × to close the comment block.

C This symbol represents your comment; click it at any time to view the comment.

What are some of the different views available in Read Mode?

To display all comments in the document, click **View** and then click **Show Comments**. To view your document as if it were printed on paper, click **View** and then click **Layout**. From the menu that appears, click **Paper Layout**.

Can I change the column width?

Yes. Click **View** and then click **Column Width**. From the menu that appears, choose **Narrow** or **Wide**; click **Default** to return to the original column view. Note that on a standard monitor, Default and Wide look the same; Wide takes effect on wide-screen monitors.

Find and Replace Text

Suppose you want to edit a paragraph in your document that contains a specific word or phrase. You can use Word's Find tool to search for the word or phrase instead of scrolling through your document to locate that paragraph.

In addition, you can use the Replace tool to replace instances of a word or phrase with other text. For example, suppose you complete a long report, only to discover that you have misspelled the name of a product you are reviewing; you can use the Replace tool to locate and correct the misspellings.

Find and Replace Text

Find Text

1. Click at the beginning of your document.

2. Click the **Home** tab.

3. Click **Find**.

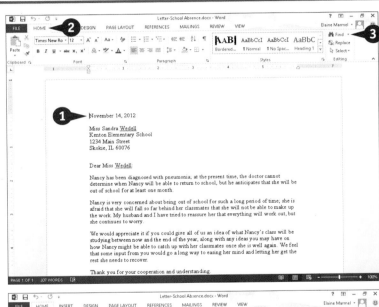

A. The Navigation pane appears.

4. Type the text that you want to find.

B. Word searches the document and highlights occurrences of the text.

C. Word also lists occurrences of the text in the Navigation pane.

5. Click an entry in the Navigation pane.

D. Word selects the corresponding text in the document.

6. When finished, click the Navigation pane's ✕.

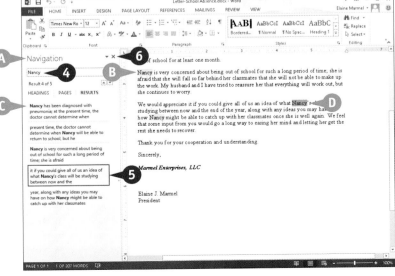

Replace Text

1 Click at the beginning of your document.

2 Click the **Home** tab.

3 Click **Replace**.

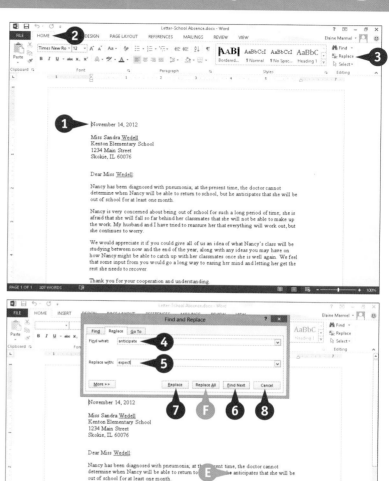

The Find and Replace dialog box opens with the Replace tab shown.

4 In the **Find what** box, type the text that you want to find.

5 Type the replacement text in the **Replace with** box.

6 Click **Find Next**.

E Word locates the first occurrence.

7 Click **Replace** to replace the occurrence.

F To replace every occurrence in the document, you can click **Replace All**.

Note: When Word finds no more occurrences, a message appears; click **OK**, and the Cancel button in the Find and Replace window changes to Close.

8 Click **Close**.

TIPS

Where can I find detailed search options?
Click **More** in the Find and Replace dialog box to reveal additional search options. For example, you can search for matching text case, whole words, and more. You can also search for specific formatting or special characters by clicking **Format** and **Special**.

How can I search for and delete text?
Start by typing the text you want to delete in the **Find what** box; then leave the **Replace with** box empty. When you search and click **Replace**, Word looks for the text and replaces it with nothing, effectively deleting the text for which you searched.

Scan Document Content

If you are working with a very long document, using the scroll bar on the right side of the screen or the Page Up and Page Down keys on your keyboard to locate a particular page in that document can be time-consuming. To rectify this, you can use the Navigation pane to navigate through a document. This pane can display all the headings in your document or a thumbnail image of each page in your document. You can then click a heading or a thumbnail image in the Navigation pane to view the corresponding page.

Scan Document Content

Navigate Using Headings

Note: To navigate using headings, your document must contain text styled with heading styles. See Chapter 6 for details on styles.

1 Click the **View** tab.

2 Select **Navigation Pane** (☐ changes to ☑).

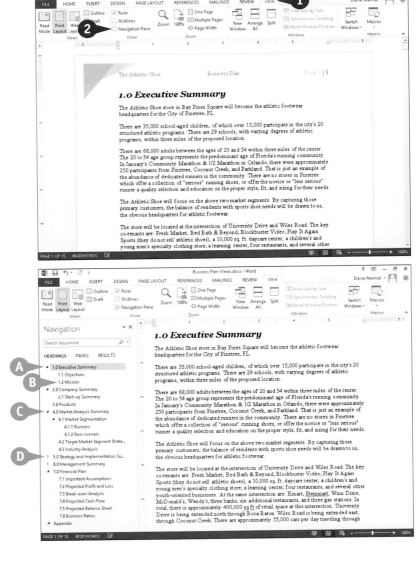

The Navigation pane appears.

A Heading1 styles appear at the left edge of the Navigation pane.

B Word indents Heading2 styles slightly and each subsequent heading style a bit more.

C This icon (◢) represents a heading displaying subheadings; you can click it to hide subheadings.

D This icon (▷) represents a heading that is hiding subheadings; you can click it to display the subheadings.

3 Click any heading in the Navigation pane to select it.

E Word moves the insertion point to this heading in your document.

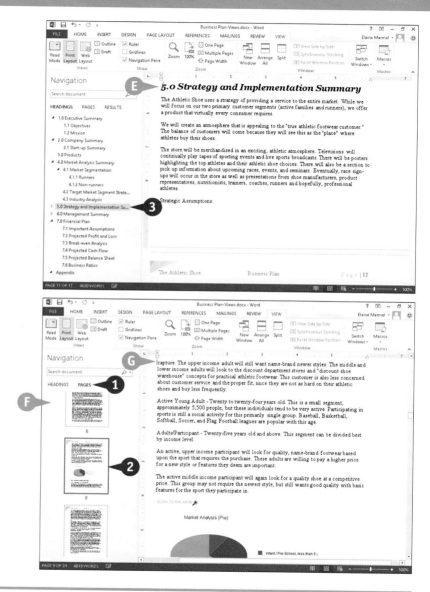

Navigate by Page

1 Click **Pages**.

F Word displays each page in your document as a thumbnail.

2 Click a thumbnail.

G Word selects that page in the Navigation pane and moves the insertion point to the top of that page. In the Navigation pane, Word surrounds the current page with a heavy blue border.

TIPS

What can I do with the Search Document box?
You can use the Search Document box to find text in your document; see the "Find Text" subsection of the section "Find and Replace Text" for details on using this box and on other ways you can search for information in your document.

Can I control the headings that appear?
Yes. While viewing headings, right-click any heading in the Navigation pane. From the menu that appears, point at **Show Heading Levels** and, from the submenu that appears, click the heading level you want to display (for example, **Show Heading 1**, **Show Heading 2**, and so on up to **Show Heading 9**).

Check Spelling and Grammar

Word automatically checks for spelling and grammar errors. Misspellings appear underlined with a red wavy line, and grammar errors are underlined with a blue wavy line. If you prefer, you can turn off Word's automatic Spelling and Grammar Check features.

Alternatively, you can review your entire document for spelling and grammatical errors all at one time. To use Word's Spelling and Grammar checking feature, you must install a dictionary; see Chapter 4 for details on downloading and installing apps for Word.

Check Spelling and Grammar

Correct a Mistake

1 When you encounter a spelling or grammar problem, right-click the underlined text.

A A menu appears, showing possible corrections. Click one, if applicable.

B To ignore the error, click **Ignore All**.

C To make Word stop flagging a word as misspelled, click **Add to Dictionary**.

Run the Spell Checker

1 Click at the beginning of your document.

Note: To check only a section of your document, select the section first.

2 Click the **Review** tab.

3 Click **Spelling & Grammar**.

D Word selects the first mistake and displays either the Spelling or the Grammar pane.

E The spelling or grammar mistake appears here.

F Suggestions to correct the error appear here.

G Definitions of the error and the highlighted suggestion appear here.

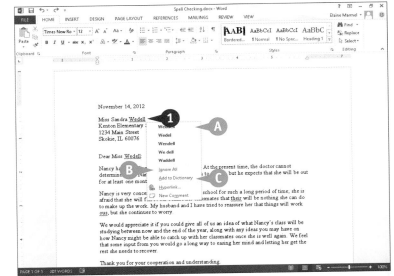

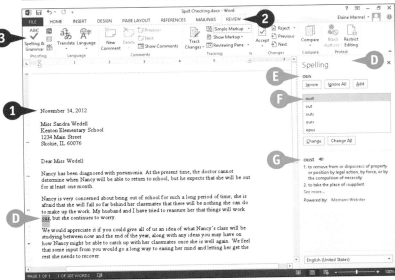

4 Click the suggestion you want to use.

5 Click **Change**.

H To correct all misspellings of the same word, you can click **Change All**.

I You can click **Ignore** or **Ignore All** to leave the selected word or phrase unchanged.

6 Repeat Steps **4** and **5** for each spelling or grammar mistake.

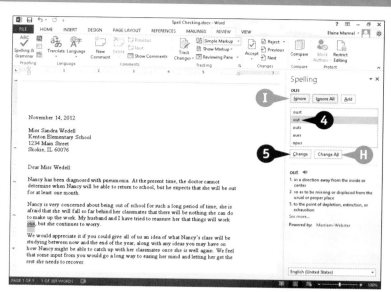

Word displays a dialog box when it finishes checking for spelling and grammar mistakes.

7 Click **OK**.

TIP

How do I turn the automatic spelling and grammar checking off?

To turn off the automatic checking features, follow these steps:

1 Click the **File** tab and then click **Options**.

2 In the Word Options dialog box, click **Proofing**.

3 In the When Correcting Spelling and Grammar in Word section, deselect **Check spelling as you type** (☑ changes to ☐).

4 Deselect **Mark grammar errors as you type** (☑ changes to ☐).

5 Click **OK**.

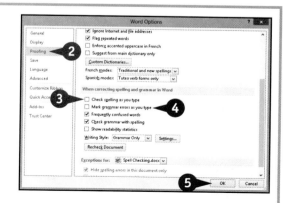

Work with AutoCorrect

As you may have noticed, Word automatically corrects your text as you type. It does this using its AutoCorrect feature, which works from a preset list of misspellings.

To speed up your text-entry tasks, you can add your own problem words — ones you commonly misspell — to the list. The next time you mistype the word, AutoCorrect fixes your mistake for you. If you find that AutoCorrect consistently changes a word that is correct as is, you can remove that word from the AutoCorrect list. If you would prefer that AutoCorrect not make any changes to your text as you type, you can disable the feature.

Work with AutoCorrect

1 Click the **File** tab.

Backstage view appears.

2 Click **Options**.

The Word Options dialog box appears.

3 Click **Proofing** to display proofing options.

4 Click **AutoCorrect Options**.

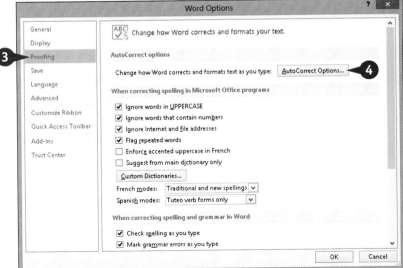

The AutoCorrect dialog box appears.

Ⓐ The corrections Word already makes automatically appear in this area.

5 Click here and type the word you typically mistype or misspell.

6 Click here and type the correct version of the word.

7 Click **Add**.

Ⓑ Word adds the entry to the list to automatically correct.

You can repeat Steps **5** to **7** for each automatic correction you want to add.

8 Click **OK** to close the AutoCorrect dialog box.

9 Click **OK** to close the Word Options dialog box.

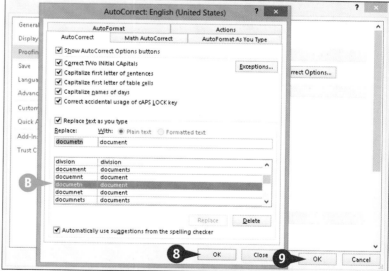

How does the automatic correction work?

As you type, if you mistype or misspell a word stored as an AutoCorrect entry, Word corrects the entry when you press Spacebar, Tab, or Enter.

What should I do if Word automatically replaces an entry that I do not want replaced?

Position the insertion point at the beginning of the AutoCorrected word and click the **AutoCorrect Options** button (🗏). From the list that appears, click **Change back to**. To make Word permanently stop correcting an entry, follow Steps **1** to **4**, click the stored AutoCorrect entry in the list, and then click **Delete**.

Using Word's Thesaurus and Dictionary

If you are having trouble finding just the right word or phrase, you can use Word's thesaurus. The thesaurus can help you find a synonym — a word with a similar meaning — for the word you originally chose, as well as an antonym, which is a word with an opposite meaning. When you use the thesaurus to look up a word, you also see the word's definition.

If you prefer, you can bypass the thesaurus and use the dictionary you download from the Office Store; see Chapter 4 for details on how to download and install an Office app.

Using Word's Thesaurus and Dictionary

Using Word's Thesaurus

1 Click anywhere in the word for which you want to find a substitute or opposite.

Note: You can press <kbd>Shift</kbd>+<kbd>F7</kbd> to display the Thesaurus pane.

2 Click the **Review** tab.

3 Click the **Thesaurus** button (▦).

The Thesaurus pane appears.

Ⓐ The word you selected appears here.

Ⓑ Each word with an arrow on its left and a part of speech on its right represents a major heading.

Note: You cannot substitute major headings for the word in your document.

Ⓒ Each word listed below a major heading is a synonym or antonym for the major heading.

Ⓓ Antonyms are marked.

4 Point the mouse at the word you want to use in your document and click the ▼ that appears.

5 Click **Insert**.

Word replaces the word in your document with the one in the Thesaurus pane.

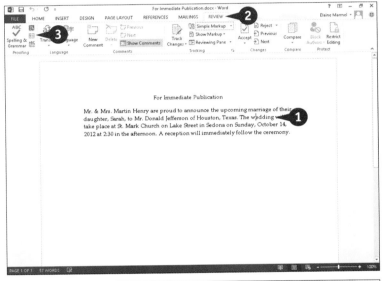

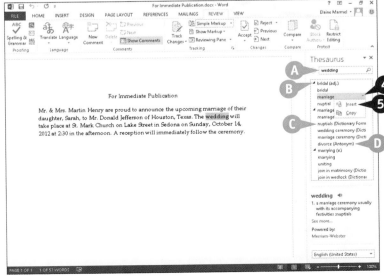

130

Using Word's Dictionary

1 Right-click the word you want to look up.

2 From the menu that appears, click **Define**.

E Word selects the word you right-clicked.

F A pane for the installed dictionary appears, displaying definitions of the word you selected.

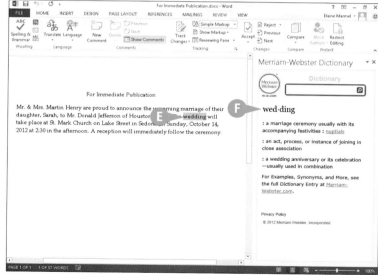

TIP

Is there a faster way I can display synonyms?
Yes. Follow these steps:

1 Right-click the word for which you want a synonym.

2 Click **Synonyms**.

3 Click a choice in the list that appears to replace the word in your document.

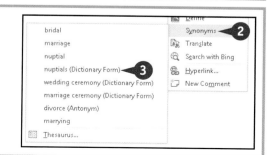

Translate Text

Yꜟou can translate a word from one language to another using language dictionaries installed on your computer. If you are connected to the Internet, the Translation feature searches the dictionaries on your computer as well as online dictionaries.

While the feature is capable of fairly complex translations, it may not grasp the tone or meaning of your text. You can choose Translate Document from the Translate drop-down menu to send the document over the Internet for translation, but be aware that Word sends documents as unencrypted HTML files. If security is an issue, do not choose this route; instead, consider hiring a professional translator.

Translate Text

Translate a Word or Phrase

1 Select a word or phrase to translate.

2 Click the **Review** tab.

3 Click **Translate**.

4 Click **Translate Selected Text**.

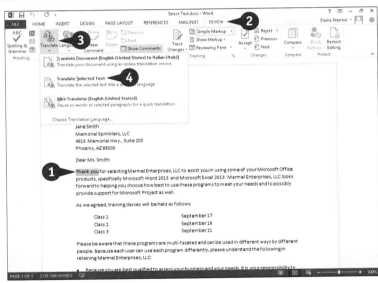

The Research pane appears.

Ⓐ The phrase you selected appears here.

Ⓑ The current translation languages appear here.

Ⓒ You can click ▼ to display available translation languages.

Ⓓ The translation appears here.

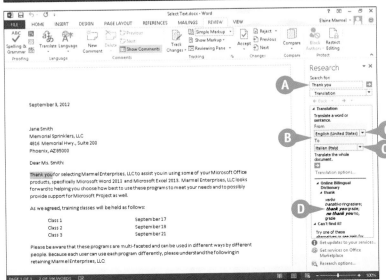

Translate a Document

1. Open the document you want to translate.

2. Click the **Review** tab.

3. Click **Translate**.

4. Click **Translate Document**.

Note: If the Translation Language Options dialog box appears, select the translation language you want to use.

The Translate Whole Document dialog box appears, notifying you that your document will be sent over the Internet for translation.

5. Click **Send**.

Your browser opens, displaying the translated document.

E. You can use these Views buttons to display the documents side by side as shown here.

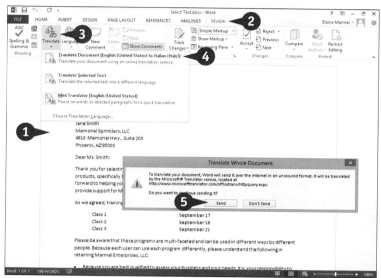

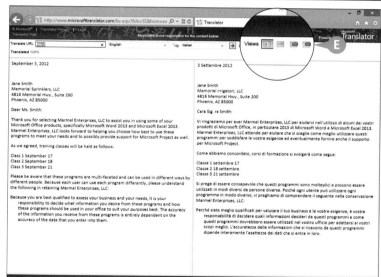

TIP

How do I choose a different language when translating the entire document?

Follow these steps. Click the **Review** tab. Click **Translate**. From the menu that appears, click **Choose Translation Language**. The Translation Language Options dialog box opens. Click the **Translate from** ⌄ and the **Translate to** ⌄ and choose languages (A). Click **OK**.

Track and Review Document Changes

If you share your Word documents with others, you can use the program's Track Changes feature to identify the edits others have made, including formatting changes and text additions or deletions. The Track Changes feature uses different colors for each person's edits, so you can easily distinguish edits made by various people. By default, Word displays changes in Simple Markup view, which indicates, in the left margin, areas that have changes. This section demonstrates how to track and interpret changes.

When you review the document, you decide whether to accept or reject the changes.

Track and Review Document Changes

Turn On Tracking

1 Click the **Review** tab on the Ribbon.

2 Click **Track Changes** to start monitoring document changes.

3 Edit the document.

A A red vertical bar appears in the left margin area to indicate that changes were made to the corresponding line.

Note: When you open a document containing tracked changes, Simple Markup is the default view. Red vertical bars appear in the left margin to indicate locations where changes were made.

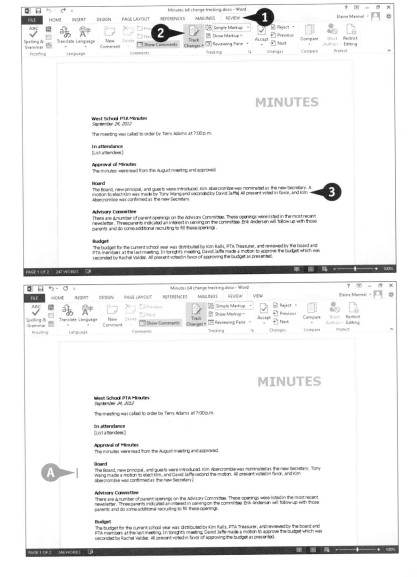

Review Changes

1 Click any vertical bar in the left margin.

All vertical bars turn gray and Word changes the view to All Markup and displays all changes in the document.

B Additions to the text appear underlined and in color.

C Deleted text appears in color with strikethrough formatting.

2 Place the insertion point at the beginning of the document.

3 Click **Next**.

D Word highlights the first change.

4 Click **Accept** to add the change to the document or click **Reject** to revert the text to its original state.

Note: To accept all changes in the document, click the down arrow under the **Accept** button and choose **Accept All Changes**.

5 Repeat Steps **3** and **4** until you have reviewed all changes.

6 When you complete the review, click **Track Changes** to turn the feature off.

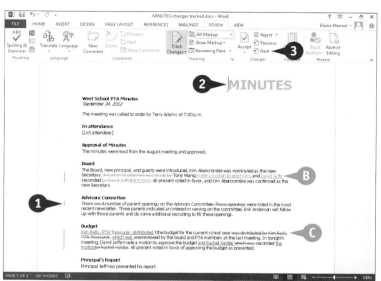

TIP

Can I see who made each change?
Yes. You can use the Reviewing pane. Follow these steps. Click the **Review** tab on the Ribbon, and then click **Reviewing Pane**. The Reviewing pane opens, summarizing the types of edits and showing each person's edits.

Revisions

∨ **17 REVISIONS**

Elaine J. Marmel Deleted
  A motion to elect Kim was made
  by

Lock and Unlock Tracking

Y ou can control who can turn tracking on and off using the Lock Tracking feature. This feature requires a password to turn off tracking. You no longer need to deal with the situation where you turn on tracking and send out a document for review, and when you get the document back, it contains no change markings because the reviewer turned the Track Changes feature off.

In the past, you needed to use the Compare Documents feature to determine how the reviewed document differed from the original. Now, you can lock tracking.

Lock and Unlock Tracking

Lock Tracked Changes

1 In the document for which you want to lock tracked changes, click the **Review** tab.

2 Click **Track Changes** to turn on tracking.

3 Click the down arrow at the bottom of the **Track Changes** button.

4 Click **Lock Tracking**.

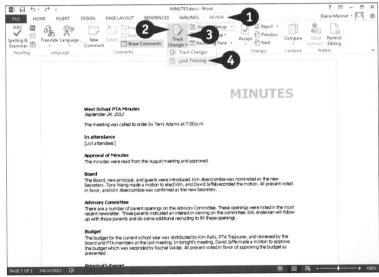

The Lock Tracking dialog box appears.

5 Type a password here.

6 Retype the password here.

7 Click **OK**.

Note: Make sure you remember the password or you will not be able to turn off the Track Changes feature.

Word saves the password and the Track Changes button appears gray and unavailable.

Unlock Tracked Changes

1 Open a document with tracked changes locked.

2 Click the **Review** tab.

3 Click the down arrow at the bottom of the **Track Changes** button.

4 Click **Lock Tracking**.

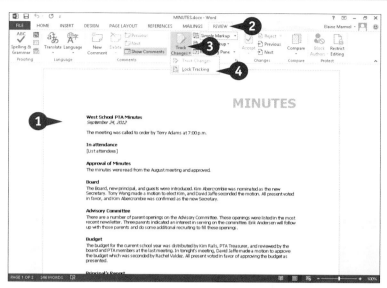

The Unlock Tracking dialog box appears.

5 Type the password.

6 Click **OK**.

The Track Changes button becomes available again so that you can click it and turn off the Track Changes feature.

TIP

What happens if I supply the wrong password?
This message box appears. You can retry as many times as you want. If you cannot remember the password, you can create a new version that contains all revisions already accepted, which you can then compare to the original to identify changes. Press **Ctrl**+**A** to select the entire document. Then press **Shift**+**←** to unselect just the last paragraph mark in the document. Then press **Ctrl**+**C** to copy the selection. Start a new blank document and press **Ctrl**+**V** to paste the selection.

Combine Reviewers' Comments

Suppose that two different people review a document, but they review simultaneously using the original document. When they each return the reviewed document, you have two versions of the original document, each containing potentially different changes. Fortunately, you can combine the documents so that you can work from the combined changes of both reviewers.

When you combine two versions of the same document, Word creates a third file that flags any discrepancies between the versions using revision marks like you see when you enable the Track Changes feature. You can then work from the combined document and evaluate each change.

Combine Reviewers' Comments

Note: To make your screen as easy to understand as possible, close all open documents.

1. Click the **Review** tab.

2. Click **Compare**.

3. Click **Combine**.

   The Combine Documents dialog box appears.

4. Click the **Open** button (📂) for the first document you want to combine.

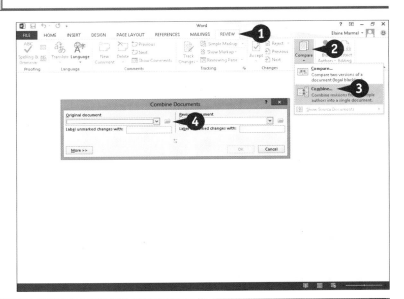

The Open dialog box appears.

5. Navigate to the folder containing the first file you want to combine.

6. Click the file.

7. Click **Open**.

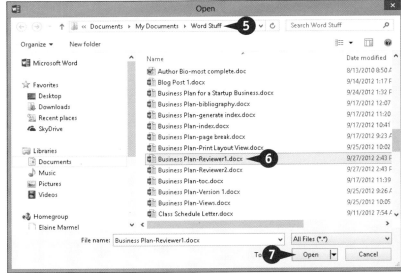

The Combine Documents dialog box reappears.

8 Repeat Steps **4** to **7**, clicking the **Open** button (📁) for the second document you want to combine.

Ⓐ You can type a label for changes to each document in these boxes.

9 Click **OK**.

Word displays four panes.

Ⓑ The left pane contains a summary of revisions.

Ⓒ The center pane contains the result of combining both documents.

Ⓓ The top-right pane displays the document you selected in Step **6**.

Ⓔ The bottom-right pane displays the document you selected in Step **8**.

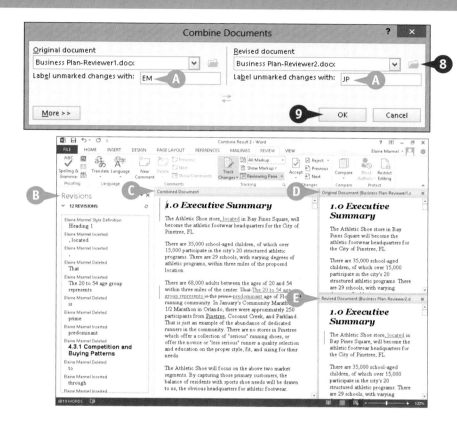

Two reviewers reviewed the same document but they forgot to track changes; can I somehow see their changes?

Yes. Follow the steps in this section, but, in Step **3**, click **Compare**. Word again displays four panes: the summary appears in the left pane; results of comparing the two documents appear in the center pane; the document you select in Step **6** appears in the top-right pane; and the document you select in Step **8** appears in the bottom-right pane.

How do I save the combined document?

The same way you save any Word document; see Chapter 2 for details.

Work with Comments

You can add comments to your documents. For example, when you share a document with other users, you can use comments to leave feedback about the text without typing directly in the document and others can do the same.

To indicate that a comment was added, Word displays a balloon in the right margin near the commented text. When you review comments, they appear in a block. Your name appears in comments you add, and you can easily review, reply to, or delete a comment, or, instead of deleting the comment, you can indicate that you have addressed the comment.

Work with Comments

Add a Comment

1 Click or select the text about which you want to comment.

2 Click the **Review** tab.

3 Click **New Comment**.

Ⓐ A comment balloon appears, marking the location of the comment.

Ⓑ A Comments block appears.

4 Type your comment.

5 Click anywhere outside the comment to continue working.

Review a Comment

1 While working in Simple Markup view, click a comment balloon.

Ⓒ Word highlights the text associated with the comment.

Ⓓ Word displays the Comments block and the text it contains.

Note: To view all comments along the right side of the document, click **Show Comments** in the Comments group on the Review tab.

2 Click anywhere outside the comment to hide the Comments block and its text.

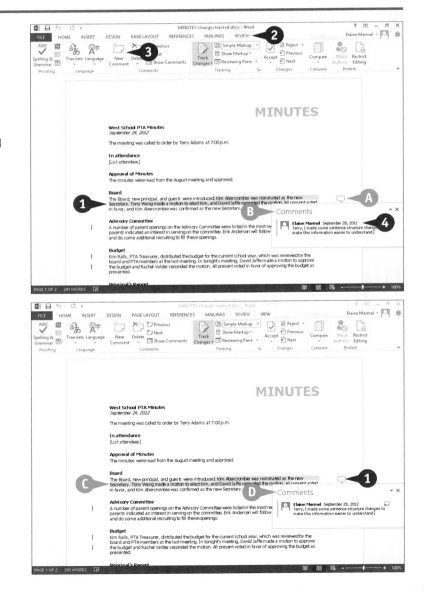

Reply to a Comment

1 While working in Simple Markup view, click a comment balloon to display its text.

2 Click the **Reply to Comment** button (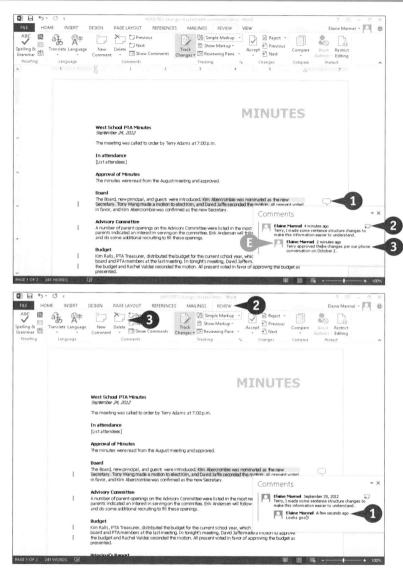).

E Word starts a new comment, indented under the first comment.

3 Type your reply.

4 Click anywhere outside the comment to continue working.

Delete a Comment

1 Click the comment that you want to remove.

2 Click the **Review** tab.

3 Click **Delete**.

Note: You can also right-click a comment and click **Delete Comment**. And, you can delete all comments in the document by clicking the down arrow at the bottom of the **Delete** button and then clicking **Delete All Comments in Document**.

Word deletes the comment.

TIP

Can I indicate that I have addressed a comment without deleting it?
Yes, you can mark the comment as done. Right-click the text of the comment and choose **Mark Comment Done**. Word fades the comment text to light gray.

PART III

Excel

Excel is a powerful spreadsheet program that you can use to enter and organize data and to perform a wide variety of number-crunching tasks. You can use Excel strictly as a program for manipulating numerical data, or you can use it as a database program to organize and track large quantities of data. In this part, you learn how to enter data into worksheets and tap into the power of Excel's formulas and functions to perform mathematical calculations and analysis.

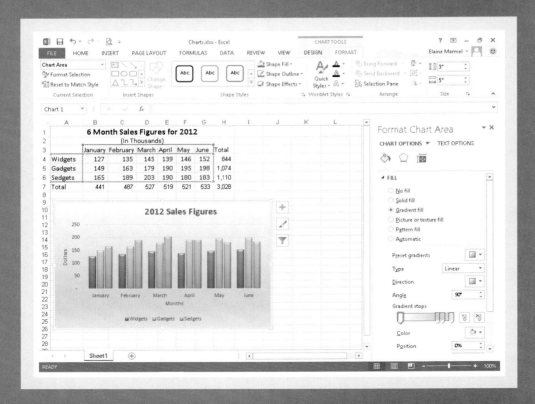

Enter Cell Data

You can enter data into any cell in an Excel worksheet. You can type data directly into the cell, or you can enter data using the Formula bar. Data can be text, such as row or column labels, or numbers, which are called *values*. Values also include formulas. Excel automatically left-aligns text data in a cell and right-aligns values.

Long text entries appear truncated if you type additional data into adjoining cells. Values that are too large to fit in a cell might be represented by a series of pound signs. But, Excel offers features to help you remedy these situations.

Enter Cell Data

Type into a Cell

1 Click the cell into which you want to enter data.

The cell you clicked is called the *active cell*. It has a thicker border around it than the other cells.

A To add data to another worksheet in your workbook, click the worksheet tab to display the worksheet.

B To magnify your view of the worksheet, click and drag the **Zoom** slider.

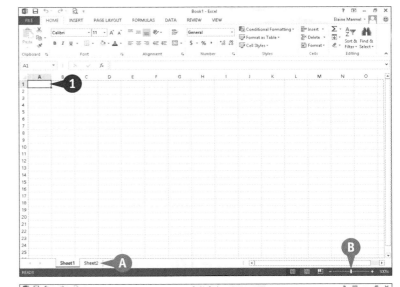

2 Type your data.

C The data appears both in the cell and in the Formula bar.

D To store the data in the cell, press Enter or click **Enter** (✓).

Note: If you press Enter, the cell pointer moves down one row. If you click **Enter** (✓), the cell pointer remains in the cell you clicked in Step **1**.

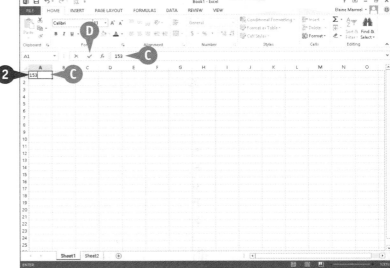

Type Data in the Formula Bar

1 Click the cell into which you want to enter data.

2 Click in the Formula bar.

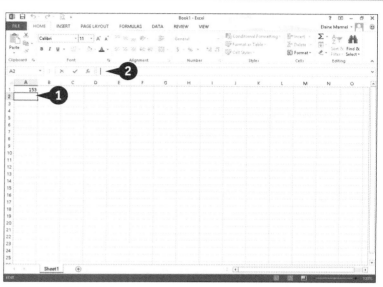

3 Type your data.

Ⓔ The data appears both in the Formula bar and in the cell.

4 Click **Enter** (✓) or press Enter to enter the data.

Ⓕ To cancel an entry, you can click **Cancel** (✗) or press Esc.

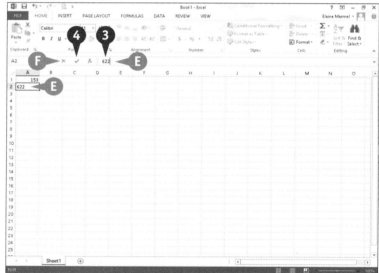

TIP

What if the data that I type is too long to fit in my cell?

In most cases, Excel expands the column to accommodate your entry. But, suppose that you type a long entry in A1 and then type information into B1. In this case, text in A1 appears truncated or, if A1 contains numbers, they appear as pound signs (#). You can remedy this behavior by resizing column A or by turning on the text wrap feature to increase column A's cell depth. To learn how to resize columns, see the section "Resize Columns and Rows." To learn how to turn on the text wrap feature, see the section "Turn On Text Wrapping."

Select Cells

To edit data or perform mathematical or formatting operations on data in an Excel worksheet, you must first select the cell or cells that contain that data. For example, you might apply formatting to data in a single cell or to data in a group, or *range*, of cells.

Selecting a single cell is easy: You just click the cell. To select a range of cells, you can use your mouse or keyboard. In addition to selecting cells or ranges of cells, you can select the data contained in a cell, as described in the tip.

Select Cells

Select a Range of Cells

1 Click the cell representing the upper-left corner of the range of cells that you want to select.

A The cell pointer (✛) appears as you move the mouse.

2 Click and drag down and to the right across the cells that you want to include in the range.

3 Release the mouse button.

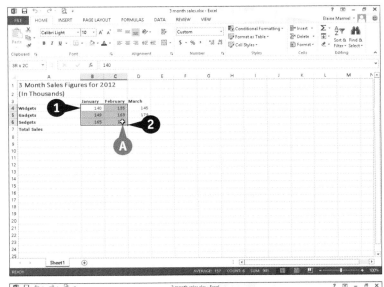

B Excel highlights the selected cells in gray.

C The Quick Analysis button (📧) appears. See Chapter 10 for details about this feature.

D To select all of the cells in the worksheet, you can click here (◢).

You can select multiple noncontiguous cells by pressing and holding **Ctrl** while clicking cells.

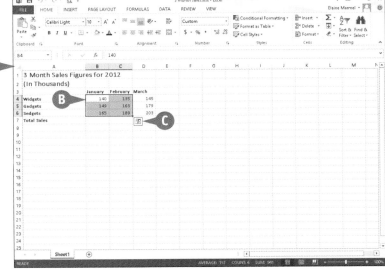

Select a Column or Row

1 Position the mouse pointer over the column letter or row number that you want to select.

The cell pointer changes from ⊕ to ↓ if you positioned the mouse pointer over a column, or → if you positioned the mouse pointer over a row.

2 Click the column or row.

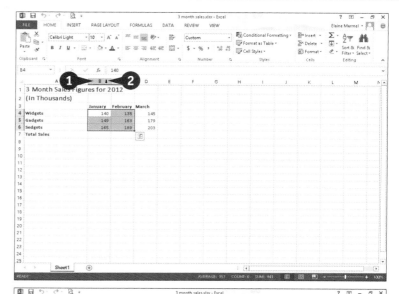

E Excel selects the entire column or row.

To select multiple contiguous columns or rows, you can click and drag across the column or row headings.

You can select multiple noncontiguous columns or rows by pressing and holding **Ctrl** while clicking column or row headings.

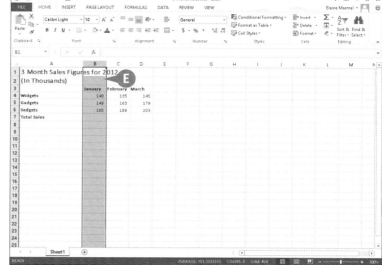

TIPS

How do I select data inside a cell?
Click the cell; then click in the Formula bar and drag over the characters or numbers you want to select. Alternatively, double-click a cell and drag to select the data.

Can I use my keyboard to select a range?
Yes. Use the arrow keys to navigate to the first cell in a range. Next, press and hold **Shift** while using an arrow key (◄ or ►) to select the remaining cells' range.

Faster Data Entry with AutoFill

You can use Excel's AutoFill feature to add a data series to your worksheet or to duplicate a single entry in your worksheet to expedite data entry. You can create number series and, using Excel's built-in lists of common entries, you can enter text series such as a list containing the days of the week or the months in the year. In addition, you can create your own custom data lists, as described in the tip.

When you click a cell, a *fill handle* appears in the lower-right corner of the cell; you use the fill handle to create a series.

Faster Data Entry with AutoFill

AutoFill a Text Series

1 Type the first entry in the text series.

2 Click and drag the cell's fill handle across or down the number of cells that you want to fill.

A ⊕ changes to the Fill handle (**+**).

If you type an entry that Excel does not recognize as part of a list, AutoFill copies the selection to every cell that you drag over.

3 Release the mouse button.

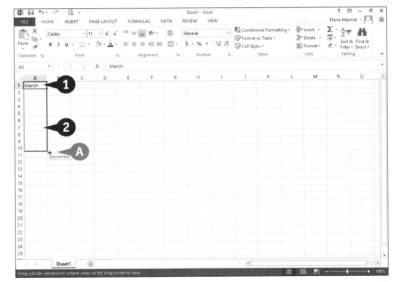

B AutoFill fills in the text series and selects the series.

C The AutoFill Options button (⊞ ▾) may appear, offering additional options that you can assign to the data.

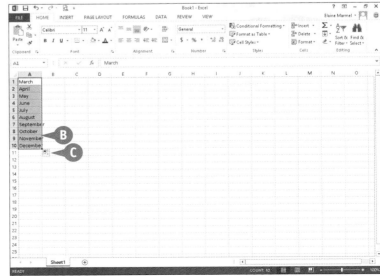

AutoFill a Number Series

1 Type the first entry in the number series.

2 In an adjacent cell, type the next entry in the number series.

3 Select both cells.

Note: See the previous section, "Select Cells," to learn more.

4 Click and drag the fill handle across or down the number of cells that you want to fill.

⇧ changes to **+**.

5 Release the mouse button.

AutoFill fills in the number series and selects the series.

D The AutoFill Options button (🖱·) may appear, offering additional options that you can assign to the data.

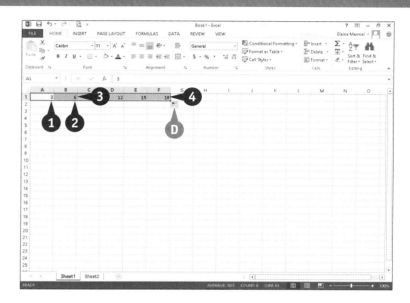

How do I create a custom list?

To add your own custom list to AutoFill's list library, first create the custom list in your worksheet cells. Then select the cells containing the list that you want to save. Click the **File** tab and then click **Options**. In the Options dialog box, click the **Advanced** tab. In the General section, click the **Edit Custom Lists** button. In the Custom Lists dialog box, click **Import**. Excel adds your list to the series of custom lists (**A**). The entries in the list appear here (**B**). Click **OK** to close the Custom Lists dialog box. Click **OK** again to close the Options dialog box.

Turn On Text Wrapping

By default, long lines of text appear on one line in Excel. If you type additional data into adjacent cells, long lines of text appear truncated, but they are not. If you select the cell and look at the Formula bar, you see all of the text.

You can display all of the text by resizing the column width (see the section "Resize Columns and Rows"). Or, you can wrap text within the cell so that some text appears on the next line. When you wrap text, Excel maintains column width and increases the height of the row to accommodate the number of lines that wrap.

Turn On Text Wrapping

1 Click the cell in which you want to wrap text.

Note: You can also apply text wrapping to multiple cells. See the section "Select Cells," earlier in this chapter, to learn how to select multiple cells for a task.

2 Click the **Home** tab.

3 Click the **Wrap Text** button (⬛).

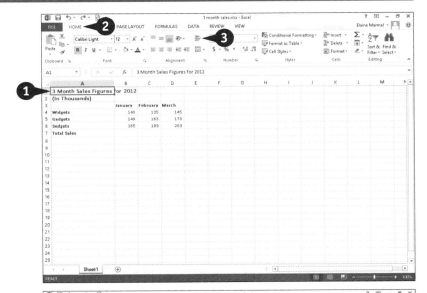

A Excel wraps the text in the cell.

Note: See the section "Resize Columns and Rows" to learn how to adjust cell depth and width to accommodate your data.

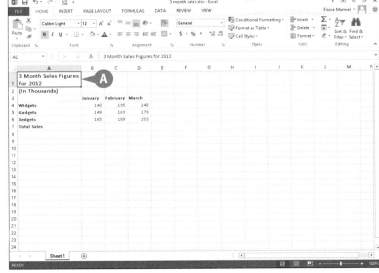

Center Data across Columns

You can center data across a range of selected cells in your worksheet. For example, you might want to include a title above multiple columns of information and center it. You can use Excel's Merge and Center command to quickly merge and center the selected cells.

Additional options appear when you click ▼ beside the **Merge and Center** button (⊞ ▾). Merge Across merges each selected row of cells into a larger cell. Merge Cells merges selected cells in multiple rows and columns into a single cell. Unmerge Cells splits a cell into multiple cells.

Center Data across Columns

① Select the cell containing the data that you want to center, along with the adjacent cells over which you want to center the data.

Note: When you merge and center, Excel deletes any data in selected adjacent cells.

② Click the **Home** tab.

③ Click the **Merge and Center** button (⊞ ▾).

You can also click the **Merge and Center** ▼ to select from several merge options.

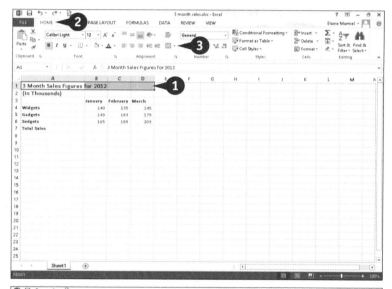

Ⓐ Excel merges the cells and centers the data.

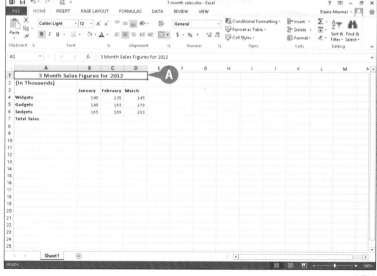

Adjust Cell Alignment

By default, Excel automatically aligns text to the left and numbers to the right of a cell. It also vertically aligns all data to sit at the bottom of the cell. If you want, however, you can change the horizontal and vertical alignment of data within cells — for example, you can center data vertically and horizontally within a cell to improve the appearance of your worksheet data.

In addition to controlling the alignment of data within a cell, you can also indent data and change its orientation in a cell.

Adjust Cell Alignment

Set Horizontal Alignment

1 Select the cells that you want to format.

2 Click the **Home** tab.

3 Click an alignment button:

Click the **Align Left** button (≡) to align data to the left.

Click the **Center** button (≡) to center-align the data.

Click the **Align Right** button (≡) to align data to the right.

Note: To justify cell data, click the dialog box launcher (⌐) in the Alignment group. In the Format Cells dialog box that appears, click the **Horizontal** ▼ and click **Justify**.

Excel applies the alignment to your cells.

A This example centers the data horizontally.

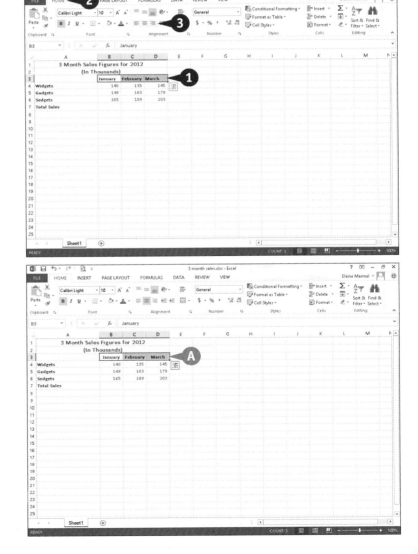

Set Vertical Alignment

1 Select the cells that you want to format.

2 Click the **Home** tab.

3 Click an alignment button:

Click the **Top Align** button (≡) to align data to the top.

Click the **Middle Align** button (≡) to align data in the middle.

Click the **Bottom Align** button (≡) to align data to the bottom.

Excel applies the alignment to your cells.

B This example aligns the data to the middle of the cell.

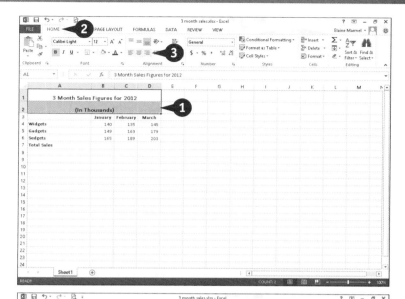

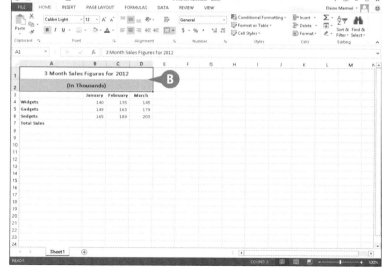

TIPS

How do I indent cell data?
To indent data, click the **Increase Indent** button (≣) on the Home tab. To decrease an indent, click the **Decrease Indent** button (≣).

Can I change the orientation of data in a cell?
Yes. For example, you might angle column labels to make them easier to distinguish from one another. To do so, select the cells you want to change, click the **Home** tab, click ▼ next to the **Orientation** button (≫ ▼), and click an orientation. Excel applies the orientation to the data in the selected cell or cells.

Change the Font and Size

You can change the font or the font size that you use for various cells in your worksheet. For example, you can make the worksheet title larger than the rest of the data, or you might resize the font for the entire worksheet to make the data easier to read. You can apply multiple formats to a cell — for example, you can change both the font and the font size of any given cell.

If you particularly like the result of applying a series of formatting options to a cell, you can copy the formatting and apply it to other cells in your worksheet.

Change the Font and Size

Change the Font

1. Select the cell or range for which you want to change fonts.

2. Click the **Home** tab.

3. Click the **Font** ▼.

   You can use ▲ and ▼ to scroll through all of the available fonts.

   You can also begin typing a font name to choose a font.

4. Click a font.

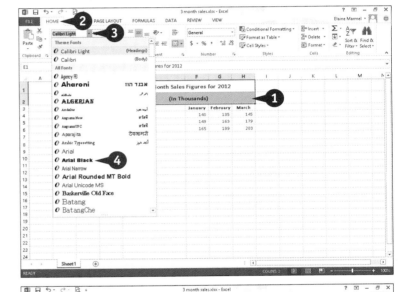

A. Excel applies the font.

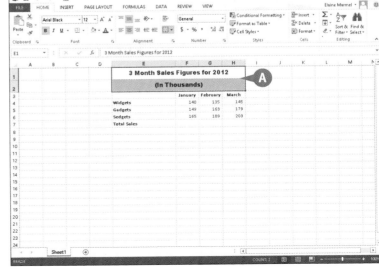

Change the Font Size

1 Select the cell or range for which you want to change font size.

2 Click the **Home** tab.

3 Click the **Font Size** ▼.

4 Click a size.

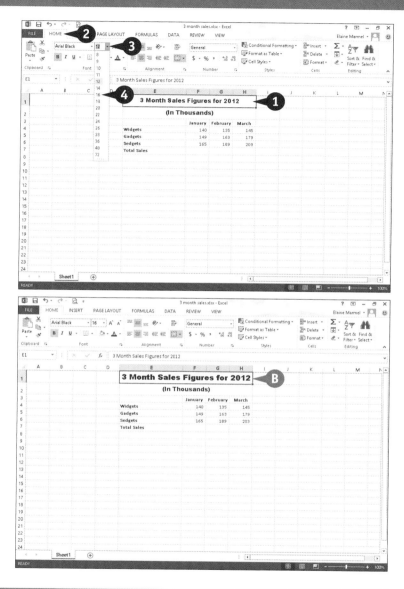

B Excel applies the new size to the selected cell or range.

Can I apply multiple formatting options at once?
Yes. The Format Cells dialog box enables you to apply a new font, size, or any other basic formatting options to selected data. To open it, click the **Home** tab and click the dialog box launcher (◨) in the Font group.

How can I copy cell formatting?
Select the cell or range that contains the formatting you want to copy. Then, click the **Home** tab, and click the **Format Painter** button (◆) in the Clipboard group. Then click and drag over the cells to which you want to apply the formatting and release the mouse button to copy the formatting.

Change Number Formats

You can use number formatting to control the appearance of numerical data in your worksheet. For example, if you have a column of prices, you can format the data as numbers with dollar signs and decimal points. If prices listed are in a currency other than dollars, you can indicate that as well.

Excel offers several different number categories, or styles, to choose from. These include Currency styles, Accounting styles, Date styles, Time styles, Percentage styles, and more. You can apply number formatting to single cells, ranges, columns, rows, or an entire worksheet.

Change Number Formats

1 Select the cell, range, or data that you want to format.

2 Click the **Home** tab.

3 Click the **Number Format** ▼.

4 Click a number format.

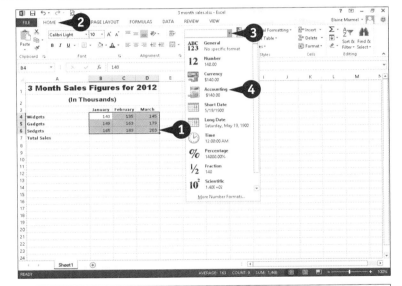

Excel applies the number format to the data.

A Click the **Accounting Number Format** button ($ ▾) to quickly apply dollar signs to your data. Click the button's ▼ to specify a different currency symbol, such as Euro.

B Click the **Percent Style** button (%) to quickly apply percent signs to your data.

C Click the **Comma Style** button (▾) to quickly display commas in your number data.

D Click the dialog box launcher (⌐) in the Number group to open the Format Cells dialog box and display additional number-formatting options.

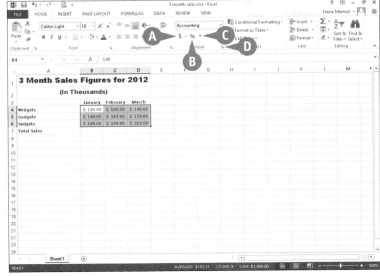

Increase or Decrease Decimals

You can control the number of decimal places that appear in numbers using the Increase Decimal and Decrease Decimal buttons. You may want to increase the number of decimal places shown in a cell if your worksheet contains data that must be precise to be accurate, as with worksheets containing scientific data. If the data in your worksheet is less precise, you might reduce the number of decimal places shown. Depending on the purpose of your worksheet's sales data, you might show two decimal places or no decimal places.

Increase or Decrease Decimals

1 Select the cell or range for which you want to adjust the number of decimal places displayed.

2 Click the **Home** tab.

3 Click a decimal button:

You can click the **Increase Decimal** button (⬆.0) to increase the number of decimal places displayed.

You can click the **Decrease Decimal** button (.00) to decrease the number of decimal places displayed.

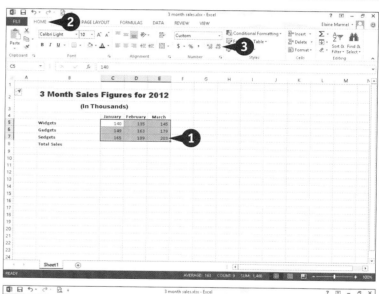

Excel adjusts the number of decimals that appear in the cell or cells.

A In this example, Excel adds a decimal place.

You can click the **Increase Decimal** button (⬆.0) again to add another decimal.

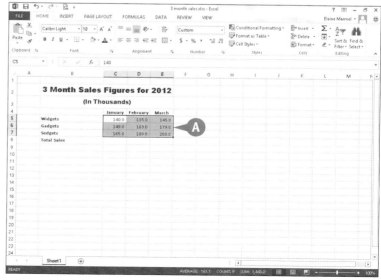

Add Cell Borders and Shading

By default, Excel displays gridlines separating each cell to help you enter data, but the gridlines do not print (also by default). You can print gridlines or hide them from view.

Alternatively, you can add printable borders to selected worksheet cells to help define the contents or more clearly separate the data from surrounding cells. You can add borders to all four sides of a cell or to just one, two, or three sides.

You can also apply shading to selected worksheet cells to help set apart different data.

Add Cell Borders and Shading

Add Quick Borders

1. Select the cell or range around which you want to place a border.

2. Click the **Home** tab.

3. Click ▼ beside the **Borders** button (⊞ ▼).

Note: To apply the current border selection shown on the button, simply click the **Borders** button (⊞ ▼).

4. Click a border style.

A. Excel assigns the borders to the cell or range.

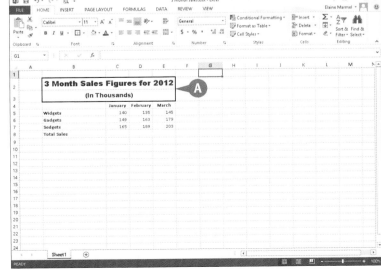

Add a Fill Color

1 Select the cells to which you want to apply a fill color.

2 Click the **Home** tab.

3 Click ▼ beside the **Fill Color** button (🖌 ▾).

4 Select a fill color.

Note: Remember, if the color you select is too dark, your data can become difficult to read.

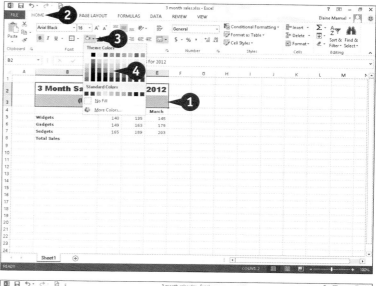

Ⓑ Excel applies the fill color to the selected cell or range.

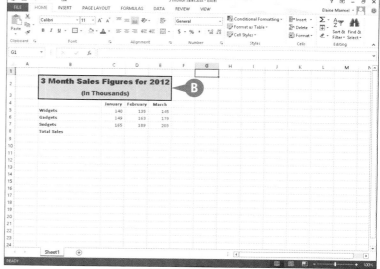

Can I turn worksheet gridlines on and off?
Yes. Printing gridlines makes worksheet data easier to read on paper. On the other hand, you might want to turn off gridlines on-screen during a presentation. To use options on the **Page Layout** tab to control the appearance of gridlines, click the **Page Layout** tab. In the Sheet Options group, deselect **View** to hide gridlines on-screen (☑ changes to ☐). Select **Print** (☐ changes to ☑) to print gridlines.

Gridlines	Headings
☑ View	☑ View
☐ Print	☐ Print
Sheet Options	⬎

Format Data with Styles

You can use the Excel styles to apply preset formatting to your worksheet data. You can apply cell styles to individual cells or ranges of cells, or table styles to a range of worksheet data. When you apply a table style, Excel converts the range into a table. Tables help you manage and analyze data independent of other data in the worksheet. For example, beside each column heading in a table, an AutoFilter ▼ appears. You can use the AutoFilter ▼ to show only certain information in the table.

You can also apply a theme — a predesigned set of formatting attributes — to a worksheet. See the tip for more details.

Format Data with Styles

Apply a Cell Style

1. Select the cell or range that you want to format.

2. Click the **Home** tab.

3. Click **Cell Styles**.

4. Click a style.

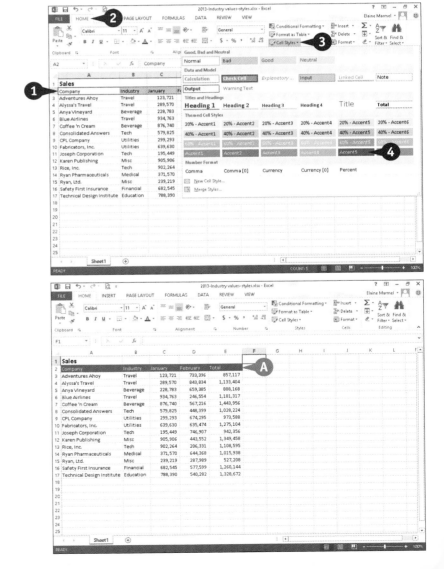

Ⓐ Excel applies the formatting to the selected cell or range.

Format as a Table

1 Select the cells that you want to format.

2 Click the **Home** tab.

3 Click **Format As Table**.

4 Click a table style.

The Format As Table dialog box appears.

5 Verify the selected cells.

6 Click **OK**.

B Excel applies the formatting style.

C AutoFilter down arrows (▼) appear in the column headings.

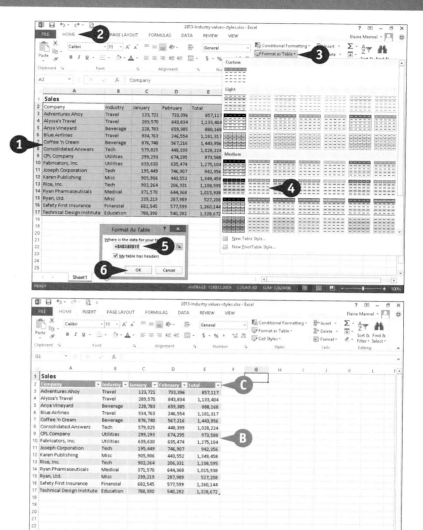

TIP

How do I apply a theme?

You can use themes to create a similar appearance among all the Office documents that you create. To apply a theme, click the **Page Layout** tab, click the **Themes** button, and select a theme from the list.

Apply Conditional Formatting

You can use Excel's Conditional Formatting tool to apply certain formatting attributes, such as bold text or a fill color, to a cell when the value of that cell meets a required condition. For example, if your worksheet tracks weekly sales, you might set up Excel's Conditional Formatting tool to alert you if a sales figure falls below what is required for you to break even.

In addition to using preset conditions, you can create your own. To help you distinguish the degree to which various cells meet your conditional rules, you can also use color scales and data bars.

Apply Conditional Formatting

Apply a Conditional Rule

1 Select the cell or range to which you want to apply conditional formatting.

2 Click the **Home** tab.

3 Click **Conditional Formatting**.

4 Click **Highlight Cells Rules** or **Top/Bottom Rules**.

This example uses Top/Bottom Rules.

5 Click the type of rule that you want to create.

A rule dialog box appears.

6 Specify the values that you want to assign for the condition.

7 Click **OK**.

A If the value of a selected cell meets the condition, Excel applies the conditional formatting.

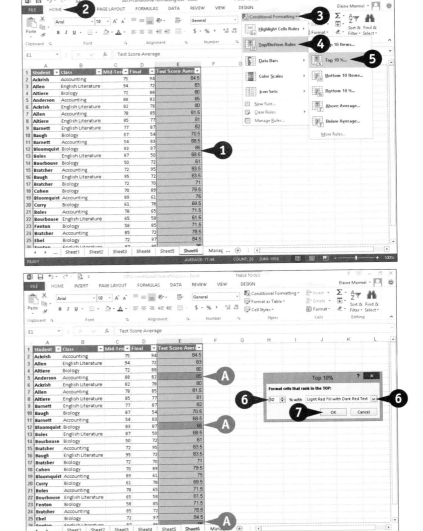

Apply Data Bars

1 Select the cell or range that contains the conditional formatting.

2 Click the **Home** tab.

3 Click **Conditional Formatting**.

4 Click **Data Bars**.

5 Click a data bar fill option.

B You can apply a color scale or an icon set instead by clicking **Color Scales** or **Icon Sets**.

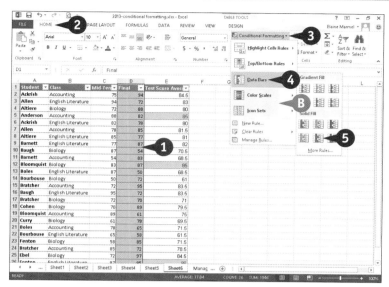

C Excel applies the data bars to the selection. Longer data bars represent higher values in your selection.

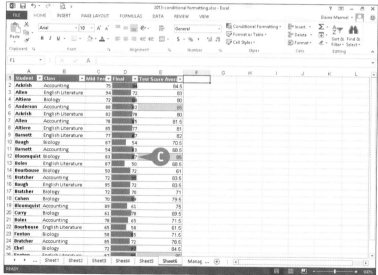

How do I create a new rule for conditional formatting?

Click the **Conditional Formatting** button on the Home tab and then click **New Rule** to open the New Formatting Rule dialog box. Here, you define the condition of the rule as well as what formatting you want to apply when the condition is met.

How do I remove conditional formatting from a cell?

Select the range that contains the formatting you want to remove, click the **Conditional Formatting** button on the Home tab, and then click **Manage Rules**. Next, click the rule you want to remove, click **Delete Rule**, and then click **OK**.

Add Columns and Rows

You can add columns and rows to your worksheets to include more data. For example, you may have typed product names in the rows of a worksheet that shows product sales over a period of time, but you did not include the region in which those products were sold. Now you find that you need to add region designations as row titles to segregate sales by region as well as by product.

You are not limited to inserting new columns and rows one at a time; if you want, you can insert multiple new columns and rows at once.

Add Columns and Rows

Add a Column

1. Click the letter of the column that should appear to the right of the new column you want to insert.

2. Click the **Home** tab.

3. Click **Insert**.

   You can also right-click a column heading and click **Insert**.

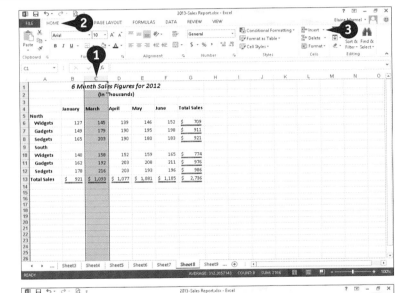

Ⓐ Excel adds a column.

Ⓑ The Insert Options button (✎ ▾) appears when you insert a column; click it to view a list of options that you can apply.

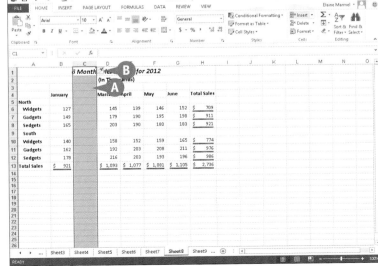

Add a Row

1 Click the number of the row that should appear below the new row you want to insert.

2 Click the **Home** tab.

3 Click **Insert**.

You can also right-click a row number and click **Insert**.

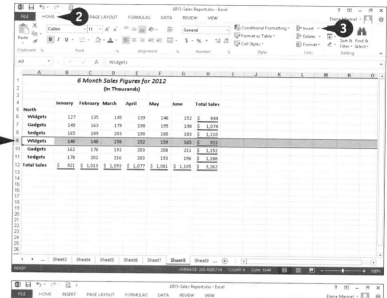

C Excel adds a row.

D The Insert Options button (✍ ▾) appears, and you can click it to view a list of options that you can assign.

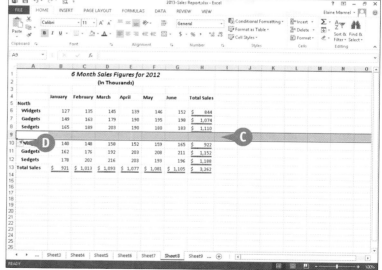

TIPS

How can I insert multiple columns and rows?
First, select two or more columns and rows in the worksheet; then activate the Insert command as described in this section. Excel adds the same number of new columns and rows as the number you originally selected.

What options appear when I click the Insert Options button?
For a new row, you can select **Format Same As Above**, **Format Same As Below**, or **Clear Formatting** (○ changes to ●). For a new column, you can select **Format Same As Left**, **Format Same As Right**, or **Clear Formatting** (○ changes to ●).

Resize Columns and Rows

Values that are too large to fit in a cell might appear as pound signs. Long lines of text appear on one line; if you type additional data into adjoining cells, long lines appear truncated, but they are not. If you select one of these cells and look at the Formula bar, you see the value or the text. To display long text in the worksheet, you can wrap it within the cell as described in the section "Turn On Text Wrapping," or you can resize the column. To display large values in the worksheet, you can resize the column. You can also resize rows.

Resize Columns and Rows

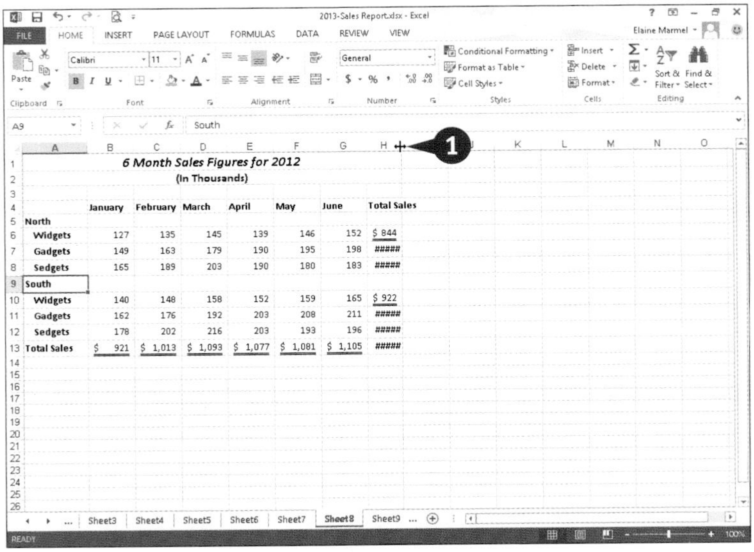

1. Position the mouse pointer on the right edge of the column letter or the bottom edge of the row number that you want to resize.

   The pointer changes to ✥ or ✥.

2. Click and drag the edge to the desired size.

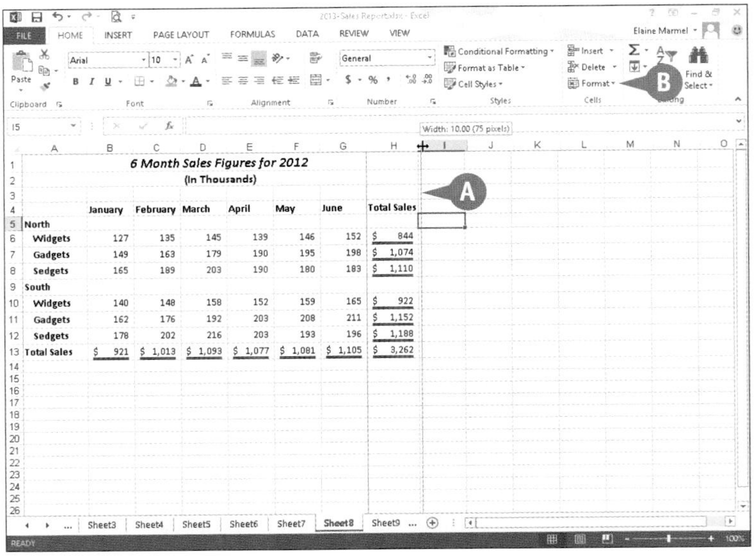

A A dotted line marks the new edge of the column or row as you drag, and Excel displays the new column width or row height.

3. Release the mouse button.

   Excel resizes the column or row.

B You can also select a column or row, click the **Format** button on the Home tab, and from the menu that appears, click **AutoFit Column Width** or **AutoFit Row Height** to resize the column or row to fit existing text.

Freeze Column and Row Titles On-Screen

When you work with a worksheet that contains more information than will fit on one screen, you can freeze one or more columns or rows to keep information in those columns and rows on-screen, regardless of where you place the cell pointer.

Freezing the top row of your worksheet is very useful when it contains headings for columns of information stored on the rows below. Similarly, freezing the leftmost column of your worksheet is very useful when titles for each row of data appear in the left column.

Freeze Column and Row Titles On-Screen

Note: To freeze both a column and a row, click the cell to the right of the column and below the row that you want visible on-screen at all times.

1 Click the **View** tab.

2 Click **Freeze Panes**.

3 Click a choice for freezing.

You can choose **Freeze Panes**, which freezes both a row of column headings and a column of row titles, or you can choose **Freeze Top Row** or **Freeze First Column**.

This example freezes the top row.

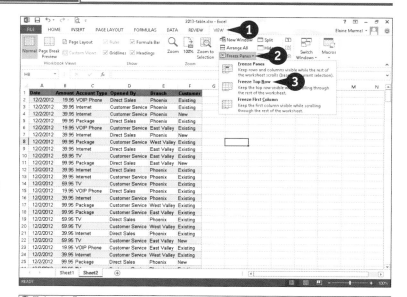

Excel freezes the areas you identified.

4 Press `Page down` or `Alt`+`Page down` to scroll down one screen or one screen to the right.

Ⓐ The frozen columns or rows remain on-screen.

Ⓑ To unlock the columns and rows, click the **Freeze Panes** ▼ and then click **Unfreeze Panes**.

Note: Freezing columns and rows only affects on-screen work; it does not affect printing.

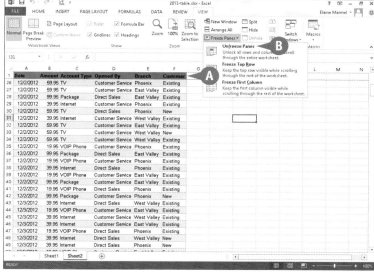

Name a Range

You can assign distinctive names to the cells and ranges of cells in a worksheet. A *range* is a rectangular group of cells; a range can also consist of a single cell. Assigning names to cells and ranges can help you more easily identify their contents. You can also use range names in formulas, which can help you decipher a formula. (Formulas are discussed later in this book.) Note that when it comes to naming ranges, you must follow some rules, as discussed in the tip at the end of this section.

Name a Range

Assign a Range Name

1 Select the cells comprising the range that you want to name.

2 Click the **Formulas** tab.

3 Click **Define Name**.

The New Name dialog box opens.

Note: Excel suggests a name using a label near the selected range. If you like the suggested name, skip Step **4**.

4 Type a name for the selected range in the **Name** field.

Ⓐ You can add a comment or note about the range here. For example, you might indicate what data the range contains.

5 Click **OK**.

Excel assigns the name to the cells.

Ⓑ When you select the range, its name appears in the Name box.

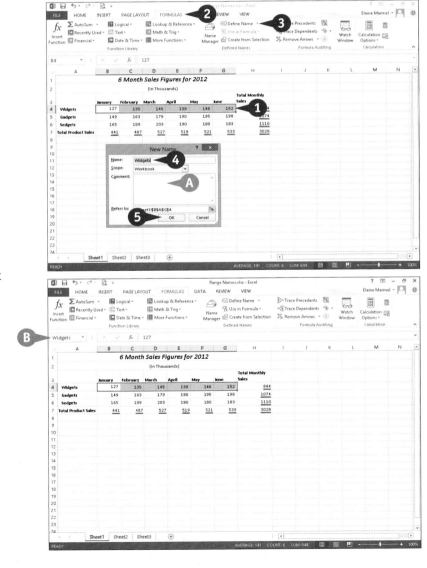

168

Select a Named Range

1 Click the **Name** ▼.

2 Click the name of the range of cells you want to select.

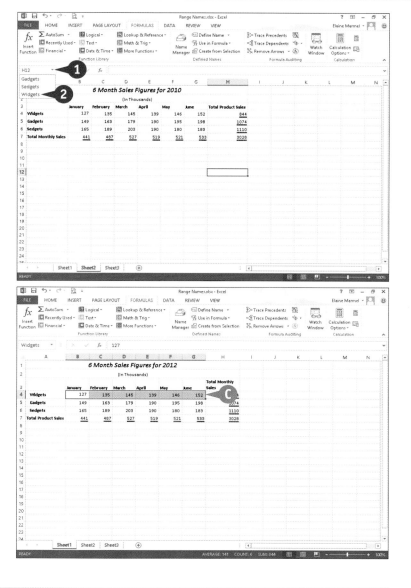

C Excel selects the cells in the range.

Note: You can use the Name Manager to make changes to your range names. Click the **Name Manager** button on the Formulas tab. You can edit existing range names, change the cells referenced by a range, or remove ranges to which you no longer need names assigned in the worksheet.

TIP

What are the rules for naming ranges?

Each name can be no more than 255 characters and must be unique. You can use uppercase and lowercase letters in a range name, but Excel ignores case — sales and SALES are the same name. The first character must be a letter, an underscore (_), or a backslash (\). You cannot use spaces in a range name; instead, substitute the underscore or the dash. You cannot name a range using cell references such as A1 or F6, nor can you name a range using either the uppercase or lowercase forms of the letters C and R.

Clear or Delete Cells

You can clear the formatting applied to a cell, the contents of the cell, any comments you assigned to the cell, any hyperlink formatting in the cell, or all of these elements. Clearing a cell is useful when you want to return the cell to its original state in Excel and you do not want to apply all of Excel's original formats manually.

You can also delete rows or columns of data. When you delete rows or columns, Excel adjusts the remaining cells in your worksheet, shifting them up or to the left to fill any gap in the worksheet structure.

Clear or Delete Cells

Clear Cells

1 Select the cell or range containing the data or formatting that you want to remove.

2 Click the **Home** tab.

3 Click the **Clear** button (✐ ▾).

4 Choose an option to identify what you want to clear.

This example clears formats.

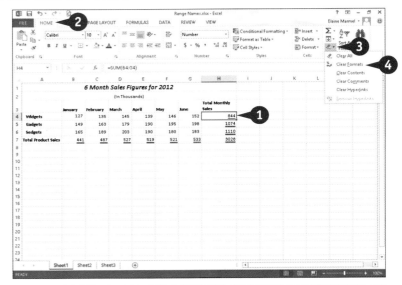

A Excel clears the cell using the option you selected in Step **4**.

In this example, Excel clears the formatting but retains the cell data.

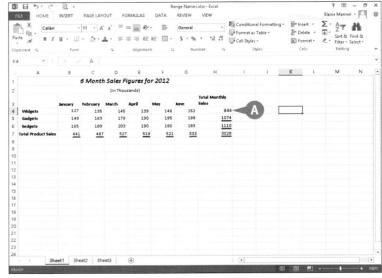

Delete Rows or Columns

1 Click the number of the row or the letter of the column that you want to delete.

This example deletes a column.

2 Click the **Home** tab.

3 Click **Delete**.

You can also right-click a row number or column heading and click **Delete**.

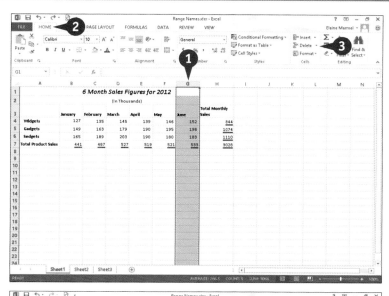

B Excel deletes the row or column and moves remaining data up or to the left to fill any gap in the worksheet structure.

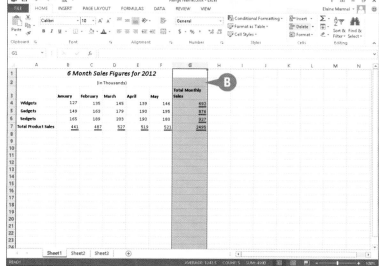

What is the difference between Clear Formats and Clear Contents?

Clear Formats removes just the formatting of a cell or range and leaves the contents of the cell or range. You retain the data and can reformat the cell or range; this command is most useful when you have applied several different formats and do not like the results. In a sense, Clear Formats lets you start over. Clear Contents, on the other hand, deletes the data in the cell but retains the cell's formatting. In this case, you can enter new data and it displays the same formatting as the data you cleared.

Split and Format a Column of Data

You can split a column of data into multiple columns. The Text to Columns feature is particularly useful when you open a list from another program. Typically, the information shows up on each row in one long string, but you want the information divided into columns.

After dividing the information, you can use the Flash Fill feature to format the data the way you want. With Flash Fill, you provide examples and, in most cases, Excel understands what you want.

Note that you can use Flash Fill in regular Excel files as well as text files you import.

Split and Format a Column of Data

Convert Text to Columns

1 Open the file containing the data you want to format.

The Text Import Wizard appears.

Note: If the Text Import Wizard does not appear, click the **Data** tab and then click **Text to Columns** in the Data Tools group.

2 Select **Delimited** (○ changes to ◉).

3 Click **Next**.

4 Select the delimiter your file uses (☐ changes to ☑).

5 Click **Finish**.

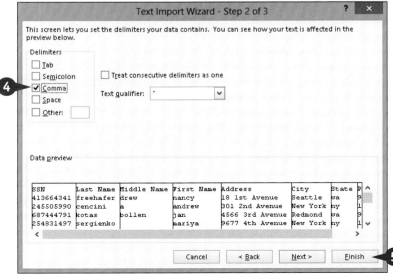

A The file appears on-screen in columnar format. You can widen the columns and, if you like, apply bold formatting to column headings.

Using Flash Fill Formatting

1 Insert a column beside the one you want to format and give it the same name as the one you want to format.

This example inserts column B.

2 Type the first entry from the original column into the inserted column using the format you want.

This example types the contents of cell A2 into cell B2, supplying dashes.

3 Start typing the second entry.

B Excel applies the formatting of the entry above to the current entry.

C Excel suggests the same formatting for all remaining entries in the column.

4 Press **Enter** to accept the formatting into the column.

5 Repeat these steps for each column you need to format. When you finish, you can delete the original columns.

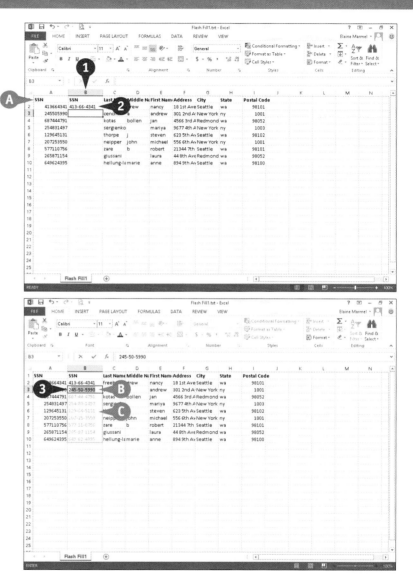

TIPS

How do I know which delimiter to select?
When you see your data separated in the Data Preview box at the bottom of the second Text Import Wizard dialog box, you know you have selected the delimiter you need.

How do I get the Flash Fill feature to insert leading zeros in a ZIP code?
Before formatting using Flash Fill, format the column you insert as a Text column; click the **Home** tab and, in the Number group, click the dialog box launcher ( ). In the Format Cells dialog box, click **Text** and then click **OK**.

Add a Worksheet

By default, when you create a new blank workbook in Excel, it contains one worksheet, which may be adequate. In some cases, however, your workbook might require additional worksheets in which to enter more data. For example, if your workbook contains data about products your company sells, you might want to add worksheets for each product category. You can easily add worksheets to a workbook.

When you add a new worksheet, Excel gives it a default name. To help you better keep track of your data, you can rename your new worksheet. For more information, see the next section, "Name a Worksheet."

Add a Worksheet

1 Click the **Insert Worksheet** button (⊕).

You can also right-click a worksheet tab and click **Insert** to open the Insert dialog box, where you can choose to insert a worksheet.

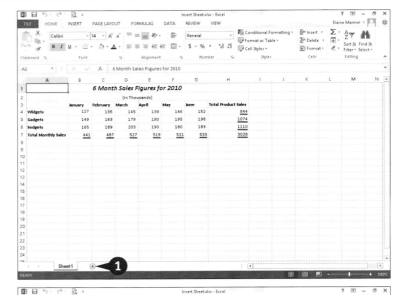

A Excel adds a new blank worksheet and gives it a default worksheet name.

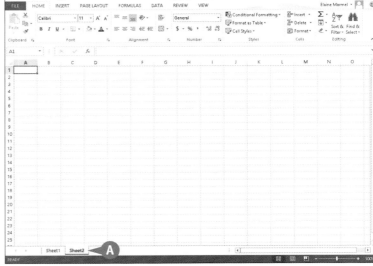

Name a Worksheet

When you create a new workbook, Excel assigns default names to each worksheet in the workbook. Likewise, Excel assigns a default name to each worksheet you add to an existing workbook.

To help you identify their content, you can change the names of your Excel worksheets to something more descriptive. For example, if your workbook contains four worksheets, each detailing a different sales quarter, then you can give each worksheet a unique name, such as Quarter 1, Quarter 2, and so on.

Name a Worksheet

1 Double-click the worksheet tab that you want to rename.

Excel highlights the current name.

You can also right-click the worksheet name and click **Rename**.

2 Type a new name for the worksheet.

3 Press **Enter**.

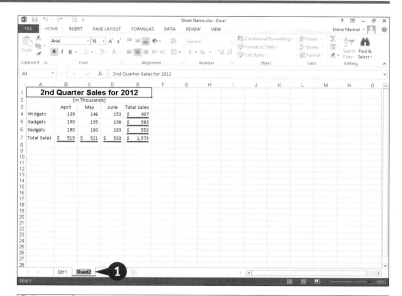

A Excel assigns the new worksheet name.

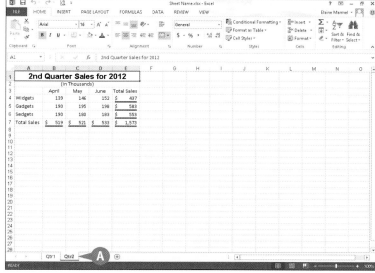

Change Page Setup Options

You can change worksheet settings related to page orientation, margins, paper size, and more. For example, suppose that you want to print a worksheet that has a few more columns than will fit on a page in Portrait orientation. (Portrait orientation accommodates fewer columns but more rows on the page and is the default page orientation that Excel assigns.) You can change the orientation of the worksheet to Landscape, which accommodates more columns but fewer rows on a page.

You can also use Excel's page-setup settings to establish margins and insert page breaks to control the placement of data on a printed page.

Change Page Setup Options

Change the Page Orientation

Ⓐ Dotted lines identify page breaks that Excel inserts.

① Click the **Page Layout** tab.

② Click **Orientation**.

③ Click **Portrait** or **Landscape**.

Note: Portrait is the default orientation.

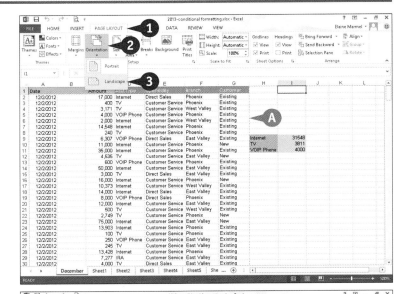

Excel applies the new orientation. This example applies Landscape.

Ⓑ Excel moves the page break indicator based on the new orientation.

Ⓒ You can click the **Margins** button to set up page margins.

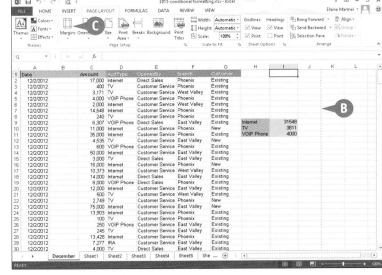

Insert a Page Break

1 Select the row above which you want to insert a page break.

2 Click the **Page Layout** tab.

3 Click **Breaks**.

4 Click **Insert Page Break**.

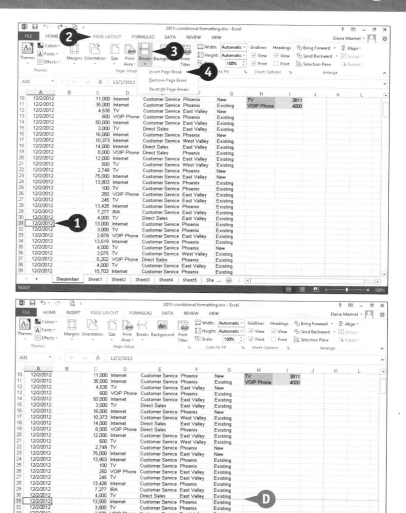

D Excel inserts a solid line representing a user-inserted page break.

How do I print just part of a worksheet?
To print only a part of a worksheet, select the cells that you want to print, click the **Page Layout** tab on the Ribbon, click the **Print Area** button, and then click **Set Print Area**. Then print as usual.

Can I set different margins for different pages that I print?
Yes. Excel assigns the same margins to all pages of a worksheet. If you need different margins for different sections that you plan to print, place each section for which you need different margins on separate worksheets and set each worksheet's margins accordingly.

Move and Copy Worksheets

You can move or copy a worksheet to a new location within the same workbook, or to an entirely different workbook. For example, moving a worksheet is helpful if you insert a new worksheet and the worksheet tab names appear out of order. Or, you might want to move a worksheet that tracks sales for the year to a new workbook so that you can start tracking for a new year.

In addition to moving worksheets, you can copy them. Copying a worksheet is helpful when you plan to make major changes to the worksheet.

Move and Copy Worksheets

1 If you plan to move a worksheet to a different workbook, open both workbooks and select the one containing the worksheet you want to move.

2 Click the tab of the worksheet you want to move or copy to make it the active worksheet.

3 Click the **Home** tab.

4 Click **Format**.

5 Click **Move or Copy Sheet**.

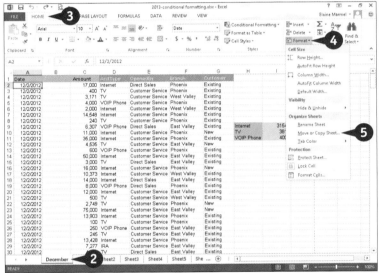

The Move or Copy dialog box appears.

Ⓐ You can click ⯆ to select a workbook for the worksheet.

6 Click the location where you want to place the worksheet that you are moving.

Note: Excel moves or copies sheets in front of the sheet you select.

Ⓑ You can copy a worksheet by selecting **Create a Copy** (☐ changes to ☑).

7 Click **OK**.

Excel moves or copies the worksheet to the new location.

Delete a Worksheet

You can delete a worksheet that you no longer need in your workbook. For example, you might delete a worksheet that contains outdated data or information about a product that your company no longer sells.

When you delete a worksheet, Excel prompts you to confirm the deletion unless the worksheet is blank, in which case it simply deletes the worksheet. As soon as you delete a worksheet, Excel permanently removes it from the workbook file and displays the worksheet behind the one you deleted, unless you deleted the last worksheet. In that case, Excel displays the worksheet preceding the one you deleted.

Delete a Worksheet

① Right-click the worksheet tab.

② Click **Delete**.

Note: You can also click the **Delete** ▼ on the **Home** tab and then click **Delete Sheet**.

If the worksheet is blank, Excel deletes it immediately.

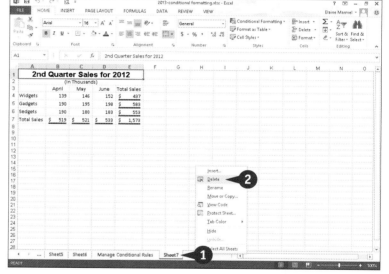

If the worksheet contains any data, Excel prompts you to confirm the deletion.

③ Click **Delete**.

Excel deletes the worksheet.

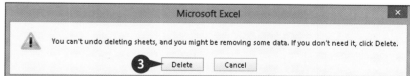

Find and Replace Data

You can search for information in your worksheet and replace it with other information. For example, suppose that you discover that Northwest Valley was entered repeatedly as West Valley. You can search for West Valley and replace it with Northwest Valley. Be aware that Excel finds all occurrences of information as you search to replace it, so be careful when replacing all occurrences at once. You can search and then skip occurrences that you do not want to replace.

You can search an entire worksheet or you can limit the search to a range of cells that you select before you begin the search.

Find and Replace Data

1 Click the **Home** tab.

2 Click **Find & Select**.

3 Click **Replace**.

Ⓐ To simply search for information, click **Find**.

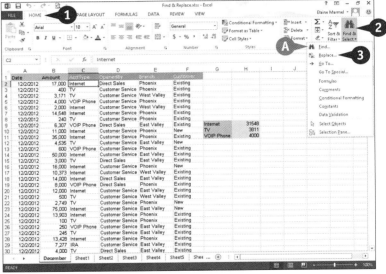

Excel displays the Replace tab of the Find and Replace dialog box.

4 Type the information for which you want to search here.

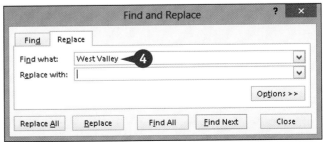

5 Type the information that you want Excel to use to replace the information you typed in Step **4**.

6 Click **Find Next**.

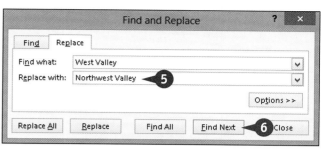

B Excel finds the first occurrence of the data.

7 Click **Replace**.

Excel replaces the information in the cell.

C Excel finds the next occurrence automatically.

8 Repeat Step **7** until you replace all appropriate occurrences.

Note: You can click **Replace All** if you do not want to review each occurrence before Excel replaces it.

Excel displays a message when it cannot find any more occurrences.

9 Click **OK** and then click **Close** in the Find and Replace dialog box.

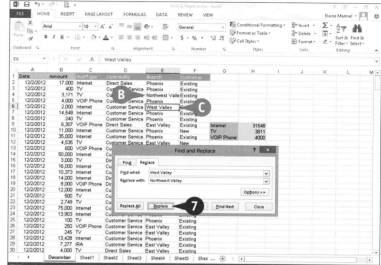

Where can I find detailed search options?
Click the **Options** button in the Find and Replace dialog box to reveal additional search options. For example, you can search by rows or columns, matching data, and more. You can also search for specific formatting or special characters using Format options.

How can I search for and delete data?
In the Find and Replace dialog box, type the text you want to delete in the **Find what** box; leave the **Replace with** box empty. When you click **Replace**, Excel looks for the data and deletes it without adding new data to the worksheet.

Create a Table

You can create a table from any rectangular range of related data in a worksheet. A *table* is a collection of related information. Table rows — called *records* — contain information about one element, and table columns divide the element into *fields*. In a table containing name and address information, a record would contain all the information about one person, and all first names, last names, addresses, and so on would appear in separate columns.

When you create a table, Excel identifies the information in the range as a table and simultaneously formats the table and adds AutoFilter arrows to each column.

Create a Table

1 Set up a range in a worksheet that contains similar information for each row.

2 Click anywhere in the range.

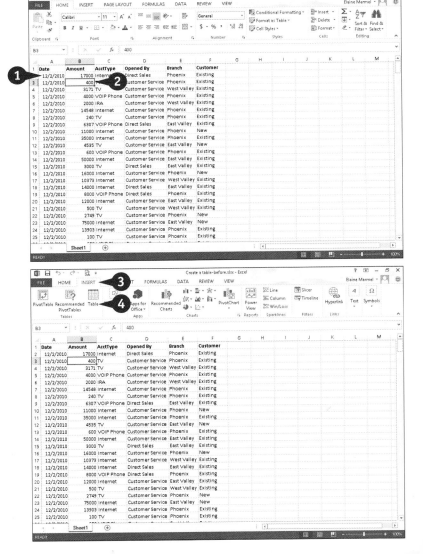

3 Click the **Insert** tab.

4 Click **Table**.

The Create Table dialog box appears, displaying a suggested range for the table.

Ⓐ You can deselect this option (☑ changes to ☐) if labels for each column do *not* appear in Row 1.

Ⓑ You can click ▦ to select a new range for the table boundaries by dragging in the worksheet.

5 Click **OK**.

Excel creates a table and applies a table style to it.

Ⓒ The Table Tools Design tab appears on the Ribbon.

Ⓓ ▼ appears in each column title.

Ⓔ Excel assigns the table a generic name.

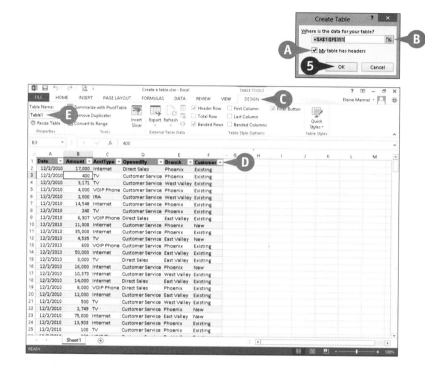

When should I use a table?

If you need to identify common information, such as the largest value in a range, or you need to select records that match a criterion, use a table. Tables make ranges easy to navigate. When you press ⌨Tab with the cell pointer in a table, the cell pointer stays in the table, moving directly to the next cell and to the next table row when you tab from the last column. When you scroll down a table so that the header row disappears, Excel replaces the column letters with the labels that appear in the header row.

Filter or Sort Table Information

When you create a table, Excel automatically adds AutoFilter arrows to each column; you can use these arrows to quickly and easily filter and sort the information in the table.

When you filter a table, you display only those rows that meet conditions you specify, and you specify those conditions by making selections from the AutoFilter lists. You can also use the AutoFilter arrows to sort information in a variety of ways. Excel recognizes the type of data stored in table columns and offers you sorting choices that are appropriate for the type of data.

Filter or Sort Table Information

Filter a Table

1 Click ▼ next to the column heading you want to use for filtering.

Ⓐ Excel displays a list of possible filters for the selected column.

2 Select a filter choice (☐ changes to ☑ or ☑ changes to ☐).

3 Repeat Step **2** until you have selected all of the filters you want to use.

4 Click **OK**.

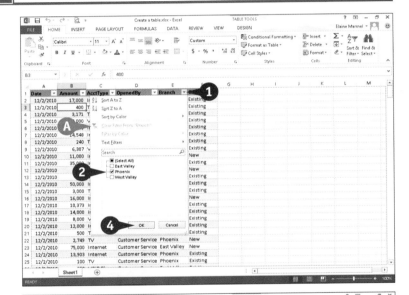

Ⓑ Excel displays only the data meeting the criteria you selected in Step **2**.

Ⓒ The AutoFilter ▼ changes to ◄▼ to indicate the data in the column is filtered.

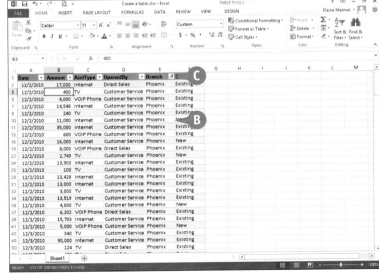

Sort a Table

1 Click ▼ next to the column heading you want to use for sorting.

Ⓓ Excel displays a list of possible sort orders.

2 Click a sort order.

This example sorts from smallest to largest.

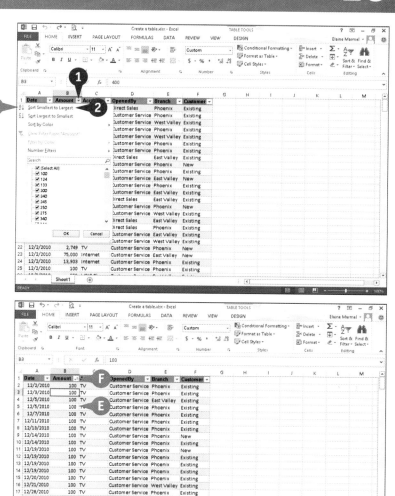

Ⓔ Excel reorders the information.

Ⓕ ▼ changes to ↓↑ to indicate the data in the column is sorted.

How does the Sort by Color option work?
If you apply font colors, cell colors, or both to some cells in the table, you can then sort the table information by the colors you assigned. You can manually assign colors or you can assign colors using Conditional Formatting; see Chapter 9 for details on using Conditional Formatting.

I do not see the AutoFilter down arrow beside my table headings. What should I do?
Click the **Data** tab and then click the **Filter** button. This button toggles on and off the appearance of the AutoFilter ▼ in a table.

Analyze Data Quickly

You can easily analyze data in a variety of ways using the Quick Analysis button. You can apply various types of conditional formatting, create different types of charts, or add miniature graphs called sparklines (see Chapter 12 for details on sparkline charts). You can also sum, average, and count occurrences of data as well as calculate percent of total and running total values. In addition, you can apply a table style and create a variety of different PivotTables.

The choices displayed in each analysis category are not always the same; the ones you see depend on the type of data you select.

Analyze Data Quickly

1 Select a range of data to analyze.

A The Quick Analysis button (🖳) appears.

2 Click 🖳.

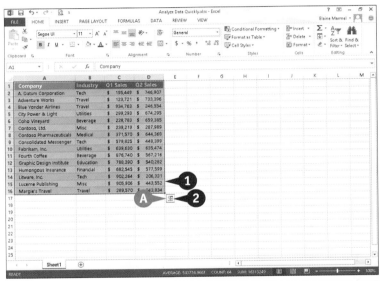

Quick Analysis categories appear.

3 Click each category heading to view the options for that category.

4 Point the mouse at a choice under a category.

B A preview of that analysis choice appears.

Note: For an explanation of the Quick Analysis choices, see the next section, "Understanding Data Analysis Choices."

5 When you find the analysis choice you want to use, click it and Excel creates it.

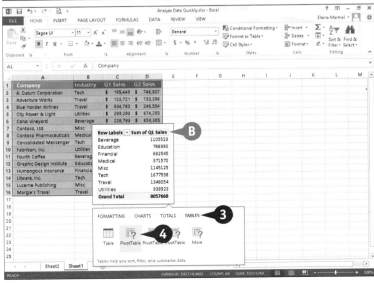

Understanding Data Analysis Choices

The Quick Analysis button offers a variety of ways to analyze selected data. This section provides an overview of the analysis categories and the choices offered in each category.

Formatting

Use formatting to highlight parts of your data. With formatting, you can add data bars, color scales, and icon sets. You can also highlight values that exceed a specified number and cells that contain specified text.

Charts

Pictures often get your point across better than raw numbers. You can quickly chart your data; Excel recommends different chart types, based on the data you select. If you do not see the chart type you want to create, you can click More Charts.

Totals

Using the options in the Totals category, you can easily calculate sums — of both rows and columns — as well as averages, percent of total, and the number of occurrences of the values in the range. You can also insert a running total that grows as you add items to your data.

Tables

Using the choices under the Tables category, you can convert a range to a table, making it easy to filter and sort your data. You can also quickly and easily create a variety of PivotTables — Excel suggests PivotTables you might want to consider and then creates any you might choose.

Sparklines

Sparklines are tiny charts that you can display beside your data that provide trend information for selected data. See Chapter 12 for more information on sparkline charts.

Track and Review Worksheet Changes

If you share your Excel workbooks with others, you can use the program's Track Changes feature to help you keep track of the edits others have made, including formatting changes and data additions or deletions. When you enable tracking, Excel automatically shares the workbook. As you set up tracking options, you can identify the changes you want Excel to highlight. When tracking changes, Excel adds comments that summarize the type of change made. Excel also displays a dark-blue box around a cell that has been changed, and a small blue triangle appears in the upper-left corner of the changed cell.

Track and Review Worksheet Changes

Turn On Tracking

① Click the **Review** tab.

② Click **Track Changes**.

③ Click **Highlight Changes**.

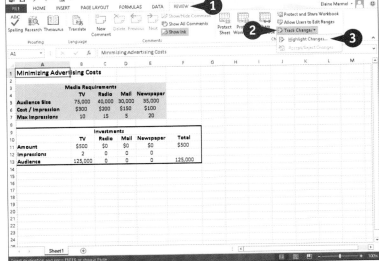

The Highlight Changes dialog box appears.

④ Select **Track changes while editing** (☐ changes to ☑).

Excel automatically shares the workbook file if you have not previously shared it.

Ⓐ You can select options to determine when, by whom, or where Excel tracks changes.

Ⓑ You can leave this option selected to display changes on-screen.

⑤ Click **OK**.

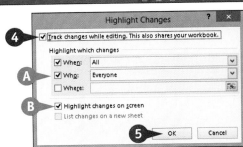

Excel prompts you to save the workbook.

6 Type a filename.

7 Click **Save**.

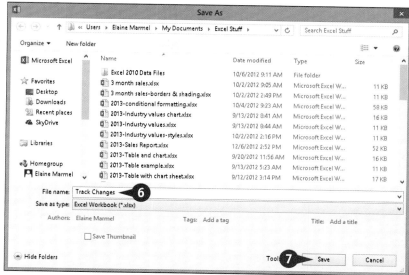

Excel shares the workbook and begins tracking changes to it.

8 Edit your worksheet.

C Excel places a dark-blue box around changed cells, and a small blue triangle appears in the upper-left corner of the changed cell.

D To view details about a change, position the mouse pointer over the highlighted cell.

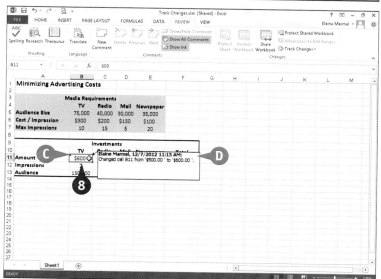

TIP

What does the Share Workbook feature do?
The Share Workbook feature enables multiple users to work in a workbook at the same time. To open this dialog box, click the **Share Workbook** button on the Ribbon. You use the Advanced tab of the Share Workbook dialog box to change various Share Workbook settings, such as when files are updated to reflect one user's changes and what should happen when changes made by two or more users conflict. You can also use this dialog box to remove a user from the shared workbook; click the **Editing** tab to find this option.

continued ▶

Reviewing edits made to a workbook is simple. When you review a workbook in which Excel tracked changes, you can specify whose edits you want to review and what types of edits you want to see. Excel automatically locates and highlights the first edit in a worksheet and gives you the option to accept or reject the edit. After you make your selection, Excel automatically locates and selects the next edit, and so on. You can accept or reject edits one at a time or accept or reject all edits in the worksheet at once.

When you finish reviewing, you can turn off tracking.

Track and Review Worksheet Changes (continued)

Review Changes

1 Click the **Review** tab.

2 Click **Track Changes**.

3 Click **Accept/Reject Changes**.

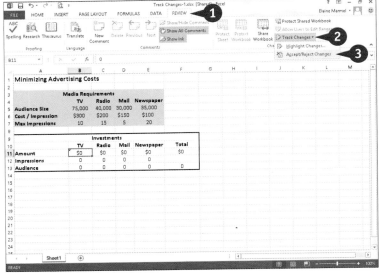

Excel prompts you to save the file.

4 Click **OK**.

The Select Changes to Accept or Reject dialog box appears.

5 Click options for which changes you want to view.

6 Click **OK**.

The Accept or Reject Changes dialog box appears.

7 Specify an action for each edit:

A You can click **Accept** to add the change to the final worksheet.

B You can click **Reject** to reject the change.

C You can click one of these options to accept or reject all of the changes at the same time.

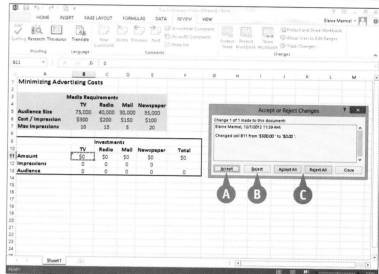

TIP

How can I stop tracking changes?

To turn off Track Changes, follow these steps:

1 Click the **Review** tab.

2 Click the **Track Changes** button.

3 Click **Highlight Changes**.

4 In the Highlight Changes dialog box that appears, deselect **Track changes while editing** (☑ changes to ☐).

5 Click **OK**. A message appears, explaining the consequences of no longer sharing the workbook; click **OK**.

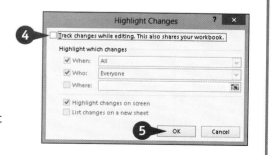

Insert a Comment

You can add comments to your worksheets. You might add a comment to make a note to yourself about a particular cell's contents, or you might include a comment as a note for other users to see. For example, if you share your workbooks with other users, you can use comments to leave feedback about the data without typing directly in the worksheet.

When you add a comment to a cell, Excel displays a small red triangle in the upper-right corner of the cell until you choose to view it. Comments you add are identified with your username.

Insert a Comment

Add a Comment

1. Click the cell to which you want to add a comment.

2. Click the **Review** tab on the Ribbon.

3. Click the **New Comment** button.

   You can also right-click the cell and choose **Insert Comment**.

A comment balloon appears.

4. Type your comment text.

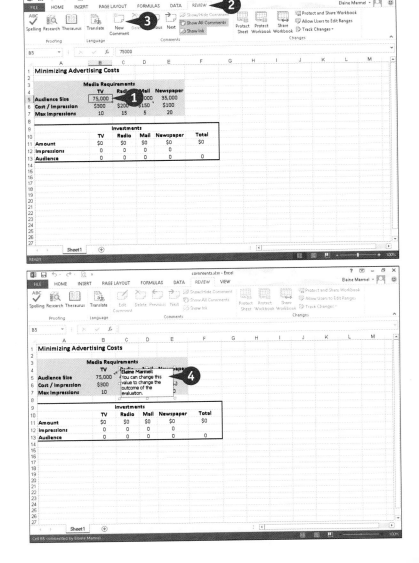

⑤ Click anywhere outside the comment balloon to deselect the comment.

Ⓐ Cells that contain comments display a tiny red triangle in the corner.

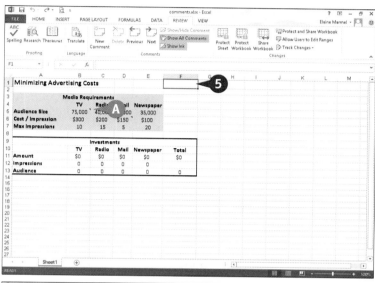

View a Comment

① Position the mouse pointer over the cell.

Ⓑ The comment balloon appears, displaying the comment.

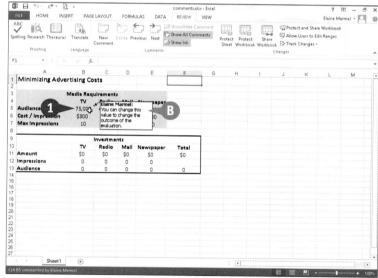

How do I view all the comments in a worksheet?
If a worksheet contains several comments, you can view them one after another by clicking the **Next** button in the Review tab's Comments area. To view a comment you have already seen, click the **Previous** button. Alternatively, display all comments at once by clicking the **Show All Comments** button.

How do I remove a comment?
To remove a comment, right-click the cell containing the comment and choose **Delete Comment** from the shortcut menu that appears. Alternatively, click the cell containing the comment and click the **Delete** button in the Review tab's Comments group.

Understanding Formulas

You can use formulas, which you build using mathematical operators, values, and cell references, to perform all kinds of calculations on your Excel data. For example, you can add the contents of a column of monthly sales totals to determine the cumulative sales total.

If you are new to writing formulas, this section explains the basics of building your own formulas in Excel. You learn about the correct way to structure formulas in Excel, how to reference cell data in your formulas, which mathematical operators are available for your use, and more.

Formula Structure

Ordinarily, when you write a mathematical formula, you write the values and the operators, followed by an equal sign, such as 2+2=. In Excel, formula structure works a bit differently. All Excel formulas begin with an equal sign (=), such as =2+2. The equal sign tells Excel to recognize any subsequent data as a formula rather than as a regular cell entry.

Reference a Cell

Every cell in a worksheet has a unique address, composed of the cell's column letter and row number, and that address appears in the Name box to the left of the Formula bar. Cell B3, for example, identifies the third cell down in column B. Although you can enter specific values in your Excel formulas, you can make your formulas more versatile if you include — that is, *reference* — a cell address instead of the value in that cell. Then, if the data in the cell changes but the formula remains the same, Excel automatically updates the result of the formula.

Cell Ranges

A group of related cells in a worksheet is called a *range*. Excel identifies a range by the cells in the upper-left and lower-right corners of the range, separated by a colon. For example, range A1:B3 includes cells A1, A2, A3, B1, B2, and B3. You can also assign names to ranges to make it easier to identify their contents. Range names must start with a letter, underscore, or backslash, and can include uppercase and lowercase letters. Spaces are not allowed.

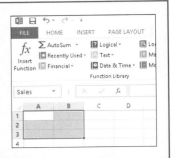

Mathematical Operators

You use mathematical operators in Excel to build formulas. Basic operators include the following:

Operator	Operation
+	Addition
-	Subtraction
*	Multiplication
/	Division
%	Percentage
^	Exponentiation
=	Equal to
<	Less than
<=	Less than or equal to
>	Greater than
>=	Greater than or equal to
<>	Not equal to

Operator Precedence

Excel performs operations from left to right, but gives some operators precedence over others, following the rules you learned in high school math:

Order	Operation
First	All operations enclosed in parentheses
Second	Exponential operations
Third	Multiplication and division
Fourth	Addition and subtraction

When you are creating equations, the order of operations determines the results. For example, suppose you want to determine the average of values in cells A2, B2, and C2. If you enter the equation =A2+B2+C2/3, Excel first divides the value in cell C2 by 3, and then adds that result to A2+B2 — producing the wrong answer. The correct way to write the formula is =(A2+B2+C2)/3. By enclosing the values in parentheses, you are telling Excel to perform the addition operations in the parentheses before dividing the sum by 3.

Reference Operators

You can use Excel's reference operators to control how a formula groups cells and ranges to perform calculations. For example, if your formula needs to include the cell range D2:D10 and cell E10, you can instruct Excel to evaluate all the data contained in these cells using a reference operator. Your formula might look like this: =SUM(D2:D10,E10).

Operator	Example	Operation
:	=SUM(D3:E12)	Range operator. Evaluates the reference as a single reference, including all of the cells in the range from both corners of the reference.
,	=SUM(D3:E12,F3)	Union operator. Evaluates the two references as a single reference.
[space]	=SUM(D3:D20 D10:E15)	Intersect operator. Evaluates the cells common to both references.
[space]	=SUM(Totals Sales)	Intersect operator. Evaluates the intersecting cell or cells of the column labeled Totals and the row labeled Sales.

Create a Formula

You can write a formula to perform a calculation on data in your worksheet. In Excel, all formulas begin with an equal sign (=) and contain the values or cell references to the cells that contain the relevant values. For example, the formula for adding the contents of cells C3 and C4 together is =C3+C4. You create formulas in the Formula bar; formula results appear in the cell to which you assign a formula.

Note that, in addition to referring to cells in the current worksheet, you can also build formulas that refer to cells in other worksheets.

Create a Formula

1 Click the cell where you want to place a formula.

2 Type =.

A Excel displays the formula in the Formula bar and in the active cell.

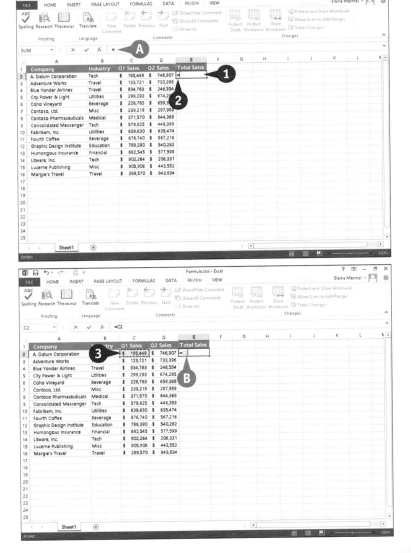

3 Click the first cell that you want to include in the formula.

B Excel inserts the cell reference into the formula.

④ Type an operator for the formula.

⑤ Click the next cell that you want to include in the formula.

Ⓒ Excel inserts the cell reference into the formula.

⑥ Repeat Steps **4** and **5** until all the necessary cells and operators have been added.

⑦ Press Enter.

Ⓓ You can also click **Enter** (✓) on the Formula bar to accept the formula.

Ⓔ You can click **Cancel** (✕) to cancel the formula.

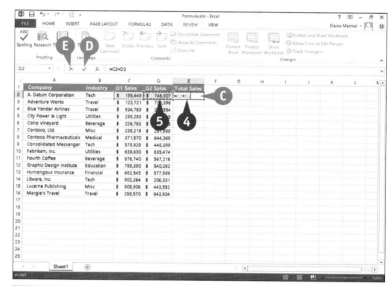

Ⓕ The result of the formula appears in the cell.

Ⓖ The formula appears in the Formula bar; you can view it by clicking the cell containing the formula.

Note: If you change a value in a cell referenced in your formula, Excel automatically updates the formula result to reflect the change.

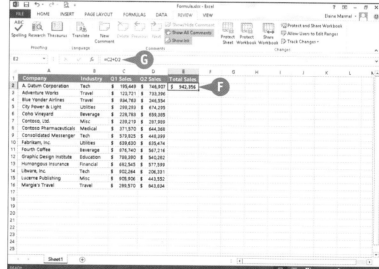

TIPS

How do I edit a formula?
To edit a formula, click in the cell containing the formula and make any corrections in the Formula bar. Alternatively, double-click in the cell to make edits to the formula from within the cell. When finished, press Enter or click **Enter** (✓) on the Formula bar.

How do I reference cells in other worksheets?
To reference a cell in another worksheet, specify the worksheet name followed by an exclamation mark and then the cell address (for example, Sheet2!D12 or Sales!D12). If the worksheet name includes spaces, enclose the sheet name in single quote marks, as in 'Sales Totals'!D12.

Apply Absolute and Relative Cell References

By default, Excel uses relative cell referencing. If you copy a formula containing a relative cell reference to a new location, Excel adjusts the cell addresses in that formula to refer to the cells at the formula's new location. For example, if you enter, in cell B8, the formula =B5+B6 and then you copy that formula to cell C8, Excel adjusts the formula to =C5+C6.

When a formula must always refer to the value in a particular cell, use an absolute cell reference. Absolute references are preceded with dollar signs. If your formula must always refer to the value in cell D2, enter D2 in the formula.

Apply Absolute and Relative Cell References

Copy Relative References

1 Enter the formula.

2 Click the cell containing the formula you want to copy.

Ⓐ In the Formula bar, the formula appears with a relative cell reference.

3 Click the **Home** tab.

4 Click **Copy** (🗎).

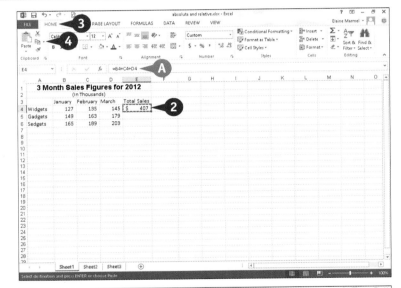

5 Select the cells where you want the formula to appear.

6 Click **Paste**.

Ⓑ Excel copies the formula to the selected cells.

Ⓒ The adjusted formula appears in the Formula bar and in the selected cells.

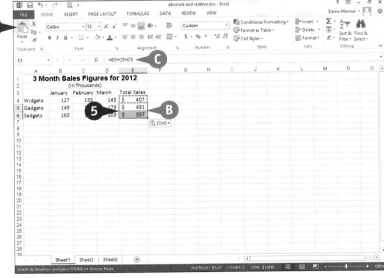

Copy Absolute References

1 Enter the formula, including dollar signs ($) for absolute addresses as needed.

2 Click the cell containing the formula you want to copy.

D In the Formula bar, the formula appears with an absolute cell reference.

3 Click the **Home** tab.

4 Click **Copy** (📋).

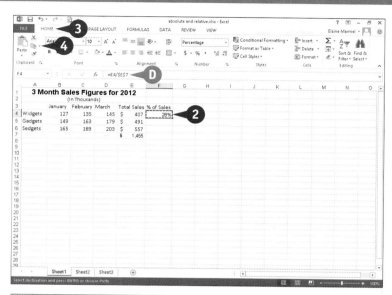

5 Select the cells where you want the formula to appear.

6 Click **Paste**.

E Excel copies the formula to the selected cells.

F The formula in the selected cells adjusts only relative cell references; absolute cell references remain unchanged.

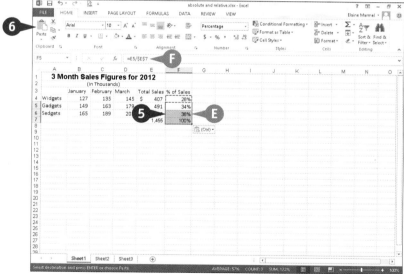

TIP

When would I use absolute cell referencing?
Use absolute cell referencing to always refer to the same cell in a worksheet. For example, suppose your worksheet contains pricing information that refers to a discount rate in cell G10. When you create a formula that involves the discount rate, that formula must always reference cell G10, even if you move or copy the formula to another cell. In this case, use G10. You can also combine absolute and relative references, creating *mixed references* that allow either the row or column to change while the other remains static if you copy the formula.

Understanding Functions

If you are looking for a speedier way to enter formulas, you can use any one of a wide variety of functions. Functions are ready-made formulas that perform a series of operations on a specified range of values. Excel offers more than 300 functions, grouped into 13 categories, that you can use to perform various types of calculations. Functions use arguments to identify the cells that contain the data you want to use in your calculations. Functions can refer to individual cells or to ranges of cells.

Function Elements

All functions must start with an equal sign (=). Functions are distinct in that each one has a name. For example, the function that sums data is called SUM, and the function for averaging values is called AVERAGE. You can create functions by typing them directly into your worksheet cells or the Formula bar; alternatively, you can use the Insert Function dialog box to select and apply functions to your data.

Construct an Argument

Functions use arguments to indicate which cells contain the values you want to calculate. Arguments are enclosed in parentheses. When applying a function to individual cells in a worksheet, you can use a comma to separate the cell addresses, as in =SUM(A5,C5,F5). When applying a function to a range of cells, you can use a colon to designate the first and last cells in the range, as in =SUM(B4:G4). If your range has a name, you can insert the name, as in =SUM(Sales).

Types of Functions

Excel groups functions into 13 categories, not including functions installed with Excel add-in programs:

Category	Description
Financial	Includes functions for calculating loans, principal, interest, yield, and depreciation.
Date & Time	Includes functions for calculating dates, times, and minutes.
Math & Trig	Includes a wide variety of functions for calculations of all types.
Statistical	Includes functions for calculating averages, probabilities, rankings, trends, and more.
Lookup & Reference	Includes functions that enable you to locate references or specific values in your worksheets.
Database	Includes functions for counting, adding, and filtering database items.
Text	Includes text-based functions to search and replace data and other text tasks.
Logical	Includes functions for logical conjectures, such as if-then statements.
Information	Includes functions for testing your data.
Engineering	Offers many kinds of functions for engineering calculations.
Cube	Enables Excel to fetch data from SQL Server Analysis Services, such as members, sets, aggregated values, properties, and KPIs.
Compatibility	Use these functions to keep your workbook compatible with earlier versions of Excel.
Web	Use these functions when you work with web pages, services, or XML content.

Common Functions

The following table lists some of the more popular Excel functions that you might use with your own spreadsheet work.

Function	Category	Description	Syntax
SUM	Math & Trig	Adds values	=SUM(number1,number2,...)
ROUND	Math & Trig	Rounds a number to a specified number of digits	=ROUND(number,number_digits)
ROUNDDOWN	Math & Trig	Rounds a number down	=ROUNDDOWN(number,number_digits)
INT	Math & Trig	Rounds down to the nearest integer	=INT(number)
COUNT	Statistical	Counts the number of cells in a range that contain data	=COUNT(value1,value2,...)
AVERAGE	Statistical	Averages a series of arguments	=AVERAGE(number1,number2,...)
MIN	Statistical	Returns the smallest value in a series	=MIN(number1,number2,...)
MAX	Statistical	Returns the largest value in a series	=MAX(number1,number2,...)
MEDIAN	Statistical	Returns the middle value in a series	=MEDIAN(number1,number2,...)
PMT	Financial	Finds the periodic payment for a fixed loan	=PMT(interest_rate,number_of_periods,present_value,future_value,type)
RATE	Financial	Returns an interest rate	=RATE(number_of_periods,payment,present_value,future_value,type,guess)
TODAY	Date & Time	Returns the current date	=TODAY()
IF	Logical	Returns one of two results that you specify based on whether the value is true or false	=IF(logical_text,value_if_true,value_if_false)
AND	Logical	Returns true if all of the arguments are true, and false if any argument is false	=AND(logical1,logical2,...)
OR	Logical	Returns true if any argument is true, and false if all arguments are false	=OR(logical1,logical2,...)

Apply a Function

You can use functions to speed up your Excel calculations. *Functions* are ready-made formulas that perform a series of operations on a specified range of values.

You use the Insert Function dialog box, which acts like a wizard, to look for a particular function from among Excel's 300-plus available functions and to guide you through successfully entering the function. After you select your function, the Function Arguments dialog box opens to help you build the formula by describing the arguments you need for the function you chose. Functions use arguments to indicate that the cells contain the data you want to use in your calculation.

Apply a Function

1 Click the cell in which you want to store the function.

2 Click the **Formulas** tab.

3 Click the **Insert Function** button.

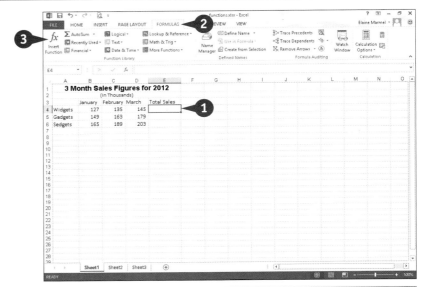

A Excel inserts an equal sign to indicate that a formula follows.

Excel displays the Insert Function dialog box.

4 Type a description of the function you need here.

5 Click **Go**.

B A list of suggested functions appears.

6 Click the function that you want to apply.

C A description of the selected function appears here.

7 Click **OK**.

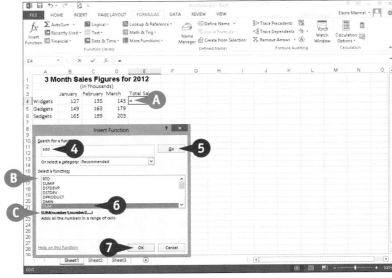

202

The Function Arguments dialog box appears.

8 Select the cells for each argument required by the function.

In the worksheet, Excel adds the cells as the argument to the function.

D Additional information about the function appears here.

9 When you finish constructing the arguments, click **OK**.

E Excel displays the function results in the cell.

F The function appears in the Formula bar.

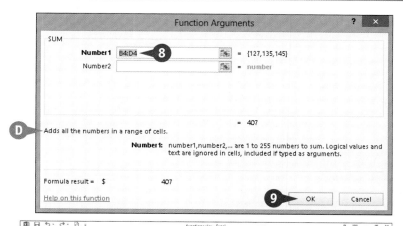

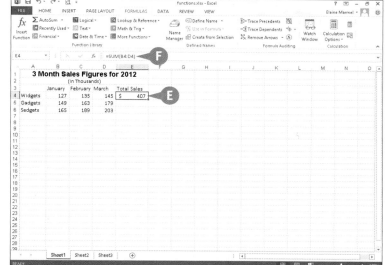

TIPS

Can I edit a function?
Yes. Click the cell containing the function, click the **Formulas** tab, and then click the **Insert Function** button. Excel displays the function's Function Arguments dialog box, where you can change the cell references or values as needed. You can also edit directly in the cell.

How can I find help with a particular function?
Click the **Help on this function** link in either the Insert Function or Function Arguments dialog box to find out more about the function. The function help includes an example of the function being used and tips about using the function.

Total Cells with AutoSum

O ne of the most popular Excel functions is the AutoSum function. AutoSum automatically totals the contents of cells. For example, you can quickly total a column of sales figures. One way to use AutoSum is to select a cell and let the function guess which surrounding cells you want to total. Alternatively, you can specify exactly which cells to sum.

In addition to using AutoSum to total cells, you can simply select a series of cells in your worksheet; Excel displays the total of the cells' contents in the status bar, along with the number of cells you selected and an average of their values.

Total Cells with AutoSum

Using AutoSum to Total Cells

1 Click the cell in which you want to store a total.

2 Click the **Formulas** tab.

3 Click the **AutoSum** button.

A If you click the **AutoSum** ▼, you can select other common functions, such as Average or Max.

You can also click the **AutoSum** button (Σ ▼) on the Home tab.

B AutoSum generates a formula to total the adjacent cells.

4 Press **Enter** or click **Enter** (✓).

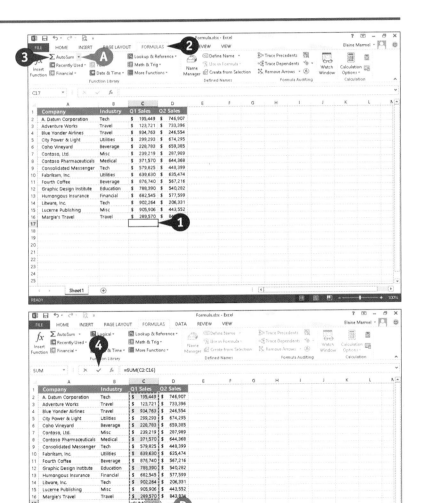

C Excel displays the result in the cell.

D You can click the cell to see the function in the Formula bar.

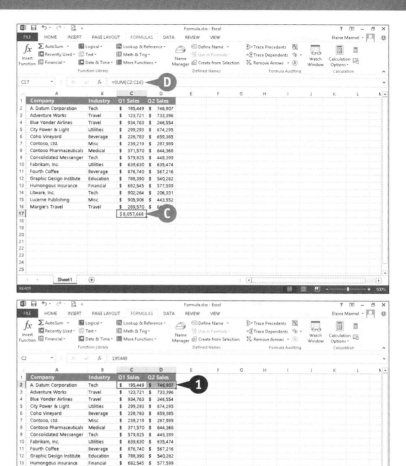

Total Cells without Applying a Function

1 Click a group of cells whose values you want to total.

Note: To sum noncontiguous cells, press and hold Ctrl while clicking the cells.

E Excel adds the contents of the cells, displaying the sum in the status bar along the bottom of the program window.

F Excel also counts the number of cells you have selected.

G Excel also displays an average of the values in the selected cells.

TIPS

Can I select a different range of cells to sum?
Yes. AutoSum takes its best guess when determining which cells to total. If it guesses wrong, simply click the cells you want to add together before pressing Enter or clicking Enter (✓).

Why do I see pound signs (#) in a cell that contains a SUM function?
Excel displays pound signs in any cell — not just cells containing formulas or functions — when the cell's column is not wide enough to display the contents of the cell, including the cell's formatting. Widen the column to correct the problem; see Chapter 9 for details.

Audit a Worksheet for Errors

On occasion, you may see an error message, such as #DIV/0! or #NAME?, in your Excel worksheet. If you do, you should double-check your formula references to ensure that you included the correct cells. Locating the source of an error can be difficult, however, especially in larger worksheets. Fortunately, if an error occurs in your worksheet, you can use Excel's Formula Auditing tools — namely, Error Checking and Trace Error — to examine and correct formula errors. For more information on types of errors and how to resolve them, see the table in the tip.

Audit a Worksheet for Errors

Apply Error Checking

1 Click the **Formulas** tab.

2 Click the **Error Checking** button ( ).

A Excel displays the Error Checking dialog box and highlights the first cell containing an error.

3 To fix the error, click **Edit in Formula Bar**.

B To find help with an error, you can click here to open the help files.

C To ignore the error, you can click **Ignore Error**.

D You can click **Previous** and **Next** to scroll through all of the errors on the worksheet.

4 Make edits to the cell references in the Formula bar or in the worksheet.

5 Click **Resume**.

When the error check is complete, a message box appears.

6 Click **OK**.

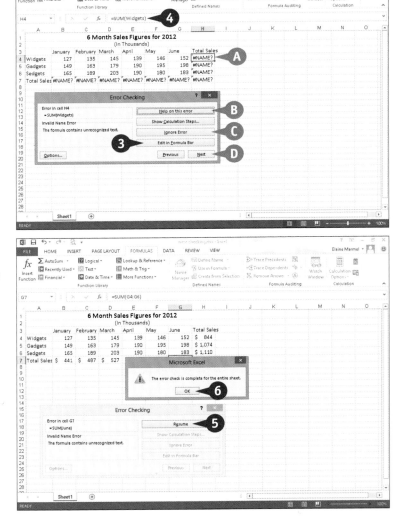

Trace Errors

1 Click the cell containing the formula or function error that you want to trace.

2 Click the **Formulas** tab.

3 Click the **Error Checking** ▼ .

4 Click **Trace Error**.

E Excel displays trace lines from the current cell to any cells referenced in the formula.

You can make changes to the cell contents or changes to the formula to correct the error.

F You can click **Remove Arrows** to turn off the trace lines.

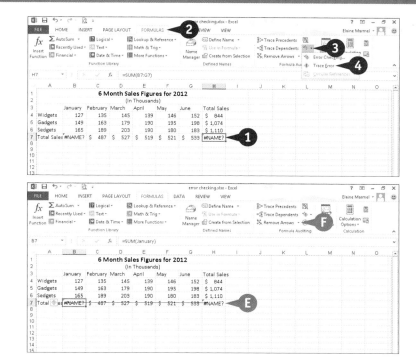

TIP

What kinds of error messages does Excel display for formula errors?

Different types of error values appear in cells when an error occurs:

Error	Problem	Solution
######	The cell is not wide enough to contain the value	Increase the column width
#DIV/0!	Dividing by zero	Edit the cell reference or value of the denominator
#N/A	Value is not available	Ensure that the formula references the correct value
#NAME?	Does not recognize text in a formula	Ensure that the name referenced is correct
#NULL!	Specifies two areas that do not intersect	Check for an incorrect range operator or correct the intersection problem
#NUM!	Invalid numeric value	Check the function for an unacceptable argument
#REF!	Invalid cell reference	Correct cell references
#VALUE!	Wrong type of argument or operand	Double-check arguments and operands

Add a Watch Window

Suppose you have a formula at the bottom of your worksheet that references cells at the top of your worksheet. Further suppose that you want to see the effects on the formula as you change cells to which the formula refers. You can create a watch window to display the cell containing the formula, no matter where you scroll. You can also use a watch window to view cells in other worksheets or in a linked workbook. You can position your watch window anywhere on-screen or dock the window to appear with the toolbars at the top of the program window.

Add a Watch Window

1 Click the **Formulas** tab on the Ribbon.

2 Click **Watch Window**.

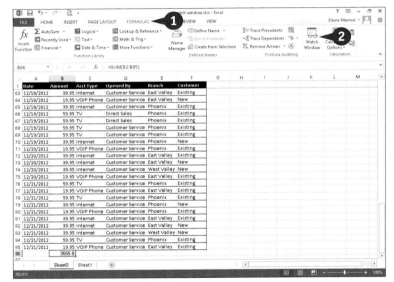

The Watch Window opens.

3 Click **Add Watch**.

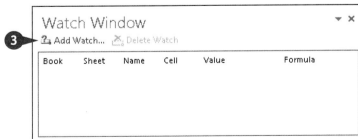

The Add Watch dialog box appears.

4 Select the cell or range that you want to watch.

5 Click **Add**.

Note: You can add multiple cells to the watch window.

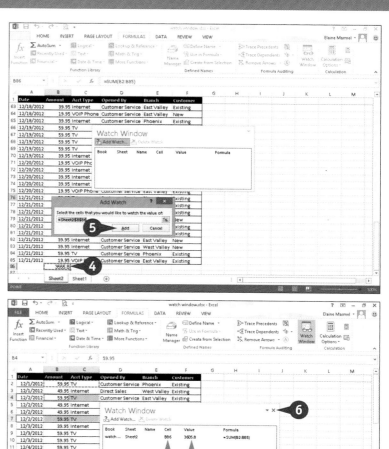

A Excel adds the cells to the watch window, including any values or formulas within the cells.

B If you scroll away from the cells included in the watch window, the watch window continues to display their contents. You can make changes and the watch window displays the updated value. In this example, Rows 4 and 7 changed, and so did the value in the watch window.

Note: To select the original cell, you can double-click anywhere on the line in the watch window.

6 Click the **Close** button (×) to close the watch window.

TIPS

How do I remove and add cells in the watch window?
To remove a cell from the watch window, click anywhere on the line for the cell in the watch window and then click the **Delete Watch** button. To add more cells, click the **Add Watch** button and select the cell that you want to add.

How can I move and resize the watch window?
To move the watch window, click and drag the window's title bar. To resize the columns within the watch window, position the mouse pointer over a column (⇩ changes to ↔), and drag to resize the column.

Create a Chart

You can quickly convert your spreadsheet data into easy-to-read charts. You can create column, line, pie, bar, area, scatter, stock, surface, doughnut, bubble, and radar charts. Excel even recommends the type of chart that works best for your data. If you do not like Excel's recommendations, you can select the chart of your choice.

You can create charts using the Ribbon or using the Quick Analysis button. After you create a chart, you can use buttons beside the chart or on the Chart Tools tabs to fine-tune the chart to best display and explain the data.

Create a Chart

Using the Ribbon

1. Select the range of data that you want to chart.

   You can include any headings and labels, but do not include subtotals or totals.

2. Click the **Insert** tab.

3. Click **Recommended Charts**.

   The Insert Chart dialog box appears.

4. Scroll through the recommended charts.

   A A preview of your data appears.

   B If you do not see the chart you want to use, click **All Charts**.

5. Click a chart type.

6. Click **OK**.

   C Excel creates a chart and places it in the worksheet.

   D Whenever you select the chart, Chart Tools tabs appear on the Ribbon.

   E You can use the **Chart Elements** (+), **Chart Styles** (/), and **Chart Filters** (▼) buttons to add chart elements like axis titles, customize the look of your chart, or change the data in the chart.

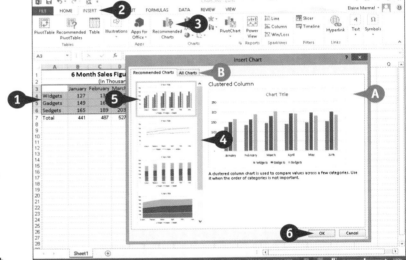

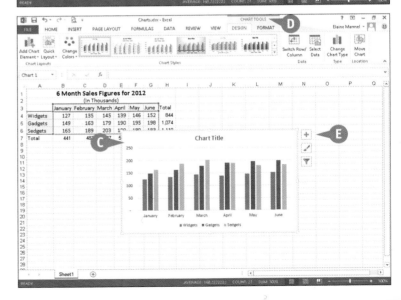

Using the Quick Analysis Button

1 Select the range of data that you want to chart.

You can include any headings and labels, but do not include subtotals or totals.

2 Click the **Quick Analysis** button (⬚).

3 From the categories that appear, click **Charts**.

4 Slide the mouse over a recommended chart type.

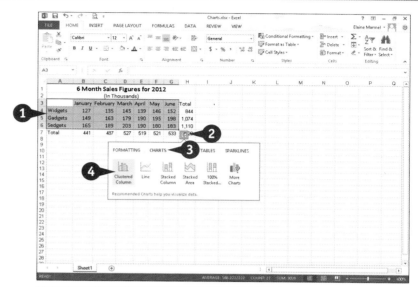

F Excel displays a preview of your data using that chart type.

G If you do not see the chart you want to use, click **More Charts**.

5 Click a chart type to insert it.

Excel inserts the chart type you selected.

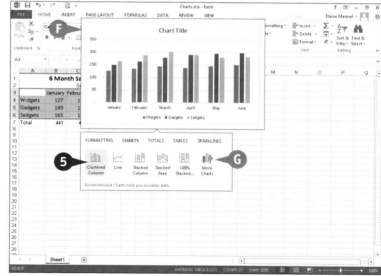

TIPS

Can I select noncontiguous data to include in a chart?
Yes. To select noncontiguous cells and ranges, select the first cell or range and then press and hold Ctrl while selecting additional cells and ranges.

In my column chart, I want bars for the elements appearing in the legend; is there an easy way to make that happen?
Yes. The legend displays the row headings in your selected data, while the bars represent the column headings. So, switch the rows and columns in the chart. Click the chart to select it. Then, click the **Chart Tools Design** tab and, in the Data group, click **Switch Row/Column**.

Move and Resize Charts

After creating a chart, you may decide that it would look better if it were a different size or located elsewhere on the worksheet. For example, you may want to reposition the chart at the bottom of the worksheet or make the chart larger so it is easier to read.

Moving or resizing a chart is like moving or resizing any other type of Office object. When you select a chart, handles appear around that chart; you use these handles to make the chart larger or smaller. Moving the chart is a matter of selecting it and then dragging it to the desired location.

Move and Resize Charts

Resize a Chart

1. Click any edge of the chart.

Ⓐ Excel selects the chart and surrounds it with handles; ✛ changes to ⇱ and ⊕, ✎, and ▼ appear.

2. Position the mouse pointer over a handle (⇱ changes to ⬉, ↕, ⬈, or ⇔).

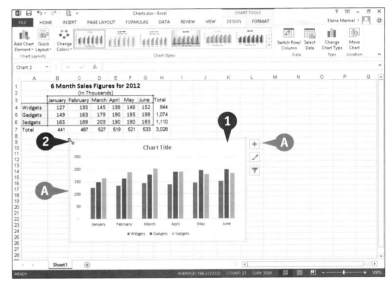

3. Click and drag a handle to resize the chart.

Ⓑ A frame appears, representing the chart as you resize it on the worksheet.

Ⓒ ⬉, ↕, ⬈, or ⇔ changes to +.

4. Release the mouse button.

Excel resizes the chart.

Move a Chart

1 Click any edge of the chart.

D Excel selects the chart and surrounds it with handles.

E ✛ changes to ‡.

F ⊞ , ✎ , and ▼ appear.

2 Position the mouse pointer over an empty area of the chart.

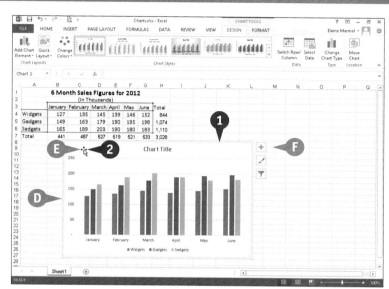

3 Click and drag the chart to a new location on the worksheet.

G ‡ changes to ✛.

⊞ , ✎ , and ▼ disappear.

4 Release the mouse button.

Excel moves the chart.

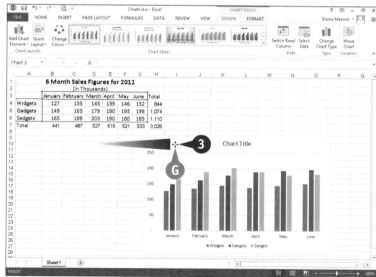

TIP

Can I delete a chart or move it to its own worksheet?
Yes. To delete a chart, right-click its edge and press
Delete . To move a chart to its own worksheet,
right-click its edge and click **Move Chart** to display
the Move Chart dialog box. Select **New sheet** (**A**)
(○ changes to ◉) and click **OK** (**B**). Excel adds a
new worksheet called Chart1 to the workbook and
places the chart in that worksheet.

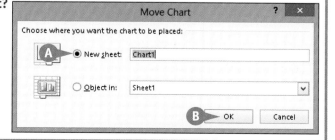

213

Change the Chart Type

Suppose you create a column chart but then realize your data would be better presented in a line chart. You can easily change the chart type. Excel recommends chart types that are suitable for your data, but you are not limited to its recommendations.

You select a new chart type using Chart Tools tabs on the Ribbon. To make these tabs available, you select the chart. You click the edge of the chart to select the entire chart or select individual elements of the chart by clicking them. As long as you click anywhere inside the chart, Chart Tools tabs appear on the Ribbon.

Change the Chart Type

1 Click an edge of the chart to select it.

A Handles surround the chart.

2 Click the **Design** tab.

3 Click **Change Chart Type**.

The Change Chart Type dialog box appears.

B To view Excel's recommendations for chart types for your data, click here.

4 Click a chart type.

5 Click a chart variation.

C A preview of your chart appears here; point the mouse at the preview to enlarge it.

6 Click **OK**.

D Excel changes the chart to the chart type that you selected.

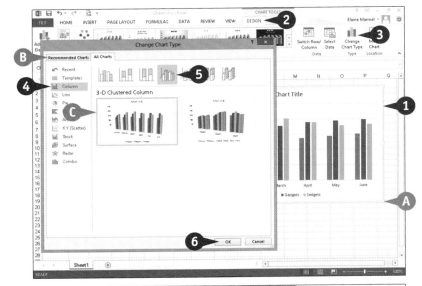

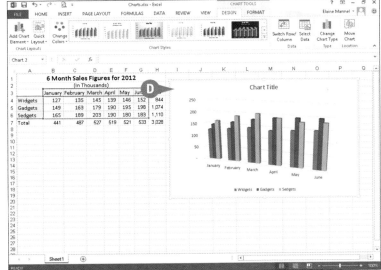

Change the Chart Style

You can change the chart style to change the appearance of a chart. You can choose from a wide variety of preset styles to find just the look you want. For example, you might prefer a brighter color scheme for the chart to make it stand out, or you might want the elements of the chart, such as the columns or pie slices, to appear three-dimensional.

You can access various preset chart styles from the Design tab or from the Chart Styles button that appears along the right edge of a selected chart. To select a chart, click along its edge.

Change the Chart Style

① Click an edge of the chart to select it.

Ⓐ Handles surround the chart.

② Click 🖊.

Ⓑ The Chart Styles pane appears.

③ Click **Style** to view available chart styles.

Ⓒ You can click 🔺 and 🔻 to scroll through available styles.

You can point the mouse at a style to preview it.

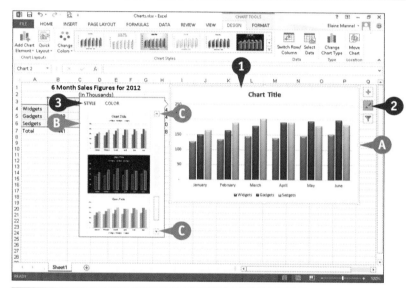

④ Click a new style.

Excel applies the new style to your chart.

⑤ Click **Color** to view color schemes for your chart.

⑥ Click a color scheme.

Ⓓ Excel applies the new color scheme to your chart.

Ⓔ You can click 🖊 again to close the Chart Styles pane.

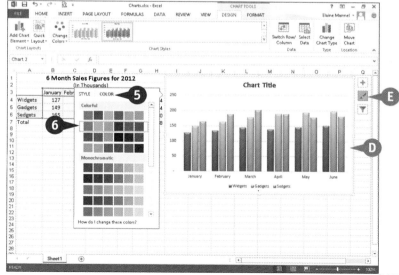

Change the Chart Layout

You can customize your chart's appearance by using Excel's preset chart-layout options to change the chart layout. Changing the chart layout changes how Excel positions chart elements. For example, you may prefer to show a legend on the side of the chart rather than on the bottom. Or, you might want a chart title to appear above the chart rather than below it. Or, you might not want to display a chart title at all.

The various preset chart layouts are available on the Design tab. To display this tab, select the chart whose layout you want to change by clicking any chart edge.

Change the Chart Layout

1 Click an edge of the chart to select it.

A Handles surround the chart.

2 Click the **Design** tab.

3 Click **Quick Layout**.

B A palette of layouts appears.

You can point the mouse at each layout to preview its appearance.

4 Click a layout.

C Excel applies the new layout to the existing chart.

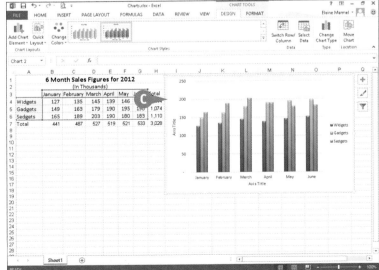

Add Chart Elements

You can add a variety of elements to your chart. For example, you can include or exclude axes, axis titles, a chart title, data labels, a data table, error bars, gridlines, a legend, and a trendline. Remember that displaying too many elements on a chart can make it hard to understand. Because a picture — a chart, in this case — is supposed to be worth 1,000 words, making a chart difficult to understand by including too many elements defeats the purpose of presenting the chart. This section shows you how to add axis titles; you use the same technique to add any chart element.

Add Chart Elements

1 Click an edge of the chart to select it.

A Handles surround the chart.

2 Click ⊞.

B The Chart Elements pane appears.

You can point the mouse at an element to preview it.

3 Select a new element to add or deselect an element to remove (☐ changes to ☑ or ☑ changes to ☐).

You can click ⊞ again to close the Chart Elements pane.

C Excel applies the change to your chart.

Note: If you add any type of title, Excel inserts dummy text representing the title.

D You can change the dummy title text. Click the title box to select it. Click again inside the box and select the dummy text. Then, type your replacement title.

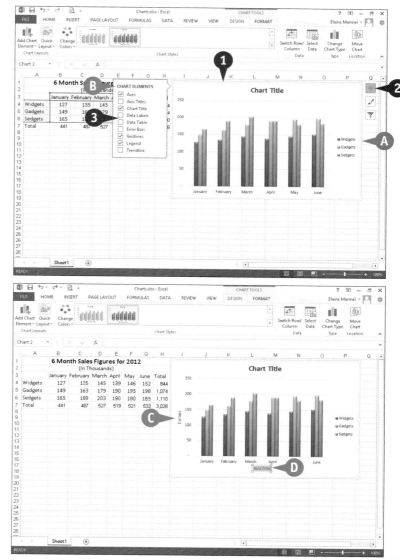

Format Chart Objects

Y ou can change the formatting of any element, or *object*, in a chart, such as the background pattern for the plot area or the color of a data series. You use the Format pane to apply formatting to selected objects. The pane appears automatically when you format an object.

The available settings in the Format pane change, depending on the object you select. This section shows you how to add a fill color to the chart area, which is the area behind your data in the chart. You can apply these same techniques to format other chart objects.

Format Chart Objects

1 Click the object that you want to format.

To add a fill to the chart area, select the chart by clicking an edge of the chart, as shown in this example.

2 Click the **Format** tab.

3 Click **Format Selection**.

A The Format pane appears.

Note: The options available in the pane change, depending on the object you selected in Step **1**.

B You can click ▼ to display other chart elements to format.

C You can click here to display chart area fill, effects, or size and properties formatting you can apply.

D You can click here to apply a variety of text formatting to the chart area.

4 Click the type of formatting that you want to change.

E Excel displays the effect.

5 Change any format settings.

6 Click × to close the Format pane.

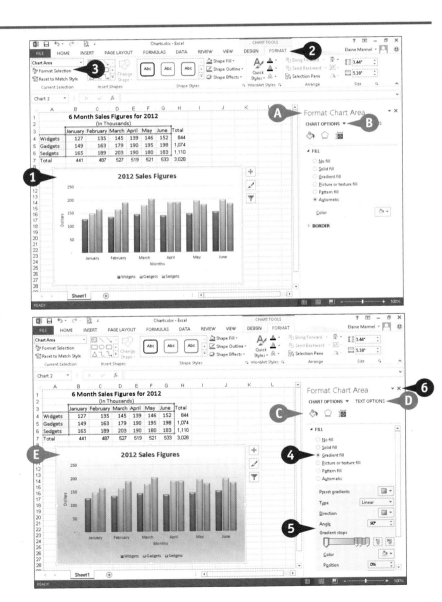

Change the Chart Data

You can quickly and easily filter the information displayed in your chart. Whenever you change data referenced in your chart, Excel automatically updates the chart to reflect your changes. But suppose that your chart shows several months of sales data for several products and you want to focus on one month only. There is no need to create a new chart; you can simply filter your existing chart. Similarly, you can display sales data for only certain products instead of all products, again, without creating a new chart. When you are ready, you can easily redisplay all data in your chart.

Change the Chart Data

1 Click an edge of the chart that you want to change to select it.

Ⓐ Handles surround the chart.

2 Click 🔽.

Ⓑ The Filter pane appears.

You can point the mouse at an element to preview it.

3 Deselect a series or category that you want to remove (☑ changes to ☐).

4 Repeat Step **3** as necessary to remove additional series or categories.

5 Click **Apply**.

Ⓒ Excel applies the change to your chart.

6 Click 🔽 again to close the Filter pane.

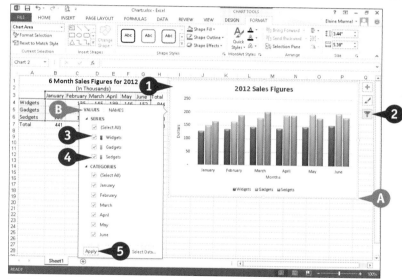

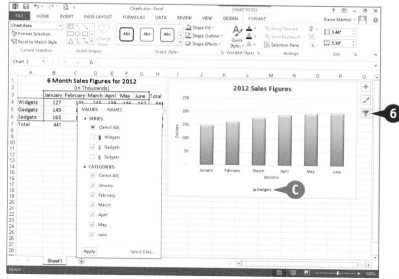

Using Sparklines to View Data Trends

You can place a micro-chart of data in a single cell in your worksheet. Excel refers to these micro-charts as *sparkline* charts.

You can create three types of sparkline charts: line, column, or win/loss. All three show you, at a glance, trend information for a range of data you select. Excel places a sparkline chart in the cell immediately beside the cells you use to create the chart; if that cell contains data, Excel places the chart on top of the data, obscuring it but not deleting it. You can then move the sparkline chart to any cell you choose.

Using Sparklines to View Data Trends

Insert a Sparkline Chart

Note: To avoid later moving a sparkline chart, make sure an empty cell appears beside the cells you intend to chart.

1 Select the cells containing the data you want to include in the sparkline chart.

2 Click 📑 to display Quick Analysis categories.

3 Click **Sparklines**.

4 Click the type of sparkline chart you want to insert.

This example creates a column sparkline chart.

A Excel inserts the sparkline chart in the cell immediately next to the selected cells.

B The Sparkline Tools tab appears.

C Any data in the cell containing the sparkline becomes obscured but remains in the worksheet, as you can see in the Formula bar.

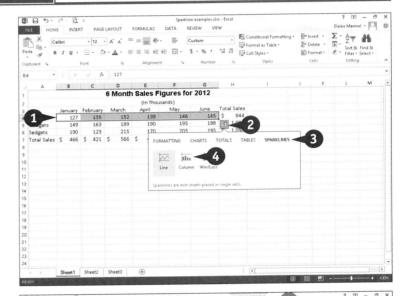

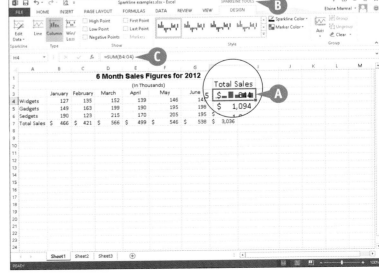

Move a Sparkline Chart

1 Click the cell containing a sparkline chart that you want to move.

2 Click the **Design** tab.

3 Click **Edit Data**.

The Edit Sparklines dialog box appears.

4 Select a new location in the worksheet for the sparkline chart(s).

Note: The number of cells you select at the new location must match the number of sparklines you want to move.

5 Click **OK**.

D Excel moves the sparkline chart(s).

E Any previously obscured data becomes visible.

Note: To delete a sparkline chart, right-click it and point to Sparklines. Then, click **Clear Selected Sparklines** or **Clear Selected Sparkline Groups**.

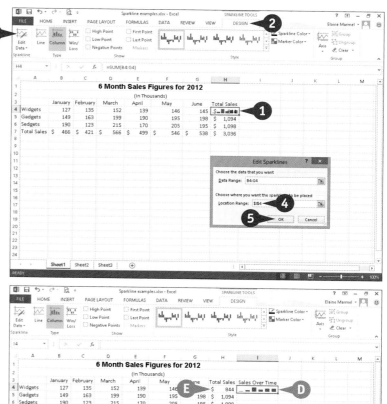

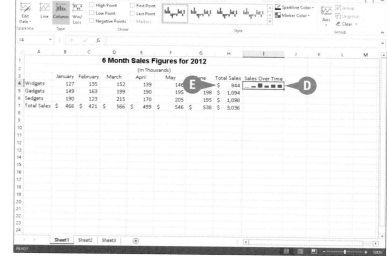

TIPS

Can I create multiple sparkline charts simultaneously?
Yes. You can select data on multiple rows; Excel creates a sparkline chart for each row and treats the sparkline charts as a group; for example, if you change the chart type of one sparkline, Excel changes the group.

Can I change the type of sparkline chart?
Yes. Click the cell containing the sparkline to display the Sparkline Tools Design tab; in the Type group, click a different chart type.

PART IV

PowerPoint

PowerPoint is a presentation program that you can use to create slide shows to present ideas to clients, explain a concept or procedure to employees, or teach a class. In this part, you learn how to create slide shows; how to add text, artwork, and special effects to them; and how to package them on a CD-ROM.

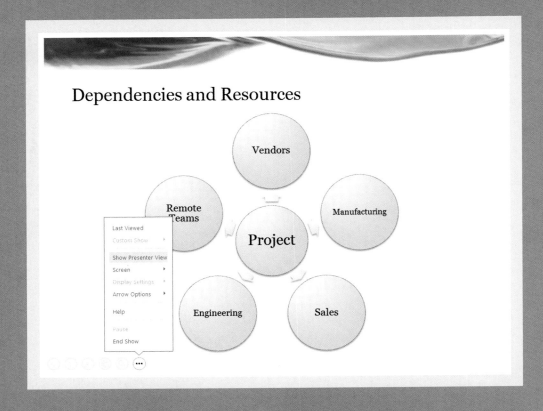

Build a Blank Presentation

When you first start PowerPoint, the PowerPoint Start screen appears. From it — or, if PowerPoint is already open, from Backstage view — you can choose to create a new blank presentation or you can search for a presentation template or theme to use as the foundation of your presentation. When you create a blank presentation, PowerPoint sets up a single slide; you can add more slides and format them as needed.

Building a presentation in this manner, rather than choosing from one of PowerPoint's existing templates, allows you the freedom to create your own color schemes and apply your own design touches.

Build a Blank Presentation

From the Start Screen

1 Start PowerPoint.

The PowerPoint Start screen appears.

2 Click **Blank Presentation**.

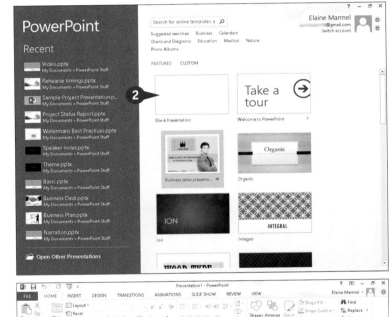

Ⓐ PowerPoint creates a new presentation with one blank slide.

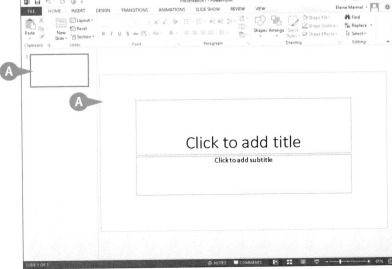

From Backstage View

1 Click the **File** tab.

2 Click **New**.

3 Click **Blank Presentation**.

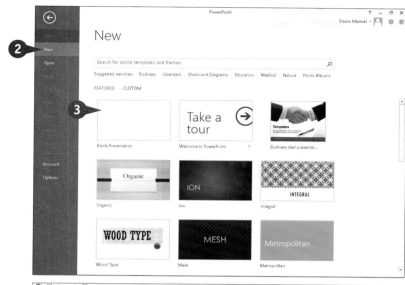

B PowerPoint creates a new presentation with one blank slide.

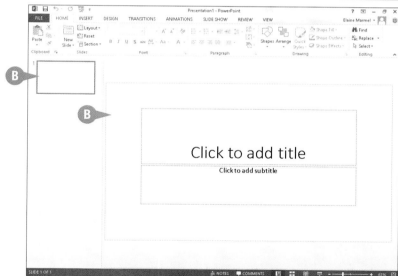

TIP

What is the default aspect ratio for PowerPoint slides, and can I change it?

The default aspect ratio is 16:9, but, if you regularly need to present using a 4:3 aspect ratio, you can change the default size for your slides by following these steps. Apply the 4:3 aspect ratio to your slides (see the section "Change the Slide Size," later in this chapter). Click the **Design** tab, and click ⊡ in the Themes group. Click **Save Current Theme**. In the Save Current Theme dialog box, type the name of the theme, and then click **Save**. In the Themes Gallery on the Design tab, right-click the saved theme. (When you point the mouse at a theme in the gallery, a tip showing the theme name appears.) Click **Set as Default Theme** from the menu that appears.

Create a Presentation Using a Template

PowerPoint templates can help you quickly create a professional-looking presentation. Templates contain *themes* that make up the design of the slide. Themes are groups of coordinated colors, fonts, and effects such as shadows, reflections, and glows. See Chapter 14 for more information on themes.

Templates contain more than just themes, though. For example, they can contain prompts to help you set up the slides in the presentation for a particular subject. In addition to a theme, a template for a scientific presentation might contain slides that prompt you to include a statement of the problem, a hypothesis, a list of variables, and so on.

Create a Presentation Using a Template

1 Click the **File** tab.

2 Click **New**.

3 Click here and type a search term and click 🔍 or press **Enter**.

Ⓐ PowerPoint displays a category list you can use to limit the search.

Ⓑ Potential templates appear here.

4 Click a template.

PowerPoint displays a preview of the template design.

ⓒ You can click these buttons to scroll through the slides in the template.

ⓓ A description of the template appears here.

ⓔ You can click these buttons to view other templates in the preview window.

5 Click **Create**.

ⓕ PowerPoint creates the presentation using the template you chose.

You can add your own text to each slide; see Chapter 14 for details.

TIP

What does the Home button on the New tab do?
Before you type a search term, a series of suggested search terms appear below the search box (ⓐ). You can click one of those search terms instead of typing in the search box. After you search for a term, you can click the **Home** button to redisplay the original suggested search terms so that you can use them again if you want.

Create a Photo Album Presentation

You can quickly turn any collection of digital photos on your computer into a slide show presentation in PowerPoint. For example, you might compile your photos from a recent vacation into a presentation. Alternatively, you might gather your favorite photos of a friend or loved one in a presentation. To liven up the presentation, you can include captions with your photos. You can also vary the layout of slides, including having one (the default), two, three, or more photos per slide. You can then share the presentation with others, or e-mail the file to family and friends.

Create a Photo Album Presentation

1 Click the **Insert** tab.

2 Click **Photo Album**.

The Photo Album dialog box appears.

3 Click the **File/Disk** button.

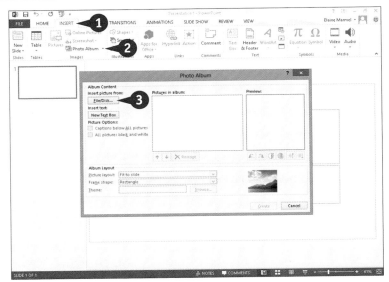

The Insert New Pictures dialog box appears.

4 Navigate to the folder or drive containing the digital pictures that you want to use.

5 Click the pictures that you want to use.

To use multiple pictures, you can press and hold Ctrl while clicking the pictures.

6 Click **Insert**.

Ⓐ You can change the picture order using these buttons.

Ⓑ To remove a picture, you can select it in the Pictures in Album list (☐ changes to ☑) and then click **Remove**.

Ⓒ You can use the tool buttons to change the picture orientation, contrast, and brightness levels.

7 Click **Create**.

PowerPoint creates the slide show as a new presentation file.

Ⓓ Each picture appears on its own slide.

Ⓔ The first slide in the show is a title slide, containing the title "Edit Photo Album" and your username.

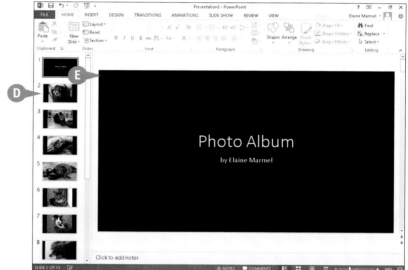

TIP

How do I fit multiple pictures onto a single slide and add captions?

Click the **Insert** tab, and then click ▼ beside **Photo Album** and choose **Edit Photo Album**. In the Edit Photo Album dialog box, click the **Picture layout** ⌄ and choose to display as many as four pictures on a slide, with or without title text (Ⓐ). Select **Captions below All pictures** (☐ changes to ☑) (Ⓑ). If this option is grayed out, choose a different Picture Layout option. Click **Update** (Ⓒ). You can type your captions after closing the Edit Photo Album dialog box.

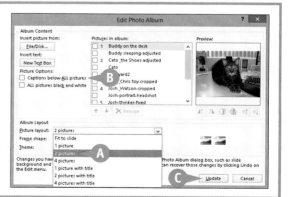

Change PowerPoint Views

You can use views in PowerPoint to change how your presentation appears on-screen. By default, PowerPoint displays your presentation in Normal view, with thumbnails of each slide showing the order of slides in your presentation. You can view the Outline tab to see your presentation in an outline format, or switch to Slide Sorter view to see all the slides at the same time.

In addition to changing PowerPoint views, you can use the PowerPoint zoom settings to change the magnification of a slide. You can also change the size of the panes in the PowerPoint window, making them larger or smaller as needed.

Change PowerPoint Views

Using Normal View

1 Click the **View** tab.

2 Click the **Normal** button.

Ⓐ You can also use these buttons to switch views.

Ⓑ Thumbnails of slides appear here.

Ⓒ The currently selected slide appears here; its thumbnail displays an orange border.

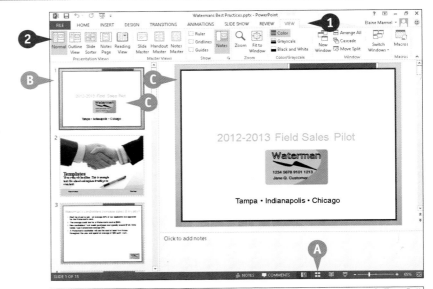

Using Outline View

1 Click **View**.

2 Click **Outline View**.

Ⓓ PowerPoint displays the presentation in an outline format.

Ⓔ You can click the outline text to edit it.

Ⓕ You can click a slide icon to view the slide.

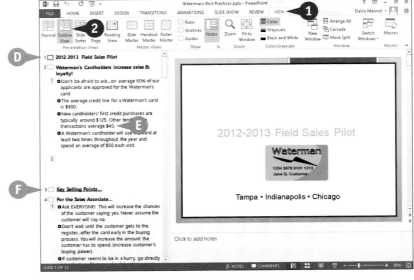

Using Reading View

1 Click 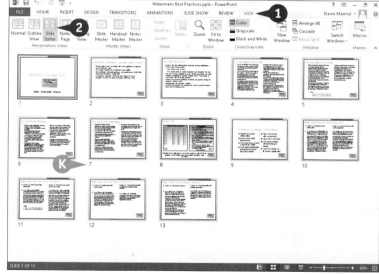.

Note: You can also click the **View** tab and then click **Reading View**.

PowerPoint hides the Ribbon and fills the screen with the first slide in the presentation.

G To view the next slide, click the slide or click .

H To view the previous slide, click .

I To display a menu of available options while reading a presentation, click .

J You can click to redisplay the presentation in Normal view.

Using Slide Sorter View

1 Click the **View** tab.

2 Click the **Slide Sorter** button.

PowerPoint displays thumbnails of all slides in the presentation.

K Under each slide is a number representing its position in the presentation.

You can drag any slide to reposition it in the presentation.

You can double-click a slide to switch to Normal view and display the slide's content.

TIPS

How do I zoom my view of a slide?
You can drag the **Zoom** slider, which appears beside the view buttons on the status bar at the bottom of the PowerPoint window. Or, you can click the **View** tab, click the **Zoom** button, and choose the desired magnification in the Zoom dialog box that opens. Click the **Fit to Window** button on the View tab to return slides to the default size for the current view.

Can I resize the PowerPoint pane?
Yes. Position the mouse pointer over the pane's border. When ⌖ changes to ⟺, click and drag inward or outward to resize the pane.

Insert Slides

PowerPoint makes it easy to add more slides to a presentation. To add a slide, you use the New Slide button on the Home tab. Clicking the top half of the New Slide button adds a slide with the same layout as the one you selected in the Slides pane; alternatively, you can click the bottom half of the button and select a different layout.

You can add and remove slides on the Slides tab in Normal view, or you can switch to Slide Sorter view and manage your presentation's slides.

Insert Slides

1 Click the thumbnail of the slide after which you want to insert a new slide.

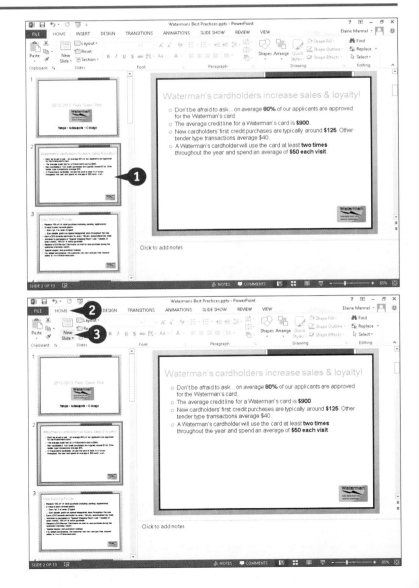

2 Click the **Home** tab.

3 Click the bottom half of the New Slide button.

Note: Clicking the top half of the New Slide button adds a slide with the same layout as the one you selected in Step **1**.

Ⓐ A gallery of slide layouts appears.

④ Click a slide layout.

Ⓑ PowerPoint adds a new slide after the one you selected in Step **1**.

Ⓒ The new slide uses the layout you selected in Step **4**.

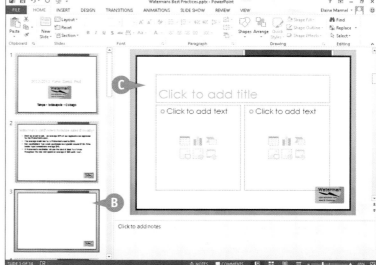

TIPS

What happens if I click the Slides from Outline command?

You can use this command to create a presentation from an outline you created in another program, such as Microsoft Word. PowerPoint creates one slide for each heading style you applied; if you did not apply heading styles to the outline, PowerPoint creates slides for each paragraph.

Can I duplicate several slides simultaneously?

Yes. Select the slides you want to duplicate; you can press and hold **Ctrl** as you click each slide. Then, click the bottom of the **New Slide** button and click **Duplicate Selected Slides**. PowerPoint inserts all of the duplicate slides after the last slide you selected.

Change the Slide Layout

PowerPoint includes several predesigned slide layouts that you can apply to your slide. For example, you might apply a layout that includes a title with two content sections or a picture with a caption.

For best results, you should assign a new layout before adding content to your slides; otherwise, you may need to make a few adjustments to the content's position and size to fit the new layout. If you find that you do not like a style element, you can make style changes to all slides in your presentation so that you maintain a uniform appearance throughout your presentation.

Change the Slide Layout

1 Click the slide whose layout you want to change in the Slides tab.

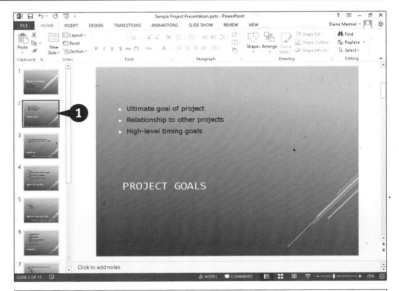

2 Click the **Home** tab.

3 Click the **Layout** button.

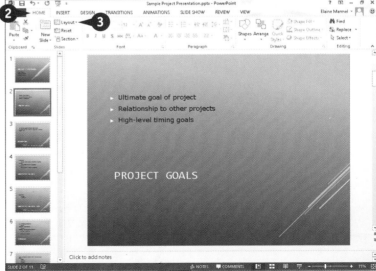

A A gallery of slide layouts appears.

B The currently selected layout is highlighted.

4 Click a layout.

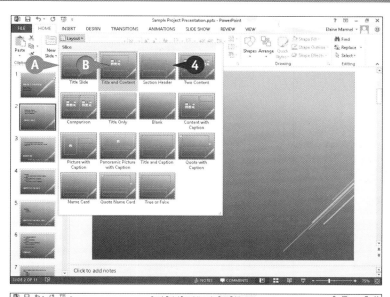

C PowerPoint assigns the layout to the slide.

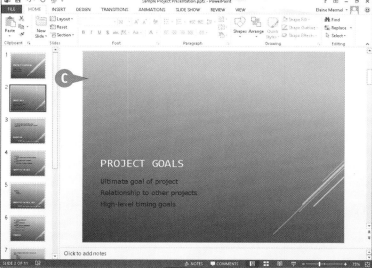

TIP

How do I make a style change that affects all slides in my presentation?
You can use the Slide Master. Suppose that you do not like the font you selected for your presentation. Using the Slide Master, you can change the font on all slides in one action. Click the **View** tab and then click **Slide Master**. PowerPoint displays the Slide Master tab. Make the changes you desire; for example, select a different font for the presentation. When you finish, click the **Close Master View** button to hide the Slide Master tab. Your new font appears on every slide in your presentation.

235

Change the Slide Size

You can easily change the size of your presentation's slides. In earlier versions of PowerPoint, slides used the 4:3 aspect ratio that was common on televisions. To accommodate widescreen and high-definition formats, PowerPoint 2013's default slide size uses an aspect ratio of 16:9.

If you change the size of a slide that contains content, PowerPoint attempts to scale your content; if it cannot, PowerPoint offers to maximize the content or ensure that it fits. If you opt to maximize the content, it is larger but may not fit on the slide. If you apply the Ensure Fit option, your content is smaller but fits on the slide.

Change the Slide Size

1 Open the presentation containing the slides you want to resize.

2 Click the **Design** tab.

3 Click **Slide Size**.

4 From the drop-down list that appears, click **Standard**.

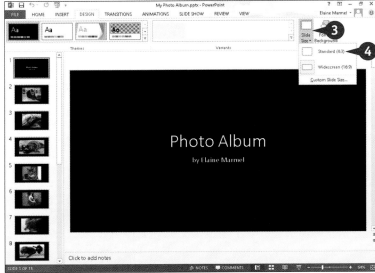

PowerPoint displays a message, asking how you want to handle content on the new slide size.

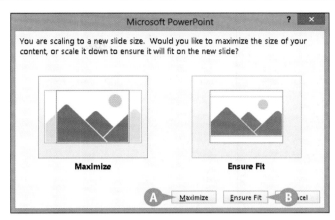

A Click **Maximize** to increase the size of the slide content when you scale to a larger slide size. Be aware that your content might not fit on the slide.

B Click **Ensure Fit** to decrease the size of your content when you scale to a smaller slide size. Although the slide content might appear smaller, you can see all content on your slide.

C PowerPoint resizes all of the slides in the presentation.

Note: You might need to reapply a theme.

TIP

Can I establish a size for my slides other than 4:3 or 16:9?
Yes. Complete Steps **1** to **3** and, from the drop-down menu, click **Custom Slide Size**. In the dialog box that appears, use the **Slides sized for** ▾ (A) to select a slide size. You can also specify slide width, height, numbering, and orientation. Click **OK** to apply your changes.

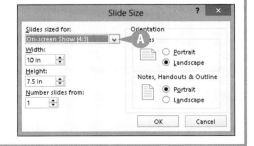

Add and Edit Slide Text

All slide layouts except for the blank slide layout are designed to automatically hold some text. To help you enter text, PowerPoint includes a text box that contains placeholder text, such as "Click to add title," "Click to add subtitle," or "Click to add text." You can replace the placeholder text with your own text by typing directly in the slide.

After you add your text, you can change its font, size, color, and more, as shown in the next section.

Add and Edit Slide Text

Add Slide Text

1 Click the text box to which you want to add text.

PowerPoint hides the placeholder text and displays an insertion point.

2 Type the text that you want to add.

3 Click anywhere outside the box to save your typing.

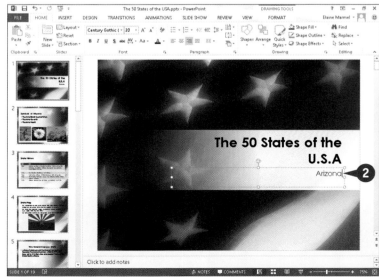

Edit Slide Text

1 Click in the text box where you want to edit the contents.

PowerPoint selects the text box and displays an insertion point in the text box.

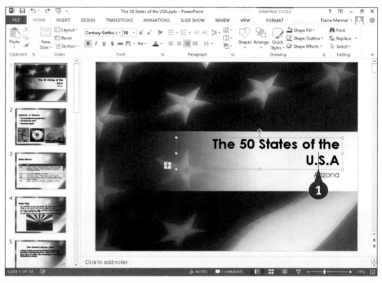

2 Make any changes that you want to the slide text.

You can use the keyboard arrow keys to position the insertion point in the text, or you can click where you want to make a change.

3 When you finish, click anywhere outside the text box.

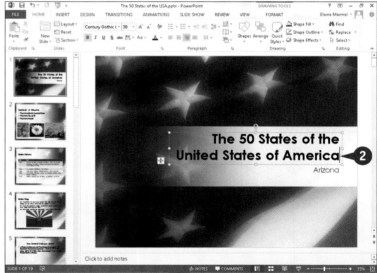

TIP

What should I do if my text does not fit in the text box, or fit the way I want?

You can resize the text, as described in the next section, or you can drag one of the handles of the text box to enlarge it, as shown here. When you position the mouse pointer over a handle, ▷ changes to ⬔, ↕, ⬈, or ↔. When you drag, the mouse pointer changes to + (Ⓐ).

- The state bird is: Cactus Wren
- The state flower is:
- The state tree is:

239

Change the Font, Size, and Color

After you add text to a slide (as described in the previous section, "Add and Edit Slide Text"), you can change the text's font, size, color, and style to alter its appearance. For example, you might choose to increase the size of a slide's title text to draw attention to it, or change the font of the body text to match the font used in your company logo. Alternatively, you might change the text's color to make it stand out against the background color. You can also apply formatting to the text, such as bold, italics, underlining, shadow, or strikethrough.

Change the Font, Size, and Color

Change the Font

1. Click inside the text box and select the text that you want to edit.

2. Click the **Home** tab.

3. Click the **Font** ▼.

4. Click a font.

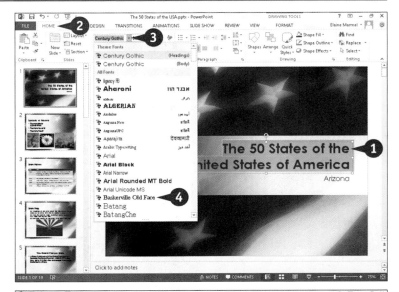

Ⓐ PowerPoint applies the font you chose to the selected text.

You can click anywhere outside the text box to continue working.

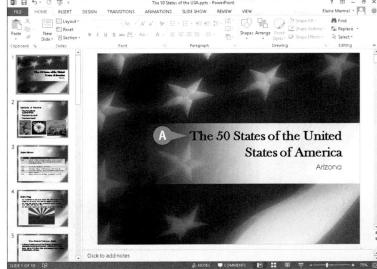

Change the Size

1 Click inside the text box and select the text that you want to edit.

2 Click the **Home** tab.

3 Click the **Font Size** ▼.

4 Click a size.

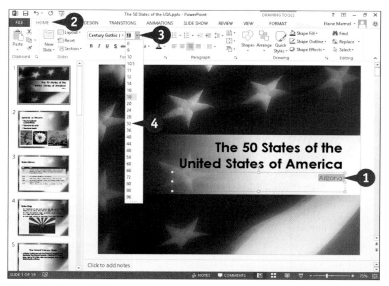

Ⓑ PowerPoint applies the font size you chose to the selected text.

You can click anywhere outside the text box to continue working.

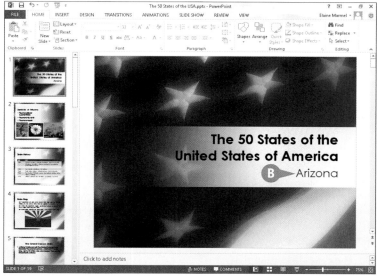

TIPS

Is there a quicker way to change the text size?
Yes. To quickly increase or decrease the font size, you can select the text you want to change and then click the **Increase Font Size** (A⁺) or **Decrease Font Size** (A⁻) button in the Home tab's Font group as many times as needed until the text is the desired size.

How do I apply text formatting?
Select the text whose format you want to change, and then click the **Bold** button (B), the **Italic** button (I), the **Underline** button (U ▾), the **Text Shadow** button (S), or the **Strikethrough** button (abc).

continued ▶

In addition to changing the text's font and size, you can change its color. You might do so to make the text stand out better against the background, or to coordinate with colors used in other slide elements such as photographs.

You can change the text color in a few different ways. For example, you can select a color from the Font Color button on the Home tab, or you can open the Colors dialog box and select a color from the palette that appears. In addition, you can apply your own custom color to text.

Change the Font, Size, and Color (continued)

Choose a Coordinating Color

1 Click in the text box and select the text that you want to edit.

2 Click the **Home** tab.

3 Click ▼ next to the **Font Color** button (**A** ▼).

A PowerPoint displays coordinating theme colors designed to go with the current slide design.

4 Click a color.

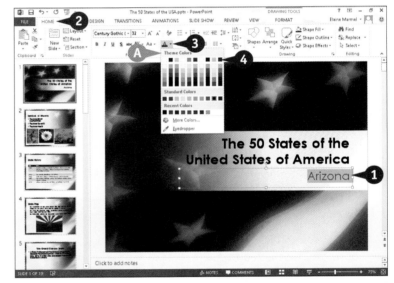

B PowerPoint applies the color you chose to the selected text.

You can click anywhere outside the text box to continue working.

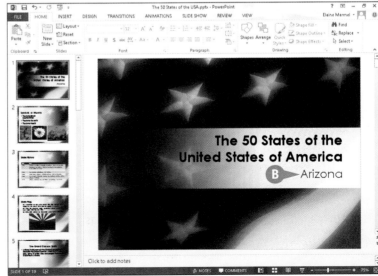

Choose a Color in the Colors Dialog Box

1 Click in the text box and select the text that you want to edit.

2 Click the **Home** tab.

3 Click ▼ next to the **Font Color** button (**A** ▾).

4 Click **More Colors**.

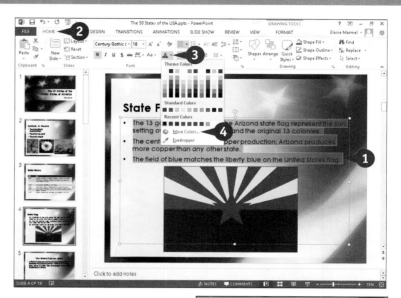

The Colors dialog box appears.

5 Click the **Standard** tab.

6 Click a color.

C A comparison between the current and new colors appears here.

7 Click **OK**.

PowerPoint applies the color you chose to the selected text.

You can click anywhere outside the text box to continue working.

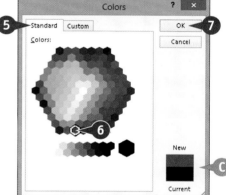

TIP

How do I set a custom color?

You can set your own custom color for use with the slide text or other slide elements. Follow these steps:

1 Open the Colors dialog box, as shown in this section, and click the **Custom** tab.

2 Click the color that you want to customize.

3 Drag the intensity arrow to adjust the color intensity.

A You can also adjust the color channel settings.

4 Click **OK**.

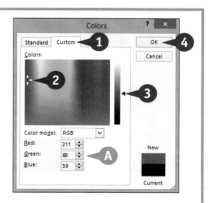

Apply a Theme

Powerpoint includes a variety of preset designs, called themes. A *theme* is a predesigned set of colors, fonts, backgrounds, and other visual attributes. When you apply a theme to your presentation, you give every slide in your presentation the same look and feel. Alternatively, you can apply a theme to selected slides in your presentation. After you apply the theme, you can use controls in the Design tab to change various aspects of the theme.

Themes are shared among the Office programs; you can use the same theme in your PowerPoint presentations that you have applied to worksheets in Excel or documents in Word.

Apply a Theme

Note: To apply a theme to selected slides, press and hold **Ctrl** as you click each slide thumbnail in Normal view.

1 Click the **Design** tab.

A In the Themes group, you can click ▲ and ▼ to scroll through the palette of themes.

B Alternatively, you can click ▼ to view all available themes.

2 Click a theme.

C PowerPoint applies the theme. Any slides you add will use the same theme.

D You can use these controls to select a color variant of the theme.

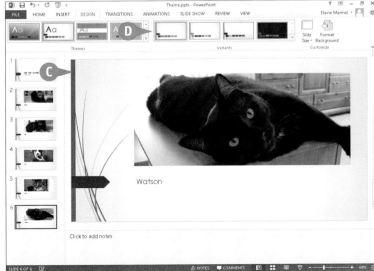

244

Set Line Spacing

You can change the line spacing in a PowerPoint slide to create more or less space between lines of text in the slide. For example, you might want to increase line spacing from the 1.0 setting to a larger setting so the text fills up more space in the text box, or to make the text easier to read. If, after increasing the line spacing, your text does not fit in the text box, you can reduce the line spacing or increase the size of the text box, as described in the tip in the section "Add and Edit Slide Text."

Set Line Spacing

1 Click in the text box and select the text that you want to edit.

2 Click the **Home** tab.

3 Click the **Line Spacing** button (‡≡ ▾).

4 Click a line spacing amount.

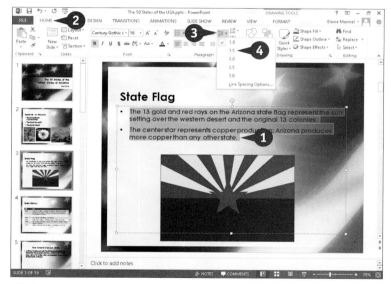

A PowerPoint applies the line spacing. This example applies 1.5 spacing.

You can click anywhere outside the text box to continue working.

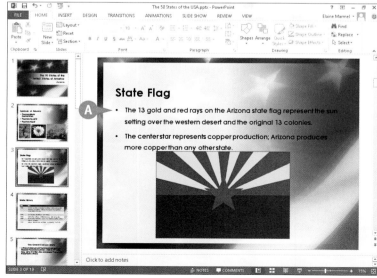

Align Text

By default, PowerPoint centers most text in text boxes (bulleted lists are left-aligned). If you want, you can use PowerPoint's alignment commands, located on the Home tab, to change how text is positioned horizontally in a text box. You can choose to center text in a text box (using the Center command), align text to the right side of the text box (using the Right Align command), or justify text and objects so they line up at both the left and right margins of the text box (using the Justify command).

Align Text

1. Click in the text box containing the text that you want to align.

2. Click the **Home** tab.

3. Click an alignment button:

   Click the **Align Left** button (≡) to align the text to the left side of the text box.

   Click the **Center** button (≡) to align the text in the center of the text box.

   Click the **Align Right** button (≡) to align the text to the right side of the text box.

   Click the **Justify** button (≡) to justify text between the left and right margins.

Ⓐ PowerPoint applies the formatting. In this example, the text is centered between the left and right margins of the text box.

   You can click anywhere outside the text box to continue working.

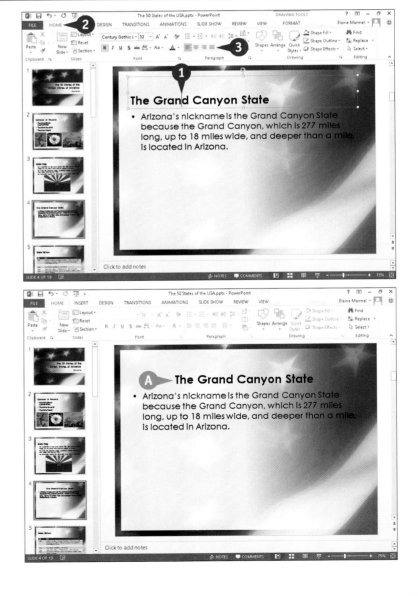

Add a Text Box to a Slide

Typically, you insert slides containing a predefined layout. You can customize the slide layout, however, by adding a new text box to it. A text box is simply a receptacle for text in a slide. (For help adding text to a text box, refer to the section "Add and Edit Slide Text," earlier in this chapter.)

When you add a new text box to a slide, you can control the placement and size of the box. (For help moving and resizing text boxes and other slide objects, see the sections "Move a Slide Object" and "Resize a Slide Object," later in this chapter.)

Add a Text Box to a Slide

1 In Normal view, click the slide to which you want to add a text box.

2 Click the **Insert** tab.

3 Click the **Text Box** button.

When you move the mouse pointer over the slide, ⬚ changes to ↓.

4 Click at the location where the upper-left corner of the text box should appear, and drag down and to the right (↓ changes to +).

Ⓐ As you drag, an outline represents the text box.

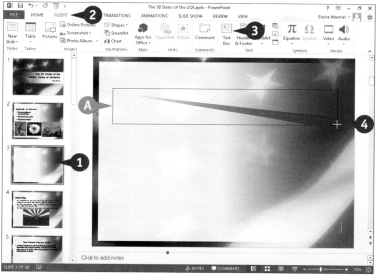

5 Release the mouse button to complete drawing the text box.

Ⓑ The insertion point appears in the new text box.

6 Type your text.

You can click anywhere outside the text box to continue working.

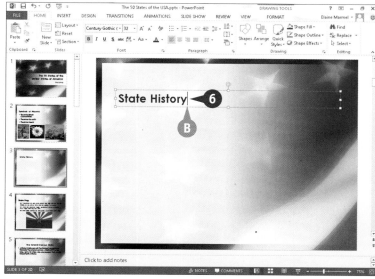

Add a Table to a Slide

You can customize the layout of a slide by adding a table to it. You can add tables to your slides to organize data in an orderly fashion. For example, you might use a table to display a list of products or classes. Tables use a column-and-row format to present information.

After you add the table to your slide, you can control the placement and size of the table. (For help moving and resizing tables and other slide objects, see the sections "Move a Slide Object" and "Resize a Slide Object," later in this chapter.)

Add a Table to a Slide

1 Click the slide to which you want to add a table.

2 If an **Insert Table** icon ( ) appears in your slide, click it.

A If an Insert Table icon does not appear in your slide, click the **Table** button on the Insert tab and choose **Insert Table**.

The Insert Table dialog box appears.

3 Type the number of columns that you want to appear in the table.

4 Type the number of rows that you want to appear in the table.

Note: If you need more rows, just press Tab in the last table cell, and PowerPoint automatically adds a row.

5 Click **OK**.

B PowerPoint inserts the table into the slide.

C PowerPoint displays the Table Tools tabs.

D You can change the table's appearance by clicking a style in the Table Styles group.

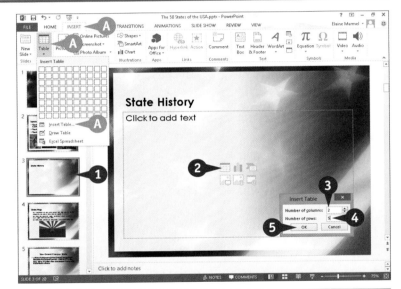

6 Click inside the first table cell and type your data.

You can press **Tab** to move to the next table cell.

7 Continue typing in each cell to fill the table.

E You can use the tools in the Layout tab to merge or split table cells, change alignment, add borders, and more.

F You can resize columns or rows by dragging their borders.

When you finish typing table data, click anywhere outside the table to continue working.

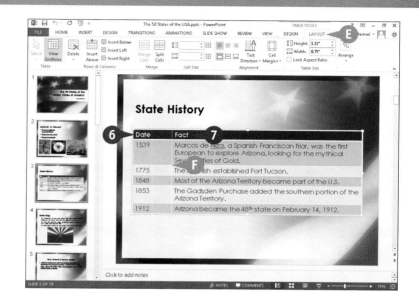

TIP

How do I add a row or column to my table?

To add a row to the bottom of the table, click in the last table cell and press **Tab**. To insert a row in the middle of the table or add a column anywhere in the table, follow these steps:

1 Click in a cell adjacent to where you want to insert a new row or column.

2 Click the **Layout** tab.

3 Click one of these buttons.

A PowerPoint inserts a new row or column.

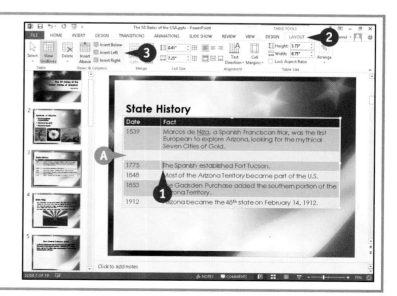

Add a Chart to a Slide

You can customize the layout of a slide by adding a chart to it. You might add a chart to a PowerPoint slide to turn numeric data into a visual element that your audience can quickly interpret and understand. When you add a chart, PowerPoint launches an Excel window, which you use to enter the chart data.

After you add a chart to a slide, you can control the placement and size of the chart. (For help moving and resizing charts and other slide objects, see the sections "Move a Slide Object" and "Resize a Slide Object," later in this chapter.)

Add a Chart to a Slide

1. Click the slide to which you want to add a chart.

2. If an **Insert Chart** icon (📊) appears in your slide, click it.

Ⓐ If an Insert Chart icon does not appear in your slide, click the **Chart** button on the Insert tab.

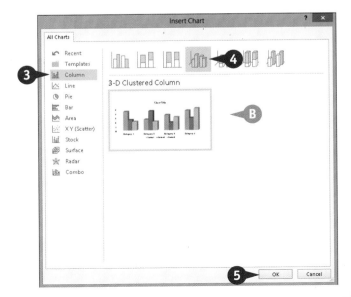

The Insert Chart dialog box appears.

3. Click a chart category.

4. Click a chart type.

Ⓑ A preview of the chart appears here.

5. Click **OK**.

C PowerPoint displays a sample chart on the slide.

D The Excel program window opens.

6 Replace the placeholder data with the chart data that you want to illustrate.

You can press `Tab` to move from cell to cell.

E PowerPoint updates the chart to reflect the data you enter.

7 Click the **Close** button (×) to close the Excel window.

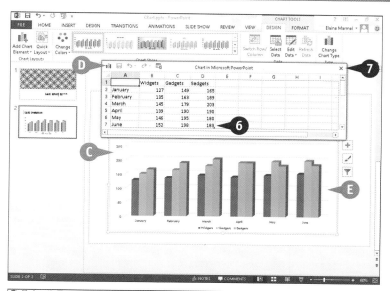

F As long as the chart is selected, PowerPoint displays the Chart Tools tabs.

8 Click the **Design** tab.

G To edit the chart data, click the **Edit Data** button.

H Click a Chart Styles button to change the chart style.

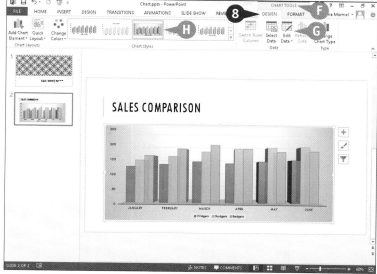

TIPS

Can I insert an existing Excel chart into my PowerPoint slide?

Yes. You can use the Copy and Paste commands to copy an Excel chart and insert it into a PowerPoint slide. To learn more about copying and pasting data between Office programs, see Chapter 2.

How do I make changes to my chart formatting?

When you click a chart in a PowerPoint slide, the Ribbon displays two tabs: **Design**, with options for changing the chart type, layout, data, elements, and style; and **Format**, with tools for changing fill colors and shape styles.

Add a Video Clip to a Slide

You can add video clips to your PowerPoint slides to play during a slide show presentation. For example, when creating a presentation showcasing the latest company product, you might place a video clip of the department head discussing the new item.

After you add a video to a slide, you can control the placement and size of the video. (For help moving and resizing video clips and other slide objects, see the sections "Move a Slide Object" and "Resize a Slide Object," later in this chapter.) You can also make certain edits to the video from within PowerPoint.

Add a Video Clip to a Slide

1 Click the slide to which you want to add a video clip.

2 If an **Insert Media Clip** icon (⬚) appears in your slide, click it.

Ⓐ If an Insert Media Clip icon does not appear in your slide, click the **Video** button on the Insert tab and choose **Online Video** or **Video on My PC**.

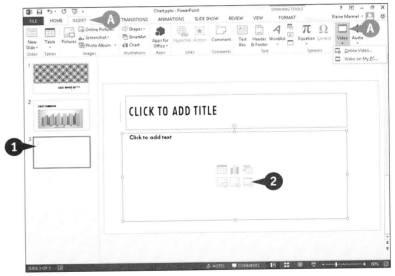

The Insert Video window appears.

Note: You can browse for videos on your computer, your SkyDrive, or using Bing Search or YouTube, or you can supply an embed code for a video stored on a website. This example browses your computer.

3 Click a location containing the video clip.

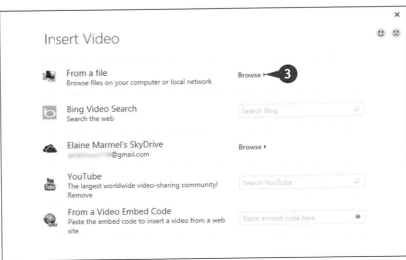

The Insert Video dialog box appears.

4 Navigate to the folder containing the video file.

5 Select the video.

6 Click **Insert**.

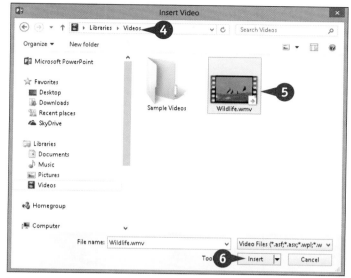

B PowerPoint inserts the clip into the slide.

C PowerPoint displays the Format tab of the Video Tools tabs.

D You can click an option in the Video Styles group to change the appearance of the video.

E You can use the options in the Size group to adjust the size of the clip on the slide.

F You can click the **Play** button (▶) to play back the clip.

TIP

What tools appear on the Playback tab?

You can use the settings in the Video Options group to specify options such as when the clip should start playing, whether it should be looped, and how loudly it should play. You can edit your video using the tools in the Editing group; using the **Fade In** and **Fade Out** fields, you can set up the clip to fade in and fade out. You can also click the **Trim Video** button to open the Trim Video dialog box, where you can change the duration of the video by trimming frames from the beginning or end of the clip.

253

Move a Slide Object

You can move any element on a slide — a text box, table, chart, picture, video clip, or graphic — to reposition it. These slide elements are often referred to as objects. For example, you might move a text box to make room for a video clip or reposition a picture to improve the overall appearance of the slide.

You can move a slide object using the standard Office Cut and Paste buttons, discussed in Chapter 2. Or, you can drag and drop the object, as discussed in this section.

Move a Slide Object

1 Click the slide containing the object that you want to move.

2 Select the slide object by clicking it (↖ changes to ✥).

Note: To select a table or a chart, slide the mouse pointer along any of the object's edges. Click when you see the ✥ mouse pointer.

3 Drag the object to a new location on the slide. As you drag, ✥ changes to ✣.

4 Release the mouse button.

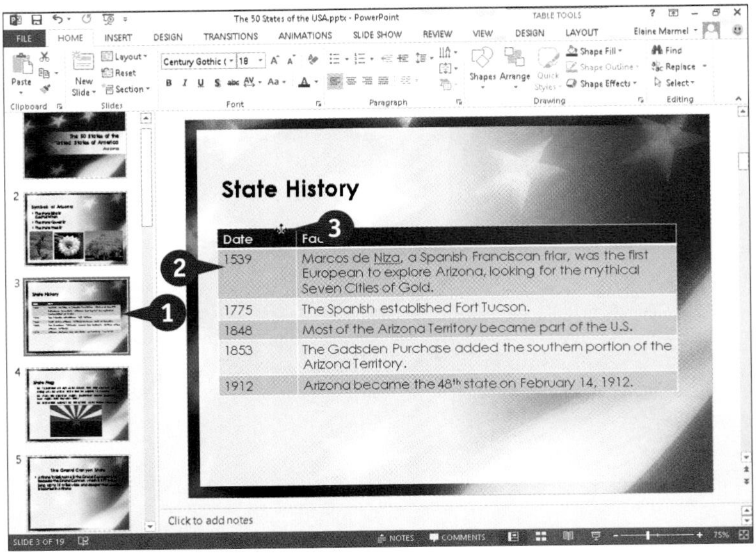

A PowerPoint repositions the object.

You can click anywhere outside the slide object to continue working.

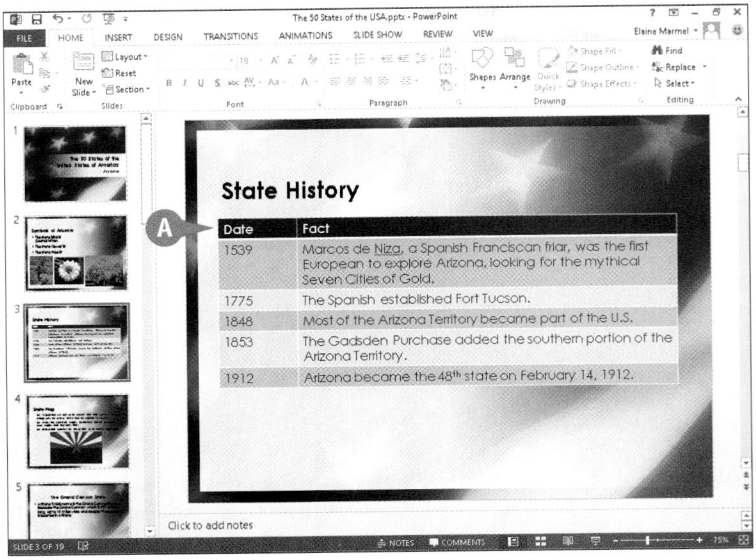

Resize a Slide Object

After you insert a slide object — a text box, table, chart, picture, video clip, or graphic — you may find that you need to make it larger or smaller to achieve the desired effect. For example, you might want to resize a text box to make room for more text or resize a picture object to enlarge the artwork. Fortunately, PowerPoint makes it easy to change the size of a slide object. When you select an object in a PowerPoint slide, handles appear around that object; you use these handles to change the object's size.

Resize a Slide Object

1 Click the slide containing the object that you want to resize.

2 Click the object to select it.

A PowerPoint surrounds the object with handles ( ).

3 Position the mouse pointer over a handle. changes to , , , or .

Use a corner handle to resize the object's height and width at the same time.

Use a side handle to resize the object along only the one side.

4 Click and drag the handle inward or outward to resize the slide object (, , , or changes to +).

5 Release the mouse button.

B PowerPoint resizes the object.

You can click outside the slide object to continue working.

Note: To delete an object that you no longer need, select the object and press Delete.

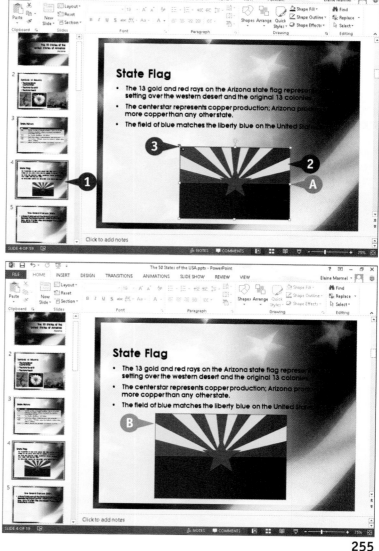

Reorganize Slides

You can change the order of the slides in your presentation. For example, you might want to move a slide to appear later in the presentation, or swap the order of two adjacent slides. You can move individual slides, or move multiple slides at once.

You can change the slide order in Slide Sorter view or in Normal view; choose the view based on the distance from the original position to the new position. If you need to move a slide only a few positions, use Normal view. Slide Sorter view works best when you need to move a slide to a new position several slides away.

Reorganize Slides

Move Slides in Normal View

1. Click ▣ to switch to Normal view.

2. Click to select the slide you want to move.

Note: To move multiple slides, select them by pressing and holding Ctrl as you click each slide.

3. Drag the slide to a new position.

Ⓐ As you drag, ↳ changes to ↳.

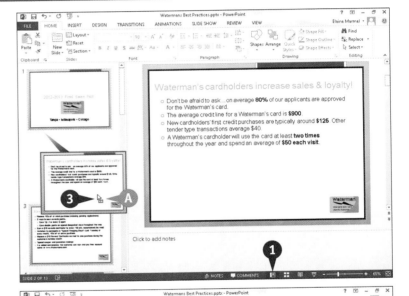

4. Release the mouse button.

Ⓑ PowerPoint moves the slide.

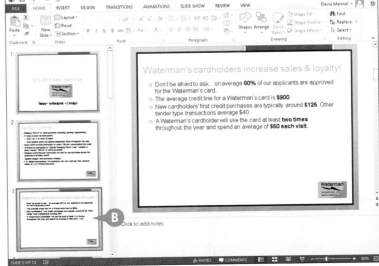

Move Slides in Slide Sorter View

1 Click ⊞ to switch to Slide Sorter view.

2 Click the slide that you want to move to select it.

Note: To move multiple slides, select them by pressing and holding `Ctrl` as you click each slide.

3 Drag the slide to a new location in the presentation.

C As you drag, ⌖ changes to ⌖.

4 Release the mouse button.

D PowerPoint moves the slide.

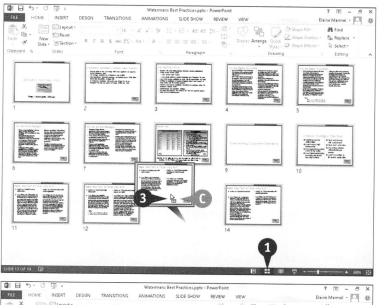

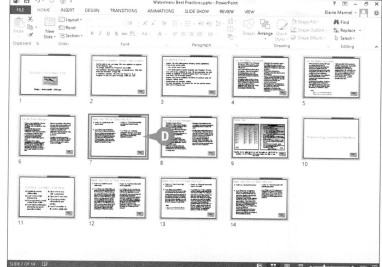

TIPS

How do I hide a slide?
Suppose you frequently give the same presentation, but your next audience does not require the information in one of the presentation slides. In that case, you can hide the slide. Click the slide, click the **Slide Show** tab, and then click the **Hide Slide** button. PowerPoint crosses out the slide. To unhide the slide, repeat these steps.

How do I delete a slide?
To delete a slide, click the slide and then click the **Cut** button (✂) on the **Home** tab, or right-click the slide and choose **Delete Slide** from the menu that appears.

Reuse a Slide

Suppose you are creating a new PowerPoint presentation, but you want to reuse a slide from an old one. Assuming the presentation containing the slide you want to reuse has been saved on your hard drive or is accessible to you via a network connection, you can easily do so. You can choose the slide you want to reuse in the Reuse Slides pane.

When you reuse a slide, PowerPoint updates the slide to match the formatting used in the new presentation. You can reuse a single slide from a presentation, multiple slides from a presentation, or all the slides in a presentation.

Reuse a Slide

① Click the slide that you want to appear before the new slide.

② Click the **Home** tab.

③ Click the bottom half of the **New Slide** button.

④ Click **Reuse Slides**.

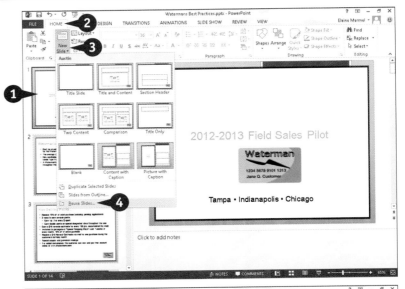

Ⓐ The Reuse Slides pane opens.

⑤ Click the **Browse** button.

⑥ Click **Browse File**.

The Browse dialog box opens.

7 Locate and select the presentation containing the slide you want to reuse.

8 Click **Open**.

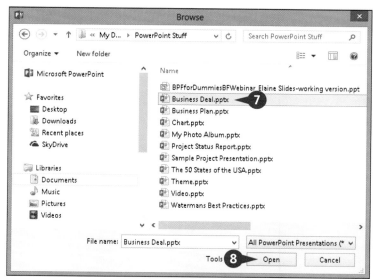

B PowerPoint populates the Reuse Slides pane with slides from the presentation you selected.

9 Click the slide you want to reuse.

C PowerPoint adds the slide to your presentation after the slide you clicked in Step **1**.

TIPS

Can I retain the reused slide's original formatting?
Yes. To retain the reused slide's original formatting, select **Keep source formatting** (☐ changes to ☑) in the Reuse Slides pane. To change all the slides in the new presentation to match the reused slide, right-click the reused slide in the Reuse Slides pane and choose **Apply Theme to All Slides**.

How do I reuse all the slides in a presentation?
To reuse all the slides in a presentation, right-click any slide in the Reuse Slides pane and choose **Insert All Slides**. PowerPoint inserts all the slides from the existing presentation into the new presentation.

Organize Slides into Sections

If your presentation has a large number of slides, keeping it organized can be difficult. To more easily manage your slides, you can organize them into sections. For example, you might group all the slides that will be displayed during your introductory speech into a section called "Introduction," place the slides that pertain to your first topic of discussion into a section called "Topic 1," and so on.

Organizing a presentation into sections can also help you move slides around in the presentation. Instead of moving individual slides, you can move sections.

Organize Slides into Sections

1 Click the slide that marks the beginning of the section you want to create.

2 Click the **Home** tab.

3 Click the **Section** button.

4 Choose **Add Section**.

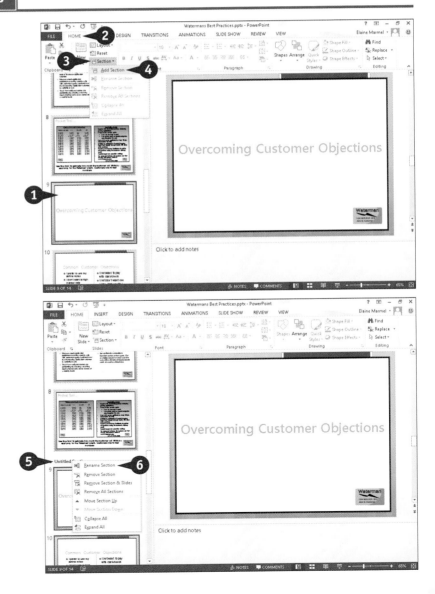

PowerPoint adds a section marker before the slide you selected, adding all slides below the marker to the section.

5 Right-click the section marker.

6 Choose **Rename Section**.

The Rename Section dialog box appears.

7 Type a name for the new section.

8 Click the **Rename** button.

A PowerPoint applies the name to the section.

9 To hide the slides in a section, click the section marker's collapse button (◢).

B PowerPoint collapses the section and identifies the number of slides in the section.

C You can click the section marker's expand button (▷) to redisplay the slides in the section.

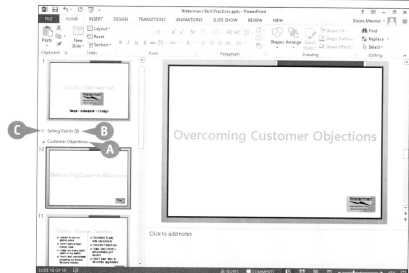

TIPS

How do I remove a section marker?
If you decide you no longer want to group a set of slides in a section, you can remove the section marker. To do so, right-click the section marker and choose **Remove Section** from the menu that appears. PowerPoint removes the marker.

How can I reorganize the sections in my presentation?
Reorganizing sections involves rearranging slides in the presentation. To reorganize the sections in your presentation, right-click a section's marker and choose **Move Section Up** or **Move Section Down** as many times as needed. PowerPoint moves the slides in the section accordingly.

Define Slide Transitions

You can add transition effects, such as fades, dissolves, and wipes, to your slides to control how one slide segues to the next. You can control the speed with which the transition appears. You can also specify how PowerPoint advances the slides, either manually using a mouse click or automatically after a time you specify passes. In addition to adding visual transition effects between your slides, you can add sound effects to serve as transitions.

Use good judgment when assigning transitions. Using too many different types of transitions might distract your audience from your presentation.

Define Slide Transitions

1 Click ⊞ to switch to Slide Sorter view.

2 Click the slide to which you want to apply a transition.

3 Click the **Transitions** tab.

A Available transition effects appear in the Transition to This Slide group. You can click ▲ or ▼ to scroll through them or click the ⊽ to view the gallery of transition effects.

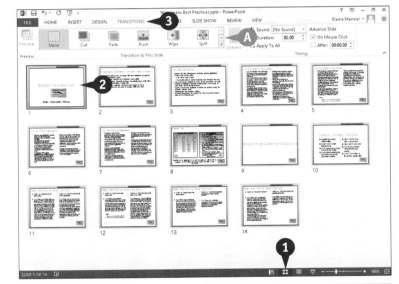

4 Click a transition.

B PowerPoint adds an animation indicator below the slide's lower-right corner.

C You can click **Preview** to display a preview of the transition effect.

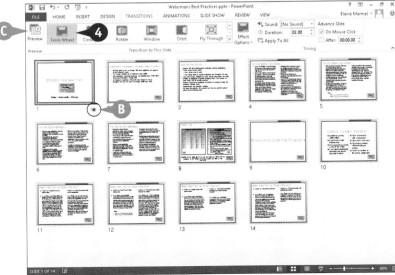

⑤ Click the **Duration** ⬍ to specify a speed setting for the transition.

Ⓓ You can click **Apply To All** to apply the same transition to the entire slide show, and PowerPoint adds the animation indicator below every slide.

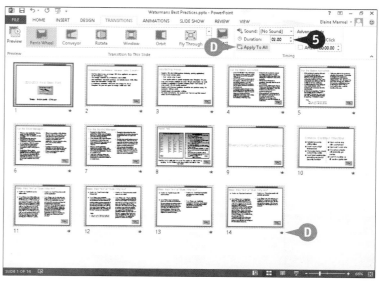

⑥ Under Advance Slide, select an advance option (☐ changes to ☑):

To use a mouse click to move to the next slide, select **On Mouse Click**.

To move to the next slide automatically, select **After** and use the spin box to specify a duration.

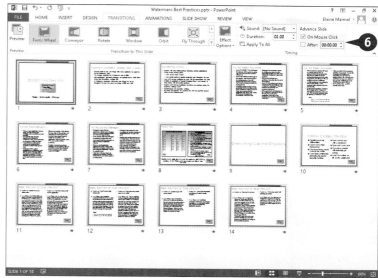

How do I remove a transition effect?
In Slide Sorter view, select the slide containing the transition that you want to remove; then click the **Transitions** tab and click the **None** option in the Transition to This Slide group. PowerPoint removes the transition that you assigned.

How do I assign a sound as a transition effect?
To assign a sound transition, click the **Sound** ▼ in the Timing group on the Transitions tab and select a sound. For example, you might assign the Applause sound effect for the first or last slide in a presentation.

Add Animation Effects

You can use PowerPoint's animation effects to add visual interest to your presentation. For example, if you want your audience to notice a company logo on a slide, you might apply an animation effect to that logo.

You can use four different types of animation effects: entrance effects, emphasis effects, exit effects, and motion paths. You can add any of these effects to any slide object. You can also change the direction of your animations. To avoid overwhelming your audience, limit animations to slides in which the effects will make the most impact.

Add Animation Effects

Add an Animation Effect

1. Click 🔲 to display the presentation in Normal view.

2. Click the slide containing the object to which you want to apply an effect.

3. Click the object.

   You can assign an animation to any object on a slide, including text boxes, shapes, and pictures.

4. Click the **Animations** tab.

Ⓐ You can click ▲ and ▼ to scroll through the available animation effects or click ▼ to view the gallery of animation effects.

5. Click an animation effect.

Ⓑ PowerPoint applies the effect and displays a numeric indicator for the effect.

Ⓒ You can click the **Preview** button to preview the effect.

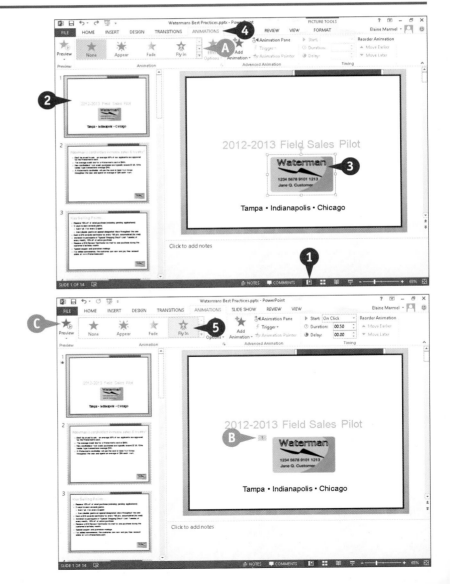

Change an Animation's Direction

1. In Normal view, click the slide element containing the animation you want to edit.

2. Click the **Animations** tab.

3. Click the **Effect Options** button.

   A list of direction options for the animation appears.

4. Select an option from the list.

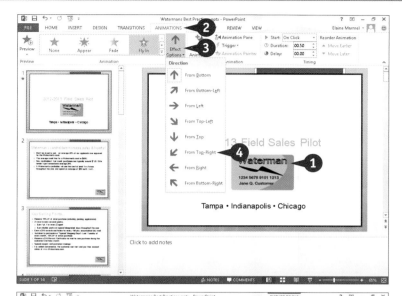

D PowerPoint applies the change; the new direction appears on the Effect Options button.

E You can click **Preview** to preview the effect on the slide.

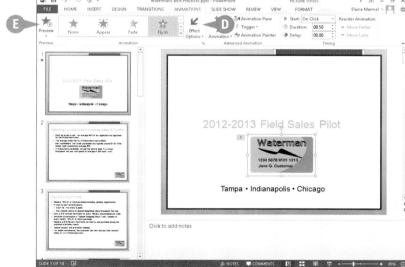

TIP

Can I copy an animation effect to another slide object?

Yes. PowerPoint's Animation Painter feature enables you to copy an animation effect applied to one slide object to another slide object. To copy an animation effect, select the slide object whose effect you want to copy; then, in the Animations tab's Advanced Animation group, click the **Animation Painter** button. Next, in the Slides tab, click the slide containing the object to which you want to apply the effect to display it; then click the object. PowerPoint copies the animation effect to the slide object.

Create a Custom Animation

In addition to applying a single animation effect to any given slide object — a text box, picture, chart, or table — you can create custom effects by applying two or more animations to a slide object. For example, you might opt to have a slide object "fly in" to the slide and then spin. You can use PowerPoint's Animation pane when you create a custom effect to help you review and reorder the effect.

To create a custom animation effect, you use a combination of the technique described in the section "Add Animation Effects" and the technique described in this section.

Create a Custom Animation

1 Click 📧 to display the presentation in Normal view.

2 Click the slide containing the object to which you want to apply an animation.

3 Click the object.

4 Click the **Animations** tab.

5 Apply an animation effect.

Note: See the section "Add Animation Effects" for details.

6 Click the **Animation Pane** button.

A PowerPoint displays the Animation pane.

B The animation you applied appears in the pane.

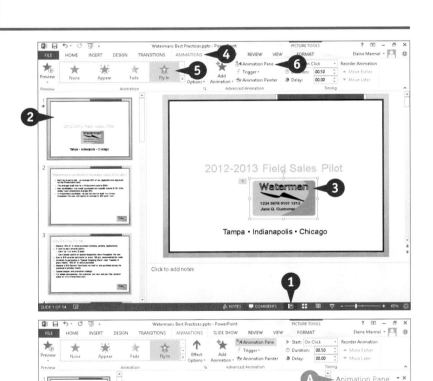

7 To add your next animation, click the **Add Animation** button.

Note: You add an animation using the **Add Animation** button; if you choose from the Animation Gallery, PowerPoint overwrites the existing animation instead of adding a new one.

8 Click an animation effect.

PowerPoint adds the effect to the Animation pane.

9 Repeat Steps **7** and **8** to add more animation effects to the selected object.

C PowerPoint places each effect in the Animation pane in the order you add them.

10 To preview your custom effect, click the **Preview** button.

D You can also click the first effect in the Animation pane and then click **Play From**.

11 To change the order in which effects appear, click an effect and then click the **Move Up** button (⬆) or the **Move Down** button (⬇).

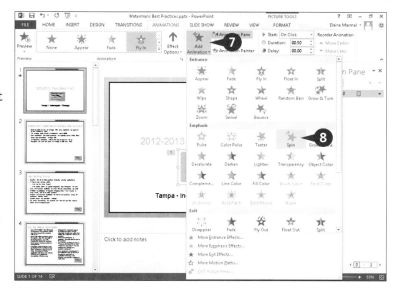

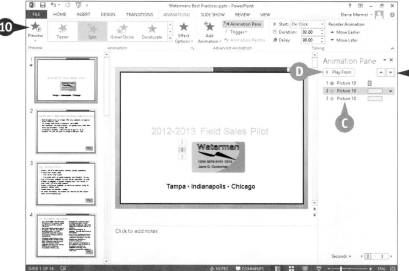

TIPS

How do I remove an animation?
Select the slide element containing the animation effect, click the **Animations** tab, and then click **None** in the Animation Gallery. If the animation is a custom animation, click the **Animation Pane** button. Then, in the Animation pane, click the effect that you want to remove, click the ▼ that appears, and click **Remove**.

Can I change the duration of an effect?
Yes. Select the slide element containing the effect, click the **Animation Pane** button, click the effect whose duration you want to change, click the ▼ that appears, choose **Timing**, and use the settings in the dialog box that opens to change the effect's duration.

Record Narration

Most presentations benefit from narration. You can speak as you present, or you can use PowerPoint's Record Narration feature to record a narration track to go along with the show. That way, you do not need to be present for your audience to receive the full impact of your presentation.

To record narration for a presentation, your computer must be equipped with a microphone. When you finish recording, an audio icon appears at the bottom of each slide for which you have recorded narration. When you save the presentation, PowerPoint saves the recorded narration along with the presentation file.

Record Narration

1 Click the **Slide Show** tab.

2 Click **Record Slide Show**.

A In the Record Slide Show dialog box, select **Narrations and laser pointer** (□ changes to ☑).

3 Click **Start Recording** to start the slide show, and speak into the computer's microphone.

B Click → to move to the next slide in the show and continue recording.

C Click ❚❚ to pause the recording. To continue recording, click **Resume Recording** in the window that appears.

D Click ↶ to start over on the current slide.

4 When you finish, right-click the last slide and click **End Show**.

An audio indicator appears in the lower-right corner on each slide for which you record narration. You can click the indicator to hear that slide's narration.

Note: You do not need to record all narration at one time. End the show; to later complete the narration, select the first slide that needs narration. Then, click the **Slide Show** tab, click the bottom of the **Record Slide Show** button and click **From Current Slide**.

Insert a Background Song

You can insert a song that plays repeatedly during your presentation. PowerPoint can play AIFF Audio (.aif), AU Audio (.au), MIDI (.mid or .midi), MP3 (.mp3), Advanced Audio Coding - MPEG-4 (.m4a, .mp4), Windows Audio (.wav), and Windows Media Audio (.wma) files.

If you choose music from a website, download it to your computer's hard drive before inserting it in your presentation; otherwise, as data flows to your computer from the Internet, your listener will experience breaks in the music.

Insert a Background Song

1 Click the first slide in your presentation.

2 Click the **Insert** tab.

3 Click **Audio**.

4 Click **Audio on My PC**.

The Insert Audio dialog box appears.

5 Navigate to and select the audio file you want to add to your presentation.

6 Click **Insert**.

Ⓐ An audio indicator and playback tools appear on the slide.

Ⓑ Audio Tools appear on the Ribbon.

7 Click **Play in Background**.

When you run your slide show (see the section "Run a Slide Show" for details), the song loops in the background from the first slide until the show ends.

Note: To decrease the size of your PowerPoint file, compress the audio file. Click **File**, click **Info**, and then click **Compress Media**. Select an audio quality and the compression automatically begins.

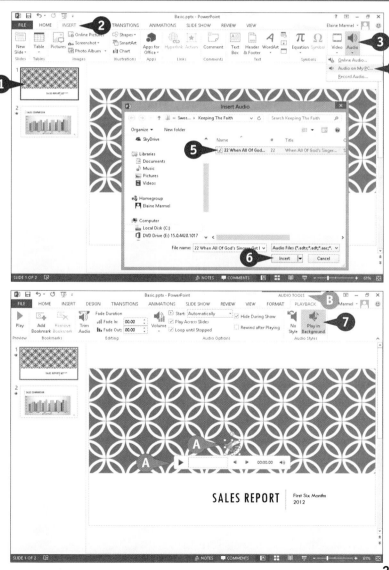

Create Speaker Notes

You can create speaker notes for your presentation. Speaker notes, also called notes pages, are notations that you add to a slide and that you can print out and use to help you give a presentation. You can also use speaker notes as handouts for your presentation. When creating notes pages, PowerPoint includes any note text that you add, as well as a small picture of the actual slide. You can add speaker notes in the Notes pane or on the Notes page.

You can print your speaker notes along with their associated slides. For details, see the tip at the end of this section.

Create Speaker Notes

Using the Notes Pane

1 Click ⬚ to switch to Normal view.

2 Click a slide to which you want to add notes.

3 Click here to display the Notes pane.

Note: The Notes pane button acts as a toggle; each click displays or hides the Notes pane.

4 Click in the Notes pane and type any notes about the current slide that you want to include.

Note: You can enlarge the Notes pane. Place ⬚ over the line separating the Notes pane from the slide (⬚ changes to ⬚) and drag up.

You can repeat Steps **2** to **4** for other slides to which you want to add notes.

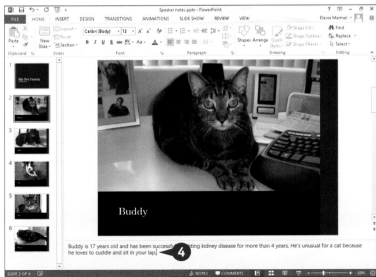

Using the Notes Page

1 Click a slide to which you want to add notes.

2 Click the **View** tab.

3 Click **Notes Page**.

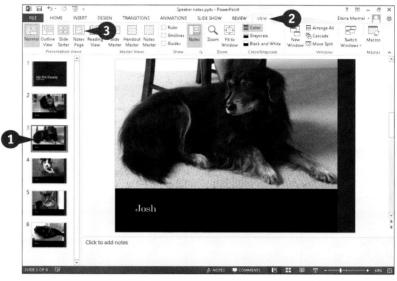

The Notes Page view opens and displays the selected slide.

4 Click in the bottom pane and type any notes about the current slide that you want to include.

Ⓐ You can click the **Zoom** button to display the Zoom dialog box and magnify the notes.

Ⓑ You can also drag the **Zoom** slider to magnify the notes.

You can edit and format your notes text using buttons on the Home tab.

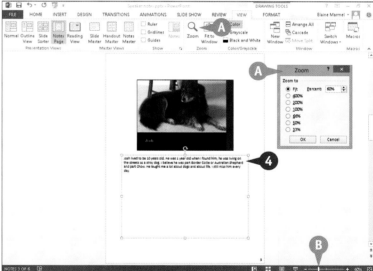

TIP

How do I print my notes with my slides?
Follow these steps. Click the **File** tab, and then click **Print**. Click to select your printer. In the Settings section, click ▾ for the second setting and click **Notes Pages** (Ⓐ). Click **Print**.

Settings

Print All Slides
Print entire presentation

Slides:

Notes Pages ◄ Ⓐ
Print slides with notes

Rehearse a Slide Show

You can determine exactly how long PowerPoint displays each slide during a presentation using PowerPoint's Rehearse Timings feature. When you use Rehearse Timings, PowerPoint switches to Slide Show mode, displaying your slides in order; you control when PowerPoint advances to the next slide in the show.

When recording how long PowerPoint displays each slide, you should rehearse what you want to say during each slide as well as allow the audience time to read the entire content of each slide. After you record the timings, PowerPoint saves them for use when you present the slide show to your audience.

Rehearse a Slide Show

1 Click ⊞ to switch to Slide Sorter view.

2 Click the **Slide Show** tab.

3 Click the **Rehearse Timings** button.

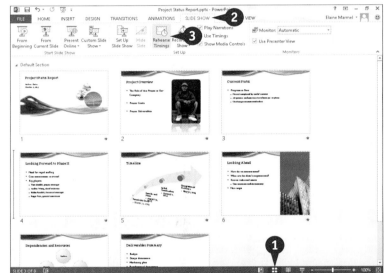

PowerPoint switches to Slide Show view and displays the first slide.

A PowerPoint displays the Record Slide Show toolbar and starts a timer.

4 Rehearse what you want to say.

B Click ❚❚ to pause the timer. To restart the timer, click **Resume Recording** in the window that appears.

C To cancel the timer on a slide and start timing that slide again, click ↶.

5 When you finish timing the first slide, click ➔ to proceed to the next slide.

PowerPoint displays the next slide.

6 Repeat Steps **4** and **5** for each slide in your presentation.

When the slide show finishes, a dialog box appears and displays the total time for the slide show.

7 Click **Yes**.

D PowerPoint saves the timings and displays them below each slide.

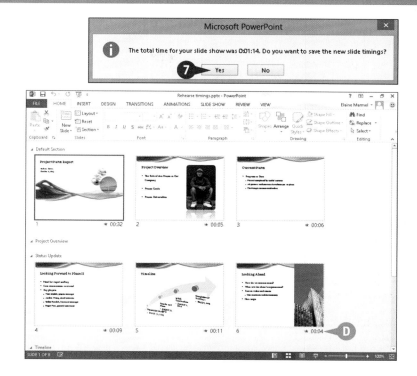

TIP

How do I create handouts for my audience?
Follow these steps:

1 Click **File**.

2 Click **Print**.

3 Select your printer.

4 In the Settings section, click ▼ for the second setting.

5 In the Handouts section, select a handout layout.

6 Click **Print**.

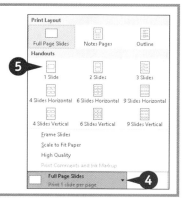

Run a Slide Show

You can run a presentation using PowerPoint's Slide Show view, which displays full-screen images of your slides. Slides advance in order, but you can, if necessary, view thumbnails of all of your slides so that you can display a particular slide out of order.

To enrich the experience for your audience, you can use PowerPoint's pointer options to draw directly on the screen. You can choose from several pen tools and colors. You can present your slide show using a single monitor or two monitors.

Run a Slide Show

Run a Presentation

1 Click the **Slide Show** tab.

2 Click **From Beginning**.

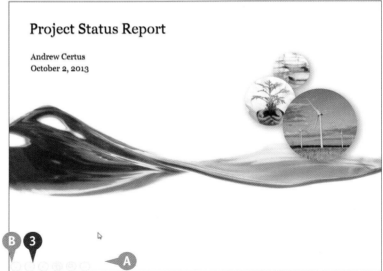

PowerPoint switches to Slide Show mode and displays the first slide.

Ⓐ When you move the mouse pointer to the bottom-left corner, faint slide show control buttons appear.

3 Click anywhere in the slide to advance to the next slide or click the **Next** button (▷).

Ⓑ To redisplay the previous slide, you can click the **Previous** button (◁).

Work with Thumbnails

1 Click the **See All Slides** button ( ).

C PowerPoint displays thumbnails of all slides in your presentation.

2 Click any slide to display it in Slide Show mode.

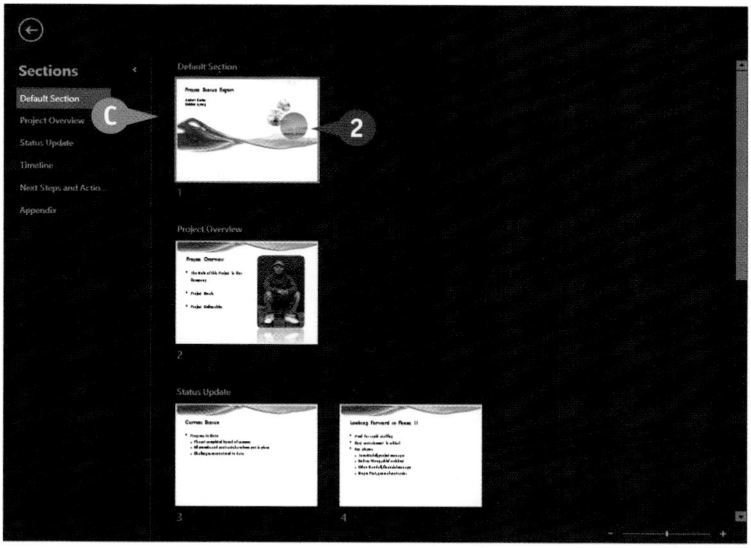

Point Out Slide Information

1 Click the **Pen and Laser Pointer Tools** button ( ).

2 Select a tool.

D When you move the mouse pointer over the slide, the mouse appears as the tool you selected.

Note: To redisplay , repeat Steps **1** and **2**, selecting the same tool.

To erase all marks, click the **Pen and Laser Pointer Tools** button ( ) and then click **Erase All Ink on Slide**.

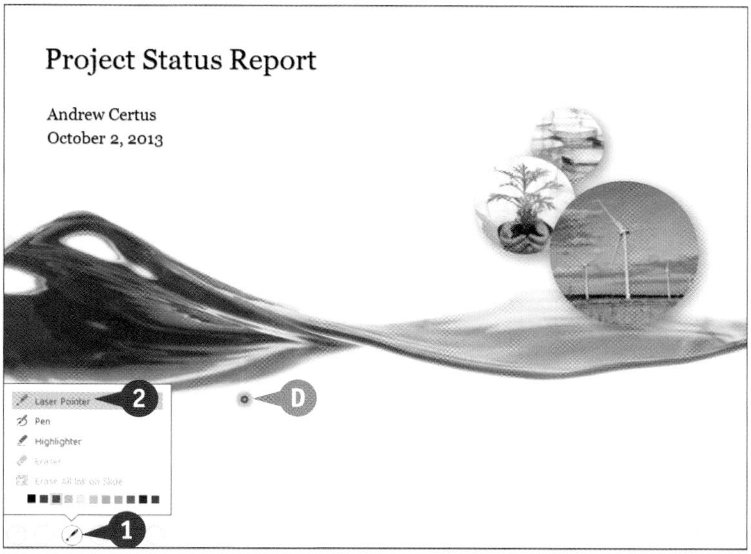

TIPS

Can I change the color of the ink I use for pen and laser pointer tools?
Yes. Follow the steps in the subsection "Point Out Slide Information" once to select a pointing tool and once again to select the tool's color. The order in which you make these selections does not matter.

Can I hide a slide while I talk?
Yes. You can do this by changing the screen color to black or white. Click the **Menu** button ( ) and point the mouse at **Screen**. Then click **Black Screen** or **White Screen**. Presenter view contains a shortcut **Black Screen** button ( ). To redisplay the slide, click anywhere on-screen.

continued

You can call the audience's attention to objects by zooming in on them. This approach can be useful if you display a slide for a lengthy time; zooming in can recapture your audience's attention.

Many people like to work in PowerPoint's Presenter view, which displays your notes as you present, but your audience sees only your slides. If you present on two monitors, PowerPoint automatically uses Presenter view to display notes and slides on separate monitors. Using only one monitor, you can still set up your presentation to use Presenter view.

Run a Slide Show (continued)

Zoom an Object

1 Click the **Zoom** button ( ).

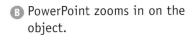

A PowerPoint grays the slide background and displays a lighted square that you can use to focus on an object.

2 Slide 🔍 over the object you want to enlarge and click.

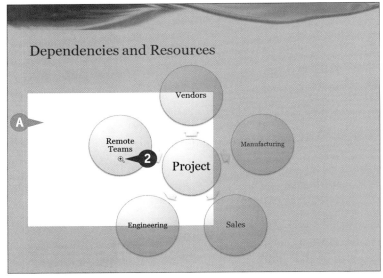

B PowerPoint zooms in on the object.

To redisplay the original size of the slide, press Esc.

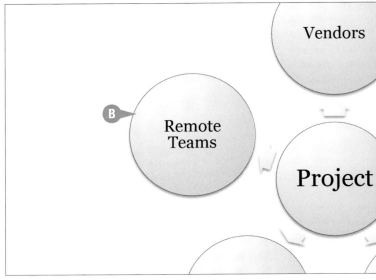

Using Presenter View

1 Click the **Menu** button (⦾).

2 Click **Show Presenter View**.

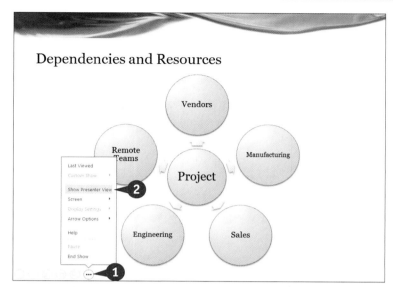

PowerPoint displays your presentation in Presenter view while your audience continues to see Slide Show mode.

C The tools to control your presentation appear here.

D You can use these buttons to increase or decrease the font size of your notes.

E You can click here to display the next or previous slide.

Note: When you display your last slide, the next slide area displays "End of slide show."

3 Press Esc or click here to end your slide show.

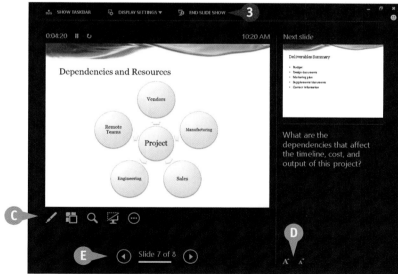

TIP

Can I display the Windows taskbar so that I can switch to another program if necessary?

Yes. When working with a single monitor, click the **Menu** button (⦾), click **Screen**, and then click **Show Taskbar** (**A**). From Presenter view, you can click **Show Taskbar** at the top of the screen.

Review a Presentation

You can use comments to review a presentation and provide feedback. Comments appear in a pane along the right side of the PowerPoint window. Small balloons appear on the slide to indicate that a comment exists, and you can click a balloon to view that comment.

PowerPoint displays comment information in the Comments pane along the right side of the PowerPoint window. In the Comments pane, you can click the New button to add another comment to the same slide, and you can view the next and previous comments using the Next and Previous buttons.

Review a Presentation

Insert a Comment

1 Click ▣ to display the presentation in Normal view.

2 Click the slide on which you want to comment.

Note: To add a general comment about the slide, skip Step **3**.

3 Click the text or object on which you want to comment.

4 Click the **Review** tab.

5 Click **New Comment**.

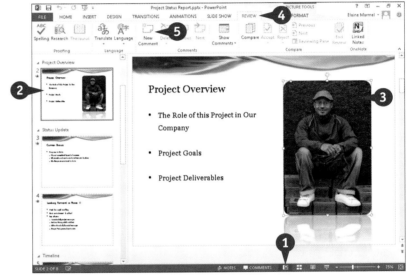

Ⓐ The Comments pane appears, containing a new comment block.

Ⓑ A comment balloon appears on the slide.

6 Type your comment here.

7 When you finish typing your comment, click outside the comment block or press Tab.

Ⓒ You can add another comment to the same slide by clicking the **New** button.

Ⓓ You can click ✕ to close the Comments pane.

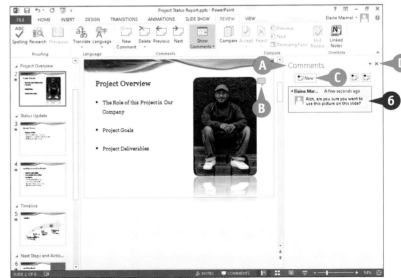

Reply to a Comment

1 Click the **Review** tab.

2 Click **Show Comments**.

The Comments pane appears.

3 Click in the **Reply** box of the comment you want to answer.

4 Type your reply.

5 Press **Tab** or click outside the Reply box.

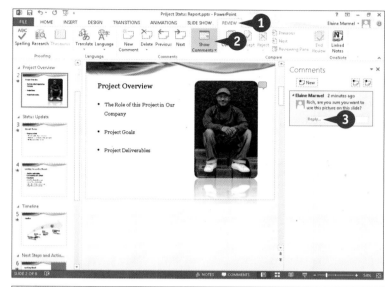

E PowerPoint stores the reply and adds another Reply box.

F PowerPoint adds another comment balloon almost on top of the original comment balloon.

G To read the next or previous comment, click 🗗 or 🗗.

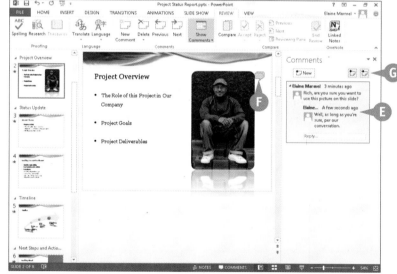

TIP

How can I edit or delete a comment?

To edit a comment, click the text of the comment that you want to edit to open a text box containing the comment. Make your changes and then click outside the comment box. To delete a comment, right-click it on the slide and then click **Delete Comment**. You can also delete it from the Comments pane. Slide ⬚ over the comment or reply until ✕ appears (**A**). Then, click ✕. Deleting a comment also deletes its replies.

Package Your Presentation on a CD

To share your PowerPoint presentation with others, you can save it to a CD. With the Package for CD feature, PowerPoint bundles the presentation along with all of the necessary clip art, multimedia elements, and other items needed to run your show, including any linked files contained in your presentation. The CD even includes a PowerPoint Viewer with the file in case the recipient does not have PowerPoint installed on his or her computer.

If you prefer, you can save your presentation as a WMV movie file that includes any narration and timings you record.

Package Your Presentation on a CD

1. Click the **File** tab.

2. Click **Export**.

3. Click **Package Presentation for CD**.

4. Click **Package for CD**.

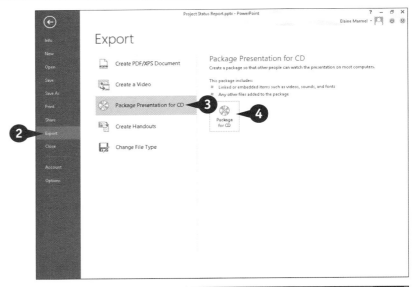

The Package for CD dialog box appears.

5. Type a name no longer than 16 characters for the CD.

6. Click **Copy to CD**.

Note: PowerPoint prompts you to insert a blank CD; do so and click **Retry**.

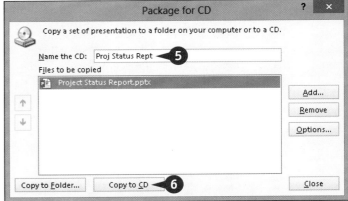

If your presentation contains linked files, PowerPoint asks you if you want to include those files on the CD.

7 If you trust the source of each linked file, click **Yes**.

PowerPoint copies the presentation files.

The size of the presentation determines how long copying takes.

When PowerPoint finishes copying the presentation, a dialog box appears.

8 Click **No**.

Note: If you want to continue packaging additional copies of the presentation, you can click **Yes**.

9 Click **Close**.

The Package for CD dialog box closes.

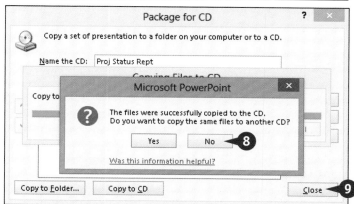

TIP

How do I save my presentation as a video?

To save your presentation as a video, follow these steps. Click the **File** tab and then click **Export**. Click **Create a Video**. Click ▼ and choose a quality level (Ⓐ). Click ▼ and specify whether PowerPoint should use recorded narration and timings (Ⓑ). Click **Create Video** (Ⓒ). In the Save As dialog box, specify the file name, type, and folder in which PowerPoint should save the video. Click the **Save** button. PowerPoint saves the presentation as a video in the folder you specified.

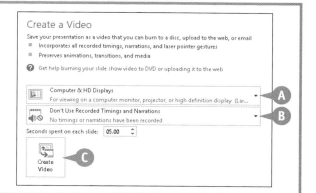

Present Online

You can deliver your PowerPoint presentation online at no cost to you by taking advantage of the free Office Presentation Service that Microsoft offers.

When you present online, members of your audience view your presentation in their web browsers. They use a link that you provide to connect to your presentation. They do not need to set up anything; they need only their browser and the link you provide.

PowerPoint generates the link for you, and you can send the link via e-mail or you can paste the link at a location where members of your audience can click it.

Present Online

1 Open only the presentation you want to share.

2 Click the **File** tab.

3 Click **Share**.

4 Click **Present Online**.

A You can click here (☐ changes to ☑) to enable your audience to download your presentation.

5 Click **Present Online**.

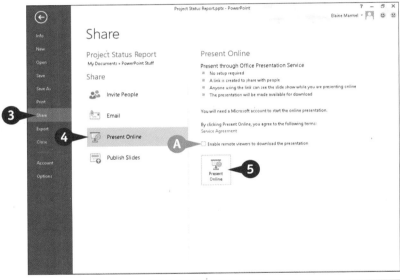

The Present Online dialog box appears.

6 Click an invitation option:

Copy Link — with this option, you need to paste the link where others can access it; or

Send in Email — this option opens an e-mail message with the link to the presentation embedded. Fill in the recipients and send the e-mail.

7 When you are ready to start your presentation, click **Start Presentation**.

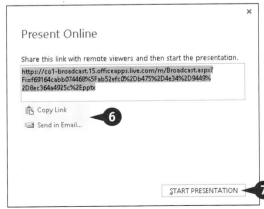

PowerPoint switches to Slide Show mode. See the section "Run a Slide Show" for details on presenting.

8 When your presentation concludes, press Esc to return to Normal view in PowerPoint.

9 Click the **Present Online** tab.

10 Click **End Online Presentation**.

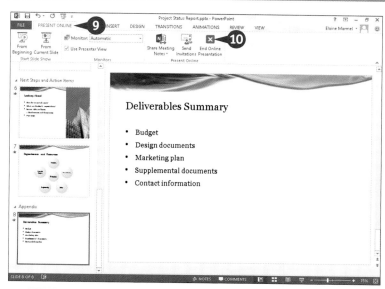

PowerPoint displays a message asking you to confirm that you want to end the presentation.

11 Click **End Online Presentation**.

PowerPoint stops the presentation and the Present Online tab disappears.

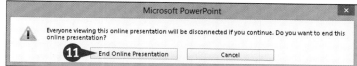

TIP

What should I do if I want to send the e-mail message with the link a few days prior to the presentation?

PowerPoint's Present Online feature assumes that you will present soon after initiating the link, so you should send an e-mail announcing that you will be presenting and provide the date and time. Tell your recipients that they will receive a link via e-mail from you approximately 30 minutes before the presentation will begin (you can choose the time, but be sure to allow enough time for the link to arrive). Then, on the day of your presentation, at the prearranged time, complete the steps in this section.

PART V

Access

Access is a robust database program that you can use to store and manage large quantities of data related to anything from a home inventory to a giant warehouse of products. Access organizes your information into tables, speeds up data entry with forms, and performs powerful analysis using filters and queries. In this part, you learn how to build and maintain a database file, add tables, create forms, and analyze your data using filters, sorting, and queries.

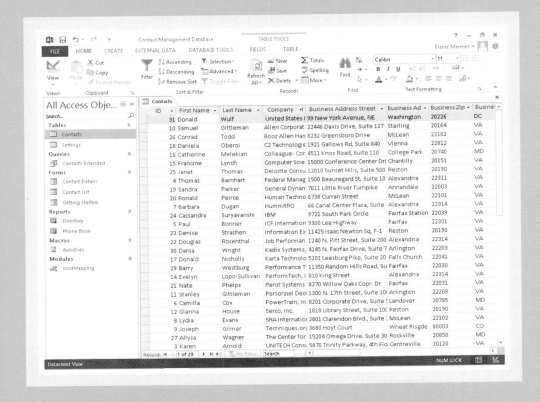

Understanding Database Basics

Access is a popular database program that you can use to catalog and manage large amounts of data. You can use Access to manage anything from a simple table of data to large, multifaceted lists of information. For example, you might use Access to maintain a list of your clients or a catalog of products you sell.

If you are new to Access, you should take a moment and familiarize yourself with the basic terms associated with the program, such as *database*, *table*, *record*, *field*, *form*, *report*, and *query*. This section contains definitions of all these key terms.

Databases

Simply defined, a *database* is a collection of related information. You may not be aware, but you use databases every day. Common databases include telephone directories or television program schedules. Your own database examples might include a list of contacts that contains addresses and phone numbers. Other examples of real-world databases include product inventories, client invoices, and employee payroll lists.

Tables

The heart of any Access database is a table. A table is a list of information organized into columns and rows. In the example of a client contact database, the table might list the names, addresses, phone numbers, company names, titles, and e-mail addresses of your clients. You can have numerous tables in your Access database. For example, you might have one table listing client information and another table listing your company's products.

ID	First Name	Last Name	State
1	Karen	Arnold	VA
2	Thomas	Barnhart	VA
3	Paul	Bonner	VA
4	Camilla	Cox	MD

Records and Fields

Every entry that you make in an Access table is called a *record*. Records always appear as rows in a database table. Every

First Name	Last Name	Company	Address	State
Donald	Wulf	Perform Tech	99 New York Avenue	VA

record consists of *fields*, which are the separate pieces of information that make up each record. Each field of a record appears in a separate column. For example, in a client contact list, each record (row) might include fields (columns) for first name, last name, company name, title, address, city, ZIP code, phone number, and e-mail address. Field names appear at the top of each column.

Forms

You can enter your database records directly into an Access table or you can simplify the process by using a *form*. Access forms present your table fields in an easy-to-read, fill-in-the-blank format. Forms allow you to enter records one at a time. Forms are a great way to ensure consistent data entry, particularly if other users are adding information to your database list.

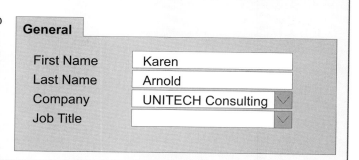

General

First Name	Karen
Last Name	Arnold
Company	UNITECH Consulting
Job Title	

Reports and Queries

You can use the report feature to summarize data in your tables and generate printouts of pertinent information, such as your top ten salespeople and your top-selling products. You can use queries to sort and filter your data. For example, you can choose to view only a few of your table fields and filter them to match certain criteria.

CONTACTS

Karen Arnold   **Dynatech Consulting**
Centreville, VA 20101   **1870 Taskey Parkway**
Phone
(703) 655-1212

Thomas Barnhart   **Management Partners Inc.**
Alexandria, VA 22311   **8522 Montegue St.**
Phone
(703) 671-6600

Plan a Database

The first step to building an Access database is deciding what sort of data you want it to contain. What sorts of actions do you want to perform on your data? How do you want to organize it? How many tables of data do you need? What types of fields do you need for your records? What sort of reports and queries do you hope to create? Consider sketching out on paper how you want to group the information into tables and how the tables will relate to each other. Planning your database in advance can save you time when you build the database file.

Tables I need:
    Contacts
Fields I need in the Contacts table:
    Name
    State
    Phone
Reports I need:
    Report that lists all fields
    Report that lists just name and phone
Forms I need:
    Contact list that shows all information for all entries
    Contact details that lists all information for one entry

Create a Database Based on a Template

You can build web apps — a new kind of database designed with Access and published online — or desktop databases based on any of the predefined Access templates. For example, you can create databases to track contact lists, assets, and task management. You can also search Office.com to find new, featured templates. This book focuses on building desktop databases.

When you create a new database using a template, the database includes pre-built tables and forms, which you populate with your own data. You control the structure of your database by modifying or eliminating preset tables and fields and adding database content such as tables, forms, and reports.

Create a Database Based on a Template

1 Start Access.

Note: You can also create a new database from within Access; click the **File** tab and then click **New**.

Ⓐ On the Access start screen or the New screen, templates appear.

Ⓑ You can search for additional templates online at Office.com by typing keywords here.

2 Click a template.

Note: To build a database, select a template that contains "Desktop" as the first word in its name. Web app template names do not contain the word "Desktop."

A window appears, displaying the template information.

Ⓒ To view the next or previous template, click these buttons.

3 Type a new name in the **File Name** field.

4 To change the folder in which you store the database file, click the **Open** button ( ).

Note: If you are satisfied with the folder Access suggests, skip to Step **7**.

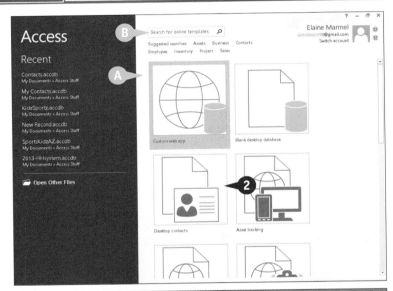

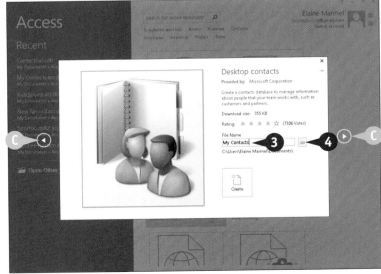

The File New Database dialog box appears.

5 Locate and select the folder in which you want to store the database file.

6 Click **OK**.

7 Click **Create**.

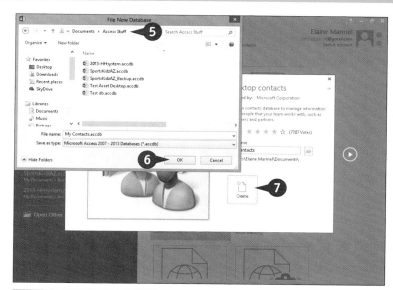

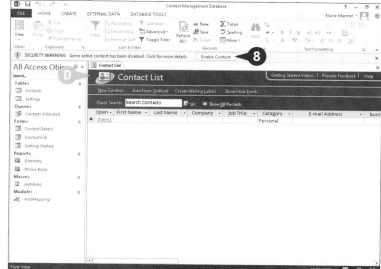

Ⓓ Access downloads the template and creates a new, blank database, ready for data.

Note: The Getting Started window for the Contacts Management Database appears. You can watch videos associated with the database or you can click × to close the window.

8 A security warning appears; to hide the warning and enable the macros in this template, click **Enable Content**.

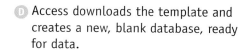

How do I know what fields to keep in or remove from my table?

To determine the fields you need in your database, decide the kinds of information you want to track in your database and the types of reports and queries you want to generate to view your data. For best results, use the suggested fields; you can always remove or hide fields that you do not use at a later time. (For help removing or hiding fields from a table, see the sections "Delete a Field from a Table" and "Hide a Field in a Table" later in this chapter.)

Create a Blank Database

Access includes many predefined database templates, including templates for creating contact lists, assets, project management, task management, and more. You can also log onto the Office.com site to find additional downloadable templates.

If you determine that none of these predesigned Access templates suits your purposes, you can create a new, blank database and then decide on the tables, fields, forms, and other objects your database will include.

Create a Blank Database

1 Start Access.

Note: You can also create a new database from within Access; click the **File** tab and then click **New**.

Ⓐ On the Access start screen or the New screen, templates appear.

2 Click **Blank desktop database**.

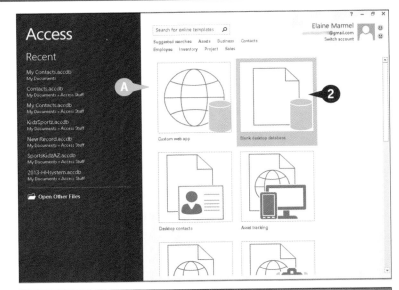

A window appears, displaying the template information.

Ⓑ To view the next or previous template, click these buttons.

3 Type a new name in the **File Name** field.

4 To change the folder in which you store the database file, click the **Open** button (📂).

Note: If you are satisfied with the folder Access suggests, skip to Step **7**.

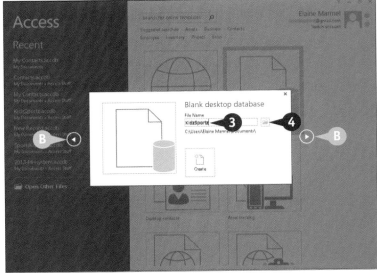

The File New Database dialog box appears.

5 Locate and select the folder in which you want to store the database file.

6 Click **OK**.

7 Click **Create**.

C Access creates a new, blank database and opens a new table, ready for data.

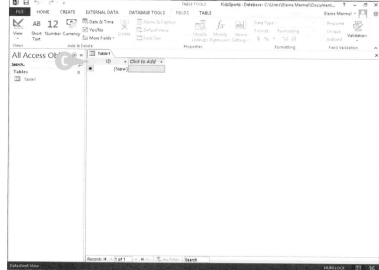

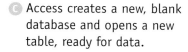

What is the pane on the left?
This is the Navigation pane, which you can use to open various database objects. Click the **Shutter Bar Open/ Close** button («) to collapse the pane; click the button again (») to expand the pane.

How do I open an existing database?
Click the **File** tab, click **Open**, click **Recent**, and then click the database in the Recent Databases list that appears. If the database does not appear in the Recent Databases list, click **Open Other Files**, click **Computer** or your SkyDrive, and then click **Browse** to display an Open dialog box. Locate and select the database file, and click **Open**.

Create a New Table

Access databases store all data in tables. A *table* is a list of information organized into columns and rows that hold data. A table might list the names, addresses, phone numbers, company names, titles, and e-mail addresses of your clients. Each row in a table is considered a *record*. You can use columns to hold *fields*, which are the individual units of information contained within a record.

If you need to add a table to a database, you can easily do so. All table objects that you create appear listed in the Navigation pane; simply double-click a table object to open it.

Create a New Table

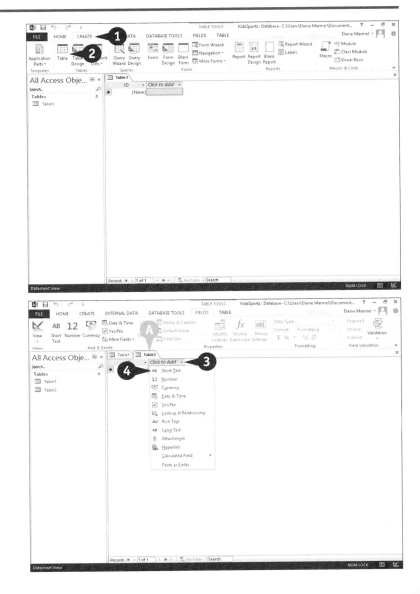

1 With your database open in Access, click the **Create** tab.

2 Click the **Table** button.

Ⓐ Access creates a new table and displays it in Datasheet view.

Note: See the next section, "Change Table Views," to learn more about Datasheet view.

3 To name a field, click the **Click to Add** link at the top of the field column.

4 Click the type of field you want to add.

In this example a Short Text field is added.

5 Type a name for the field and press **Enter**.

6 Repeat Steps **4** to **5** to create more fields for the table.

7 When you are finished adding fields, close the table by clicking the **Close** button (×).

Access prompts you to save the table changes.

8 Click **Yes**.

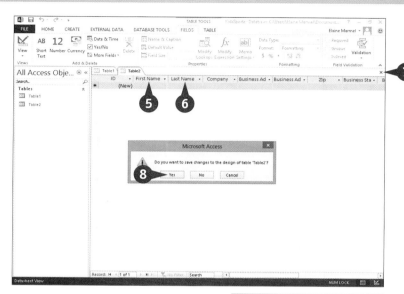

The Save As dialog box appears.

9 Type a name for the table.

10 Click **OK**.

Access lists the table among the database objects in the Navigation pane.

Note: After you save a table, you can reopen it by double-clicking it in the Navigation pane.

Can I rename table fields?

Yes. You can rename fields in any table. To do so, double-click the field label and type a new name. When you finish, press **Enter**.

How do I remove a table that I no longer want?

Before attempting to remove a table, ensure that it does not contain any important data that you need. To delete the table, select it in the Navigation pane and press **Delete**. Access asks you to confirm the deletion before permanently removing the table, along with any data that it contains.

Change Table Views

You can view your table data using two different view modes: Datasheet view and Design view. In Datasheet view, the table appears as an ordinary grid of intersecting columns and rows where you can enter data. In Design view, you can view the skeletal structure of your fields and their properties and modify the design of the table.

In either view, you can add fields by typing new field names in the Field Name column, or change the field names. In Design view, you can also change the type of data allowed within a field, such as text or number data.

Change Table Views

Switch to Design View

1 Open any table by double-clicking it in the Navigation pane.

A Access displays the table in the default Datasheet view.

2 Click the **Home** tab.

3 Click the bottom half of the **View** button.

4 Click **Design View**.

Note: You can quickly toggle between Datasheet view and Design view by clicking the top half of the **View** button.

B Access displays the table in Design view.

C The bottom of the view displays the properties of the field you select in the top of the view.

D Access displays the Table Tools Design tab.

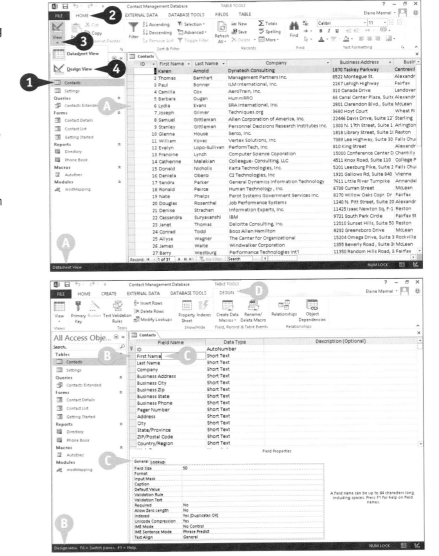

Switch to Datasheet View

1 Click the **Home** tab.

2 Click the bottom half of the **View** button.

3 Click **Datasheet View**.

Note: You can quickly switch from Design view to Datasheet view by clicking the top half of the **View** button.

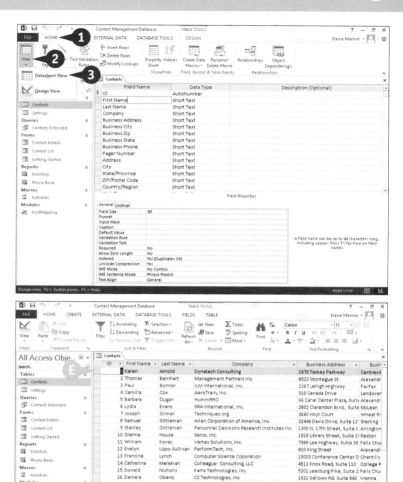

Ⓔ Access displays the default Datasheet view of the table.

TIPS

Do all Access objects have the same views?
No. All Access objects have a Design view, but other available views depend on the object you select in the Navigation pane. For example, in addition to a Design view, reports have a Report view, a Print Preview, and a Layout view, and forms have a Form view and a Layout view.

What is the purpose of the Field Properties area in Design view?
The Field Properties area enables you to change the design of the field, specifying how many characters the field can contain, whether fields can be left blank, and other properties.

Add a Field to a Table

You can add fields to your table to include more information in your records. For example, you may need to add a separate field to a Contacts table for mobile phone numbers. Alternatively, you may need to add a field to a table that contains a catalog of products to track each product's availability.

After you add a field, you can name it whatever you want. To name a field, double-click the field label in Datasheet view, type a new name, and press the Enter key. Alternatively, you can change the field name in Design view.

Add a Field to a Table

1 Double-click to open the table to which you want to add a field in Datasheet view.

2 Click the column heading to the left of where you want to insert a new field.

Note: Access adds the column for the new field to the right of the column you select.

3 Click the **Fields** tab.

4 In the Add & Delete group, click the button for the type of field you want to add.

In this example, a Short Text field is added.

A Access adds the new field.

Note: You can rename the field by typing a new name and pressing **Enter**.

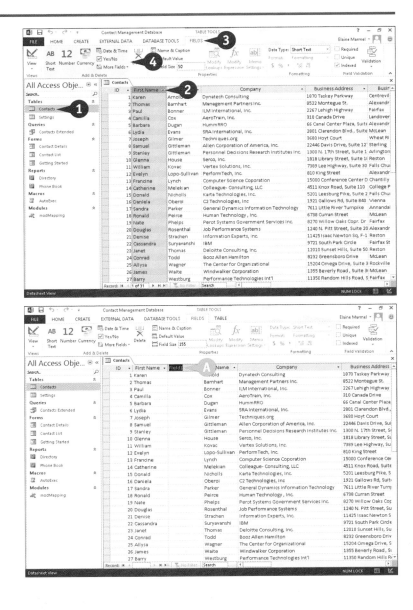

Delete a Field from a Table

You can delete a field that you no longer need in a table. For example, if your employee contact information database contains a Pager Number field, you might opt to delete that field.

When you remove a field, Access permanently removes any data contained within the field for every record in the table. If you do not want to delete the information in the field, you might choose to hide the field. For information, see the next section, "Hide a Field in a Table."

Delete a Field from a Table

1 Double-click to open the table that you want to edit in Datasheet view.

2 Click the column header for the field you want to remove.

Ⓐ Access selects the entire column.

3 Click the **Fields** tab.

4 Click the **Delete** button.

Ⓑ Access prompts you to confirm the deletion.

5 Click **Yes**.

Note: You might also see a message warning you that deleting the field will also delete an index; click **Yes**.

Ⓒ Access removes the field and any record content for the field from the table.

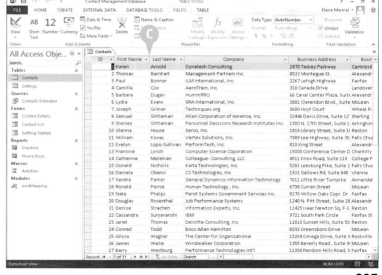

297

Hide a Field in a Table

Suppose your table contains fields that you do not want to view on a regular basis, but that you do not want to delete from the table. For example, a table containing a catalog of products might include a field indicating the country in which the product was manufactured — information that you might not need to view on a regular basis but still need occasionally. You also might hide a field to prevent another user on your computer from seeing the field. Whatever the reason, you can hide the field. When you are ready to view the field again, you can easily unhide it.

Hide a Field in a Table

1 Double-click the table that you want to edit to open it in Datasheet view.

2 Right-click the column heading of the field you want to hide.

3 Click **Hide Fields**.

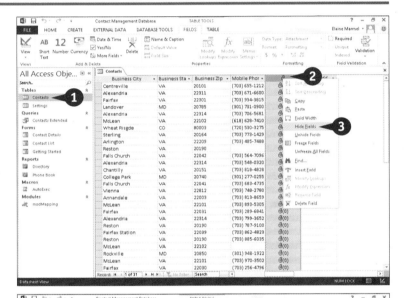

A Access hides the field.

Note: To view the field again, right-click any column heading and click **Unhide Fields**. In the Unhide Columns dialog box that appears, select the column that you want to display again (☐ changes to ☑), and click **Close**. Access displays the hidden field as the last column in the table.

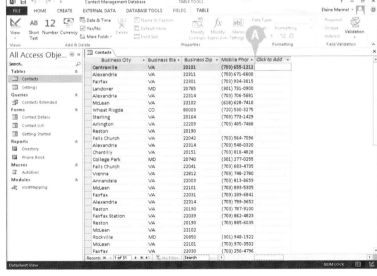

Move a Field in a Table

You can change the order of fields in a table. Moving fields is particularly useful if you built your database from a predesigned template, because you may want to reorder fields to suit the way you enter data for each record.

Moving a field changes its position in Datasheet view but does not change the order of the fields in the table design. If you create a form after reordering fields, the form fields appear in their original position.

Move a Field in a Table

① Double-click the table that you want to edit to open it in Datasheet view.

② Click the column heading of the field you want to move.

Ⓐ Access selects the entire column.

③ Drag the column to a new position in the table (ↆ changes to ↆ).

Ⓑ A bold vertical line marks the new location of the column as you drag.

④ Release the mouse button.

Ⓒ Access moves the field to the new location.

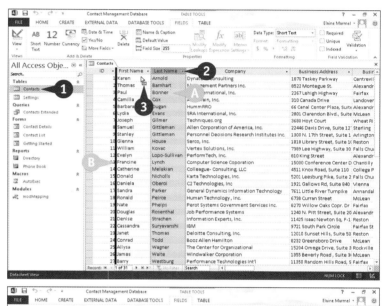

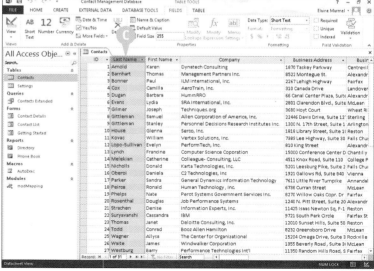

Create a Form

Although you can enter data into your database by typing it directly into an Access table, you can simplify data entry, especially if someone else will be entering the data, by creating a form based on your table. Forms present your table fields in an easy-to-read, fill-in-the-blank format. When you create a form based on a table, Access inserts fields into the form for each field in the table.

Forms, which enable you to enter records one at a time, are a great way to help ensure accurate data entry, particularly if other users are adding information to your database.

Create a Form

1 Double-click the table that you want to edit to open it in Datasheet view.

2 Click the **Create** tab.

3 Click the **Form** button.

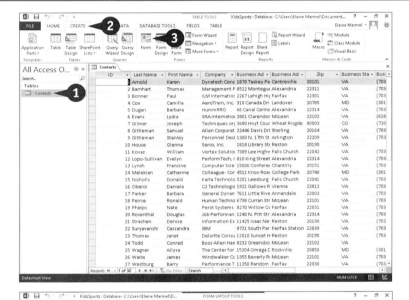

A Access creates the form.

4 Click the **Close** button (×) to close the form.

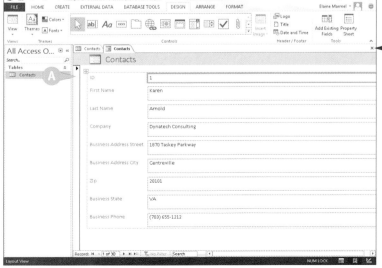

Access prompts you to save your changes.

5 Click **Yes**.

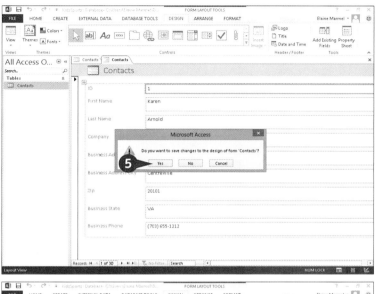

The Save As dialog box appears.

6 Type a name for the form.

7 Click **OK**.

Access lists the form among the database objects in the Navigation pane.

Note: After you save a form, you can reopen it by double-clicking it in the Navigation pane.

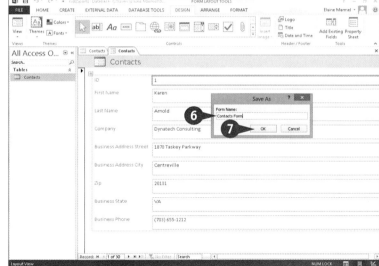

How do I delete a form that I no longer need?

To delete a form, click it in the Navigation pane, and then press Delete or click the **Delete** button on the Home tab. Access asks you to confirm the deletion; click **Yes**.

Can I create a blank form?

Yes. Click the **Blank Form** button on the Create tab to open a blank form. A field list appears, containing all the fields from all of the tables in the database. To add a field to the form, drag it from the list onto the form. You can populate the form with as many fields as you need.

Change Form Views

You can view your form using three form views: Form view, Design view, and Layout view. Form view is the default; in this view, you can simply enter data. In Design view, each form object appears as a separate, editable element. For example, in Design view, you can edit both the box that contains the data and the label that identifies the data. In Layout view, you can rearrange the form controls and adjust their sizes directly on the form. Access makes it easy to switch from Form view to Design view to Layout view and back.

Change Form Views

Switch to Design View

1. Double-click the form that you want to edit to open it in Form view.

2. Click the **Home** tab.

3. Click the bottom half of the **View** button.

4. Click **Design View**.

Ⓐ Access displays the form in Design view.

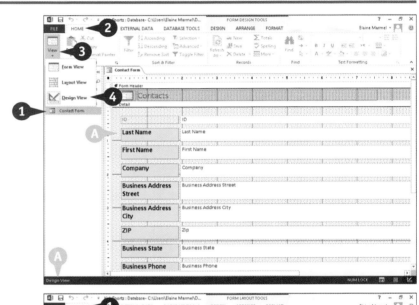

Switch to Layout View

1. Click the **Home** tab.

2. Click the bottom half of the **View** button.

3. Click **Layout View**.

Ⓑ Access displays the form in Layout view.

To return to Form view, you can click the bottom half of the **View** button and then click **Form View**.

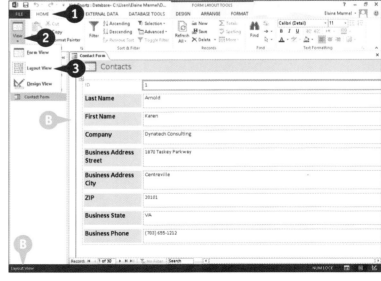

Move a Field in a Form

You can move a field to another location on your form. For example, you might move a field to accommodate the order in which data is entered in the form. When you click a field label to select it, Access selects only the field label. Because you will probably want to move both the field label and the field contents, you can more easily move both of them if you select both at the same time.

Although you can move a field in either Design view or Layout view, you might find it easier to make changes to your form in Layout view.

Move a Field in a Form

1 Double-click the form that you want to edit to open it in Form view.

2 Switch to Layout view (see the previous section, "Change Form Views," for details).

3 Click the label of the field that you want to move (⌖ changes to ⌖).

4 Press and hold **Ctrl** as you click the contents of the field.

5 Click and drag the field label and contents to the new location on the form.

Ⓐ This symbol identifies the proposed position of the field label and contents.

Ⓑ When you release the mouse button, Access repositions the field.

You can click anywhere outside the field label and contents to deselect them.

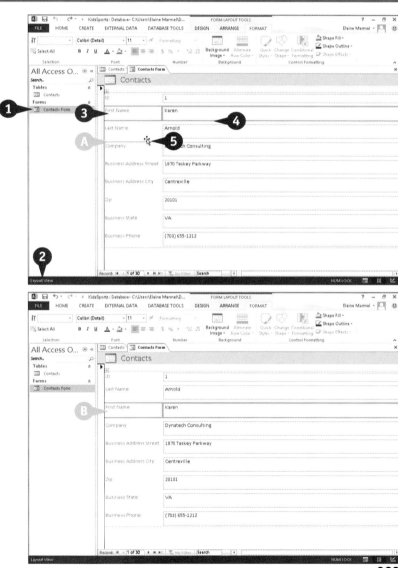

Delete a Field in a Form

Y ou can delete a field that you no longer need in a form. When you remove a field, you need to remove both the data box and the field label. Although you can delete a field in Design view or in Layout view, you might find it easier to do this in Layout view.

Note that removing a form field does not remove the field from the table upon which the form is originally based or any of the data within that field; it simply removes the field from the form.

Delete a Field in a Form

1 Double-click the form that you want to edit to open it in Form view.

2 Switch to Layout view (see the section "Change Form Views" for details).

3 Click the label of the field that you want to delete (changes to).

4 Press and hold **Ctrl** as you click the contents of the field.

5 Press **Delete**, or click the **Home** tab and then click the **Delete** button.

A Access removes the field and label from the form.

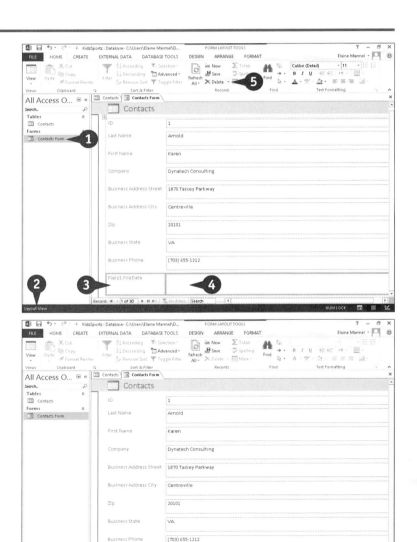

Apply a Database Theme

A *theme* is a predesigned set of color schemes, fonts, and other visual attributes. Applying a theme to an Access database is a quick way to make it more visually appealing. When you apply a theme to an Access database, that same theme is applied to all forms and tables in your database.

Themes are shared among the Office programs; you can use the same theme in your Access database that you have applied to worksheets in Excel, documents in Word, or slides in PowerPoint.

Apply a Database Theme

1 Double-click the form that you want to edit to open it in Form view.

2 Switch to Layout view (see the section "Change Form Views" for details).

3 Click the **Design** tab.

4 Click the **Themes** button.

5 Click the theme you want to apply.

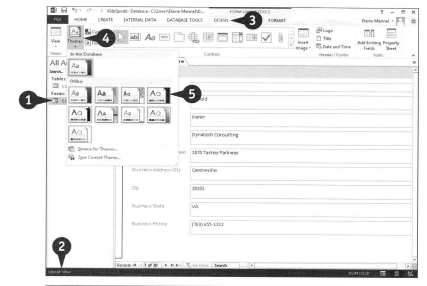

A Access applies the theme to all forms in the database, changing colors and fonts.

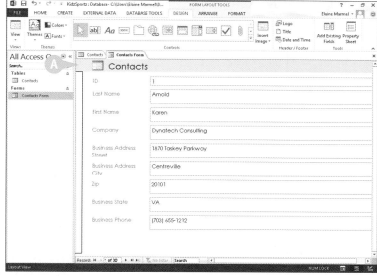

Format Form Fields

To change the look of a form, you can apply formatting to fields in the form. You might format a form field to draw attention to it in order to make it easier to locate that field for data-entry purposes. Or, you might opt to change the font of all field labels, make them larger, and change their color, to make them stand out on the form for those who enter data.

You can apply the same types of formatting to form fields that you apply to words in Word documents, PowerPoint presentations, Publisher publications, Outlook messages, and Excel cells.

Format Form Fields

1 Double-click the form that you want to edit to open it in Form view.

2 Switch to Layout view (see "Change Form Views" for details).

3 Click to select the field whose text you want to format.

Ⓐ To select multiple fields, you can press and hold **Ctrl** as you click additional fields.

4 Click the **Format** tab.

5 Use these tools to format the fields:

Click the **Font** ▼ and choose a font.

Click the **Font Size** ▼ and choose a font size.

Click ▼ to the right of the **Font Color** button (**A ▼**) and choose a color.

Click ▼ to the right of the **Background Color** button (**🖉 ▼**) and choose a color.

Ⓑ Access formats the text in the selected fields.

You can click anywhere outside the selected fields to deselect them.

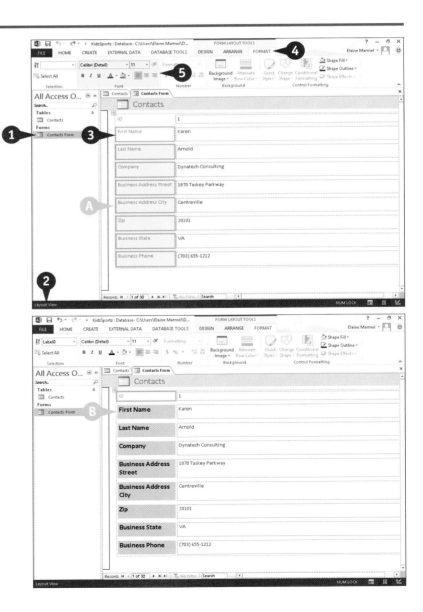

Add a Background Image

You can add a background image to a form to make it more pleasant to view. For example, you could add a company logo or a photograph that appears in your company's marketing materials. A background image, while not necessary or essential to a form, can make data entry a bit more interesting, simply because the form looks less form-like. And, when data entry is less boring and more interesting, the person entering the data is less likely to make mistakes. A background image on a form remains fixed, even as you change records.

Add a Background Image

1 Double-click the form that you want to edit to open it in Form view.

2 Switch to Layout view (see the section "Change Form Views" for details).

3 Click the **Format** tab.

4 Click the **Background Image** button.

5 Click **Browse**.

The Insert Picture dialog box opens.

6 Locate and select the image you want to use.

7 Click **OK**.

A Access adds the image to the form background.

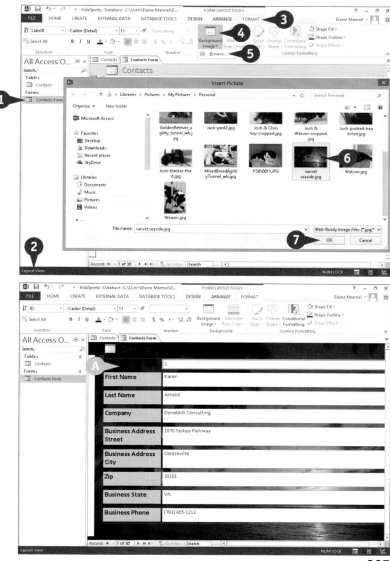

Add a Record to a Table

You build a database by adding records to a table in the database. Any new records that you add appear at the end of the table. You add records to a table in Datasheet view. As your table grows longer, you can use the navigation buttons on your keyboard to navigate it. You can press `Tab` to move from cell to cell, or you can press the keyboard arrow keys. To move backward to a previous cell, press `Shift` + `Backspace`.

After you enter a record in a database table, you can edit it in a table in Datasheet view.

Add a Record to a Table

1 In the Navigation pane, double-click the table to which you want to add a record.

Ⓐ Access opens the table, placing the cell pointer in the first cell of the first row.

Ⓑ By default, the first field in each table is a unique ID number for the record. Access sets this value automatically as you create a record.

2 Click in the second cell of the first empty row.

3 Type the desired data in the selected cell.

4 Press `Tab`.

Access fills in the ID number to add the new record.

5 Repeat Steps 3 and 4 until you have filled the entire row.

6 Press `Enter` or press `Tab` to move to the next row or record.

C The new record appears here.

D Access moves the cell pointer to the first cell in the next row.

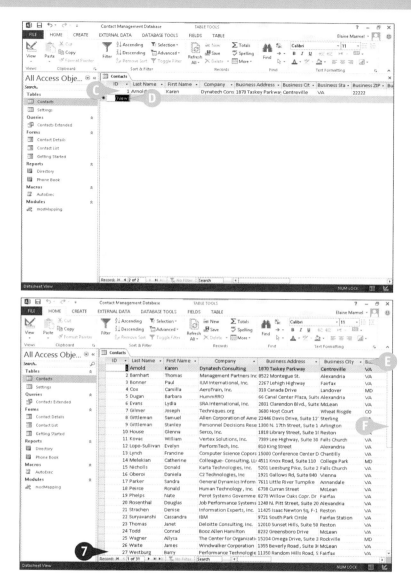

7 Repeat Steps **3** to **6** to add more records to the table.

Access adds your records.

E You can resize a column by dragging the column border left or right.

F You can use the scroll bars to view different parts of the table.

What is a primary key?

A *primary key* uniquely identifies each record in a table. For many tables, the primary key is the ID field by default. The ID field, which Access creates automatically, stores a unique number for each record as it is entered into the database. If you want, however, you can designate another field (or even multiple fields) as a primary key. To do so, switch the table to Design view, select the field that you want to set as the primary key, and click the **Primary key** button on the Design tab.

Add a Record to a Form

You can use forms to quickly add records to your Access databases. Forms present your record fields in an easy-to-read format. When you use a form to add records, the form presents each field in your table as a labeled box that you can use to enter data.

After you enter a record in a form, you can edit it if necessary. (See the tip for more information.) For help locating a particular record in the form window in order to edit it, see the next section, "Navigate Records in a Form."

Add a Record to a Form

1. In the Navigation pane, double-click the form to which you want to add a record.

   Ⓐ Access opens the form.

2. Click the **Home** tab.

3. Click the **New** button in the Records group.

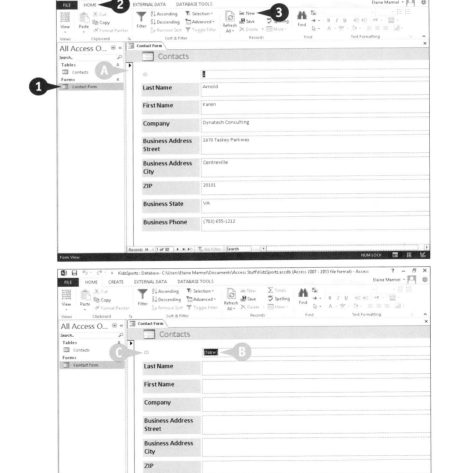

   Ⓑ Access displays a blank form, placing the insertion point in the first field.

   Ⓒ By default, the first field in the table associated with this form is a unique ID number for the record. Access sets this value automatically.

4. Press Tab .

Access moves the insertion point to the next field in the form.

⑤ Type the desired data in the selected field.

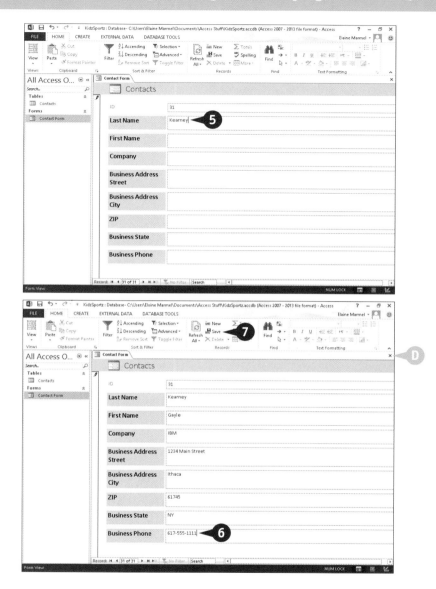

⑥ Repeat Steps **4** and **5** until you have filled the entire form.

⑦ Click **Save** or press Enter and press Tab.

Access saves the record and displays another blank form, ready for data.

Ⓓ To close the form window, you can click the **Close** button (×).

Are there other ways to insert a new record?

Yes. You can click the **New (Blank) Record** button (▸) on the form window's navigation bar, located along the bottom of the form.

How do I edit a record in a form?

You can reopen the form, navigate to the record that you want to change, and make your edits directly to the form data. When you save your changes, Access automatically updates the data in your table. To learn how to display a particular record in a form, see the next section, "Navigate Records in a Form."

Navigate Records in a Form

You may find it easier to read a record using a form instead of reading it from a large table containing other records. Similarly, editing a record in a form may be easier than editing a record in a table. You can locate records you want to view or edit using the navigation bar that appears along the bottom of the form window. This navigation bar contains buttons for locating and viewing different records in your database. The navigation bar also contains a Search field for locating a specific record. (You learn how to search for a record in a form in the next section.)

Navigate Records in a Form

1 In the Navigation pane, double-click the form whose records you want to navigate.

A Access displays the form.

B The Current Record box indicates which record you are viewing.

2 Click the **Previous Record** (◀) button or **Next Record** (▶) button to move back or forward by one record.

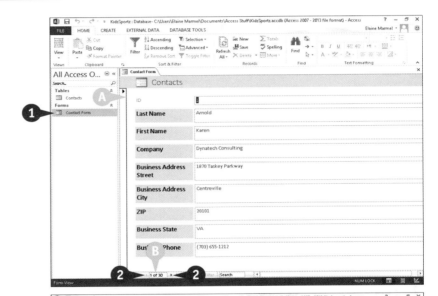

C Access displays the previous or next record in the database.

D You can click the **First Record** (◀) button or **Last Record** (▶) button to navigate to the first or last record in the table.

E You can click the **New (Blank) Record** button (▶) to start a new, blank record.

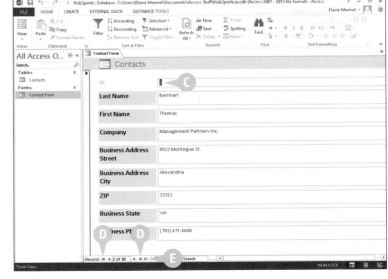

Search for a Record in a Form

You may find it easier to read and edit records in a form than in a large table containing other records. As described in the previous section, you can locate records you want to view or edit by using the various buttons in the navigation bar, such as the Previous Record button, the Next Record button, and so on. However, that method can become time-consuming if the table associated with the form contains many records. This section describes how to search for the record — an easier approach to finding a record while using a form. You search using the form's navigation bar.

Search for a Record in a Form

1 In the Navigation pane, double-click the form containing the record you want to find.

A Access displays the form.

2 Click in the **Search** box.

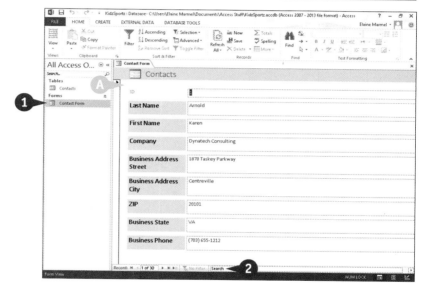

3 Type a keyword that relates to the record you want to find.

In this example, a search for a person's last name is performed.

B As you type, Access displays the first matching record.

4 After you finish typing your keyword, press Enter to display the next matching record, if any.

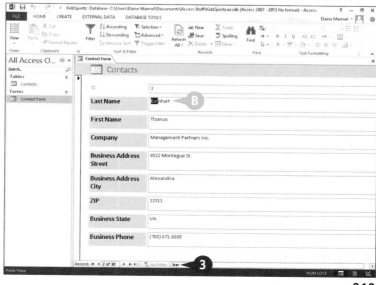

Delete a Record from a Table

You can remove a record from your database if it holds data that you no longer need. Removing old records can reduce the overall file size of your database and make it easier to manage. When you delete a record, all of the data within its fields is permanently removed.

You can remove a record from a database by deleting it from a table or by deleting it from a form. This section shows you how to delete a record from a table. (For help deleting a record from a form, see the next section, "Delete a Record from a Form.")

Delete a Record from a Table

1 In the Navigation pane, double-click the table that contains the record you want to delete.

A Access opens the table.

2 Position your mouse pointer over the gray box to the left of the record that you want to delete (⟲ changes to ➡) and click.

B Access selects the record.

3 Click the **Home** tab.

4 Click **Delete**.

Note: You can also right-click the record, and then click **Delete Record**.

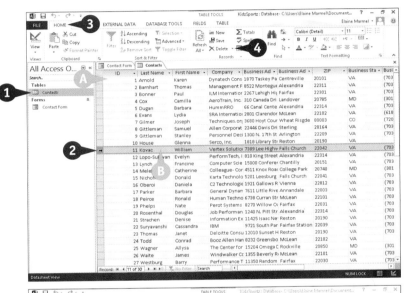

Access asks you to confirm the deletion.

5 Click **Yes**.

C Access permanently removes the row containing the record from the table.

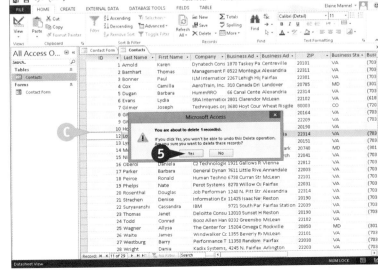

Delete a Record from a Form

I n addition to removing records directly from a table, as described in the previous section, you can remove records that you no longer need by using a form. Removing old records can reduce the overall file size of your database and make it easier to manage. When you delete a record, whether from a table or a form, Access permanently removes all the data within its fields.

The first step is to locate the record you want to delete; refer to the sections "Navigate Records in a Form" and "Search for a Record in a Form" for help locating the record.

Delete a Record from a Form

1 In the Navigation pane, double-click the form containing the record you want to delete.

Ⓐ Access displays the form.

2 Navigate to the record you want to delete.

3 Click the **Home** tab.

4 Click ▼ beside the **Delete** button.

5 Click **Delete Record**.

Access asks you to confirm the deletion.

6 Click **Yes**.

Access permanently removes the record.

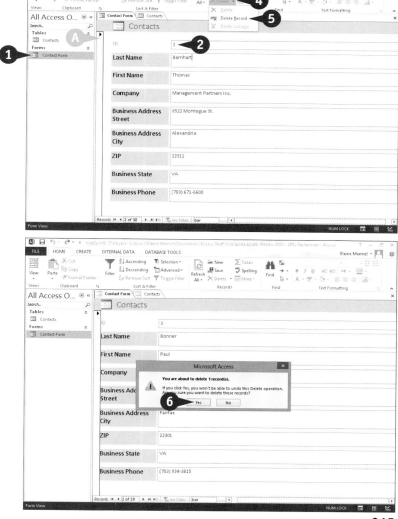

315

Sort Records

Sorting enables you to arrange your database records in a logical order to match any criteria that you specify. By default, Access sorts records in ID order. However, you may want to sort the records alphabetically or based on the ZIP code. You can sort in ascending order or descending order.

You can sort records in a table, or you can use a form to sort records. Sorting records in a table has no effect on the order in which records appear in an associated form; similarly, sorting in a form has no effect on the records in an associated table.

Sort Records

Sort a Table

1 In the Navigation pane, double-click the table you want to sort.

2 Position your mouse pointer over the column heading for the field by which you want to sort (⌖ changes to ↓) and click to select the column.

3 Click the **Home** tab.

4 Click a sort button:

Click **Ascending** to sort the records in ascending order.

Click **Descending** to sort the records in descending order.

Access sorts the table records based on the field you choose.

Ⓐ In this example, Access sorts the records alphabetically by company name in ascending order.

5 Click × to close the table.

Ⓑ In the prompt box that appears, you can click **Yes** to make the sort permanent or **No** to leave the original order intact.

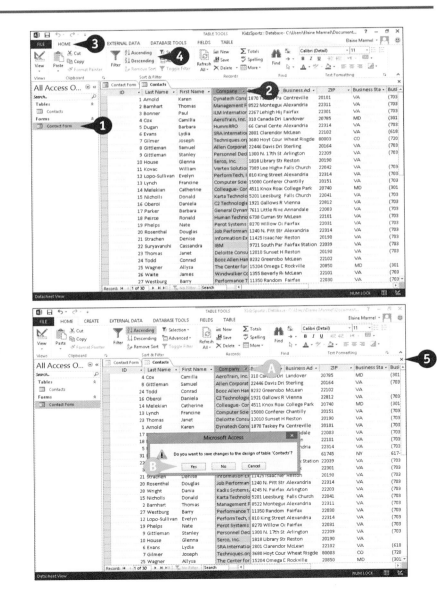

Sort Using a Form

1 In the Navigation pane, double-click the form you want to use to sort records.

2 Click in the field by which you want to sort.

3 Click the **Home** tab.

4 Click a sort button:

Click **Ascending** to sort the records in ascending order.

Click **Descending** to sort the records in descending order.

Access sorts the table records based on the field you chose.

C In this example, Access sorts the records alphabetically by company name in ascending order.

D You can use the navigation buttons to view the sorted records.

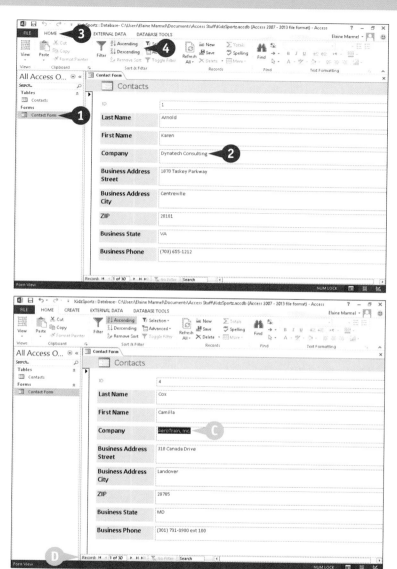

How are empty records sorted?
If you sort using a field for which some records are missing data, those records are included in the sort; they appear first in an ascending sort, or last in a descending sort.

How do I remove a sort order?
With the sorted table or form open, click the **Remove Sort** button in the Sort & Filter group on the Home tab. This returns the table to its original sort order. You can also use this technique to remove a sort from a query or report. (Queries and reports are covered later in this chapter.)

Filter Records

You can use an Access filter to view only specific records that meet criteria you set. For example, you may want to view all clients buying a particular product, anyone in a contacts database who has a birthday in June, or all products within a particular category. You can also filter by exclusion — that is, filter out records that do not contain the search criteria that you specify.

You can apply a simple filter on one field in your database using the Selection tool, or you can filter several fields using the Filter by Form command.

Filter Records

Apply a Simple Filter

1 In the Navigation pane, double-click the form you want to use to filter records.

2 Click in the field by which you want to filter.

3 Click the **Home** tab.

4 Click the **Selection** button.

5 Click a criterion.

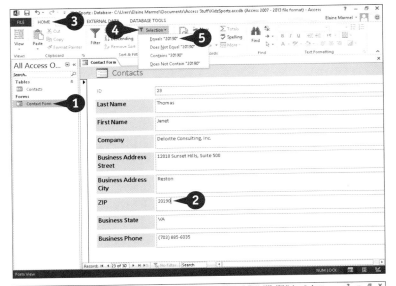

A Access filters the records.

B In this example, Access finds three records matching the filter criterion.

C You can use the navigation buttons ◄, ►, ◄, and ►◄ to view the filtered records.

D To remove the filter, you can click the **Toggle Filter** button.

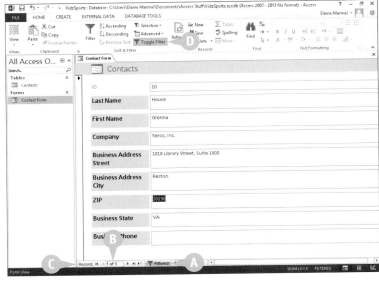

Filter by Form

1 In the Navigation pane, double-click the form you want to use to sort records.

2 Click the **Home** tab.

3 Click the **Advanced** button.

4 Click **Filter By Form**.

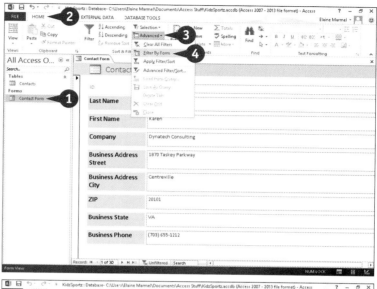

E A blank form appears.

5 Click in the field by which you want to filter.

6 Click the 🔽 that appears and choose a criterion.

7 Repeat Steps **5** and **6** to add more criteria to the filter.

F You can set OR criteria using the tab at the bottom of the form.

8 Click the **Toggle Filter** button to filter the records.

To remove the filter, you can click the **Toggle Filter** button again. Then, click the **Advanced** button and click **Clear All Filters**.

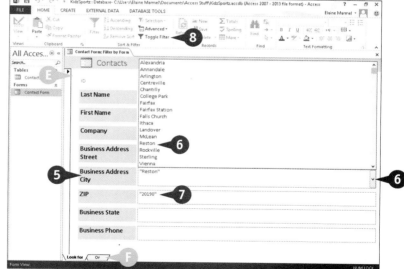

How do I filter by exclusion?

Click in the field that you want to filter in the form, click the **Selection** button on the Home tab, and then click an exclusion option.

What are OR criteria?

Setting OR criteria enables you to display records that match one set of criteria or another. For example, you might set up your filter to display only those records with the value 46989 OR 46555 in the ZIP field. After you set a criterion, Access adds an OR tab. If you set an OR criterion using that tab, Access adds another OR tab, and so on.

Apply Conditional Formatting

You can use Access's Conditional Formatting tool to apply certain formatting attributes, such as bold text or a fill color, to data in a form when the data meets a specified condition. For example, if your database tracks weekly sales, you might set up the Conditional Formatting feature to alert you if sales figures fall below what is required for you to break even.

You apply conditional formatting by creating a rule that specifies the criteria that the value in a field must meet. Access formats values that meet the criteria using settings you specify.

Apply Conditional Formatting

1 In the Navigation pane, double-click the form to which you want to apply conditional formatting.

2 Switch to Layout view.

Note: For details on switching form views, see Chapter 16.

3 Click the field to which you want to apply conditional formatting.

4 Click the **Format** tab.

5 Click the **Conditional Formatting** button.

The Conditional Formatting Rules Manager dialog box opens.

6 Click the **New Rule** button.

The New Formatting Rule dialog box opens.

7 Set the criteria you want to use to apply conditional formatting.

8 Specify how values that meet your criteria should be formatted.

9 Click **OK**.

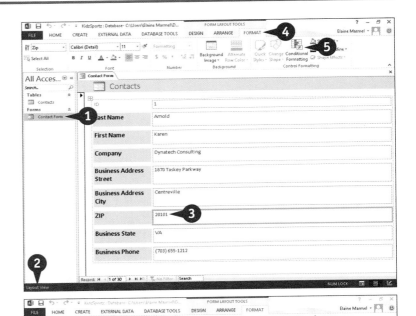

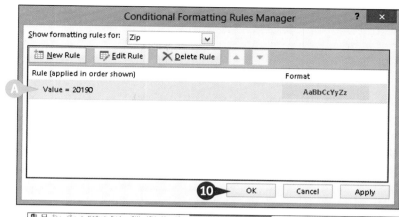

Ⓐ Access creates a rule based on the criteria you set.

⑩ Click **OK**.

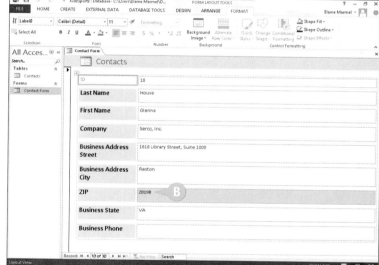

Ⓑ Access applies the conditional formatting.

TIP

How do I remove conditional formatting?
To remove conditional formatting complete Steps **1** to **5** in this section to open the Conditional Formatting Rules Manager dialog box. Click the conditional formatting rule you want to remove (Ⓐ), and click the **Delete Rule** button (Ⓑ). Click **OK**. Access removes the conditional formatting.

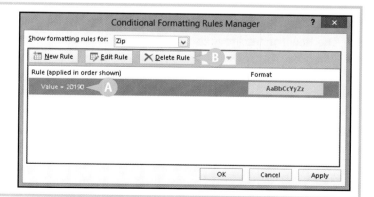

Perform a Simple Query

You can use a query to extract information that you want to view in a database. Queries are similar to filters but offer you greater control. You can use the Query Wizard to help you select the fields you want to include in the analysis. There are several types of Query Wizards. This section covers using the Simple Query Wizard.

Although beyond the scope of this book, queries also can help you collect information from multiple tables that you can then use to perform a mail merge; see *Teach Yourself VISUALLY Access 2013* for details on using Access data with Word's mail merge feature.

Perform a Simple Query

Create a Query

1. In the Navigation pane, double-click the table for which you want to create a simple query.

2. Click the **Create** tab.

3. Click the **Query Wizard** button.

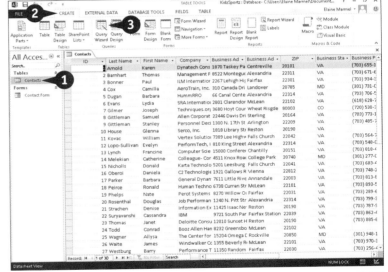

The New Query dialog box appears.

4. Click **Simple Query Wizard**.

5. Click **OK**.

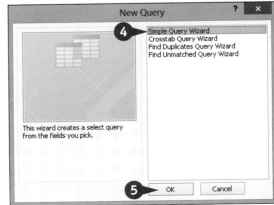

The Simple Query Wizard opens.

6 Click the **Tables/Queries** ☑ and choose the table containing the fields on which you want to base the query.

7 In the Available Fields list, click a field that you want to include in the query.

8 Click the **Add** button (>).

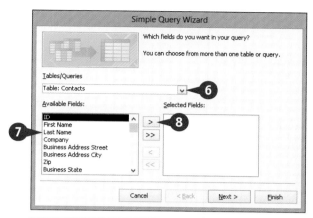

A The field appears in the Selected Fields list.

9 Repeat Steps **7** and **8** to add more fields to your query.

You can repeat Step **6** to choose another table from which to add fields.

Note: When using fields from two or more tables, the tables must have a relationship.

10 Click **Next**.

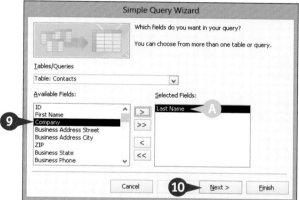

TIP

What is a table relationship?
A table relationship enables you to combine related information for analysis. For example, you might define a relationship between one table containing customer contact information and another table containing customer orders. With that table relationship defined, you can then perform a query to, for example, identify the addresses of all customers who have ordered the same product. To access tools for defining table relationships, click the **Database Tools** tab on the Ribbon and then click **Relationships**. If you created your database from a template, then certain table relationships are predefined.

continued ▶

During the process of creating a new query, the Query Wizard asks you to give the query a unique name so that you can open and use the query later. All queries that you create appear in the Navigation pane; you can double-click a query in the Navigation pane to perform it again.

If, after creating and performing a query, you determine that you need to add more criteria to it, you can easily do so. For example, you may realize that the query needs to include an additional table from your database or additional criteria to expand or limit the scope of the query.

Perform a Simple Query (continued)

11 Type a name for the query.

12 Select **Open the query to view information**
(○ changes to ●).

13 Click **Finish**.

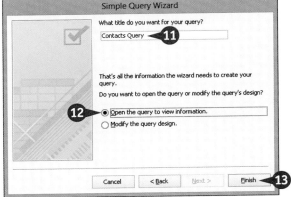

Ⓐ A query datasheet appears, listing the fields.

Ⓑ The query appears in the Navigation pane.

Add Criteria to the Query

1 If necessary, double-click the query in the Navigation pane that you want to modify to open it.

2 Click the **Home** tab.

3 Click the bottom half of the **View** button.

4 Click **Design View**.

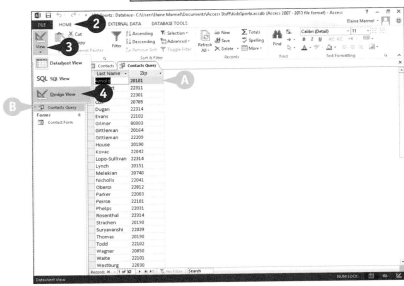

C Access displays the Query Tools Design tab.

5 Click in the **Criteria** box for the field you want to use as a criterion and type the data that you want to view.

This example specifies a ZIP code as the criterion.

6 Click the bottom half of the **View** button.

7 Click **Datasheet View**.

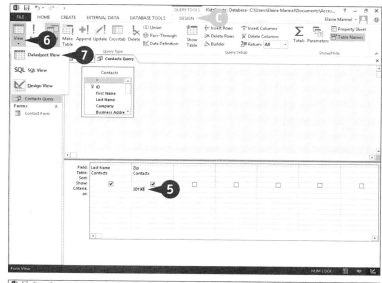

D The table now shows only the records matching the criteria.

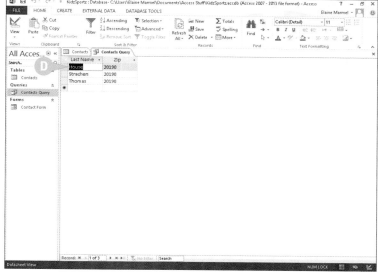

TIPS

How do I add another table to my query?

Switch to Design view, click the **Design** tab on the Ribbon, and then click the **Show Table** button to open the Show Table dialog box, where you can add another table to the query.

What kinds of queries do the other wizards in the New Query dialog box create?

The Crosstab Query Wizard's query displays information in a spreadsheet-like format, the Find Duplicates Query Wizard's query finds records with duplicate field values, and the Find Unmatched Query Wizard's query finds records in one table with no related records in another table.

Create a Report

You can use Access to create a report based on one or more database tables. You can create a simple report, which contains all the fields in a single table, or a custom report, which can contain data from multiple tables. To use fields from two or more tables, the tables must have a relationship. See the tip "What is a table relationship?" in the previous section for more information.

To create a custom report, you can use the Report Wizard; it guides you through all the steps necessary to turn complex database data into an easy-to-read report.

Create a Report

Create a Simple Report

1. In the Navigation pane, double-click the table for which you want to create a simple report.

2. Click the **Create** tab.

3. Click the **Report** button.

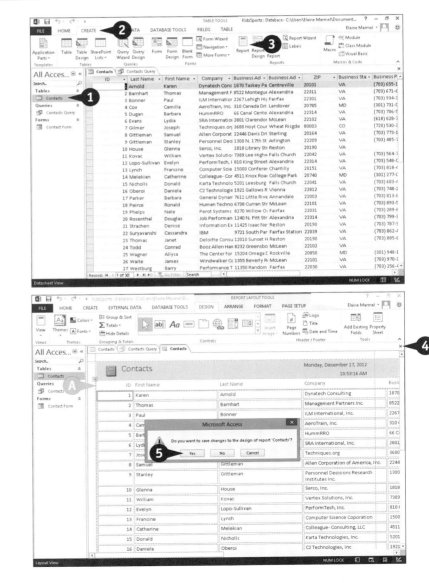

A. Access creates a simple report based on the table you selected.

4. Click × to close the report.

   Access prompts you to save the report.

5. Click **Yes**.

6. In the dialog box that appears, supply a report name and click **OK**.

B The report appears in the Navigation pane.

Create a Custom Report

1 In the Navigation pane, double-click the table for which you want to create a simple report.

2 Click the **Create** tab.

3 Click the **Report Wizard** button.

The Report Wizard opens.

4 Click the **Tables/Queries** ☑ and choose the table containing the fields on which you want to base the report.

5 In the Available Fields list, click a field that you want to include in the report.

6 Click the **Add** button (>).

C The field appears in the Selected Fields list.

7 Repeat Steps **5** and **6** to add more fields to your report.

8 Click **Next**.

9 Optionally, click the field you want to use to group the data.

10 Click the **Add** button (>).

D A preview of the grouping appears here.

11 Click **Next**.

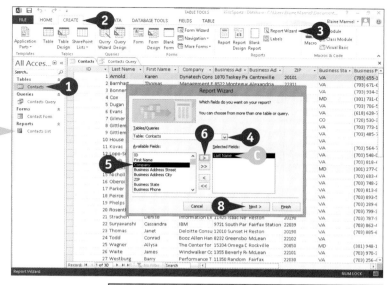

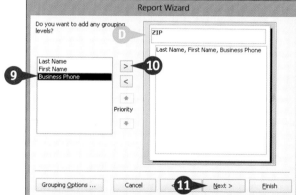

TIPS

How do I choose fields from different tables in a custom report?
Repeat Step **3** in the subsection "Create a Custom Report" for each additional table that contains fields you want to include.

How do I remove a field from a custom report?
If you have not yet completed the wizard, you can remove a field from the report by clicking the **Back** button until you reach the wizard's first screen. Then click the field you want to remove in the **Selected Fields** list and click the **Remove** button (<) to remove the field. To remove all the fields, click the **Remove All** button (<<).

continued ▶ 327

As you walk through the steps for building a report, the Report Wizard asks you to specify a sort order. You can sort records by up to four fields, in ascending or descending order. The wizard also prompts you to select a layout for the report. Options include Stepped, Block, and Outline, in either portrait or landscape mode.

Note that you can change other design aspects of the report by opening it in Design view. And, after you create the report, you can print it. For more information, see the tips at the end of this section.

Create a Report (continued)

12 To sort your data, click the first ⌄ and click the field by which you want to sort.

You can add more sort fields as needed.

Note: Fields are sorted in ascending order by default. Click the **Ascending** button to toggle to descending order.

13 Click **Next**.

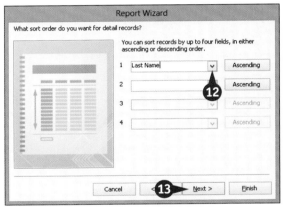

14 Select a layout option (○ changes to ◉).

Ⓐ You can set the page orientation for a report here (○ changes to ◉).

15 Click **Next**.

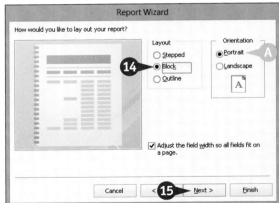

16 Type a name for the report.

17 Select **Preview the report**
(◯ changes to ◉).

18 Click **Finish**.

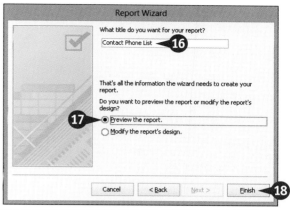

Ⓑ Access creates and displays
the report.

Ⓒ The report appears in the
Navigation pane.

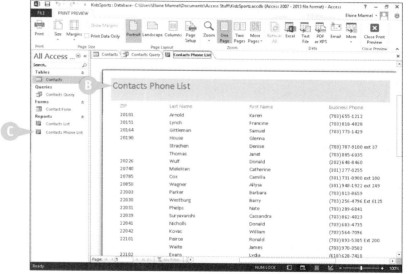

TIPS

How do I print a report?
To print a report from Print Preview
view, click the **Print Preview** tab and
click the **Print** button. Alternatively,
click the **File** button and click **Print** to
open the Print dialog box, where you
can select various printing options.

How can I customize a report in Access?
You can customize a report using Design view. You can change
the formatting of fields, move fields around, and more. You
can even apply conditional formatting to the report by
clicking the **Conditional Formatting** button on the Format
tab. For more about conditional formatting, refer to the
section "Apply Conditional Formatting" earlier in this chapter.

PART VI

Outlook

Outlook is an e-mail program and a personal information manager for the computer desktop. You can use Outlook to send and receive e-mail messages, schedule calendar appointments, keep track of contacts, organize lists of things to do, and more. In this part, you learn how to put Outlook to work for you using each of its major components to manage everyday tasks.

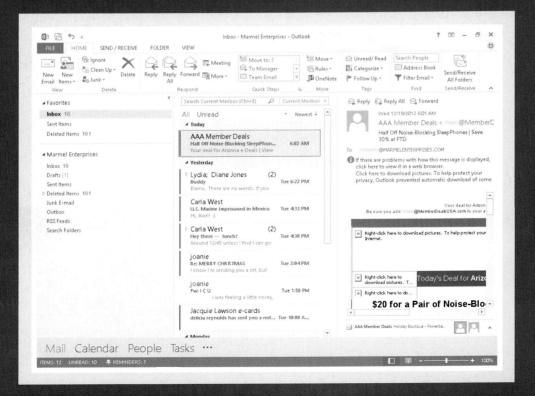

Navigate in Outlook

Outlook functions as a personal organizer, with Mail, Calendar, People, Tasks, and Notes components. You switch between these components using the Navigation bar.

Mail appears by default when you open Outlook and enables you to send and receive e-mail messages. Calendar enables you to keep track of appointments. People enables you to maintain a database of your contacts and include those contacts in e-mail messages you send and appointments you schedule. Tasks enables you to keep a to-do list.

Navigate in Outlook

Note: When Outlook opens, the Mail component appears by default. You can read more about using the Mail component in Chapter 19.

1 Click **Calendar** on the Navigation bar.

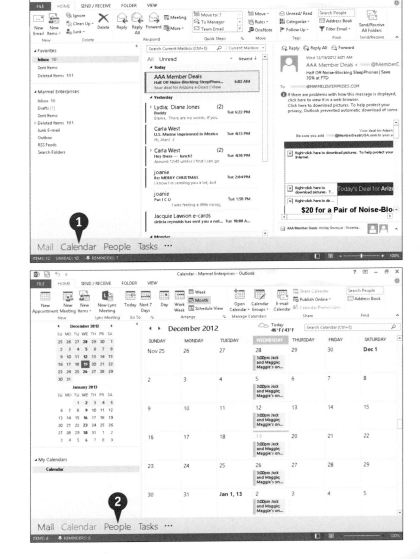

Outlook displays the Calendar component.

2 Click **People** on the Navigation bar.

Outlook displays the People component.

③ Click **Tasks** on the Navigation bar.

Outlook displays the Tasks component.

How do I change which component opens by default when I start Outlook?

To start with a different Mail folder or another component, such as Calendar, perform the steps that follow. Click the **File** tab, and click **Options** to display the Outlook Options dialog box. Click **Advanced**. In the Outlook Start and Exit section, click the **Browse** button to display the Select Folder dialog box. Click the component or Mail folder that you want to set as the default component (Ⓐ). Click **OK** twice to close both dialog boxes.

Schedule an Appointment

You can use Outlook's Calendar component to keep track of your schedule. When adding new appointments to the Calendar, you fill out appointment details, such as the name of the person with whom you are meeting, the location and date of the appointment, and the start and end times of the appointment. You can also enter notes about the appointment, as well as set up Outlook to remind you of the appointment in advance. If your appointment occurs regularly, such as a weekly department meeting, you can set it as a recurring appointment. Outlook adds recurring appointments to each day, week, or month as you require.

Schedule an Appointment

1 Click **Calendar** on the Navigation bar.

2 Click the date for which you want to set an appointment.

Ⓐ You can click here to navigate to a different month.

Ⓑ You can click here to select a different calendar view, such as a daily or weekly view.

3 Click the **New Appointment** button to display the Appointment window.

4 Type a name for the appointment; Outlook adds the name to the window's title.

Ⓒ You can type the appointment location here.

5 Click the **Start time** ▼ and set a start time.

Note: By default, Outlook allots 30 minutes for an appointment.

Ⓓ You can click the **End time** ▼ and change the end time.

Ⓔ Outlook automatically sets a reminder. You can click ▼ to change the reminder setting.

Ⓕ You can type notes about the appointment here.

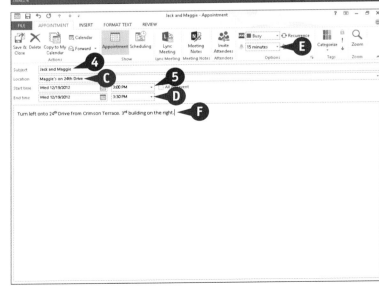

6 If your appointment occurs regularly, click the **Recurrence** button. Otherwise, skip to Step **9**.

The Appointment Recurrence dialog box appears.

7 Select the recurrence pattern.

G In the Range of Recurrence section, you can limit the appointments if they continue only for a specified time.

8 Click **OK**.

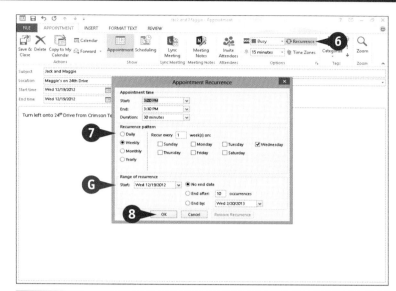

H Outlook marks the appointment as a recurring appointment.

9 Click the **Save & Close** button.

Outlook displays the appointment in the Calendar. To view the appointment details or make changes, double-click the appointment. To delete an appointment, right-click it and click **Delete**.

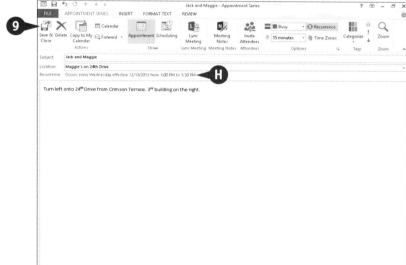

TIPS

Can I schedule an all-day event?
Yes. In the Appointment window, select **All day event** (☐ changes to ☑) beside the Start Time boxes.

Why do certain dates on the navigation calendars appear in bold?
Dates that appear in bold indicate that you have appointments scheduled on those days.

Create a New Contact

You can use Outlook's People component to maintain a list of contact information. You can track information such as your contacts' home and business addresses; e-mail addresses; instant message address; company information; home, work, fax, and mobile phone numbers; and social media updates. You can also enter notes about a contact.

By default, Outlook displays contact information using the People view, where you can edit contact information. You can also switch to other views such as the Business Card or List view.

Create a New Contact

Create a Contact

1 Click **People** on the Navigation bar.

2 Click the **New Contact** button.

Outlook opens a Contact window.

3 Fill in the contact's information.

You can press **Tab** to move from field to field.

Ⓐ You can click **Show** and then click **Details** to fill in additional information about the contact.

4 Click the **Save & Close** button.

Ⓑ Outlook saves the information and displays the contact in the People view.

Ⓒ You can click ⊡ to see available views and switch to one.

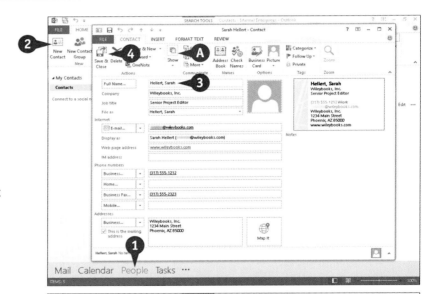

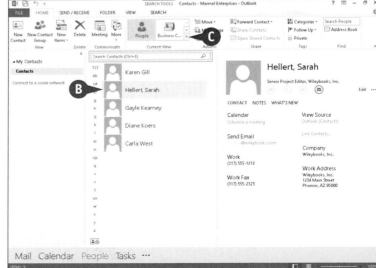

Work with the People Card

1 Click a contact.

D You can click here and type a part of the contact's name.

E Information about the contact appears here.

F You can click these links to set up an appointment or meeting with the contact or send an e-mail to the contact.

G You can click this link to reopen the window shown in the subsection "Create a Contact" to edit the contact's information.

2 To edit using the People card, click here.

Outlook displays People card fields in an editable format.

3 Make any changes.

H You can click ⊕ to add information.

4 Click **Save**.

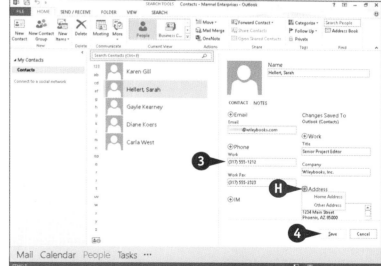

Is there an easy way to set up an appointment or e-mail one of my contacts if I am using Business Card view?

Yes. Right-click the contact and click **Create**. Click **Email** or **Meeting** (**A**). If you click **Email**, Outlook opens a Message window containing the contact's e-mail address in the To field; see Chapter 19 for details on completing the message. If you click **Meeting**, a Meeting window appears, where you can enter appointment details and e-mail a meeting request to the contact.

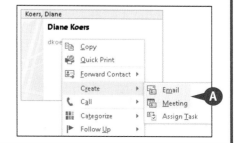

Create a New Task

You can use Outlook's Tasks component to keep track of things that you need to do; for example, you can create tasks for a daily list of activities or project steps that you need to complete. You can assign a due date to each task, prioritize and categorize tasks, and set a reminder date and time. You can set up a recurring task and even assign tasks to other people.

When you finish a task, you can mark it as complete. Depending on the current view, completed tasks may appear with a strikethrough on the Tasks list or they may not appear at all.

Create a New Task

1 Click **Tasks** in the Navigation bar to open the Tasks component.

2 Click the **New Task** button.

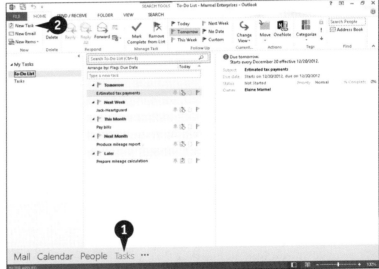

Outlook displays a Task window.

3 Type a subject for the task.

A You can click 🔲 to enter a due date.

B You can type notes or details about the task here.

C You can set a priority for the task using the **Priority** ▼.

D You can select **Reminder** (☐ changes to ✔) and then set a reminder date and time.

4 If your task occurs regularly, click here; otherwise, skip to Step **7**.

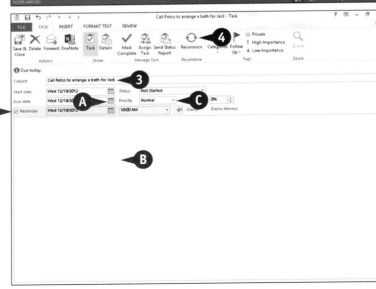

338

The Task Recurrence dialog box appears.

5 Select the recurrence pattern.

E In the Range of Recurrence section, you can limit the tasks if they continue only for a specified time.

6 Click **OK**.

7 Click the **Save & Close** button.

F Outlook displays the task in the list.

G Details of the selected task appear here.

To edit a task, you can double-click the task to reopen the Task window.

H This indicator (🔔) represents a reminder.

I This indicator (🔄) represents a recurring task.

J You can click a task and mark it complete by clicking the **Mark Complete** button.

K You can click the **Change View** button and choose a different view of tasks.

TIP

What happens if I click Tasks on the left side of the Tasks component?

When you click **Tasks**, you see an alternative view of your tasks. From the To-Do List view (shown throughout this section), you see only outstanding tasks you have not yet completed. From the Tasks view, you see all your tasks; the ones you have completed (**A**) appear with a strikethrough line and a check mark to indicate they are complete.

Add a Note

Outlook includes a Notes component, which you can use to create notes for yourself. Much like an electronic version of yellow sticky notes, Outlook's Notes component enables you to quickly and easily jot down your ideas and thoughts. You can attach Outlook Notes to other items in Outlook, as well as drag them from the Outlook window onto the Windows desktop for easy viewing.

Add a Note

1 Click here to display a pop-up menu.

2 Click **Notes** to open the Notes component.

A Notes appear in Icon view.

3 Click the **New Note** button.

B Outlook displays a yellow note.

4 Type your note text.

5 When you finish, click the note's **Close** button ( ).

C Outlook adds the note to the Notes list.

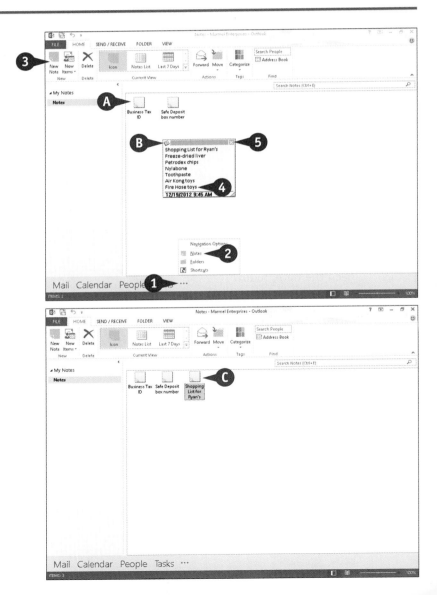

To view the note again or to make changes, you can double-click it.

D To change your view of notes in the Notes list, you can click an option in the Current View group.

This example displays the Notes List view.

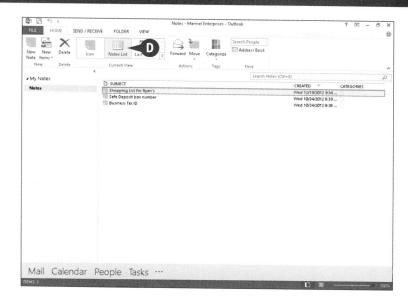

TIP

How do I delete a note that I no longer want?

Click the note in the Notes list and then press [Delete]. To delete multiple notes at the same time, press and hold [Ctrl] while clicking the notes. Once you delete a note, Outlook places it in the Deleted Items folder. If you accidentally delete a note, you can click the **Undo** button (⤺) immediately after you delete the note. If you discover later that you need the note, follow these steps:

1 Click here.

2 Click **Folders**.

3 Click **Deleted Items**.

4 Find the note and drag it to the Notes folder.

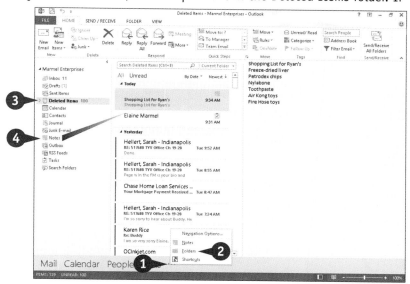

Customize the Navigation Bar

You can control the appearance of the Navigation bar, displaying fewer items or more items to suit your needs. For example, suppose that you use the Notes component regularly. You can save mouse clicks if you display the Notes component as part of the Navigation bar.

In addition to determining which components appear on the Navigation bar, you can control the order in which they appear. You can also control the size of the Navigation bar by choosing to display buttons that represent each component instead of displaying the component name.

Customize the Navigation Bar

1 From any Outlook component, click here.

A A pop-up menu appears.

2 Click **Navigation Options**.

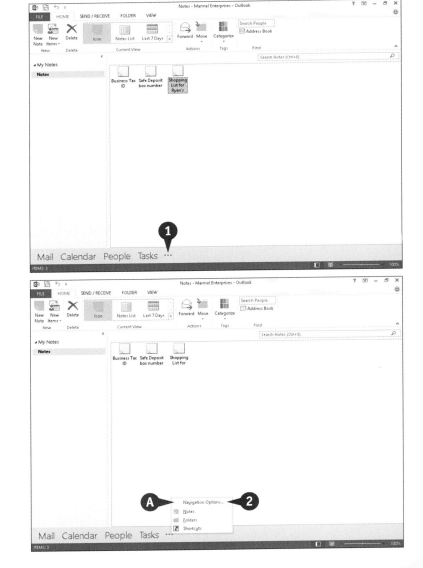

The Navigation Options dialog box appears.

3 Click ↕ to specify the number of items you want visible on the Navigation bar.

4 To reorder the Navigation bar entries, click an item and then click the **Move Up** or **Move Down** button.

B You can click **Reset** if you want to return the Navigation bar to its original state.

5 Click **OK**.

C The Navigation bar appears with your changes.

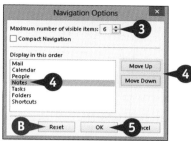

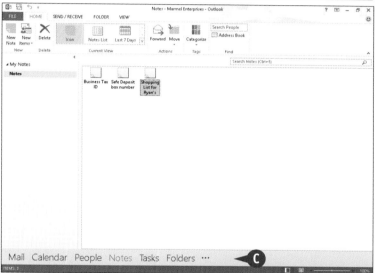

TIP

How can I reduce the size of the Navigation bar?

Perform Steps **1** and **2** to display the Navigation Options dialog box. Then, select **Compact Navigation** (☐ changes to ☑). Click **OK**, and your Navigation bar appears more compact because buttons represent the components. You might need to widen the left pane in Outlook to see all the Navigation buttons. Slide the mouse pointer over the pane divider (↳ changes to ↔) and drag the pane divider to the right.

Peek at Appointments and Tasks

From any Outlook component, you can take a peek at today's appointments and at your task list. You do not need to select Calendar or Tasks to view appointments or tasks.

The Calendar peek view displays the current month, and today's appointments appear below the monthly calendar. The Task peek view displays upcoming tasks not only for today but also for the week, for next week, and for next month. In the Task peek window, you can scroll through tasks and create a new task. You can also pin a peek view to any component so that it remains visible.

Peek at Appointments and Tasks

1 To peek at your appointments, slide the mouse pointer over **Calendar** on the Navigation bar.

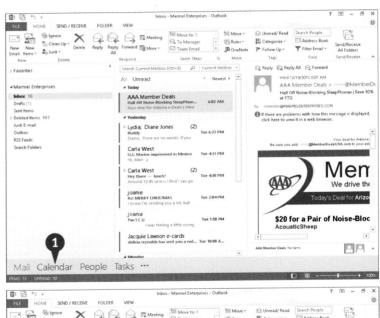

Ⓐ Outlook enables you to "peek" at your calendar.

Ⓑ Point your mouse at any day to view that day's appointments here.

2 To peek at your tasks, slide the mouse pointer over **Tasks**.

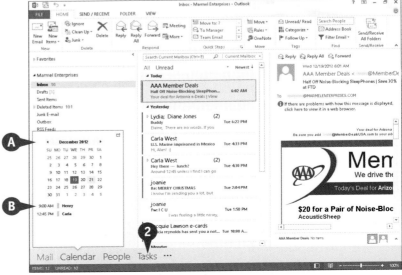

C Outlook displays a list of your tasks.

D You can click ▲ and ▼ to scroll through your task list.

E You can click here and type a name for a new task.

Note: When you press **Enter** to add the task, Outlook adds the task to your list as a task for today. See the section "Create a New Task" for details on editing the task.

3 To pin a peek view so that it is permanently visible, click the docking button (▭).

F Outlook pins the tasks or appointments to the right side of the current component's window.

Note: The pinned peek view appears only in the component you were viewing when you pinned it.

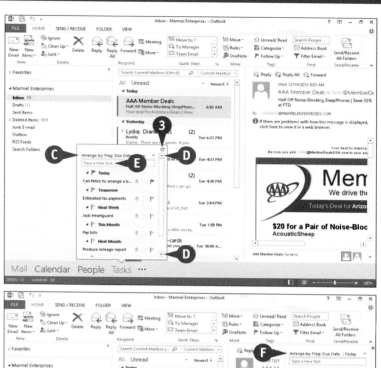

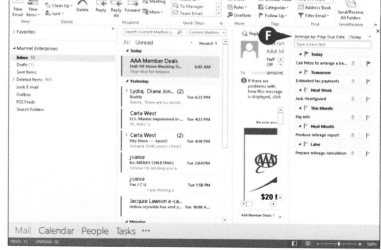

Search for Outlook Items

Suppose you need to locate an Outlook item, such as an e-mail message about a project you are working on, an item on your to-do list that you need to review, or the contact record for a co-worker that you need to call. Instead of sifting through your Outlook folders to locate it, you can use Outlook's Search tool to quickly find it. Each component includes a Search box; you simply enter a keyword or phrase, and Outlook searches for a match, even displaying items that match your criteria as you type.

Search for Outlook Items

Perform a Basic Search

1 Click the Outlook component you want to search.

Note: This example uses the Tasks component.

2 Click in the **Search** box.

A Outlook displays a Search tab, with several search-specific tools.

B You can click **All Outlook Items** to search all Outlook folders instead of just the current component's folder.

C These tools change, depending on the component you selected in Step **1**.

③ Type your keyword or phrase.

Ⓓ As you type, Outlook displays items that match your entry.

You can double-click an item to view it in its own window.

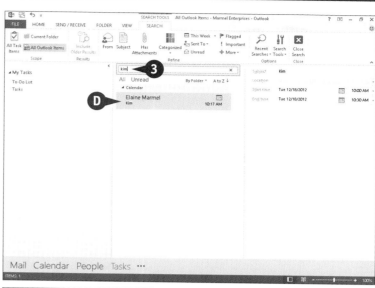

Using Advanced Search Criteria

① Click in any component's search box.

② On the Search tab, click **Search Tools**.

③ Click **Advanced Find**.

Ⓔ In the Advanced Find window that appears, specify your search criteria at the top of the window and on the Any Items tab. More options appear on the More Choices tab and the Advanced tab.

④ Click **Find Now** to search.

Ⓕ Results appear in the bottom of the window.

⑤ Click ✕ to close the window when you finish.

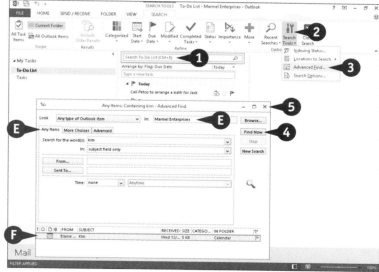

TIP

Can I control search options?

Yes. Perform Steps **1** and **2** in the subsection "Using Advanced Search Criteria." Then click **Search Options** to display the search options available in the Outlook Options dialog box. You can, for example, improve search speed by limiting the number of results Outlook displays, and you can control the color Outlook uses to highlight terms that match your search criteria. Make any necessary changes and click **OK**.

Work with the To-Do Bar

Outlook's To-Do Bar can display a monthly calendar and appointments, your favorite contacts, or your tasks. You can choose to show all or any combination of these elements. The To-Do Bar appears along the right side of the Outlook window.

To-Do Bar elements can appear in any Outlook component. Note that displaying To-Do Bar elements in one Outlook component does not display them in any other Outlook component. You can, however, display To-Do Bar elements individually in each Outlook component.

Work with the To-Do Bar

1 On the Navigation bar, click the Outlook component in which you want to display To-Do Bar elements.

2 Click the **View** tab.

3 Click **To-Do Bar**.

4 Click the To-Do Bar element you want to display.

In this example, Outlook displays the calendar.

Ⓐ The To-Do Bar appears along the right side of the Outlook window, displaying the element you selected in Step 4.

5 Repeat Steps 3 and 4 to display another To-Do Bar element.

6 Repeat Steps 1 to 5 to display To-Do Bar elements in another Outlook Component.

Ⓑ To hide an individual To-Do Bar element, click × for the element.

Note: To hide the entire To-Do Bar in a particular Outlook component, repeat Steps 2 and 3 and then click **Off**.

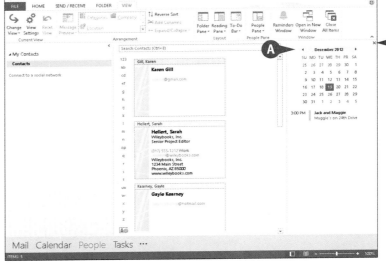

Link Contacts

You can link two contacts so that, in the People view of your contacts, you can see all information for the linked contacts on one card.

For example, suppose that you set up two cards for one contact because you want to be able to easily e-mail that person at two different e-mail addresses. If you link the two cards, you can still e-mail to whichever address you want, but you have the added benefit of viewing all of the person's contact information on one card in the People view. You can unlink the contacts at any time.

Link Contacts

1 Click **People** on the Navigation bar.

2 Click **People**.

3 Click a contact you want to link.

4 Click here.

5 Click **Link Contacts**.

6 In the Linked Contacts dialog box, type another contact's name.

7 Click the search result you want to link.

Ⓐ Outlook moves the contact you selected in Step **7** above the search box.

8 Click **OK**.

Outlook links the contacts.

9 Click either contact card.

Ⓑ Outlook displays all contact information for the contact on both contact cards.

Ⓒ To unlink the contacts, click here and then click **Link Contacts** to redisplay the Linked Contacts dialog box; click the Contact you want to unlink and click **OK**.

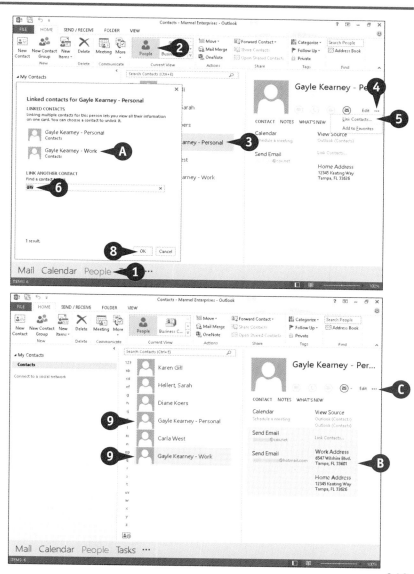

Compose and Send a Message

You can use Outlook to compose and send e-mail messages. When you compose a message in Outlook, you designate the e-mail address of the message recipient (or recipients) and type your message text. You can also give the message a subject title to identify the content of the message for recipients.

You can compose a message offline, but you must be working online to send it. If you do not have time to finish composing your message during your current work session, you can save the message as a draft and come back at a later time to finish it.

Compose and Send a Message

1 On the Navigation bar, click **Mail** to display the Mail component.

2 Click the **Home** tab.

3 Click the **New Email** button.

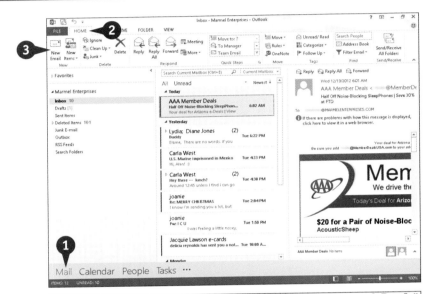

Outlook opens an untitled message window.

4 Type the recipient's e-mail address.

Ⓐ If the e-mail address is already in your Address Book, you can click the **To** button and select the recipient's name.

If you enter more than one e-mail address, you must separate each address with a semicolon (;) and a space.

5 Type a subject title for the message.

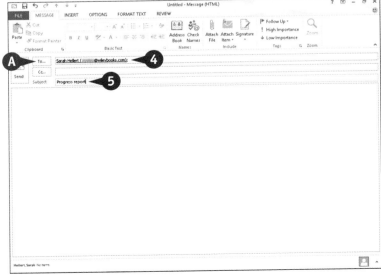

6 Type the message text.

B You can use the formatting buttons to change the appearance of your message text.

C To set a priority level for the message, you can click **High Importance** or **Low Importance**.

Note: By default, the message priority level is Normal.

7 Click **Send**.

Outlook places the message in your Outbox.

Note: You might need to press **F9** or click the **Send/Receive** tab and click **Send All** or **Send/Receive All Folders** to send the message.

8 Click the **Sent Items** folder.

D The message you sent appears in the Item list; Outlook stores a copy of all messages you send in the Sent Items folder.

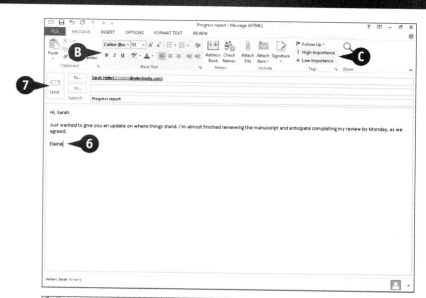

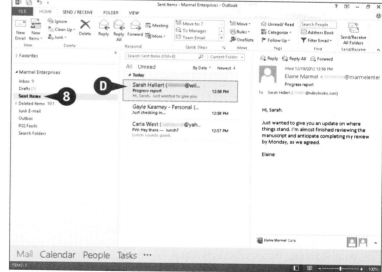

TIPS

How do I save a message as a draft?

Click the message window's × and click **Yes** when prompted to save the message. Outlook saves the message in the Drafts folder. When you are ready to continue composing your message, click the **Drafts** folder and double-click the saved message to open it.

How do I send a copy of my message to someone?

To copy or blind copy the message to another recipient, either type the recipient's e-mail address directly in the field or click the **Cc** or **Bcc** button to select the address from your contacts.

Send a File Attachment

You can send files stored on your computer to other e-mail recipients. For example, you might send an Excel worksheet or Word document to a work colleague or send a digital photo of your child's birthday to a relative. Assuming that the recipient's computer has the necessary software installed, that person can open and view the file on his or her own system.

Note that some e-mail systems are not set up to handle large file attachments. If you are sending a large attachment, check with the recipient to see if his or her system can handle it.

Send a File Attachment

1 Create a new e-mail message, entering the recipient's e-mail address, a subject title, and the message text.

Note: Refer to the previous section, "Compose and Send a Message," for help creating a new e-mail message.

2 Click the **Message** tab.

3 Click the **Attach File** button.

The Insert File dialog box appears.

4 Locate and select the file you want to send.

5 Click **Insert**.

A Outlook adds the file attachment to the message, displaying the filename and file size.

6 Click **Send**.

Outlook sends the e-mail message and attachment.

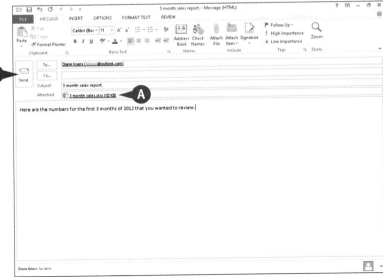

Read an Incoming Message

You can use Outlook's Mail feature to retrieve new e-mail messages that others have sent you and view them on-screen. You can view a message in a separate message window or in the Reading pane, as described in this section. By default, the Reading pane appears beside the list of messages, but you can place it below the message list.

Note that you must be connected to the Internet to receive e-mail messages.

Read an Incoming Message

1 Click **Mail**.

2 Click the **Home** tab.

3 Click the **Send/Receive All Folders** button.

Outlook retrieves new e-mail messages.

4 If the Inbox is not selected, click the **Inbox** folder.

Ⓐ Messages appear in the Message list pane, with a preview.

Ⓑ You can filter the list to show all or only unread messages.

Ⓒ Messages you have not opened display a vertical bar.

5 Click a message.

Ⓓ The contents of the message appear in the Reading pane.

Note: You can double-click a message to open it in a message window.

Ⓔ Messages containing attachments display a paper clip; double-click it to open the attachment. A warning dialog box appears; click **Open** to view or click **Save** to save the attachment. Never open a file unless you trust the sender.

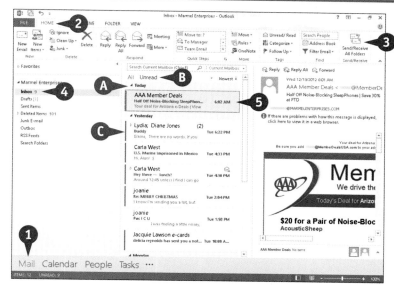

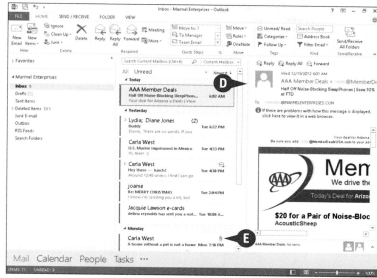

Reply To or Forward a Message

Y ou can reply to an e-mail message by sending a return message to the original sender. For example, if you receive an e-mail message containing a question, you can reply to that e-mail with your answer. When you reply to an e-mail, the original sender's name is added to the To field in the message.

You can also forward the message to another recipient. For example, you might forward a message that you receive from one co-worker to another co-worker who will find its contents useful.

Note that you must be connected to the Internet in order to send replies or forward e-mail messages.

Reply To or Forward a Message

Reply To a Message

① In the Message list pane, click the message to which you want to reply.

② In the Reading pane, click **Reply** to reply to the original sender.

Ⓐ To reply to the sender as well as to everyone else who received the original message, you can click **Reply All**.

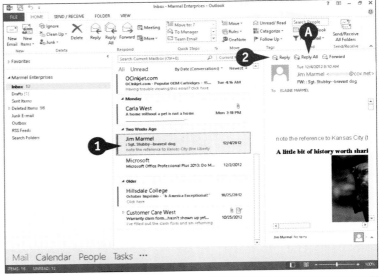

Ⓑ The original sender's address appears in the To field.

Ⓒ You can click **Pop Out** to open your reply in its own message window.

③ Type your reply.

Ⓓ If you change your mind and do not want to reply to the message, you can click **Discard**.

④ Click **Send**.

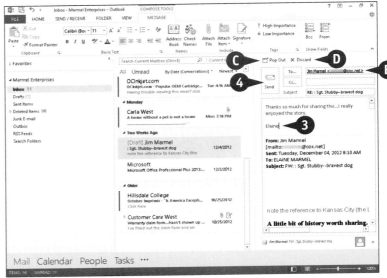

E Outlook places the e-mail message in the Outbox.

F Outlook sends the message at its next automatically scheduled send/receive action; to send the message, click the **Send/Receive All Folders** button on the Home tab.

Forward a Message

1 In the Message list pane, click the message that you want to forward.

2 In the Reading pane, click **Forward**.

3 Type the recipient's e-mail address in the **To** field.

G You can click **Pop Out** to open your message in its own window.

4 Perform Steps **3** and **4** in the previous subsection, "Reply To a Message."

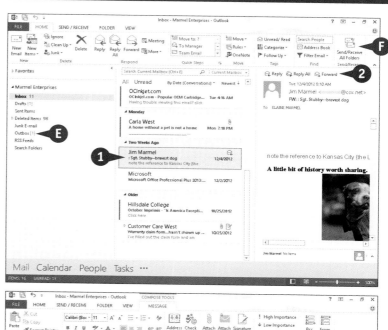

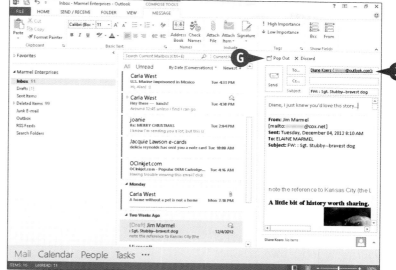

TIP

How do I look up an e-mail address when forwarding a message?

Perform Steps **1** and **2** in the subsection "Forward a Message." Click the **To** button to display a list of your contacts. Type a few letters to identify the contact. Outlook highlights the first contact that matches what you typed. If necessary, use the arrow keys to highlight the correct contact. Press Enter to display the contact in the To field. Click **OK** and Outlook places the contact name in the To field of your message.

Add a Sender to Your Outlook Contacts

Suppose you receive an e-mail message from someone with whom you expect to correspond regularly, but you do not have a record for that individual in Outlook contacts. You can easily add the contact information of the sender of any message you receive to your Outlook contacts, directly from the message. If, at a later time, you want to send a new message to that person, you can click the To button and choose his or her name from the Select Names: Contacts dialog box, as described in the tip in the previous section, "Reply To or Forward a Message."

Add a Sender to Your Outlook Contacts

1 In the Message list pane, click the message from the sender you want to add as a contact.

2 In the Reading pane, right-click the sender's name.

3 Click **Add to Outlook Contacts**.

A A window opens with the sender's e-mail address already filled in.

4 Type a name for the contact.

B You can click any ⊕ to add additional information.

5 Click **Save**.

Outlook saves the contact information.

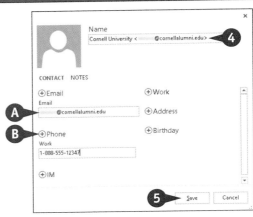

Delete a Message

As you receive e-mail messages, you can eliminate clutter if you delete messages you no longer need from your Inbox and other Outlook folders.

Note that when you delete a message from your Inbox or any other Outlook folder, Outlook does not remove it from your system. Rather, it moves it to the Deleted Items folder. To permanently remove deleted messages from your system, thereby maximizing your computer's storage capacity, you should empty the Deleted Items folder on a regular basis.

Delete a Message

1 In the Message list pane, click the message you want to delete.

2 Make sure the mouse pointer remains over the message you clicked in Step **1**.

✕ appears.

3 Press **Delete**, or click ✕ in the Message list pane, or click **Delete** on the Home tab.

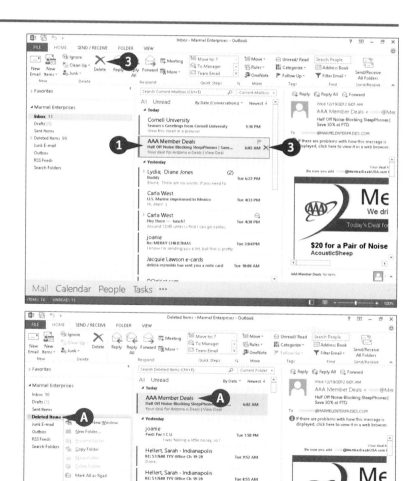

Outlook deletes the message from the Inbox and the Message list pane and adds it to the Deleted Items folder.

Ⓐ You can click the **Deleted Items** folder to view the message that you deleted.

Ⓑ To empty the Deleted Items folder, right-click it and click **Empty Folder**.

Work with Conversations

You can view your e-mail messages as conversations in Outlook. In Conversation view, Outlook groups related messages that are part of the same conversation, or *thread*, in the Message list pane.

Using Conversation view, all related messages, including messages that you have sent as replies or forwarded to others, appear under a single heading — typically the subject of the message. You expand a thread to view its related messages. By default, Outlook displays all messages in the Message list pane of the Inbox in Conversation view.

Work with Conversations

View a Conversation

1 In the Message list pane, click a conversation entry.

Note: You can identify a conversation because ▷ appears on the left side of the entry. If your messages do not appear as conversations, click the **View** tab and then select **Show as Conversations** (☐ changes to ☑).

Ⓐ The number of messages in the conversation appears here.

2 Click ▷ to expand the conversation.

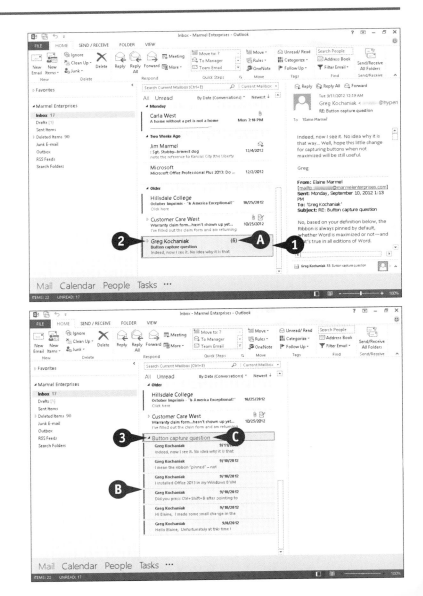

Ⓑ Outlook expands the conversation, displaying all the related messages (▷ changes to ◢).

Ⓒ Outlook displays the conversation using the subject as a heading.

3 Click ◢ to close the conversation (◢ changes to ▷).

Outlook closes the conversation, displaying a single entry for the conversation as it appeared before you opened the conversation.

Clean Up a Conversation

1 Perform Steps **1** and **2** in the previous subsection, "View a Conversation."

2 Click a message in the conversation you want to clean up.

3 Click the **Home** tab.

4 Click the **Clean Up** button in the Delete group.

5 Click **Clean Up Conversation**.

The Clean Up Conversation dialog box opens.

6 Click **Clean Up**.

D Outlook removes redundant messages from the conversation.

E Outlook places the removed messages in the Deleted Items folder.

Note: To permanently remove the messages, right-click the **Deleted Items** folder and click **Empty Folder**.

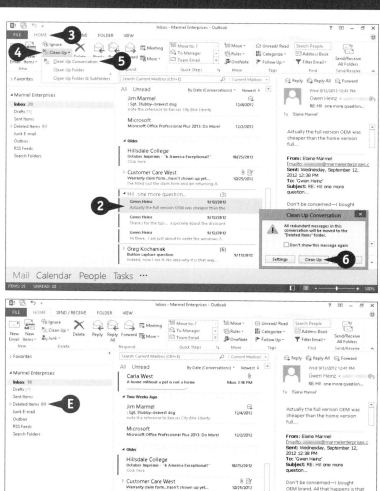

TIP

Is there a way to ignore conversations where I am included but they are not relevant to me?

Yes. Perform Steps **1** and **2** in the subsection "View a Conversation." Click the **Home** tab, and then click the **Ignore** button. In the message box that appears, click **OK**. Outlook removes the conversation and places it in the Deleted Items folder. If you realize you have ignored a conversation in error, you can stop ignoring it. Click the **Deleted Items** folder, repeat Steps **1** to **3** in this tip, and then click **Stop Ignoring Conversation**.

Screen Junk E-Mail

Junk e-mail, also called *spam*, is overly abundant on the Internet and often finds its way into your Inbox. You can safeguard against wasting time viewing unsolicited messages by setting up Outlook's Junk E-mail feature. This feature enables you to make sure that Outlook bypasses e-mail from specific web domains and instead deposits those messages into the Outlook Junk E-mail folder.

Outlook might erroneously place e-mail that is *not* spam in the Junk E-mail folder. Periodically scan the contents of this folder to ensure that it does not contain any messages you want to read.

Screen Junk E-Mail

View Junk E-Mail Options

1 Click the **Home** tab.

2 Click the **Junk** ▼.

3 Click **Junk E-mail Options**.

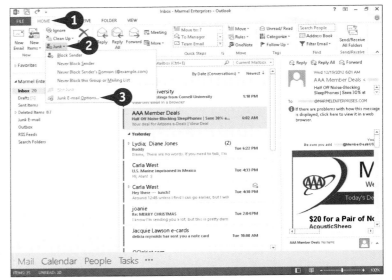

The Junk E-mail Options dialog box appears.

Ⓐ You can use the various tabs to view junk e-mail settings, blocked domains, and safe senders.

Ⓑ You can click one of these options to control the level of junk e-mail filtering that Outlook applies.

4 Click **OK**.

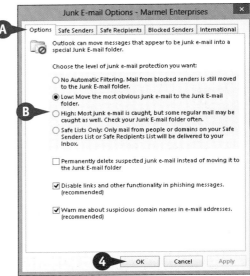

Designate a Message as Junk

1 Click the message in the Message list pane.

2 Click the **Home** tab.

3 Click the **Junk** ▾.

4 Click **Block Sender**.

A prompt box appears.

5 Click **OK**.

C Outlook adds the sender's e-mail address to the list of filtered addresses and moves the message to the Junk E-mail folder.

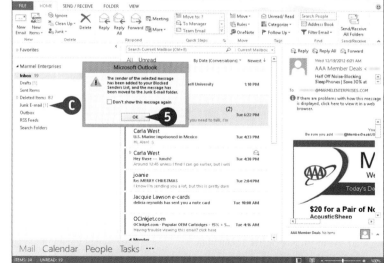

How can I restore a junk e-mail to my safe list?

Right-click the message in the Junk E-mail folder and, from the menu that appears, point at **Junk** and click **Not Junk**. Outlook alerts you that it will move the message back to its original location and gives you the option of removing the sender from the filter list; click **OK**.

Does Outlook empty the Junk E-mail folder?

No. To empty the folder, right-click it and click the **Empty Folder** button. Outlook permanently removes all items in the Junk E-mail folder.

Create a Message Rule

You can use rules to determine what Outlook does when you receive a message that meets a specific set of conditions. For example, you might create a rule that ensures that any message from a certain sender is placed directly into a folder of your choosing as soon as Outlook downloads the message. Alternatively, you might set up Outlook to play a certain sound when you receive a message that meets the criteria you set.

You can set rules that are quite simple, as outlined in this section, or rules that are very complex — involving various criteria, exceptions to the rule, and so on.

Create a Message Rule

1. Click the message on which you want to base a rule.

2. Click the **Home** tab.

3. Click the **Rules** ▼ .

4. Click **Create Rule**.

   The Create Rule dialog box appears.

5. Select the conditions that you want to apply (☐ changes to ☑).

6. Specify the actions to take when the conditions are met. In this example, select the **Move the item to folder** check box (☐ changes to ☑).

7. Click the **Select Folder** button.

   The Rules and Alerts dialog box appears.

8. Click the folder where you want Outlook to move the messages.

9. Click **OK**.

10. Click **OK**.

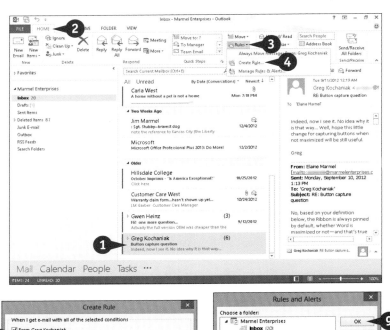

362

Outlook prompts you to run the rule now.

11 Select the check box (☐ changes to ☑).

12 Click **OK**.

Ⓐ Outlook runs the rule; in this example, Outlook moves any existing messages to the folder you specified.

The next time you receive a message matching the criteria you set, Outlook runs the rule.

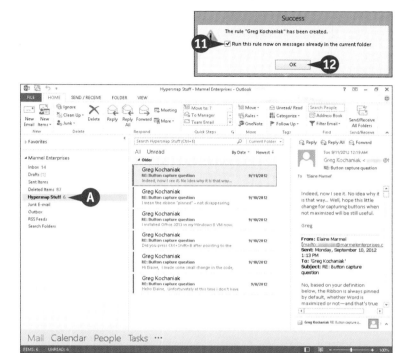

TIPS

How do I add more criteria to a message rule?
Perform Steps **1** to **4**. Then, click the **Advanced Options** button to display the Rules Wizard, which includes several sets of criteria that you can specify, such as exceptions to the rule, actions, and even a dialog box for naming the rule.

How do I remove a rule?
Click the **Home** tab, click the **Rules** ▼, and then click **Manage Rules & Alerts.** In the dialog box that appears, click the rule you want to delete and click the **Delete** button.

PART VII

Publisher

Publisher is a desktop publishing program that you can use to design and produce a variety of publications. Publisher installs with a large selection of predesigned publications that you can use as templates to build your own desktop publishing projects; additional templates are available from Office.com. In this part, you learn how to build and fine-tune publications, tapping into Publisher's formatting features to make each document suit your own design and needs.

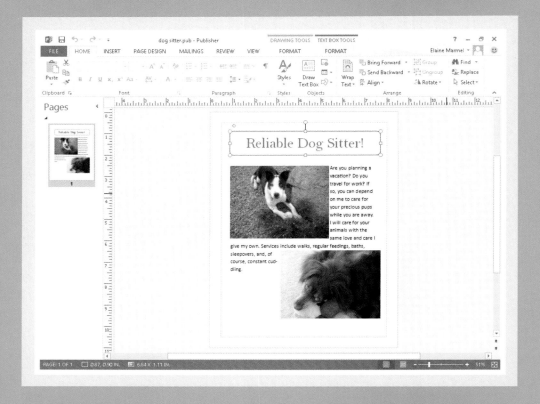

Create a Publication

You can use Publisher to create all kinds of publications, such as brochures, flyers, newsletters, and letterhead stationery. Publisher installs with a wide variety of publication design templates, and you can search for templates at Office.com.

If none of Publisher's predesigned publication templates suits your needs, you can create a blank publication, populate it with your own text boxes, and design your own layout. For example, you might want to create your own brochure or invitation and customize it.

Create a Publication

① Open Publisher.

The Publisher Start screen appears.

Note: If Publisher is already open, click the **File** tab and then click **New**.

② Use ▲ and ▼ to scroll through the available publication templates.

③ Click a publication design to preview it.

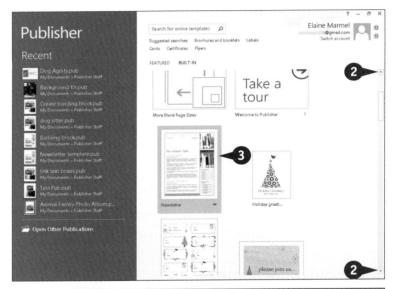

Ⓐ Publisher displays a preview of the selected design template.

Ⓑ A description of the template appears here.

Ⓒ You can click these buttons to view more images of the template.

Ⓓ You can click these buttons to preview the next or previous template design.

④ Click **Create**.

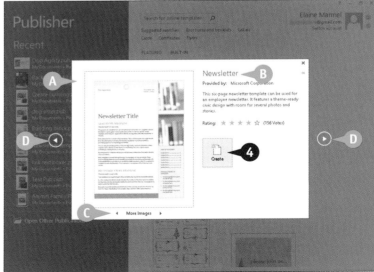

Publisher creates the publication.

E Thumbnail images of each page of the publication appear here.

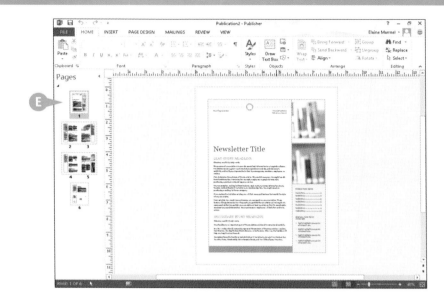

How can I search for additional templates?

Follow these steps:

1 In the search box at the top of the Publisher Start screen or the New screen, type a keyword that describes the type of publication template you want to find.

Note: Click **File** and then click **New** to display the New screen.

2 Click 🔍.

A You can now filter the search results by clicking a category. Each category you click reduces the search results further.

B If nothing appeals to you, click **Home** and then click a blank template.

Zoom In and Out

You can use Publisher's Zoom feature to control the on-screen magnification of your publication. By default, Publisher displays your document in a zoomed-out view so that you can see all the elements on a page. When you begin adding text and formatting, you can zoom in to better see what you are doing.

There are a few ways to zoom in and out of your publication. One is to use the Zoom settings on the View tab. Another is to use the Zoom buttons. A third is to use your keyboard.

Zoom In and Out

Specify a Magnification

1 Click the area of the publication where you want to change the zoom magnification.

A When you click an object on the page, Publisher surrounds it with selection handles (↔ and ◯).

2 Click the **View** tab.

3 Click the **Zoom** ▼.

4 Click a percentage.

B You can also type a value in the **Zoom** field.

C Publisher changes the magnification setting for your publication.

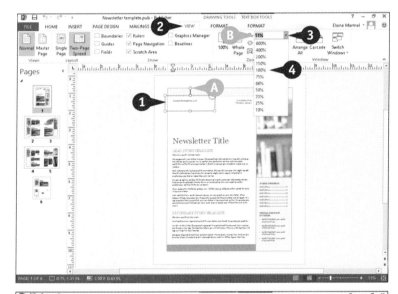

Using Zoom Buttons

1 Click the area of the publication where you want to change the magnification.

D Publisher surrounds the area with selection handles (⊡ and ○).

2 Click a magnification button to zoom in or out.

You can click the Zoom buttons multiple times to change the level of magnification.

E You can also click and drag the slider to change the level of magnification.

F Publisher changes the magnification setting for your publication.

G You can see the current magnification level here.

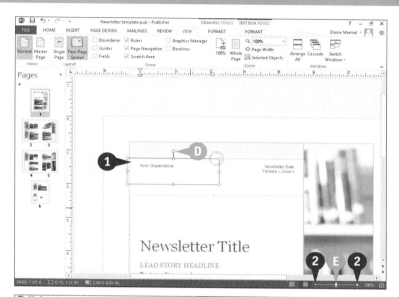

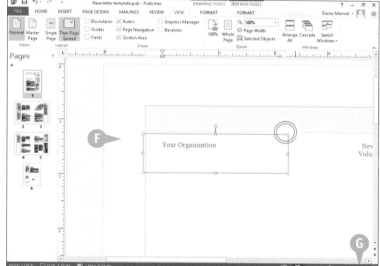

TIP

Are there other ways to zoom my publication?
Yes, there are several shortcuts you can use to quickly zoom a publication. For example, you can press F9 on the keyboard to quickly zoom in and out of a publication. To quickly zoom to 100 percent, you can click the **View** tab and, in the Zoom group, click the **100%** button. To quickly view the whole page, click the **Whole Page** button in the same Zoom group. You can click the **Page Width** button in the Zoom group to match the width of the page to the width of the Publisher window.

Add Text

When you create a new publication based on a design, Publisher inserts a layout for the text and displays placeholder text in the text boxes, also called *objects* or *frames*. The placeholder text gives you an idea of the text formatting that the design applies and what sort of text you might place in the text box.

As you build your publication, you replace the placeholder text with your own text. After you add your text, you can apply formatting to it, as well as move and resize it, as discussed in Chapter 21.

Add Text

1 Click the text object that you want to edit.

You may need to zoom in first to see the text object.

A Publisher surrounds the selected object with selection handles (⬜ and ⬤).

2 Select the placeholder text within the object.

3 Type your own text.

Publisher replaces any placeholder text with the new text that you type.

Note: To apply formatting to text and to move and resize text box objects, see Chapter 21.

You can click anywhere outside of the text object to deselect the text box.

To edit the text at any time, you can click the text box and make your changes.

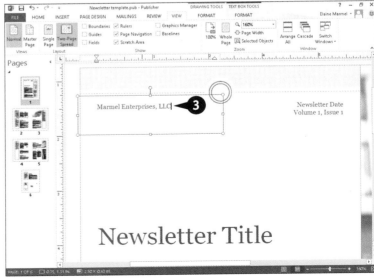

Add a New Text Box

You can add new text boxes to a publication and type your own text. For example, you might need to add a new text box to an empty area in your layout to include additional information, or you might need to add new text boxes to a blank publication.

When you add a text box to a publication, Publisher does not supply any placeholder text. Therefore, when you fill the text box with your own text, you do not replace any existing text. After you enter text, you can format it or move and resize it as described in Chapter 21.

Add a New Text Box

1 Click the **Home** tab.

2 Click **Draw Text Box**.

changes to +.

3 Click at the spot that represents the upper-left corner of the text box.

4 Drag down and to the right until the text box is the size that you need.

5 Release the mouse button.

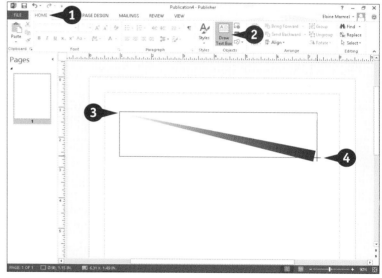

A The text box appears on-screen, with the insertion point inside (+ changes to I).

6 Type the text that you want to insert into the text box.

Note: To apply formatting to text and to move and resize text box objects, see Chapter 21.

7 Click anywhere outside the text object to deselect the text box.

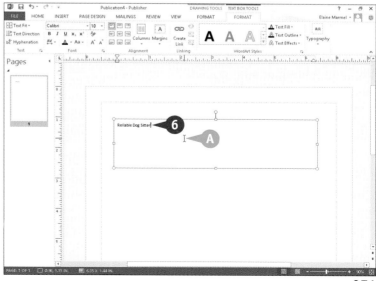

Swap Pictures

You can add pictures to your publication — pictures stored on your hard drive or pictures you download from the Internet — as described in Chapter 3. Publisher's Swap Pictures feature enables you to insert several pictures simultaneously into the *scratch area*, a space outside the publication page. Then, you can drag one picture onto your publication and, if necessary, you can swap it for another picture in the scratch area. You can continue substituting different pictures until you find the right one for your publication.

Swap Pictures

1 Click the **Insert** tab.

2 Click **Pictures**.

Note: To use online pictures, download them to your computer, as described in Chapter 3.

The Insert Picture dialog box appears.

3 Navigate to and select the pictures you want to consider.

You can select multiple pictures by holding Ctrl as you click each one.

4 Click **Insert**.

Ⓐ The pictures appear in the scratch area outside your publication page.

Note: Publisher surrounds each picture you insert with selection handles (⋤ and ◯).

5 Click anywhere in the scratch area outside the pictures so that none are selected.

6 Point at a picture you want to place on the publication page.

Ⓑ A button containing an image of a mountain (▣) appears in the center of the picture.

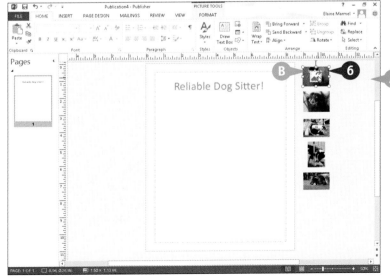

372

7 Drag 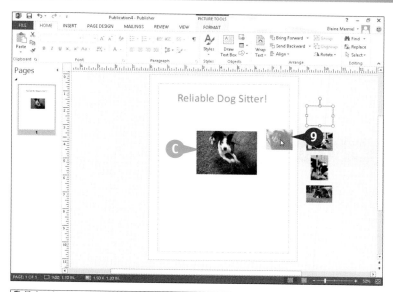 to place the picture on the publication page.

C The picture disappears from the scratch area and appears on the publication page.

8 Click anywhere outside the picture to deselect it.

9 To swap the image with another one, point at the picture you want to use as a replacement and drag until the new picture appears close to the existing picture on the publication page.

10 Release the mouse button when a pink outline appears.

D Publisher swaps the original picture for the new one.

Save a Publication for Photo Center Printing

Publisher enables you to save each page of a publication as an image that you can print as a photo using any photo printing method. Publisher saves each page of the publication as a JPEG or TIFF image — using the best possible resolution for photo printing — in a folder on your hard drive, and Publisher names the folder using the name of your publication.

You can print photos from your own printer, take a CD of photos to a photo printing location like Costco or Walgreens, or upload photos to commercial websites that will prepare printouts.

Save a Publication for Photo Center Printing

1 Open the publication containing the pictures you want to save for photo center printing.

Note: Publisher saves each page of the publication as a separate image.

2 Click the **File** tab.

Backstage view appears.

3 Click **Export**.

4 Click **Save for Photo Printing**.

5 Click ▼ and choose whether you want to create JPEG images or TIFF images.

6 Click **Save Image Set**.

The Choose Location dialog box appears.

7 Navigate to the folder where you want Publisher to save your images.for photo printing.

8 Click **Select Folder**.

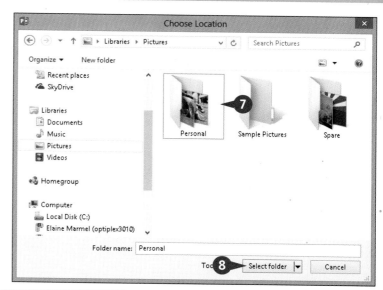

Publisher displays a progress bar as it saves your images. When it finishes, your publication reappears on-screen.

9 You can view the folder using File Explorer (Windows Explorer for Windows 7 users). Click the **Explorer** button on the Windows taskbar.

10 Navigate to the folder in which you chose to save your images.

A Publisher saves the images in a folder using the name of your publication.

B Publisher assigns image names to each page based on the page number in the publication.

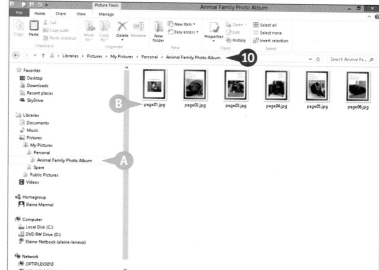

TIP

Can I change the names that Publisher assigns to each image?
Yes. You can change them in File Explorer after Publisher creates them, or you can change them in Publisher before creating them by performing the steps that follow. In the Pages pane on the left side of the Publisher window, right-click a page. From the menu that appears, click **Rename**. In the Rename Page dialog box, type the name you want to use for the photo image (**A**) and click **OK**. Repeat these steps for each page in the publication. When you create photos for printing, Publisher names the photos using the page names you provided.

Change the Font, Size, and Color

You can control the font, size, and color of the text in your publication. By default, when you assign a publication design, Publisher uses a predefined set of formatting for the text, including a specific font, size, and color. You may need to change the font or increase the size to suit your publication's needs. For example, you might change the font, size, and color of the publication's title text to emphasize it. In addition, you can use Publisher's basic formatting commands — Bold, Italic, Underline, Subscript, and Superscript — to quickly add formatting to your text.

Change the Font, Size, and Color

Change the Font

1 Select the text that you want to format.

2 Click the **Home** tab.

3 Click the **Font** ▾.

4 Click a font.

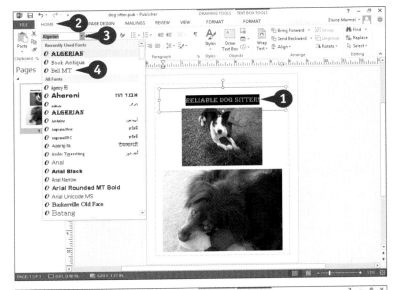

Ⓐ Publisher applies the font to the text.

Change the Font Size

1 Select the text that you want to format.

2 Click the **Home** tab.

3 Click the **Font Size** ▾.

4 Click a size.

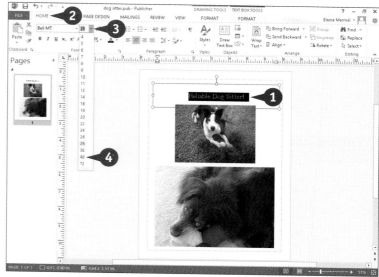

Ⓑ Publisher applies the font size to the text.

This example applies a 48-point font size.

Note: You can also change the font size by clicking the **Grow Font** and **Shrink Font** buttons (A˄ and A˅) on the Home tab. Publisher increases or decreases the font size with each click of the button.

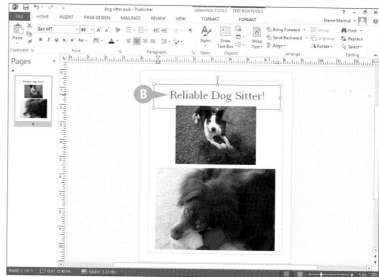

TIPS

How do I apply formatting to my text?
Select the text you want to format, click the **Home** tab, and click the **Bold** (B), **Italic** (I), **Underline** (U ▾), **Subscript** (x₂), or **Superscript** (x²) buttons.

What is the toolbar that appears when I select text?
When you select text, the Mini toolbar appears, giving you quick access to common formatting commands. You can also right-click selected text to display the toolbar. If you want to use any of the tools on the toolbar, simply click the desired tool; otherwise, continue working, and the toolbar disappears.

continued ▶

Changing the text color can go a long way toward emphasizing it in your publication. For example, if you are creating an invitation, you might make the description of the event a different color to stand out from the other details. Likewise, if you are creating a newsletter, you might make the title of the newsletter a different color from the information contained in the newsletter or even color-code certain data in the newsletter. Obviously, when selecting text colors, you should avoid choosing colors that make your text difficult to read.

Change the Font, Size, and Color (continued)

Change the Color

1 Select the text that you want to format.

2 Click the **Home** tab on the Ribbon.

3 Click ▼ next to the **Font Color** button (**A** ▾).

A In the color palette that appears, you can click a color to apply to the selected text and skip the rest of these steps.

4 Click **More Colors**.

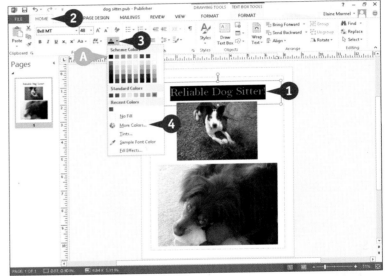

The Colors dialog box opens.

5 Click the **Custom** tab.

6 Click a color in the Colors field.

7 Click a shade to refine your selection.

8 Click **OK**.

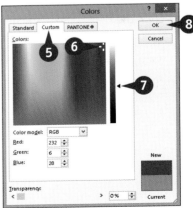

B Publisher applies the color to the text.

This example applies a red color.

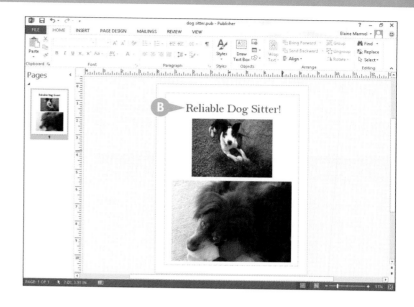

TIP

Is there another way to change font characteristics?
Yes. You can also change font characteristics using the Font dialog box. Follow these steps:

1 Select the text that you want to format.

2 Click the **Home** tab on the Ribbon.

3 Click the dialog box launcher (🔲) in the Font group.

4 In the Font dialog box, click the font, style, size, color, underline style, or effect that you want to apply.

5 Click **OK**.

Apply a Text Effect

In addition to changing the font, size, and color of text in your publication, you can also apply text effects. These include a shadow effect, a reflection effect, a glow effect, and a bevel effect. Text effects can go a long way toward making your newsletter, brochure, postcard, or other type of publication appear more professional.

You apply text effects from the Format tab, under Text Box Tools. This tab appears on the Ribbon when you click in a text box or select text in your publication.

Apply a Text Effect

1. Select the text that you want to format.

2. Click the **Text Box Tools Format** tab.

3. Click **Text Effects**.

4. Point at the type of effect you want to apply to view a gallery of choices.

   This example shows shadow effects.

5. Click an effect.

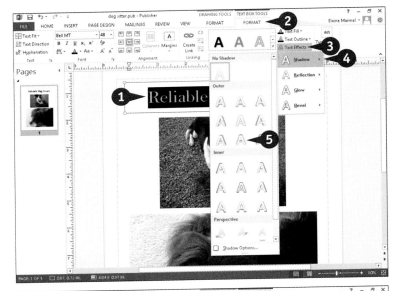

A. Publisher applies the text effect.

Change Text Alignment

Although each publication design automatically establishes an alignment to best suit the design, you can change the alignment to suit your own needs. You can use Publisher's alignment commands to change the way in which text is positioned both horizontally and vertically in a text object box. For example, you might choose to align text in the bottom-right corner of the text object box. There are nine alignment options: Align Top Left, Align Top Center, Align Top Right, Align Center Left, Align Center, Align Center Right, Align Bottom Left, Align Bottom Center, and Align Bottom Right.

Change Text Alignment

1 Select the text that you want to format.

2 Click the **Text Box Tools Format** tab.

3 Click a button in the Alignment group.

Ⓐ This example uses the **Align Bottom Left** button (▣).

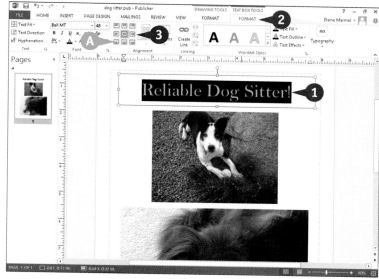

Ⓑ Publisher applies the new alignment.

Add a Border

You can add a border to any object in a publication, including text boxes, clip art, and pictures, to add emphasis or make the publication more aesthetically appealing. Publisher comes with several predesigned border effects that you can apply to your publication. These include borders of various colors, shapes, and thicknesses, with or without background shading. If none of these suit you, you can create your own custom borders — for example, making each border line a different color or thickness.

Add a Border

1 Select the text or object to which you want to apply a border.

2 Click the **Drawing Tools Format** tab.

3 Click a border style.

A You can click ▾ to display a gallery of borders from which to choose.

B You can click the **Shape Outline** button to make selections from available line styles, colors, and weights.

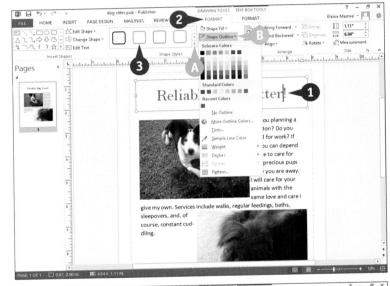

C Publisher applies the border to the object.

D You can click the **Change Shape** button to view available shapes for the border.

Control Text Wrap

To add visual interest, many publications include text as well as objects, such as photographs, clip art images, tables, charts, or other visual elements. You can control the way in which text wraps around a picture, table, chart, or any other object in a publication. For example, you may want a column of text to wrap tightly around an object, to appear above and below the object but not on the sides, and so on. Alternatively, you might want the text to simply appear on top of the object.

Control Text Wrap

1 Create a text block and type text into it. (See Chapter 20 for details.)

2 Insert a picture or other object inside the text block. (See Chapter 3 for details.)

Note: The picture might temporarily obscure some of your text. When you finish these steps, all text will be visible.

3 Click the picture object or other object inside the text block to select it (⬥ and ◯ appear around the picture).

4 Click the **Picture Tools Format** tab.

5 Click the **Wrap Text** button.

6 Click a text wrapping option.

Publisher applies the text wrapping.

A This example applies square text wrapping.

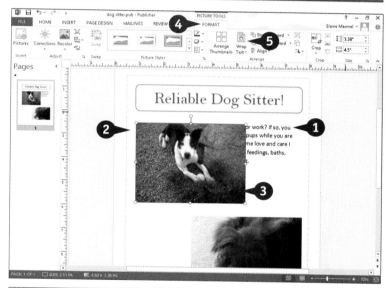

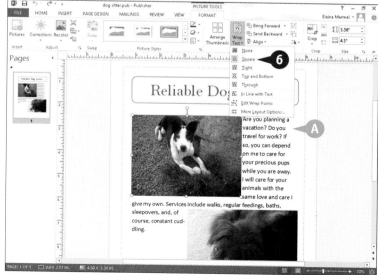

Link Text Boxes

When you add too much text to a text object, any text that does not fit in the text box is called *overflow*. In some cases, Publisher attempts to correct this problem with its AutoFit feature, which reduces the size of your text to make it fit. Alternatively, you can correct the problem of overflow text by creating a new text box adjacent to the existing one, linking the two text boxes, and flowing the extra text into the new text box. You use the Linking tools on the Text Box Tools Format tab to navigate and connect text boxes in a publication.

Link Text Boxes

Link Text Boxes

1 Create a text block and type text into it. (See Chapter 20 for details.)

Note: Type all the text you need, even though you cannot see all of it.

2 Create another text box; you will place the overflow text into this box.

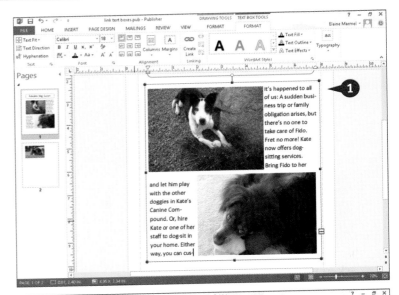

③ Click in the text box that contains the overflowing text.

④ Click the **Text Box Tools Format** tab.

⑤ Click the **Create Link** button (⌖ changes to ✍).

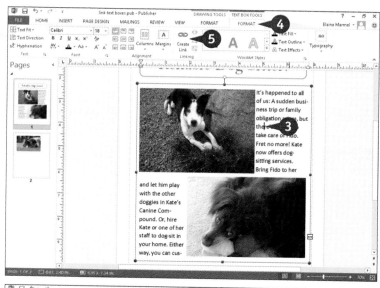

⑥ Click in the text box you created in Step **2** for the text overflow.

Ⓐ Publisher links the two boxes, and moves any extra text from the first text box into the second text box.

Ⓑ You can click the **Previous** button (◀) to return to the previous text box, which contains a **Next** button (▶) that you can use to switch back to the overflow text box.

Note: You can turn off the AutoFit feature by selecting the text object to which AutoFit has been applied, clicking the **Text Box Tools Format** tab, clicking the **Text Fit** button, and clicking **Do Not Autofit**.

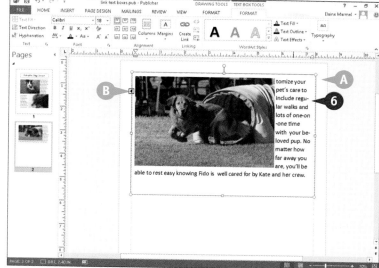

TIPS

How do I break a link?
Click in the first linked text box, click the **Text Box Tools Format** tab, and then click the **Break** button (⛓).

Are there other ways to handle overflow?
Yes. You can also use Publisher's Text Fit tools to auto-fit your text into the text box. Click the text box to select it, click the **Text Box Tools Format** tab, click the **Text Fit** button, and choose **Best Fit**.

Move and Resize Publication Objects

When you insert an object, such as a text box, photograph, table, and so on, into a publication, you might need to make it larger or smaller, or you might need to move it to achieve the effect you want. For example, you may want to resize a text object or move or resize a picture you place in a text box to fit more text into the box. When you select an object, an outline and handles appear around it. You can drag the handles to make the object larger or smaller, and drag the outline to move the object.

Move and Resize Publication Objects

Move an Object

1 Click the object that you want to move.

A Publisher surrounds the selected object with handles (⬚ and ◯).

2 Position the mouse pointer over the edge of the object until it changes from ⬚ to ✥ .

3 Drag the object to a new location.

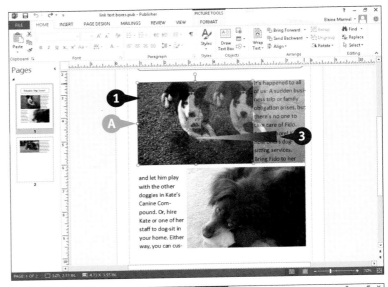

Publisher moves the object.

B This example moves a picture object.

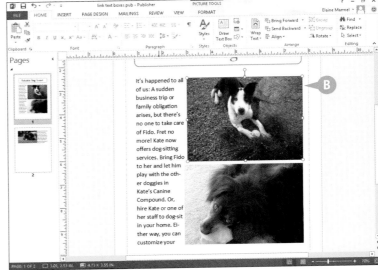

Resize an Object

1 Click the object that you want to resize.

C Publisher surrounds the selected object with handles (⬜ and ◯).

2 Position the mouse pointer over the edge of the object until it changes from ⇖ to ⬉, ↕, ⬈, or ⟷.

Note: To maintain an object's perspective, drag a corner using ⬉ or ⬈.

3 Click and drag a handle inward or outward to resize the object.

D A dotted line represents the object's proposed size.

When you release the mouse button, Publisher resizes the object.

E This example resizes a picture.

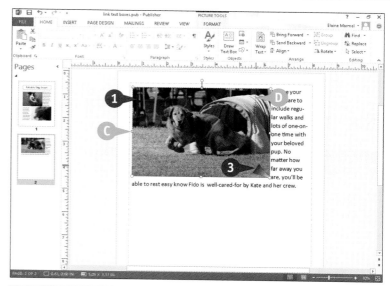

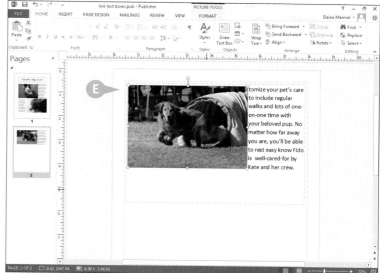

Can I rotate an object?
Yes. Click the object to select it, and then click the green rotation handle at the top of the selected object and drag it in the direction you want to rotate the object. When you have rotated the object to the desired degree, release the mouse button.

How do I delete an object?
To remove an object from a publication, click the object to select it and press **Delete**. Publisher removes the object from the page. You can select more than one object to delete by pressing and holding **Ctrl** as you click each object.

Edit the Background

You can add visual interest by changing the background of your publication page. You can assign a new background color, gradient effect, or texture. If you decide you no longer want a background, you can remove it.

Clicking the Background button in the Page Design tab enables you to quickly choose from among several solid backgrounds and gradient backgrounds; alternatively, you can choose from a variety of textures, patterns, and tints, or even add one of your own photographs, from the Fill Effects dialog box.

Edit the Background

Apply a Background

1 Click the **Page Design** tab.

2 Click the **Background** button.

3 Click the background that you want to apply.

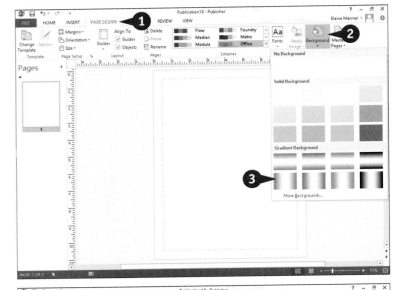

Ⓐ Publisher applies the background.

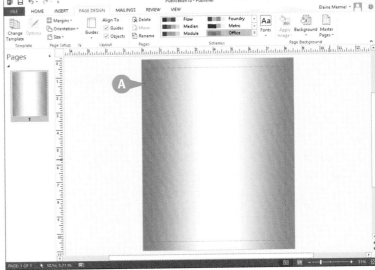

Create a Picture Background

① Select the page you want to fill with a background picture.

② Insert the picture you want to use into your publication and drag it to the scratch area.

Note: See Chapter 3 for details on inserting a picture, and Chapter 20 for details on using the scratch area.

③ Right-click the picture.

④ Point the mouse at **Apply to Background**.

⑤ Click either **Fill** or **Tile**.

This example uses Fill.

Ⓑ Publisher fills the page you selected in Step **1** with the photo or tiles of the photo.

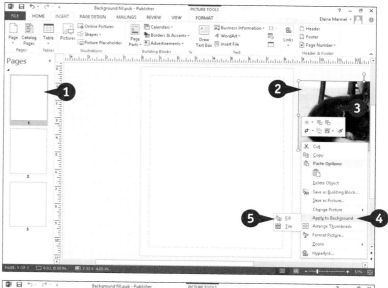

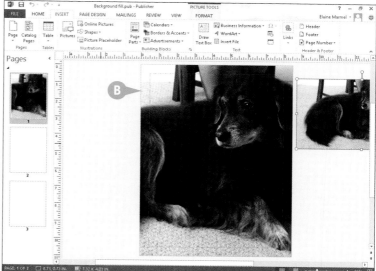

How do I remove a background?
Click the **Page Design** tab, click the **Background** button, and click at the left edge of the gallery under **No Background**. The option for no background is white and fades into the gallery, but as you move the mouse, the white square becomes visible.

Can I apply a custom background?
Yes. You can assign a one-color or two-color gradient background using colors you choose. You can also apply a texture, a pattern, or your own custom tint. You access these options from the Format Background dialog box. To open this dialog box, click the **Page Design** tab, click **Background**, and choose **More Backgrounds**.

Add a Building Block Object

You can use Publisher's Building Block objects to add all kinds of extra touches to your publication projects. For example, you can add a calendar to a newsletter or a graphical marquee to a letterhead. The Building Block objects encompass a wide variety of design objects, such as mastheads, borders, boxes, and even coupons and logos. You can customize the design of a Building Block object as needed — for example, you might change the border or fill color of an object. You can also change the text in a Building Block object by selecting it and typing over it.

Add a Building Block Object

1 Click the **Insert** tab.

2 Click a button in the Building Blocks group.

This example chooses **Calendars**.

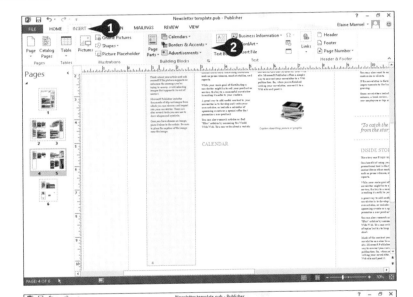

3 Click the Building Block object you want to insert.

A Publisher adds the object to your publication.

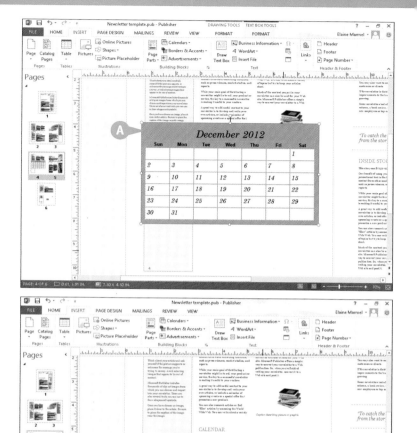

B You can move and resize the object to suit your layout.

Note: Refer to the section "Move and Resize Publication Objects," earlier in this chapter, to learn more.

TIP

How do I customize a Building Block object?

Many of the Building Block objects are composed of simple lines and shapes. You can customize the appearance of an object by selecting individual parts of it and making changes to the selection's formatting. Note that you may need to ungroup an object to edit its individual elements. To do so, click the object, click the **Home** tab, and then click the **Ungroup** button (🔲) as many times as necessary to free all of the object's individual elements. When you finish making your edits, click the **Group** button (🔲) to turn the elements back into a single object.

Create a Building Block Object

If you find yourself using an object you have created over and over, you can save that object as a Building Block object and reuse it as needed. For example, if you use the same headline in every publication you create, you can save it as a Building Block object; then, you can insert it into a publication anytime you need it (simply follow the steps in the previous section, "Add a Building Block Object," to insert it). Anything you save as a Building Block object is accessible from any other Publisher files you open.

Create a Building Block Object

1 Click the element that you want to save.

2 Click the **Insert** tab.

3 Click a button in the Building Blocks group:

Click **Page Parts** if the Building Block object you want to create is a heading, sidebar, or something similar.

Click **Calendars** if the Building Block object you want to create is a calendar.

Click **Borders & Accents** if the Building Block object you want to create is a border or accent.

Click **Advertisements** if the Building Block object you want to create is a coupon or other advertisement.

In this example, a **Page Parts** building block is created.

4 Click **Add Selection to *Building Block* Gallery**.

Note: The precise name of this option varies, depending on the button you click in Step **3**.

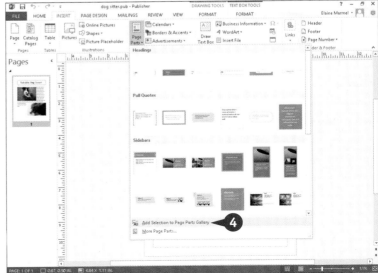

The Create New Building Block dialog box appears.

5 Type a name for the item.

6 Type a description for the item.

7 Click ⌄ to choose a category for the item.

8 Type keywords describing the item.

9 Click **OK**.

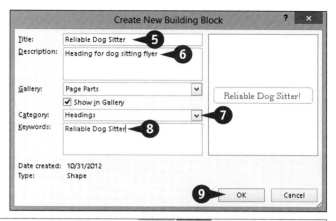

Publisher creates the Building Block object.

Ⓐ You can view the item by clicking the button you clicked in Step **3**.

TIPS

How do I remove a Building Block object?
Click the **Insert** tab and click the appropriate button in the Building Blocks group. Then right-click the Building Block object you want to delete, choose **Delete**, and click **OK** to confirm the deletion.

Are there more Building Block objects?
Yes. To access more Building Block objects, click the appropriate button in the Building Blocks group and choose **More *Building Blocks*** from the menu that appears. (The precise name of this option varies, depending on what button you click.) The Building Block Library window opens, displaying all Building Block objects of the type you selected.

PART VIII

OneNote

OneNote acts like a digital notebook, enabling you to jot down ideas, sketch out plans, brainstorm business strategies, and compile scraps of information in one searchable, shareable, easy-to-access location. You might use OneNote to take notes during meetings and lectures, collect research materials from the web, gather information about an upcoming trip, assemble ideas for a home improvement project, and more.

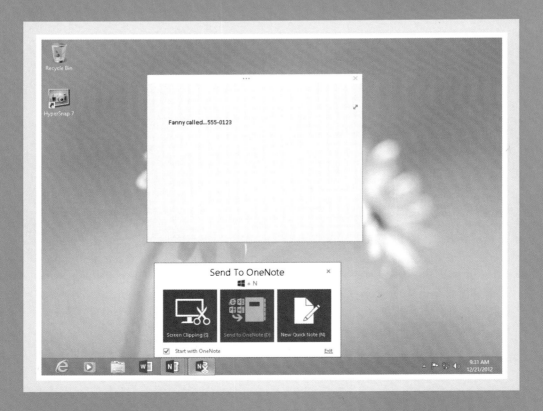

Navigate OneNote

You can digitally use OneNote the same way that you use physical binders, with the added improvement of being able to easily search and share your notes.

In OneNote, you can create notebooks in which you type, write, and draw your ideas; compile scraps of information; create tables; and paste in digital images such as a screenshot of a web page or a photograph. You can divide notebooks into sections — represented as tabs — to organize them, and you can group sections containing related information together, as described in Chapter 23.

Navigate OneNote

1 Click ▼ to display a list of notebooks that you can open.

2 Click the notebook you want to open.

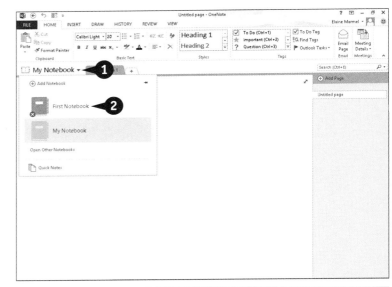

Ⓐ OneNote opens the notebook you clicked.

3 Click a section tab.

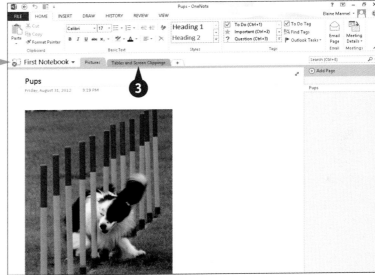

B OneNote displays the section tab you clicked.

4 Click a page in the tab.

C OneNote displays the page you clicked.

TIP

Can I keep all my notebooks visible at all times?
Yes. You can use the OneNote Navigation bar. Click ▼ beside your notebook's name. Then, click the pushpin (➤) to pin the OneNote Navigation bar on the left side of the window. Beside each notebook, the **Expand Notebook** button (⌄) appears; click it to view the notebook's sections. Click the **Collapse Notebook** button (⌃) to collapse the notebook and hide its sections. To hide the Navigation pane, click the pushpin (📌).

Type and Draw Notes

You can jot down ideas in OneNote in a few ways. For example, you can type them using your keyboard. You can then format your text as desired, changing the font, size, and color; applying bold, italics, underline, subscript, or superscript formatting; and more.

Alternatively, you can use OneNote's drawing tools to sketch drawings, such as a map. And, on touch devices, you can use drawing tools to hand-write notes and then convert them to typewritten notes.

Regardless of the method you use, you can move the notes you create around on the page as desired.

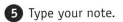

Type Notes

1 Click a section and a page on which you want to type a note.

2 Click the **Draw** tab.

3 Click **Type**.

4 Click the spot on the page where you want to type.

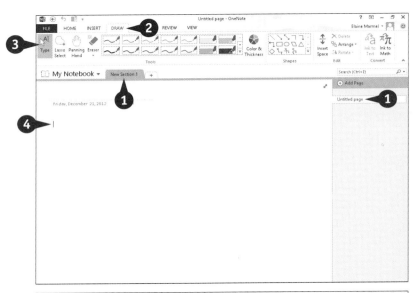

5 Type your note.

Note: When you finish, click anywhere outside the box containing the note.

Note: Using the tools on the Home tab, you can change the text font, size, and color, and also apply bold, italics, underline, subscript, or superscript formatting and more.

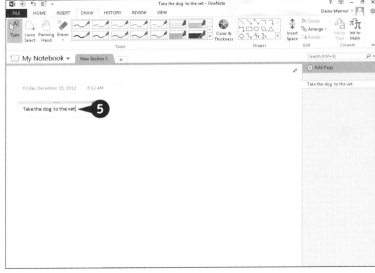

Draw Notes

1 Click a section and a page on which you want to draw a note.

2 Click the **Draw** tab.

3 In the Tools group, click a drawing tool.

A You can click ⊡ to view all available drawing tools.

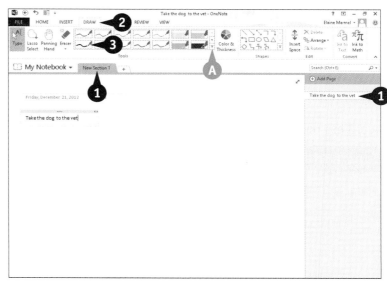

4 Draw or handwrite your note.

Note: When you finish, click **Type** to stop drawing.

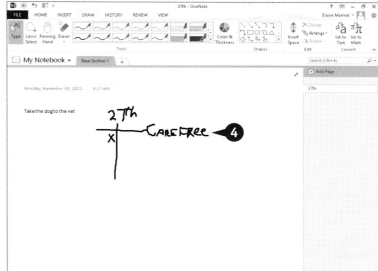

How do I move a note?

To move a typed note, position the mouse over the text; the note container appears. Position the mouse pointer over the container's top; when ꞮꞮ changes to ✥, click and drag the container to the desired location. To move a drawing, click the **Lasso Select** button on the Draw tab and draw a box around the drawing. Then click **Type** and move the mouse over the drawing (Ꞇ changes to ✥); drag the drawing.

Can I convert handwriting to typing?

Yes. Click **Type**, drag the mouse pointer over the handwriting to select it, and click **Ink to Text**.

Insert and Format a Table

You can create sophisticated-looking tables in your notes. In addition to inserting and deleting rows in tables as needed, OneNote supports formatting options for cells, including shading them and hiding their borders. You can also align cell information to the left or right edge of the cell or center it within the cell. In addition, you can sort data in your table so you can organize and display information the way you want. You can also convert a table in OneNote to an Excel spreadsheet if you need to perform detailed analysis on the table data.

Insert and Format a Table

Insert a Table

① Click in the notebook where you want the table to appear.

② Click the **Insert** tab.

③ Click **Table** to display a table grid.

④ Slide the mouse pointer across the squares that represent the number of rows and columns you want in your table.

⑤ Click the square representing the lower-right corner of your table.

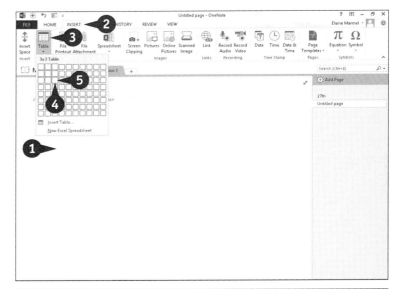

The table appears in the location you selected in Step **1**.

Ⓐ The insertion point appears in the upper-left corner of the table, ready for you to type.

Ⓑ Table Tools appear on the Ribbon.

Apply Table Formatting

6 Click the **Layout** tab.

C You can select any of these options to format your table.

7 Click a cell in the table or select multiple cells.

8 Click an option on the Ribbon.

Note: In this example, OneNote applies shading. For shading, you can click the bottom half of the **Shading** button to display and select from a palette of shading colors.

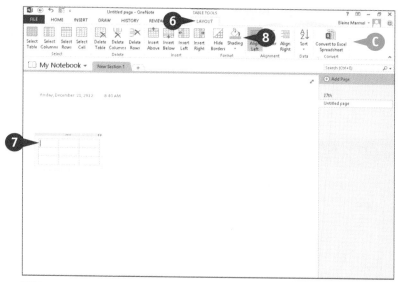

D OneNote applies the option you selected in Step **8** to the cell you selected in Step **7**.

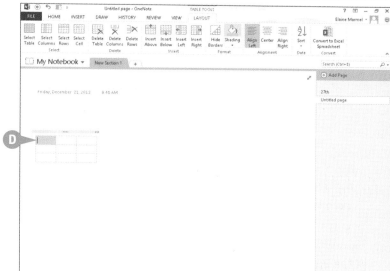

TIPS

How do I select more than one cell?
Selecting multiple cells is useful when you want to apply the same option to several table cells. Click in the first cell you want to select and drag either across or down to select adjacent cells. You can select non-adjacent cells if you press and hold Ctrl+Shift as you drag across each cell you want to select.

How do I delete a table?
Click in the table, click **Layout** on the Ribbon, and then click the **Delete Table** button.

Attach Files to Notes

Sometimes it is helpful to attach a document or other file to a page in OneNote. For example, suppose you have created a spreadsheet for expense account transactions in Microsoft Excel; you can attach that spreadsheet to a OneNote page devoted to work. Likewise, you could attach a PowerPoint presentation to a OneNote page devoted to a business meeting that you plan to attend.

When you attach a file to a note in a OneNote notebook, an icon for that file appears on the note; you can double-click the icon to open the file from within OneNote.

Attach Files to Notes

1 Click a section and a page on which you want to attach a file.

2 Click the place on the page where you want the file attachment to appear.

3 Click the **Insert** tab.

4 Click **File Attachment**.

The Choose a File or a Set of Files to Insert dialog box opens.

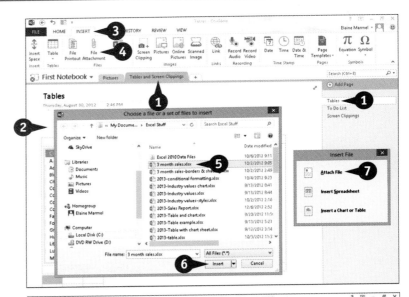

5 Locate and select the file you want to insert.

6 Click **Insert**.

OneNote displays the Insert File window.

7 Click **Attach File**.

A OneNote inserts an icon for the file.

You can move the shortcut icon as needed by dragging it.

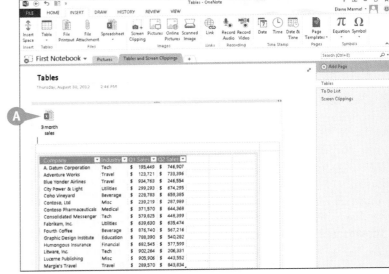

Send Information to OneNote

Suppose that you have composed a letter in Word or created a worksheet in Excel. You can send a copy of your work in a OneNote notebook using the OneNote Clipping Tool.

You can think of using the OneNote Clipping Tool to place information from another program into OneNote as a quick and easy way to copy and paste information. If you have multiple documents open in multiple programs, the OneNote Clipping Tool copies the last document you viewed in another program to OneNote.

Send Information to OneNote

1 Open any document in any Office program.

This example uses a letter in Word.

2 On the Windows taskbar, click the **Send To OneNote** button.

3 Click **Send to OneNote**.

The Select Location in OneNote dialog box appears.

4 Click a location in the notebook where you want to place the document.

5 Click **OK**.

Ⓐ The document appears in OneNote.

Note: If you use these steps for an Excel workbook, OneNote prompts you to choose between inserting a file attachment icon, a spreadsheet, or a chart or table.

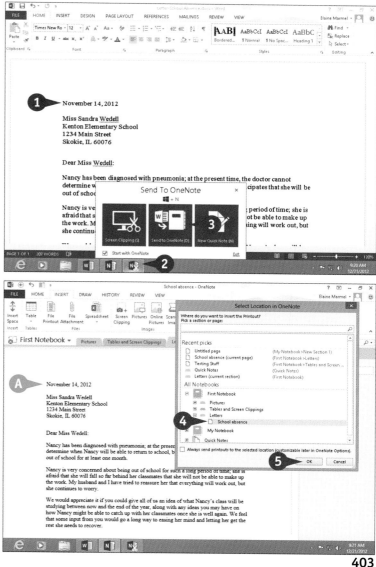

Insert a Screen Clipping

You can use OneNote's Screen Clipping tool to capture parts of anything you can view on-screen — including documents and web pages — and paste them into OneNote. For example, you might clip an image of a web page devoted to a car you are interested in buying, or a price sheet for a service you are considering using. You can move a screen clipping the same way you move a note. For more information, refer to the tip "How do I move a note?" in the section "Type and Draw Notes," earlier in this chapter. This section demonstrates clipping from a web page.

Insert a Screen Clipping

1 Open the document or page that contains the item you want to clip.

This example clips a part of a web page.

2 On the Windows taskbar, click the **OneNote Clipping Tool** button.

3 Click **Screen Clipping**.

The screen dims and ⟍ changes to +.

4 Click and drag from the top-left corner to the bottom-right corner of the area you want to clip.

Note: The part of the screen you select no longer appears dimmed.

5 In the Select Location in OneNote dialog box, click a location for the clipping.

6 Click **Send to Selected Location**.

Ⓐ The clipping appears in OneNote.

Ⓑ The clipping includes the date and time you created it.

Note: You can move a screen clipping the same way you move a note. For more information, refer to the tip "How do I move a note?" in the section "Type and Draw Notes."

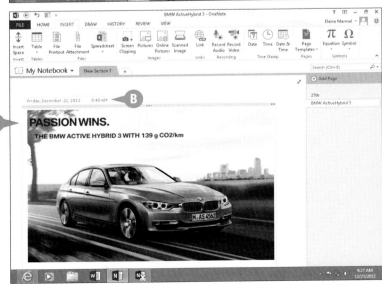

Create a Quick Note

Even if OneNote is not open, you can create a Quick Note to quickly jot down information. You can think of Quick Notes as electronic, yellow sticky notes. You can position Quick Notes anywhere on your screen and leave them there for as long as you need to refer to them. When you no longer need a particular Quick Note, you can close its window. As soon as you create a Quick Note, OneNote saves it to your OneNote notebook, so you can view it again from OneNote. You can also search and organize Quick Notes the same way you search and organize regular notes.

Create a Quick Note

1 Press ⊞+N to display the OneNote Clipping Tool window.

2 Press N or click **New Quick Note**.

A A Quick Note window appears.

3 Type your note.

Note: To format note text, select it and use the commands on the Mini toolbar.

4 Click × to close the note.

You can click × in the OneNote Clipping Tool window to hide it.

5 Launch OneNote.

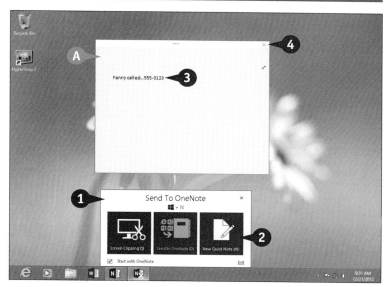

6 Click ▼.

7 Click **Quick Notes**.

B Your Quick Notes section appears.

C OneNote displays the most recent Quick Note you created.

D You can click here to review other Quick Notes.

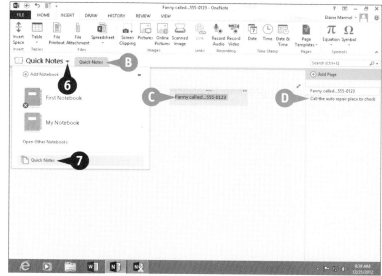

Record an Audio Note

If you are attending a significant meeting or participating in an important conference call, you can use OneNote to record it and store the recording as part of your notes. As you record, you can type notes into OneNote; when you do, OneNote links the note to the recording, displaying a small icon alongside it. You can then click this icon to listen to the audio that was recorded at the time you typed the note.

To record audio, you must have a microphone. Ask permission before recording someone.

Record an Audio Note

1 With the page to which you want to attach a file open in OneNote, click the **Insert** tab.

2 Click the **Record Audio** button and begin speaking.

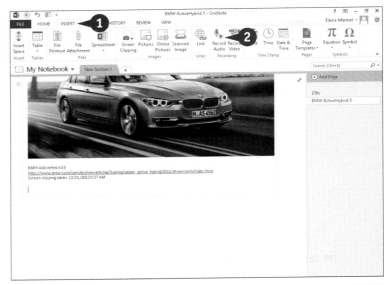

OneNote begins recording.

A A shortcut icon for the audio file appears.

B The Audio & Video Recording tab appears, displaying playback controls.

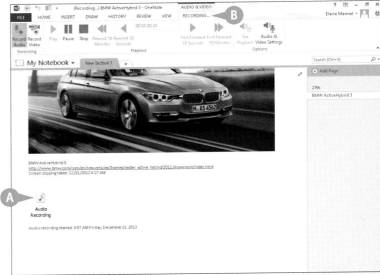

C You can type a note as you record, and OneNote links the note to the recording.

3 To stop recording, click the **Stop** button.

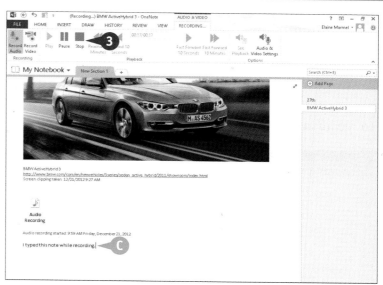

OneNote stops recording.

D To listen to the recording, double-click the **Audio Recording** icon.

E You can point the mouse at a note you typed during recording to see ⊙ beside it, indicating the note is linked to the recording.

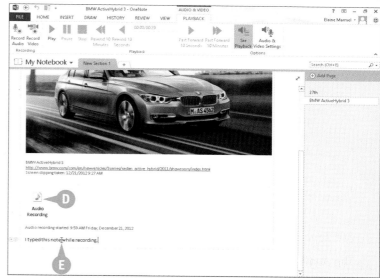

TIPS

Why do I care if OneNote links a typed note to an audio recording?

The link gives you another way to play the audio. When you slide the mouse pointer over the note you typed while recording, OneNote displays ⊙ beside the note; click ⊙ to listen to the recorded audio.

Can I record video notes?

Yes, if your computer features a webcam. Click the **Record Video** button on the Insert tab. OneNote displays the Audio & Video Recording tab and launches a video screen in which you can view the footage as it is recorded. To stop recording, click the **Stop** button on the Ribbon.

Create a New Notebook

You can create as many notebooks as you want. For example, you might create a notebook to hold notes for a trip you are planning or a notebook to hold information relating to a home project.

New notebooks contain one section and one page by default; you can add more sections and pages as needed. See "Create a New Section" and "Create a New Page" for details.

When you create a new notebook, you specify where the notebook should be stored — on the web, on a network, or on your computer.

Create a New Notebook

1. Click the **File** tab.

2. Click **New**.

3. Choose a place to store the notebook.

   In this example, OneNote saves the notebook to the computer's hard drive.

4. Type a name for the notebook.

   Ⓐ To save the notebook somewhere other than the default folder, click **Create in a different folder** and select the folder in which to save the notebook.

5. Click **Create Notebook**.

   Ⓑ OneNote creates a new notebook.

   Ⓒ The new notebook contains one section.

   Ⓓ The section contains one page.

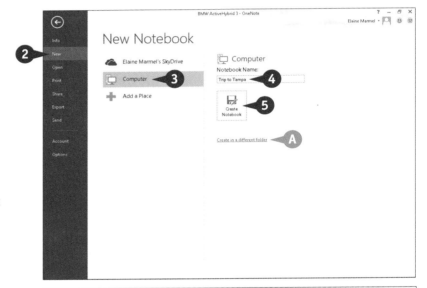

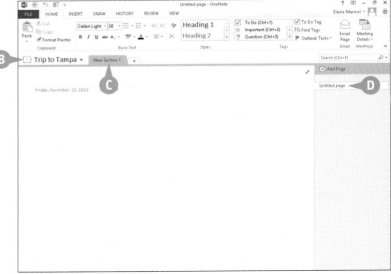

Create a New Section

You can use sections in notebooks to help you organize information. For example, if you are planning a trip to multiple cities, you might want to create sections for each city. Or, if you are planning a trip to one city, you might want to create separate sections for travel arrangements, hotel arrangements, and sites to see during your stay. OneNote names each new section as New Section 1, New Section 2, and so on, by default, but you can rename the sections. For help renaming sections, see "Rename a Section or Page," later in this chapter.

Create a New Section

1 Click ▼ to display a list of notebooks that you can open.

2 Click the notebook you want to open.

3 Click the **Create a New Section** tab (+).

Note: For help opening a notebook, see Chapter 22.

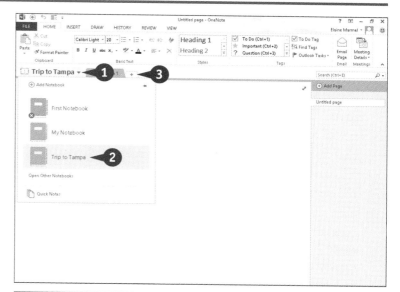

A OneNote creates a new section tab and selects its name.

Note: You can type a new name and press Enter or you can just press Enter or click anywhere to accept the default name.

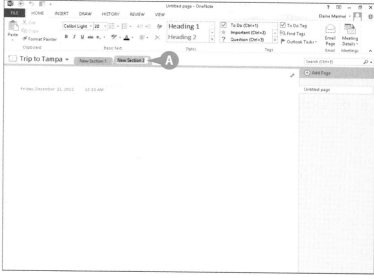

Create a New Page

You can easily add new pages to a notebook section. For example, if you are using OneNote to plan a vacation, you might create a notebook with one page for each phase of the trip or for travel arrangements, hotel arrangements, and sites to visit. Or if you are using OneNote to plan a meeting, you might create a notebook with one page for each topic the meeting will cover.

When you create a new page, you can opt to create a blank page, or you can create a page using a template — for example, to create a to-do list.

Create a New Page

1 Click the **Insert** tab.

2 Click the bottom half of the **Page Templates** button.

3 Click **Page Templates**.

Ⓐ The Templates pane appears.

4 Click the name of a category to reveal templates available in that category.

5 Click a template.

Ⓑ OneNote creates a new page based on the template you selected.

Ⓒ The page title appears here.

Ⓓ To close the Templates pane, click ✕.

Ⓔ To create a blank, untitled page, simply click the **Add Page** ⊕.

Note: To move a page to a different section or notebook, right-click the page title and choose **Move or Copy**. In the Move or Copy Pages dialog box, click beside the notebook in which you want to store the page, click the desired section, and then click **Move** or **Copy**.

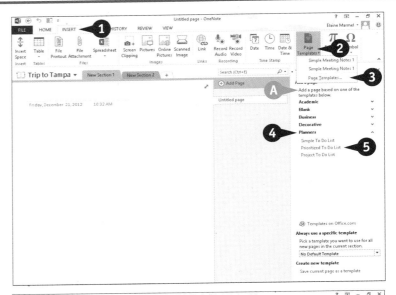

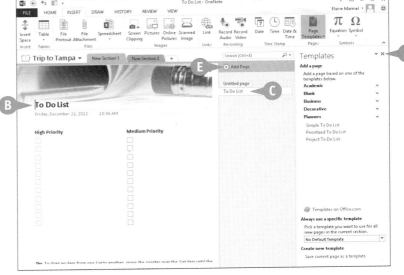

410

Rename a Section or Page

OneNote assigns new section names, such as New Section 1, New Section 2, and so on, by default. OneNote also assigns default names to pages.

You can assign your sections and pages more descriptive names to keep better track of where you have stored various pieces of information. For example, if your notebook relates to a project, you might create sections for each phase of the project and assign section names accordingly.

Rename a Section or Page

1 Right-click the tab for the section you want to rename.

A To rename a page, right-click the page's name.

2 Choose **Rename**.

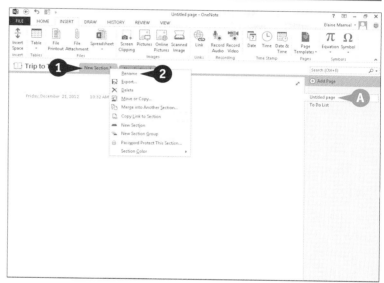

OneNote selects the current section or page name.

3 Type the new name and press **Enter**.

B OneNote applies the name you typed to the section tab or the page.

Note: You can delete a section or a page by right-clicking its title and choosing **Delete** from the menu that appears.

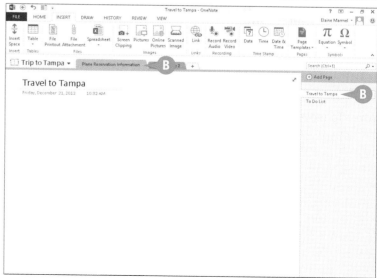

Group Sections

If your notebook contains several related sections, you can gather those sections into a group to make it easier to locate the section you need. For example, suppose that you are planning a vacation and have created a OneNote notebook to keep track of your research. You might gather the notebook's transportation-related sections — one with flight information, one for rental cars, one for hotel information, and so on — into a group. Or if you are using OneNote to jot down ideas for your business, you might gather all the sections that pertain to a particular project in one group.

Group Sections

1. Right-click any section.

2. Click **New Section Group**.

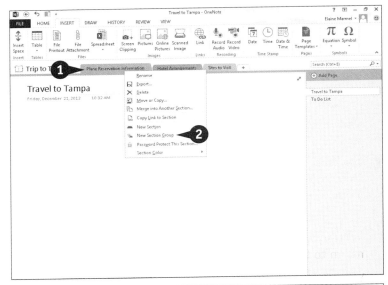

OneNote creates a new section group.

3. Type a name for the section group and press Enter.

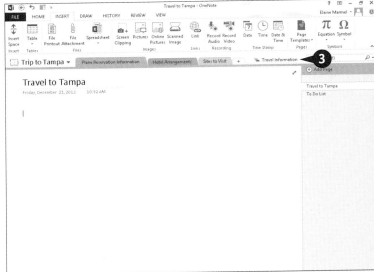

④ Click a tab.

⑤ Drag the tab to the section group (↖ changes to ↗).

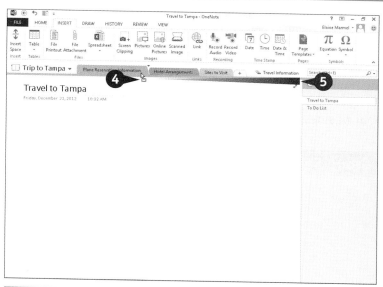

OneNote moves the tab to the section group and displays the section group.

Ⓐ The section tab you moved in Step **5** appears in the section group.

Ⓑ Click the **Navigate to Parent Section Group** button (⑤) to return to the regular view.

You can click the section group at any time to see its contents.

Note: Repeat Steps **4** and **5** to add additional section tabs to the section group.

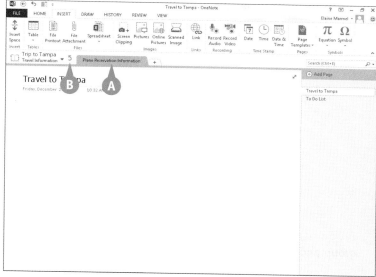

Can I remove a section tab from a group?
Yes. Open the section group, click the tab you want to move, and drag it to the **Navigate to Parent Section Group** button (⑤).

Can I change the order in which sections appear?
Yes. Click the tab for the section you want to move, drag the tab to the desired position among the sections, and release the mouse button. You can also change the order of pages in a section; to do so, click the page title and drag it up or down to the desired position among the pages.

Search Notes

As you enter more notes into OneNote, you may find it difficult to locate the information you need. Fortunately, OneNote offers a robust search function. Using it, you can locate any text in your OneNote notebooks — even text found in graphics. You can limit your search to a particular notebook or section or search all notebooks and sections. If you have enabled OneNote's Audio Search feature, you can also search audio and video for spoken words. Note that in order to search audio and video, you must enable the Audio Search function. For help, see the tip at the end of this section.

Search Notes

Set Search Scope

1 Click the **Search** ▼.

A A list of OneNote elements that you can search appears.

2 From the list, click the OneNote element you want to search.

This example uses **All Notebooks**.

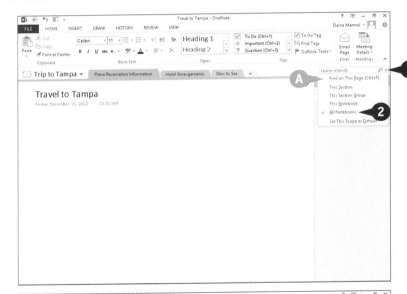

Conduct a Search

1 Click in the OneNote **Search** field.

B A drop-down list appears, displaying options for searching as well as previous search results.

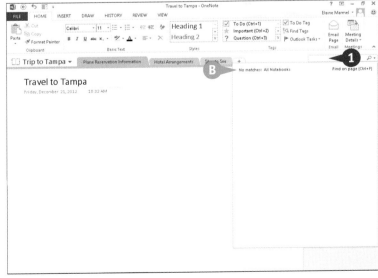

2 Type your search text.

C As you type, potential matches to your search criteria appear.

3 Click a match to view the page.

D OneNote displays the page.

E OneNote highlights the search text.

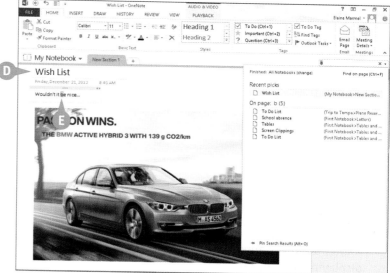

How do I search audio and video?

To search audio and video, you must enable OneNote's Audio Search function. To do so, click the **File** tab and choose **Options**. In the OneNote Options dialog box that appears, click **Audio & Video** and select **Enable searching audio and video recordings for words** (□ changes to ☑). The Audio Search dialog box appears; click the **Enable Audio Search** button. Finally, click **OK** to close the OneNote Options dialog box.

Search for Recent Edits

Y ou can search for recent changes that you have made in OneNote. Suppose that you made a change to your notebook that you want to view, but you cannot remember exactly where in your notebook you made the change. You can search the current notebook, section, section group, or all notebooks. You can search for any change you might have made today, since yesterday, within the last seven, 14, or 30 days, within the last three months, or within the last six months. Or, you can search for changes made to all pages sorted by date.

Search for Recent Edits

1 Click the **History** tab.

2 Click **Recent Edits**.

3 Click a timeframe.

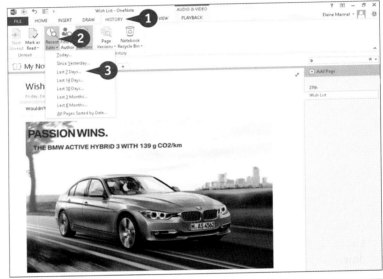

Ⓐ OneNote opens the Search Results pane and displays pages in the current notebook that you have edited in the timeframe you selected in Step **3**.

You can click any page in the list to view that page; edits appear highlighted in yellow.

Ⓑ You can click ▼ to change the elements OneNote searches.

Ⓒ You can click ▼ to control the order in which the search results appear.

4 Click ✕ to close the Search Results pane.

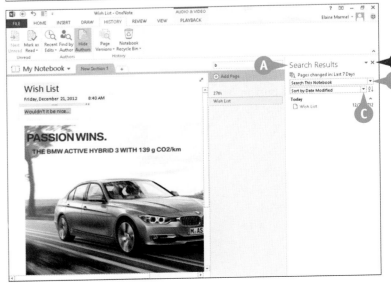

Set Synchronization Options

OneNote enables you to store your notebooks in the cloud, and, when you do, OneNote keeps them synchronized and up-to-date by default. You can access them using the OneNote web app, any computer running Windows 7 or Windows 8, and many mobile devices.

But there may be times when you want or need to synchronize changes manually. For example, suppose that you want to synchronize notebook changes to the cloud before you shut down your computer. OneNote enables you to check sync status as well as synchronize your changes manually.

Set Synchronization Options

1 Click the **File** tab.

2 Click **Info**.

3 Click **View Sync Status**.

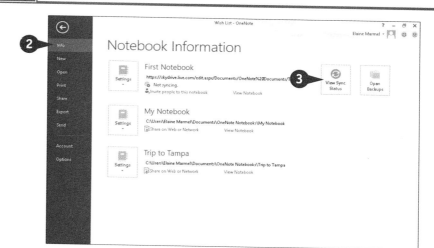

OneNote displays the Shared Notebook Synchronization window.

4 Select a synchronization method (○ changes to ●).

This example uses the **Sync manually** option.

5 Click the **Sync All** button or an individual notebook's **Sync Now** button.

OneNote synchronizes changes to the cloud.

Note: To continue automatic synchronization, click **Sync automatically whenever there are changes**.

6 Click **Close**.

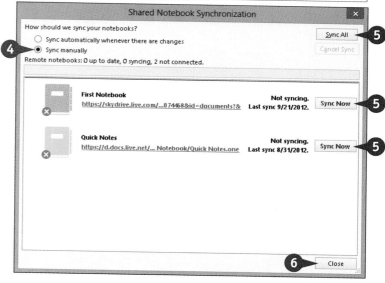

Share Notes with People Who Do Not Have OneNote

You can share pages in your OneNote notebooks with others who do not have OneNote by e-mailing the pages or by converting them to PDF or XPS files. When you e-mail pages from OneNote, it starts your e-mail program, creates a new message window containing the OneNote page in HTML format, and applies the page's title to the message's Subject line. You simply enter the recipient's address and any additional text and send the message as normal. You can also convert note pages, sections, or entire notebooks into PDF or XPS format so that you can distribute them to others who do not have OneNote.

Share Notes with People Who Do Not Have OneNote

E-Mail a Note Page

1 Display the page you want to e-mail in OneNote.

2 Click the **Home** tab.

3 Click the **E-mail Page** button.

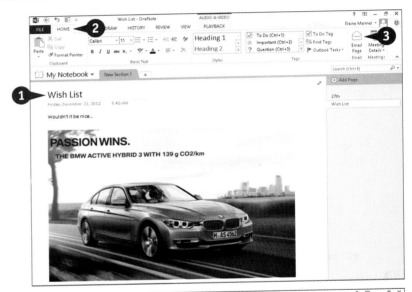

Ⓐ OneNote launches your e-mail program, displaying a new message window containing the OneNote page.

Ⓑ The message's Subject line contains the page's title.

Ⓒ Any audio attached to the page appears as an e-mail attachment.

4 Type the recipient's e-mail address in the **To** field.

5 Click **Send**.

Your e-mail program places the message in your Outbox and will send the message when you initiate sending and receiving messages.

Convert Notes to PDF or XPS Format

1 Display the page, section, or notebook you want to convert.

2 Click the **File** tab.

3 Click **Export**.

4 Click **Page**, **Section**, or **Notebook**.

5 Click **PDF (*.pdf)** or **XPS (*.xps)**.

6 Click **Export**.

The Save As dialog box opens.

Ⓓ The name of the page, section, or notebook appears in the File Name field.

7 Locate and select the folder in which you want to save the page, section, or notebook.

8 Click **Save**.

OneNote saves the page, section, or notebook in the format you specified.

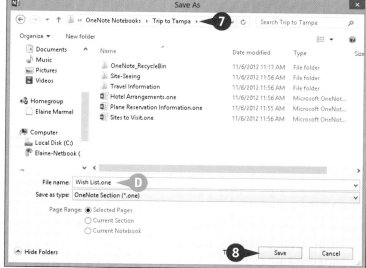

TIP

Can I send a OneNote page as a PDF attachment to an e-mail message?
Yes. Display the page. Click the **File** tab, click **Send**, and click **Send as PDF**. Your e-mail program opens and displays a message with the OneNote page attached as a PDF file, and the page name appears in the Subject line. Type a recipient name and send the message.

419

Index

Index